GLOBAL
MISSIOLOGY
FOR THE
21ST
CENTURY

GLOBAL MISSIOLOGY FOR THE 21ST CENTURY

The Iguassu Dialogue

Edited by
William D. Taylor

Baker Academic
A Division of Baker Book House Co
Grand Rapids, Michigan 49516

Technical editor: Susan Peterson
Cover design: Cheryl Van Andel
Cover photos: Jackie Gibson and William D. Taylor

© 2000 by World Evangelical Fellowship

Published by Baker Academic
a division of Baker Book House Company
P.O. Box 6287, Grand Rapids, MI 49516-6287

Second printing, August 2001

Printed in the United States of America

Unless otherwise noted, Scripture quotations are taken from the HOLY BIBLE, NEW INTERNATIONAL VERSION®. © 1973, 1978, 1984 by the International Bible Society. Used by permission of Zondervan Publishing House. All rights reserved.

Library of Congress Cataloging-in-Publication Data

Global missiology for the 21st century: the Iguassu dialogue / edited by William D. Taylor.
    p.   cm.
Includes bibliographical references and index.
ISBN 0-8010-2259-2
    1. Missions—Theory—Congresses. I. Taylor, William David.
BV2063.G56 2000
266—dc21   00-058583

For information about academic books, resources for Christian leaders, and all new releases available from Baker Book House, visit our web site:
http://www.bakerbooks.com

Contents

In appreciation

I AM PROFOUNDLY GRATEFUL to many colleagues who joined me in doing missiology.

First, there are the brothers Bertil and Leif Ekström, Brazilian-Swedes, who made the Iguassu Consultation happen administratively. Joining them in Brazil were Mark Orr and David Ruíz. The four were a quiet, efficient, and servant-hearted team.

Thanks too to my World Evangelical Fellowship Missions Commission staff colleague, Jon Lewis, and our Chairman, David Tai-Woong Lee, who understood the entire concept of our "process." Together we envisioned a process that would flow from consultation to publication and then to further work on global missiological concerns.

Special thanks to the Iguassu Affirmation team. Nobody knows how many hours they worked, late at night and early in the morning, listening, writing and re-writing, editing and re-editing. Thank you, David Tai-Woong Lee (Korea) and Jim Stamoolis (USA) as co-leaders, Rose Dowsett (Scotland), Abel Ndjerareou (Chad), David Neff (USA), Kang San Tan (Malaysia), and Tonica van der Meer (Brazil).

Many Iguassu participants have encouraged me and made recommendations since Brazil, including: Paul, Rose, Bob, Cliff, K, Jim, Paula, Stewart, Richard, Stanley, Jonathan, Jason, Alex, John, Barbara, Jeff, David, Jorge, Stan, Hans, Kathy, Norbert, Francis, Rosifran, Gary, Dave. You know who you are.

Susan Peterson again has taken on the task as our technical editor. Her eagle eye has shaped all our Missions Commission books. This volume has been a special challenge, and without her patience, keen sense for language, and accuracy, we would not have the editorial quality we have sought over the years.

And finally, let me publicly express my thanks to Yvonne, my wife. Her conceptual thinking helped shape the Iguassu Consultation itself in many ways. Her editorial gifts clarified a number of the chapters, including my own. Called by vocation to the contemplative life, she has served unseen, quietly, and deeply as my "silent partner."

To all of you, a thousand steadfast thanks.

— *William D. Taylor*

Foreword

I WILL NEVER FORGET the first missionary conference I ever attended. The year was 1966. My brother and I had just arrived in Canada as immigrants from India and happened to walk into a church that was beginning its week of missions emphasis. As it turned out, the opening speaker was an American missionary who had been serving in India for many years. I had never been at such a conference before. In a new church, in a new country, and experiencing a new theme, I sat there awaiting the missionary's address. When he was through, I was quite shaken, wondering if all of his descriptions of the land of my birth were exactly the way *I* had seen them. Both my brother and I left that service somewhat perplexed by it all. Not only was I a relatively new Christian, but I was now going through an identity crisis. I was not sure if I was inside looking out or outside looking in. It took a few years for me to realize what had happened.

When I made my first trip back to India five years after this event, its sights and sounds caught my attention in a way that had never registered with me before. Yes, there was the nostalgia and the thrill of using the language in which so much of my cultural memory was enshrined. But there was the staggering experience of surprise, even shock. I was reminded of the old Chinese proverb: "If you want to know what water is, don't ask the fish." The point is well taken. When we are immersed in an environment, we do not see it for what it really is. It takes an outsider's glimpse to bring a visceral response to that for which proximity only brought familiarity without emotion.

But something fascinating happened as a sequel. Years later, when I was preaching in India alongside that very missionary who was hosting my meetings, he made a comment that brought laughter to all of us. When I told him of my initial reaction when I heard him years ago, he told me of his memory of seeing us walk into the sanctuary. It gave him a great deal of unease, he said. Not knowing who we were—friend or foe—he had held back from many things that he had wanted to say.

This simple episode may well capture our fears and agonies in finding a meaningful response to a world in need of the gospel of Jesus Christ. Many of us have become so immersed in our present contexts that we are not able to be objective judges of our failures and our shortcomings. At the same time, cultural sensitivities are running so deep that we are fearful of saying the wrong thing and bringing unwarranted offense. How do we understand the need, the demands, the methods, and the commitments that will be needed to bring the message to the whole world? Change is in the air.

For that alone, I am deeply grateful to the men and women who gathered at the Iguassu Missiological Consultation to share from their hearts and their convictions for the cause of Jesus Christ. Listening to this diversity of voices and having our eyes opened to the vastness of the need are the first steps to grasping the urgency of the response. I for one will always be grateful to the Lord for the missionary call and burden that brought the gospel to my native land. Because of the passion of William Carey, the devotion of Amy Carmichael, and the sensitivity of the missionary I just mentioned, there are millions today who call the Lord Jesus their Savior. They were missionaries who loved the people and lived the message.

One of the key sentiments voiced at this historic consultation was that of kairos—the timing of God's working. I believe this is real, not just imagined. May I add another slant to this? An English writer years ago penned an essay that he titled, "The Candle and the Bird," in which he contrasted the light of a candle with the song of a bird. If you extinguish a candle, he said, the light goes out. On the other hand, if you chase a bird away, "it just goes and sings its song on another bough." The gospel as carried by the Holy Spirit, he mused, is not just a candle. It is also akin to a bird's song. At times, it has seemed as the though the bird were silent in a land because it has been frightened away. But, he said, if you follow the bird, you will find that it is just singing in a different land.

What a wonderful metaphor that is for the proclamation and timing of God's work around the world! It was not accidental, for example, that in the late 18th century, at the very moment that the French mob was tearing the cross off Notre Dame Cathedral in Paris, France, William Carey was setting foot on Indian soil. No, the bird had not been silenced. It had just moved its music elsewhere. If we track the history of missions, we will see that just as one nation seemed harder to reach, another one was opening its arms. The writer summarizes that theme by saying, "There is a divine element in the church—an element that no persecuting fires can devour and that no convulsion can destroy." That is a glorious reminder that the light never goes out and the song of the soul set free is ever being sung in some land somewhere. We must be in tune with the kairos of God for such music.

I commend this book to you who long to know what you can do to hear these strains. I commend it to you who may be getting weary in well doing. I commend it to the Christian who needs to get a glimpse of the convulsion in some parts and the exultation in others. Oh, that we might hear his voice and say, "What will you have me to do, Lord?" When the famed missionary Robert Jaffray was offered an enormous sum of money by an oil company to work for them rather than as a missionary, he answered, "Your salary is big, but your job is too small." How marvelous is the example of those who knew what the real cost was and what the real inheritance is. Are we surprised at the result of such commitment?

Let us who are immersed in familiar air breathe in these thoughts. I have no doubt that we will be stirred within by a counter-perspective impelling us to capture the moment with eternity in sight.

When our task is done, with the hymn-writer we can beckon:

Let every creature rise and bring
Peculiar honors to our king
Angels descend with songs again
And earth repeat the long Amen.

— *Dr. Ravi K. Zacharias*
President
Ravi Zacharias
International Ministries

Part 1

Setting the stage

WE BEGIN WITH AN INVITATION to the global Evangelical "reflective practitioners." These are women and men of both action and study; rooted in the Word of God and the church of Christ; passionately obedient to the fullness of the Great Commandment and Great Commission; globalized in their perspective, yet faithful citizens of their own cultures.

This book emerges from the Iguassu Missiological Consultation, held in Brazil in October 1999. The World Evangelical Fellowship Missions Commission leaders convened this strategic event because we perceived the need to pause at this historical hinge of both century and millennium to examine our missiological foundations, commitments, and practices. That event and this book initiated an ongoing process that purposes to release further serious and practical global missiology at the service of the borderless church.

The structure of this publication in part parallels that of the Iguassu Consultation. Of the 41 chapters, only 13 were commissioned after Iguassu, primarily to fill in some gaps and address other major global challenges that Christians face. Only two of the 41 writers were unable to attend the consultation itself—Howell and Engqvist. Escobar had to cancel at the last moment due to his wife's health, but his papers played a central role in the Consultation.

The Iguassu Affirmation "began" months before the consultation, when the WEF Missions Commission leadership

asked David Tai-Woong Lee (Missions Commission Chair) and Jim Stamoolis (WEF Theological Commission Executive Director) to coordinate the composition of a document that would reflect the Consultation itself and point to new directions of our globalized Evangelical missiology.

Lee, who had read many of the papers prior to Iguassu, began structuring the missiological concerns in a draft form. By the time it was given to the Team of Seven, the document had gone through six initial revisions. The Team of Seven members were drawn Europe, Southeast Asia, Northeast Asia, North America, South America, and Africa. Together they crafted a broad-based document, carefully studied two cycles of written and oral suggestions from the participants, and presented the final copy for participants to affirm. The Iguassu Affirmation comes as a working document, forged in the warmth, collegiality, and discussion of a very intense week of doing missiology in Brazil.

The Iguassu program was designed to be rooted in worship and prayer, followed by the models of mission that flow from spirituality and community, then Fernando's expositions; from there we transitioned into the missiological themes during morning and afternoon sessions. These in turn led to group interactions and discussion, further prayer and worship, with the evenings primarily open for networking and relationships.

One mid-week highlight came with Steuernagel's poignant introduction to the movie *The Mission*, followed by viewing the film. Many scenes from that movie had been filmed at the Iguassu Falls, and hence when we visited them the next morning, they had been transformed from a natural wonder of the world into missiological waterfalls of historic significance for the church in mission.

From Iguassu to the reflective practitioners of the global family of Christ

WILLIAM D.
TAYLOR

OUR NEW CENTURY and millennium present a *kairos* moment of unparalleled magnitude and opportunity for the borderless church of Christ. However, the global *chronos* moment will not make it easy for the Christian movement. Externally and internally, we grapple with a spectrum of significant and unrelenting challenges: globalization with its mixed blessings and curses; the global AIDS tragedy; the information technology revolution; unrelenting urbanization and the economic crises it presents; the massive refugee highway movement; and a new pluralism that challenges our Christian concept of truth, our hermeneutic of Scripture, our Christology, and our understanding of what it means to be human. Multifaceted persecution unleashes its violence against Christians in many areas of the world; yet, ironically, we discover that we have a deficient theology of suffering and martyrdom. The worldwide worldview transformation—pre-modernity to modernity to post-modernity—does not allow us to rest on our past accomplishments.

The church struggles to define truth and the authority of Scripture. It also grapples with the nature of the transforming gospel of Jesus, with what it means to be "Christian" and "Evangelical," with what it means to "be" and "do" church, with the international anemia that characterizes the church, and with what it means to be obedient to the kingdom of God regarding our mission in the world and within our diverse mission movements. We still have not understood how modernity has misshaped our church and missions "enterprise."

In light of these challenges, many insightful and courageous observers of the international arena felt it vital that we as Evangelicals pause and gather together a group of women and men who, as reflective practitioners, could consider how these complex trends and realities affect us as we project mission and missions into the century before us.

In light of this *kairos* hinge-moment of history, therefore, the World Evangelical Fellowship Missions Commission convened an international missiological consultation held in the historic city of Iguassu, Brazil, October 10-16, 1999. There 160 church, theological education, and mission leaders met for an intense week of worship, prayer, relationship-building, and missiological reflection. We had six stated purposes:

1. A call to international reflection in order to identify and carefully evaluate the radical global and cultural changes which have shaped our contemporary world history as well as the church and its mission.

2. An occasion that allows us to begin the process of identifying and seeking definitions of the key concepts and terminology of globalized Evangelical missiology, faithfully representing the diverse and biblical perspectives from West and non-West, North and South. From one or two dominant centers of Christianity, the Spirit has now created a rich panoply of centers of globalized Christianity.

3. An initial creation of a mosaic/profile of this international Evangelical missiology, and then the effective communication of its content and import to the borderless church and mission community.

4. An opportunity to help shape global missiological foundations which are both biblical and culturally appropriate and which will undergird us for the long-term future.

5. An occasion that encourages us to broker and invest in a process of globalized missiology that returns us to our grassroots, to our cultures, to our home churches, and to our ministries and networks.

6. A "moment of time" that allows us to evaluate/critique the prime missiological emphases and currents that influenced the missionary movement in the last 50 years of the 20th century.

The Danger of Over-Simplification of a Complex Assignment

Following up on the last item above, we realized that during the last decades of the 20th century, an unfortunate over-emphasis on pragmatic and reductionist thinking came to pervade the international Evangelical missionary movement. Whether we wish to recognize it or not, we must acknowledge that this emphasis has seeped into the church around the world. The results have not been healthy or encouraging (see Engel & Dyrness, 2000).

What are some of the over-simplifications that have been made? They include the following:

• The crippling omissions in the Great Commission—reducing it to proclamation alone—which lead to only a partial understanding of the mission of the church, resulting in spiritual anemia and a thin veneer of Christianity, regardless of culture or nation.

• The absence of a robust gospel of the kingdom which calls us to radical commitment and discipleship to Christ.

• An inadequate theology of suffering and martyrdom.

• The use of emotive slogans to drive the missions task, leading to a false understanding of both task and success in our mission.

• The application of simplistic thinking and methodologies to the Great Commission, which are guided too much by marketing strategies and secular concepts of what it means to be effective and efficient.

- The reduction of world evangelization to a manageable enterprise with an over-emphasis on research, statistics, quantifiable objectives, and desired outcomes.
- A focus on a limited geography of the world and an excessive emphasis on the year 2000, generating unrealistic expectations and leading to profound disappointment.
- An over-emphasis on short-term missions that minimizes longer-term service, and an inadequate biblical theology of vocation.
- The illusion by some that mass media is the final answer to world evangelization or the suggestion that "the church finally has the technology to finish the Great Commission," whether the Internet, mass communications, publication, or other media. The danger is obvious, for it disregards the sacrificial, incarnational calling of God into our world of profound personal, familial, socio-economic, cultural, and environmental crises.

Inviting the Reflective Practitioners of the Evangelical World

The search for "reflective practitioners" guided us in formulating the roster of participants who were invited to the consultation. These women and men of both action and reflection are committed to God's truth; obedient in the power of God's Spirit to the Great Commission in all its fullness; servants who are globalized in perspective; citizens of their own culture but also of the world; leaders who are passionate of heart and who also reflect the heart of Christ. Of the 160 participants at Iguassu, half came from Latin America, Asia, Africa, the Middle East, and the Islands; the other half came from North America, Europe, Australia, and New Zealand. This balance of West and the "Great Rest of the World" contributed

to the spice and diversity of Iguassu. All of us were challenged, even forced, to listen to and engage with perspectives that graciously and at times sharply questioned some missiological presuppositions. There were lively discussions and even disagreements between colleagues of West and non-West, East and East, South and South. It was a free-flowing and dynamic week.

The venue of the consultation was selected by our Brazilian colleagues, the city of Iguassu, Brazil, a few short kilometers from the majestic falls of the same name. Those who have seen the movie, *The Mission*, will remember well the scenes filmed on site at the falls. Halfway through our consultation, Valdir Steuernagel presented an eloquent talk on the historic and contemporary significance of that film; then we viewed the movie on a large screen. It was a powerful evening. The next morning, we took a break from heavy discussions and traveled the short distance to the falls themselves. We saw them not only as one of the seven natural wonders of the world, but also in missiological context. Steve Sang-Cheol Moon, one of our Korean colleagues, came up to me in the spray of the falls to say with a touch of Asian humor, "Bill, Niagara Falls is a modernity worldview cataract—one huge flow in the same general direction. But Iguassu Falls is a post-modernity cataract—three kilometers of 265 different falls, flowing in so many directions!"

This publication has been written by and for the global community of reflective practitioners—men and women engaged in the trans-cultural mission of God, whether students or veterans, female or male, younger or older, activists or missiologists, regardless of geography or culture. Samuel Escobar's definition of missiology (see page 101) has been very helpful in the shaping of this book. For him, missiology is "… an interdisciplinary approach to understand missionary action. It looks at missionary facts from the perspective of the biblical sciences, theology, history, and the social sciences." The consultation as well as this book flow in the strength of this definition, and we intentionally emphasize a globalization dimension.

The borderless body of Christ in recent years has experienced a massive epicenter shift—from the centers of the North to the many centers of the South. No single center from now on will dominate the agenda of our dialogue and reflection. Nobody knows for certain, but estimates suggest that 75% of the family of Jesus is found in the non-Western nations (Asia, Africa, Latin America, South Pacific, Caribbean, Middle East). This transformation does not spell the end of the West as a center of God's church and its leadership. It simply means that the Spirit of God has created many centers where he is at work, and it provides rich soil from which new kinds of strategic thinking and long-term commitment to service will germinate, flower, and transform the global church.

We are all familiar with the historic three "selfs" of the church: self-supporting, self-propagating, self-governing. But today's reality is more complex, richer, and more challenging, for there are really five "selfs." These include the known three, plus self-theologizing and self-missiologizing. These latter two by definition will challenge the established verities of older theology and missiology, including theological and missiological approaches and categories and the historic ways of conceptualizing and doing theology and missiology. Guided by the Spirit, faithful to Scripture, within the community of faith, and graciously reflecting the marvelous diversity of culture and church permutations, the future is bright and encouraging. However, the outcomes may be radically different from those that are currently known.

Learning From Valuable Missiological History

Further background for the Iguassu Consultation came as we read our missiological church history. As far as we in the WEF Missions Commission knew, this consultation, coming upon the eve of the year 2000, was the primary Evangelical global event of such a theological-missiological nature. This realization was disturbing, for it seemed that the major Evangelical international structures, networks, and theological institutions were focusing on their own particular tasks and were perhaps more concerned about their own projects, programs, curricula, and organizational future. There was relatively little interest in substantial theological and missiological reflection or in a sober self-evaluation that would lead to a revised way of going about our task in the world—a revitalized praxis.

Looking back to the historic World Missionary Conference of Edinburgh (1910) at the beginning of the 20th century, we realized there were lessons we needed to heed. That international event, the fourth of its kind in the West, had been very carefully conceived and prepared "... in its character as an assembly for careful and scientific thought and not merely for the edification of the faithful and the expression of Christian enthusiasm; and in the steps which it took to secure the permanence of Christian cooperation in the future ..." (Neill, 1986, p. 393).

Edinburgh's driving slogan, coined and given currency by John Raleigh Mott (1865-1955), was, "The Evangelization of the World in This Generation." Actually, as Neill (1986, p. 394) reports, "The slogan was based on an unexceptional theological principle—that each generation of Christians bears responsibility for the contemporary generation of non-Christians in the world, and that it is the business of each such generation of Christians to see to it, as far as lies within its power, that the gospel is clearly preached to every single non-Christian in the same generation."

Edinburgh's leaders understood the continual growth of missionary outreach in the world and the hope that it would increase. Neill lists 12 great achievements in the preceding century, and the conference convened serious men and women for a landmark event. However, most significantly, he notes:

"There had been little discussion of theology at the Edinburgh Conference of 1910. There had seemed to be little need for it, when all were at one on all the fundamentals. All were agreed that Jesus Christ the Son of God was the final and decisive Word of God to men; that in him alone is the certainty of salvation given to men; that this gospel must be preached to every living human soul, to whom God has given the freedom to accept or to reject and who must stand by that acceptance or rejection on the last day. The delegates differed somewhat in their attitude towards the non-Christian religions, but all were agreed that, as the Lordship of Christ came to be recognized, these others religions would disappear in their present form—the time would come when Shiva and Vishu would have no more worshippers than Zeus and Apollo have today.

"But in these years of rapid missionary expansion, a very different gospel had been growing up and taking hold of the minds of a great many Christians, especially in America. The liberal was not by any means so sure that Jesus Christ was the last Word of God to man. He was repelled by the exclusive claim to salvation through Christ alone. He tended to take a much more favourable view of the other religions than his more conservative colleagues, and to look forward to some kind of synthesis of religions rather than to the disappearance of any of them. The real enemy is secularism. Adherents of all the great religions should stand together in defence of the spiritual reality of man's life. There should be no hostility between them, the spirit of proselytism being replaced by the willingness to learn from one another" (Neill, 1986, pp. 454-455).

As we approached the Iguassu Consultation, at the end of the 20th and the beginning of the 21st century, we members of the international body of Christ recognized that it behooved us to listen to and learn from our history. We did not want to repeat the errors that have come from not revisiting the theological and biblical underpinnings of our mission. For that reason, we felt it imperative to engage in serious and substantive reflection and analysis. For our own good as reflective people of God in global mission, we must strive to be thoughtful and grounded practitioners and visionaries.

Revisiting a Relevant and Poignant Gospel Narrative

Having studied the various papers prior to the consultation and pondering the issues and trends with which we would be grappling, I felt the Spirit of God calling me to Matthew 11:1-12 as a reference point for our days together in Iguassu. During the last decade, I have pondered this story, mining it time and time again for its richness and finding its application so relevant for our lives and ministry. Following are some of the reflections that flow from this narrative, with its power to shape our lives and ministry.

Matthew 11:1-12

[1] After Jesus had finished instructing his twelve disciples, he went on from there to teach and preach in the towns of Galilee.

[2] When John heard in prison what Christ was doing, he sent his disciples [3] to ask him, "Are you the one who was to come, or should we expect someone else?"

[4] Jesus replied, "Go back and report to John what you hear and see: [5] The blind receive sight, the lame walk, those who have leprosy are cured, the deaf hear, the dead are raised, and the good news is preached to the poor. [6] Blessed is the man who does not fall away on account of me."

[7] As John's disciples were leaving, Jesus began to speak to the crowd about John: "What did you go out into the desert to see? A reed swayed by the wind? [8] If not, what did you go out to see? A man dressed in fine clothes? No, those who wear fine clothes are in kings' palaces. [9] Then what did you go out to see? A prophet? Yes, I tell you, and more than a prophet. [10] This is the one about whom it is written: 'I will send my messenger ahead of you, who will prepare your way before you.'

"[11] I tell you the truth: Among those born of women there has not risen anyone greater than John the Baptist; yet he who is least in the kingdom of heaven is greater than he. [12] From the days of John the Baptist until now, the kingdom of heaven has been forcefully advancing, and forceful men lay hold of it."

Mission is carried out in the context of change, crisis, and the unexpected turns of life.

In the time of Jesus

We observe our Lord in the previous two chapters encountering the swelling wave of opposition that would soon explode against him. We contemplate his heart for the sick and the dead, the aged and the children, the oppressed and the demonized, the helpless and the shepherdless. We see his commitment to prayer. We note his selection and commissioning of the Twelve to a first-time, strategic, short-term mission project. Now, in chapter 11, Matthew introduces John the Baptizer into the story. Jesus uses that occasion for penetrating and enigmatic statements about the times of opportunity and violence, about true meaning in life and ministry.

Little could the disciples have imagined what Jesus was referring to as he spoke of personal and ministry significance and of the future. But they would discover and experience those realities very soon. And then the task would be theirs, empowered by the Spirit, to impact their own historical moment.

In our times, today

We stand at the start of this uncertain new century, this new millennium. New language and categories have entered our lives. We speak of globalization, and we witness the worldview transitions from pre-modernity to modernity to post-modernity with their respective blessings and curses. Regardless of our culture, our gender, our geography, and our ministry, the times have radically changed, requiring a serious re-evaluation of why we do the things we do in ministry—whether personal or organizational.

Mission is worked out in the context of questions and doubt.

In the time of Jesus

The Baptizer's existential crisis has become painfully real. He had no idea that his prophetic ministry would land him in jail or of the kind of death that would come to him with such violence. Grappling from prison with profound doubts ("Did I misunderstand history, God, and you, Jesus?"), he sends a delegation of his last disciples to ask Jesus that very hard question. However, our Lord sends him an oblique answer, inviting the disciples only to report to John what they had heard and seen of the signs of the kingdom. It's only *after* they leave that Jesus gives his verdict—an unprecedented accolade—of John as a person with a mission. Why did Jesus not encourage John more by sending word of his now public evaluation and affirmation of John? Notably, Jesus did not condemn John for his doubts.

In our times, today

We must feel free to ask each other, and God, the dangerous and presuppositional questions: Where is the power of the gospel and the church today? Has something gone wrong with the harvest? What kind of gospel have we transported around the world? Why Rwanda, Ireland, Bosnia? Why such a post-Christian and anti-Christian Europe and North America? What does it mean to see the presence of the kingdom of heaven today in our world? Has there been an excessive export/import business of theology, missiology, and church and educational structures, primarily from the West to the rest of the world?

On a more personal level, why are we followers of Jesus the Christ? How have we uncritically allowed our own cultures to shape and misshape our worldview, our relationship with the supernatural God, our theological structures, and our missiological reflection and action? What would it mean to become practicing supernaturalists today?

Mission must be carried out in the context of downward mobility, not upward success.

In the time of Jesus

The great Forerunner would soon face a stunning and ignominious death. What's more, he never heard what Jesus had said about him on that occasion, for Jesus talked about him after John's disciples left. John apparently died without explanation and without comfort from God. But then, Jesus himself would die a brutal and seemingly pointless death. In time, all of the apostles except John would be subsequently martyred. Worldly success, triumphalism, and popular acclaim were definitely not written into the contract of their spiritual journey.

In our times, today

The majority of Christians—whether in the West or the non-West—do not have an adequate theology of suffering, much less of persecution and martyrdom. But we must develop one soon! The Iguassu Consultation purposefully did not convene the powerful, the network controllers, the wealthy, or the high-profile people. Those present were primarily lower-profile servant-leaders. And if we don't place ourselves in the category of the powerless and the nameless, we need to revisit what we think it means to walk with Jesus on the path of downward mobility.

Perhaps the late Henri Nouwen (1989, p. 62) says it best, with direct application to our Evangelical world and its fascination with leadership and power: "The way of the Christian leader is not the way of upward mobility in which our world has invested so much, but the way of downward mobility ending on the cross. This might sound morbid and masochistic, but for those who have heard the voice of the first love and said 'yes' to it, the downward-moving way of Jesus is the way to the joy and the peace of God, a joy and peace that is not of this world."

Mission is worked out in the bipolar context of gospel advance and persecution.

In the time of Jesus

Matthew's narrative notes how the kingdom of heaven had advanced forcefully through the life and ministry first of John (Matt. 3:5-8) and then of Jesus (Matt. 4:23-25). Yet we note the enigma of verse 12, an ambiguity that is reflected in different translations. The first part is clear: the kingdom of heaven would advance forcefully, as in the ministry of John and Jesus. But the second part is simply unclear. The Greek text allows us to translate it two ways. One idea is that some would forcefully want to get into the kingdom. The second possibility is a very different idea, that others would forcefully attack the kingdom itself. The account in Luke 16:16 emphasizes the first option. In the time of Jesus, some people were pushing their way in, even tearing up the roof-tops of homes to get to Jesus. But at the same time, the opposition to Jesus would grow into the plot to eliminate him. Ultimately, the converged adversarial forces would kill both John and later Jesus. Was our Lord playing with words, preparing the disciples (and us) for both options?

In our times, today

World population stands today at about the 6 billion mark. We saw the addition of 2 billion in the 20th century alone. This is the global arena of the church of Christ. The task is almost overwhelming!

We are encouraged as we witness and read of the advance of the gospel. We rejoice in each report—assuming the information is verifiable—that marks the advance of the kingdom message. We live in the remarkable day of the globalization of both the church and the missions movement—from every nation and every continent to every nation and every continent. This is good news and challenging news. We also live in a day of instant communication through the Internet. Not every report is truly true. So we must ask hard questions: What does it mean to be the church? What kind of gospel have we exported and communicated around the world?

We rightfully must be wary of the "Christian numbers game," such as this statement which I recently read in a fund-raising letter: "More than 100,000 people a day are choosing to follow Christ in Asia, Africa, Latin America, East Europe, and the former Soviet Union." Where does this number come from? How do we acquire and believe rounded-off figures? Is the truth being told, or are we being sold a successful package of guaranteed religious projects and programs? More significantly, have we assumed that God promises that a majority of the world's population will be found in the church?

Even as we celebrate the growth of the Christian faith, we also witness the revival and expansion of a well-funded and intensely expansionist Islam, the new missionary vision of Buddhism and Hinduism, as well as the plethora of smaller evangelistic religious groups. The New Age networks have spread throughout the world, offering an especially appealing religious soup that allows one to be both spiritual and materialistic at the same time. These religious alternatives have joined the forces of anti-Christian secularism, modernity, and post-modernity to challenge Christians today as never before. It is the best of times and the worst of times for the church. And this is the arena into which the Spirit invites Evangelical reflective practitioners to serve, suffer, and die.

While some of the opposition is subtle and non-violent, we have documented the growing wave of persecution against Christians. Significantly, the theme of suffering and martyrdom emerged many times during the Iguassu Consultation. Ajith Fernando's expositions, plus reports from specific geographies—the Middle East, India, and other areas—were a sobering reminder of the suffering church.

Ironically—and sadly—we know that some of the persecution of Christians is precipitated by Christians using language and missions metaphors that rely heavily on military terminology: target, conquer, army, crusade, mobilize, beachhead, advance, enemy, battle, spiritual warfare, capture the city for Christ. Thankfully, the movement to eliminate inappropriate language is growing, but much damage has been done (see Mission Leaders, 2000).

How Might One Read This Book With Profit?

This book emerges primarily from the Iguassu Consultation, where the majority of the chapters were presented there in some form. Of the 41 writers, all but three were with us in Iguassu. Another 13 chapters were commissioned afterward to fill in missing themes. Three of the major papers, the two by Samuel Escobar and the one by Chris Wright, had been circulated by e-mail for the participants to read prior to our gathering.

How might a person work through this compendium? Some courageous ones might want to read from start to finish. Congratulations if you do so!

Here are some other possible approaches:

First, review the table of contents to get a sense of the overall flow of categories and topics. Note the structure of the book and its major categories:

- Establishing the global arena
- Setting the macro context and raising major issues
- Grounding trinitarian missiological reflections in Scripture
- Addressing issues of globalized Evangelical missiology
- Responding to major challenges
- Listening to mission that rises from community and spirituality
- Engaging the commitments flowing from the Iguassu Affirmation
- Concluding with final challenges

Second, read and evaluate the Iguassu Affirmation (chapter 2), for much of the book will echo these themes. This missiological statement summarizes the issues of the Iguassu Consultation. But keep in mind that not all of your concerns will emerge in this short document.

Third, remember that this book reflects a globalized missiology. Represented here are many voices speaking from within orthodox Christianity and the authority of Scripture, rooted in history and committed to serious contextualization of the gospel and church.

Fourth, trace some of the key themes of personal interest through the index. For example, note the references to trinitarian missiology.

Fifth, don't get sidetracked with things with which you disagree. Examine everything and attempt to read through the eyes of the writer. If what is said about managerial missiology irritates you, don't worry; you are not alone. At the same time, listen to the challenge, for it comes from your colleagues and friends. If you are concerned about what "should" have been said, fine. At the same time, listen to the godly and creative voices that may offer a healing critique to mission that flows from the worldview of modernity and is too dependent upon marketing techniques. Ask the Holy Spirit to allow you to listen and learn, even when you disagree.

Sixth, keep in mind the diversity of the writers: ethnicity, gender, age, perspective, formal education, experiences in life and ministry, and style of writing. Almost half of the writers would not consider English their first language, and for many of them this was their first venture into print.

Finally, read away! Stretch your mind, your heart, and your theological and missiological categories. Read together and perhaps out loud with a group of reflective practitioners, whether younger or older, students or those experienced in ministry. In a spirit of receptivity, ask the Triune God what he has to teach you through this publication.

Metaphors That Draw to a Close This Invitation to Read

The Iguassu Missiological Consultation and this book remind me of my first trip to Singapore and a late-night visit to that city-nation's Newton Circus hawkers center—the open-air culinary feast at the intersection of Scott's, Bukit Timah, and Newton Roads. Surrounded by a dizzying array of food booths, we were invited to savor the unusual diversity of foods, textures, tastes (and after-tastes)—Chinese, Malay, Indian, and all of Southeast Asia. In a similar way, Iguassu and this book offer a feast of the globalized body of Christ. This book also allows participants and readers to share in the multifaceted exchange and contribution to the mission of the church that took place as we sat together around the table as equal partners in mission.

Likewise, Iguassu and this book offer us the gift of a tapestry, multi-colored and multi-textured, but all part of the same weaving. From below, the pattern may be confusing; but from above, one discerns the rich integration and harmony of the tapestry. What's more, there are key colors, fabrics, and designs. This book is complex and challenging. However, the key

elements reveal that all of the writers had a commitment to think Christianly about their world and the diverse challenges before us. The publication uniquely contributes to the robust Evangelical missiology we need for the future.

Finally, this book is like a prism refracting light. The resultant colors depend on the angle, but all come from a single beam of light focused on the prism. In a similar way, light emanating from God's full revelation is refracted through the prism of the magnificent diversity of culture, language, gender, and ministry of the writers of this book. All of the authors share a deep commitment to the authority of Scripture, and all are deeply involved in ministry, most of them in cross-cultural service. The result is a singular sample of Evangelical and global missiological reflection.

I close with the powerful prayer that has come to us from the heart of Jim Engel (Engel & Dyrness, 2000, pp. 24–25).

A Prayer for Renewal and Restoration

Heavenly Father,
our Lord and giver of life,
forgive us for the extent to which
we have naively succumbed
to the spirit of the age,
for our preoccupation with
false measures of success,
for a sense of triumphalism
which replaces
humble dependence on you,
and for our blindness in avoiding
those parts of your Word
which do not fit neatly
into our theology.
We humbly confess our total
dependence on you
as the Lord of life.
Let us see a lost world afresh
through your eyes
and give us discernment

through your Spirit.
Share with us your priorities
and give us the courage to be
responsible stewards
of our obligation
to take the whole gospel
to the whole world.
Speak, Lord, for your servants
are listening.
To you we give all glory,
honor, and praise.
Amen.

So to our colleagues, sisters and brothers in the global task, may the blessing and empowering presence of the Sacred Three be upon you all.

References

Engel, J. F., & Dyrness, W. A. (2000). *Changing the mind of missions: Where have we gone wrong?* Downers Grove, IL: InterVarsity Press.

Mission leaders urge end to "fighting" words. (2000, August 4). *World Pulse*, pp. 6-7. Report and formal statement from the Consultation on Mission Language and Metaphors held at the School of World Mission, Fuller Theological Seminary, Pasadena, California, June 1-3, 2000.

Neill, S. (1986). *A history of Christian missions*. New York: Penguin Books.

Nouwen, H. J. M. (1989). *In the name of Jesus: Reflections on Christian leadership*. New York: Crossroad.

***William D. Taylor** is Executive Director of the WEF Missions Commission and has coordinated the ministries of the MC since 1986. He was born in Costa Rica of missionary parents and has lived in Latin America for 30 years, 17 of them with his family as a long-term missionary with CAM International, serving on the faculty of the Central American Theological Seminary. Married to Yvonne, a native Texan, he has three adult children who were born in Guatemala. He has edited **Internationalizing Missionary Training** (1991), **Kingdom Partnerships for Synergy in Missions** (1994), and **Too Valuable to Lose: Exploring the Causes and Cures of Missionary Attrition** (1997). He co-authored with Emilio Antonio Nuñez, **Crisis and Hope in Latin America** (1996), and with Steve Hoke, **Send Me! Your Journey to the Nations** (1999). He also serves as visiting faculty at seminaries in various countries.*

The Iguassu Affirmation

FROM IGUASSU, BRAZIL, to the missions movement around the world, October 17, 1999:

The WEF Missions Commission has just concluded the historic Iguassu Missiological Consultation in the city of Foz do Iguassu, Brazil, October 10-15. With gratitude to God, the Missions Commission leadership commends a crucial outcome of this singular week to the mission movement around the world, in particular the missions networks.

We are profoundly thankful to our Lord for those who in recent decades have sustained the passion for world evangelization. There are many women and men, organizations and movements which have done all in their power to focus our attention on the unfinished task, to understand the vast unreached world of peoples and cities, and to underscore the vital necessity of obedience to Christ's final charge to the apostles. For this we are grateful, and we are indebted to them. We are also grateful to God for the growing body of women and men who are seriously reflecting on just what it means to do biblical missiology in this complex world. Just as the epicenter of the global church has shifted from the North to the South, in the same way the epicenter of creating and doing theology and missiology is changing. We rejoice in the former shift and realize that the second one invites us to greater missiological partnership. The Triune God has many "centers" from which to work now.

As we face the unique turn of a century/millennium, the 160 participants at the Iguassu Missiological Consultation have also sensed the need for a serious analysis of the challenges we face in a radically changing world—in the sociological, cultural, philosophical, economic, and spiritual arenas. We came together to contribute to the development and application of a biblical missiology which represents with authenticity the national and cultural diversity of God's people in mission. And then we came together to affirm the foundational commitments we make as mission practitioners, missiologists, and church leaders. We also worshiped and prayed together all through the week.

With this backdrop, we present to you the Iguassu Affirmation, a statement of context, declaration, and commitment as we look to the Spirit's empowering presence in our mission task, regardless of geography, culture, or ministry.

The Iguassu Affirmation emerged from the process of the week in Brazil. A "Team of Seven" was given an initial draft (based on the plenary papers already in distribution) for discussion, and then they went to work. The 160 participants were able to study three drafts of the document, giving scores of serious recommendations to the team. Friday the 15th found us meeting for a three-hour session to finalize changes and emerge with a strong consensus of the direction of the Lord on the Affirmation.

The Iguassu Affirmation is to be received as a working document to stimulate serious discussion around the world. We desire that it will become a point of dialogue that will help shape both missiology and strategy into the next century/millennium. The first phase of our work took place in Brazil, the second phase followed the consultation, and now the third phase begins—the release of this major book. We pray that this process—international and contextualized—will facilitate the flow of the Iguassu Affirmation down into our regional/national networks and organizations, and into the grassroots life of the churches.

This local, regional/national, and organizational contextualization invites discus-

sion, modification, and adaptation of the document for the diverse realities we live in mission. The invitation is to the global missions community, and that can also include mission societies, as well as theological and missiological training institutions. We will focus on Evangelicals whose roots are linked to the churches and whose members share our deep passion for serious world evangelism.

We invite each participating network and organization to communicate to us your discussion of this document. We release the Affirmation to you for translation into any language, and we ask that you send us a copy for our own records, verification, and information.

Respectfully submitted,
The Team of Seven and the
WEF Missions Commission
Executive Commission

The Affirmation team:
David Tai-Woong Lee (Korea), co-leader
Jim Stamoolis (USA), co-leader
Rose Dowsett (Scotland)
Abel Ndjerareou (Chad)
David Neff (USA)
Kang San Tan (Malaysia)
Tonica van der Meer (Brazil)

The Iguassu Affirmation

Preamble

We have convened as 160 mission practitioners, missiologists, and church leaders from 53 countries, under the World Evangelical Fellowship Missions Commission in Foz do Iguassu, Brazil, on October 10-15, 1999 to:

1. Reflect together on the challenges and opportunities facing world missions at the dawn of the new millennium.

2. Review the different streams of 20th century Evangelical missiology and practice, especially since the 1974 Lausanne Congress.

3. Continue developing and applying a relevant biblical missiology which reflects the cultural diversity of God's people.

We proclaim the living Christ in a world torn by ethnic conflicts, massive economic disparity, natural disasters, and ecological crises. The mission task is both assisted and hindered by technological developments that now reach the remotest corners of the earth. The diverse religious aspirations of people, expressed in multiple religions and spiritual experimentation, challenge the ultimate truth of the gospel.

In the 20th century, missiology witnessed unprecedented development. In recent years, reflection from many parts of the church has helped missions to continue shedding paternalistic tendencies. Today, we continue to explore the relationship between the gospel and culture, between evangelism and social responsibility, and between biblical mandates and the social sciences. We see some international organizations—among them World Evangelical Fellowship, the Lausanne Committee for World Evangelization, and the AD 2000 and Beyond Movement—that have begun a promising process of partnership and unity.

Increased efforts at partnership have been catalyzed by an emphasis on methodologies involving measurable goals and numerical growth. Flowing from a commitment to urgent evangelization, these methodologies have shown how our task might be accomplished. However, these insights must be subject to biblical principles and growth in Christlikeness.

We rejoice in diverse missiological voices emerging around the world, but we confess that we have not taken them all into our theory and practice. Old paradigms still prevail. Participation by and awareness of the global church, as well as

mission from people of all nations to people of all nations, are needed for a valid missiology in our time.

Our discussions have invited us to fuller dependence on the Spirit's empowering presence in our life and ministry as we eagerly await the glorious return of our Lord Jesus Christ.

In the light of these realities, we make the following declarations:

Declarations

Our faith rests on the absolute authority of the God-breathed Scriptures. We are heirs of the great Christian confessions handed down to us. All three Persons of the Godhead are active in God's redeeming mission. Our missiology centers on the overarching biblical theme of God's creation of the world, the Father's redeeming love for fallen humanity as revealed in the incarnation, substitutionary death, and resurrection of our Lord Jesus Christ, and ultimately of the redemption and renewal of the whole creation. The Holy Spirit, promised by our Lord, is our comforter, teacher, and source of power. It is the Spirit who calls us into holiness and integrity. The Spirit leads the church into all truth. The Spirit is the agent of mission, convicting of sin, righteousness, and judgment. We are Christ's servants, empowered and led by the Spirit, whose goal is to glorify God.

We confess the following themes as truths of special importance in this present age. These themes are clearly attested to in the whole of the Scriptures and speak to the desire of God to provide salvation for all people.

1. *Jesus Christ is Lord of the church and Lord of the universe.*

Ultimately every knee will bow and every tongue confess that Jesus is Lord. The Lordship of Christ is to be proclaimed to the whole world, inviting all to be free from bondage to sin and the dominion of evil in order to serve the Lord for his glory.

2. *The Lord Jesus Christ is the unique revelation of God and the only Savior of the world.*

Salvation is found in Christ alone. God witnesses to himself in creation and in human conscience, but these witnesses are not complete without the revelation of God in Christ. In the face of competing truth claims, we proclaim with humility that Christ is the only Savior, conscious that sin as well as cultural hindrances often mask him from those for whom he died.

3. *The good news of the salvation made possible by the work of Jesus Christ must be expressed in all the languages and cultures of the world.*

We are commanded to be heralds of the gospel to every creature so that they can have the opportunity to confess faith in Christ. The message must come to them in a language they can understand and in a form that is appropriate to their circumstances. Believers, led by the Holy Spirit, are encouraged to create culturally appropriate forms of worship and uncover biblical insights that glorify God for the benefit of the whole church.

4. *The gospel is good news and addresses all human needs.*

We emphasize the holistic nature of the gospel of Jesus Christ. Both the Old Testament and the New Testament demonstrate God's concern with the whole person in the whole of society. We acknowledge that material blessings come from God, but prosperity should not be equated with godliness.

5. *Opposition to the spread of the gospel is foremost a spiritual conflict involving human sin and principalities and powers opposed to the Living God.*

This conflict is manifested in different ways, e.g., fear of spirits or indifference to God. We recognize that the defense of the truth of the gospel is also spiritual warfare. As witnesses of the gospel, we announce that Jesus Christ has power over all powers and is able to free all who turn to him in faith. We affirm that in the cross, God has won the victory.

6. *Suffering, persecution, and martyrdom are present realities for many Christians.*

We acknowledge that our obedience in mission involves suffering and recognize that the church is experiencing this. We affirm our privilege and responsibility to pray for those undergoing persecution. We are called to share in their pain, do what we can to relieve their sufferings, and work for human rights and religious freedom.

7. *Economic and political systems deeply affect the spread of God's kingdom.*

Human government is appointed by God, but all human institutions act out of fallenness. The Scriptures command that Christians pray for those in authority and work for truth and justice. Appropriate Christian response to political and economic systems requires the guidance of the Holy Spirit.

8. *God works in a variety of Christian traditions and organizations, for his glory and the salvation of the world.*

For too long believers, divided over issues of church organization, order, and doctrine—such as the gifts and ministry of the Holy Spirit—have failed to recognize each other's work. We affirm, bless, and pray for authentic Christian witness wherever it is found.

9. *To be effective witnesses of the Holy God, we need to demonstrate personal and corporate holiness, love, and righteousness.*

We repent of hypocrisy and conformity to the world, and we call the church to a renewed commitment to holy living. Holiness requires turning from sin, training in righteousness, and growing in Christlikeness.

Commitments

We commit ourselves to continue and deepen our reflection on the following themes, helping one another to enrich our understanding and practice with insight from every corner of the world. Our hearts' desire is the discipling of the nations through the effective, faithful communication of Christ to every culture and people.

1. *Trinitarian foundation of mission*

We commit ourselves to a renewed emphasis on God-centered missiology. This invites a new study of the operation of the Trinity in the redemption of the human race and the whole of creation, as well as to understand the particular roles of Father, Son, and Spirit in mission to this fallen world.

2. *Biblical and theological reflection*

We confess that our biblical and theological reflection has sometimes been shallow and inadequate. We also confess that we have frequently been selective in our use of texts rather than being faithful to the whole biblical revelation. We commit ourselves to engage in renewed biblical and theological studies shaped by mission, and to pursue a missiology and practice

shaped by God's Word, brought to life and light by the Holy Spirit.

3. *Church and mission*

The church in mission is central to God's plan for the world. We commit ourselves to strengthen our ecclesiology in mission, and to encourage the global church to become a truly missionary community in which all Christians are involved in mission. In the face of increasing resistance and opposition from political powers, religious fundamentalism, and secularism, we commit ourselves to encourage and challenge the churches to respond with a deeper level of unity and participation in mission.

4. *Gospel and culture*

The gospel is always presented and received within a cultural context. It is therefore essential to clarify the relationship between gospel and culture, both in theory and practice, recognizing that there is both good and evil in all cultures. We commit ourselves to continue to demonstrate the relevance of the Christian message to all cultures, and ensure that missionaries learn to wrestle biblically with the relationship between gospel and culture. We commit ourselves to serious study of how different cultural perspectives may enrich our understanding of the gospel, as well as how all worldviews have to be critiqued and transformed by it.

5. *Pluralism*

Religious pluralism challenges us to hold firmly to the uniqueness of Jesus Christ as Savior even as we work for increased tolerance and understanding among religious communities. We cannot seek harmony by relativizing the truth claims of religions. Urbanization and radical political change have bred increased interreligious and ethnic violence and hostility. We commit ourselves to be agents of reconciliation. We also commit ourselves to proclaim the gospel of Jesus Christ in faithfulness and loving humility.

6. *Spiritual conflict*

We welcome the renewed attention given in recent decades to the biblical theme of spiritual conflict. We rejoice that power and authority are not ours but God's. At the same time, we must ensure that the interest in spiritual warfare does not become a substitute for dealing with the root issues of sin, salvation, conversion, and the battle for the truth. We commit ourselves to increase our biblical understanding and practice of spiritual conflict while guarding against syncretistic and unbiblical elements.

7. *Strategy in mission*

We are grateful for many helpful insights gained from the social sciences. We are concerned that these should be subject to the authority of Scripture. Therefore, we call for a healthy critique of mission theories that depend heavily on marketing concepts and missiology by objectives.

8. *Globalized missiology*

The insights of every part of the church are needed, and challenges encountered in every land must be addressed. Only thus can our missiology develop the richness and texture reflected in the Scriptures and needed for full obedience to our risen Lord. We commit ourselves to give voice to all segments of the global church in developing and implementing our missiology.

9. *Godly character*

Biblical holiness is essential for credible Christian witness. We commit ourselves to renewed emphasis on godly living and servanthood, and we urge training institutions, both missionary and ministerial, to include substantive biblical and practical training in Christian character formation.

10. *The cross and suffering*

As our Lord called us to take up our crosses, we remind the church of our Lord's teaching that suffering is a part of authentic Christian life. In an increasingly violent and unjust world with political and economic oppression, we commit to equip ourselves and others to suffer in missionary service and to serve the suffering church. We pursue to articulate a biblical theology of martyrdom.

11. *Christian responsibility and the world economic order*

In a world increasingly controlled by global economic forces, Christians need to be aware of the corrosive effects of affluence and the destructive effects of poverty. We must be aware of ethnocentrism in our view of economic forces. We commit ourselves to address the realities of world poverty and oppose policies that serve the powerful rather than the powerless. It is the responsibility of the church in each place to affirm the meaning and value of a people, especially where indigenous cultures face extinction. We call all Christians to commit themselves to reflect God's concern for justice and the welfare of all peoples.

12. *Christian responsibility and the ecological crisis*

The earth is the Lord's, and the gospel is good news for all creation. Christians share in the responsibility God gave to all humanity to care for the earth. We call on all Christians to commit themselves to ecological integrity in practicing responsible stewardship of creation, and we encourage Christians in environmental care and protection initiatives.

13. *Partnership*

As citizens of the kingdom of God and members of Christ's body, we commit ourselves to renewed efforts at cooperation, because it is our Lord's desire that we be one and that we work in harmony in his service so that the world will believe. We acknowledge that our attempts have not always been as equals. Inadequate theology, especially in respect to the doctrine of the church, and the imbalance of resources have made working together difficult. We pledge to find ways to address this imbalance and to demonstrate to the world that believers in Christ are truly one in their service of Christ.

14. *Member care*

Service of the Lord in cross-cultural environments exposes missionaries to many stresses and criticisms. While acknowledging that missionaries also share the limitations of our common humanity and have made errors, we affirm that they deserve love, respect, and gratitude. Too often, agencies, churches, and fellow Christians have not followed biblical guidelines in dealing with cross-cultural workers. We commit ourselves to support and nurture our missionary workers for their sakes and for the gospel witness.

Pledge

We, the participants of the Iguassu Missiological Consultation, declare our passion as mission practitioners, missiologists, and church leaders for the urgent evangelization of the whole world and the discipling of the nations to the glory of the Father, the Son, and the Holy Spirit.

In all our commitments, we depend on the Lord who empowers us by the Holy Spirit to fulfill his mission. As Evangelicals, we pledge to sustain our biblical heritage in this ever-changing world. We commit ourselves to participate actively in formulating and practicing Evangelical missiology. Indwelt by the Spirit, we purpose to carry the radical good news of the kingdom of God to all the world. We affirm our commitment to love one another and to pray for one another as we struggle to do his will.

We rejoice in the privilege of being part of God's mission in proclaiming the gospel of reconciliation and hope. We joyfully look to the Lord's return and passionately yearn to see the realization of the eschatological vision when people from every nation, tribe, and language shall worship the Lamb.

To this end may the Father, the Son, and the Holy Spirit be glorified. Hallelujah! Amen.

Part 2

Establishing the macro context of the major issues

THIS MEATY SECTION requires careful study. Escobar's two papers and Wright's one were circulated via e-mail prior to Iguassu, enabling participants to start reflection as they prepared for the event, and also provide feedback to the writers prior to the Consultation.

Escobar's double challenge was to read both the global scenario as well as current Evangelical missiology. Due to his absence, Bonk and Steuernagel were drafted at a late date to engage thought-provoking challenges. Hiebert's presentation was directed at the delicate yet crucial issue of spiritual warfare and worldview. In this section, four writers who were present at Iguassu—Araujo, Lee, van der Meer, and Roxburgh—were asked later to write chapters that addressed crucial issues.

Araujo presents a well-researched discussion of the controversial issues swirling around globalization. Even as I write these words from Malaysia, news from Melbourne, Australia, reports the organized protests against the World Economic Forum Asia/Pacific Economic Summit—sequels to the violent protests in Seattle in late 1999 and Washington, D.C. in early 2000. But globalization must be evaluated from a Christian perspective, for we cannot accept uncritically the

dictums of the dominant global financial institutions. How should thoughtful Christians respond to the journalist who declares, "That the world is moving towards globalization is as inevitable as the sun rises each morning"?

Wright presented a masterful exposition of the pluralisms before us—hermeneutical (Scripture), religious (Jesus), and ethical (humanity). His consultation draft had a "pregnant" footnote on the subject of eternal destinies, which fostered discussion and controversy in small groups and hallways. Due to the complexity of this subtopic, Wright's final chapter does not explore the options that godly Evangelicals have taken on this theme, and it remains a future agenda item.

One element of Escobar's second paper critiqued "managerial missiology," and this generated another wave of discussions. In light of these issues, Lee was asked to write his own evaluation of contemporary Evangelical missiology, offering another perspective from the Two-Thirds World.

Van der Meer focused on the church and its mission, and Roxburgh offered another perspective on the vital subject of trinitarian missiology.

Iguassu reminded us that we live in a complex world. Some of our colleagues serve in the context of three overlapping worldviews: pre-modernity, modernity, and post-modernity. While some participants at Iguassu felt that too much emphasis was given to post-modernity, the fact is that this worldview has traveled at warp speed through the world— through modern media, the Internet, the arts world, and globalizing economies. While around the world the transition from pre-modernity to modernity to post-modernity is patchy, nevertheless it is taking place, whether we realize it or want it.

The global scenario at the turn of the century

SAMUEL **E**SCOBAR

THE END OF A CENTURY and the beginning of a new one, which in this case is also the beginning of a new millennium, lend themselves not only to an inventory of opportunities and resources, but also to a balance of where things stand at the point at which we have arrived. As I try to sketch an outline of the way ahead for Christian mission, I am aware that as a Christian in 1999, I have a way of looking at reality grounded in the memory and the experience of my own Christian generation: I stand on ground that represents the sacrificial work of many missionary generations that have preceded us.

The balance of that missionary work has been positive, in spite of the paradoxes of this century. Unbelievable scientific and technological prowess has gone hand in hand with the regression to refined forms of cruelty and barbarism in totalitarian revolutions and wars. Rapid and efficient communication that has turned the planet into a global village has gone hand in hand with intolerance and tribalism that hinder the pacific coexistence of peoples that have been neighbors for centuries. In a relentless movement of urbanization, the cities with their accumulation of intellectual sophistication, wealth, and educational and medical services have attracted masses; but the same greed, injustice, and abuse that were the marks of feudal structures in the rural world have turned the hearts of these cities into a jungle of concrete and asphalt, where humans live in alienation and despair. However, in the midst of these processes that reflect so well the fallenness of human beings, Christian mission has advanced in this century, and the balance is positive for the cause of God's kingdom. I feel it is only appropriate that I try to express some convictions that come from the reflection about this positive balance of the century that is coming to an end. These are some notes of what is involved in the way I look at the world from a missionary stance. These are the notes from what I might call an Evangelical outlook on mission from a Latin American missiologist.

A Translatable Gospel

I start with doxology, with thanksgiving to God for the mystery and the glory of the gospel. The missionary facts of our time make me pause in wonder. Jesus Christ, Son incarnate of God, is the core of the gospel that as a potent seed has flourished in a thousand different plants. We can name a place and a time on earth in which Jesus lived and taught. In other words, we can place him in a particular culture at a particular moment in history. "The Word became flesh and lived for a while among us" in Palestine during the first century of our era. After that, the story of Jesus has moved from culture to culture, from nation to nation, from people to people. And something strange and paradoxical has taken place. Though this Jesus was a peasant from Palestine, everywhere he has been received, loved, and adored, and people in hundreds of cultures and languages have come to see the glory of God in the face of Jesus Christ. Moreover, they have come to feel that he is "theirs," so that they say, "Jesus is one of ours." At this end of the century, the global church stands closer than ever to that vision of the seer in Revelation: "A great multitude that no one could count, from every nation, tribe, people, and language, standing before the throne and in front of the Lamb" (Rev. 7:9).

I cannot but wonder in amazement at the fact that the message of Jesus Christ is "translatable." This means that the gospel dignifies every culture as a valid and acceptable vehicle for God's revelation. Conversely, this also relativizes every culture; there is no "sacred" culture or language that may be considered as the only vehicle that God might use. Not even Hebrew or Aramaic is "sacred," because the original documents of the gospel that we possess are already a translation from those languages to that form of popular Greek that was the *lingua franca* of the first century, the *koiné*.[1] Thus it is clear that the God who revealed himself in Jesus Christ intended his revelation to reach all of humankind, as Jesus stated it so clearly in the Great Commission, and Paul expressed it in sweeping statements: "... God our Savior, who wants all men to be saved and to come to a knowledge of the truth" (1 Tim. 2:3-4).

My Evangelical outlook starts with commitment to the authority of God's Word, and in the contemporary situation I have become aware that understanding of God's Word requires cultural awareness. The new global dimension of Christianity has brought this new sensitivity to the fact that the text of Scripture can only be understood adequately within its own context, and that the understanding and application of its eternal message demand awareness of our own cultural context. From a global Evangelical dialogue about this issue after Lausanne came this illuminating statement: "Today's readers cannot come to the text in a personal vacuum and should not try to. Instead they should come with an awareness of concerns stemming from their cultural background, personal situation, and responsibility to others. These concerns will influence the questions which are put to the Scriptures. What is received back, however, will not

---

[1] For a fascinating development of the theological consequences of these facts, see Walls (1996) and Sanneh (1989).

be answers only, but more questions. As we address Scripture, Scripture addresses us. We find that our culturally conditioned presuppositions are being challenged and our questions corrected. In fact, we are compelled to reformulate our previous questions and to ask fresh ones. So the living interaction proceeds" (Willowbank Report, 1996, p. 84).

An adequate training provides the Bible scholar with a working knowledge of the cultural world of the Middle East and the Mediterranean basin during the time span covered by the Old and New Testaments. It also must provide a high degree of cultural awareness to the evangelist or teacher in the church, who must move meaningfully from the questions of our post-modern culture to the answers that the gospel has for them.

A Global Church

Work in WEF activities and in several of the Evangelical organizations related to it that provide its capable international leadership have made me aware of the reality of a global church. At this end of a century, facilities for travel, the flow of information at a global scale through the media, as well as colossal migration movements caused by economic change allow Christians and churches in the West and everywhere else to see and experience the amazingly rich and diverse varieties of expression of the Christian faith. I have met with amazement wandering prophets of independent African churches, native storytellers from Latin American Pentecostal Movements, tireless missionary entrepreneurs spreading through the world from their Korean homeland, Orthodox priests regaining political weight in the lands which used to be part of the Soviet Empire. Their images fill the pages of our missionary books and the screens of our VCRs. They are also a living testimony to

the remarkable variety of human cultures and the uniqueness of the gospel of Jesus Christ, which is the one seed of a thousand different plants.

Migration patterns and refugee movements have also brought the great variety of cultures from this planet, as well as the different forms that the Christian church has taken among them to Europe, the United States, and Canada. At the heart of European and North American cities, there are now growing pockets of Third World cultures, as well as varied expressions of the global church. From the missionary perspective, indigenous churches from faraway places have become sister churches down the street, and growing Muslim communities have become a new evangelistic challenge that put to the test the quality of our Christian lives, as well as our ability to communicate the gospel. In the case of the United States, while at the beginning of this century many churches and denominations were committed to the task of "Americanizing" the immigrants, today the same churches have to grapple with multiculturalism.

This phenomenon also has a consequence for Christians in these Western nations, because the form of Christianity that has grown more in the Southern hemisphere and has come now to the great Western cities could be described as a "popular" form of both Catholicism and Protestantism that we might well call "grassroots Christianity." It is marked by the culture of poverty: an oral liturgy, narrative preaching, uninhibited emotionalism, maximum participation in prayer and worship, dreams and visions, faith healing, and an intense search for community and belonging. Sensitivity to this form of Christianity is especially necessary for Evangelical leaders who have always emphasized the clear and correct intellectual expression of Christian truth and the rationality of the Christian faith.

A New Balance of Christian Presence

Through the reality of the global church, we have also become aware of the new balance of numerical and spiritual strength in the Christian world.[2] As we look at the religious map of the world today, we find a marked contrast between the situation at the beginning of this century and the present situation. Scottish missiologist Andrew Walls has described it as a "massive southward shift of the center of gravity of the Christian world." He understands the history of Christian mission—and of the church, in fact—as a sequence of phases, each one of which represents the embodiment of Christianity in a major culture area, and the movement forward through transcultural mission in such a way that when that major culture declines, Christianity continues to flourish, now in a different setting. In our times, Walls (1996, p. 22) reminds us, "... the recession of Christianity among the European peoples appears to be continuing. And yet we seem to stand at the threshold of a new age of Christianity, one in which its main base will be in the Southern continents, and where its dominant expressions will be filtered through the culture of those countries. Once again, Christianity has been saved for the world by its diffusion across cultural lines."

The new situation has been hailed by a Swiss missiologist who was a missionary in Africa as "the coming of the Third Church" (Bühlmann, 1986, p. 6). He points to the fact that the first thousand years of church history were under the aegis of the Eastern Church in the eastern half of the Roman Empire, and the second millennium the leading church was the Western Church in the other half.

Those familiar with the history of theology also perceive to what degree theological themes, language, and categories reflected this historical situation. Bühlmann (1986, p. 6) goes on to say, "Now the Third Millennium will evidently stand under the leadership of the Third Church, the Southern Church. I am convinced that the most important drives and inspirations for the whole church in the future will come from the Third Church."

Drive and inspiration to move forward and take the gospel of Jesus Christ to the ends of the earth, crossing all kinds of geographical or cultural barriers, are the work of the Holy Spirit. There is an element of mystery when the dynamism of mission does not come from above, from the expansive power of a superior civilization, but from below, from the little ones, those that do not have abundance of material, financial, or technical resources, but are open to the prompting of the Spirit. It may not be entirely coincidental that the form of Christianity that has grown more during this century, especially among the poor urban masses, is that which emphasizes the presence and power of the Holy Spirit. It was by 1912 that Roland Allen first coined the expression "the spontaneous expansion of the church," and in this year 1999 we can measure the incredible extent to which a Christian testimony among the masses of this planet has been the result of such spontaneous expansion, especially in China, Africa, and Latin America. In many cases, such expansion was only possible when indigenous Christians became free from the stifling control of foreign missionary agencies.

Another aspect of this reality is that while many non-Western cultures are very receptive to the gospel of Jesus Christ,

---

[2] Helpful data on which many statements of this paper are based can be found in Myers (1996).

paradoxically it is within the Western culture that we find less receptivity to it. Lesslie Newbigin (1986, p. 3), who was a missionary in India for 30 years and later on went back to minister among working class people in England, wrote, "The most widespread, powerful, and persuasive among contemporary cultures ... modern Western culture ... more than almost any other is proving resistant to the gospel." Patterns of church growth prove the validity of this observation in the case of North America and Europe today. Several of the old mainline denominations show decline and fatigue with significant numerical losses. We could well ask the question if here we are confronted with the resistance of Western culture or with the impotence of the Western churches. In many cases, ethnic churches of the same denominations are growing vigorously. This constitutes a tough challenge for partnership in mission.

Precisely at the point in which the influence of Christianity declines in the West, which turns into a hard mission field because its culture resists the gospel, the new global order has brought the so-called Third World into the heart of North America, Europe, and Japan. Within that environment, Christians from old and new churches are called to new partnerships. For the old traditional denominations, partnership with the new immigrant churches will bring the need for serious self-appraisal. This is not easy for respectable, middle class, Evangelical churches that have a more steady, institutionalized, well-mannered, predictable kind of church. "Mission at our doorstep" is the new training ground for the new partnerships that will also carry on mission around the world. Such partnerships will have as an aim the proposal advanced by the Lausanne Covenant: "Missionaries should flow ever more freely from and to all six continents in a spirit of humble service" (LC, par. 9).

These are some of the missionary realities of today, which allow us to believe that the balance of mission in this century has been positive. It has been the result of God's initiative revealed in his Word, and human obedience that responded to that Word. They are the ground from which we peer into the future in an effort to figure out the special challenges to missionary obedience in the coming century.

Globalization and Contextualization

Empires have always been the sociohistorical frame for the development of Christian mission, as the Pax Romana was in the first century, the Pax Hispanica in the 16th, or the Pax Britannica in the 19th. Since 1955,[3] the way in which we used to look at the world was influenced by the idea of three worlds: the Western capitalist world, the socialist world, and the emerging "Third World" of new nations. In many ways, this perspective affected missionary concepts and practices. Well into the 1980s, U.S. President Ronald Reagan referred to the Soviet Union as "the evil empire." With the collapse of the Soviet empire, bipolar thinking has become obsolete, and there is only one world power with several poles connected to it.

There is a growing awareness that the most recent form of capitalism is now embracing all nations in the planet through a sophisticated system of communication that takes the latest aspects of Western culture as merchandise to the most remote corners of the world. "It is every day more and more evident," said Jacques Attali (1991, pp. 8-9), "that the

---

[3] That year during the Bandung conference of "non-aligned" nations, a French journalist coined the expression "Third World."

central organizing principle of the future, whatever happens at the margins, will be economic. This will become increasingly apparent as we approach the year 2000. The rule of military might that characterized the Cold War is being replaced by the reign of the market." Like an irresistible wave, the market is the main force behind this process of globalization. The market is even giving a new language to the way some Christians in the North speak about the church: "marketing your church." Howard Snyder (1995, p. 46) has very aptly summarized this trend: "Global integration and networking are now the driving force in business and economics. The world is becoming one vast marketplace, not a patchwork of local markets. Economic integration on a world scale is reshaping society in a process that will reach well into the 21st century." A key question to be asked is, Should Christian mission simply ride on the crest of this wave?

Missiologists who have reflected about this globalization process point to its ambiguities. Schreiter (1997, p. 9), for instance, analyzes the modern values of "innovation, efficiency, and technical rationality" that drive the global systems. But he states that though innovation connotes improvement, "without a clear goal [it] becomes change for its own sake, or change to create new markets or to stimulate desire." Think for a moment on how this kind of innovation may create havoc for missionary organizations that make computer technologies indispensable for their task. In the same way, "Efficiency can mean less drudgery; but efficiency without effectiveness can become narrow and abstract, even deadly. Technical rationality has the advantage of providing clear purpose and procedure, but it can become profoundly dehumanizing" (Schreiter, 1997, p. 9). I have observed this in missionary life: ideological pressure to make

numerical growth the only standard of correct missionary practice is destroying the ability of churches to develop pastoral responses to sweeping cultural transformations. My attention has also been called to another fact. Instant global communication through the Internet provides sometimes a selfish way of escape to a fictitious "global village," for missionaries who refuse to work in the difficult task of contributing to build up fellowship with those that live around them day after day.

If we trace back the globalization movement, we may connect it with the expansion of Europe that took place after Columbus came to the American continent in 1492. It accelerated in the 19th century, and in both cases Christian missionary work accompanied it. In the 16th century, Iberian Catholic mission transported to the Americas, some parts of Africa, and the Philippines the feudal medieval social and economic order that was disappearing in Europe. Two centuries later, on the wake of British imperialism and U.S. "manifest destiny" advance, Protestant missions had a modernizing component by their insistence on Bible translation, literacy, leadership training for the laity, and also by their use of modern medicine and the communication of basic technology. Aspects of globalization such as efficient communication at a global level or facilities for exchange within an increasingly connected economic system could be neutral factors from which Christian mission may benefit. Therefore, it becomes more difficult to review critically the past and present associations of mission to globalization.

The culture of globalization as it has been pointed out creates attitudes and a mental frame that may be the opposite of what the gospel teaches about human life under God's design. If mission simply rides on the crest of the globalization wave, it might end by changing the very nature of the gospel. Coming from the experience of evangelistic movements that wanted to pattern their missionary activity according to biblical standards, in 1974 at Lausanne, René Padilla (1985, pp. 16-17, notes) criticized the total identification of modern Western values (the American way of life) and the gospel that was propagated in the name of Christian mission. He called it "culture Christianity" and commented: "In order to gain the greatest possible number of followers, it is not enough for 'culture Christianity' to turn the gospel into a product; it also has to distribute it among the greatest number of consumers of religion. For this the 20th century has provided it with the perfect tool—technology. The strategy for the evangelization of the world thus becomes a question of mathematical calculation."

The criticism is still valid today and a good warning against contemporary trends. Let me give an example. Precisely at the point in which religiosity has returned to be a mark of our post-modern culture, organizations in the U.S. have turned prayer for mission into an industry in which teachings and methodologies are packaged and marketed. The quantifying rationality of American technological culture has been uncritically applied even to the understanding of demonic activity. Nations that are at odds with the foreign policies of the United States have been represented in maps as "windows" in which we are told that through spiritual mapping it is possible to detect a more intense demonic activity than in other parts of the earth. Without any care for theological consistency, the warlike language of the Old Testament permeates liturgy and worship to an intolerable degree.

In tension with the globalization process, we have the rise and expansion of a movement that seeks to affirm local cultures in their search for autonomy and full expression. This may be described as a contextualization movement, and Christian mission has also played an important part in it. Through Bible translation, Protestant missions have contributed to the preservation, recognition, and evaluation of native tongues and cultures. The historical significance of this movement has been the subject of research and writing by African scholar Lamin Sanneh (1989, p. 2). His thesis is that "particular Christian translation projects have helped to create an overarching series of cultural experiences with hitherto obscure cultural systems being thrust into the general stream of universal history." Conversely, Bible translation into the vernacular has been a decisive factor in the strengthening of a sense of identity and dignity of peoples and nations, thus preparing them to struggle against colonialism. On the basis of his research in Africa, Sanneh (1989, p. 138) says, "When we look at the situation, we are confronted with the paradox of the missionary agency promoting the vernacular and thus inspiring indigenous confidence at a time when colonialism was demanding paternal overlordship."

The great challenge to Christian mission at this point is for missionaries to be messengers of Jesus Christ and not just harbingers of the new globalization process. The biblical perspective on mission has a global vision and a global component that comes from faith in God the creator and his intention to bless all of humankind through the instruments that he chooses. The contemporary globalization process has to be evaluated from that biblical perspective. Missionaries will be caught in the tension between globalization and contextualization, and they also have to avoid a provincialist attitude that exaggerates contextualization to the detriment of a biblical global awareness.

The Growth of Poverty and Inequality

The economic side of the globalization process has accentuated social disparities in the world. On the one hand, it has generated new wealth and unprecedented comfort, placing the most sophisticated technologies within the reach of the average citizen in the rich nations and of the elites in the poor nations. On the other hand, figures indicate that a larger proportion of people are being driven into extreme forms of poverty. According to Schreiter (1997, p. 7), "This is caused partially by global capitalism's quest for short-term profit, a quest that precludes long-term commitment to a people and a place; and partially by the destruction of traditional and small-scale societies and economies by the centrality of the market."

This process has brought uncertainty, suffering, and decline in the quality of life for people whose welfare depends on public institutions, such as older and retired people, children, and poor students. Christian missionaries become conversant with the subject because of their firsthand experience with the victims of this process. Long-term Christian endeavors such as theological education and institutional development necessary for the fulfillment of the church's mission have been affected by the collapse of financial supporting structures in some Latin American nations, due to growing unemployment brought by privatization of health, social security, and education.

An analyst of the scene in the U.S. has stressed the social transformation that is taking place in North America. Peter Drucker (1994) describes this as the post-capitalist society in which "knowledge workers" are replacing industrial workers. He stresses the fact that this shift to knowl-edge-based work brings enormous social challenges that will transform the lives of people—for instance, by the disappearance of old communities, such as family, village, and parish. For Drucker, neither government nor the employing organizations, the classic "two sectors" that hold power in post-capitalist America, are able to cope with the effects of this massive social change, what he calls "social tasks of the knowledge society." These tasks include "education and health care; the anomies and diseases of a developed and, especially, a rich society, such as alcohol and drug abuse; or the problems of incompetence and irresponsibility such as those of the underclass in the American city."

Drucker places the agenda of assuming those tasks in the hands of what he calls "the third sector" in U.S. society, which is made up of churches and of a myriad of voluntary organizations that he calls "parachurches," because they have modeled themselves following the nonprofit pattern provided by the churches. He assigns to this "social sector" two responsibilities. One is "to create human health and well-being," and the other is "to create citizenship." Of course, a presupposition behind Drucker's scheme is the tremendous volunteerism that characterizes American society, and which has definitely Protestant roots, though its contemporary manifestations may be secular in outlook and intention. His formula, however, may not work in societies that have totally different structures, worldviews, and attitudes.

From the perspective of mission, particularly in the Evangelical world, we have lately observed the mushrooming of holistic mission projects, in which a social component becomes indispensable.[4] In

---

[4] Agencies such as World Vision, MAP, Food for the Hungry, Habitat for Humanity, MEDA, and World Concern have grown significantly in recent years. Several volumes in the series *Cases in Holistic Ministry* from MARC (Monrovia, California) provide a helpful overview.

Latin America, for instance, the number of street children who are victims of all forms of exploitation is the result of family disintegration, loss of basic Christian values, and growing poverty. A good number of missionary projects have developed as a response, and there is now a network trying to give a measure of coordination to them. Services to the material needs of people are in some places the only way through which missionaries can obtain a visa to enter a country. Mission projects of this kind are not just the result of a new awareness among Christians about a biblically based social responsibility. They are also the inevitable response to worsening social conditions that have created many victims, becoming a new challenge to Christian compassion.

It will be a fact, however, that in the coming century Christian compassion will be the only hope of survival for victims of the global economic process. The challenge for missionaries will be how to avoid the pitfalls of missionary paternalism on the one hand and the failed secular welfare system on the other. Only the redemptive power of the gospel transforms people in such a way that it enables them to overcome the dire consequences of poverty. Sociological studies of Christianity in the 1960s and '70s were usually hostile against churches. The scenario has changed today. As social planners and city governments acknowledge the problems generated by the current economic system, sociologists in places as distant as the city of Philadelphia, Pennsylvania (Stafford, 1999), the urban world of Brazil (Mariz, 1994), South Korea, or South Africa (Martin, 1990)[5] have come to see churches as the source of hope from which the urban poor gain strength, courage, and a language to cope

with poverty. Just as in New Testament times, even among the poorest the gospel brings a measure of prosperity. This prosperity is totally different from the kind of blessed consumerism known as "prosperity theology," which is being propagated from the United States, Germany, and South Africa. One of the main differences is that Christian prosperity goes always hand in hand with ethical responsibility and with an intentional solidarity: "He who has been stealing must steal no longer, but must work doing something useful with his own hands, that he may have something to share with those in need" (Eph. 4:28).

There is a related factor that seems a paradox from a purely human perspective. It is precisely among the poor where we find people open to the gospel and enthusiastic about their faith. Churches are growing with incredible vitality in this world of poverty, while churches in other segments of society tend to decline. In Asia, Africa, and Latin America, Evangelicals have found receptive hearts among the millions who have moved from rural areas to the cities. Even in North America and Europe, popular forms of Protestantism are growing. These churches of the poor have learned to respond to the urban challenge; they speak the language of the masses and offer fellowship in the impersonal city. The urban frontier presents a challenge for holistic witness. Neighborhood associations, the mass media, schools, medical services, and the war on drugs await the presence of Christians with a sense of mission.

Moreover, missionary initiative expressed in numbers of persons volunteering for missionary work seems to be passing from North to South at a time

---

[5] Martin (1990) uses studies about Pentecostal growth in South Africa and South Korea for comparison with his massive study about Latin America.

when the South is increasingly poor. Within this context of poverty, two models of mission activity have developed that provide keys for the future. In the *cooperative model*, churches from rich nations add their material resources to the human resources of the churches in poor nations in order to work in a third area. Some specialized Evangelical organizations or ministries such as YWAM, OM, and IFES have experience with this model, forming international teams to carry on transcultural mission in very different settings. Several other missionary organizations are moving in this direction, but the model poses some practical questions for which there are no easy answers, one of them being the raising of support for non-Western participants. The traditional Catholic missionary orders such as Franciscans or Jesuits, which are supranational, provide the oldest and more developed example, facilitated by the vows of poverty, celibacy, and obedience. However, they presuppose concepts of missionary vocation, church order, and ministry which are totally different from the Evangelical ones.

The *migration model* has also functioned through the centuries. Migrants from poor countries who move in search of economic survival carry the Christian message and missionary initiative with them. Moravians from Curazao moved to Holland; Jamaican Baptists emigrated to England; Filipino Christian women go to Muslim countries; Haitian believers went to Canada; and Latin American Evangelicals are going to Japan, Australia, and the United States. This missionary presence and activity has been significant, though it seldom gets to the records of formal institutional missionary activity. Some denominational mission agencies as well as faith missions are trying to set up connections that will allow them to serve within the frame of this migration movement.

They will need to exercise much care to avoid stifling the lay initiative and spontaneity that characterize it.

The End of Christendom

I would venture to say that the unbalanced economic growth that has widened the gap between rich and poor may well be an evidence of the degree to which Western culture has lost the veneer of Christian values that it used to keep. The position of the church in society evolved from the time that Emperor Constantine made Christianity official: "The church was blended into a half-civil, half-religious society, *Christendom*. It has covered a whole civilization with its authority, inspired a politic, and had become an essentially Western reality" (Mehl, 1970, p. 67). Christendom presupposed the predominance of Christianity in Western societies and a certain degree of influence of Christian ideas and principles on the social life of nations and on their international policies. However, it is important to remember what historian Latourette (1948, p. 8) said: "No civilization has ever incorporated the ideals of Christ." Today the influence of Christianity has declined, and not even lip service is paid to elements such as compassion and fairness in the national or international policies of the rich and developed nations where Christianity still may be an established religion.

In the post-Christendom situation, Christians cannot expect society to facilitate through social mechanisms the kind of life that abides by the qualities of Christian ethics. Legislation in Western countries of Europe or North America continues to lose Christian values. Today the Christian stance in the West has to become a missionary stance in which the quality of Christian life goes "against the stream" to the point that to be a Christian is equivalent to being a "resident alien"[6] (Hauerwas & Willimon, 1989). The same qualities that were required of the pioneers that went to plant Christianity in mission fields have come to be required for the Christian who stays at home in a Western nation and wants to be a faithful witness of Jesus Christ. Missionaries have learned and have been inspired by the way in which Christians live their lives in the hostile environment where they are a tiny minority. Western Christians can learn much from Christians in situations of minority and hostility, where every day they practice an alternative lifestyle.

Within this situation, missionaries will have to expect less and less in terms of support or protection from their governments as they travel and engage in mission. At the same time, it becomes necessary for missionaries to go back to the fundamentals of the gospel and to disengage themselves from the Western cultural trappings that consciously or unconsciously characterized mission during the imperial era in the 19th and early 20th centuries. The Lausanne Covenant expresses this conviction forcefully when it says: "The gospel does not presuppose the superiority of any culture to another but evaluates all cultures according to its own criteria of truth and righteousness, and insists on moral absolutes in every culture. Missions have all too frequently exported with the gospel an alien culture, and churches have sometimes been in bondage to culture rather than to the Scripture. Christ's evangelists must humbly seek to empty themselves of all but their personal authenticity in order to become the servants of others, and churches must seek to transform and enrich culture, all for the glory of God" (LC, par. 10).

Movements that minister among young people and students have been more open to take risks, creating models of sensitive multicultural missionary teams. Participants in them have been able to look at their own culture from a critical distance. This has been facilitated also by the mobility and simple lifestyle of the teams. Through experience and reflection in light of God's Word, this has been an important training ground for mission. I believe that this type of experience gives participants a taste of some of the positive characteristics of the traditional monastic orders that have remained in the Catholic church as instruments for mission across cultural and social frontiers. Evangelical movements could have a systematic exchange of experiences along these lines. Much could be gained from the experience of movements such as Operation Mobilization, Mennonite Central Committee, YWAM, and IFES.

A Post-Modern Culture

Not only Christianity has lost a grip on contemporary Western societies. The rejection of Christian values could be understood within the larger frame of a rejection of ideologies and worldviews that had been shaped by the ideas of the Enlightenment, what is usually known as "modernity." Now we see in Europe and North America the rise of a culture and attitudes that might be described as "post-modern," because they express a revolt against some of the key points of modernity. Thus we have the predominance of feeling and the revolt against reason, the revival of paganism in elements such as the cult of the body, the search for ever more sophisticated forms of pleasure, and the ritualization of life. Sports and popular artistic shows take the shape of reli-

---

[6] This is the title of a very helpful book that deals with the issue in the United States context.

gious celebration and substitute religious services to provide relief from the drudgery of routine work and duty.

An important aspect of post-modernity is the glorification of the body. Post-modern culture depicts the body in all forms and shapes and offers thousands of products to beautify, perfume, modify, improve, and perfect the body, even to the point of promising ways to overcome the inroads of natural decay. There are products, methods, and stimuli for enhancing physical pleasure in all its forms. This search for pleasure has become a mark of contemporary life that, coupled with the hopelessness brought by the collapse of ideologies, becomes pure and simple hedonism. Globalization through communications generates another imbalance here. The media portray this hedonistic way of life and thought and propagate it across the globe. Incitement to expensive pleasure fills the screens of TV sets in poor societies, and young people specially crave the symbols and instruments of a sophisticated hedonistic West, while not having met some of the basic necessities of their own material life, such as adequate housing and running water.

Another important mark of modernity was that its myths provided hope and a sense of direction to the masses. Some of us remember well how the Marxist dream of a classless utopia fostered political militancy in several generations of students that were ready to give their lives for the cause of the proletariat. When some of us attended high school, we were required to memorize the political liberal discourses of the French Revolution and the dreams of unlimited progress. Later on came Marxism, and the words of Argentinian medical doctor Che Guevara painted in the walls of the University of Cordoba in Argentina come to mind as an illustration: "What does the sacrifice of a man or a nation matter if what is at stake

is the destiny of humankind?" A mark of post-modernity is precisely the loss of those dreams. No one has a clue to the direction of history nowadays, and it does not matter anymore. For post-modern generations of students, the philosophy of life may be embodied in those words that Paul quotes from Isaiah to describe the materialism of his own day: "Let us eat and drink for tomorrow we die" (1 Cor. 15:32).

Such materialism lies behind the attitude that turns consumption into the main determinant value of the average citizen in the developed world. The incredible abundance of consumer goods generated by modern economy is met by the passion for buying and using, the ideology of consumerism. The great shopping malls that are open seven days a week have become the new temples of a post-modern religion, and it is not difficult to detect the vacuum in the lives of its worshipers. Jacques Attali (1991, p. 5) describes them as modern nomads with their Walkmans, laptops, and cellular phones that "will roam the planet seeking ways to use their free time, shopping for information, sensations, and goods only they can afford, while yearning for human fellowship and the certitudes of home and community that no longer exist because their functions have become obsolete."

Statements like this from secular sources about the human condition in the post-modern culture come close to the theological description of the symptoms of the fallen condition of human beings. Post-modern literature in both North and South evidences the cynicism and bitter disillusion brought by the end of modern myths and ideologies. This is the condition of the "unreached peoples" of affluent post-modern societies, which are also a challenge to Christian compassion. Prayer is required here, along the lines of what Jesus taught us when he looked at the "harassed and helpless" masses of his day (Matt. 9:35-38). Compassion and prayer are needed, more than a kind of triumphalistic apologetics that seems to be saying, "I told you so," from the distance of a self-righteous aloofness. Missionary obedience at this frontier is mandatory for Evangelical churches and is as urgent as missionary obedience to go to "unreached peoples" in exotic jungles or remote rural areas.

It is also important to reconsider the lifestyle of Jesus himself. Maybe our images of him and of what the Christian life is have been conditioned by the rationalism of modernity. We have made him look more as a somber and serious professor of theology than as a popular teacher and storyteller who was committed to his Father's will but also able to enjoy creation, human friendship, good meals, and playing children. In contrast with the darkness of deconstruction and hopelessness that permeates what media moguls and intellectuals try to sell to young people around the world, how important it is to have in every level of society Christian fellowships that are communities of faith, love, and hope, able to express uninhibitedly the joy of salvation and new life.[7] Those that go to work as missionaries among the poor confess that many times they receive back the gift of joy from Christians who have an abundance of it in the midst of dire poverty and persecution.

A New Religiosity

Modernity in both its liberal as well as its Marxist versions operated with the "enlightened" presupposition that religion was in the process of waning away. At this end of the century, however, we find ourselves in a more religious world. This trend started in the 1960s and surprised alert missionaries, especially on the university campuses around the world. During the first part of the century, Christian thinkers were confronted in cultural circles by a hostile rationalism nourished by the three "masters of suspicion": Marx, Nietzsche, and Freud. From the perspective of Christian mission, the return of an attitude of openness to the sacred and the mysterious looked at first sight as a sign of improvement. Soon it became evident that Christians were being confronted with a new and more subtle challenge. Our apologetics needed serious refurbishing, and the plausibility, authenticity, and quality of our faith were now being questioned from a different angle.

As a student evangelist on campuses of different parts of the world, already in the late '70s I had a chance to lecture or to dialogue with students who showed this new openness to the religious. In many cases, it allowed Christians to demonstrate in the open air a freer and uninhibited expression of Christian faith through prayer, song, and drama. I found myself engaged in dialogues with people whose language was strangely similar to the language of some forms of evangelicalism: joy in the heart, a feeling of self-realization, a sense of peace and harmony, a feeling of goodwill towards all human beings, including animals and planet earth. However, when I pushed some specific issues such as suffering, death, compassion, final hope, failure, and sin, this new religious mood became hollow and empty. And when I talked of the cross, evil, sin, redemption, and Christ, I could see hostility developing against what was considered my exclusivism and intolerance.

The new attitude towards religion and the proliferation of religious practices has to be understood as part of the revolt

---

[7] For a well-informed and theologically based book on discipleship on North American campuses along these lines, see Garber (1996).

against modernity. The modern ideologies of indefinite progress and social utopia were actually myths that attracted and mobilized masses for action. Their failure and collapse have brought awareness of a vacuum and disillusionment about the ability of human reason to give meaning to life and provide answers for deep existential questions. This is at the root of the search for alternatives, for a contact with the occult, for an ability to handle mystery, for a connection with extra-rational forces that may influence the course of human events, both in individual lives as well as in communities and nations.

It is helpful to remember that in the days of the New Testament, the message of Jesus Christ confronted not only the challenges of Greek philosophy and Roman politics, but also the questions that came from the mystery religions that pervaded especially the ideas and practices of popular culture. Mystery religions in the first century claimed to help people with their daily problems, to give them immortality, and to enable them to share their lives with the god. They promised cleansing to deal with guilt, security to face fear of evil, power over Fate, union with gods through orgiastic ecstasy, and immortality (Green, 1970). The way in which the Apostolic message and practice developed in the New Testament was the response to these needs of the human heart, stemming from the basic fact of Jesus Christ.[8]

Missionaries today are being driven to restudy the New Testament teaching about religiosity, as well as about the presence and power of the Holy Spirit. Communication technology and techniques, as well as an intellectually reasonable faith, are not enough. Spiritual power and disciplines such as prayer, Bible meditation, and fasting are necessary for mission across this new religious frontier. Evangelicals must be open to the ministry of persons who are gifted to minister in these areas. On the other hand, the Apostle Paul, writing to the Corinthians, recognized also that there could be worldliness, abuses, and manipulation even within a context of spiritual gifts. Eastern European theologian Peter Kuzmic has said, "Charisma without character leads to catastrophe."

This warning has a particular relevance as we consider the phenomenon of new megachurches that have developed in the most recent decades. Some of them follow what we might call the Willow Creek pattern, in which the marks of classical evangelicalism are evident in doctrine and liturgy, in spite of the fact that they studiously avoid names that would indicate a denominational origin. Others, especially in Latin America, have come from Catholic charismatic movements and show in their preaching, lifestyle, and liturgy some of the marks of the middle class Catholic culture from which they proceed. What they have in common is the ability to respond positively to the needs, attitudes, and outlook generated by the market culture in a post-modern society. There are logical reasons to understand why prosperity teaching, developed within popular Protestantism in the U.S., attracts people to these megachurches that have developed adequate techniques to "market" their church.

While Protestants in general and Evangelicals in particular have emphasized *true doctrine* as a mark of the church, they have been weak in their understanding of *ritual and symbol* as well as *church structure* as equally important components in the religious life of people, and consequently in the formation of disciples of Jesus Christ. The new religiosity demands

---

[8] Helpful at this point is the article by Drane (1998).

a better understanding of how these elements relate, that will allow for better pastoral and teaching practices. Megachurches have learned how to use these elements, though sometimes they may cross the thin line that divides an adequate use from sheer manipulation. The fact that so many Evangelicals are attracted to Catholic spirituality in North America is another indication of the limitations of excessive concentration on correct doctrine at the expense of the other dimensions of the Christian life.

Old Religions and Fundamentalist Wars

Besides the new religiosity, there is the resurgence of old religions. In the streets of Western cities, you see now the shapes of mosques and Hindu temples being built not as exotic ornaments for casinos, but as places of worship for communities that sometimes outdo Christians in their missionary zeal. With the end of Christendom, many societies face the thorny issue of religious pluralism. The West with the Protestant ideals and practice of democracy and tolerance was intellectually prepared. Nations where Catholicism and the Orthodox church predominated have found it more difficult to come to terms with it. All Christians, however, are faced with the need to review their attitudes; a more alert form of apologetics must be matched by spiritual discernment.[9]

One of the most significant trends in recent years is the resurgence of Islam. Islam has become one of the greatest missionary challenges of today. It is now a rival faith in Indonesia, several African countries, the Middle East, and even at the heart of cities in Europe and the United States. Islam's success turned it into a thriving, conquering faith that remained in the Iberian peninsula for eight centuries and could barely be stopped at the Pyrenees. Within the frame of a Christendom mentality, Europeans later organized aggressive wars called "Crusades." Christian mission at that time became a holy war against the Moors. Unfortunately, many Christians still operate within those categories. The rhetoric of some Christian mission promoters during the Gulf War in 1990-1991 reflected more the propaganda of the United States government than the spirit of Christ. Criticizing that type of discourse during the 1990 Urbana missionary convention, an IVCF staff wrote: "Foreign policy is couched in spiritual conflict terms, and militaristic attitudes are baptized in the name of Christ. Haven't we learned anything from history?" (Escobar, 1991).

There is, however, an alternative way to relate to Islam that reflects more the spirit of Christ. At the time of the Crusades, Francis of Assisi dared to cross the battle lines peacefully in order to share the gospel with the Sultan of Egypt, showing him a different Christian approach. The same attitude was exemplified by Raimon Lull, the Spanish mystic and missionary who made four trips to North Africa in order to preach the gospel and who died as a result of persecution in 1315. Evangelical missionaries I have known, such as William Miller, Dennis Clark, Margaret Wynne, and Phil Parshall, have taught me that the key to mission in the Muslim world is a spirituality of the cross, readiness for suffering, and a respectful acquaintance with the Muslim faith.

---

[9] We are indebted to Vinoth Ramachandra (1997) for his excellent book *The Recovery of Mission*. It is an example of an Evangelical approach to other religions in a post-Christendom situation.

What is a more difficult reality to face is the phenomenon of fundamentalism. This term was coined to refer to the conservative reaction against theological liberalism among Protestants in the U.S. at the beginning of this century. What started as a theological effort to reformulate and defend the fundamentals of Evangelical faith became dominated by what Carl Henry (1957, pp. 43, 33) called "a harsh temperament, a spirit of lovelessness and strife." Its anti-intellectualism degenerated into "a morbid and sickly enthusiasm," and it became a reactionary cultural phenomenon associated with the defense of a conservative political agenda in the United States and with racism, nationalism, blind anti-Communism, and the arms race.

When in the 1980s a resurgent Islam came to power in Iran, the religious/political phenomenon that followed in several other countries of the Middle East and North Africa came to be known as Muslim fundamentalism. It was around the same time that Protestant Fundamentalists in the U.S. came again to political prominence through the Moral Majority. It is this reaction against modernity and secularism from a conservative alliance of religious conviction and political interests that today is known as fundamentalism. There is Hindu fundamentalism in India, Jewish fundamentalism in Israel and the United States, and Catholic fundamentalism in Mexico and Argentina. Other religions such as Buddhism have also fundamentalist forms. From a missiological perspective, the problem is the confusion this might create. Protestant fundamentalism in the form of religious/political alliances such as the media empires of Pat Robertson and Jerry Falwell in the United States tends to mix evangelism with the promotion of a variety of political causes in different parts of the world. These fundamentalists seem committed to attract national Evangelical leaders from other countries to their educational institutions in the U.S.

The Pentecostal Phenomenon

It is a well-known fact today that during this century there has been a relentless process of urban accumulation that has turned old cities into urban labyrinths and has given birth to new cities around the world. This has brought to light the emergence of new segments of population, especially those with low education or those that belong to ethnic minorities that in the past could be hidden in distant rural areas but now have invaded massively the streets of capitals in six continents. The expansion of popular Protestantism in the form of Pentecostal and Pentecostal-like churches among these emerging masses has been one of the surprising phenomena of our century.

These churches may be described as forms of "popular Protestantism" because they have taken roots among the *populus*, the social stratum at the base, which almost everywhere constitutes the majority of the population. During our century, the form of popular Protestantism known as Pentecostalism has become a new force to be reckoned with in the Christian religious scene. Some observers predict that this will become the predominant religious force in Latin America at the eve of the Third Millennium. These churches are indigenous in nature and inspired by a contagious proselytistic spirit. They show some of the marks of the early Pentecostal Movement in North America that Hollenweger (1997) also associates with indigenous non-white churches in other parts of the world, namely, glossolalia, oral liturgy, a narrative style in the communication of their message, maximum participation of all the faithful in prayers and worship, inclusion of dreams and visions in public meetings, and a unique understanding of the body/mind relationship applied in healing by prayer.[10]

In the case of Latin America, these Pentecostal churches grew especially among the most marginalized social groups in the urban areas, usually unnoticed during their first decades. However, in some cases political circumstances brought them to public attention, especially when governments had tensions with the Roman Catholic Church and looked for other sources of religious legitimation. When the Billy Graham Evangelistic Association sponsored the great Congress on Evangelism in Berlin (1966), one of the most difficult decisions that Graham himself faced was the admission of Pentecostals to the platform and the leadership of the congress (see Martin, 1992, especially chap. 20, pp. 331-335). Those of us who attended the congress will never forget that when reports about evangelization were presented, country after country and continent after continent, the story was frequently the same: "Pentecostals number more than all other Protestants put together."

At the middle of the 20th century, the great historian of missions, Kenneth Scott Latourette (1948, p. 147) presented a series of lectures assessing the state of Christianity at that point and trying to understand trends that could help foresee the future. As he drew the panorama with rough strokes, Latourette kept asking the question, "What forms will Christianity take in the far future?" His balance of facts and trends was mostly positive about the contribution of Protestantism and its future. He answered the question in this way: "The Protestantism of the future will not be the Protestantism of the past. We cannot yet clearly discern what that Prot-

estantism is to be. We can, however, perceive something of the direction which is being taken and from it may be able to forecast in part what is to come. The very fact that we cannot foretell the precise or even the general features of the Protestantism of the future is probably evidence of vitality in that branch of Christianity."

Latourette said almost nothing about Pentecostals. However, the marks of missionary Protestantism that he stressed, such as active lay participation in mission, indigenous leadership, poor ecclesiology, and a sectarian trend of separation from the world, are precisely the marks of Pentecostalism. Less than five years after Latourette wrote what I quoted above, Lesslie Newbigin (1954) was calling all Protestants to acknowledge the reality of Pentecostalism and the missiological and theological contributions it was making to Christianity. Recently, in a report about conversations between Pentecostals and Catholics, a well-known Catholic author stated clearly that the importance of these conversations was due to the fact that "Catholics and Classical Pentecostals [are] the two largest bodies of Christians in the world" (McDonnell, 1999, p. 11).

Latin American Pentecostalism has been studied intensely in recent years, partly because of its explosive numerical growth and partly because of its political significance. David Martin (1990) offers a massive summary of his own research and that of many others and compares American Pentecostalism with other forms of Pentecostalism in other parts of the world. It could be said that these popular Protestant churches have become alternative societies where urban poor people are accepted and become actors, not on the basis of what gives people status in the

---

[10] This description comes from Walter J. Hollenweger, considered an authority in the missiological study of Pentecostals. His most recent book (1997) is a good summary of key points in a long-standing life of research around the world.

world, but on the basis of values that come from their vision of the kingdom of God. A new generation of social scientists working at the micro level have brought to light the transforming nature of the spiritual experience offered by these churches.[11] Martin (1990, p. 284) finds that the massive migration from countryside to megacity is the background for the religious transformation: "The new society now emerging in Latin America has to do with movement, and Evangelicals constitute a *movement*. Evangelical Christianity is a dramatic migration of the spirit matching and accompanying a dramatic migration of bodies."

Observers and scholars have had to come to terms with the fact that in spite of all good theory and good intentions, many actions in favor of the poor were tainted by a paternalistic approach. Social and political conscientization took the form of a struggle for the poor, trying to create a more just society *for* them rather than *with* them. Historical churches connected to world communities and denominational families had access to funds, foreign press, and even diplomatic ties that were used in an effort to help the victims of poverty or state terrorism. Incarnation among the poor has been many times the source of these movements, but they have failed in mobilizing the poor themselves. By contrast, the popular Protestant churches are popular movements in themselves. Their pastors and leaders do not have to identify with the poor; *they are the poor*. They do not have a social agenda but an intense spiritual agenda, and it is through that agenda that they have been able to have a social impact. As Martin (1990, p. 284) observes about the impact of the Pentecostal experience, "Above all it renews the innermost cell of the fam-

ily and protects the woman from the ravages of male desertion and violence. A new faith is able to implant new disciplines, reorder priorities, counter corruption and destructive machismo, and reverse the indifferent and injurious hierarchies of the outside world."

Any missiological outlook has to ask questions about the significance of what sociology has now described and interpreted. Both the redemptive nature of the Pentecostal experience and its indigeneity are key factors for mission in the future. They throw light on our understanding of what is the gospel and the mission of the church? I have also posed elsewhere (Escobar, 1996) the way in which these facts throw us back to understand the New Testament church as a model for mission in our times. For non-Pentecostals, and especially for those Evangelicals that have seen their task as guarding the integrity of a biblical gospel, a great question is how their own contribution to Protestantism will match the vitality and Spirit-filled sense of mission that Pentecostalism is contributing. They must learn to apply a "hermeneutic of charity" instead of a "hermeneutic of suspicion," as theologian Richard Mouw (1994, pp. 15-19) has so ably reminded us. The future demands a common walk of mutual understanding and learning for mission.

Recovery of Biblical Patterns for Mission

As we have moved through this quick overview, it has become evident that the new century will require a return to biblical patterns of mission. Radical shifts in culture, politics, and economics, as well as the growth of Christianity in the Southern hemisphere, have brought new sce-

---

[11] The conflicting approaches to popular Protestantism are studied in Escobar (1994).

narios. Traditional mission models inherited from the Christendom mentality and the colonial era are now obsolete. It is time for a paradigm change that will come from a salutary return to the Word of God. As South African missiologist David Bosch (1993, p. 177) said, "Our point of departure should not be the contemporary enterprise we seek to justify, but the biblical sense of what being sent into the world signifies."

The new perspective requires a firm commitment to the missionary imperatives that are part of the very structure of our faith and at the same time a serious work of biblical scholarship and interpretation. Here we have a key to understand the long-term impact of the Lausanne Movement. An antecedent of the Lausanne Congress (1974) was the Berlin Congress on Evangelism that I have already mentioned. It was called by Billy Graham to commemorate 10 years of the periodical *Christianity Today*. The vision for this periodical came from the desire to keep together the evangelistic thrust of Billy Graham with the scholarly work of leading Evangelical theologians. The revival of Evangelical scholarship in the English-speaking world, after the controversies of Fundamentalism, came from vigorous Evangelical student movements. It was not purely academical, but it had a missionary thrust, thanks to the connection with the missionary life of those movements.

Mission has to be acknowledged as God's initiative coming from God's love for his creation, and from his design of choosing some instruments to use them for the salvation and blessing of all of humankind. When the old way of doing mission needs to be reviewed, we can see to what degree it had become just a human enterprise, maybe the religious side of the expansion of one culture and one empire. At the point at which we recover a biblical vision, we come to experience the awe and wonder of being invited to enter into God's plan, which is far more than choosing a career or going for a nice trip abroad. We experience what Moses felt before the burning bush (Ex. 3:11), and Peter when Jesus invaded his boat (Luke 5:8), and Saul when he was met by Jesus on the road to Damascus (Acts 22:8-10).

John Stott opened for us another dimension of the biblical agenda: "mission in Christ's way."[12] Already in 1966 he shifted our attention from the classic passage of the Great Commission in Matthew 28:18-20 to the almost forgotten text of John 20:21. Here we have not only a mandate for mission, but also a model of mission style: in obedience to the loving design of the Father, patterned by the example of Jesus Christ, and driven by the power of the Holy Spirit. In the cross, Jesus Christ died for our salvation and also left a pattern for our missionary life. Before any "practical" training for mission in the use of methods and tools for the verbal communication of a message, it is imperative to form disciples for *a new style of missionary presence*. Mission requires orthopraxis as well as orthodoxy.

This Christological model that was also the pattern under which Paul and the other apostles placed their own missionary practice could be described as "mission from below."[13] At the beginning of the 20th century, a great missionary gathering such as the Edinburgh 1910 Conference represented the triumphant spirit of a church identified with Christendom and

---

[12] I refer here to the 1966 Berlin Congress on World Evangelism that preceded the Lausanne Movement. Stott presented there the Bible expositions about the Great Commission that became very influential afterwards.

[13] For an excellent theological meditation about this point, see Tomlin (1997).

the rich and developed West; it was "mission from above." The trends we have described make it necessary to consider a new paradigm, because the dynamism for mission is coming now from the periphery of the world, from the churches of the poor, as well as from Christians in the West that have to live as "resident aliens" in a post-modern culture. This Christological paradigm is only possible by the power of the Holy Spirit.

I think it is very important to remember at this point that Protestant missions came from the Evangelical movements in Europe. The missionary movement after Carey was more inspired by the Wesleyan revivals and the Moravian pioneers of mission than by the 16th century magisterial Reformers. The dynamism of missionary Protestantism came from the renewal movements of the 18th and 19th centuries. They had grasped truth about the Holy Spirit which then began to make sense. This, however, is not the whole picture. The readiness of men like John Wesley and Count Zinzendorf to abandon old church structures and their creativity in developing new structures for mission were made possible because they were open to the movement of the Spirit. Such an attitude of openness to the Spirit is what Brazilian missiologist Valdir Steuernagel (1993) calls for: "Mission understood in pneumatological language is one act with two steps. It is first to perceive the blowing of the Spirit and the direction from which it comes. And then it is to run in the same direction to which the Spirit is blowing."

Conclusions

Contemporary trends place a demanding agenda for missionaries and mission organizations in the new millennium. The pace of change is such that we may better limit ourselves to think of the next decade.

By way of conclusion, I would like to suggest some notes about the direction to which we should be moving in light of the trends I have outlined.

As in the first century, when Paul engaged in mission in the context of the Roman Empire, mission today should use the means provided by globalization, without falling prey to the spirit of the globalizing age. Paul used the means provided by the Pax Romana without ever appearing in style, intention, or method as a representative of Rome. Paul also affirmed and defended the freedom of Gentiles from the burdens that the Judaizers wanted to impose on them. As missionaries today, we must be open to respect the many contextual expressions of the faith that are developing around the world.

Existing missionary models among Evangelicals have not been able to overcome the distances and barriers created by the comparative affluence of missionaries and agencies. The frequent tendency of Western mission agencies to bypass their indigenous partners and to perpetuate their own "independence" is an indication of failure, and growing poverty exposes that failure. The missionary dynamism of churches in the South could well be stifled and misdirected by an imitation of the expensive Western models of missionary organization. The future demands more models of non-paternalistic, holistic missions. An incarnational approach modeled by Jesus and Paul is the key. Gross inequalities make partnership impossible.

A church that lives comfortably in the post-Christian West is unable to respond to the pain and the spiritual need of postmodern generations. It is interesting to see how spiritual vitality can foster a missionary stance in Western societies that expresses itself also in an ability to partner with churches abroad. It seems to me that churches that look successful (because they give the people in North America the kind of domesticated Christianity they are asking for) become the supporters of the most traditional forms of global mission, the ones that prolong the old colonial situation.

In the face of growing religiosity, mission in the next decade will require spiritual revitalization at the base. There must be a more humble attitude of dependence on the Holy Spirit and a renewed understanding of the gifts and the fruit of the Spirit as they manifest themselves in mission. The question is not so much to market "spiritual" packages that have no theological or biblical basis, but to walk alongside churches everywhere that engage in mission from the base of a simple but real spiritual vitality.

Traditional missionary practice among Evangelicals reflects a very weak and undefined concept of the church. This explains the sectarian trends, the competitive spirit, the waste of resources that we all know and lament, and the tendency to practice proselytism instead of evangelism. As missionaries and missiologists, we need to tackle seriously the task of understanding the church, in order to understand better what we expect as a long-term outcome of our mission activity. Not to do so is to content ourselves with irresponsible activism. Such understanding of the church is also indispensable in order to know better how to do mission in the face of the great traditional religions.

I have tried to outline the missionary challenge ahead of us in this century and the resources of our trinitarian faith for responding to this challenge. God's Spirit is at work in the world in many different ways. During the past half century, the Evangelical Missionary Movement has been an instrument of God to keep a biblical missionary vision alive within Protestantism. After Lausanne, the Evangelical Movement—or at least some sectors

within it—were able to appreciate the distinctives and the unique contextual identity of the growing churches in the world outside North America and Europe. At the same time, this new appreciation came from a firm stand on the biblical basis for understanding and articulating the Christian message. This combination of firmness and flexibility will allow the rise of creative partnerships that are required in order to respond to the new missionary situations around the world.

References

Attali, J. (1991). *Millennium*. New York: Times Books.

Bosch, D. (1993). Reflections on biblical models of mission. In J. M. Phillips & R. T. Coote (Eds.), *Towards the 21st century in Christian mission: Essays in honor of Gerald H. Anderson* (p. 177). Grand Rapids, MI: Wm. B. Eerdmans Publishing Co.

Bühlmann, W. (1986). *The church of the future: A model for the year 2001*. Maryknoll, NY: Orbis Books.

Drane, J. W. (1998, February). Methods and perspectives in understanding the New Age. *Themelios, 23*(2), pp. 22-34.

Drucker, P. F. (1994, November). The age of social transformation. *The Atlantic Monthly*, p. 73.

Escobar, S. (1991). The significance of Urbana '90. *Missiology, 19*(3), pp. 333-338.

———. (1994). The promise and precariousness of Latin American Protestantism. In D. R. Miller (Ed.), *Coming of age: Protestantism in contemporary Latin America* (pp. 3-35). Lanham, MD: University Press of America.

———. (1996, October–December). Mañana: Discerning the Spirit in Latin America. *Evangelical Review of Theology, 22*(4), pp. 312-326.

Garber, S. (1996). *The fabric of faithfulness: Weaving together belief and behavior during the university years*. Downers Grove, IL: InterVarsity Press.

Green, M. (1970). *Evangelism in the early church*. Grand Rapids, MI: Wm. B. Eerdmans Publishing Co.

Hauerwas, S., & Willimon, W. H. (1989). *Resident aliens: Life in the Christian colony*. Nashville, TN: Abingdon Press.

Henry, C. F. H. (1957). *Evangelical responsibility in contemporary theology*. Grand Rapids, MI: Wm. B. Eerdmans Publishing Co.

Hollenweger, W. J. (1997). *Pentecostalism: Origins and developments worldwide*. Peabody, MA: Hendrickson Publishers.

Latourette, K. S. (1948). *The Christian outlook*. New York: Harper & Brothers.

Mariz, C. (1994). *Coping with poverty*. Philadelphia, PA: Temple University Press.

Martin, D. (1990). *Tongues of fire*. Oxford, England: Basil Blackwell.

Martin, W. J. (1992). *A prophet with honor: The Billy Graham story*. New York: William Morrow.

McDonnell, K. (1999, March 6). Pentecostals and Catholics on evangelism and sheep-stealing. *America*, p. 11.

Mehl, R. (1970). *The sociology of Protestantism*. Philadelphia, PA: Westminster Press.

Mouw, R. J. (1994). *Consulting the faithful: What Christian intellectuals can learn from popular religion*. Grand Rapids, MI: Wm. B. Eerdmans Publishing Co.

Myers, B. L. (1996). *The new context of world mission*. Monrovia, CA: MARC.

Newbigin, L. (1954). *The household of God: Lectures on the nature of the church*. New York: Friendship Press.

———. (1986). *Foolishness to the Greeks: The gospel and Western culture*. Geneva: World Council of Churches.

Padilla, C. R. (1985). *Mission between the times: Essays*. Grand Rapids, MI: Wm. B. Eerdmans Publishing Co.

Ramachandra, V. (1997). *The recovery of mission: Beyond the pluralist paradigm*. Grand Rapids, MI: Wm. B. Eerdmans Publishing Co.

Sanneh, L. O. (1989). *Translating the message: The missionary impact on culture*. Maryknoll, NY: Orbis Books.

Schreiter, R. J. (1997). *The new Catholicity*. Maryknoll, NY: Orbis Books.

Snyder, H. A. (1995). *Earthcurrents: The struggle for the world's soul*. Nashville, TN: Abingdon Press.

Stafford, T. (1999, June 14). The criminologist who discovered churches. *Christianity Today, 43*, pp. 35-39.

Steuernagel, V. R. (1993). *Obediencia missionária e prática histórica: Em busca de modelos*. São Paulo, Brazil: ABU Editora.

Tomlin, G. (1997, October). The theology of the cross: Subversive theology for a postmodern world? *Themelios, 23*(1), pp. 59-73.

Walls, A. (1996). *The missionary movement in Christian history: Studies in the transmission of faith*. Maryknoll, NY: Orbis Books.

The Willowbank report on gospel and culture. (1996). In J. R. W. Stott (Ed.), *Making Christ known: Historic mission documents from the Lausanne Movement 1974-1989*. Grand Rapids, MI: Wm. B. Eerdmans Publishing Co.

Samuel Escobar and his wife Lilly are Peruvians. From 1959 to 1985, they were missionaries among university students in Peru, Argentina, Brasil, Spain, and Canada, under the International Fellowship of Evangelical Students. Samuel's missiological thinking developed as reflection on praxis in evangelism and through mission conferences such as the Urbana Missionary Convention, CLADE I Bogota (1969), and Lausanne (1974). Samuel was a founder of the Latin American Theological Fraternity and served as its president (1970–1984). He has an earned Ph.D. from Universidad Complutense, Madrid, Spain, and an honorary D.D. from McMaster University, Canada. He is an ordained Baptist minister. Presently he teaches at Eastern Baptist Theological Seminary in Wynnewood, Pennsylvania, during the fall and serves the rest of the year as Consultant for Theological Education with Baptist International Ministries, based in Lima, Peru. He and Lilly have a daughter who teaches in Spain and a son who works as agricultural economist with MEDA in Lancaster, Pennsylvania.

O NE OF THE MOST CRYPTIC descriptions of the century just passed has been provided by Robert Conquest (1999), for whom the 100 years of life on our planet from 1900 to 1999 are reducible to three T's: total war, totalitarianism, and terror. For all of humankind's astounding technical accomplishments—indeed, to some extent *because* of them—the human slaughter that wiped out an estimated 200 million human beings, a majority of these civilians, may well be the 20th century's most enduring legacy. Samuel Escobar's 11-part discussion of themes which distinguish our globe as it embarks upon a new millennium constitutes a similarly sobering inventory. Because both the present and the future grow out of the past, these themes mark the contours of the macro context in which Christian missionaries are formed and in which they must function.

Escobar (page 26) begins with praise to God for the mystery and the glory of the translatable gospel. It is of course absolutely appropriate to begin with what Escobar refers to as "a potent seed" that has "flourished in a thousand different plants [soils?]." "Seed" is a wonderfully biblical metaphor, but it is sobering too, because it reminds us that fruit from any seed comes only with the death of that seed. This is one of the great themes in our Lord's teaching. One of the great missiological books of the past decade is Lamin Sanneh's (1989) *Translating the Message: The Missionary Impact on Culture*, to which Escobar alludes. This book is notable because it offers an articulate, dissenting point of view to the commonly held notion that Christianity destroys culture, arguing rather that with its insistence on providing the Scriptures in the vernacular, Christianity has provided otherwise oral cultures with a means of recollecting their stories.

Engaging Escobar ... and beyond

JONATHAN BONK

These stories—which would otherwise suffer obliteration by the inexorably homogenizing forces of modernity—thus affirm, strengthen, and enrich cultural identities in ways which Islam, with its insistence upon Arabic, cannot. The translatability of the gospel is an appropriate theme with which to begin any missiological discussion, but it must also be the last word, and I shall return to the theme in my conclusion.

Escobar next addresses the global church, the new balance of Christian presence, and globalization and contextualization, three naturally intersecting and overlapping themes. I begin with the reminder that this global church is diverse— so kaleidoscopic in its variety as sometimes to prevent one part of the church from recognizing its counterpart. Andrew Walls (1996, pp. 3-15) has steadily reminded us that the gospel is at once the prisoner and liberator of culture and that one will look in vain for an "historic Christian faith." Walls takes his readers on an imaginary journey through Christian time, in company with a scholarly space visitor, a professor of comparative inter-planetary religions, who is engaged in the study of Christians over the centuries and whose research grant enables him to visit this planet every few centuries to conduct his research. After two millennia of study, involving field visits to Jerusalem in 37 CE, Nicea in 325 CE, Ireland in 650 CE, Exeter Hall in 1840, and Lagos in 1980, Walls' imaginary scholar is able to distill several seminal continuities from the plethora of conspicuous discontinuities. These continuities are that Jesus the Christ has ultimate significance; the same sacred writings are employed; all use bread, wine, and water in similarly significant ways; and each group believes itself to be part of the same Christian continuity, which in turn is in some strange way linked to that of ancient Israel. Our professor concludes that while each of these groups is "cloaked with such heavy veils belonging to their environment that Christians of different times and places must often be unrecognizable to others, or indeed even to themselves," they must nevertheless be regarded as "manifestations of a single phenomenon" (Walls, 1996, p. 7). It is the presence of these elements which marks the faith community as Christian.

In terms of both demographics and evangelistic vigor, the Christian center (but not the money center) has moved from the North to the South, from the rich to the poor, from the centers of power to the slums of the periphery (see Barrett & Johnson, 2000). While the profound ramifications of this shift have yet to be adequately reflected in Euro-American missiological theory and practice, we are beginning to understand that Eurpoean and North American churches no longer command the heights when it comes to theological, ecclesiastical, or missiological agendas. Their fiscal, organizational, and print resources are significant, but as the surprised and somewhat chagrined North American bishops attending the 1998 Lambeth conference discovered, there is a big difference between the agendas of the two hemispheres. While prim, politically correct bishops, presiding over their older, somewhat theologically agnostic, declining ecclesiastical domains might regard ordination of homosexuals and the blessing of same-sex marriages as central to the 21st century church's task, to African and Asian bishops representing more youthful, vigorously reproductive churches, it was clear that evangelism was paramount.

Our Scriptures remind us that God has always found it difficult to work with or through comfortably secure people. There seems to be something spiritually corrosive about the kind of security to which we who inhabit the hemisphere of privilege have come to assume entitlement. We Western theologians and missiologists have, to all appearances, become accustomed to thinking like the Laodicean church: we "have need of nothing," and we think that the flow of missiological and theological benefits, insights, personnel, and agendas is a one-way flow, with *rich* churches providing out of their largess for the *poor* churches. Recognition that our relative affluence may have made us impervious to our wretched, poor, blind, and naked state is rare, despite the fact that of the seven churches described in St. John's Revelation, the most desperately needy church was the Laodicean church—a "Christian" faith community with Christ on the outside, trying to get in. This being so, it can come as no surprise that the church in affluent lands, seemingly secure with its economies of plenty, its culturally driven entitlements to more and more of this world's goods, and its participation in the Western engines of the global economy, desperately needs its materially poorer counterpart.

Escobar is right to warn us of the insidious effects of globalization upon those of us who actually benefit from it. "The culture of globalization," he warns (pages 30-31), "creates attitudes and a mental frame that may be the opposite of what the gospel teaches about human life under God's design. If mission simply rides on the crest of the globalization wave, it might end by changing the very nature of the gospel." There can be no doubt that missionaries must inevitably be carriers of more than the gospel of our Lord! They are also powerful advocates of those values, orientations, and privileges which they themselves incarnate and value. I have written on this extensively (Bonk, 1991) and need not belabor it in this context. The awkward question which must be raised, but to which no sure answer can be provided, relates to the speed and

inevitability of the corrosive effects of secularism upon the emerging centers of Christian faith. This is something that our brothers and sisters in the South, not we in the North, will need to address on their own terms and within their own contexts.

Given the importance of evolving technologies in the global culture and the ease with which technological luxuries become technological "needs" in Western missiology, Escobar is right to remind us that technology will not save the world. Only the imitable gospel, incarnate at the level of person to person, will spare us from the pitfalls of propaganda and jingoism that sometimes substitute for genuine Christian mission. The extent to which we who are part of the Western mission establishment have embraced the power and the convenience provided by the new technologies, on the one hand, and the essentially relational nature of our faith and its transmission, on the other, make Ruth Conway's (1999, p. 18) observations both apt and timely: "One much trumpeted feature of modern information and communications technologies," she observes, "is their ability to span geographical distance."

But we should not be fooled into substituting information exchange for genuinely Christian mission. Conway (1999, pp. 18-20) continues, "We can exchange a flood of information but remain aloof from the personal experience and feelings, the genuine hopes and fears of other people who are briefly 'on line.'" Technology-reliant communication can thus become "... a distancing power that undermines real understanding, solidarity, and commitment one to another. Preoccupation with disembodied instantaneous messages prevents a fully sympathetic response to actual pressing human needs.... It is this distancing power that contributes a lethal element to globalization: it makes possible the gathering of data, the transfer of capital, the control of markets, the bureaucratic communications within global institutions, and the management of structural adjustment programs, all without any 'feel' for the highly varied, unique local situations affected."

In anticipation of missiology's tendency toward Walter Mittyism, more needs to be said concerning the globalization juggernaut sweeping our globe. No one can avoid being swept along by this tidal wave. Like the proverbial "flies on a chariot wheel," we find ourselves "perched upon a question of which we can neither see the diameter, nor control the motion, nor influence the moving force."[1] Christian missionaries are at once caught up in and contribute to this irresistible force for change, and like virtually everyone else on our planet, they are deeply affected by the impact of values, images, goods, and weapons which emanate from the West and which are mediated through tourism, media images, Western-style education, global economy, the substitution of artificial needs for real needs, the generational and economic division of once coherent families and peoples, and the widespread and seemingly indiscriminate use of frighteningly destructive Western weapons against largely civilian populations all over the world. Missiology needs to ask deeply theological questions about prevailing notions of progress—notions whose roots extend to the old, discredited white man's burden, to a time when it was unabashedly assumed that a part of the missionary's task was to "civilize." The term's

metamorphosis into the word "develop" provides only the most threadbare of disguises, certainly not sufficient to conceal its fundamental Eurocentrism, and its effects are the same everywhere, with the West both its measure and its motor (see, for example, Norberg-Hodge, 1996).

It is within this context of chronic uncertainty and endemic mayhem that Escobar's stress on the authority of the Word of God is significant, offering us an understanding of ourselves, our times, and our destiny within the context of humankind's individually short and sometimes brutal sojourn on this planet. The Word of God is both a compass and a handbook, providing reliable direction regardless of where its readers might be located in time, culture, or circumstance.

In his fifth section, accenting the growth of poverty and inequality, Escobar rightly reminds us of the fact that the prospect of material, economic, and technological progress—once thought to be an inevitable outcome of social and economic organization along capitalist lines—has proven to be an illusory and fundamentally false dream. The relative proportion of impoverished people around the world is increasing, not diminishing. At the same time, the relative proportion of very rich persons is diminishing, while the percentage of the planet's material resources which they control is increasing.

A recent *United Nations Human Development Report*[2] provides some perspective on just what this means:

---

[1] This image comes from the colorful Sydney Smith, in his 1823 counter-petition to the several emancipating bills brought before the British Parliament in the first quarter of the 19th century—bills which alarmed his fellow Anglican clergymen. Smith suggested an alternative petition, asking "for an inquiry into all laws affecting the Roman Catholics of Great Britain and Ireland," in the hope that "only those which were absolutely necessary to the safety of Church and State might be suffered to remain." The quotation above was a part of his speech in support of his motion. Despite his eloquence, his motion was soundly defeated by his fellow Anglicans (see Russell, 1905, pp. 106-109).

[2] As summarized in *The New York Times* (September 27, 1998, p. 16).

1. The world's 225 richest individuals, of whom 60 are Americans with total assets of $311 billion, have a combined wealth of over $1 trillion—equal to the combined wealth of the poorest 47% of the entire world's population.

2. The three richest people in the world have assets that exceed the combined gross domestic product of the 48 poorest countries.

3. The average African household is some 20% poorer today than it was 25 years ago.

4. The richest 20% of the world's people consume 86% of all goods and services. The poorest 20% consume 1.3%.

5. Americans and Europeans spend $17 billion a year on pet food. This is $4 billion more than the estimated annual total needed to provide basic health and nutrition for everyone in the world.

6. Americans spend $8 billion a year on cosmetics—$2 billion more than the estimated annual total needed to provide basic education for everyone in the world.

Even in the United States, the gulf between rich and poor is growing. In comparing the change in relative wealth of the wealthiest and the poorest U.S. citizens between 1977 and 1999, Congressional Budget Office figures indicate that the poorest 20% of the U.S. population earned 5.6% of all income in 1977 but only 4.2% in 1999. Their after-tax income averaged $10,000 in 1977 but only $8,800 in 1999, a 12% decrease. The richest 1% of the U.S. population earned 7.3% of all income in 1977 and 12.9% in 1999. Their after-tax income amounted to $234,700 in 1977 and $515,600 in 1999, an increase of 119.7%.[3]

Evangelicals have responded to these realities by becoming more involved in "holistic mission projects," Escobar points out. This is appropriate, being the way of obedience, and it will need to be a continuing and growing priority if the gospel is to be comprehensible and meaningful. Partial obedience has always been lumped with disobedience in the Scriptures, and the line between "evangelism" and the so-called "social gospel" has always been an excuse for selective obedience. For Evangelicals, partial obedience is not an option.

The fact that the capacity for vital missionary initiative is passing from the North to the South at a time when the South's financial ability to engage in missions or theological education as modeled by the North is diminishing has serious implications, some of which we are just beginning to grasp. Escobar advocates an international model of mission which for many Western agencies will require a rethinking of their fundamental structures.

It has been common for missiologists and mission strategists to speak of "partnership." This is a useful term, but it has its roots in the cognitive domains of management and business and allows us to remain somewhat remote from the one

---

[3] These figures appeared in *The New York Times* (September 5, 1999, p. 16). See also Zuckerman (1999, p. 108). Zuckerman, the Editor in Chief of *U.S. News and World Report*, points out that the U.S. itself is becoming two nations. "The prosperous are rapidly becoming more prosperous, and the poor are slowly getting poorer." Even though the American economy continues to experience dramatic growth, according to New York University economist Edward Wolff, "the top 20% of Americans account for more than 100% of the total growth in wealth from 1983-1997, while the bottom 80% lost 7%." Zuckerman cites another study that found that "the top 1% saw their after-tax income jump 115% in the past 22 years. The top fifth have seen an after-tax increase of 43% during the same period, while the bottom fifth of all Americans—including many working mothers—have seen their after-tax incomes fall 9%." The result is that 4 out of 5 households are relatively worse off than they were 22 years ago.

with whom we partner. As the social and economic disparity between erstwhile "partners" increases, partnership becomes more and more complicated and to some extent unworkable, since in managerial terms a partnership between unequals always favors the more powerful partner. The term is to some extent satisfactory, so long as our ecclesiology stresses the *independence* of individual churches, in consonance with the tried and true "three-self" formula. But when we begin to apply a more biblically satisfactory set of metaphors to the relationship—organic metaphors that will not allow us to think of being "independent" from one another, but as *interdependent* members of the same body with limbs, torso, head, eyes, ears, etc.—it becomes more difficult to use the term. After all, what does it mean for a hand to be in partnership with a leg or a foot or an eye? All members are a part of the same body, and *partnership* in that context surely requires as a minimum a permanent sharing of resources, experiences, and agendas. We need an ecclesiology and a missiology that more aptly reflect the language, the intent, and the reality of God's view of the church as the body of Christ.

As a Mennonite, I heartily endorse what Escobar has written about the "end of Christendom," his sixth point. The funeral dirge of Christendom is one at which Christians should join in lifting their voices in praise to God, since we humans so easily confuse self-serving ends with God-tolerated means. I can think of only one social aggregate than can be more mindlessly self-serving than the nation-state, and that is the ethnic group. The notion that any nation-state ever has or indeed *can* manifest the self-giving, self-sacrificing spirit of Christ has been one of the great delusions of Christendom and of much of its missionary expression. The idea that the West in particular has been

somehow more "Christlike" than those other expressions of collective ego that we have come to call "nations" continues to result in great confusion in its inevitable conflation of human culture with Christian gospel.

Escobar's comments on post-modern culture and a new religiosity go naturally together, and I do not have time to dwell on them. I note only that resurgence of religious interest is not necessarily a hopeful sign, although it might be. To use a rather crude analogy, preoccupation with one's body is usually a sign of ill health or old age, not a sign of health. It may be that Western interest in religion is simply a symptom of that fatal malaise marking the approaching end of life. On the other hand, the disillusionment and hopelessness of post-modernism are quite consonant with observations of God's messengers nearly 3,000 years ago. The prophets were deeply disillusioned because they could see their societies as God saw those societies. If there is anything positive about the culture of post-modernity, it is that people now have the capacity to see themselves and their cultural contexts for what they really are—without God, hopeless, and in desperate need of redemption. This is a good starting point for conversion.

Jesus was no stranger to either old religions or fundamentalism, Escobar's ninth point. In the end, it was those bent on protecting the "old religion" who arranged for Jesus' execution. Jesus showed his followers the way to deal with this: the way of the cross, the way of the seed falling into the ground, the way of love for enemies, the way of forgiveness, the way of refusing to respond in kind. All of this takes place only at the level of everyday relationships with real people. It is risky, of course, but there is no other way.

The Pentecostal phenomenon is perhaps the most remarkable evidence that the gospel is still good news for the poor and not simply a secret passage into Western consumer culture and, in the sweet by and by, a comfortable "middle class" existence. It is only natural that there should be a surge in the Pentecostal phenomenon, since its concerns and expressions have always resonated with the poor—and most Christians around the world are now poor.

Escobar's conclusions begin with his appeal for a recovery of biblical patterns for mission. His four concluding observations—each of which suggests the "new" direction required if our missionary endeavors are to maintain or regain relevance—can be little improved upon within the confines of this short response.

That neither the present nor the future is very different from the past may be the most appropriate vantage point from which to contemplate the new century. Despite what appear to be remarkable changes at the turn of the century, the famous lament of the author of the book of Ecclesiastes provides a helpful perspective. After a lifetime in close pursuit of novelty, he observed that there is nothing new under the sun. This is at once comforting and disconcerting. Comforting, because we know that the eternal revelation of God transcends culture and time, addressing the sad realities of the human condition which, while expressing itself in various cultural contexts, remains essentially the same. We need peace with God. We need redemption. We cannot save ourselves. We need a Savior.

While it is not a little fascinating to look at the macro trends affecting persons, tribes, nations, continents, and the entire globe at the end of the century, it is entirely possible for us as missiologists and missionaries to become, in Walker Percy's (1983) words, "lost in the cosmos"—so caught up in the big picture that we lose sight of the particular. Missionary action always takes place at the micro level. The macro level is simply context. But the gospel is always mediated through and to specific persons, families, communities, and contexts. An understanding of global trends can be helpful only if it helps us to incarnate the gospel right where we are. If Evangelical missiology is to keep in touch with the really big issues, it must think small.

A theme implicit in much of what Escobar has written, but which we who fashion our livelihoods from thinking "missiologically" can inadvertently overlook, needs to be highlighted: God's people are never instructed or urged to love the world or large segments of populations within it. God can and does love the world, but human beings are so constituted that they cannot. When we try, our expressions of love for the multitudes inevitably degenerate into pious posturing. We are called upon to love one another, spouse, neighbor, stranger, and enemy—whatever the cultural or cross-cultural context. This is challenge aplenty for even the most pious among us. Wherever the context of our missionary work, unless we fall into the ground and "die" at this personal level, our missiology means nothing. Given the ways in which we missiologists have come to envision and project the Christian task, this fact is of profound missiological import.

When God sent his Son to save the world, he sent him to live in a small backeddy of the Roman Empire—in an occupied country, traveling on foot, never wandering very far beyond a 30-mile radius from where he grew up. It is good to recall that Jesus never even rode a bicycle, let alone flew in a jet! The Son of God, when he came to save the world, walked at three miles per hour (Koyama, 1980) and was constantly interrupted by the petty, intensely personal needs of individuals who could not realize what an important agenda he had personally—to save the world.

The most significant discussion in which we can engage involves this question: What does it mean to do missionary work in ways congruent with biblical patterns and models? Are there some constants that transcend time and culture and society? I believe there are:

1. We need a missiology that recaptures the servant mode—not the servant with an *a priori* agenda, but the servant who lets his or her master set the tasks.

2. We need a missiology that recaptures the corn of wheat principle—the "he saved others, he cannot save himself" approach to mission modeled and mandated by Jesus.

3. We need a missiology that distinguishes between mere motion and actual accomplishment, between slick organization and costly incarnation, between believable propaganda and true communication, between self-serving career and self-giving service.

4. We need a missiology that moves us away from "efficiency" and teaches us to walk with the poor.

5. We need a missiology that forces us to think small, that encourages us to recognize that each human being lives at the level of micro-context, that this is the level at which the good news transforms and transfigures, and that this is the Great Commission.

6. We need a missiology that translates the good news—a missiology that recognizes that any gospel not made visible in the living flesh of another human being is no gospel at all. It is simply noise.

References

Barrett, D. B., & Johnson, T. M. (2000, January). Annual statistical table on global mission: 2000. *International Bulletin of Missionary Research*, *24*(1), pp. 24-25.

Bonk, J. J. (1991). *Missions and money: Affluence as a Western missionary problem*. Maryknoll, NY: Orbis Books.

Conquest, R. (1999). *Reflections on a ravaged century*. New York: W. W. Norton & Company.

Conway, R. (1999). *Choices at the heart of technology: A Christian perspective*. Harrisburg, PA: Trinity Press International.

Koyama, K. (1980). *Three mile an hour God: Biblical reflections*. Maryknoll, NY: Orbis Books.

Norberg-Hodge, H. (1996). The pressure to modernize and globalize. In J. Mander & E. Goldsmith (Eds.), *The case against the global economy and for a turn toward the local* (pp. 33-46). San Francisco: Sierra Club Books.

Percy, W. (1983). *Lost in the cosmos: The last self-help book*. New York: Farrar, Straus & Giroux.

Russell, W. E. (1905). *Sydney Smith*. London: MacMillan & Co.

Sanneh, L. O. (1989). *Translating the message: The missionary impact on culture*. Maryknoll, NY: Orbis Books.

Walls, A. F. (1996). *The missionary movement in Christian history: Studies in the transmission of faith*. Maryknoll, NY: Orbis Books.

Zuckerman, M. B. (1999, October 18). A nation divided: What to do about the ever widening gulf between rich and poor? *U.S. News and World Report*, p. 108.

Jonathan J. Bonk, formerly Professor of Global Christian Studies at Providence College and Seminary in Canada, has served as Associate Director of the Overseas Ministries Study Center in New Haven, Connecticut since 1997. He became Director of OMSC and Editor of the International Bulletin of Missionary Research in July of 2000. He grew up in Ethiopia, where he and his wife also served as missionaries. He is an ordained Mennonite minister, has served as President of both the American Society of Missiology and the Association of Professors of Mission. He is the author of numerous articles and reviews and has published four books, the best known of which is Missions and Money: Affluence as a Western Missionary Problem (Orbis, 1991), now in its sixth printing. He is Project Director for the multilingual (English, French, Portuguese, Swahili) electronic Dictionary of African Christian Biography. He graduated from Trinity Evangelical Divinity School and the University of Aberdeen.

5

Globalization and world evangelism

ALEX
ARAUJO

H OW CAN A BRAZILIAN ministry leader obtain funds from a multi-national corporation like Microsoft? Simple, according to an electronic message I received recently. Microsoft offered to send someone a reward for testing one of its software products, this person writes. All one has to do, he explains, is send a particular e-mail message to as many friends as possible, as a test of a new Microsoft product. This person claims to have received several thousand dollars already, and he encourages all of us to participate in this product test to raise funds for our ministries. Anyone anywhere in the world can participate through e-mail, at no cost and in only a few minutes. I have not been able to verify this message, but the amazing thing is that the message was written by a sincere Christian leader at all.

Globalization permits the merging of widely disparate interests from any place on earth by any person with access to modern technology. It permits, even invites, as in the real-life example above, the merging of world evangelization and the marketing plans of a multi-national corporation. For some, as with this Brazilian friend, globalization seems to be a welcome development, because it offers new ways to find and apply resources for ministry. Others have serious misgivings, suspecting that there is a hidden danger when such disparate interests as the profit strategies of a multi-national corporation and the evangelism strategies of a missions agency come together.

The difference of perspective between those Christians who are willing to seize the benefits of globalization for missions purposes and those who see or at least strongly suspect something wrong with this approach defines the essence of relevant discussions about globalization and missions.

Is there something inherently bad or practically harmful to missions in the globalization phenomenon? Are there safe ways to take advantage of elements of globalization without at the same time being exposed to its harm? Perhaps more important still, is globalization merely a neutral realignment of socio-economic mechanisms, or does it have inherent ethical errors and weaknesses?

These questions cannot be ignored, because globalization itself cannot be ignored. It is shaping how we think and function in missions. Either we know what it is and how to control what it does to us and through us, or we will simply be shaped by it according to its own impersonal forces and agenda. The missions movement today already relies extensively on electronic mail, for example, one of the more ubiquitous tools made available worldwide by globalization. E-mail has made it possible for Christians from very different countries and socio-economic contexts to participate in dialogue about the theology and practice of missions. It has also begun to divide us into those who have access to electronic mail and those who don't. Some precious believers, toiling under harsh conditions, blessing many by their sacrificial service, are excluded from the rich mission dialogue the rest of us enjoy because they do not have effective access to e-mail.

Globalization of information not only permits wider participation in the dialogue, but also provides avenues for worldwide dissemination of prevailing ideas and methods concerning missions. While on the one hand it gives Christians of non-Western countries an opportunity to join the dialogue, it also provides new avenues for the better resourced Western Christians to promote and disseminate their own already-developed ideas through Internet-ready literature, courses, and activity reporting. These activities are extremely relevant to the question of better involvement of non-Western missions thinkers and practitioners in the worldwide missions movement, because they maintain and even increase the gap between the more affluent and less affluent churches, independently of spiritual worth and effectiveness of ministry.

Defining Globalization

How should Christians think about globalization?

Globalization is, at the practical level, a way of describing the manner in which socio-economic interaction is carried on. At this level, some would argue that it is ethically neutral. The rice I eat is just rice, whether it is produced by the local tenant farmer or by an international agro-business concern. At another level, globalization represents a way of thinking about the world, a worldview. It is a way of organizing priorities, thus establishing a scale of values for determining what is more important. "How is economic globalization likely to change our common future and particularly our view of what is important and of value?" asks Tom Sine (1999, p. 49).[1] Globalization, like any other worldview, has serious ethical implications. While it may not be a fully developed system of thought such as Marx-

---

[1] Sine's book *Mustard Seed versus McWorld* (1999) provides very practical approaches to understanding and responding to the pressures of globalization. The book is especially useful for American Christians, although non-Americans will also find it helpful as a tool for better understanding their American colleagues and their challenges. The book can also be used to identify some of the main issues of globalization that need to receive more specific treatment in each cultural context.

ism, socialism, or Western democracy, it does provide ethical themes, which we will discuss below. Christians eager to take advantage of the new tools of globalization must first reflect seriously about these less obvious ethical implications. My purposes in this essay are to identify and introduce for the larger discussion some of these themes and to suggest some questions Christians need to ask of one another concerning the implications of globalization for world missions.

What is globalization?

Globalization is a complex phenomenon that can be approached from many different directions. Thomas Friedman provides one of the best secular analyses in his book *The Lexus and the Olive Tree*. He offers the following as three key elements to a definition of globalization:

- Democratization of technology, finance, and information. "This means that it is now possible for hundreds of millions of people around the world to get connected and exchange information, news, knowledge, money ... financial trades ... in ways and to a degree never witnessed before" (Friedman, 1999, p. 45).
- Free-market capitalism as the organizing principle of world economics. "The more you let market forces rule and the more you open your [national] economy to free trade and competition, the more efficient and flourishing your economy will be. Globalization means the spread of free-market capitalism to virtually every country in the world" (Friedman, 1999, p. 8).
- A specific cultural bias. "... globalization has its own dominant culture, which is why it tends to be homogenizing.... Culturally speaking, globalization is largely, though not entirely, the spread of Americanization ... on a global scale" (Friedman, 1999, p. 8).

"The strongest advocates for a new global economic order," writes Tom Sine (1999, p. 50), "... have been schooled in a worldview that defines what is best largely in terms of economic growth and efficiency. And they have concluded that the best way to achieve those outcomes is through the creation of a borderless economic order."

Edward Luttwak (1999, p. 222) writes, "Everywhere the logic of turbo-capitalism [Luttwak's concept for what drives globalization] is that nothing should stand in the way of economic efficiency ... for nothing must hinder competition, which alone enforces efficiency by impoverishing less efficient individuals, firms, industries, local communities, and countries—and sometimes all of them at once." Another way to put this is that growth and change *must* occur because they *can* occur. The idea echoes the evolutionary view that a thing's existence is its own justification and that the possibility of growth and change is sufficient reason for that growth and change to occur. C. S. Lewis (1946, p. 295) anticipated this in the mid-1940s, when he put in the mouth one of his characters the following words: "... is justified by the fact that it is occurring, and it ought to be increased because an increase is taking place."

It seems, from these examples and from the writings of other students of globalization, that this complex reality contains the following key elements:

1. It is fueled primarily by economic considerations.

2. It is inspired by rapid economic growth and efficiency as the best foundation for solving humanity's problems.

3. It has a strongly Western, primarily American cultural imprint.

4. It is highly dependent on recent developments in communication technology.

5. It favors those who have a longer tradition in free-market capitalism and who lead in communication technology.

We will look at some of the implications of globalization to the Christian missions movement, but first we need to consider globalization in relation to the church.

Globalization and Christ's Church

The growth of the church around the world, in contrast to globalization, is an expression of eternal principles set in motion by God in Christ through the Holy Spirit. It is not a product of recent secular historical movements and trends.

The church was meant to become global even if the world remained forever provincial. Since Abraham, God has been speaking explicitly about the gathering of all nations into one people. The Psalmist writes, "The nobles of the nations assemble as the people of the God of Abraham, for the kings of the earth belong to God; he is greatly exalted" (Ps. 47:9).[2] And the writer of Revelation proclaims that the new Jerusalem, representing God's kingdom on earth, "does not need the sun or the moon to shine on it, for the glory of God gives it light, and the Lamb is its lamp. The nations will walk by its light, and the kings of the earth will bring their splendor into it…. The glory and honor of the nations will be brought into it" (Rev. 21:23, 24, 26).

We often hear the question these days how we should face globalization. It seems that we feel the church may be left behind if it doesn't adapt and adapt speedily. Globalization, the experts tell us, is the only boat available for mankind today. If we don't get into it, we will be left behind. Globalization is this inexorable force that

is sweeping the world like a tidal wave. Those who learn quickly to ride the wave will survive, and those who don't will perish. This idea seems to have infected some in the missions movement, to judge by the optimism and eagerness of some mission agencies in adapting to globalization's hopes and promises.

The question of how the church should face globalization is misplaced. From a biblical perspective, it is globalization that has to face the church. We must judge the "pattern of this world" and decide under the counsel of the Holy Spirit what is good and what is not good about it. As the Apostle Paul puts it, "Do not conform any longer to the pattern of this world, but be transformed by the renewing of your mind. Then you will be able to test and approve what God's will is—his good, pleasing, and perfect will" (Rom. 12:2).

The key principle for Christians looking at globalization, then, is to refuse to be lured, intimidated, or pressured by it. Globalization is the current strategy that a secular and lost humanity has developed to cope with an existence devoid of faith and hope in God. World evangelization is essentially the reality of which globalization is merely and ineffectively a shadow. In this sense, missions has the answer to the question that gave birth to globalization. The church does not need to learn how to adjust to globalization. It is called to speak to people caught up in globalization's tidal wave, just as it did with all the previous tidal waves in human history.

Jacques Ellul (1989, p. 4) has eloquently stated this point. Speaking of the church in society, he writes, "This 'light of the world' is that which gives meaning and direction to the history of the world, and thus explains it. In the succession of events which the course of history pre-

---

[2] See also Gen. 12:1-3; Isa. 49:6; 66:18-21; Matt. 28:19; Eph. 2:15-19; Rev. 5:9-10; 7:9; 11:15.

sents, there is no logic, no certitude, but this logic is supplied by the presence of the church, however strange this may seem ... the Christian ... reveals to the world the truth about its condition." The Christian, Ellul (1989, p. 39) continues, "judges the present time in virtue of a meta-historical fact, and the incursion of this event into the present is the only force capable of throwing off the dead weight of social and political institutions which are gradually crushing the life out of our present civilization."

This view does not give us license to be aloof or proud, nor to ignore the significant and occasionally beneficial changes brought about by globalization. It simply establishes a right order of relationship between the church and the current "pattern of this world."

Understanding Globalization

With the above discussion in mind, we must set ourselves to the task of understanding globalization and its implications to the work of missions.

First, the balance between nation-states has changed. In the present globalization system, the United States is the sole and dominant superpower, and all other nations are subordinate to it to one degree or another (Friedman, 1999, p. 11). In some ways and in a parallel sense, the situation resembles for the current American missions movement the colonial days of William Carey and Hudson Taylor. Just as Carey and Taylor rode on the wings of the British economic empire, with all its facilities and power of projection, American missionaries today ride on the global expansion of American economic activities and accompanying cultural exports. This is not a criticism of American missionaries. In some ways, Americans have no choice, just as Carey and Taylor did not. In fact, Taylor fought hard to shed his

Britishness. Yet even to the degree that he succeeded, he had to direct a fair amount of energy to that issue. So, to the extent that globalization today carries a strong American flavor, American missionaries have to face similar tensions. Conversely, non-Americans on the field have to contend with this American cultural overlay as they seek to work in cooperation with their American colleagues. The sooner both sides recognize this reality and discuss it openly, the better it will be for truly cooperative missions work.

Second, the balance between nation-states and global markets has changed. These global markets are made up of millions of investors moving money around the world instantly through their computers and from the privacy of their homes. Friedman calls them the "electronic herd." This "herd" cannot be tightly controlled by national governments. The national economy can be severely affected by this activity, whether or not it fits national policy. Like swarming bees, this herd cannot be controlled by governments, because they gain access to a nation's economy from any place in the world through electronic transactions. And they can force governments to make decisions and adopt policies by the simple threat of taking their investments from one country and instantly placing them in another. This weakens national sovereignty and erodes democratic processes. Voters may elect their leaders, but the international economy may dictate the leaders' policies.

Third, the balance between nation-states and individuals has changed. Individuals and their wealth—particularly very rich individuals—can move across national boundaries with increasing freedom. That means that financially powerful individuals such as Osama Bin Laden and Bill Gates may find themselves negotiating directly with governments of sovereign states, striking deals that their own countries' governments may not approve, yet are powerless to prevent.

Implications for Missions

What are the implications of this turn of events to the missions movement? The challenge of globalization intersects with the Christian missions movement in a variety of ways.

The theology of the church

We need to reflect on the current state of our theology of the church and of missions. The church, to be true to its nature, must be distinct, separate from any current human trend and condition, so that it can speak to humanity and to its condition. The Apostle Paul tells us that "God placed all things under [Christ's] feet and appointed him to be head over everything for the church, which is his body, the fullness of him who fills everything in every way" (Eph. 1:22-23). And God's "intent was that now, through the church, the manifold wisdom of God should be made known to the rulers and authorities in the heavenly realms, according to his eternal purpose which he accomplished in Christ Jesus our Lord" (Eph. 3:10-11). Unless we see the church as greater than the human condition at any point in history, it does not have a message. It must be "in" the world, in order to speak intelligibly to the world. But if it is "of" the world, it is part of the problem, however conscientious it tries to be in preaching the gospel.

The church is not supposed to cope with globalization, but rather to judge globalization and offer itself as the real global community. The church is what a globalized society can never be, "a chosen people, a royal priesthood, a holy nation, a people belonging to God, that you may declare the praises of him who called you out of darkness into his wonderful light" (1 Pet. 2:9). Peter, along with Paul, helps

us understand how the church stands as prophet and priest to the world. But in order to exercise its prophetic and priestly role effectively, the church cannot be or act like a mere religious segment of the world. The church is not part of the globalization phenomenon, needing to learn how to ride its wave, as human institutions must, in order to survive.

As Peter puts it, we are "aliens and strangers in the world" (1 Pet. 2:11). It seems, at times, that our local churches resemble more and more a religious version of business enterprises. We compete for customers by improving the marketing of our Christian product. We look to the business gurus to help us recreate our churches and agencies in terms that make sense within modern economic trends. The more our ecclesiology resembles in practice the commercial world around us, the more it fits the terminology and worldview of global economic trends. Unless we review our ecclesiology and restore it to its biblical foundations and conceptual language, we will not be able to judge the trends that surround us, and the churches may in fact become simply one of the many sub-elements of that trend. We have already seen the development of a school of thought that promotes the marketing of the church. Soon we may see the next development, the globalization of the church, along the same driving concepts of economic globalization: rapid numerical growth and efficiency defined by return on missions dollars.

Non-numerical language

We must rediscover the non-numerical language of the gospel. Evangelicalism has flourished predominantly in Western and North American societies during the last two centuries. This flourishing coincides with the development of the free-market capitalism that is now both the driving force and the essence of globalization. It has given Western society a numerical language that is particularly suited to business transactions, but terribly poor to describe the worth and experience of the gospel. Recently I attended a missions consultation that focused on a region of the world where the growth of the church is modest in comparison to certain places in Asia and Latin America. At least in two instances, speakers described the success of the mission in a given area by indicating the percentage of growth of the church in the last 10 years. It was interesting that this growth was described in percentages rather than absolute numbers, which allowed them to say the church grew 28 times in 10 years—an impressive growth rate. This way of reporting growth has a much greater impact on the churches back home than if the growth were described in absolute numerical terms: from 50 to a few thousand in 10 years.

Would the disciples in the early church have thought in terms of numerical valuation of the church? After all, the Lord Jesus used very different language, perhaps shocking to our ears, when he said that there is more joy in heaven for one sinner who repents than for 99 righteous; and he considered the widow's mite a greater offering than the larger offerings of the Pharisees. He also gave us a very humbling picture of the growth of the gospel in the parable of the narrow way and the broad way. And he never promised that Christians were to become a national majority population.

I am not arguing for a total abandonment of numbers in assessing and reporting our missions work, but I suggest that statistics and numbers for the most part be presented as footnotes to our field reports, since they seem to be given only marginal significance in the Scriptures. The actual language with which Christ described matters of the kingdom was quite different, and we need to rediscover it.

Conceptual language is powerful in shaping how we think and eventually what we believe. I recently attended another regional-focused missions consultation. In the midst of field reports by various missionaries, a woman believer from the region was asked to give her testimony. She spoke from the podium about how the gospel came to her family. As she elaborated on the biblical metaphor of the light of the gospel shining to the darkness of her people, her testimony became increasingly an emotional expression of deep gratitude to the Lord and to the missionaries he had sent to her country. She finished unable to speak, her eyes flooded with tears of gratitude to her gracious God.

I was myself deeply moved by such a beautiful reminder of the reason for missions, which is precisely to make the wonderful light of Christ to shine and deliver people from darkness. In my heart I deeply hoped the moderator would interrupt the formal agenda with a time of praise to God. Instead, as soon as this sister finished, the moderator announced the next presenter, and we went on with the report. Where was the rejoicing in the church for the one sinner who had repented? Can it be that we have become so shaped by the pattern of this world that we don't even recognize the full impact of our own service to God in the lives of those we touch? Therefore, this matter of language is very important. How can we judge the spirit of the age, the "pattern of this world," if we do not have an independent, biblically based conceptual language with which to describe it?

Exporting distortions

The church in mission-sending countries must be careful not to export such culturally generated distortions to emerging churches. Yet the Western church may not be able to escape the strong grip of economic globalization without the help of the emerging church. What does the church look like when it is not so heavily influenced by material affluence and driven by the mechanistic values of growth and efficiency? How do brothers and sisters who live at the margins of this worldwide globalization pattern experience communion with Christ and his family? We must learn to listen to and learn from them.

Redefining what it means to be human

Since globalization is essentially driven by economic forces, it must redefine what it means to be human in terms that are compatible to the structures, mechanisms, and outcomes of a free-market economy. We attribute to the economist Adam Smith much of the foundation of today's Western version of a market economy. Theologian Timothy Gorringe (1999, p. 30), discussing this point, writes, "Aristotle believed that speech was given us to form community, but for Smith speech was part of our 'property to barter, truck, and exchange one thing for another.' So for Smith it was not the polity [community] which came first, but the market. We see how the community that nourishes the virtues is displaced by this loose agglomerate of individuals in trade. Doubtless led on by the flow of his argument, Smith abandoned the elaborate cautions of his moral philosophy and famously observed that it is not to the benevolence of the butcher that we owe our dinner, but to the appeal to his self-interest."

Thus, Gorringe (1999, p. 30) goes on to say, "*Homo sapiens* is reduced to *Homo economicus*, the rational utility maximizer, of whom it is assumed that self-interest, expressed primarily through the quest for financial gain, is his main concern." Since globalization is primarily a globalization of the Western free-market economy, the market view of humans is that they are consumers—buyers and sell-

ers. Though people who are in the vanguard of globalization may deny that this is their view of human beings, in practice it really doesn't matter since they assume (whether implicitly or obviously) that in the end every consumer will eventually find space within the global economy and benefit from it.

The church, in contrast, must affirm the biblical view of human beings as *Homo spiritualis*, created male and female, in the image of God, not reducible to *Homo economicus* or any other variant.

Competition and Change

The free-market economic model is marked by the need for constant competition and change. Wealth, in this system, is created by competition and innovation. It is not a maintenance economy but a growth economy. "Today," writes Friedman (1999, p. 41), "there is no more First World, Second World, and Third World. There is now just the Fast World—the world of the wide open plain—and the Slow World—the world of those who either fall by the wayside or choose to live away ... in some walled-off valley of their own." Market economies have thrived for centuries by ruthless competition, in an economic Darwinism where the strongest survive by devouring the others. Globalization, says Friedman (1999, p. 41), "... put this process into hyperspeed in the 1980s, requiring companies and countries to move much faster in order to avoid disaster."

The reduction of humans to *Homo economicus* does not alleviate the anguish that a global free-market system driven by constant change at ever-increasing speed generates. Surely we must recognize that competition as a way of life is ultimately destructive and in contradiction to the life of the gospel. A socio-economic system that thrives only when there is fierce competition may indeed generate better medical treatment and improved food production. But its longer-term implications need serious and continuous assessment. Its implicit moral tenet is that each of us must fend for ourselves because there is no one else who is for us.

Effects on American Culture

We have seen that globalization is not culturally neutral. It is heavily marked and shaped by American culture, as Friedman points out. Various authors have extensively documented this fact, and I will not elaborate on it, except as it relates to the Christian missions movement. In summary, all we have to do is to travel to any country in the world, including some small towns in under-developed countries, to see the presence of American culture, whether in the music coming out of radio boxes, the brand names found in sports shoes and tee-shirts (in fact, the practice of wearing sports shoes and tee-shirts merely as fashion is itself an Americanism), the long lines of applicants for visas in American consulates, and the billboards advertising American products. Again, globalization is not neutral. It has given all of us, regardless of nationality, the wonders of the portable computer. Yet, it is American-based Intel and Microsoft which make it possible for us to use it. This means that globalization provides a home-culture flavor for American mission personnel that is not experienced by missionaries of any other country. This reality says that the role of Americans in missions is not simply that of just another cultural group, but of a group whose culture and values have a major influence in shaping the trend and values of globalization.

More specific to our missions topic, we note the predominance of American authors in Christian bookstores throughout the world, of American worship music CD-ROMs and tapes, and the trend toward "seeker friendly" services copied from America. While other societies have international projection and influence, none comes close to matching the extent of American influence. But does this projection of American Christianity worldwide result in the global church being enriched by deeper spirituality and more serious missiology?

I must make the following caution at this point. It is very important that the reader not conclude that this is merely a generalized criticism of American believers or specifically of American missionaries. It is simply a factor to take into account as we consider the impact of globalization on world missions. It would be unprofitable and unjust to fault all American believers for what obviously is not of their doing. Neither does their cultural locus disqualify them for effective participation in the international missions enterprise. My point is simply to say that the role of Americans in missions requires a more complex self-assessment in light of their society's place in the globalization phenomenon.

Implications of Cultural Bias

What are the implications for missions of this cultural bias in favor of the United States? First of all, a missions movement so steeped in the dominant culture that drives globalization is bound to reflect, consciously or unconsciously, elements of the prevailing value system. It is easy to discern in American missions thinking certain traits that reflect the economic globalization mindset, things such as numerical thinking, pragmatism, efficiency, and continuous quantifiable growth, to name the more obvious.

Second, the American church has been predominant in leading and shaping the modern missions movement, at least since the end of World War II. That means that for much of the promising emerging missions movements from Latin America, Africa, Asia, and even Eastern Europe today, the most visible missions model is American. In this sense, American missions leaders have a burden that they may not have chosen to carry, but it is theirs nevertheless. They must pay particular attention to how globalization trends, so closely tied to American culture as it is projected around the world, shape their missions model and how this model is unwittingly reproduced.

Third, missions thinkers and practitioners from the emerging missions movements around the world, and even from Western Europe, can in good faith help Americans see beyond their cultural blind spots (all cultures have them). But Americans must be helped to divest themselves of undue valuation derived from the free-market globalization, values such as the primacy of efficiency, continuous quantifiable growth, excessive pragmatism, and numerical thinking as applied to the work of missions.

Unequal Distribution

Though signs of a global economy and accompanying value systems can be seen nearly everywhere, it is important to understand that globalization is not experienced equally by everyone. It is possible to believe that globalization has made us all equal in the face of the market forces that shape us. But this is not true. As we pointed out before, globalization has expanded the free-market economy into world scale. That means that those societies with a longer history of an innovative free-market economy have a decided advantage. They set the pace, and the others

must work very hard simply not to fall further behind. Americans, we have seen, are at the front of the tidal wave, with some European and Asian countries close behind and matching the pace. But the vast majority of the peoples of the world are lumped together in a very distant third place. Though people from all countries can experience globalization, not all can participate in shaping it or reaping its benefits.

Globalization is experienced differently by people near its front and people at the rear. Like the paralytic at the pool of Siloam, those in weaker and less stable economies are too far from the water's edge, and there is always someone who plunges in first whenever the angel stirs the water. That someone will most likely be an American, Japanese, or Northern European. It is easy to say that with globalization we are all part of the same reality. Yet some Christians live in a Western country with a negligible unemployment rate, while others live where unemployment reaches 50% to 60%. In countries near the front of the globalization tidal wave, the church parking garages are full of relatively new automobiles. Churches in countries at the rear may not even have paint on the walls, much less own a parking garage or have members who drive cars.

Implications for missions

For the missions movement, it is significant that most of the still unreached peoples of the earth belong to countries that bring up the rear of globalization. What are some of the implications of this reality?

First, we must discern this fact beyond superficial appearances. When I traveled through the rural communities of Chiapas in southern Mexico, I was intrigued by the extensive Coca-Cola distribution network. Coca-Cola signs appeared frequently along the roads, and occasionally I saw Coca-

Cola warehouses and trucks, reflecting a fairly extended distribution system. Signs of Western commercialism in places like Chiapas, Mexico, may give the impression that globalization is more evenly spread than is true.

In Chiapas, rural peasants still cultivate small plots of land for daily survival. In West Kalimantan, among the Dayaks I visited two years ago, the drink offered to us was not Coca-Cola but coconut milk, which our host obtained by climbing one of the coconut trees on his property, harvesting a few coconuts, opening them with a machete, and serving the nourishing, fresh, cool liquid to us. These people are a little farther away from the reach of globalization. With or without Coke, the least reached peoples of the world—with the exception of a small elite—still do not directly participate in the global economy. It can be argued that indirectly or not, they are part of it. But the fact that a Chiapas Indian may have become addicted to Coca-Cola does not mean that he is ready to understand the new language of globalization.

Second, failure to recognize the uneven impact of globalization around the world has implications for missionary training. The preparation and training of missionaries to reach the remaining unreached may not need to differ very much from the way pioneering missionaries were trained. Yet the pace of socio-economic development in mission-sending countries may pressure mission agencies into more sophisticated and complex models of ministry, which make heavy use of technology and may be less effective in the host countries.

Third, the unevenness with which globalization distributes resources and allocates control of decision-making, favoring those near the front of the trend, means that Western mission efforts will continue to have a disproportionately greater influ-

ence in the world missions movement unless we find a way to shift the weight away from globalization-generated values. What adjustments can Western believers make to minimize this imbalance?

The view from the rear

Significantly, globalization is predominantly a Western concept, and from there it spreads to other economically powerful nations. It was primarily born of a Western reality and shaped and defined by Western paradigms. Paradigms define the nature of problems and limit the range of solutions. It is not surprising, then, that it is the Westerners in the missions movement that seem more at home with the subject and more likely to engage it. What does globalization look like to those near the rear? What perspective can they bring to the missions movement and the remaining task of world evangelization? Perhaps they can help us see world evangelization as more than a task we must accomplish. They can help us to see where the competitive urge of free-market economics contradicts the Scriptures and can help us to correct our thinking. They may also help us, among other things, to see that things that seem like virtues for those living at the front end of globalization may not look like virtues at all from a biblical perspective. And the fact is that both in Scripture and history, most of the advance of the people of God has taken place in contexts of weakness, poverty, and uncertainty.

It is essential for the health of the missions movement that we really listen to Christians from the rear. Those at the front may not be able to see and value the wonderful things God is doing through his church elsewhere.

Missions as an Antidote

Missiologist, missionary, and anthropologist Don Richardson faced criticism from non-Christian anthropologists that he and all missionaries are harmful to the culture of the people they seek to evangelize. Some secular anthropologists charge that the introduction of a new religion disrupts benevolent age-old beliefs and customs that define the values of persons within that culture, thus creating insecurity and leading to the breakdown of the cultures altogether. Richardson ably corrects the critics by pointing out that long before the missionary comes to a people, their doom is already sealed by the incursion of profiteers and adventurers (including the anthropologists who supposedly study these peoples in supposed neutrality), who introduce destructive new elements such as destruction of the environment, liquor abuse, and new forms of diseases. Missionaries, on the other hand, actually bring to the peoples of the world a set of values that are much more likely to enable them to resist the incursions of this incipient globalization. Though accelerated to the point where it covers the globe and is making itself nearly irresistible to any human culture, globalization has manifested itself to some degree for centuries.

One of my favorite books is the biography of John Paton, missionary to the New Hebrides more than a century ago. One of his frustrations was the fact that British colonial authorities did nothing to police the European merchants and profiteers who introduced the liquor, diseases, and firearms that caused irreparable damage to the indigenous peoples to whom he ministered. Over 100 years ago, Paton, like Richardson, worked hard to prepare these people for the growing, irreversible onslaught of globalization in its earlier expressions. As Richardson (1992, p. C-144) states: "There are reasons why missionaries had to go into isolated areas like Irian Jaya as soon as they could. History has taught them that even the most isolated minority cultures must eventually be overwhelmed by the commercial and political expansion of the majority peoples."

Missions today still can perform a significant service to the nations by giving them a new set of values—God-given values with which they can judge all economic systems, including the alien incursions of global market forces. Are new believers resulting from our missions work becoming equipped to judge the pattern of this world, or is our missions work merely helping make them more compliant with it? This equipping of the new saints is not a peripheral by-product of missions, but central to it. But in order to equip effectively, we must ourselves:

1. Understand the nature and power of globalization, not merely separating the products that are beneficial from those that are harmful, but discerning the value system that is communicated by globalization's very existence and nature.

2. Recognize the degree to which globalization may have already begun to reshape our worldview and take steps to renew our minds through the Scriptures.

3. Reaffirm (for some of us, perhaps even rediscover) a biblical worldview that places Christ and his church above world trends, whether economic, political, cultural, or religious.

Mission Partnerships and Globalization

The face of the church today has changed dramatically since 100 years ago.

• The church has changed geographically: In 1900, most Evangelical believers were in North America, England, and Northwest Europe. Today, these regions comprise perhaps only 25% of the worldwide Evangelical church.

• The church has changed ethnically: The church the Lord sees from his throne today has many more people from Asia,

Africa, and Latin America than from North America and Europe.

• The church has changed intellectually: No longer are theological thinking and understanding coming predominantly from North America and Europe. Godly men and women from other continents are studying, researching, writing, and teaching on an equal footing with their North American and European colleagues.

• The church has changed dynamically: Today, most of the growth of the church worldwide is generated locally and nationally, rather than provoked and led by expatriates.

We would be seriously mistaken if we assumed that these factors are just another expression of some religious version of the wider globalization trend. They are, rather, the expression of the sovereignty of God in Christ, manifest in his church to fulfill his Great Commission.

Back to the Beginning

This encouraging state of the borderless church of Christ today offers us a marvelous opportunity to learn new ways of working together. We must abandon, through newly acquired mental and spiritual disciplines, any trace of paternalism, cultural resentment, or cultural blinders that might cause us to miss the blessing that comes from brothers and sisters from other cultures. Nigerians and North Americans, Koreans and Brazilians, Filipinos and Chinese, Swedes and Malays, and believers in every nation on earth form the one universal church, the people of the God of Abraham, "a holy nation, a people belonging to God" (1 Pet. 2:9). In contrast to the doomed Babel of our day, we live like strangers in a foreign country, looking forward together to the "city with foundations, whose architect and builder is God" (Heb. 11:10).

Finally, we must return to the beginning. Globalization is a logical development of a secular world system. It is the best one can expect of a world resistant to the love and the kingdom of God. As such, it is grossly inadequate to answer the pressing deepest anxieties and despair of humanity. The church must be careful not to be too comfortable in the company of globalization. The church is the worshiping community of God, the one legitimate unifying structure for the peoples of the world. I believe the history of Babel was recorded precisely to help us understand this. It was humankind's best effort to unite all peoples into one world community. God rejected it as unfit for the purpose. He offers instead a new community through the seed of Abraham, the church. We are the alternative. The church today must stand to globalization as Abraham stood to Babel (see Gen. 11:1-8; 12:1-3). Globalization is not the enemy, but it is a bad answer to the problem of the fall and fragmentation of humanity, and it will fail, just as Babel failed.

"Woe! Woe, O great city, O Babylon, city of power! In one hour your doom has come! The merchants of the earth will weep and mourn over her because no one buys their cargoes anymore ... articles of every kind ... and bodies and souls of men" (Rev. 18:10-13).

Our mission remains, as always, to bring to the stranded peoples of the world the invitation to join the community of the God of Abraham and become the kingdom of the Lord and of his Christ, who shall reign forever and ever in a truly universal kingdom.

References

Ellul, J. (1989). *The presence of the kingdom.* Colorado Springs, CO: Helmers & Howard.

Friedman, T. L. (1999). *The Lexus and the olive tree.* New York: Farrar, Straus & Giroux.

Gorringe, T. J. (1999). *Fair shares: Ethics and the global economy*. New York: Thames & Hudson.

Lewis, C. S. (1946). *That hideous strength: A modern fairy-tale for grown-ups*. New York: The Macmillan Company.

Luttwak, E. N. (1999). *Turbo-capitalism: Winners and losers in the global economy*. New York: HarperCollins Publishers.

Richardson, D. (1992). Do missionaries destroy cultures? In R. D. Winter & S. C. Hawthorne (Eds.), *Perspectives on the world Christian movement: A reader* (rev. ed.) (pp. C-137–C-148). Pasadena, CA: William Carey Library.

Sine, T. (1999). *Mustard seed versus McWorld: Reinventing life and faith for the future*. Grand Rapids, MI: Baker Books.

Alex Araujo was born in Brazil. His parents were among the first-generation Evangelicals in his home town. Alex and his wife Katy have three children. Araujo has become bicultural after many years in the United States. He has served with the IFES in Portugal and with the COMIBAM 87 steering committee in Brazil. He served for 10 years as Director of International Operations with Partners International and is currently serving with Interdev as a consultant in contextualization and cross-cultural partnership dynamics. Araujo has a bachelor's degree in political science and a master's in international relations from San Jose State University, California.

I N JANUARY 1999, England reeled under the shocking news
that Glen Hoddle, the coach of the England national football team, had been sacked. This was not for failure on the
football field (though that would have been justified enough!)
but because of remarks he made about the disabled. Hoddle
had a Christian religious experience some years ago which
led to his being called a "born-again Christian." However,
more recently he has embraced a form of New Age spirituality under the influence of a spiritual faith-healer, Eileen
Drewery. He expressed the view that the disabled are as they
are because of their karma from previous lives. It was, indirectly, their own fault.[1] This statement outraged public sentiment in Britain and produced a fascinating clash of cultural
and ethical worldviews. Hoddle's view, of course, comes
straight from the Hindu roots of much New Age philosophy
(though he did not go on to include women as also "suffering" the results of their karma, perhaps fortunately for him,
even though that is also part of the re-incarnational Hindu
worldview).

Interestingly, the response to Hoddle shows up a contradiction in secular pluralism. On the one hand, a "politically correct" ideology wants to affirm the validity of Hindu
and New Age "alternative" spiritualities and reject allegedly
"absolutist" and "arrogant" Christian claims. Yet on the other

Christ and the mosaic of pluralisms

C HRIS
W RIGHT

---

[1] Hoddle's words, in an interview with *The Times*, were, "You
have to come back [in another lifetime] to learn and face some of
the things you have done, good and bad. There are too many injus-
tices around. You and I have been physically given two hands and
two legs and half-decent brains. Some people have not been born
like that for a reason. The karma is working from another lifetime....
It is not only people with disabilities. What you sow, you have to
reap."

hand, it is also very "politically correct" to affirm and defend the disabled (or more "correctly," the "differently abled").

What the Hoddle affair shows up is that in the latter case, the "politically correct" attitude itself is the legacy of a Christian worldview which affirms the value of every unique individual human being and denies the debilitating and imprisoning doctrine of karma. This contradiction within popular religious and moral belief was not much noticed, however. Pluralism does not foster clear thinking about the inconsistencies it is happy to live with. One version of popular pluralism says, "It doesn't matter what you believe so long as you are sincere." Another version seems to say, "It does matter what you believe if it means insulting the weak." But those who so vociferously adopt the latter view would probably not like to be told that such a view is itself strongly indebted to the biblical and Christian worldview.

This example from recent British life illustrates how popular spirituality and opinions about ethical and social issues are profoundly influenced by a great plurality of religious worldviews, some being new forms of pre-Christian paganism, others being very ancient Oriental religious fundamentals re-packaged in Western forms.

The Task

My understanding of the task assigned to me in this paper is two-fold:

1. To survey some of the forms of pluralism that lie behind the pluralities of our world as we enter the new millennium.[2]

2. To suggest what will be key tasks for Evangelical missiology in relation to them. It is not my brief, as I understand it, to propose what new *mission strategies* may be needed in relation to global pluralities, but rather to focus on what will be the issues needing to be addressed by Evangelical *theological* reflection that should undergird our mission activity.

I have chosen three examples of pluralism that I see as particularly challenging to Evangelical missiology: hermeneutical, religious, and ethical.[3] Part of the reason for this selection is that these three forms of pluralism directly challenge three of the defining marks of Evangelicalism—our concern for the authority of the Bible, for the uniqueness of Jesus Christ, and for transformed living according to biblical ethical standards. These three are also central to an Evangelical understanding of mission, which flows from our understanding of the scriptural mandate, proclaims that Jesus Christ alone is Lord and Saviour, and aims to produce transformed human lives and communities.

I fully realise that this is an inadequate selection—there is a plurality of pluralisms! Even pluralism itself is changing. However, it is hoped that those reading this sketch will helpfully fill out the gaps in my own presentation, and that other paper writers will address issues that I am well aware of but have not felt able to address in the confines of this paper. This would especially include the plurality of contextualized Christologies and the missiologies that flow from them. I have also chosen not to discuss the inner plurality

---

[2] I will use the term *plurality* to denote the empirical phenomena of social, political, ethnic, religious, etc. variety. *Pluralism* denotes the usually relativistic ideologies that support or respond to those phenomena. Plurality is simply an observable fact of life. Pluralism is a philosophy. I shall try to maintain this distinction.

[3] In the first draft of this paper, I also included ethnic/political pluralism, but I have omitted that variety now, since some aspects of that phenomenon are discussed in Samuel Escobar's paper (see chapter 3), under the heading "Globalization and Contextualization."

to be found within Evangelical missiology itself (though I refer briefly to it under "Religious Pluralism" below).

An Age of Enormous Transition

Finally, by way of introduction, it is vital that we give full recognition to the transition from modernity to post-modernity that is taking place in a very patchy way around the world, together with the implications not only for the practice of Christian mission, but also for the task of missiology. This is not to ignore the fact that in some parts of the world, the transition is still more from pre-modernity into modernity itself. However, it is the case that some forms of pluralism that Christian missiology must address are the product of post-Enlightenment modernity, whereas others are the product of the post-modern reaction to modernity itself. Religious pluralism, for example, actually exhibits a variety of forms that have roots in the intellectual and cultural soil of *both* modernity and post-modernity. Missiological response, as we shall see below, must discern and distinguish these different roots when confronting different brands of religious pluralism.

By *modernity* I am referring to the epoch of Western civilization that began with the Renaissance, flourished in the wake of the Enlightenment, and has reached its zenith in 19th and 20th century cultures dominated by the triumphs of science and technology. Its dominant characteristic has been the exaltation of autonomous human reason and the application of reason to every realm of life. There are many excellent analyses of modernity's characteristics and history.[4] Among the features of modernity that are particularly relevant to the Christian confrontation with various pluralisms are those listed by Andrew Walker (1996, ch. 5): the rise of the nation-state, the establishment of functional rationality, the emergence of structural (epistemological) pluralism, the emergence of cultural pluralism, a worldview dominated by science and the idea of progress, and the growth of individualism.

By *post-modernity* I am referring to the shift in Western intellectual and popular culture that began in the 1960s and 1970s. It is helpful to distinguish the intellectual and the popular forms of post-modernity and, furthermore, in each case to observe that there are negative and positive aspects to the form.[5]

Intellectual post-modernism

Intellectually, through the work of such as Foucault, Lyotard, Derrida, and Baudrillard, the whole Enlightenment project was exposed as having faulty foundations. The negative or "deconstructing" acids included the observation that so-called "objective and factual truth" depends on all kinds of assumptions, which are themselves relative and questionable. Foucault pointed out that these hidden assumptions also frequently functioned as an inherent ideology of Euro-centric power and hegemony. Language itself is no longer seen as referential (referring to real objects) but symbolic (a system of signs). The post-modern intellectual world is characterized by relativism, with all attempts at finding meaning doomed to being nothing more than arbitrary and changing social constructions.

---

[4] See, for example, Sampson, Samuel, & Sugden (1994); Giddens (1990); and Walker (1996).

[5] In the section that follows, I am dependent on the helpful outline that explores these distinctions provided by Craig Van Gelder (n.d.).

Not all intellectual post-modern culture is negative in this way, however. There are those who helpfully explore the *relativity* of all our knowing, without accepting utter *relativism*. The position known as *critical realism* accepts that there is an objective real world out there (physically and historically) which we can know, but it insists that we need to be constantly critical of our own capacity to know it with any finality or completeness. All our knowing is embedded in culture, history, and community, but that does not *invalidate* it. We may never be able to know fully or perfectly, but that does not mean we cannot know anything. So we need to be humble (shedding Enlightenment arrogance) but not despairing.[6]

In another way also, post-modernity returns to perspectives on human life and history which have been and still are held by substantial sections of the human race who have not yet been engulfed by the Enlightenment assumptions of Western-style modernity. I quote here from helpful comments made on the first draft of my paper by Miriam Adeney:

"Post-modernism has a number of aspects which may have positive dimensions. For example: (1) Subject and object cannot be disconnected. (2) Fact and value cannot be disconnected. (3) History is not necessarily progressing. (4) Cultures are not necessarily ranked. (5) Truth is experienced in multiple and incomplete ways, including paradox and ambiguity. (6) If there is a meta-narrative, it is not based on Enlightenment categories.

"Post-modernism is not really a problem for much of the world, who always have seen the sense of the above six perspectives and so are not disturbed by their rise in the post-modern period."

It may well be, therefore, that Christian mission in the 21st century will find that some aspects of the post-modern worldview are more compatible with bringing the gospel to certain cultures than the values of modernity, which have unfortunately characterized much Western mission.

Popular post-modernism

Turning to the popular side of post-modernity, popular culture manifests the same ambiguity of negative and positive forms of post-modernity. Negatively, there is the brutal nihilism of some forms of art and cinema. Life is meaningless: so what? The failure and emptiness of so much of the promise inherent in the mythology of modernity have led to a great deal of pessimism in Western life, as well as a very shallow attitude of "get what you can from the present: there isn't much future to look forward to."

But post-modernity has its positive side in popular culture as well. There are the more vibrant forms of playfulness, collage, irony, and symbolism of much contemporary culture. Mix and match; switch images; plunder the past and mix it with the present and future; don't look for depth but enjoy the surface; life is a carnival to be enjoyed, not a drama to be understood. Furthermore, post-modernity celebrates diversity of culture, whereas modernity pushes for uniformity and homogenization of human life into secular, scientific, and materialistic categories.

Again, Miriam Adeney in her comments on the earlier draft of this paper warned against regarding plurality as a bad or bewildering thing. She says, "I like to think of God's glorious multicultural kaleidoscope. I view cultures as treasure chests

---

[6] See Best & Kellner (1991, pp. 256-304). A helpful exposition of "critical realism" in relation to biblical history is provided by the outstanding Evangelical New Testament scholar N. T. Wright (1992, pp. 31-46).

of symbols for exuberant expression of the image of God. It's true that people (as sinners) create patterns of idolatry and exploitation in every culture. Equally, however, people (in God's image) create patterns of beauty, wisdom, and kindness in every culture."

I fully agree and would say that post-modernity's celebration of cultural diversity is a lot closer to the Bible's own affirmation of "every tribe and nation and language" than is the homogenizing anti-culture of modernity.

It is important, then, to be aware of the fact that we live in an age of transition—and it is not neat. People and societies do not go to bed one night "modern" and wake up the next day "post-modern." There is an inter-layering between modernity, late or hyper-modernity (the "McWorld" phenomenon (Sine, 1999) of the globalized, multi-national, capitalist world), and post-modernity. At the same time, of course, large sections of humanity are bound to a religious worldview in which the philosophical issues of modernity and post-modernity are largely irrelevant or are treated with scathing dismissal as evidence of the poverty of "Western religion." The challenge to missiology is to know which world we are addressing in any given context, which world the church itself is identified with, and what challenges the gospel presents to each of the interwoven worldviews.[7]

Hermeneutical Pluralism

The transition from modernity to post-modernity is producing some fascinating effects in the world of biblical hermeneutics, which have knock-on effects in missiology, since so many missiological issues are hermeneutical in essence. This is especially so for Evangelicals, because of our commitment to attaining a theology of mission that can be defended as "biblical." The problem is, what does it mean to be "biblical," and who decides when you are or are not being "biblical"?

Enlightenment modernity constrained biblical hermeneutics into the straitjacket of the historical-critical method and a form of "modern scientific exegesis" that excluded the transcendent from Scripture as sharply as autonomous rationality excluded it from the natural sciences. But, as Brueggemann and others have pointedly made clear, the myth of neutrality, of scientific objectivity, concealed a Western hegemony in biblical studies that tended to stifle all other voices or readings.

Post-modernity, with its rejection of all hegemonies and deep suspicion of all claims to "scientific objectivity," finality, and universality, has challenged the critical hermeneutical consensus on Scripture as well and has opened up a world of almost infinite plurality of readings and interpretations. At one level, this has had the exhilarating effect of giving a place in the sun to a great variety of contextual readings of the Scripture which are not bound to the historical-critical method. There is value in recognizing the *relativity* of all hermeneutics. A positive benefit of the post-modern shift in biblical studies is that you don't have to submit your interpretation of Scripture to a single accrediting agency—the Western critical guild of scholarship. On the other hand, the post-modern rejection of any foundation or grounds on which we might affirm a reading of the biblical text to be *right or wrong* opens up an uncontrolled *relativism*. The plurality of contexts in which the text is read and heard becomes a pluralism of approach that has no limits or controls in

---

[7] Helpful discussion of these interwoven phenomena is to be found in Van Gelder (1996).

relation to the truth of the text. Indeed, such an approach questions whether the very concept of "the truth of the text" is meaningful. The text can have as many meanings as there are readers and contexts.

I believe 21st century missiology will have to wrestle with a *doctrine of Scripture* that moves beyond the way Evangelical scholarship has tended to defend the inspiration and authority of the Bible with the concepts and methods of modernity itself, towards a more dynamic understanding of the authority and role of the Bible in a post-modern world. And I think this will be one of the biggest challenges for Christian theology in the 21st century, since there is no mission without the authority of Christ himself, and our access to that authority depends upon the Scriptures. *So, a major missiological task for Evangelical theology will be a fresh articulation of the authority of the Bible and its relation to Christ's authorization of our mission.*

Faced with the basic hermeneutical question, "What does this biblical text mean?" scholars have tended to focus on one of three possible locations for the real source of "meaning" in texts: (1) the author(s), (2) the text itself, or (3) the reader(s). I would like to look at each of these three focal points. First, I will very briefly describe each one and evaluate some key strengths and weaknesses. Then I would like in each case to explore not only how they relate to the contemporary plurality of cultures and religions, but also how cultural and religious plurality was actually a major factor in the *ancient biblical context* in which the text emerged and which it addressed.

Author-centred focus

This hermeneutical approach, which is common to Evangelical as well as more critical interpretation, assumes that the meaning of any biblical text is to be found by going back to the origins of the text. Exegesis is fundamentally based on recovering the author's intent. This then involves the grammatico-historical method. By means of textual criticism, lexical and semantic study, words, syntax, and grammar, the exegete seeks to answer the question, "What did this author actually say, and what did the words mean at the time?" A vital step in this process is to "set the text in its context" or rather, its contexts, which will include canonical, historical, social, and cultural contexts. Then, further, all the tools of critical study, sometimes collectively described as the historico-critical method, will be employed to explore the origins of the text before us. These include source criticism, form criticism, redaction criticism, etc. The common aim is to get as close as possible to understanding what the original author(s) of the text meant to communicate through its production, collection, and preservation.

There are several obvious strengths in such an approach:

- It seems to be the "common sense" approach. It assumes that meaning starts in the mind of the author; when somebody speaks or writes, he or she intends to communicate some meaning which the hearer/reader is meant to understand. This approach respects the priority of author-intent.

- Author-centred focus tries to take an objective approach, arguing for some core of stable meaning in each text, which is in principle recoverable by the exegete.

- This approach offers some control over the hermeneutical process by setting limits/boundaries to possible meanings. It enables some adjudication of legitimate and illegitimate interpretations. We may agree that a text could have several possible meanings but also agree that some meanings are impossible. This does not guarantee "certainty"—there is always room for disagreement among readers. But there is an assumption that we *can* know enough to get a reasonably close approximation to what the author probably meant to say.

• The importance of paying attention to the authors of biblical texts also lies in their character as witnesses (directly or indirectly) to the story of salvation. It is assumed that biblical texts are referential. That is, they actually refer to real events in the real world—events in which God has acted for our salvation. The world of the biblical authors is the world where things happened that constitute the gospel. The biblical text is like a window to that world. Using the Bible among the religions must therefore mean telling the story which makes it good news, not merely treating it as a quarry of religious ideas and ideals for comparison, admiration, or exchange.

• This last point highlights the futility of the question, "Is there salvation in other religions?" Such a question overlooks the primary nature of salvation in the Bible, namely, as something that God has done in and through the story which the Bible relates. Other religions do not save, not because they are inferior as religions in some way, but because religion itself does not save anybody. God does. Other religions do not tell the story, this story. This is also why we cannot accept the substitution of the scriptures of other religions for the Old Testament.

But there are also some dangers if we focus exclusively on the search for the original author's intent:

• Obsession with origins can obscure the purpose of the text. The expression "modern scientific criticism" reveals the fact that the rise of the critical approach to the text went hand in hand with Enlightenment modernity's preference for explaining everything by finding causes at

the expense of teleology (i.e., at the expense of seeking the purpose of something). Science explains by reducing phenomena to their smallest parts and by seeking causes of how things have become what they are. It does not ask, "What is this *for*?" Similarly, some critical exegesis of the Bible breaks the text up into ever smaller sources and then explores the origins, history, and structure for the smallest possible units of the text, but it does not answer the question, "Yes, but what is this book as a whole actually *saying*? What is this text *for*? What does it *do*?"

• Author-centred focus treats the text as a window, through which we can gain access to the authors' own world. However, exclusive attention to that world ("the world behind the text") can obscure the fact that the purpose of a window is also to let the light shine into the room of the observer—i.e., it can overlook (or exclude) the revelatory function of the biblical text. The text is not there simply to shed light on the world of ancient Israel or the early church, but to be "a light to *my* path." In other words, an Evangelical approach to the Bible recognizes that "author-intent" is not confined to the human author but must also include the intent of the divine Author whose message addresses every human context through these inspired texts.

In what way, then, does an author-centred focus relate to religious plurality? It is vital to remember that the biblical authors did not speak or write in a vacuum: religious plurality was often a factor in their contexts just as much as ours. Their "intended meaning" was related to their world. We do not just look for a sealed package of "original meaning" and *then* seek to apply it to our context of mission in the midst of plurality; we need to recognize that what they meant in their context was itself shaped by the missional engagement of God and God's people with the world around them.

Here are a few examples in which religious plurality is clearly part of the context of the author's world and needs to be taken into account when interpreting the text in question:

- **Exodus 15**, the song of Moses. The polemical affirmation of the kingship of Yahweh is made in the context of a power encounter with Pharoah's claim to divinity.

- **Joshua 24:14f.** "Choose today …," whether Mesopotamian gods of the ancestors or the gods of Egypt or of Canaan. The monotheistic covenantal choice of Yahweh was made in the context of acknowledged religious plurality which was part of the roots and background of the people of Israel.

- **Hosea**, confronted with the syncretism of Baal cults with Yahwism, takes the offensive by using the sexual nature of the former as a source of language and imagery to portray the "married" relationship of Yahweh and Israel. By presenting the covenant relationship as a marriage, he can then portray Israel's covenant unfaithfulness as adultery and prostitution. But in doing so, he is exploiting the sexual imagery of the very religious corruption he is attacking.

- **Isaiah 40–55.** The great affirmations of Yahweh's sovereignty over nations, history, and "the gods" are made against the background of the grand claims of Babylonian gods—especially the astral deities (40:26) and state gods (46:1-2).

- **Genesis 1.** Israel's monotheistic understanding of creation is affirmed against contemporary Ancient Near Eastern mythology, polytheism, astrology, etc.

- **John.** The conflict with elements of Judaism that rejected the messianic claims of Jesus and his early followers is portrayed.

- **Colossians.** The uniqueness and supremacy of Jesus Christ are upheld, in the midst of the surrounding mixture of paganism, early Gnosticism, Jewish rituals, and mystery cults.

- **Revelation.** Jesus is limned as the Lord of history, against a background of the sinister threat of emperor worship and the state cult of Rome.

So, it seems to me that we will get a closer understanding—a better understanding—of the author's original meaning when we actually take into account the worlds of religious plurality in which they lived and therefore *feel* the contrast, *feel* the way in which these words are being emphasised. Our use of the Bible in the world of modern religious pluralism will be greatly helped in its missional sharpness if we give more attention to the religious pluralism that was part of the world of the biblical authors themselves.

Text-centred focus

This approach believes that meaning is to be found in the text itself. The meaning is regarded as an artifact, that is, something of human construction—like a painting, a piece of music, or a sculpture, which can be appreciated for itself, no matter who produced it or why. The text is not so much a window that we look through to some world beyond itself as it is a painting that we look at. A painting can even be made to look exactly like a window, giving the illusion of some objective reality outside itself, but it is still merely a painting, a work of human artistry. So, as applied to biblical texts, this approach pays little attention to the author and his or her intentions (which we cannot know for certain anyway). The text now has an existence and a meaning of its own, to be appreciated for its own sake as a work of literary art and craft.

This approach has developed the use of many helpful tools of literary analysis and tends to engage in close reading of texts, paying careful attention to all the fine detail of a narrative or poem, in the same way that an art connoisseur will appreciate every brush stroke of a master painter. Literary appreciation of biblical literature will include, for example:

• Genre identification – What kind of literature is this, and how is it to be read?

• Literary conventions – How do stories, poems, etc., actually work? How do they engage and affect us when we read them?

• Narrative art – Setting, plot, characters, suspense, irony, perspective, gapping, patterning, word-play, etc.

• Poetic art – Economy of words, imagery, metaphor, parallelism, poetic figures, chiasmus/concentricity, climax, contrast, symbolism, etc.

Literary approaches to the biblical text often bring out all sorts of layers of meaning and significance that have been embedded by the skill, the thought, the art, and the craft of the human author to whom God was entrusting the message that was to be conveyed by the medium of literature.

In evaluating this text-focused, literary approach to biblical hermeneutics, we may observe several strengths and values: ·

• The Bible *is* great literature: it can and should be appreciated at that level. There is no necessary conflict between believing in divine inspiration and appreciating human artistry.

• Literary approaches tend to be more wholistic (that is, they tend to treat passages or books as a whole), yet at the same time they pay very close attention to the fine details of the text. This is consonant with an Evangelical commitment to

verbal inspiration; the choice of words matters.

• A literary approach helps us to understand how meaning is carried by the form of a text and not just by its content. We need to look not only at *what* is written, but also at *how* it has been written.

• Paradoxically also, a text-centred approach respects the author, not so much on the assumption that we can recover the author's intended meaning, but that we can admire the author's artistry.

• Such an approach can go along with the conviction that, strictly speaking (e.g., 2 Tim. 3:16), inspiration is a property of the *texts* of Scripture, not of the authors or of the pre-canonical sources, etc. Therefore, indirectly, a close literary reading of the biblical texts is a compliment to the divine Author as well (on an Evangelical understanding).

• A text-centred approach treats the great variety of biblical texts with integrity by genuinely listening to their pluri-vocality—i.e., the internal dialectic of views and perspectives, which often seem in uncomfortable opposition to one another. It resists flattening everything out or squeezing everything into a univocal system. This is a major emphasis in recent post-modern hermeneutics.[8]

But there are also, of course, dangers in a literary approach which focuses exclusively on the text itself without concern for the identity or the world of the author. ("Never mind the history; feel the art.")

• Literary approaches to the text can sometimes totally ignore history. If the fascination with literary art leads us to dismiss the historical question, "Did it really happen?" then we have problems with the biblical faith, which is actually rooted in

---

[8] Cf. especially the later work of Brueggemann (1997a, 1997b), who rightly highlights how the Bible itself has counter-pointing voices and traditions (exodus and exile, covenant and judgement, hymn and lament, etc.), which need to be given their full expression and not explained, excused, or excluded.

history. Now we may make allowances for "narrative liberty"—that is, we may be willing to accept that not every single detail in the way a story has been told mirrors precisely "what actually happened if you'd been there." But it is possible for real history to be told as a good story and for a good story to be grounded in real history. The "having-happenedness" of the biblical story is very important and should not be lost sight of when we look at the art by which that story was written.

• A purely literary approach can lead to texts being read without reference to their place in the canon and therefore in the story of Scripture as a whole. One can focus on a text and appreciate its literary qualities and even be moved by it, yet remain untouched by its significance as part of the whole word of God to humanity.

• Unbalanced commitment to unresolved plurivocality of the texts (favoured by post-modern interpretation) results in the loss of any real finality or normativity: all we have is a constant oscillation of perspectives. This seems to me an abuse of the plurality of the Bible's texts. It is the opposite danger to the tendency to flatten the whole Bible out into a single monotone message. This is the tendency never to allow the Bible to say anything with finality at all.

Now, what about the religious plurality aspect of this focus? It is important to recognise—and I think sometimes Evangelical scholarship does *not* adequately recognise—that the biblical texts themselves do use religious language, metaphors, and symbolism that are drawn from the plurality of religions that surrounded the authors, yet without sharing the polytheistic worldview that supported such religion.

• As noted in the previous section, **Hosea**, confronted with the syncretism of Baal cults with Yahwism, takes the offensive by using the sexual nature of the former as a source of language and imagery to portray the "married" relationship of Yahweh and Israel. By presenting the covenant relationship as a marriage, he can then portray Israel's covenant unfaithfulness as adultery and prostitution. But in doing so, he is exploiting the sexual imagery of the very religious corruption he is attacking.

• Some **Psalms** make use of Canaanite mythology. For example, Psalm 48:1-3 uses the mythological "city of the great king," which in Baal epics was situated in the far north, to describe the historical city of Yahweh, Jerusalem. Other psalms employ Canaanite poetic metres, such as Psalm 93, which also portrays Yahweh as triumphant over the mighty mythological enemy, the sea.

• **Isaiah 51:9-10** and **Ezekiel 29:1-6** make use of Ancient Near Eastern dragon/monster mythology to describe Yahweh's judgement on Egypt, both in the Exodus and in the defeat by Babylon.

• **Ezekiel 1** uses familiar Ancient Near Eastern religious art and statuary, but he transcends these objects in portraying the dynamic sovereignty and glory of Yahweh (e.g., four-headed, bull-legged, winged creatures who held up the thrones of gods or rode on wheeled chariots were well known in Ancient Near Eastern iconography).

• **Paul in Athens** uses Greek poets, yet subverts their religious worldview (Acts 17:24-31).

• **John's *Logos*** was a familiar term in Greek philosophy, but John harnesses it to full-scale Christological and incarnational significance (John 1).

Such examples raise the age-old missiological question of whether or how far biblical texts can be preached and taught, making use of contemporary religious concepts and symbols in our day. Can we re-contextualize the biblical text from an ancient to a modern religious milieu, without dissolving the text into syncretism? If the Bible itself could utilize a plurality of pagan words, symbols, myths, etc., to communicate its mono-theistic and saving message, why should not the church in mission, and in transla-tion, do the same? But what are the limits and controls? Again, the hermeneutical task is fundamentally a missiological one, and pluralism is the operating context at both ends of the task, for both the biblical text and the modern world.

It needs to be stressed that biblical texts emphatically reject idolatry in all its forms, throughout a very wide span of historical and cultural contexts: Egyptian, Canaan-ite, Babylonian, Persian, Greek, and Ro-man idolatry are all condemned in the course of biblical history. In fact, although biblical texts obviously do describe the religious practice of God's own people (i.e., of Old Testament Israel and of the New Testament church), there is a strong textual tradition that is "anti-religious." The Bible undermines the idea that religion itself is the solution to human problems. More often (in the prophetic perception), it was the most virulent form of the problem itself. (cf. Isa. 1, Jer. 7, Amos 5, Hos. 6, etc.).

Some biblical texts make remarkable universal claims, in the midst of surround-ing religious plurality, in relation to the revelatory and salvific significance of par-ticular key events (e.g., Deut. 4, Psalm 33, Psalm 24, Isa. 40–55, John 1, Phil. 2, Heb. 1, etc.). The great claim made for Jesus, for example, in Philippians 2:10-11, was made in its own context, against the wor-ship of Caesar (Caesar is not Lord; Jesus is). But it is made on the basis of quoting a text from Isaiah 45:22-24 which is actu-ally a claim for *Yahweh* in the context of *Babylonian* pluralism: "I am God, and there is no other. By myself I have sworn, my mouth has uttered in all integrity a word that will not be revoked: Before me

every knee will bow; by me every tongue will swear. They will say of me, 'In the Lord alone are righteousness and strength.'" So, the Philippians 2 passage is affirming the uniqueness of *Jesus* in the context of *Cae-sar* worship (religious plurality of the first century) and building it on the founda-tion of the uniqueness of *Yahweh* in the context of *Babylonian* religious plurality in the sixth century B.C. Both texts derive their sharpness and significance from the plurality of the contexts in which and against which they were uttered. From a missiological perspective, we need to see their monotheistic meaning as sharply defined because of the pluralism that they so vigorously deny.

Reader-centred focus

Let us move on finally, then, to the third main focus—a reader-centred focus. This is a more recent approach, in which people bring into the foreground the role of the reader(s) in active interpretation of the Bible.

Under an author-centred approach, we looked at the text as a *window* through which we have access to the other world— the world of the ancient author. Under a text-centred approach, we looked at the text as a *painting*—that is, as a product of human art and skill, which needs to be appreciated and understood for its own sake. Here, under a reader-centred ap-proach, we are thinking more of the text as a *mirror*. What can be seen in a mirror depends on who is standing in front of it. The "contents" of the mirror, in a sense, reflect who is looking into it or what ob-jects are before it. And so, in this view, the *meaning* in the text is not something fixed and final in the text—some sort of objective reality. The meaning of the text actually only arises in the act of reading. It is when the reader *reads* that the text *means*, just as it is only when you look in a mirror that the mirror reflects you. So meaning is the interaction between text and reader.

Now this approach also reflects the shift from a modernity paradigm of exegesis to a post-modernity paradigm. Under modernity, the reader, rather like a scientist, was simply the neutral observer of a fixed reality which was external to himself or herself. An objective "real meaning," like the "real world," was assumed to exist; the task of the interpreter, like the task of the scientist, was merely to uncover the meaning. The more post-modern view is to say, "Well, actually, even in science the subjective observer is part of the reality under observation and, indeed, may change it in the act of observing it." And so the myth of the "objective neutral observer" has been somewhat demoted in newer forms of science and is similarly also being lost in hermeneutics. The *reader* as subject also is a significant part in the whole process. There is no independent, final, fixed meaning. And of course, we are not the only readers of the biblical text. There are also the original readers to whom the text was first addressed; the later biblical readers who collected these texts, edited them into books, built the books into collections, and built the collections into a canon; the whole long chain of Jewish and Christian readers down through the centuries since the Bible reached its final form; and finally, modern readers in multiple global contexts around our world today.

So, a reader-centred focus urges us to take all these readers seriously. We need to recognise that the meaning of the text does relate to and cannot ignore *who* is doing the reading and *what* they bring to their reading from their own cultural background, presuppositions, assumptions, and so on. (Nobody reads just as a blank sheet; we always read with something else in our minds.) We also need to take note of *where* readers are reading—that is, their position geographically (where they live); their culture; their position within the culture (whether at the top or the bottom); their social, economic, and political interests, and so on. All of these aspects of the readers' contexts will affect the way in which the meaning is articulated and applied. There is no such thing as "contextless, presuppositionless" exegesis or interpretation.

How do we evaluate this reader-centred approach? As before, there are positive things to be said, first of all:

• There is no doubt, I think, that focusing on the reader has facilitated fresh ways of discovering the relevance of the text in many modern contexts. The reality of "contextualised theology" is now taken for granted, provided we recognise that we are *all* interpreting contextually, because all of us interpret in a particular context! Western biblical interpretation has no right to assume that all its insights are "the standard," while those from other continents are "contextualised." The West is also a context—and not necessarily a better or a worse context for understanding and interpreting the text of the Scriptures than anywhere else on the planet.

• Recognizing this fact has led somewhat to the demise of Western hegemony over exegesis and hermeneutics. We recognise the relativity of all hermeneutics and the fact that we all need one another. In fact, for Westerners to hear the Bible interpreted, understood, and preached by African, Latin, or Asian brothers and sisters in Christ, and vice versa, and then to see the perspectives that others are bringing are often very enriching experiences.

• Attention to the context of the reader(s) has unleashed the power of the biblical text into contexts of human need, conflict, or injustice—e.g., in liberationist, feminist, and other "advocacy" hermeneutics. We may not always agree with where such readers want to take us, but we cannot deny the validity of reading the text in and into such contexts and issues. Meaning *is* affected by who you are and what agenda you have. As Anthony Billington once put it, "If you are a feminist, pacifist vegetarian, the text may show up different meanings as *you* read it than if you are a male-chauvinist, war-mongering carnivore."

There are, of course, dangers in an unbalanced emphasis on the role of the reader in determining the meaning of the biblical text:

• A reader-centred approach can degenerate into pure subjectivism if it is not carefully watched. It reverses the priority of author intent as the determinant factor in a text's meaning. In fact, in some cases, reader response theory goes so far as virtually eliminating the author altogether: "It doesn't really matter who said this or what they meant by saying it; what matters is what it means to me. That's all that really counts." So the reader is prioritised over the author, and the *authority*, therefore, lies not with the author or with the text but with the reader, the reader's self— and that, again, is very reflective of a postmodern kind of worldview. One has to say that it is not far removed either from some popular forms of Evangelical Bible reading, which arrogantly exclude any tradition of scholarly study of the text and are content only to ask, "What does this text mean for me?"

• A reader-centred approach also means, of course, that all sense of objective or external controls is lost. If there is *no* assumption of some fixed or stable core of meaning in the text itself deriving ultimately from the author's intention, then pluralism rules: there is no such thing as a "right" or a "wrong" reading, a "legitimate" or "illegitimate" reading—some may be better than others, but it is difficult to know who has the right to say so.

Effects on interpretation

How then is the interpretation of the Bible affected by the religious plurality of contemporary readers? How do the multiple cultural and religious contexts of people reading the Bible today affect how they understand its meaning? This of course is a question as old as the Bible itself. The Hebrew Scriptures were translated into Greek long before the New Testament was written, so that culturally and contextually Greek-speaking people could read them. A few examples will suffice to illustrate how the reading of the Scriptures is affected by the cultural and religious pre-understandings of the readers.

The Islamic world

There are obvious difficulties in the Bible for Muslims: God as Father, Jesus as the Son of God, the story of the Conquest, and the treatment of Ishmael. More subtle difficulties include the biblical record of the "sins of the prophets," such as Abraham's lies, Moses' murder, and David's adultery. These human failings—things which Jews and Christians accept as encouraging evidence of the humanity of the Old Testament saints—are for Muslims further proof that Christians have tampered with the Bible.

Positive aspects of interpretation in the Islamic world include the Arab/Islamic appreciation of stories (cf. the work of Kenneth Baillie). Parables are quite powerful in this culture, and the parabolic method is helpful in circumventing certain theological objections and blindspots.

The Hindu world

Some biblical language and imagery is very open to misunderstanding within the Hindu worldview, such as "born again," avatar/incarnation, "abide in me," etc.

The apostles could freely use pagan words that had different connotations in the Greek world, such as *theos*, *kyrios*, *logos*, *soter*, and *mysterion*, in order to re-shape and use them for Christian purposes. But there is the danger of liberal Indian theologies that syncretise biblical categories into the Hindu worldview and then dissolve the vital distinctions.

African Independent Churches (AICs)

Because of their practice of reading the whole Bible "flat" (i.e., assigning equal authority to all parts, with no regard for historical development in the canon), some AICs have picked out some very odd and exotic aspects of, for example, Old Testament ritual. They have then not only continued these practices, but also exalted them as "biblical."

Sometimes, as an indirect result of translation policies, young churches have had only the New Testament for almost a generation before the Old Testament becomes available. The Old Testament, coming later, is viewed as *superior* (like *secondary* education), so some Old Testament practices are regarded as privileged. Furthermore, the long delay in translating the Old Testament means that sometimes the underlying worldview of the traditional religion has not been challenged or replaced by a fully biblical one encompassing creation, the fall, the history of salvation from Israel through Jesus, and the eschatological hope of a new creation.

Conclusion

The thrust of my argument in this section is that Evangelical missiology will have to take as a major task in the 21st century a fresh articulation of our doctrine of Scripture. In doing so, we shall have to take more account of the plurality (cultural and religious) that is to be found at every level of the hermeneutical process—in the world of the author; in the language, idiom, and imagery of the text; and in the contexts of the readers.

Religious Pluralism

Features and roots

It is not the facts, statistics, and challenges of the plurality of religions which are at issue here. Obviously, it is a task for practical mission strategy to address the multiplicity of specific religious contexts in which ambassadors for the Christian gospel must witness. What the missiologist must address is the challenge of the philosophy of pluralism which presents itself as a powerful and dominant response to that religious plurality. Pluralism, briefly defined, is the view that "salvation/enlightenment/liberation is said to be a reality in all major religious traditions, and no single religion can be considered somehow normative or superior to all others. All religions are in their own way complex historically and culturally conditioned human responses to the one divine reality" (Netland, 1991, p. 26).

Elsewhere, pluralism is defined as "the belief that there is not one, but a number of spheres of saving contact between God and man. God's revealing and redeeming activity has elicited response in a number of culturally conditioned ways throughout history. Each response is partial, incomplete, unique; but they are related to each other in that they represent different culturally focused perceptions of the one ultimate divine reality" (Race, 1982, p. 78).

Religious pluralism of the variety that has emerged from the cradle of modernity is primarily an *epistemological* pluralism. That is, it has to do with the question of how we can (or cannot) *know* the truth-value of religious claims. It is based on a key feature of the Enlightenment transformation of Western thinking—namely, the cleavage or gulf that was inserted into human knowing in the wake of Descartes and Kant in particular. The whole sphere of Western life and culture was divided into two hemispheres—public and private. The public world is the world of so-called objective facts, which are discovered by empirical enquiry and by the application of reason by a detached, neutral observer. The private world is the world of subjective beliefs, personal morality, family values, religion, etc. In this structural dichotomy, one can only really "know" what is in the public hemisphere, because knowledge has to be based on "scientific" proof. Only that which can be empirically proved can be taken as true and therefore can be known. Everything else is a matter of opinion or faith, but it cannot be a matter of truth and knowledge. Any appeal to authoritative divine revelation is ruled out as a source of truth and knowledge. Therefore, religion, since it cannot be "proved" empirically and rationally, is removed from the arena of public truth and relegated to the zone of private belief.

Western culture thus embraced a dualism. On the one hand, there was a kind of secular monism—a commitment to the sole objective truth of all things scientific and rational. In that "hemisphere," intolerance ruled: you don't argue with the objective facts of science. On the other hand, there developed religious pluralism—the refusal to accept that any single set of religious beliefs could be proved to be solely true. Since religious beliefs cannot be known or proved by the exercise of reason alone, we have to allow for a variety of opinions. It is important to understand that this is an epistemological form of pluralism. It does not assert that there is no such thing as truth at all (that is the more post-modern brand of *ontological* pluralism). Rather, it limits the

boundaries of what can be known to be true to the realm of materialistic science and applied rationality. Then, by excluding all religious belief from any valid claim to knowable truth, it argues that the only valid stance in relation to conflicting religious beliefs is to allow the possibility of some truth in all of them and to exercise a tolerant pluralism.

Along with this epistemological pluralism goes that other fruit of modernity—a consumerist, supermarket approach to everything at the popular level. In a supermarket, you don't look for the breakfast cereal that is "right" or "true." You just choose what you like. The same goes for religion and morality and all the values that go with them. Since they fall into the hemisphere in which objective knowledge is said to be impossible in principle, you just choose what suits you best.

Missiological response

The missiological task in relation to the kind of pluralism that stems from modernity roots has to be to attack those roots themselves. That is, we must carry forward the critique of Enlightenment modernity assumptions that have made pluralism the dominant philosophy of Western culture, both intellectually and in popular plausibility. Easily the most pioneering voice in this task has been that of Lesslie Newbigin. Along with other participants in the Gospel and Culture Movement in Britain, he has exposed the fallacies and false trails of modernity's epistemological dichotomy and arrogance.[9] He has shown that the task for the church in Western societies, where religion has been privatized and marginalized by the dominance of scientism and materialism, is to re-affirm the gospel as "public truth." By that he means that Christians must assert their claim that

---

[9] See Newbigin (1989, 1991, 1995). Another key work from the Gospel and Culture Movement is Walker (1996).

the biblical story of God's redemptive engagement with the world he created is the universal story, that it can be known and affirmed as truth, and that it constitutes a valid starting point for other truth-seeking and knowing. We must reject the narrow, shallow reductionism that tells us we can only "know" what we can discover with our senses and demonstrate with our rationality. We must get the claims of Christian truth back into the public hemisphere from which modernity banished them. Furthermore, we must point out more aggressively that even scientific knowing also starts out from some enormous faith commitments. As Newbigin says, all knowing starts from believing something—in the world of science as much as religion. The Enlightenment dichotomies of objective-subjective, public-private, and knowledge-faith are built on very shaky foundations.

Ironically, in confronting the falsehoods of modernity, Christian missiology now has an ally in the post-modern critique that has arisen from the contradictions of late modernity itself. Postmodernity attacks the presuppositions of modernity, just as many Christians do (though many Evangelical Christians, including many mission strategists, still operate within paradigms profoundly shaped by modernity). However, while postmodernity certainly helps us to dispense with the arrogant claim that scientific truth is the only truth worth knowing or capable of being known at all, it throws up what is probably an even more serious challenge to the Christian worldview—that is, the assertion that there is no ultimate or universal truth to be known about anything

at all, science included. When this postmodern mindset comes to deal with religions, it moves beyond the epistemologically based religious pluralism we have just considered ("we cannot *know* which religion gives us the real truth, so we must allow for something true in all of them and seek the truth in dialogue together") to a more ontological religious pluralism ("there is no universal truth, in religion or anywhere else; what matters is not what may or may not be universally true, but what is locally or temporarily true for *you*; religion is little different from therapy for the self—if there is such a thing").

It seems to me that Evangelical missiology will have to continue to tackle both kinds of religious pluralism—modernity based epistemological pluralism and postmodern ontological pluralism—well into the 21st century, since both forms will co-exist during the era of cultural transition we have entered.

What's Wrong With Pluralism? [10]

Superficially, pluralism can seem plausible and attractive. After all, it still talks about God and is willing to keep Christ in the picture somewhere, so what more do you need? You are allowed to keep Christ as the focus of your own religion, so long as you make room for the other "planets" in the religious solar system. Isn't that fair enough? It also seems to relieve us of all that worry about what will happen to those who never hear the gospel of Christ. They have their own religion which puts them in touch with God, so that's all right then too. And most of all, it fits so perfectly with the "supermarket mentality"

---

[10] This section is substantially an extract from Wright (1997). In that volume, I seek to define and critique the three major Christian responses to the reality of religious plurality—exclusivism, inclusivism, and pluralism—and to provide further biblical reflection on the uniqueness of Christ in that context.

that characterizes the modern and post-modern Western mind. However, underneath all these attractive features, pluralism has some major implications that set it totally at odds with biblical Christianity and make it actually a particularly dangerous philosophy for Christians to toy with. My dominant criticisms are directed at what pluralism does to our understanding of God, Jesus, and the worship of Christians themselves.[11]

Pluralism reduces God to abstractions

John Hick is one of the leading pluralist theologians. He has argued for what he calls "pluralist theocentrism"—that is, we should no longer put Christ or the church at the centre of the religious universe, but only God. "God" is like the sun at the centre of the solar system, and Christianity along with all the other religions are like the orbiting planets, all attracted by the gravity of the sun, but each in its own unique orbit. However, one marked feature of this "Copernican revolution," as Hick called it, is that the *theos* ("god") who is finally left at the centre becomes utterly abstract. Clearly "he" cannot be identified or named in terms of any particular deity known within the different world faiths, for they are all only partial responses to this mysterious being. In fact, Hick is quite insistent on this. Names like Yahweh,

Jesus, Vishnu, Allah, Brahman, etc., are simply human cultural constructs by means of which people within a particular religious community give expression to their experience of the divine. Whatever those believers may think or claim, the names of their gods are not to be identified with the actual divine reality. (It is important to realize that what pluralism does to Christianity, it also does to all religions; none of them has access to the ultimate truth about God as God really is.) Those names or concepts found in the various religions are like humanly constructed "masks"[12] by which the divine reality is thought to be encountered by devotees of those religions. But none of them is ultimately true in the way their worshippers claim. Thus, for example, Hick (1992, pp. 130-131) says about the Jewish view of God: "The concrete figure of Jahweh is thus not identical with the ultimate divine reality as it is in itself but is an authentic face or mask or *persona* of the Transcendent in relation to one particular human community." He then goes on to say that this is how he regards the ultimate names of deity in other religions: "For precisely the same has to be said of the heavenly Father of Christianity, of the Allah of Islam, of Vishnu, of Shiva, and so on."[13]

So one finds that the "sun at the centre" is given other "names," which are in

---

[11] I am confining myself here to some fundamental theological issues raised by pluralism. There are many other aspects in which pluralism is open to profound criticism and which are tackled by other scholars (cf. Newbigin, 1989; Netland, 1991; Kirk, 1992; Carson, 1996).

[12] Hick uses the term *personae* for this, which originally in Latin referred to the mask that ancient actors wore. Thus, what the worshippers of a particular deity "see" as they contemplate their particular god is not the divine reality as it really is in itself (the actor), but only the "mask" as a kind of interface between the hidden divine reality (the actor) and the worshipper (the spectator). This assumes, of course, that although the different religions have manifestly different and grossly contrasting "masks," it is the same actor behind all of them. Then Hick goes on to suggest using *impersonae* for the non-personal understandings of the ultimate as found, for example, in philosophical advaita Hinduism and Buddhism.

[13] A fuller explanation of Hick's thinking in this area will be found in Hick (1989, especially part 4, pp. 233-296).

fact not names at all but abstract "undefinitions." "Ultimate Divine Reality" is Hick's favourite. Then you will often read of "Transcendent Being" or even simply "The Real." And if you ask what this "Being" is like, you will be told that you cannot know. It is beyond description or knowing as it is in itself. But all the religions have some partial view of it through the "lens" of their culturally particular religion.

By using this kind of language, you can also avoid having to decide whether this divine being is personal or impersonal. This is very convenient, since that is precisely the point of conflict between, say, Hinduism and Christianity, and even within different schools of Hinduism. But the language of the pluralists certainly tends towards an *impersonal* view of deity. There is little of the living warmth of the biblical language of the personal characteristics of God. Most ordinary people find the abstract concepts of philosophers rather difficult to understand and even more difficult to believe in for their salvation. As Newbigin (1995, pp. 165-167) has put it so strongly, why should we have to believe that an impersonal, indefinable abstraction has any better claim to be the centre of the religious universe than a known person who stands revealed in recorded history? Why should such an abstract philosophical concept be regarded as a more reliable starting point for discovering the truth and finding salvation than commitment to a personal God in Christ?

Pluralism diminishes Jesus

God or Christ at the centre?

The pluralists want us to be theocentric (God-centred) but to give up being Christocentric (having Christ at the centre). The trouble is that it seems impossible to do this and stay within the framework of New Testament faith. There are some scholars, however, who try to drive a wedge between the fact that Jesus preached the kingdom of *God* (i.e., a theocentric proclamation) and the fact that the church preached *Jesus* (thus shifting the focus to a Christocentric proclamation, which then became the church's dominant position). However, this will not do. Certainly Jesus preached the kingdom of God—a very theocentric thing to do. But the kingdom of God, as preached by Jesus, centred on himself—who he was and what he had come to do. In fact, it was precisely because he so persistently put himself at the centre of his teaching about God and about God's kingdom that Jesus aroused such hostility.

There was nothing at all scandalous about simply being theocentric in Jewish society! God was at the centre of everybody's religious "universe" in one way or another. But for a man to claim that scriptures concerning the future work of God were fulfilled in himself, that he had power to forgive sins, that he was Lord over the Sabbath, that he was the Son of Man to whom eternal dominion would be given, and many other such claims was simply blasphemy—and these claims were indeed reckoned to be blasphemous by his contemporaries. That was why they crucified him—not for being theocentric, but for putting himself in that centre where they knew only God should be. Blasphemous it certainly was—unless, of course, it was true.

In the same way, the first Christians, who were Jews and therefore strict monotheists, already lived in a thoroughly theocentric universe. They were shaped to the core by the central affirmation of Jewish faith: "Hear, O Israel: the LORD our God, the LORD is one. Love the LORD your God with all your heart and with all your soul and with all your strength" (Deut. 6:4-5). But with considerable struggle and often at great personal cost, these believers deliberately put their contemporary, the man

Jesus of Nazareth, right at the centre of that majestic Old Testament faith. They did so every time they made the crucial affirmation, "Jesus is Lord." That did not mean they had given up or diluted their theocentrism. On the contrary, their faith in God at the centre of the religious universe was as strong as ever. But now it was filled out, re-defined, and proclaimed in the light of their encounter with God in the person and action of Jesus, the Christ. So Paul could write what is virtually an expansion of the great Jewish creed to include Jesus Christ alongside the creator God: "For us there is but one God, the Father, from whom all things came and for whom we live; and there is but one Lord, Jesus Christ, through whom all things came and through whom we live" (1 Cor. 8:6).

The New Testament writings are a constant reflection of the struggle by which the God-centred faith of the Old Testament was seen to be Christ-centred in reality. This was not a perversion nor an exaggeration born out of human hero-worship. It was the calm conviction that Jesus of Nazareth, in the light of his life, death, and resurrection, was indeed the centre and key to the whole redemptive work of God, past, present, and future. He was at the centre of their theocentric religious universe because he was Immanuel, no less than *God with us.*

A relativized Jesus?

Following from the above point, it seems to me that the pluralist view cannot be reconciled with authentic Christianity, because to relativize Jesus Christ is to deny him. By "relativizing Jesus," I mean regarding him as only one among many great religious figures through whom we can know about God and find salvation. It means regarding him as one of the orbiting planets of world religions, not as the one and only absolute source

of life and light as, for example, John 1 presents him.

However, if the New Testament is taken even as a reasonably reliable source, then it is unquestionable that Jesus made some astounding and absolute claims for himself. It is equally clear that his immediate followers in the early Christian church made similar claims concerning him, both explicitly in their preaching and implicitly in their worship and prayer through his name. So since biblical and historical Christianity makes such affirmations about Jesus, it follows that whatever kind of "Christianity" is put into orbit around the "sun of ultimate divine reality," it is not the Christianity of Christ and his apostles.

Jesus only for Christians?

Now pluralists will reply that Jesus still remains central *for Christians* and that nothing need change that. As such, they say, Jesus is the distinctive Christian gift to the inter-religious dialogue. But, we are told, we should only come to the dialogue table once we have renounced those absolute claims to the uniqueness or finality of Christ, for those claims are regarded by pluralists as arrogant and intolerant and therefore out of place in genuine dialogue. Jesus may be decisive and authoritative for those who have chosen to follow him (Christians), but he need not be imposed on others as unique or universal. Thus Race (1982, p. 136) says, "Jesus is 'decisive,' not because he is the focus of all the light everywhere revealed in the world, but for the vision he has brought in one cultural setting.... Jesus would still remain central for the Christian faith." In other words, the great New Testament affirmation, "Jesus is Lord," is reduced to meaning, "Jesus is Lord for us because we have chosen to regard him as such; his Lordship is relative to our acceptance of him." It no longer means, "Jesus is objectively and absolutely the universal Lord to whom alone we submit and to whom ultimately all creatures in heaven and earth will bow."

A deluded Jesus or a deluded church?

But even supposing we were to go along with the pluralists at this point and accept that Jesus is unique only in the sense that he is relatively special for Christians but not the supreme Lord of all, we then have to ask what kind of "gift to interfaith dialogue" this relativized Jesus actually is. If Jesus Christ was not God incarnate, if he was not the final revelation of God and the completion of God's saving work for humanity, if he is not the risen and reigning Lord, then we are faced with two possibilities: The first is that Jesus himself was mistaken in the claims he made concerning himself, in which case he was either sadly deluded or an arrogant boaster. Certainly, if his enormous claims were actually false, he would not be a worthy religious figure whom we could bring to the dialogue table with any confidence. We would need to apologize, not evangelize.

The second possibility is that the church from its earliest period (including the generation of Jesus' own contemporaries, who were the first witnesses to him) has grossly misunderstood him, inflated his claims, and exaggerated his importance. Pluralists require us to accept that the church throughout its history (until its rescue by late 20th century pluralist Enlightenment) has propagated, lived by, and based all its hope upon a massive, self-deluded untruth. A deluded Jesus or a deluded church or both—this seems to be the unavoidable implication of the pluralists' insistence on relativizing Jesus.

The dismal results of this view are quickly clear. A. G. Hunter, for example, argues that Jesus was, in fact, not more than human but was elevated to divine status only by the church and was installed

in the Trinity only at the Council of Chalcedon. Somehow, Hunter (1985, p. 55) simply *knows* that it was "psychologically and religiously impossible for Jesus [to have claimed divinity], and it is historically false to say that he did." When you can be so confidently and dogmatically negative about the "historical" Jesus, you have to be equally negative and uncertain about what value he has for faith. Hunter (1985, p. 76) concludes: "What emerges is that though we are agreed that Jesus is at the heart of our faith as Christians, it is hard to find any clear consensus as to the precise delineation of his importance."

If such paralysed agnosticism is all we are left with, is it worth contributing to religious dialogue at all? Is that what representatives of other world faiths want to hear from us? If, as pluralists say, we have to relativize Jesus before we can come to the dialogue, then we had better not come at all. All we have to bring with any integrity would be a repentant confession that we belong to a worldwide faith which throughout the whole of its history has had an illusion and a falsehood at its fundamental heart and core.

Pluralism renders Christian worship idolatrous

Religious pluralists say that Jesus cannot stand at the centre of the religious universe. He cannot be equated or identified with the God (however described) at the centre. We must not look at Jesus "from above," so to speak, as God incarnate, but rather see him as essentially one of us (which he was, of course) and do our Christology "from below." There are many shades of opinion among scholars who prefer this approach, but in the end what it means is that, whatever else Jesus may have been, he was ultimately not more than human. Certainly he was not God incarnate in any ontological sense. He may have been a vehicle or agent of

God's activity for revelation and salvation, but only as a man. That is, he may have been one of those exceptionally special human beings through whom the rest of us can come to a deeper and clearer understanding of God, but the language about his being "of God, with God, or from God" is simply the understandable exaggeration that gives voice to faith and adoration and gratitude.

Many who take this view would agree that Jesus was unique in some sense: for example, in the depth of his own relationship with God and the extent to which he mediated God to others, including ourselves. But they would see this as a uniqueness of degree, not of essence. God may have been very specially present and active through Jesus of Nazareth, but Jesus was not (and therefore is not) God. He cannot stand at the centre of the religious universe. Even in his uniqueness as defined, he must go into orbit around the

centre along with other great religious figures who all have their own unique features also.

The more I reflect on this view, the more surprised I am at how reluctant its advocates seem to be to draw the ultimate conclusion from it, which seems quite inescapable—that is, that Christianity is and always has been the worst form of idolatry ever practised on earth.[14] The most serious charge which Jews and Muslims[15] have levelled against Christians all through the centuries would actually be true: we have elevated a human being to the place of God and have worshipped him there. For that is what we do and what we have been doing ever since the book of Acts. We ascribe to Jesus honour and glory that belongs only to God; we call on his name in prayer as God; we call him Lord and refuse to acknowledge any other; we claim that through Jesus and Jesus alone God has acted to save humanity and there is

[14] Some pluralists are indeed prepared to say that the worship of Christ is actually idolatry, though they carefully re-define idolatry in a positive light and tend to be very dismissive of how the Bible talks of it. Wilfred Cantwell Smith (1987), for example, in a carefully argued re-assessment of what, based on a pluralist understanding, actually constitutes idolatry, says that it should only be used negatively when describing religious positions which regard themselves as ultimate and then negate the value of others. On such grounds, "For Christians to think that Christianity is true, final, or salvific is a form of idolatry," if by that they mean to deny that God has also inspired Islam, Hinduism, etc. Smith goes on to ask whether "the figure of Christ served as ... an idol through the centuries for Christians?" and essentially answers that it has, but there is nothing wrong with that, since the best meaning of idols in all religions is something earthly or material in itself, which becomes the channel of transcendence. See Smith (1987) and also the comments of Tom F. Driver in the same volume: "I think it necessary to say that the idolization of Christ—let us call it 'christodolatry'—is not only possible but in fact frequent. Indeed I would go further and say that there is even such a thing as an idolatrous devotion to God" (pp. 214-215). I still prefer to maintain a biblical understanding of the category of idolatry as meaning the action of giving ultimate and divine status to anything or anyone that is not in reality the living God—meaning the God as revealed in the Bible, not the characterless abstract "Transcendent" of the pluralist hypothesis. According to this understanding, the worship of anything or anyone other than God as revealed in Christ *is* idolatry, but the worship of Christ himself as not merely the one through whom we can "see" God, but ontologically God-in-humanity, is assuredly *not* idolatry.

[15] Muslims are well aware of the implications of the pluralist developments in Christian theology. A friend from Singapore has told me that *The Myth of God Incarnate* (Hick, 1977) is required reading for Muslim missionaries. I was told by Indian Christian missionaries in India that even in remote rural villages, Muslims can counter the Christian gospel with the riposte that even bishops in the Church of England now believe what Muslims have always believed—that Jesus was not really God and did not really rise again.

no other way; we apply to him the most solemn scriptures that Israel used concerning Yahweh; we sing to him songs of worship and praise that were originally sung to Yahweh and have made up bookfuls of our own. All these things we have done for 2,000 years but with no justification at all, if the pluralists are right. For, no matter how remarkable he was, no matter what God did in and through him, if Jesus was not more than a man, then the whole Christian faith and all the generations of Christian worship have been a monstrous idolatry.

Conclusion

So we arrive at the end of the pluralists' road. At best, "Christ" becomes so universal as to be of no real value except as a symbol. At worst, he is exposed as an idol for those who worship him and as dispensable by those who don't.

The discussion above has been limited to the internal Christian debate about the plurality of religions and has not even begun to focus on the challenges presented by the great world religions themselves to Christian mission and missiology. Each of them would need a separate paper, since the contexts they represent are so unique. Obviously, Christian missiological response to each of the great faiths will remain a major challenge in the 21st century. But Evangelical missiology will have to continue to confront that brand of Christian pluralism which undermines the uniqueness of Christ and subverts the challenge of the gospel from within.

Ethical Pluralism

Features and roots

We live in a world of ethical plurality and confusion. Even in the West, it seems a long way, both historically and culturally, from the apparent "self-evident truths" of the American Declaration of Independence, which included basic statements about human equality and proclaimed ideals of life, liberty, and the pursuit of happiness. Universal statements of ethical rights and duties, such as the various United Nations declarations on human rights, command less respect, in spite of continued lip service and the moralizing of Western politicians.

On the one hand, such universal declarations are challenged by countries and cultures whose moral views come from a radically different religious worldview from the broadly Christianized context out of which the U.N. Declaration of Human Rights, for example, arose. Islamic states have protested at being judged by moral standards which they see as not founded in the principles of Islam, especially since the very nations which "preach" those standards at Islamic countries are guilty of manifest hypocrisy in their own moral failures. Similarly, in India, militant Hinduism sees no ethical hindrance to its exclusion of lower caste and non-caste Indians from social participation or political rights; the caste system, allied to the religious philosophy of karma and reincarnation, provides plenty of ethical justification for the status quo. This philosophy, which turns up in the West as somewhat outlandish but malice-free views on the lips of Glen Hoddle, is the religious worldview that undergirds the oppression currently resurgent in the largest democracy on earth.

On the other hand, universal moral declarations are under challenge in the cultures which produced them in the first place—within the West itself. In the postmodern, post-imperial climate, any claim regarding universally valid morality is rejected as cloaked imperialism. To say that something is an absolute human right or duty is simply to impose our cultural values on others. If there is no transcendent authority behind morality, then we have no right to choose one set of values that appeal to us and insist that the rest of the world abide by them. This is a problem faced not just by Christians. Some Western secular companies with a concern for business ethics are conscious of the following dilemma, which I read in a secular business magazine on an international flight: When you are operating in a non-Western country where accepted practices clash with your own ethical standards (e.g., as regards human rights violations in working conditions, etc.), do you adopt the view, "When in Rome do as the Romans do," and call it "cultural sensitivity and respect for others" (in which case you will have a struggle with your own integrity and conscience), or do you make a fuss and insist on certain ethical standards as a precondition of doing business at all (in which case you may be accused of neo-colonial imposition of Western cultural values or, even worse, of missionary arrogance and intolerance)?

Again, the roots of ethical pluralism can be traced both to modernity and to the post-modern reaction.

Modern ethical pluralism

We recall that Enlightenment modernity introduced structural dualism—the division of life into public and private hemispheres. This had the effect of consigning ethics as well as religion to the hemisphere of privatized belief, as distinct from public knowledge. Even if some moral absolute did exist (as Kant continued to assert with his "categorical imperative"), it could not be *known* by the only mechanism capable of knowing anything, autonomous *reason*. It could only be *recognized and responded to* through the *will*. But what if human wills differ? Morality becomes merely a fragile matter of social consensus, for as long as it lasts. And if the consensus of will breaks down, then morality will be determined, for good or

ill, by the most powerful will, or the more sinister "will to power" that Nietsche envisaged. Since "God is dead," then there is no transcendent, revealed, and authoritative basis for ethics. In such a climate, ethics either fragments into private value preferences or succumbs to the tyranny of "might is right."

Part of modernity's attractiveness, however, was its optimism. The myth of inevitable progress that would follow on the heels of scientific advance led generations to believe that somehow things were getting better and better. Human beings could eventually achieve sufficient ethical consensus to engineer a future that would be both good and happy. The trouble was that autonomous reason seemed capable of generating widely conflicting ethical visions, depending, it seems, on what scientific approach one regarded as primary or, to be more precise, what particular scientific reductionism governed one's view of the fundamental essence of humanity.

What is the essential nature of human life? Different life sciences and social sciences came up with different answers—all of them partially true but inadequate as full explanations of what it is to be human. These answers then became the basis for similarly inadequate ethical theories. Thus, biology produced a version of ethics based on evolution. This itself bifurcated into a positive form, which enthused about our ability to control our own evolution as a human species for good, and a more cynical form, which asserted that if survival of the fittest is the game, then everyone should try to be among the fittest and, if possible, engineer the genetic or genocidal non-survival of the least fit. Biology also produced the behaviourist ethic of the human zoo: ethics is nothing more than socialized and rationalized animal instincts. Psychology reduced ethics to health or sickness of the mind and replaced repentance with therapy. Sociology reduced ethics to a function of social interaction; Marxism, to economic determinism, and so on.

Such ethical reductionisms stem from modernity's insistence on analysing and describing *human* life by means of the same kind of allegedly neutral scientific tools as were applied to the rest of the *material* universe. They then tried to come up with some account of the "laws" governing human behaviour that would be as universal as the laws of physics, chemistry, or biology which appeared to govern the universe.

Post-modern ethical pluralism

The post-modern reaction has been to reject the idea of any absolute and final explanation of human reality, of any universal moral framework that can be epistemologically grounded in some objective or scientific "truth." Not only is there no transcendent authority to provide ethical universals (a denial common to modernity and post-modernity); neither is there any universal truth to be found in modernity's pursuit of scientific objectivity—in the human and social sciences any more than in the physical sciences. Modernity rejected transcendent authority but tried to preserve some universal moral criteria. Post-modernity rejects both transcendent authority *and* the possibility or even desirability of universal moral grounds. So no ethical stance can be deemed final and universal on the basis of any allegedly scientific description of the human being. Historical and cultural relativism pervades human ethics as much as human religion.

As we noticed in the earlier discussion of post-modernity, there are negative and positive aspects of this feature of ethics in a post-modern context. On the one hand, there is a cynical nihilism at the more intellectual end of the post-modern cultural spectrum: If no culture has the "right" answer to ethical questions, then why bother wrestling with the questions at all? All that counts in the end is the will to power. It seems sometimes that ethics, not just power, comes out of the barrel of a gun. Or if we are too refined to impose our will by might, there is always manipulation by propaganda, persuasion, and image-massaging. Never mind the ethics; watch the spin.

On the other hand, there is the more cheerful celebration of plurality that comes at the popular end of post-modern culture: let's not only respect, but also enjoy the wide divergences of values that are to be found in today's multi-cultural society. Western "soap operas" often tackle ethical issues in their story lines. The most popular British "soap," Eastenders, in recent years has included racism, homosexuality, AIDS prejudice, adultery, incest, wife-battery, alcoholism, child abduction, and murder. But the dominant impression in responding to many of these situations, especially the sexual ones, is a non-judgemental individualism ("you just do what is right for you; nobody can tell you otherwise"). The trouble is that "multi-culturalism" as espoused, for example, in Australia and Canada, generates an ethic of political correctness which can be oppressive in its hidden absolutisms. It also has no means of dealing with (or even actually recognizing) the kind of paradoxical clash of values illustrated by the Hoddle case above. As another British commentator has said, "We're all ethical pluralists now ... until we meet a paedophile."

Missiological response

The Christian missiological response to ethical pluralism needs to start from the same place as for religious pluralism—namely, by identifying and attacking the roots. We must follow the same agenda of critiquing Enlightenment modernity's relegation of ethics to the hemisphere of privatized belief, as Newbigin has so effectively done for religion. This has two effects. First of all, we must firmly challenge the epistemological arrogance that claims to outlaw all ethical matters from the realm of genuine knowledge, on the grounds that only scientific "facts" can be regarded as objectively true. This "reality filter" needs to be exposed as the deception it really is. Secondly, those ethical stances that are based on the variety of scientific reductionisms in relation to human life also need to be challenged—whether biological evolutionism or behaviourism, psychology, sociology, economics, or more recently, geneticism as preached by Richard Dawkins. Whenever we are told that human ethics is "nothing but ...," we should be on the alert and expose the poverty of all attempts to reduce human life to partial and materialistic explanations.

In fact, I would urge that Evangelical mission theology must address afresh the question of our doctrine of humanity. At the heart of so much of the fragmentation in human societies today lies the loss of human identity or the struggle (often violent) for identity to be recognized or recovered. Where is it to be found? Modernity located human identity in the autonomous rational self. Post-modernity dethrones reason and goes on to decentre and dissolve the self. What is there left that is distinctly human, or are we left with only the kaleidoscopic relativities of cultures and histories? Culture and history enrich human life and identity, but according to Christian understanding they do not constitute or exclusively define it. I believe that 21st century Evangelical missiology must address the question of *what it means to be human* and must seek to give a genuinely biblical answer. As we observed in the section on religious plural-

ism, the 20th century battle over Christology and soteriology will doubtless continue. But if God became incarnate in Jesus in order to save humanity, what was it that he became in becoming truly human, and what is it that is saved through his death and resurrection?

Returning to ethical pluralism, postmodernity will certainly help us to challenge the dominance of scientific reductionism, but unfortunately it also presents an even more dangerous kind of relativism at the ontological level. How should we respond to the post-modern assertion that there are simply *no foundations* for any common human morality? Must we accept that uncontrolled ethical variety is inevitable because of the plurality of cultures and perspectives and that there is no possibility of any "standing ground" outside all cultures, from which anyone can have the right to adjudicate ethically between them?

A very interesting attempt to address this problem from within the religious pluralist camp has come from Paul Knitter (1992, pp. 111-122). Recognizing the strength of the "anti-foundationalist" case, as expressed in the last paragraph, Knitter asks if there is any way that the different religions can overcome the impasse of utter relativism, any way in which they can find some "common ground" (even though the term is out of favour). He believes it is important to do so, because of the dangers of succumbing too easily to post-modern relativism. He pin-points two dangers: First, full-blown relativism gives you no grounds to criticize even your own culture, let alone other cultures, and it produces an "ethical toothlessness brought about by the lack of any basis on which to validly and coherently resist what appears to be intolerable in other cultural-linguistic systems." Secondly, it offers no basis for moral resistance to naked power: "In arguing that we must simply rejoice in plurality without ever allowing the possibility that some truth claims may prove to have intrinsic or universal validity, postmoderns allow the warning of Michael Foucault to become reality: the verdict on differing truth claims will be decided not on any mutually reached judgments (since they are impossible) but on the basis of who has the economic or military power.... The criteria will be determined ... by those who have the dollars or the guns" (Knitter, 1992, p. 114).

Knitter's answer to the dilemma is to suggest that rather than looking in vain for common *ground* at the start of the dialogue, the different religions should get stuck into making a common *response* to human problems. Then, hopefully, in the process and praxis of making that response, some patches of common ground may emerge between them. He then identifies what he regards as the two most urgent problems facing the world: *human poverty* ("the millions who because they are deprived of such basic needs as food, drinking water, shelter, and medical care are prevented from living a human life") and *ecological damage* ("the victimized planet earth which, as its life-giving and sustaining gifts of air, water, and soil are devastated and drained, becomes the domain of ever more human victims"). He goes on, "I am suggesting that the reality of suffering due to oppression and victimization—both human and ecological—calls for a common response that can become a common ground for cross-cultural and inter-religious understanding" (Knitter, 1992, p. 118).

Knitter seems almost embarrassed by the glimpse of an ethical universal lurking in such a proposal. So he backs off it somewhat: "One must be careful of speaking of an ethical imperative to confront such issues, since morality is so culture-bound. And yet, it does seem evident that today followers of almost all the religious

paths—from Eastern to Western to so-called primal spiritualities—are recognizing that their own spiritual traditions require them to respond to the reality of human and planetary oppression" (Knitter, 1992, p.119). But do they? It is seriously questionable, I would argue, whether most religions would take the same view of human and planetary suffering as Knitter does, and even more questionable that "within all religious traditions there seems to be a "soteriocentric core" of concern for human well-being *in this world*" (Knitter, 1992, p.119, emphasis added).

So the weakness of Knitter's proposal is that it wants to find common ground, while simultaneously denying that any ground can be or has been provided by a transcendent or trans-cultural source—such as the biblical revelation. Yet the issues he chooses to see as primary and the response he sees as needing to be made to them are actually only *ethical* issues and responses within certain worldviews (such as Christianity). Even identifying the issues to which we call for a response requires standing on *some* ground.

Missiologically, however, in my view, we can turn Knitter's weakness into a strength. We can certainly agree with his identification of two major evils in today's world—poverty and ecological destruction. And we can certainly also challenge and invite the wider non-Christian human community to address them. However, in doing so, we ought to make prominently clear the *Christian* "ground" on which we do so. That means telling the story, which in the Christian worldview both *explains* the problems in terms of humanity's rebellion against God and consequent fracture of all relationships, including that with the planet itself, and also *proclaims* the redemptive action that God himself initiated in the history of Israel and the saving work of Christ. Indeed, we can go further than a liberationist response, because the full biblical story illuminates wider aspects and deeper roots of the problems than the presenting symptoms themselves. At the Rio de Janeiro Earth Summit, it was said that the intense "green" concern for ecological action was "an ethic in search of a religion." Yet the Christian voice was muted, leaving the "religion" to be provided by the New Age Movement.

Human and planetary oppression are major examples, but they are only part of the total spectrum of ethical issues that societies will face in this new millennium. The missiological challenge to our ethics must be:

- That we seek to show how a *biblically* grounded ethic is valid in theory and works in practice.
- That we also tell the story in which that ethic is grounded and without which it is empty moralism.
- That we ensure that the telling of that story preserves the central focus of Jesus Christ.

We need, in other words, a *missiologically framed and motivated ethical engagement with the world*. Such is the plea of Andrew Walker (1996, p. 170) as he urges Christians to remember and re-tell the story of the biblical gospel, which modernity has marginalized by its epistemological arrogance and which post-modernity threatens to swamp by the way it relativizes and equalizes all narratives: "Christian activism is not a question of creating a programme for government: it is about standing up in the public square to be counted. Do the public know what the Christian story has to say about moral behaviour? Have we taken the time to tell the story often enough so that people can see that from it flow economic and social consequences? Lesslie Newbigin appears to be right about Christian witness. It is

because we have grown timid, lost faith in the gospel, or even forgotten it, that we do not rush forward for our voices to be heard amidst the clamour of competing interests. We must avoid the vain temptation to build another Christendom; but equally we must not shirk our duty to stir the conscience of our nations for as long as they last."

Finally, the missiological challenge of ethical pluralism is, of course, practical. If we proclaim that the Christian ethical vision is distinctive and that it is grounded in the true story of God, the universe, human history, and salvation through Christ, are we able to demonstrate that it is so? The church, as Newbigin again so effectively argued, must be the "plausibility structure" for the gospel and the ethic that flows from it.

Concluding Challenges

What are the major issues for our missiological reflection and work? Here are some suggested questions arising out of each of the main sections above.

Hermeneutical pluralism

1. How can a missiologically framed re-shaping of the Evangelical doctrine of Scripture better equip us to discern, articulate, and apply the authority of the Bible in the cultural plurality of the 21st century and especially in a world increasingly affected by post-modernity?

2. How can we make room for the multiplicity of readers' contexts in the global hermeneutical community and especially climb down off the pedestal of Western dominance, without either surrendering to subjectivism, relativism, and the loss of any commitment to a stable core meaning in biblical texts or substituting the authority of readers/contexts for the authority of the biblical text itself?

Religious pluralism

1. Are there ways in which Evangelical Christians can harness the energy of post-modernity in its critique of Enlightenment modernity's arrogance, without submitting to the ontological relativism that comes with post-modernity?

2. Are there positive and gospel-friendly categories/symbols/perspectives within post-modern consciousness that can be harnessed in order to re-conceptualize and communicate the uniqueness of Jesus in the midst of religious plurality and in polemical engagement with religious pluralism?

Ethical pluralism

1. What will a missiological approach to ethics look like? How can we demonstrate (intellectually and existentially) that the Christian ethic is actually "best," because it most closely relates to the "way things are," according to the biblical story and revelation?

2. Is it our Christian task in the 21st century with its post-modern perspectives to work out fresh ways to enshrine and advocate our understanding of biblical ethics, rather than simply repeating the classical formulations of Western universal declarations?

3. What is a more biblical understanding of *humanity*, which can go beyond the reductionisms of modernity but avoid the narcissism of post-modernity? What theological understanding of human/ethnic identity can provide a missiology that then generates appropriate missional responses to the fragmentation, anger, and despair that seem likely to afflict increasing numbers of human communities in the 21st century?

And finally...

In training people adequately for mission in the 21st century, we shall be handling young adults who are themselves culturally and probably intellectually shaped by *post-modernity*, yet whose education and worldview has largely been shaped by the paradigms of *modernity*, and whose future ministry may well be in cultures that are as yet effectively *premodern*. How can we prepare them adequately to understand the cultural identity crisis they themselves are living through, as well as the one they are heading into? Missionaries in the 21st century will need to be the Christian and cultural equivalent of Olympic triple-jumpers.

References

Best, S., & Kellner, D. (1991). *Postmodern theory: Critical interrogation.* New York: Guilford Press.

Brueggemann, W. (1997). *Biblical Theological Bulletin, 127,* pp. 4-8.

———. (1997). *Theology of the Old Testament: Testimony, dispute, advocacy.* Minneapolis, MN: Fortress Press.

Carson, D. A. (1996). *The gagging of God: Christianity confronts pluralism.* Downers Grove, IL: InterVarsity Press.

Giddens, A. (1990). *The consequences of modernity.* Stanford, CA: Stanford University Press.

Hick, J. (1989). *An interpretation of religion: Human responses to the transcendent.* London: Macmillan.

———. (1992). A religious understanding of religion. In D. Cohn-Sherbok (Ed.), *Many mansions: Interfaith and religious intolerance* (pp. 122-136). London: Bellew.

Hick, J. (Ed.). (1977). *The myth of God incarnate.* London: SCM Press.

Hunter, A. G. (1985). *Christianity and other faiths in Britain.* London: SCM Press.

Kirk, J. A. (1992). *Loosing the chains.* London: Hodder & Stoughton.

Knitter, P. (1992). Common ground or common response? Seeking foundations for interreligious discourse. *Studies in Interreligious Dialogue, 2,* pp. 111-122.

Netland, H. A. (1991). *Dissonant voices: Religious pluralism and the question of truth.* Grand Rapids, MI: Wm. B. Eerdmans Publishing Co.

Newbigin, L. (1989). *The gospel in a pluralist society*. London: SPCK.

———. (1991). *Truth to tell: The gospel as public truth*. Grand Rapids, MI: Wm B. Eerdmans Publishing Co.

———. (1995). *The open secret: An introduction to the theology of mission* (2nd ed.). Grand Rapids, MI: Wm. B. Eerdmans Publishing Co.

Race, A. (1982). *Christians and religious pluralism: Patterns in the Christian theology of religions*. Maryknoll, NY: Orbis Books.

Sampson, P., Samuel, V., & Sugden, C. (Eds.). (1994). *Faith and modernity*. Oxford, England: Regnum.

Sine, T. (1999). *Mustard seed versus McWorld: Reinventing Christian life and mission for a new millennium*. Crowborough, England: Monarch.

Smith, W. C. (1987). Idolatry in comparative perspective. In J. Hick & P. F. Knitter (Eds.), *The myth of Christian uniqueness: Toward a pluralistic theology of religions* (pp. 53-68). Maryknoll, NY: Orbis Books.

Van Gelder, C. (1996). Mission in the emerging postmodern condition. In G. H. Hunsberger & C. Van Gelder (Eds.), *The church between gospel and culture: The emerging mission in North America* (pp. 127-133). Grand Rapids, MI: Wm. B. Eerdmans Publishing Co.

———. (n.d.). *Shaping ministry in a post-modern world: Building bridges with the gospel to a changed context*. Unpublished manuscript.

Walker, A. (1996). *Telling the story: Gospel, mission and culture*. London: SPCK.

Wright, C. (1997). *Thinking clearly about the uniqueness of Jesus*. Crowborough, England: Monarch.

Wright, N. T. (1992). *The New Testament and the people of God*. London: SPCK.

Chris Wright, born of missionary parents in Belfast, North Ireland, obtained his doctorate in Old Testament economic ethics from Cambridge University in 1977. Ordained in the Church of England, he spent several years in pastoral ministry. For five years he taught at the Union Biblical Seminary, Pune, India, as a missionary with the Anglican mission agency Crosslinks (formerly BCMS), of which he is now Honorary President. In 1988 he returned to the U.K. as Director of Studies at All Nations Christian College, the largest Evangelical mission training institution in Europe. He was appointed Principal there in September 1993. He has written several books, including Knowing Jesus Through the Old Testament (Marshall Pickering and Inter-Varsity, 1992) and Thinking Clearly About the Uniqueness of Jesus (Monarch, 1997). His life's passion is bringing to life the relevance of the Old Testament for Christian mission and ethics. He and his wife Liz have four children, two of whom are now married.

Evangelical missiology: peering into the future at the turn of the century

T HE HISTORY OF CHRISTIAN mission during the 20th century could be summarized in the words of Latourette as the story of "advance through storm." Thinking especially about Evangelical missions, Ralph Winter has used the expression "unbelievable years" for the explosion of American missionary activity during the 25 years that followed World War II. As we come to the start of a new century, there are clear signs that a new age of missions has come, to be marked by the new face of global Christianity and the engagement of the churches of the Southern hemisphere in the fulfillment of the Great Mandate and the Great Commission. There was an old way of doing mission developed during the age of the European empires and the United States era of "Manifest Destiny." It has become obsolete, even though its patterns endure to the point of being imitated by Third World agencies. At the close of my first paper (see chapter 3), I outlined the missiological recovery of biblical patterns for mission that will be developed in this paper.

I define missiology as an interdisciplinary approach to understand missionary action. It looks at missionary facts from the perspectives of the biblical sciences, theology, history, and the social sciences. It aims to be systematic and critical, but it starts from a positive stance towards the legitimacy of the Christian missionary task as part of the fundamental reason for the church's "being." A missiological approach gives the observer a comprehensive frame of reference in order to look at reality in a critical way. Missiology is a critical reflection on praxis, in light of God's Word. One could say that in that regard a significant portion of the writings of the Apostle Paul is missiological in nature. Think, for instance, of 2 Corinthians and the way in which Paul refers

SAMUEL
ESCOBAR

to his own missionary practice, pointing to Old Testament teachings as well as the living revelation of God in Jesus Christ through the Spirit. The Spirit-inspired missionary acts of Jesus, Paul, and the apostles, as well as their Spirit-inspired reflection on their practice, are authoritative for us in a way in which no other post-apostolic missionary practice or reflection is authoritative.

As the Spirit drives God's people to missionary obedience today, we have the light of God's inspired Word to continually check and evaluate our actions. David Bosch (1993, p. 177) has very aptly referred to the critical spirit in which the missiological task is to be approached: "... if we wish to reflect on 'biblical foundations for mission,' our point of departure should not be the contemporary enterprise we seek to justify, but the biblical sense of what being sent into the world signifies." I would add that theology, history, and the social sciences are useful as tools for a better understanding of God's Word and of contemporary missionary action, but only the Word is inspired and always fertile to renew the church in mission. Moreover, there is another proviso from Bosch (1993, p. 177) which we must take into account: "... however important single biblical texts may [seem to] be, the validity of mission should not be deduced from isolated sayings but from the thrust of the central message of Scripture."

During the last quarter of the 20th century, Evangelical missiologists embarked on a concerted effort to reflect on the massive experience of Evangelical missionary activity. Honest evaluation of missionary activism in light of God's Word, theological truth, and new missionary challenges becomes an effort to envision new models of missionary obedience. In this paper, I will summarize developments in Evangelical missiology during the second part of the 20th century, outlining

three trends that have developed during this period. I will then outline a trinitarian direction in which I think the missiological agenda should be pursued in order to meet the challenges posed by the kind of developments in the church and in the world that I have outlined in my first presentation.

Two cycles of Protestant mission developed during the 20th century. Before World War II, mainline Protestant denominations played a key role both in the practice of mission and in the theologizing about it. It was a period still marked by significant activity from European as well as North American churches and by theological debate about the nature of the Christian mission and the identity of the young churches that were growing in Africa, Asia, and Latin America. After the War, there was a decline of traditional Protestant activity and a marked growth of activity and influence from conservative Protestant agencies in the United States. There was also an explosive growth of faith missions and parachurch agencies that spread missionary concepts, along with methodologies that reflected American cultural values and mores. Through massive use of Christian media, theological institutions, and missionary conferences, its influence was felt not only in countries receiving missionaries but also in the old sending countries of Europe.

I think it is important to acknowledge the fact that new generations of missionaries without an adequate historical awareness or biblical training were condemned to repeat the mistakes of the past. It became necessary for theologians to embark anew in the search for a missiological reflection. This is what historian William H. Hutchison (1987, p. 176) has called "familiar debates in an unfamiliar world." As an Evangelical, I find comforting the fact that the explosion of Evangelical missionary activity after 1945—criticized by missiologists from the previous half of the century—provided a bulk of new practice, on the basis of which it was possible to reflect and formulate new theories. Commenting on critical remarks from missiologist R. Pierce Beaver, Dana Robert (1994, p. 146) has described the situation in which a renewed effort has come at the level of scholarship from the missionary activity of conservative Evangelicals: "The 'sectarian' evangelicals that Beaver had excoriated in 1964 reached such a level of institutional maturity and ecclesiastical dominance that critical historical analysis became possible and necessary." At the same time, I also find sobering the remark of Joel Carpenter (1990, p. 131) pointing to the Evangelical isolation from previous missionary practice and experience: "When a post-fundamentalist, 'neo-Evangelical' theological movement appeared in the 1950s and 1960s, it virtually had to reinvent Evangelical missions theology."

Missiological reflection has experienced sustained growth in both quantity and quality because of the widening and deepening of its agenda, the growing dialogue of different traditions, and the emergence of missiologists from the younger churches of Asia, Africa, and Latin America. Evangelicals kept a very focused missionary activity, even at periods in which such activity declined in other sectors of Christendom. Their reflection was made possible in part by the new developments in theological scholarship within the Evangelical camp and by the growth towards maturity of Evangelical churches in those lands that used to be called mission fields. Towards the end of the third quarter of the 20th century, Evangelical missiological reflection gathered momentum, and the 1974 Lausanne Congress became a rallying point to promote Christian mission but also to reflect about it. The Lausanne Covenant became at the same time a summary and an agenda.

Background of Missiological Developments Among Evangelicals

Within the second half of the 20th century, we can place events such as the birth of World Evangelical Fellowship, the growth of an American Evangelical missionary vitality, the development of the World Council of Churches and its eventual merge with the International Missionary Council, the Vatican II Council, and the increasing growth and recognition of the Pentecostal Movement. I will refer specially to the Lausanne Movement because of the missiological trends it synthesized and sparked.

Lausanne was preceded by three vigorous Evangelical Movements following World War II. First, there was the renewal of mass evangelism that reached public notice with Billy Graham in Los Angeles in 1949. Some classic elements of revivalistic Protestantism, combined with the use of mass media, shook the dormant religious routine of people, especially in the big cities, first in North America and then in Europe. The type of evangelistic organization represented by Billy Graham put in evidence the fact that in those countries there was a new awareness of spiritual needs and a religious vacuum that was not being filled by the routine life of institutionalized Christianity. Second, there was a renewal of serious Evangelical scholarship in biblical studies and theological reflection, following a renewal of Evangelical university life in Europe and especially Great Britain. This was related to the Evangelical student work of InterVarsity, that had managed to keep together missionary zeal and concern for theology and scholarship. Third, strong Evangelical churches and movements had emerged around the world, connected to Protestant missionary work of the pre- and post-World War II streams of missionary fervor and activity from Europe and North America. Independent "faith missions" had played an important role in this emergence, representing a new generation that threw itself with great vigor into the task of planting churches, translating Scripture, and reaching the restless masses of the Third World through evangelism.

These three movements exemplify the type of Evangelical churches, missionary organizations, and denominational renewal groups that find a way of expressing their concern for Christian unity and cooperation in alliances such as WEF or the Lausanne Movement. Their variety also explains the tensions that develop within those alliances or umbrella movements, which sometimes are unable to contain them. The volunteerism which is the genius of Evangelical life and mission is a key factor in understanding these developments. The "faith mission" type of missionary activity contributes to the rise of vigorous Evangelical churches in the Third World, which are independent and have no connection with the historic Protestant denominations. Ecclesiology is undefined in these independent churches. Their participation in Evangelical alliances brings them into contact with Evangelicals inside the mainline churches. The encounter is mutually enriching, but it also accounts for a long and difficult process of theological dialogue and definition. There is a dialectical interaction between the vitality that comes from these movements at the grassroots and the direction and stimulation that the alliances themselves provide. In order to understand Evangelical missiological developments, both the promise and the precariousness of this interaction have to be appreciated, and its historical significance has to be evaluated theologically.

The three movements mentioned above converged in the Berlin 1966 World Congress on Evangelism, convened under the leadership of Carl F. H. Henry, to celebrate the 10th anniversary of the magazine *Christianity Today*. Henry was a theologian and journalist who had articulated with clarity the theological agenda for an Evangelicalism that wanted to distance itself from the Fundamentalist trap. As editor of *Christianity Today*, he was in contact with a new generation of Evangelical scholars that were not afraid to dialogue in the academic world and had gone beyond the narrow anti-intellectualism of fundamentalists. This scholarship, however, was matched by an evangelistic and missionary thrust and a global perception that Billy Graham's ministry had made possible.

The vision of the Berlin congress was summarized in its motto, "One Race, One Gospel, One Task." One important fact about Berlin is that Evangelicals acknowledged and accepted the validity and significance of the Pentecostal Movement. The follow-up congresses after Berlin were platforms of convergence not only for reaffirming Evangelical truth, but also for sober consideration of the spiritual needs of the world. The pragmatic concerns of Evangelicals from North America and the theological and missiological acumen of European Evangelicals were matched by the restless sense of mission of Evangelicals in the young churches of the Third World or among the oppressed minorities. The agenda of the ongoing reflection had to make room for the burning questions of those who were witnessing to their faith in Jesus Christ within situations where the ferment of nationalism, social upheaval, and ideological conflict were testing the theological depth of both Evangelical and non-Evangelical missionaries and churches. The Berlin follow-up regional congresses in Singapore (1968), Minneapolis (1969), Bogotá (1969), Ottawa (1970), Amsterdam (1971), and Madrid (1974) were steps in the building-up process that culminated in Lausanne 1974. Because of this preceding process, Lausanne was not the missiological and theological monologue of European or North American Evangelicals, but a brotherly global dialogue of a community that had grown beyond expectations all over the world: a dialogue in search of ways of obedience to the missionary imperatives of Jesus, our Savior and Lord.

The Lausanne Covenant expresses this unique missiological moment. Precisely at the point in time in which Evangelical Christianity was joyfully aware of its global dimension, it also became painfully aware of its serious shortcomings. Liberated by its missionary thrust from the bonds of sterile fundamentalism, Evangelicalism was able again to rediscover the holistic dimensions of the Christian mission that are clearly presented in the Bible. The Lausanne Covenant restates convictions that are characteristic of Evangelicalism. It starts with a trinitarian confession, a statement about the authority of the Bible, and an expression of Christological conviction (LC, par. 1-3). At the same time, the Covenant expresses repentance for what was wrong or missing in the way in which Evangelicals had been accomplishing their missionary task.

I think it possible to summarize in four points the direction of the process of the Lausanne 1974 event, as well as the content of the Covenant it issued. They express a forceful challenge to adopt a new form of missionary practice for world evangelization and a corresponding call for new theological formulation.

First, there was a commitment to a concept of *holistic* mission that retains the Evangelical emphasis on proclamation of the gospel of Jesus Christ while also describing the kind of missionary presence it requires, and the call to discipleship and incorporation into the church (LC, par. 4). Inherent in this is self-criticism of the type of dualistic spiritualization that had come to be prevalent in the practice of Evangelical missionaries. Mission relates to every area of human need. For the majority of Evangelicals, however, holistic mission has evangelism as a key and primary component: "In the church's mission of sacrificial service evangelism is primary" (LC, par. 6).

Second, there was the call for *cooperation* in the mission task—between church and parachurch, mainline and Evangelical, Pentecostal and Reformed—based solely on the missionary passion shared in the Lausanne event and the basic theological consensus reached in the Covenant itself. The sheer magnitude of the task of world evangelization, along with the scandal of sterile division and competition among missionary agencies, demanded a new attitude. The sense of urgency of reaching those still unreached even makes room for the type of concern that had been underlying the call for a "moratorium" (LC, par. 7, 8, 9).

Third, and closely related to the previous point, was the awareness that in the post-imperial era in which we live, the missionary and the theological tasks have a *global* dimension. Christians and missionaries from the European and North American regions, once strongholds of Evangelical faith in the past, had to acknowledge the spiritual decline in those regions and the rise of new thriving churches in Africa, Asia, and Latin America. Thus, neither imperialism nor provincialism could be tolerated.

Fourth was the commitment to consider seriously the *context* of mission. Issues such as culture, education of leaders, spiritual conflict, and persecution were addressed (LC, par. 10-13). The need was recognized for an evaluation of the social, ideological, and spiritual struggles that surround and condition the missionary enterprise, in order to design a relevant type of discipleship for our own times.

From Lausanne I to Lausanne II in Manila

After the Lausanne Congress, Evangelical missionary action was more visibly accompanied by a process of reflection and clarification. A series of consultations was sponsored by the Lausanne Committee, with the participation of missionaries, pastors, mission executives, and missiologists from World Evangelical Fellowship, Latin American Theological Fraternity, Fuller School of World Mission, World Vision International, Evangelicals for Social Action, and many other Evangelical bodies. These gatherings became the platform in which practitioners and theoreticians of mission engaged in the task of "doing theology" together, at a global scale. In one of the first of those consultations, an agreement was reached and a commitment expressed: "We should seek with equal care to avoid theological imperialism or theological provincialism. A church's theology should be developed by the community of faith out of the Scripture in interaction with other theologies of the past and present, and with the local culture and its needs" (Willowbank Report, 1978).

Some Evangelicals (notable among them is Johnston, 1978) became very critical of the kind of missiological and theological agenda expressed by the Covenant. Others tried to narrow and reduce the Lausanne Movement to a fundamentalistic program. For some, it was impossible to accept the commitment to globalism and respect the legitimacy of Third World concerns and challenges.[1] In spite of all these objections, between Lausanne I in 1974 and the second conference sponsored by the Lausanne Committee, Lausanne II in Manila in 1989, a good degree of missionary activity and reflection was sparked, encouraged, oriented, or fostered by the Lausanne Movement. The balance of cooperation and global dialogue achieved was very delicate and fragile, and in many instances it almost came to breaking points. However, it was kept, thanks to the maturity and diplomatic ability of Evangelical statesmen such as John Stott, Leighton Ford, Emilio Núñez, Bishop Jack Dain, Gottfried Ossei-Mensah, Dick Van Halsema, and others like them. As the date for Lausanne II approached, several missionaries and theologians, especially in the Third World, expressed apprehension about the direction that the movement seemed to be taking. They detected a mood of retreat from the territory gained in 1974 to narrower and "safer" positions. They perceived what appeared as an effort to avoid controversial issues and speakers, and a tendency to use Lausanne II as a marketing launch for missionary packages devised in North America.[2]

Lausanne II was held in Manila, Philippines, July 11-20, 1989, 15 years after the first conference. Chris Sugden and Valdir Steuernagel (1990) have interpreted this second event in the pages of *Transformation*.[3] Robert T. Coote (1990) wrote an excellent interpretative chronicle of the event in the *International Bulletin of Missionary Research*. From my own perspec-

---

[1] The best study of this aspect of the post-Lausanne process is the Ph.D. dissertation of Brazilian missiologist Valdir Steuernagel (1988).

[2] As an example of this perception, René Padilla, who was a speaker at Lausanne I, did not accept the invitation to Lausanne II. See his editorial comments in Padilla (1989).

[3] This issue also contains the text of several presentations and documents from the Lausanne II Conference.

tive, in Lausanne II we had a clear demonstration that at grassroots level, across the world, significant progress has been made in the practice of mission following the agenda of Lausanne I. Voices like those of Caesar Molebatsi from South Africa, Valdir Steuernagel from Brazil, Peter Kuzmic from Yugoslavia, and Jovito Salonga from the Philippines could not be barred from the platform. But there were also hundreds of practitioners of holistic forms of mission sharing their experience, their joys, their pain, their frustration, and their hope in seminars and workshops. However, this progress in the application of Lausanne I has come in tension with Evangelical forces that seem committed to pull the movement backwards, towards mission styles of the Cold War era and imperial marketing of theological and missiological packages created within the frame of the present North American society.

Three Missiological Trends

I think that in the Lausanne II process through the most recent years we have seen the development of three different missiological schools or approaches currently present in the Evangelical world. They have gone their own parallel ways within the Evangelical Movement, and it would benefit greatly the cause of mission if they could interact adequately. This is especially important as a new missionary thrust develops in the churches of the Third World, which are in search of models for their participation in the global missionary task of the coming decades. However, the Lausanne consensus has been a fragile platform, and constructive interaction has not been easy and sometimes seems impossible. Coexistence has not developed into cooperation. Given the urgency of the tasks ahead and the growing scarcity of resources, we should try our best to have a real dialogue and come to

new forms of cooperation. Here I offer an outline of the three missiological approaches that I see at work.

Post-imperial missiology

This is the missiology coming from Evangelicals in Great Britain and Europe, and it is characterized by a clear post-imperial stance. By this I mean an awareness that the imperial domination they used to exert is gone and new patterns of relationships have developed. For this missiology there are two sources of serious questions about mission: on the one hand, the decline of Christian churches in Europe and their loss of influence on shaping values and attitudes in their societies, and on the other hand, the emergence of new forms of Christianity in the Third World.

The practice and the theory of mission have to deal with these facts as part of the new frame of reference for mission. Consequently, missiological research and reflection have moved in at least three directions. First, there is a renewed search for biblical patterns to correct and illuminate contemporary mission activity. The field was pioneered by John Stott (1967, 1975) in his biblical studies about the Great Commission and his definition of key words such as salvation, conversion, evangelism, dialogue, and mission. Another systematic contribution that focused on evangelism came from Michael Green (1970), in a book that summarized the findings of contemporary scholarship from the perspective of an evangelist. Other Evangelical contributions exploring the New Testament material have important missiological consequence as they clarify the relevance of New Testament ethical teaching (especially Yoder, 1972) or social practice (a good summary is given in Tidball, 1983). Missionary practice, especially its social and political dimension, has been the source of the questions brought by these scholars to the exploration of the biblical material, and there has been a significant growth of scholarship around the world.[4]

The second direction taken by this missiological approach has been the critical work of writing and interpreting the history of missionary activity, taking very seriously the ambiguities of the Western imperial enterprise and trying to detach missionary obedience from it. This view of history uses critical insights from the sociology of knowledge and the sociology of religion. However, it does not reduce missionary history to a form of class struggle or imperial advance, as some liberation theologians do.[5] Missiologists from the Ecumenical Movement that are taken seriously by Evangelicals, such as Max Warren (1967) and Stephen Neill (1966), pioneered this effort of missiological clarification. An excellent methodological introduction was provided by Roger Mehl (1970, especially chaps. I, II, and 8), himself a theologian and a sociologist, and some valuable Evangelical contributions have been added recently.[6]

One important consequence of this approach has been to clarify the degree to which missionary ideas and practices were influenced by the social context from which missionaries came. In this way, it is possible to distinguish the biblical content of their teaching from the trappings of their class attitudes and their national idiosyncrasies. This is especially helpful as a generation of leaders in the younger churches give themselves to the theological task of contextualizing the Christian

faith in their own cultures. The contribution of Max Warren (1967) in his analysis of the British missionary movement was very valuable in this regard. American missionary anthropologist Jacob Loewen (1975) has been one of the most consistent scholars in his use of insights from anthropology to evaluate critically the missionary enterprise from North America.

The third direction of this missiological exploration is the visualization of the future of mission as a global task in which the churches of the North Atlantic world enter into creative patterns of partnership with churches in the Third World. In relation to this, Andrew Walls (1996) has explored the missiological significance of what he calls "the massive southward shift of the center of gravity of the Christian world," and the theological consequences that such a shift has for the self-image of churches in both North and South. Excellent introductions to mission from this perspective have been written by Maurice Sinclair (1988) and Michael Nazir-Ali (1991). What is distinctive of the partnership proposed by this missiology is that the Third World churches are seen as agents and originators of a missionary effort and a missiological reflection that is valid in its own right. They are not simply being asked to join the missionary enterprise devised in a mission center of North America or Europe. This point becomes especially important because the missionary agenda in the Third World cannot avoid the issues linked to Christian mission and social transformation—issues such as human rights, the socio-political

---

[4] The field was pioneered by E. A. Judge (1960) and followed by authors as diverse as Wayne Meeks, Alan Kreider, and Derek Tidball.

[5] This kind of reductionism was expressed, for instance, in the WCC-sponsored "Declaration of Barbados," which caused an uproar in the 1970s. See *International Review of Mission*, July 1973, and my discussion of this matter in Escobar (1978).

[6] See Stanley (1990) and Carpenter & Shenk (1990). These books are truly historical essays and go beyond the naïve chronicles or memories that we commonly call "mission history."

consequences of missionary action, the ideological use of the Christian message for political aims, and the religious sanction for contemporary forms of economic or cultural colonialism.

What characterizes this missiology is that the traditional Evangelical missionary zeal is matched with a disposition to take courageously the lessons of history and explore God's Word using the best tools of biblical scholarship at the service of mission. More than a closed package that is to be protected from the tough questions that come from life, mission theology is grounded on basic convictions, but it is also an open enterprise so that missionary practice is open to correction. One could also say that missionary practices of British and European agencies tend to express these convictions and that agencies like Tear Fund, South American Missionary Society, Overseas Missionary Fellowship, or Latin Link try to shape their policies according to biblical principles more than mere pragmatic considerations.

Managerial missiology

The distinctive note from the missiology that has developed especially around the cluster of Evangelical institutions in Pasadena, California, connected to the Church Growth School and movements such as the AD 2000 and Beyond Movement, is the effort to reduce Christian mission to a manageable enterprise. Every characteristic of this missiology becomes understandable when perceived within the frame of that avowed quantifying intention. Concepts such as "people groups," "unreached peoples," "10/40 window," "adopt a people," and "territorial spirits" express both a strong sense of urgency and an effort to use every available instrument to make the task possible. As a typical school of thought coming from modern United States, the quantitative approach is predominant and the pragmatic

orientation well defined. One way of achieving manageability is precisely to reduce reality to an understandable picture and then to project missionary action as a response to a problem that has been described in quantitative form. Missionary action is reduced to a linear task that is translated into logical steps to be followed in a process of management by objectives, in the same way in which the evangelistic task is reduced to a process that can be carried on following marketing principles.

Movements that express this approach proliferated as we were approaching the end of the century. Organizations and strategies using the year 2000 A.D. as a date to complete evangelization were given prominent publicity during the Lausanne II gathering, in which an array of "arresting but mystifying statistics" were offered in highly promoted packages (see Coote, 1990, pp. 15-16). The use of statistical information in order to visualize the missionary task, as well as of key dates in order to motivate missionaries, is not something new in the history of missions. The famous "Enquiry" written by William Carey in 1792 in order to promote Protestant missions devoted a good number of pages to statistical charts about the population of the world and the religious affiliation of the peoples. In preparation for some of the great missionary conferences of our century, similar statistical information was compiled in order to communicate the nature of the missionary effort that was required and to promote a sense of urgency about it.

Within managerial missiology, statistical analysis was used first as a way of measuring the effect of missionary action, in an effort to reduce the lack of clarity that surrounded it and the fuzziness in the traditional way of defining and evaluating it. This evaluative methodology was at the service of a narrowly defined concept of mission as numerical growth of the church, coupled with an insistence about the unfinished evangelistic task among those that had not yet heard or accepted the message of the gospel. Donald McGavran was the champion of this position, which he presented in contrast to more inclusive definitions of mission that were predominant, especially in the conciliar Ecumenical Movement. In one of his last writings, McGavran (1989, p. 338) posed the dilemma very clearly: "In short, is mission primarily evangelism, or is it primarily all efforts to improve human existence?" His choice is clear: "Winning many to the Christian life must be the dominant concern of all Christians. All those engaging in missiology need to be all things to all people in order to lead some to believe in Christ and receive everlasting life. Once that is done, then limitation of population, feeding the hungry, healing the sick, developing just forms of government, and other steps toward the better life will become much more possible and more permanent" (McGavran, 1989, p. 340).

Extreme forms of managerial missiology as we know it may have not been what McGavran intended to develop, but it came to happen in any case. Some acts of verbal communication of the gospel, such as distribution of the printed page, hours of broadcasting through radio or TV, massive gatherings for evangelism, and groups of new believers organized into churches, are all activities that can be counted and registered. It is not difficult to see how such a narrowed-down concept of mission has given birth to a managerial approach to the missionary task. It is at this point that this missiology has been subject to severe criticism, because it has yielded to the spirit of the age. It is interesting that as the influence of market economy ideas becomes pervasive in society, authors from this movement are writing now about marketing the church.

Anyone who has engaged in mission in the Third World or among the poor in the First World knows that the neat distinction established by McGavran is artificial. It was good for debate against exaggerations, but it does not function in practice. In the United States or in Europe, middle class churches can keep a neat distinction between "spiritual" needs and "social" needs, and they can specialize in the former. In most African American or Hispanic churches of the U.S. or in churches of immigrants in Europe, such distinction is impossible. On the other hand, there are some aspects of missionary work that cannot be reduced to statistics. Managerial missiology has diminished those aspects of missionary work which cannot be measured or reduced to figures. In the same way, it has given predominance to that which can be reduced to a statistical chart.

The second important note that reflects managerial missiology's origins is the pragmatic approach to the task, which de-emphasizes theological problems, takes for granted the existence of adequate content, and consequently majors in method. An enterprise that presupposes that the theoretical questions are not important will be by force anti-theological. It is the kind of process that demands a closed view of the world, in which the tough questions are not asked because they cannot be reduced to a linear management-by-objectives process. This system cannot live with paradox or mystery. It has no theological or pastoral resources to cope with the suffering and persecution involved many times in mission, because it is geared to provide methodologies for a guaranteed success. However, only categories like paradox, mystery, suffering, and failure can help us grasp something of the depth of the spiritual battle involved in mission. In this way, an important aspect of the history of missions is either silenced or underestimated, because it would not fit the mathematical categories of so-called "church growth."

The pragmatic bias accounts also for the reductionist theological foundation of this missiology. If the missionary effort is reduced to numerical growth, anything that would hinder it has to be eliminated. If the struggle for obedience to God in holistic mission involves costly participation in the processes of social transformation, it is simply eliminated. The slow process of development of a contextual theology for a young church tends to be considered inefficient and costly, and it is easy to substitute prepackaged theologies translated from English. Efficient educational techniques like "extension" have been developed within the frame of managerial missiology, but there has not been much success in the production of contextual textbooks. Charles Taber (1983, p. 119) points to the Evangelical origins of the theological presuppositions of the Church Growth School, but he proves that its foundation is a "narrowed-down version of the evangelical hermeneutic and theology."

In the third place, the strong influence of the American functionalist social sciences on managerial missiology accounts for an important deficiency when we come to the transformative dynamism of the gospel. The structural-functional model of cultural anthropology is based on a static view of the world for which, as Taber (1983, p. 119) says, "'Cultural givens' take on permanence and rigidity; it suggests that whatever is endures. This cannot help but undermine the hope of transformation which is central to the gospel." Peruvian missiologist Tito Paredes (1986) has developed this critical point, showing how the way in which managerial missiologists read Scripture is affected by this socially conservative approach, which takes them to reductionist understanding of the gos-

pel and Christian mission. Harvie Conn (1983) has studied the development of the missiological thought of Donald McGavran in relation to this area, especially the concepts about discipling and perfecting as phases and moments of the missionary process.

Proponents of this missiology that entered in a global dialogue after Lausanne 1974 have worked critically to develop the best of its insights. On the other hand, Conn suggests that McGavran's evolution and self-correction have not been always adequately noticed or followed by his students and defenders. As an insider in the movement, Arthur Glasser (1986) provided a brief and clarifying evaluative chronicle. Some anthropologists of this school, especially Alan Tippett (1987), Charles Kraft (1979), and Paul Hiebert (1986), worked patiently in a clarification of methodologies from the social sciences as they are applied to missiological work. Missiologist Charles Van Engen (1991) has worked systematically in an effort to incorporate key concerns from the Church Growth School into a full-fledged theology of the church in mission.

A more recent movement that embodies in an extreme form all the characteristics we have outlined above is the so-called Spiritual Warfare Movement. While no one would deny the reality of spiritual life and the spiritual battles involved in missionary work, this American-based movement provides maps and statistics of demons in cities and regions. It majors in offering methodologies for which there is no biblical or theological basis, and it handles Scripture in an arbitrary way. It comes in packages of literature, video, songs, and methodologies that are being propagated with the best use of marketing techniques. The Evangelical Missiological Society has provided a careful theological and biblical evaluation of this movement (Rommen, 1995).

The enthusiastic fervor and the militancy of some proponents of managerial missiology, as well as the great amount of material and technical resources with which they promote their cause, has created a suspicion about motivation, especially in the Southern hemisphere. The idea that an accumulation of material resources is bound to produce certain effects has reflected itself in the constant preoccupation with augmenting the missionary force quantitatively, without much debate about the quality of that missionary action. The suspicion of some Third World Christians is that they are being used as objects of a missionary action that seems to be directed to the main objective of enhancing the financial, informational, and decision-making power of some centers of mission in the First World. The first rule of missionary life is that embodied in the model proposed by the Lausanne Covenant of emptying ourselves, and there is a right to suspect motivation. However, that is precisely the aspect that cannot be grasped by simple statistical analysis. Properly speaking, more than a missiology, this is a methodology for mission, and if it limits itself to that realm, accepting the need to enter into dialogue with theology and other missiologies, it could make its valuable contribution to mission in the third millennium.

A critical missiology from the periphery

From the lands which used to be missionary territories, a new missiology has started to develop and is letting its voice be heard. Lausanne I was characterized by the openness to hear from that new reflection, at the same time contextual and engaged. We could say that the basic thrust of this missiology is its critical nature. The question for this missiology is not *how much* missionary action is required today but *what kind* of missionary action is necessary. And the concern with quality links naturally with the questions about the social dynamism of the gospel and that transformative power of the experience of conversion to Jesus Christ.

What characterizes Evangelical churches in the Third World, especially in Africa, Latin America, and Asia, is their evangelistic and missionary dynamism. And that is clearly reflected in the missiology that comes from them. None among the pastors, missionaries, and theologians from the Third World that spoke at Lausanne I or Lausanne II proposed a moratorium of evangelization or a concept of mission that would deny the priority of announcing the message of salvation in Jesus Christ as Savior and Lord. Most of them, however, would agree about the need to distinguish between the gospel and the ideologies of the West, between a missionary action patterned by the model of Jesus Christ and one that reflects the philosophies and methodologies of the multi-national corporations. Probably the Latin Americans René Padilla and Orlando Costas are the theologians that have done more to provide a solid biblical foundation to the twofold missiological approach of Evangelicals from the Third World: the criticism of existing patterns of mission and the proposal of a missiology that corresponds to the missionary challenges of the day.

Costas' (1983) approach was Evangelical in its inspiration and emphasis, and he tried to formulate basic missiological concepts that would incorporate some insights from liberation theologies as well as others from church growth methodologies. His holistic concept of church growth is an excellent summary of his efforts towards a synthesis that could be communicated and implemented at the level of the local church. His missiological exploration into biblical themes is specially valuable in his posthumous work, *Liberating*

News (Costas, 1989). His study of the significance of the ministry of Jesus in Galilee and from Galilee provides a paradigm for mission from the Third World that he describes as "a model of contextual mission from the periphery." In light of it, Costas (1989, p. 67) believes that, "The global scope of contextual evangelization should be geared first and foremost to the nations' peripheries, where the multitudes are found and where the Christian faith has had the best opportunity to build a strong base." Many historical examples as well as the tremendous dynamism of churches in Africa and parts of Asia and Latin America today prove his point and mark some guidelines for the future of mission, not so much as churches adopt managerial plans from the North, but as they develop their own missionary projects that express their genius and ethos.

Padilla also offers a missiological reflection that is especially committed to take seriously the biblical text. His most complete proposal thus far is in his book *Mission Between the Times* (Padilla, 1985). Padilla finds in the biblical text solid ground for a concept of the gospel and Christian commitment, in which the socially transformative dimensions are unavoidable. Conn (1983, p. 85) thinks that Padilla's dealing with issues like the "homogeneous unit principle" provides "a powerful model of exegetical interaction with the church growth paradigm" and "an articulate example of the way in which these questions ought to be approached from a biblical-theological perspective." What this example offers to missionaries is an exploration into the depths of the social significance of the basic Christian truths. Precisely it is this kind of Evangelical depth that is missing in managerial missiology and that makes sense to those who minister in the name of Jesus Christ, in the midst of poverty and with the pain of social transitions.

Three collective volumes contain some of the missiological contributions from Evangelical theologians of the Third World to the ongoing dialogue, with special reference to the relation between mission and social transformation. A careful consideration of their content will show that this missiological concern is not something added artificially to what otherwise would be purely evangelistic emphasis. It is a concern that comes from the demands of both the evangelistic and the pastoral activity which these practitioners of mission cannot avoid. What is at stake every day and every week in the ministry of these men, be it in the ghettos of North American cities or in the dusty roads of Latin America, Asia, and Africa, is their credibility as messengers of Jesus Christ. Thus a renewed Christology is essential for their mission (Samuel & Sugden, 1983), as well as the way in which churches can respond to human need (Samuel & Sugden, 1987) or proclaim Christ among those that have not come to saving knowledge of him (Samuel & Hauser, 1989).

Contributions from missiologists like Kwame Bediako and David Gitari in Africa or Vinay Samuel and David Lim in Asia to the above-mentioned volumes posed special questions in the area of the relationship between gospel and culture and the way in which Evangelicals rooted in the context of non-Christian cultures will deal with their historical memory and their own religious past. From the Catholic context of popular religiosity and syncretism in Latin America, these questions have a different twist in the work of men like Tito Paredes and Key Yuasa. In all these contexts, the religious experience cannot avoid reference to its social conditioning and its social impact. As militant social scientists put missionary work in the Third World under the microscope of their research, missiologists have to come to terms with the lights and the shadows of a missionary enterprise made up of human frailties and ambiguities. The missiologist in the Third World cannot avoid the evaluative questions not only for the defense of missionary work as it stands today, but also for the formulation of a missionary strategy for the coming decades.

Trinitarian Missiology

In the final section of this paper, I want to outline some notes of a trinitarian missiology that may give us clues in relation to the challenges of the future. Evangelical missiological reflection has been strong in its Christology, because Evangelicals in mission have usually been Christocentric in their spiritual life and their concept of mission. I have the conviction that the times call for a new understanding of the Triune God as we think about mission in light of God's Word. This is not to detract from a Christ-centered stance but to look at our Lord the way Scripture presents him in relation to the Father and the Spirit. I will refer to several documents that have been produced by conferences and consultations, because many times they reflect the consensus of practitioners and missiologists as a result of exercises in dialogue. Missiology is the reflection of the people of God, not only of bright, specialized scholars.

God's mission in all of Scripture

Because Evangelicals have the highest regard for the Word of God, they see the Bible as the norm for faith and practice. It is therefore the norm for our way of thinking and acting in mission. Documents such as the Lausanne Covenant and those produced by working groups and consultations of the World Evangelical Fellowship in dialogue with different Christian interlocutors reflect this biblical conviction (Stott, 1996; Meeking & Stott, 1986;

Schrotenboer, 1987). In all these documents, the concept of mission is grounded on Scripture, both Old and New Testament: "Mission arises from the self-giving love of the Triune God himself and from his eternal purpose." From Scripture comes the conviction that "the arrival of the messianic Kingdom through Jesus necessitates the announcement of the Good News, the summons to repentance and faith, and the gathering together of the people of God."

This effort to find the missionary imperative in the great lines of God's revelation in both Testaments is part of an ongoing rediscovery of the missionary theme that runs through the Bible. Here we come to a point Evangelicals must acknowledge: they themselves have a long way to go in terms of deepening their understanding of the biblical basis of mission, in order to establish its validity not on isolated sayings but on the general thrust of biblical teaching. As an Evangelical from Latin America, I have found especially significant the fact that Catholic scholars have produced books that have become standard works in the field of the biblical basis of mission. South African missiologist David Bosch (1993, p. 178) referred to this reality in an eloquent comment: "One might even say that by and large, Catholic biblical scholars are currently taking the missionary dimension of Scripture more seriously than their Protestant counterparts."

In the WEF Perspective (Schrotenboer, 1987) there is also a note of self-criticism about this point: "We must acknowledge that often we have also set our Evangelical traditions above Scripture. In many instances our lip service to biblical authority contradicts the predominant place we give to our denominational and historical baggage." With this note comes also an important commitment to enter into a global inter-Evangelical dialogue to better understand the biblical teaching on missions: "The time has come for Evangelicals around the world to work together in a contextual hermeneutics that will benefit from the rich expressions of Evangelical faith that are now taking root in so many nations and cultures."

Some of the more difficult dialogues and debates within the Evangelical Movement are related to the corrective role of Scripture in relation to missionary practice. I have referred to the missionary strategy known as Spiritual Warfare developed in relation to the Church Growth Movement. At a time in which there is a resurgence of religiosity in many parts of the world, Spiritual Warfare has contributed to a renewed awareness of the spiritual dimension of the missionary task. The Lausanne Covenant had a clear reference to it: "We believe that we are engaged in constant spiritual warfare with the principalities and powers of evil" (LC, par. 12). However the Spiritual Warfare Movement has taken extreme and confusing directions. The Lausanne Committee (1992) issued a statement warning about this development and recommending some antidotes: "There is a danger that we revert to think and operate on pagan worldviews or on undiscerning application of Old Testament analogies that were in fact superseded in Jesus Christ. The antidote to this is the rigorous study of the whole of Scripture always interpreting the Old Testament in the light of the New."

The return to Scripture in Evangelical missiology, especially to the New Testament patterns, means a continual rediscovery of how mission was carried on by the pre-Constantinian church. Sometimes the understanding of this may not give adequate regard to historical developments. This lack of historical awareness mixed with Evangelical zeal may account for some ways of doing mission that may well be labeled as proselytism. Dialogue has to make room for understanding this, as one of the joint groups working on the issue of proselytism came to acknowledge, affirming that most persons engaged in proselytism "do so out of a genuine concern for the salvation of those whom they address" (quoted in Robeck, 1996, p. 6).

The Christological center and model

McGrath (1995, p. 65) has reminded us recently that the Evangelical stance is radically Christ-centered. He relates this to the high view of Scripture to which Evangelicals are committed: "Christology and scriptural authority are inextricably linked, in that it is Scripture and Scripture alone that brings us to the true and saving knowledge of Jesus Christ." One could describe the development of Evangelical missiology after Berlin 1966 as the search for a new Christological paradigm. Traditionally, the Great Commission of Jesus Christ in Matthew 28:18 had been the motto of Evangelical missions, stressing the imperative of Jesus' command to go and evangelize the nations. In Berlin, John Stott started his Bible expositions with the Gospel of John and emphasized that in it we have a model for mission ("As my Father hath sent me"), as well as a missionary imperative ("even so send I you"). Many came to agree with Stott (1967, p. 39) that "although these words represent the simplest form of the Great Commission, it is at the same time its most profound form, its most challenging and therefore its most neglected."

The Christological paradigm of mission found in the Gospels is incarnational and is marked by a spirit of service. Its roots are in the message of prophets such as Isaiah as well as in the theological elaboration of the Christology of Paul, Peter, John, and other apostolic writers. It came to be understood as a corrective to Evangelical triumphalism, and consequently taken very seriously by Evangelicals around the world (see, for instance, Padilla, 1976; Samuel & Sugden, 1983). From the shift of attention to the Johannine version of the Great Commission came a new appreciation of the humanity of Jesus Christ and the importance of his incarnational style of mission. This may be an adequate source for evaluation and self-criticism within the Evangelical missionary enterprise. One finds it as a theme in the Lausanne Covenant and as a hermeneutical key in several documents produced later on by the Lausanne Movement and WEF.

René Padilla (1982) has expressed well an Evangelical perspective recovered from a fresh reading of the Gospels: "Jesus Christ is God's missionary par excellence, and he involves his followers in his mission." As we find it in the Gospels, Jesus' mission includes "fishing for the kingdom," or, in other words, the call to conversion to Jesus Christ as the way, the truth, and the life. It is this conversion to Jesus which stands as the basis upon which the Christian community is formed. Mission also includes "compassion" as a result of immersion among the multitudes. It is neither a sentimental burst of emotion nor an academic option for the poor, but definite and intentional actions of service in order to "feed the multitude" with bread *for* life, as well as bread *of* life. Mission includes "confrontation" of the powers of death with the power of the Suffering Servant, and thus "suffering" becomes a mark of Jesus' messianic mission and a result of this power struggle and of human injustice. Through creative contextual obedience, Jesus' mission becomes a fertile source of inspiration. It contains the seeds of new patterns being explored today through practice and reflection—patterns such as simple lifestyle, holistic mission, the unity of the church for mission, the pattern of God's kingdom as

missiological paradigm, and the spiritual conflict involved in mission.

Within the Evangelical missionary stance, the theme of *imitatio Christi* was given a missiological dimension, and one could say that in the case of Latin America there were in this process some convergences with certain forms of liberation theology. For Evangelicals, however, it is clear that biblical Christology also includes an unequivocal reference to the atoning work of Jesus Christ on the cross and the need of every person to respond to it. There cannot be an imitation of Christ in the biblical sense without a new birth. In response to liberation theologians who would stress the socio-political dimension of the death of Jesus, Padilla, for instance, accepts the truth based on examination of the texts of the Gospels that the death of Jesus was the historical outcome of the kind of life he lived, and that he suffered for the cause of justice and challenges us to do the same. But a warning is necessary, because: "Unless the death of Christ is also seen as God's gracious provision of an atonement for sin, the basis for forgiveness is removed and sinners are left without the hope of justification ... salvation is by grace through faith and ... nothing should detract from the generosity of God's mercy and love as the basis of joyful obedience to the Lord Jesus Christ" (Samuel & Sugden, 1983, p. 28).

Here we can appreciate better an Evangelical conviction that distinguishes Evangelicals from others (Catholics, for instance), as we see in the section on the biblical basis of mission in the ERCDOM Report (Meeking & Stott, 1986). First we find a summary of agreements and disagreements in a crisp sentence: "While both sides affirm that the pilgrim church is missionary by its very nature, its missionary activity is differently understood." It goes on to explain the Vatican II definition of the church as "sacrament of salvation ... the sign and promise of redemption to each and every person without exception." It then states that most Evangelicals have a contrasting position: "The church is the beginning and anticipation of the new creation, the first born among his creatures. Though all in Adam die, not all are automatically in Christ. So life in Christ has to be received by grace with repentance, through faith. *With yearning, Evangelicals plead for a response to the atoning work of Christ in his death and resurrection.* But with sorrow, they know that not all who are called are chosen" (emphasis added). This conviction is then reflected in missionary activity: "Evangelization is therefore the call to those outside to come as children of the Father into the fullness of eternal life in Christ by the Spirit, and into the joy of a loving community in the fellowship of the church."

This call to conversion is crucial for Evangelical mission. Personal encounter with Jesus Christ changes people radically, and there is a component of moral transformation in this concept of conversion. As an historian observed, in the Evangelical revival of John Wesley we could see both the pessimism about human nature characteristic of Calvin's biblical anthropology and the optimism about divine grace from Evangelical Arminianism that matched it (Rupp, 1952). I would say that this balanced but tense vision has been one of the marks of Evangelical missionary and evangelistic efforts. There is power in the blood of Jesus Christ to regenerate persons by the power of the Holy Spirit. This conviction was forcefully restated in 1988 by a joint group of WEF and the Lausanne Committee (Hong Kong Call, 1992, p. 264): "Conversion means turning from sin in repentance to Christ in faith. Through this faith believers are forgiven and justified and adopted into the family of God's children and heirs. In the turning process, they are invited to the crucified and risen Christ by the Holy Spirit who prompts them to die to the sinful desires of their old nature and to be liberated from Satanic bondage and to become new creatures in him. This is their passage from spiritual death to spiritual life, which Scripture calls regeneration or new birth (John 3:5)."

Because mission involves frequently a transcultural action, it is important to be alert against forms of evangelism and conversion that appear more as the imposition of foreign cultural patterns on the receptors of the gospel. The Lausanne Covenant had a warning reminding us that, "Missions have all too frequently exported with the gospel an alien culture, and churches have sometimes been in bondage to culture rather than to Scripture" (LC, par. 10). The Hong Kong Call (1992, pp. 264-265) offers a more specific reminder: "There is a radical discontinuity in all conversions, in the sense that the convert 'turns from darkness to light and from the power of Satan to God' (Acts 26:18)." However, it also tries to make clear that: "Conversion should not 'de-culturise' the converts. They should remain members of their cultural community, and wherever possible retain the values that are not contrary to biblical revelation. In no case should the converts be forced to be 'converted' to the culture of the foreign missionary."

The radical Christocentrism of Evangelicals accounts also for their stance in relation to other religions. The WEF Perspective (Schrotenboer, 1987) uses strong language when it criticizes syncretistic practices. At Lausanne II in Manila (1989), Canon Colin Chapman, who had been a missionary among Muslims, acknowledged the fact that Evangelicals had still much to learn in their understanding of how the Bible deals with the issue of religion in general. The question has become more urgent in recent times, in view of the increase of religiosity in the West and the tension between growing pluralism on the one hand and fundamentalisms on the other hand in many parts of the world.

The way ahead is being opened by the work of theologians from those parts of the world where the encounter with other faiths is part of the daily life of the missionary and the Christian community. Asian and African Evangelicals are contributing to a better understanding of the uniqueness of Jesus Christ. There is firmness in their Evangelical conviction, but there is also an awareness of the dangers of Western triumphalism that may have tainted Evangelical positions in the past. Thus, for instance, Vinoth Ramachandra (1996, p. 275), an Evangelical from Sri Lanka, examines critically the missiological approach of three Asian Catholic theologians: Samartha, Pieris, and Pannikar. Then he offers a careful development of orthodox Christology in dialogue with religions and modernity. From his Christology comes a position that avoids arrogance: "This kind of theological position, which seeks a biblical balance of confidence and humility, defies classification under the customary categories of exclusivist, pluralist, and inclusivist, where Christian views on the world religions are concerned."

During the most recent decade in Latin America, there has been much pastoral and theological work (and very little dialogue) in the area of popular religion among both Catholics and Evangelicals. On the one hand, there is the effort of the Catholic Church to understand critically the syncretistic forms of Christianity, especially among the indigenous peoples, what is now being called "the Indian face of God." On the other hand, there is the existence of popular forms of Protestantism that have grown beyond all expectations. Anyone familiar with the situation

of the continent knows that the question of popular religiosity does not only have a pastoral angle but also a political one, which may be the source of most serious disagreements.

A Methodist theologian who has insisted on affirming his Evangelical stance, José Míguez Bonino (1997, p. 120), has written recently, challenging Latin American Evangelicals to take seriously the issue of other religions. He believes that a trinitarian Christological focus can serve as our guide. "We must not separate the Jesus Christ of the New Testament from the Word 'that was from the beginning' 'with God and was God,'" and he invites us to see in human experiences the presence of that Word and that Spirit. This is not "to 'give in' to paganism but rather to confess the One 'without (whom) not one thing came into being'(John 1:3)." His Evangelical warning comes then loud and clear: "It is no less true, however, that Christian theology cannot disengage the Word and the Spirit of God from the 'flesh' of the son of Mary—of his teaching, his message, his life and his death, his resurrection and Lordship. It is there where we can find the marks of the authentic Word and Spirit of the God of the covenant. By the yardstick of the presence of God in Jesus one measures all presumed presence of that God in human history."

The power of the Holy Spirit

Since Anglican missiologist Roland Allen, former missionary in China, published his book *The Spontaneous Expansion of the Church* in 1912, the question of a return to New Testament patterns of mission has been pursued in Protestant missiology. Allen started with methodological questions but soon found that he also had to give serious consideration to the presence and power of the Holy Spirit in mission. Actually, he was returning to a key point in the practice and theology of both Pietists and Revivalists in the history of missions. It was an important theme for Evangelical champions of missions linked to the Holiness Movements, with persons such as A. B. Simpson, A. J. Gordon, and A. T. Pierson. In the second part of the 20th century, the growth of the Pentecostal Movement, which had had a strong missionary thrust from its inception, eventually forced the question from the missiological level into the realm of historical and biblical studies. The Pentecostal Movement in itself became a vast field for research (Dempster, Klaus, & Petersen, 1991).

The understanding of the initiative of the Holy Spirit in relation to mission has been enriched by the contributions of several Evangelical scholars. Their works provide a solid foundation for a better understanding of the Evangelical practice of mission.[7] In his book *Pentecost and Missions*, Harry Boer (1961) reminded us that the use of the "Great Commission" as the imperative motto for Evangelical missionary work was actually a relatively recent development. The biblical pattern stresses the presence and power of the Holy Spirit in the life of the church as the source of missionary dynamism—not a new legalism, but the free and joyous expression of a renewed experience of God's grace. Here we have a better key to understand what may be the source that inspires the spontaneous missionary thrust in Evangelical missions and churches around the world.

As has already been noted, there are many types of Pentecostals within the Evangelical ranks of both WEF and the Lausanne Movement. However, the acknowledgment of their specific contributions as movements inspired and empowered by the Holy Spirit was not easy to accept by

other Evangelicals. In this area we have witnessed significant advance in recent years. An important section in the ERCDOM Report (Meeking & Stott, 1986) is given to the work of the Holy Spirit in mission, and it is one of the sections in which there are also significant points of agreement among Catholics and Evangelicals. At the same time, it is surprising how very little space is given to the work of the Holy Spirit in the WEF Perspective (Schrotenboer, 1987). In contrast with this, the Summary Reports of the 1995 consultation of the WEF Theological Commission about "Faith and Hope for the Future" are permeated by a trinitarian affirmation and confession of faith and hope in the work of the Holy Spirit (WEF Theological Commission, 1997).

At the end of my previous paper, I recalled the fact that Evangelical missions in our century were more inspired by the Wesleyan revivals and the Moravian pioneers of mission than by the 16th century magisterial Reformers. The dynamism that nurtured missionary Protestantism came from renewal movements that emphasized personal, living faith and disciplined life rather than confessional conformity. Not that intellectual understanding of orthodox faith was not important. Men like Wesley or Zinzendorf were theologically articulate. But it was their living experience that enabled them to abandon old church structures that were obsolete and gave them creativity in developing new structures for mission. In this they were open to the movement of the Spirit. After Lausanne, Howard Snyder has been the missiologist who has contributed more to our understanding of this relationship between spiritual renewal and new patterns of missionary action which is part of our Evangelical heritage.

---

[7] I think of Harry Boer (1961), John V. Taylor (1973), several works by James D. G. Dunn, and, more recently, Gordon Fee (1994).

I quote again Brazilian missiologist Valdir Steuernagel (1993): "Mission understood in pneumatological language is one act with two steps. It is first to perceive the blowing of the Spirit and the direction from which it comes. And then it is to run in the same direction to which the Spirit is blowing." Some Evangelicals like myself think that discernment of the blowing of the Spirit requires an open attitude and sensitivity, which acknowledge that behind those things that appear as something new and unusual, the strength and vigor of the Spirit may be at work. The act of obedience demands creativity in order to shape new structures that will be adequate instruments for missionary action in a particular historical moment.

In Pauline missionary practice we find this pattern. Paul's Christology is the development of pastoral, doctrinal, and ethical teaching that stems from the fact of Christ. Paul elaborates his Christology as he responds to the needs and the questions of churches which were born from the Spirit and which showed evidence of new life, but which had not yet articulated their belief in a meaningful way. The recipients of these letters were people who had grasped the Lordship of Christ and whose eyes had been opened by the Spirit to see the glory of God in the face of Jesus Christ, but they did not have yet a clear Christology. What we have in the world today are churches in which people may repeat weekly the minutiae of a Christological creed but who do not have the new life in Christ that the Spirit begets. On the other hand, we have growing churches where there are the signs of the power of the Spirit at work, but where a basic theological task is necessary, along the lines of what Paul did in his ministry.

Evangelical theology has been an effort to keep both a missiological thrust and faithfulness to revealed truth. Our emphasis has not been in a continuity expressed by an earthly hierarchical institution, but in a continuity made possible by God's Word revealed to human beings. In all the crossing of missionary frontiers, and in all the efforts at contextualization, Evangelical missiology has stressed a continuity of faithfulness to the Word. In the contemporary situation, we also need to pay heed to what Emil Brunner (1953, p. 47) wrote at the middle point of the 20th century: "It is not merely a question of the continuity of the word—the maintenance of the original doctrine—but also of the continuity of a life; that is life flowing from the Holy Ghost. The fellowship of Jesus lives under the inspiration of the Holy Spirit; that is the secret of its life, of its communion and of its power."

I hope and pray that this missiological conference called by the Missions Commission of WEF may become one of the foci where Evangelicals looking at mission in the 21st century may experience an encounter of the continuity in truth and the continuity in life, for the glory of God.

References

Boer, H. R. (1961). *Pentecost and missions*. Grand Rapids, MI: Wm. B. Eerdmans Publishing Co.

Bonino, J. M. (1997). *Faces of Latin American Protestantism*. Grand Rapids, MI: Wm. B. Eerdmans Publishing Co.

Bosch, D. (1993). Reflections on biblical models of mission. In J. M. Phillips & R. T. Coote (Eds.), *Toward the 21st century in Christian mission: Essays in honor of Gerald H. Anderson*. Grand Rapids, MI: Wm. B. Eerdmans Publishing Co.

Brunner, E. (1953). *The misunderstanding of the church*. Philadelphia, PA: Westminster Press.

Carpenter, J., & Shenk, W. (Eds.). (1990). *Earthen vessels*. Grand Rapids, MI: Wm. B. Eerdmans Publishing Co.

Conn, H. M. (1983). Looking for a method: Backgrounds and suggestions. In W. R. Shenk (Ed.), *Exploring church growth* (pp.

EVANGELICAL MISSIOLOGY: PEERING INTO THE FUTURE 121

79-94). Grand Rapids, MI: Wm. B. Eerdmans Publishing Co.

Coote, R. T. (1990, January). Lausanne II and world evangelization. *International Bulletin of Missionary Research*, *14*(1), pp. 10-17.

Costas, O. E. (1983). A wholistic concept of church growth. In W. R. Shenk (Ed.), *Exploring church growth* (pp. 95-107). Grand Rapids, MI: Wm. B. Eerdmans Publishing Co.

———. (1989). *Liberating news*. Grand Rapids, MI: Wm. B. Eerdmans Publishing Co.

Dempster, M. A., Klaus, B. D., & Petersen, D. (Eds.). (1991). *Called and empowered: Global mission in Pentecostal perspective*. Peabody, MA: Hendrickson Publishers.

Escobar, S. (1978). *Christian mission and social justice* (ch. 3). Scottdale, PA: Herald Press.

Fee, G. D. (1994). *God's empowering presence: The Holy Spirit in the letters of Paul*. Peabody, MA: Hendrickson Publishers.

Glasser, A. F. (1986). Church growth at Fuller. *Missiology*, *14*(4), pp. 401-420.

Green, M. (1970). *Evangelism in the early church*. Grand Rapids, MI: Wm. B. Eerdmans Publishing Co.

Hiebert, P. G. (1986). *Anthropological insights for missionaries*. Grand Rapids, MI: Baker Book House.

The Hong Kong call to conversion. (1992). *Evangelical Review of Theology*, *16*(3), pp. 262-270.

Hutchison, W. H. (1987). *Errand to the world: American Protestant thought and foreign missions*. Chicago: University of Chicago Press.

Johnston, A. P. (1978). *The battle for world evangelism*. Wheaton, IL: Tyndale House Publishers.

Judge, E. A. (1960). *The social pattern of Christian groups in the first century*. London: Tyndale Press.

Kraft, C. (1979). *Christianity in culture*. Maryknoll, NY: Orbis Books.

Lausanne Committee on World Evangelization. (1992, August 27). Lausanne Committee issues statement on spiritual warfare. *World Evangelization Information Service* (Press release, p. 3).

Loewen, J. A. (1975). *Culture and human values: Christian intervention in anthropological perspective*. Pasadena, CA: William Carey Library.

McGavran, D. (1989). Missiology faces the lion. *Missiology*, *17*(3), pp. 338-340.

McGrath, A. (1995). *Evangelicalism and the future of Christianity*. Downers Grove, IL: InterVarsity Press.

Meeking, B., & Stott, J. R. W. (Eds.). (1986). *The Evangelical-Roman Catholic dialogue on mission 1977-1984*. Grand Rapids, MI: Wm. B. Eerdmans Publishing Co.

Mehl, R. (1970). *Sociology of Protestantism*. Philadelphia, PA: Westminster Press.

Nazir-Ali, M. (1991). *From everywhere to everywhere: A world view of Christian mission*. London: Collins.

Neill, S. (1966). *Colonialism and Christian mission*. New York: McGraw Hill.

Padilla, C. R. (1985). *Mission between the times*. Grand Rapids, MI: Wm. B. Eerdmans Publishing Co.

———. (1982). Bible studies. *Missiology*, *10*(3), pp. 319-338.

———. (1989, December). Mision y compromiso social. *Misión*, Buenos Aires, *8*(4), pp. 120-121.

Padilla, C. R. (Ed.). (1976). *The new face of evangelicalism*. Downers Grove, IL: InterVarsity Press.

Paredes, T. (1986). *El evangelio en platos de barro*. Lima, Peru: Ed. Presencia.

Ramachandra, V. (1996). *The recovery of mission*. Grand Rapids, MI: Wm. B. Eerdmans Publishing Co.

Robeck, C. M., Jr. (1996, January). Mission and the issue of proselytism. *International Bulletin of Missionary Research*, *20*(1), p. 6.

Robert, D. L. (1994). From missions to mission to beyond mission: The historiography of American Protestant foreign missions since World War II. *International Bulletin of Missionary Research*, *18*(4), p. 146.

Rommen, E. (Ed.). (1995). *Spiritual power and mission: Raising the issues*. Pasadena, CA: William Carey Library/Evangelical Missionary Society.

Rupp, E. G. (1952). *Principalities and powers: Studies in the Christian conflict in history* (pp. 76-93). New York: Abingdom Cokesbury.

Samuel, V., & Hauser, A. (1989). *Proclaiming Christ in Christ's way: Studies in integral evangelism*. Oxford: Regnum Books.

Samuel, V., & Sugden, C. (Eds.). (1983). *Sharing Jesus in the Two Thirds World*. Grand Rapids, MI: Wm. B. Eerdmans Publishing Co.

———. (1987). *The church in response to human need*. Grand Rapids, MI: Wm. B. Eerdmans Publishing Co.

Schrotenboer, P. G. (Ed.). (1987). *Roman Catholicism: A contemporary Evangelical perspective*. Grand Rapids, MI: Baker Book House.

Sinclair, M. (1988). *Ripening harvest, gathering storm*. London: MARC.

Stanley, B. (1990). *The Bible and the flag*. Leicester, England: InterVarsity Press.

Steuernagel, V. (1988). *The theology of missions in its relation to social responsibility within the Lausanne movement*. Chicago: Lutheran School of Theology.

———. (1993). *Obediencia missionária e prática histórica: Em busca de modelos*. São Paulo, Brazil: ABU Editora.

Stott, J. R. W. (1967). The Great Commission. In C. F. H. Henry & S. Mooneyham (Eds.), *One race, one gospel, one task* (Vol. 1). Minneapolis, MN: World Wide Publications.

———. (1975). *Christian mission in the modern world*. Downers Grove, IL: InterVarsity Press.

Stott, J. R. W. (Ed.). (1996). *Making Christ known: Historic mission documents from the Lausanne Movement 1974-1989*. Grand Rapids, MI: Wm. B. Eerdmans Publishing Co.

Sugden, C., & Steuernagel, V. (1990, January–March). *Transformation, 7*(1).

Taber, C. R. (1983). Contextualization. In W. R. Shenk (Ed.), *Exploring church growth*. Grand Rapids, MI: Wm. B. Eerdmans Publishing Co.

Taylor, J. V. (1973). *The Go-between God*. Philadelphia, PA: Fortress Press.

Tidball, D. (1983). *An introduction to the sociology of the New Testament*. Exeter, UK: Paternoster.

Tippett, A. R. (1987). *Introduction to missiology*. Pasadena, CA: William Carey Library.

Van Engen, C. (1991). *God's missionary people: Rethinking the purpose of the local church*. Grand Rapids, MI: Baker Book House.

Walls, A. F. (1996). *The missionary movement in Christian history: Studies in the transmission of faith*. Maryknoll, NY: Orbis Books.

Warren, M. (1967). *Social history and Christian missions*. London: SCM Press.

WEF Theological Commission. (1997, January). Faith and hope for the future. *Evangelical Review of Theology, 21*(1), pp. 5-40.

Willowbank Report. (1978). In J. R. W. Stott & R. T. Coote (Eds.), *Down to earth studies in Christianity and culture*. Grand Rapids, MI: Wm. B. Eerdmans Publishing Co.

Yoder, J. H. (1972). *The politics of Jesus*. Grand Rapids, MI: Wm. B. Eerdmans.

Samuel Escobar and his wife Lilly are Peruvians. From 1959 to 1985, they were missionaries among university students in Peru, Argentina, Brasil, Spain, and Canada, under the International Fellowship of Evangelical Students. Samuel's missiological thinking developed as reflection on praxis in evangelism and through mission conferences such as the Urbana Missionary Convention, CLADE I Bogota (1969), and Lausanne (1974). Samuel was a founder of the Latin American Theological Fraternity and served as its president (1970–1984). He has an earned Ph.D. from Universidad Complutense, Madrid, Spain, and an honorary D.D. from McMaster University, Canada. He is an ordained Baptist minister. Presently he teaches at Eastern Baptist Theological Seminary in Wynnewood, Pennsylvania, during the fall and serves the rest of the year as Consultant for Theological Education with Baptist International Ministries, based in Lima, Peru. He and Lilly have a daughter who teaches in Spain and a son who works as agricultural economist with MEDA in Lancaster, Pennsylvania.

IT WAS MY FIRST TRIP ABROAD, and I was about to turn 22 years old. Catching a bus in Southern Brazil, at a city called Porto Alegre, and aiming to reach Buenos Aires, I had 24 hours to become acquainted with some words in Spanish. With a dictionary in hand, I tried my best.

Arriving in Buenos Aires, I still had before me an overnight train journey. I spent the night sitting on the floor of a crowded train car. But reaching that small town called Villa Maria was exciting, and I was looking forward to the month-long training program. It was there that I first met that smiling character and loaded "book man" called Samuel Escobar. As I respond to Escobar's paper, I would like for us to keep a mental image of him before us. His ready smile would call us to participate in the present reflection and discussion. And his long bibliographical notes would tell us that he continues to be a loaded book-man who certainly does his homework!

At his age, Escobar no longer needs to carry all those books along, throwing them on the table, as he did in Villa Maria and quite impressing a young fellow like me. And I can tell you, he did impress me! More than that, he helped to "transform" me. From that time on, my eyes and ears have been wide open to learn from him and to try to follow in some of his footsteps.

A few years had passed by, and Villa Maria was a distant memory. Now I was about to turn 25. This time I was in Lima, Peru. To me, Samuel Escobar had become a more familiar figure and had grown in stature. After all, he had spoken at that "Mecca" event called Lausanne 1974. He had done it meaningfully, and those of us from Latin America were proud of him. And there I was, close to this "statesman." It

Learning from Escobar ... and beyond

VALDIR STEUERNAGEL

was there that Samuel departed from his notes for a while and did some personal sharing of life experience. Profound life sharing, I would say.

Emerging from Lausanne as a worldwide Evangelical figure, he was also a beaten human being. He had been applauded and criticized, and he saw himself being evaluated and judged from here and there. Looking at those Evangelical tendencies and pressures, he was asking the key questions about the really important and substantial things in life. And there he was, telling us that he had known the Evangelical machinery from within. He had seen it, so to speak. And after having seen it, he concluded that this was not what he wanted, what he was dreaming about! His desire, he told us, was to be known by the Lord. To have his name written in God's book, as Scripture tells us.

Can you imagine the scene? Can you picture our lost and puzzled faces, usually hungry to receive yet one more bibliographical reference? But here we were witnessing a very human confession and sharing a very real moment in life. Samuel, I suspect, did not imagine how much he impacted me that day by his open and vulnerable life-sharing. There I was being confronted with the really important things in life! That experience I've never forgotten.

And there is a third vignette. Not a story really, but an observation. The fact is that Samuel knows my wife's name. He recognizes her and calls her by name. The other day he sent me a picture of the three of us when we were together in Guatemala. It's something small, but actually quite important. Do we know one another's spouse and children's names?

Starting With Conclusions

As I looked into the task of responding to Samuel Escobar's paper, I began to remember him and some of the opportunities I had to get to know him and to be influenced by him. And this I would say is very important: By approaching the themes of his paper, "Evangelical Missiology: Peering Into the Future," I suggest that besides sharing ideas, it is equally important that we also tell stories and share our lives. Therefore, I'd like to outline some conclusions at the beginning of this response.

The important things should come first. We might somehow be well known, and some people at Iguassu might be quite important. A few books might have been translated into several languages, and someone might be a "must" author of today. His/her name may be in every bibliography and in the program of every missiological consultation. But all of this means so little if God has difficulty knowing how to spell our names and if our friends don't know our spouse's name. They might not even know if we are married or if we have children.

If the truly important things come first with us, then our greatest desires will point us in the direction of God: "Please, Lord, write my name into that book of yours!" And if Jesus tells us that yes, our name is there, let's walk away smiling and embrace one another, sharing those things that matter the most in life.

I have seen some of Escobar's older friends calling him Sammy. But this is not something for me. I cannot step in and say something like, "Come on, Sammy." But I do consider him a friend. If he ever comes to Curitiba, I would like to host him at my home. My wife and I would open the kitchen door for him, invite him to have a cup of coffee at the kitchen table, and ask the boys to clean their room for him to sleep there.

Good missiology is made at the kitchen table. Meaningful missiology is made in the context of relationship. Should we not confess that so much of our missiology is library-made, and so many of our consultations are head-encounters? Relationship-building is an essential part of our journey towards tomorrow.

Have you had the opportunity to meet Samuel a few times? It looks as if he is always "humbly smiling." First, it must be said that it is not easy to find a good smile in some of our consultations. We might find some smiling, but so often it is a kind of "well behaved" smiling. And what we find very often is "bibliographical seriousness" in an attempt to show off our intellectual achievements.

Is it possible to look into the challenging issues of our times with a sense of grace? Is it possible to smile while walking towards our *gegenüber*, enriching our lives and task? And would it be possible to do some laughing as we look into the mirror, not taking ourselves too seriously? Our aim should be to be known for "humbly smiling" while embracing our task and walking together into the future. We should be enjoying life and building up meaningful relationships.

I still remember how excited and challenged I was when I returned from my first meetings of the Latin American Theological Fraternity. And I must tell you that I was quite impressed by some of those fellows' knowledge, by the number of books listed in their bibliography, by the depth of their discussions, and by the size of their "behind"—after all, it was not in vain that they sat for so many hours. With them, I learned that to be a responsible Christian, a meaningful citizen, and a somewhat "good theologian" meant hard work. There is no other way to do missiology today and tomorrow. But I noticed also that they were good friends and enjoyed a good meal together.

Advancing Through Storm Once More

At the beginning of his paper, Escobar recovers Latourette's expression "advance through storm" by describing the history of Christian mission in the 20th century. And by using Eric Hobsbawn's categories, we could say that it was mission in a short century in between the two world wars. Escobar also recovers Ralph Winter's expression "unbelievable years" when he describes the growing presence of the North American missionary movement, especially after World War II. But even though Winter looked specifically at the increasing impact of the North American missionary movement, I could say the same about the Brazilian church, which is my church. Especially the latter decades of the 20th century were, to us, unbelievable years that were characterized by three trends.

First, we saw the emergence worldwide of a strong evangelistic focus and advance. This movement generated, in some places, substantial church growth. Thus, the church became significantly bigger and stronger.

Second, we saw the church not only grow in numbers but also become much more universal. The church can now be found on every continent and every political nation. It is a global church whose numbers are expressive, for we have created a worldwide movement. One of the consequences of this development is that the church is less white and more like a mosaic of colors, races, tastes, and languages. Another consequence has been the emergence of a new and heterogeneous missionary movement. Some decades ago, according to Andrew Walls, every missionary was North American until identified differently. But today the missionary movement is much more international in its outlook, if not yet global in its philosophy.

Third, there has been the emergence of a theological trend that tries to say that our particular cultures and geographies will help to determine our perception and understanding of reality and truth. Therefore, every theology must be contextual and should reflect its own local flavor. As a consequence, the import/export business of theology must be questioned, and in its place we must create an open arena where we all share in the creation of Christian theology.

Creative Tensions

Those were unbelievable years, and so many of us had the privilege of being active witnesses to them. Yet this was not a clean and straightforward process. The tensions and difficulties could be seen in different places. I had the opportunity of seeing them as I did my research on the Lausanne Movement. It would even be possible to outline some of the tensions that were building up during that second half of the century.

First, it could be said that mission had to be re-worked, as it moved away from the old colonial era and point of reference. What then emerged was a heavily dominated North American mission initiative. Escobar will say that in later years that trend could be called managerial missiology, strongly determined by the cultural values of North America: practical and efficient, technical and result oriented. And the motto "let's just do it" became a key slogan of this initiative.

However, as the church experienced growth, visibility, and activity outside of the North American and European setting, new theological and missiological voices began to emerge. And, in Escobar's words, "a critical missiology from the periphery" began to question the system, raising its hand and wanting to be a part of the mission awakening and initiative.

But it has to be said, secondly, that this tension and development cannot be understood apart from the North-South paradigm. And the poor South, when it saw that the rich North was calling all the shots and controlling the game and playing field, said that it also wanted to play in the game and not serve the role of the "ball boy"—the one who chases after the ball when it goes off the field but who never plays on the field with the team. This tension, which could very often be seen ideologically along political and theological lines, became quite evident in the prolonged discussions on the tension of evangelism vis-à-vis social action. A lot of people were hurt, walls were built, paper was used up, and adrenaline was expended in a discussion that so very often impoverished the gospel itself.

Thirdly, we could say also that our divisions along ecclesiastical lines were quite evident. Old churches were struggling to survive, new churches were emerging, and competition was the name of the game. The movement surrounding the issue of the Holy Spirit, labeled Pentecostal or charismatic, brought such new and necessary life and vitality, while at the same time generating too much division and misunderstanding in too many places.

Those were, in fact, unbelievable years! And they also became equally unbelievable when viewed from the opposite side. At the latter part of the century, Lesslie Newbigin began to ask the puzzling but legitimate and necessary question: "Can the West be converted?" The former harvest place for mission had become profoundly secular and was crying out for new and meaningful ways to communicate the gospel. Some stormy resistance could be seen there, and it was "raining" heavily on our heads. We again need to say, "Let's advance through storm!" That is, after all, the only way to do mission.

As we move into a new century, I share the conviction that we need to reposition ourselves and to work once again on the agenda. Let's celebrate the unbelievable things God has done, recognize the open doors and the heavy storm all around us, while we search for paths of obedience in our generation.

Facing This Generation With Joy!

Returning to Brazil after four years of study in the U.S., I thought I had by then filled up a good deal of my mental "storage room." After all, I had been studying for four years and should have learned something! But then I noticed that while I was gone the agenda had changed, and I was left alone with my already-filled mental storage room. Moving one step further, I came to the conclusion that even I was getting tired of my own discourse. I had worked on the relationship between evangelization and social responsibility, and I should have grasped the issue at some depth. But examining the challenges of my new time, with the emergence of a new generation, a new environment, and new questions, I felt somehow empty handed and realized that I had to go back and do my homework.

Samuel says in his paper that missiology is an "honest evaluation of missionary activism in light of God's Word," and we would all agree with him. But he also alludes to the fact that new models of missionary obedience should be a result of a good and necessary perception of new missionary challenges. Samuel himself has been addressing that issue as he talks about the new missionary frontiers.

I would stress that one of the tasks of missiology is to read the signs of the times. When describing the "men armed for battle who came to David at Hebron" (1 Chron. 12:23), the writer describes the men of Issachar as being those "who understood the times and knew what Israel should do" (1 Chron. 12:32). From within the church and looking into the always-present, new missionary challenges, missiology should be able to help us to understand the times and respond with a sense of vocation and service.

I return to my own story in this moment of my life. I had to recognize that I had done my doctoral studies in the twilight of that high season of the study and hermeneutical centrality of ideology, and of the dreams of social and political revolutions. Coming back to Brazil in a time of significant and worldwide changes, I had to face a new reality: the Berlin wall had come down; the ideological situation was changing; the Enlightenment crisis was overwhelming society. The younger generation was asking different questions and using a new language; meanwhile, the church was becoming much more pragmatic and market oriented. Doing my homework again, I had to try to understand my new times and try to spell out some of the frontiers that I saw emerging.

It is impossible here to address fully the challenges of our times. First, because they are quite complex and multiform. Second, because the task of doing this goes beyond one person's capacity, and the job needs both a team and an interdisciplinary approach. Third, because to do that goes far beyond the limits of this paper. But Evangelical missiology has to spell out the key distinctives, characteristics, and challenges of this emerging era. Therefore, by simply highlighting some of those distinctives, I want to say that I am impressed by their magnitude and concerned with the map of challenges of our time. May I try to outline what I see emerging and, in part, what I see that is already among us?

The map of challenges

• Is there a friend around? The search for relationship in an environment of loneliness.

• I am all alone, without "a father or a mother." The crisis of the state.

• Democracy with disenchantment. The political crisis and the imposition of chaos and disintegration.

• Is there any work for me, please? The emergence of professional Darwinism. The changing work market.

• The security crisis in an environment of fear. The absence of frontiers.

• Tell me what your price is! The supremacy of the market.

• Let's buy a new one. A discarding mentality.

• The nature of today's conflict. The fight over resources and the law of destruction.

• The savage urbanization process and the absence of sanctuary. Urbanism is a mindset.

• From communication to propaganda. Everything, after all, is a question of good marketing.

• Instant poverty and the intensification of vulnerability. Destitution can happen in hours.

• Ethics and the new challenges. Are there any limits for bio-ethics?

• How do you feel about it? The predominance of the subjective and intuitive.

• The re-emergence of idolatry. The irruption of the religious and of mysticism.

• Christendom is dying. Should we cry or laugh?

Just to enumerate those characteristics and challenges is overwhelming. And I would not even begin to comment on any of them. But we cannot just stop at those dimensions. We also have to look at the church as a part not only of our own reality but also as a cultural and even political factor in so many of our societies. We should start first with a prophetic analysis

of our own culture and ecclesiastical home. In prophetic terms, it is impossible to look "out there" and not look at what we are as the church.

The Mirror Called Our Church

But the church is quite complex and varied as well. It can be so different from one cultural setting and tradition to another. However, I don't want to pass over the difficult task of looking into the mirror and sharing a little of what I see. What I want to share are some of the yellow and red lights that I see as I look into that mirror called "our church." In fact, we should try to build a bridge between some of the characteristics of our time and some of the present marks of the church. We will conclude that the church is also a child of our times, struggling with the call to be distinctly different as it faces the pressure to conform to the surrounding culture. Let me, once more, share a mere outline of concerns about the direction I see the church heading into. And I can only do this from my own perspective, which is shaped by a Christianized environment and a growing church.

1. The church is being viewed through the lenses of progress and success. Within this view, the church must always grow and be bigger tomorrow than it is today.

2. The church is understood according to the criteria of numbers and a political as well as marketing perception of "space to be occupied."

3. The church tends to be managed from a business and bureaucratic approach. The church is being run as a corporation—small or large.

4. There is a tendency to view worship according to a "showtime" mentality.

5. There is a challenge and an invitation to communicate the gospel as a propaganda tool in a "war of communication."

6. There is an insistent presence of the theology of prosperity, as a by-product of the law of the market, with an emphasis on individualism, well-being, and success.

7. The school of spiritual warfare is prominent, with its mystifying and magic emphasis of reality and of the Christian faith itself.

8. There is danger of the emergence of a new type of charismatic Constantinianism, as well as of an Evangelical syncretism.

Finding Ways to Walk Into the Future

As we proceed with an analysis of the present and some of the tendencies and challenges of tomorrow, it is important to remember that we must resist the temptation to dream nostalgically about a romantic past that has never existed. There should be a sense of peace and celebration about the privilege of being called by God to live today. We are challenged to walk today, stretching out towards tomorrow, seeking to obey God's calling, and also drinking from the fountain of service.

In his address at the synagogue in Pisidian Antioch, Paul finds himself heavily involved in a mission enterprise. He obviously wants people to believe in Jesus. In his contextual discourse, Paul goes through the history of salvation and mentions King David on two occasions. At one point he says that David "served God's purpose in his own generation" (Acts 13:36). This word has been a source of challenge and encouragement to me, pointing to the task of serving God in one's own generation. In fact, every generation is called by God to serve him in his or her own moment of history—rejoicing in God's calling, understanding the times, and facing the challenges as they create conflicts, hardships, and opportunities.

At another reference to David, Paul mentions him as a man according to God's heart and obedient to his will. He refers to God, saying, "I have found David, son of Jesse, a man after my own heart; he will do everything I want him to do" (Acts 13:22). This is a very caring and touching statement. It is worthwhile to seek to follow and aim for David's example.

We have transformed missiology into a science and mission outreach into an activity. There is high value in these accomplishments. We have to have a good foundation, based on necessary and accurate information. We also have to be practical, knowing how and when to do mission. But let's never forget that the voice of God wants to reach our heart. Knowing and doing must be surrounded by a spirituality of the heart whereby we know to whom we belong and what God wants us to do. The voice of God gives meaning and direction to our life. By conquering our heart, God enables us to walk out into the world with the conviction of being embraced by God and, therefore, embracing others.

By going back to Acts 13 and encountering Paul and his companions at the synagogue, it is possible to hear the rulers of that synagogue calling to them and meaningfully saying, "Brothers, if you have a message of encouragement for the people, please speak"(Acts 13:15). To be involved in mission is not only to speak. It also refers to the art of positioning oneself and waiting for the right questions to come. The right questions echo the search for meaning and a longing for salvation. In our days, we certainly need a "message of encouragement for the people."

Road Signs to Look Out For

Therefore, to be continuously working on an Evangelical missiology of today and tomorrow means to intentionally follow the heart of God, to willingly serve him in this generation, and to sensibly hear the verbal and non-verbal questions of today. In order to do these things, I would like to try once more to outline an agenda that will address some of the road signs of today, as I see them.

1. **We need to rescue the centrality of the Word of God based on a "hermeneutics of enchantment."** To value and stress the centrality of the Word of God is part of our tradition. In the recent past, we have even developed some fighting skills concerning the nature and character of the Word of God. Today, however, it is possible to notice that the reference to God's Word becomes a kind of hermeneutic of cosmetics, whereby the important thing is to feel good and to have fun. We need to rescue the centrality of God's Word. This, however, has to be done based on a hermeneutic that will take us to God's heart and captivate our own hearts.

2. **We must constantly look out of the window and face the missionary task of the church.** Being constantly challenged to be involved in mission is a part of the task of the church and a sign of its health. But let's not forget that this is the task of the whole church called to serve Christ in the whole world. Therefore, the church is called always to be involved in mission. Look out of the window; witness what is going on, hear the cry for help, and discern the questions of salvation in order then to share Christ.

3. **We must always emphasize our commitment to evangelism and must reinvent how we do it.** Isn't there always the temptation to skip over evangelism in the agenda? The trend of accommodation is always one of the church's key temptations. Evangelism, therefore, must be the conscious decision of each group in each generation at every place, because evan-

gelism is the entrance point in the open door of salvation.

4. **We need to rediscover the role of the community in the life of the church.** It looks as if the church is becoming bigger in so many places. It is even fashionable to be part of a megachurch. And the risk of anonymity always surrounds such a church; people will come and go without being noticed (and they sometimes don't even want to be noticed!). Some of these groups are trying to break the cycle by talking about home churches or by embracing other attempts to put people together in small groups. These days, the word "community" is not used very much, but the church has to help recover it. It is at the level of community that people and situations become real. God always wants to know about the real things. To experience community is, therefore, part of the nature of the church.

5. **We must not avoid the path of martyrdom.** "Sacrifice" is an absent word in the vocabulary of our days. Well-being is a "must" category in our consumer society and mentality. The church runs the risk of being an extension of such a mentality. But we need to recover the conviction that there is no Christian life without sacrifice, and martyrdom is always a possibility in a witnessing context. But martyrdom is not a category in itself. It goes hand in hand with a search for meaning that overcomes a traditional sense of belonging.

6. **We must commit to relationship rather than hierarchical submission and administration.** The church needs to be relational, and mission involvement and practice need to be born out of and to point to relationality. Hierarchy and even administration are being put under some level of suspicion and need to be understood as being instruments of service. We need hierarchy and we can use good administration, but the aim is

to build relationships with God and with each other.

7. We need to relearn how to say "NO" and how to spell out the word "justice." I come out of a tradition where I was taught to say "NO" and to spell out a clear claim for justice. An indifferent and silent church was seen as a weak church, a compromising church. But when the Berlin wall fell down and everything became so monolithically capitalist and pragmatic—so market, success, and image oriented—the word "justice" seemed to disappear from our vocabulary. The process of doing theology was affected. The church followed the market so much that it did not know how and/or did not want to say "NO." But it is time to breathe deeply, to practice saying "NO" again, and to search for justice intensively. There is no other way to be the church than by serving God and people, and by doing so with justice.

8. We need to be part of a reshaping process of state and politics, as a step of missionary obedience. Even as the word "justice" tended to disappear from our vocabulary, all of us witnessed the state running out of ideological motifs and becoming utterly pragmatic. The political system fell into a deep credibility crisis. Many had the clear perception that the state and the political system were having a very hard time adapting to another time and to new challenges. They even continued to dance to the melody of yesterday. But the young people, many poor communities, and part of the intelligentsia were asking for another tune in order for their dance to find some rhythm and meaning to life.

This is a dangerous time of philosophical and political emptiness, where the church does not have the luxury of being silent or simply following the dance of the marketplace. The church must be a creative force in society, joining efforts with others who want a political system that is able to hear and to respond to the claims of today, especially the claims of the poor.

9. We need to allow local initiatives to replace centralized activities. Not only is the state dancing according to the tune of another time, but the church with its structures and traditions is also. It has not been easy for the church, including mission agencies, to acknowledge structural crises and the weakening influence of centralized pronouncements. Sometimes the church continues to embrace a mega-discourse, issuing pronouncements here and there, without noticing that there are so few people paying attention to what is being said.

One of the signs of our times is that this is a season of local initiative. People want to own and personally participate. They don't want, for example, just to give money to some distant agency. They want to go where their money goes and want to know the people they are helping. This is a time of partnership and participation—which should be celebrated.

Poetry Walking Alongside Prose

I had never suspected that I could and would, someday, write some poetry. This wasn't me, I thought. I was only trained to write prose—logical and systematic sentences. So I studied and did theology, borrowing the framework, concepts, and language from philosophy and later from social sciences. But in the process we all became too abstract, elitist, dry, and discursive.

However, in the recent years of my life journey and accompanied by friends, I discovered that I could write some poetry. Even if it was only poor poetry, it was very important. It challenged me to do theology with my heart and take my soul, my feelings, and my intuition seriously. I still write prose as you can see, but not only prose and not only as I once did.

I share the awareness that we still need good theology written in prose. But we need more poetry in order to become more human, to take our soul seriously, and to talk meaningfully in our days and to our people and cultures. In order to do that, we need not only to do our homework in systematic ways. We need to learn how to do poetry and to recover the art of telling stories.

Never forget the small things, because life goes on. I first dealt with the idea of smallness when looking into the Anabaptist tradition, where purity and commitment were more important than numbers and growth. Largeness was even put under suspicion. Then economy came into the picture with Schumacher's (1975) famous book *Small Is Beautiful*, with a whole new setting of possibility coming into view. But lately it was Eugene Peterson who brought it to my attention by once again pointing out that life consists so much of the small things. Small things that make such a significant part of our everyday life. Washing, cooking, greeting, and that same meal-time table talk that occurs everyday: "How was school today? Mom is still sick!" A good theology knows how to integrate the small everyday aspects of life, and a good spirituality is for table talk.

The end of all things is near. Let's not forget it. Not too long ago we were inundated by sermons about eschatology. I was even running away from that issue and from a tendency to be categorized in this or that eschatological box. But today it is difficult to find someone talking about the end of all things. Now we are much more concerned about giving people tools for well-being and success in the here and now. Much of our eschatology has become materialized; one measures God's blessing by getting a new car.

I share the conviction that we need to recover the eschatological dimension of the gospel. We must re-visit our approach to hope that is shaped today mostly in material terms. By recovering eschatology, we allow it to shape our life in such a way that we see ourselves and are recognized by others as incarnational citizens of God's future, the first fruits of the kingdom to come.

As I come to the end of this conversation with Samuel Escobar, I would like to thank him for his paper and to walk with him in the way he concludes it:

- Missiology is inspired by the Triune God.
- All Scripture is pregnant with God's mission.
- To do mission is to focus on Christ … and to be inspired by his model.
- Let's be blessed and challenged by the power of the Holy Spirit.
- And let's receive God's hug as we peer into the future.

References

Schumacher, E. F. (1975). *Small is beautiful: economics as if people mattered*. New York: Harper & Row.

Valdir R. Steuernagel is married to Sileda Silva, and they have four grown children. A Lutheran pastor, he is also the director of the Centro de Pastoral e Missão in the city of Curitiba, Brazil. He completed his doctoral studies at the Lutheran School of Theology, Chicago, Illinois, with a concentration in missiology. Author of a number of books in Portuguese, Spanish, and English, he has provided leadership for many years to the Latin American Theological Fraternity. He is the current Chair of World Vision International.

TO WRITE AN EVALUATION of Evangelical missiology (hereafter referred to as EM) of the past half century is a formidable job. For the sake of limiting the scope of our argument to guidelines given by such documents as the Lausanne Covenant, this chapter will apply the Iguassu Affirmation and the so-called "main axioms" delineated by Donald McGavran (Glasser & McGavran, 1983, pp. 100-112). It will then become somewhat clear that the EM that this writer aims to evaluate consists of a body of missiological materials that have been produced after the mid-20th century in alignment with the contemporary Evangelical Movement, expressed through such Evangelical gatherings as the International Congress on World Evangelization at Lausanne, Switzerland in 1974 (Lausanne Congress hereafter). This date conveniently coincides with greater participation of Two-Thirds World Evangelicals in formulating EM.[1] First, an attempt will be made to sort out different streams that have merged to create a modern EM. As a summary statement, a chronological perspective of the development of EM will follow. Finally, an evaluation will be made of this missiology.

A Two-Thirds World evaluation of contemporary Evangelical missiology

David Tai-Woong Lee

Major Influences in the Development of Evangelical Missiology

Historically, a number of factors have influenced the formulation of Evangelical missiology. It is important that we take a look at some of the major factors that have helped to shape EM in order to evaluate them properly.

---

[1] Although missionary work from the Two-Thirds World began much earlier, it was in the 1970s that we find Western missiologists becoming aware of the new movement, with such activities as the All-Asia Mission Consultation in Seoul, Korea in 1973 (see Nelson, 1976, p. 109ff.).

First, the European missionary movement and its missiology must be mentioned. European missiology has its roots in European missionary work, which began as early as the 17th century (Rommen, 1991). The study of mission began in 1622 with the very practical purpose of training missionaries for service in the East Indies. In 1702, another attempt to formulate missiology emerged with the founding of Halle University, which was established for the purpose of training missionaries. Gustav Warneck was their missiologist, and by his effort missiology began to take shape (Thomas, 1989, p. 103). By the time the center of the missionary movement began to shift from Europe to North America in the early 20th century, European missiology seemed to have gained its own characteristics. However, in an attempt to be accepted as a part of the academic discipline in the university, it became scientific and theoretical.[2] We shall see that this trend in missiology continued even in North America, when in the 1970s EM began to gain its own identity (Scherer, October 1987, p. 508).[3]

Second, the Edinburgh missionary conference in 1910 and subsequent major conferences held by the International Missionary Council (IMC hereafter) and the World Council of Churches (WCC hereafter) assemblies have influenced EM in one way or another. Until the Evangelicals began to hold their own missionary conferences in the late 1960s, both Evangelicals and non-Evangelicals had worked together to formulate missiology (Scherer, 1987, pp. 39, 165; Scherer & Bevans, 1992, p. xvi). Even after Evangelicals withdrew from ecumenical circles, a number of the same themes found their way into EM,[4] such as gospel and culture, contextualization, a trinitarian concept of mission, the relationship between evangelism and social responsibility, and dialogue as a form of evangelism.[5]

Third, after the 1960s, Evangelical missionary conferences and consultations have tremendously influenced the formulation of EM. The Lausanne Congress in 1974 and the subsequent Lausanne Movement have probably influenced the shaping of EM more than any other single

---

[2] Edward Rommen (1987) insists that "German missionary theory first embraced and later eschewed the social science" in the 19th century and up to the middle of the 20th century.

[3] This trend in missiology roughly coincides with the period when the American Society of Missiology was admitted into the Council on the Study of Religion. Louis Luzbetak said on this occasion: "On this day missiology becomes a fully recognized academic discipline." There is also "a qualitative ... and a quantitative increase in teaching programs related to missiology, particularly in Evangelical seminaries and schools of world mission, especially between 1975 and 1985." The number of missiological issues that have surfaced also warrants this view. Scherer (1987, p. 35) argues, "Before 1950, the study of the 'theology of mission' in today's sense hardly existed. It is even later for the Evangelicals in my opinion." See also Glasser & McGavran (1983, p. 8).

[4] See Utuk (1994, p. 110). Utuk argues that the Ecumenical Movement has been one of the influences in the shift of the Evangelical position in mission from 1966 to 1974.

[5] The ecumenical circle had the IMC and the WCC as their forum to dialogue regarding cultural issues. For Evangelicals, it was after the Lausanne Congress in 1974 that the relationship between gospel and culture received attention (see Scherer & Bevans, 1999, pp. 4-5). For example, "*Missio Dei*" was the theme of the 1952 Willingen conference, and "Contextualization" was the theme of the 1972 TEF report of the WCC. Evangelicals were introduced to contextualization at the Lausanne Congress, and it was in 1982 that a consultation on "Contextualization" was convened at Trinity Evangelical Divinity School campus (see Hesselgrave, 1978, p. 87; *Trinity World Forum*, Spring, 1982; Scherer & Bevans, 1992, pp. 263ff, 276ff; Thomas, 1995, p. 117).

movement in the history of Evangelical- ism.[6] Some of the outspoken missiological voices came from the more radical dis- cipleship camp. These voices have particu- larly affected the Lausanne Movement to no small degree.[7] Meanwhile, the WEF Missions Commission and the AD 2000 and Beyond Movement, with their own re- spective missiological position, have also added richness to EM, as we shall see in the evaluation section below.[8]

Fourth, the Two-Thirds World mission- ary movement began to take shape in the 1970s. By the end of the 1980s, it began to draw the attention of some Western missiologists. In the 1990s, it was well es- tablished as a strong and newer mission- ary force.[9] Its influence on the formulation of EM may have been meager in the past, with the exception of some of the outspo- ken voices representing the "radical dis- cipleship" camp. Some of the Two-Thirds World leaders from more independent groups such as the Third World Mission Association (TWMA) have also been active. One can predict that the contributions from Two-Thirds World missionaries will increase significantly in the new millen- nium. By the 1990s, EM began to take a global character. Missiology done from the

West alone is no longer adequate. As we enter the new millennium, we will see yet another paradigm shift in EM as mission- aries from the Two-Thirds World exceed in numbers the force from the West (Pate, 1991, p. 59; Anderson, 1988, p. 114).

Participation of the Two-Thirds World mission force in the formulation of missi- ology began early in the ecumenical camp. With the birth of the IMC and the WCC, a forum was provided for their participation. Through conciliatory effort, ecumenical missiology began to emerge (Lossky et al., 1991, p. 529; Bosch, 1980, pp. 180-181). For Evangelicals, it was not until the Lausanne Congress in 1974 that the Two- Thirds World began to be active in the world-class missionary conferences con- tributing towards the formulation of EM. Since then, in virtually all of the ecumeni- cal world missionary conferences, the Two-Thirds World has had a lion's share in the formulation of EM. Some observers even predict that with the drastic changes taking place in the new millennium and the rapid growth of the Two-Thirds World missionary force, most of the missiological textbooks written from the Western per- spective will become obsolete.[10] This may mean that we have to write a whole new

---

[6] Scherer & Bevans (1992, p. xviii) state, "Lausanne 1974 'marks the high point in the develop- ment of Evangelical mission theology.'"

[7] These voices represent the position that has demanded that greater prominence be given to social concerns (see Scherer, 1987, pp. 194-195; Scherer & Bevans, 1992, p. xviii).

[8] Glasser (1993, p. 19) argues that the AD 2000 and Beyond Movement had the desire for a "last big push" to evangelize the world. Many of the WEF Missions Commission's recent member- ship would identify with that goal, unlike the "radical discipleship" camp. A series of publications include Taylor (1991, 1997), Harley (1995), Ferris (1995), and this volume. Most significant about these is that all of them were the joint product of both Western and Two-Thirds World mission leaders. The AD 2000 and Beyond Movement had their major congress in Seoul, Korea in 1995 and in South Africa in 1997. The majority of the participants were from the Two-Thirds World.

[9] Three important research projects attest to this development. James Wong (1976), Marlin Nelson (1976a, 1976b), and Larry Pate (1989) have contributed towards helping both the West and the Two-Thirds World discover the new missionary movement.

[10] This voice was raised by some of the Evangelical leaders from the Two-Thirds World who attended the Iguassu Consultation on Missiological Issues in October 1999.

series of missiological textbooks that include the Two-Thirds World perspectives.

Fifth, at least two things should be mentioned in relation to North America's role in the formulation of EM. One is the number of missionaries that have been dispatched. Beginning in 1956, two-thirds of the entire missionary force came from North America. After reaching its plateau in the 1970s, this missionary force sustained its momentum for three decades. Keeping in step with this unprecedented growth, there was tremendous development both in mission structures as well as in missiology.[11] The missionary work has provided field tests for the missiologist. Furthermore, missionaries themselves became the missiologists. The missionaries who had first-hand knowledge of cross-cultural work wrote many missiological books.

The other item of note regarding North America is the proliferation of mission schools. After the 1910 Edinburgh missionary conference, a number of missionary schools sprouted in North America. The Kennedy School of World Mission, Disciples of Christ College of Missions, and Union Theological Seminary were some of the schools that either taught mission or were founded as missionary training schools. By 1934, most of the theological schools taught some subjects related to missions or comparative religions (Thomas, 1989, p. 104). It was, however, after the 1960s and '70s, with the emergence of schools such as the Fuller School of World Mission and the School of World Mission and Evangelism of Trinity Evangelical Divinity School, that the impact on EM was most evident.[12] These schools and others like them have played a key role in creating a consensus on what the modern curriculum of the Evangelical missiological discipline would look like.[13] This period during the 1970s coincides with a period in which missiology was accepted as a separate discipline on its own by the academia (Thomas, 1989, p. 105). It was probably scholars from these schools that formulated the modern version of a philosophy of education in mission for the first time in the history of Evangelical mission.[14] Donald McGavran and Alan Tippett from Fuller School of World Mission and David Hesselgrave and Herbert Kane from Trinity Evangelical Divinity School are some of the representatives in this effort who laid the foundations for their schools.[15] This period probably marks the most significant time in the development and re-

---

[11] See Anderson (1988, pp. 113-114). According to Coote (1982), "EFMA/IFMA taken as a whole, 1968 marked the beginning of a plateau, and this plateau has prevailed for almost two decades." This is the period when the Two-Thirds World missionary movement began to gain its momentum. See also Scherer (1999, pp. 10-11).

[12] These schools are used as representatives of the school of world mission.

[13] See Anderson (1988, pp. 111-112). A survey indicates that nearly 1,000 Ph.D., Th.D., S.T.D., and Ed.D. related dissertations in mission were accepted during 1945-1985. Alan Tippett (1987, pp. xi-xxv) argues that the 1960s and early 1970s were the formative years in missiology. He then goes on to introduce a philosophical background for mission curriculum design.

[14] It was the Evangelical schools that kept intact. For the non-Evangelicals, "They were less able, however, to impact the curricular changes of the 1960s and 1970s except in Evangelical seminaries in which the missionary mandate remained strong" (Thomas, 1989, p. 106).

[15] See Scherer (October 1987, p. 512) and Tippett (1974). See also Anderson (1988, p. 110), relating to Herbert Kane.

birth of EM.[16] In this regard, the integration of social science and traditional biblical themes such as evangelism and the church has acted as a catalytic agent.[17] EM has now begun to comprise both theory and practice, but it would be inappropriate to call this body of missiological literature "managerial" (we shall address some of the reasons for this objection in the evaluation section of this paper).[18]

Missiology that began with the birth of European mission has had a number of paradigm shifts, with the convergence of these influences creating EM in North American soil. For the last half century, we have witnessed tremendous progress and change, both positive and negative. More recently, the missionary movement from the Two-Thirds World contributed towards adding a significant new perspective by reflecting on its own missionary experiences. We will mention some of the details in the evaluation below.

A Summary Statement to This Point

Prior to the Lausanne Movement, missiology was predominantly Western in its character. European missiology had become the foundation upon which the International Missionary Council and the World Council of Churches would build their own missiology.[19] These would later develop into what we now know as ecumenical missiology, which was a missiology formulated with the concept of the West moving to the non-West. We will see that the subsequent missiological trends continued to hold this view. In this stage, there was no significant development in EM. It was still in its infant stage, for as of yet there was no consensus on what missiology was, let alone what EM was.

After the Lausanne Congress, Evangelicals from both the West and the Two-Thirds World increasingly worked together to formulate EM. This has helped to highlight the contribution from both perspectives. One of the most significant changes in EM after the Lausanne Congress has been in opting for holistic missiology.[20] As early or late as the Berlin World Evangelization Congress in 1966, EM had a single focal point: evangelization of the world was what the purpose of mission was all about.

After Lausanne, EM crossed the "Rubicon." Since then, at least two camps have

---

[16] Arthur Glasser (1985, p. 10) argues that with his epochal work, *The Bridges of God*, Evangelicals were stimulated to begin "evangelical theologizing." It was during this period that widely read textbooks such as *Christian Missions in Biblical Perspective* by J. Herbert Kane (1976) also appeared, along with a host of other books by the same author in the 1970s. Anderson (1988, pp. 110-111) claims that "spin-offs from McGavran's movement" include a series of other missiological developments.

[17] Tim Stafford (1986) claims that social science was integrated with evangelism.

[18] Samuel Escobar (see chapter 7) uses the term "managerial missiology" to describe the Church Growth School represented by McGavran and others.

[19] See Verkuyl (1978). Hartenstein, Freytag, Hendrik Kraemer, J. C. Hoekendijk, Max Warren, and Lesslie Newbigin are some of the popular names that appear in the history of the Ecumenical Movement prior to the Lausanne Congress. Except for some of the Latin American theologians and missiologists, activities of Evangelical missiologists from the rest of the world were still in the embryonic stage. See also Kinnamon & Cope (1997, pp. 9-40). Western voices were still dominating the platform at least until the 1970s.

[20] Utuk (1994) argues that at Lausanne the "two-mandate view" was affirmed.

coexisted in Evangelical circles. Both are holistic in their approach. One camp stresses intentional equality between evangelism and social responsibility. This view is represented by John Stott and some Latin Americans, Asians, and Africans such as Samuel Escobar, René Padilla, Orlando Costas, and Vinay Samuel.[21] The other position has the evangelization of the world as its primary focus. This camp is represented by those who later helped to stage the AD 2000 and Beyond Movement, plus some from the World Evangelical Fellowship Missions Commission.[22] The rest of Evangelicals will be found in between these two poles. Although there was active participation by the Two-Thirds World through different consultations and missionary congresses, the make-up of EM was still very North American. However, inevitable changes began to take place with the rapid growth of the Two-Thirds World missionaries and the shift of the Evangelical population from the West to the Two-Thirds World in the 1980s and '90s. Only two significant paradigm shifts will be mentioned here.

First is the change from theory based missiology to social science based missiology. In the beginning of the study of missiology, the theory of mission was a prominent factor (Shenk, 1996). More recent EM then took another sharp turn. With the coming of the modern Church Growth Movement ushered in by Donald McGavran, Peter Wagner, and others, social science became an important component of EM. There was an emphasis on the "harvest field," based on homogeneous principles. Subsequent "frontier missiology" dominated agendas for EM in the last three decades of the 20th century. Therefore, it would be absurd to speak about modern EM without mentioning a very large segment of missiological literature representing this trend.

Second, a change from general missiology to contextual missiology and then to global missiology took place. Western EM opened the way for doing missiology from a different context, as the concept of contextualization became a prominent missiological motif in the last two decades in Evangelical circles. This is particularly true in the Two-Thirds World. Not only missiology, but also the whole of the theological method has been affected by this phenomenon. More recently, there is new interest in the formulation of a globalized perspective of missiology, keeping step with broader currents of globalization. It is important to note that it was during this period that EM began to show its distinct identity. Therefore, we will refer back to this period as we evaluate EM.

World evangelization again received attention, especially with the birth and growth of the AD 2000 and Beyond Movement in the 1990s. Strategies of mission have received much attention in conjunc-

---

[21] Utuk (1994, p. 107) argues that although there were other "interest" groups, "some combined their efforts with the Radical Discipleship group to produce a Covenant that, for the first time in the Evangelical Movement, affirmed in unambiguous tone that 'biblical evangelism is inseparable from social responsibility,'" quoting Padilla (1976, p. 11). See also Stott (1975, pp. 23, 27), quoted by Utuk.

[22] Those representing opposite poles would be persons such as Donald McGavran, David Hesselgrave, and J. Robertson McQuilken. See McGavran (1996, pp. 252-253) and McQuilkin (1993, p. 175). There are also exchanges between Hesselgrave and Stott on this issue in *Trinity World Forum* (Spring 1990 and Spring 1991). This issue was also featured in the *Evangelical Missions Quarterly* (July 1999). There seems to be consensus on "holism" itself among Evangelicals, as the recent Iguassu Affirmation proclaims. Nevertheless, in terms of giving equal status or refusing to interlock both evangelism and social responsibility, Evangelicals are still polarized.

tion with the AD 2000 Movement and the optimism that came as a result of this strategical understanding. Such concepts as the "10/40 window" have received special attention. In addition, various forms of the theory of "unreached people groups" became the dominant theme for EM, at least in some sectors of both the West and the Two-Thirds World. This theory coincided with the strategy of discontinuity. It was during this period that the concept of "power encounter" began to occupy a prominent position in EM (see Warner, 1985, and Wagner, 1986). It was introduced in order to bring balance to EM, which was clouded with social science. Now it occupies a permanent place in EM. It is, therefore, not unfair to characterize the EM of this period as being practical in its essential nature.

We have so far looked at how EM took its shape in the last half century. We have for the sake of convenience used landmarks such as the Lausanne Congress as reference points upon which to hang different missiological developments. We will now attempt to evaluate EM from a Two-Thirds World perspective.

An Evaluation of Evangelical Missiology From a Two-Thirds World Perspective

EM as a discipline

Like the rest of the academic disciplines, missiology was also developed in the undercurrents of the Modernity Movement (Lee, 1997). Missiology in this form had its strength in theologizing and "principlizing" mission. For those with "intuitional" and "concrete-relational"[23] worldviews from some parts of the Two-Thirds World, this was too theoretical, and

it also came at an odd period of time. The Two-Thirds World missionary movement was still in the infant stage of growth.

It was probably after this period that EM as we now know it began to be profiled with various influences merging in a great stream. At least two distinct changes were favorable to the Two-Thirds World missionaries. First, some sort of consensus was reached among Evangelicals on the philosophy of education in studying missiology. Thus the schools of world mission with well-developed curricula began to sprout in different parts of North America and other parts of the world. It was this form of EM that was spread to the Two-Thirds World through at least three ways. Students who came to study in North America from the Two-Thirds World were the major means of exportation. Missiological literature that was distributed to the rest of the world was another means of spreading this form of EM. Finally, Western missionaries who were serving in the Two-Thirds World have also significantly contributed to this end.

The second change in EM that favored Two-Thirds World missionaries was the integration of social science and pragmatism in the 1970s. Without such measures, EM might have ended up as just another academic acrobatic, which the Two-Thirds World finds less relevant.

Samuel Escobar (see pages 107-109) gives us some helpful insights when he mentions three directions of what he calls "post-imperial missiology." These are the renewed search for biblical patterns, the critical work of writing and interpreting the history of missionary activity, and entering into partnership with churches in the Two-Thirds World. I would add a fourth key ingredient, the integration of

---

[23] I am using Hesselgrave's (1991, pp. 305-340) division of different cognitive styles in accordance with different worldviews here. He gives at least two different worldviews with their cognitive processes in addition to the more conceptual thinking of the West.

missiology with the social sciences. This latter component would be an additional important direction that EM has taken since the Lausanne Congress. These four seem to be the general description of the direction of EM as a whole. Therefore, if Escobar's intention was to dichotomize missiology that has integrated social science with missiology not so integrated, his divisions are inappropriate.

Furthermore, closely following his argument, one cannot but conclude that one of his most important criteria for deciding the kind of missiology is how one views "social/human needs." Escobar has an obvious preference for "a critical missiology from the periphery," represented by such persons as René Padilla and Orlando Costas from Latin America. They claim to take the biblical text more seriously than others. What this actually means is "an exploration into the depths of the social significance of the basic Christian truths" (see page 113). People with this presupposition claim that "Evangelical depth" is missing in "managerial missiology" and that such depth is what makes sense to those who minister "in the midst of poverty and with the pain of social transitions" (page 113). Thus the "Evangelical depth" is none other than social concern for them. In the 1976 post-Lausanne symposium, Padilla (1976, p. 192) goes one step further in the following remarks: "Lausanne had updated the Evangelical agenda by eliminating North American pragmatism, returning biblical theology to its proper basis, giving a deathblow to superficial church planting, eliminating the dichotomy between evangelism and church renewal, and refusing to separate conversion from a radical change in lifestyle." Scherer's comment (see Padilla, 1976, p. 192) is incisive: "In his [Padilla's] view, biblical evangelism is *inseparable* from social responsibility and church renewal" (emphasis added).[24]

Not all Evangelicals from the Two-Thirds World will agree with this theological position. Needless to say, neither will all Evangelicals from the Two-Thirds World agree with the way the term "managerial" is utilized. This, however, does not mean that EM that has mostly been nurtured in North America is faultless. On the contrary, it has a number of shortcomings. This aspect is expressed in the Preamble of the Iguassu Affirmation approved during the WEF Missions Commission's Missiological Consultation held October 10-15, 1999, attended by 160 key Evangelical leaders from 53 nations. Some of the methodologies of mission seem to be based on inadequate exegesis. Others use a few proof texts but do not make an effort to synchronize those emphases with the greater biblical story.[25]

Since the Lausanne Congress, as Escobar (page 113) has aptly mentioned, EM has taken on a holistic character, among other things. Two radically different kinds of holism seem to exist in tension. The one that emphasizes "a concept of the gospel and Christian commitment, in which the socially transformative dimensions are unavoidable" is represented by the "radical discipleship" advocates, the ones mostly cited by Escobar in his paper (see Anderson, 1988, p. 113). The other group is equally concerned with biblical wholism yet

[24] There is ample biblical and theological support for the opposing view. We do not have space to go into any in-depth argument in this paper.

[25] See the Preamble of the Iguassu Affirmation. It says, "Flowing from a commitment to urgent evangelization, these methodologies have shown how our task might be accomplished. However, these insights must be subject to biblical principles and growth in Christlikeness."

does not automatically interlock it with social activism.[26] It was leaders with this theological preference that led the Lausanne Continuation Committee to work on such strategies as "people group theory," "unreached people," "adopt a people," and so on. A movement such as AD 2000 and Beyond was born particularly to meet the urgent need of those whose focus was on the evangelization of the world. Movements such as COMIBAM I and II also seem to have been led with this kind of theological inclination.[27]

Both of the camps will continue to exist in tension among Evangelicals, while attempts to seek biblical answers for the support of two conflicting positions will proceed well into the new millennium. In the Iguassu Affirmation, however, the weight seems to have slightly tilted toward the latter position. The urgent need for the proclamation of the gospel to the whole world was stated categorically. At the same time, a strong emphasis was placed on the necessity for meeting human needs as a central Christian value. Holism is simply there in the Bible, though not as a prerequisite for evangelism.[28]

Having said these things, we must go on to mention some of the problems in EM as a discipline. Only a few basic ones will be cited here. More specific issues will be dealt with under separate headings. The difficulty seems to be evident in at least two ways. First, we mention the claims, which have in fact much truth in them, of critics who argue that EM has been excessively preoccupied with social science for the past several decades, dealing less with theological issues and integrating less with biblical content.[29] This preoccupation obviously brings imbalance to the discipline as a whole. For example, the felt need of Western missionaries is cultural adjustment as they move out of their own comfort zone. It is taken for granted that Western missionaries already know how to minister, as most likely they would have had a theological education in a seminary. This may not always be the case for missionaries from the Two-Thirds World. These servants need not only a similar cultural adjustment, but most often the greater need is for a missiology that guides them in how to integrate biblical themes so that greater ministry power will be exhibited.

Furthermore, when missiology is done only by the West, it lacks the global perspective. Greater contributions from the Two-Thirds World must come in the future. This is required both by

---

[26] There is a whole range of people within this camp, including persons such as David Hesselgrave and Bryant Myers. See Hesselgrave (1999) and Myers (1999). In the book of Acts and the synoptic Gospels, at least the following three things are evident: (1) There were no attempts to systematize between proclamation of the gospel and social action. (2) Holism was taken for granted throughout these books. Even the Great Commissions found in these books presuppose holism. (3) All of the Great Commissions focus on the proclamation of the gospel. To go beyond what the writers of these books try to say is not being faithful to the intention of the original authors. Concerning the Johannine version of the Great Commission, refer to the recent argument between John Stott and David Hesselgrave in *Trinity World Forum*, Spring 1990 and Spring 1991. Hesselgrave seems to be closer to the intention of the original author.

[27] This is the conclusion drawn from the *Report on Global Consultation on Worldwide Evangelization* in May 1995 and COMIBAM II in 1997. See also Neff (1999).

[28] See the Iguassu Affirmation, especially items 3 and 4 in the Declarations section.

[29] See Rommen (1987, 1993) and Netland (1994). These articles all have warnings about an unhealthy relationship with social science. These warnings, however, are not meant to deny the integration itself.

the rapid changes taking place as a result of globalization, as well as by a shift of the Evangelical population to the Two-Thirds World. There is an urgent need for the formulation of a "global Evangelical missiology." The answer does not consist merely of moving further from the West towards the Two-Thirds World, as we find in mission history and general missiology.[30]

Shift from theory and practice to practical strategy

A gradual shift from theory and practice to more practical strategy has taken place in the last two decades. Concepts such as strategy with "closure" as a presupposition have contributed toward this end. Such visual concepts as the 10/40 window and unreached people groups, combined with modern statistical research methodology, have helped us see the world in black and white in terms of where the greatest needs are. In conjunction with such movements as AD 2000 and Beyond, tremendous strides have been taken in pushing beyond new frontiers, especially in parts of Asia, Central Asia, and North African countries. For the new sending countries such as Korea, Singapore, Japan, and parts of Latin America and Africa, this strategy has helped to guide and dispatch their new missionaries for the past several decades.[31]

The downside dimension of what has happened is that this kind of strategy has shortcomings. First, it is too simplistic in terms of an ongoing missiological guiding principle. For the North American and European based missionary agencies, it provided opportunities for redirecting the missionary force to the unreached peoples in some of the least evangelized areas of the world. Before such redirection, at one time it was estimated that more than 90% of the entire North American/European missionary force was still in the so-called evangelized zone (Winter, 1976, p. 167).

Yet when this strategy of targeting unreached people groups in the 10/40 window was applied by some of the Two-Thirds World countries in an unfiltered and unevaluated form, it had a number of negative effects. The Two-Thirds World countries have dispatched a majority of their new missionaries to the 10/40 window, without weighing other alternative strategies and missiological theories. This was the case in Korea.[32] Granted, there may be other causes of attrition, such as lack of training, undeveloped structure, and lack of member care. Still, this deployment strategy may be one of the major causes of unnecessary attrition of missionaries in Korea. It would have been better if some of the more experienced Western missionaries had been redirected to go to the hard fields in the 10/40 window and not the younger mission force from some of the new send-

---

[30] See Noll (1996). Recently there have been a number of attempts to write a church history that is global. But so far it is the West trying to include the Two-Thirds World. Missiology also has been moving in this direction. Only a few examples will be cited here. See Verstraelen et al. (1995) and Pittman, Habito, & Muck (1996).

[31] Virtually all of the Korean nationwide missionary conferences have dealt with reaching unreached people in the last decade.

[32] The *Korean Mission Handbook 1998-2000* (p. 40), published by Global Missionary Fellowship Press, indicates that roughly 56.5% of Korean missionaries are working in the 10/40 window. This is apparently good news. But this statistic does not show what avoidable attrition the Korean church has suffered. In addition, there is no indication of how many more workers could have been sent out if the church had adopted a more comprehensive deployment strategy.

ing countries, who were less experienced and not well-equipped to tackle some of the difficult tasks of pioneering that needed tremendous sensitivity. Because of this mission strategy, there have been more casualties than were expected, which naturally has brought discouragement to new missionary movements. Furthermore, the strategy seems to have produced a bottleneck effect on some of the new missionary force. For example, in Korea many young people have dedicated themselves for missionary service. Yet when they look at the fields where they might serve, especially in the 10/40 window, there are very few openings. Consequently, many have not been able to take any further steps and have remained in their own countries. This situation might have been prevented if other equally valid strategies of mission had also been consulted.

Reactionary missiology

As we follow the development of the important missiological themes, we cannot help but notice that EM has been a step behind the Ecumenical Movement in terms of dealing with some of the key missiological issues. Only a few examples will be cited here. The trinitarian base of missiology was first discussed in the 1952 Willingen Conference of the International Missionary Council. *Missio Dei*, as it was coined at the conference, quickly began to dominate the agenda for ecumenical missiology, changing its meaning many times. It was incorporated into EM first as a part of the biblical basis of mission in the 1970s; still later, David Bosch (1980, 1991) has theologized the same theme in both of his major works. A voice was again raised in the 1999 World Evangelical Fellowship Missions Commission Missiological Consultation to base EM more firmly on a trinitarian foundation.[33]

Contextualization is another case in point. While its roots return us to the creation of the theological education fund in the 1958 Ghana IMC conference, contextualization surfaced as a crucial missiological theme in 1972 through the "Ministry in Context" report of the WCC. Evangelicals, for example, held a consultation at Trinity Evangelical Divinity School to debate the same subject as late as 1982. Since then, the subject has dominated the EM agenda for the past two decades, and it is still an item for discussion. Other similar themes include social responsibility in mission, dialogue as a method of doing evangelism, theological issues in the encounter with non-Christian religion, and mission "from six continents to six continents." Evangelical missiologists and the mission community need to take the initiative to discern key missiological and contextual issues in the third millennium, both in the West and in the Two-Thirds World. Then they must creatively missiologize these areas.[34]

Missiology still largely with a Western perspective

In past eagerness to translate EM into a more academic discipline, there was a tendency toward overdependence on social science, paying only lip service to Scripture. In the future, EM must strive to base its theory not on just a few relevant texts from the Scriptures; rather, EM must be synchronized with the whole of the biblical narrative. This also summarizes one of the commitments in the Iguassu Affirmation.

To meet the felt needs of the Two-Thirds World missionaries, there must be greater breakthroughs than we have seen to this point in EM. Merely being biblically and theologically sound is still not ad-

---

[33] See the Declarations and Commitments sections of the Iguassu Affirmation.

[34] A think-tank session was held at the Iguassu Missiological Consultation for this purpose.

equate. There must be one more step taken towards the integration of biblical content with missiological principles so that missionaries on the field know how to teach the Bible effectively in cross-cultural situations. For example, the book of Romans must be taught from a cross-cultural perspective. Missiology thus gives us concrete guidance in teaching the biblical text in all contexts.

At the present, except for a select number of countries, the majority of the Two-Thirds World countries seem to send their missionaries to their own region or to different people groups within their own nation. This may be the case with the majority of the African, Latin American, and Indian missionaries, primarily because of the vast cross-cultural spiritual need within each region. Cultural understanding is always vital for situations like these. However, it is less urgent for workers staying within their own region than for Western missionaries going to some of the Two-Thirds World countries. Missionaries from the Two-Thirds World will inevitably have different needs. Future EM will have to deal with these different needs that Two-Thirds World missionaries are facing in their own region. One of these needs is dealing more with how best to transmit biblical content so that it will be contextually appropriate. Another area of concern is prayer in mission. Not much has been written on this subject. Training, partnership, and member care in mission are other areas of need. Fortunately, the WEF Missions Commission has done the lion's share of work in these areas in the past 10 years. For the first time in the history of mission, we now have good missiological literature dealing with some of these themes.

In the final analysis, it is essential that a greater number of missiologists from the Two-Thirds World take the initiative and make their contribution in creating a new and global Evangelical missiology. Only then will EM become truly globalized. The Two-Thirds World mission community is now ready to contribute as a full partner in the task of international mission as we enter the new millennium.

As We Look to the Future

EM is facing another critical period in the history of mission as we enter the new millennium. This is due first to the revolution of the information technology era that is upon us all. Information now flows with astonishing speed to the remotest parts of the world. Information technology is also creating a great deal of anxiety and uncertainty. Yet, to shut ourselves out from the changes that are taking place and go our own way will not bring any better results. The future of EM will depend largely upon how it will meet this challenge, with all of the implications of postmodernity and the pluralistic context of the West and segments of the Two-Thirds World. We may have to drastically reconceptualize a major part of EM, if not its entirety.[35]

Second, by the end of the 20th century, EM seemed to have lost the vitality it once had some three decades ago. The lack of interest in mission in the Western church and the decline of the Western missionary movement may be the major reasons for this phenomenon. As a result, several observations can be made. EM seems to have lost the direction it once had in the 1970s and '80s. During that period, there was a measure of consensus among missiologists about EM. Currently, needs seem

---

[35] This sentiment was voiced by more than one person in the think-tank session at the Iguassu Missiological Consultation.

to dictate the content of EM. EM resembles somewhat the path that the ecumenical missiologists took in the last half century. For them, the world set the agenda for mission. Unless we come again to the Bible and define what mission is, in the new millennium we will increasingly widen the agenda for mission just as ecumenical missiology did. More conservative Evangelicals of the Two-Thirds World will not agree with this trend.

Third, Patrick Johnstone (1999) has recently written a book entitled *The Church Is Bigger Than You Think*.[36] He has brought to our focus the reality of the global church. When the West began its missionary movement, it began with the free volunteer missionary society. With the coming of the global church, the scene has changed drastically. We can no longer do mission without considering the place of the local and world church in mission. There are other reasons why we need to take a serious look at the church in mission. For one, in the West the churches are no longer satisfied with their passive role in doing mission. Also, in the Two-Thirds World, churches play a much more dominant role in mission, especially in countries such as India, Korea, and Japan. Some of the Latin American and African countries are also in this category. In many cases, they do not have elaborate missionary societies to do mission. Instead, the churches send their missionaries by themselves. These and other theological concerns, such as the place of the church in mission, require us to give greater attention to the existence of the global church in the formulation of EM.[37]

Fourth, Western Evangelicalism itself has been threatened in the past three decades. In the past, it was largely forces from without that endangered Evangelicalism. The difference is that the recent threats have come from within the "family." One example has to do with the nature of the eternal punishment of God for those who have not heard the gospel proclamation. Some of these issues and discussions could change the face of Evangelicalism in the new millennium to the degree that the line that once divided non-Evangelicals from Evangelicals will no longer exist. We already find this trend in some Evangelical missiological writings. This will widen the chasm between Western and Two-Thirds World mission communities, unless leaders from both of these sectors dialogue and battle to return to the biblical position.

A Final Reflection

In this regard, I suggest that the Iguassu Affirmation can give guidelines as to where Evangelical missiology should go in the new millennium. This document states the focus of mission as the proclamation of the gospel of Jesus Christ to every creature in a culturally appropriate manner. But the totality of the declaration gives an unusual balance to the mission given to us by God. Some of the important areas were also mentioned without trying to systematize or unnecessarily lock things in that the Bible does not lock in. While the Iguassu Affirmation does not claim to offer an exhaustive list in our missiology for Evangelicals, it has the potential to

---

[36] Already in 1977, the Swiss Catholic missiologist, Walbert Bühlmann (1978, p. 131; quoted in Anderson, 1988, p. 114), predicted the coming of the "third church" as "the epoch-making event of current church history."

[37] Johannes Blauw (1962) and Charles Van Engen (1991) have done us a great service by their writings. We need to go further. Not only the factors affecting the church of the Two-Thirds World should be brought into focus, but also the church theme should pervade every aspect of our EM.

guide the global church as it missiologizes with the required focus and yet without losing other important agenda items for the future. In the process, a true "global Evangelical missiology" could emerge to the benefit of both the West and the Two-Thirds World to the glory of the Father, the Son, and the Holy Spirit. Amen.

References

Anderson, G. H. (1988, July). American Protestants in pursuit of mission: 1886-1986. *International Bulletin of Missionary Research, 12*(3), pp. 98-102, 104-118.

Blauw, J. (1962). *The missionary nature of the church: A survey of the biblical theology of mission.* New York: McGraw-Hill.

Bosch, D. J. (1980). *Witness to the world: The Christian mission in theological perspective.* Atlanta, GA: John Knox Press.

———. (1991). *Transforming mission: Paradigm shifts in theology of mission.* Maryknoll, NY: Orbis Books.

Bühlmann, W. (1978). *Courage, church! Essays in Ecclesial spirituality.* Maryknoll, NY: Orbis Books.

Coote, R. T. (1982, July). The uneven growth of conservative Evangelical missions. *International Bulletin of Missionary Research, 6*(3), pp. 118-123.

Ferris, R. W. (Ed.). (1995). *Establishing ministry training: A manual for programme developers.* Pasadena, CA: William Carey Library.

Glasser, A. F. (1985, January). The evolution of Evangelical mission theology since World War II. *International Bulletin of Missionary Research, 9*(1), pp. 9-13.

———. (1993). Evangelical missions. In J. M. Phillips (Ed.), *Toward the 21st century in Christian mission.* Grand Rapids, MI: Wm. B. Eerdmans Publishing Co.

Glasser, A. F., & McGavran, D. A. (1983). *Contemporary theologies of mission.* Grand Rapids, MI: Baker Book House.

Harley, D. (1995). *Preparing to serve: Training for cross-cultural mission.* Pasadena, CA: William Carey Library.

Hesselgrave, D. J. (1978). *Theology and mission.* Grand Rapids, MI: Baker Book House.

———. (1991). *Communicating Christ cross-culturally: An introduction to missionary communication* (2nd ed.). Grand Rapids, MI: Zondervan Publishing House.

———. (1999, July). Redefining holism. *Evangelical Missions Quarterly, 35*, pp. 278-284.

Johnstone, P. (1999). *The church is bigger than you think: Structures and strategies for the church in the 21st century.* Pasadena, CA: William Carey Library.

Kane, J. H. (1976). *Christian missions in biblical perspective.* Grand Rapids, MI: Baker Book House.

Kinnamon, M., & Cope, B. E. (1997). *The ecumenical movement: An anthology of key texts and voices.* Grand Rapids, MI: Wm. B. Eerdmans Publishing Co.

Lee, Hyun-Mo. (1997, July). The influence of post-modernism on the contemporary theology of mission. *Current Mission Trends* (Korean ed.), No. 10, p. 34.

Lossky, N., et al. (Eds.). (1991). *Dictionary of the ecumenical movement.* Geneva, Switzerland: World Council of Churches.

McGavran, D. A. (1996). Contemporary Evangelical theology of mission. In D. A. Pittman, R. L. F. Habito, & T. C. Muck (Eds.), *Ministry and theology in global perspective: Contemporary challenges for the church.* Grand Rapids, MI: Wm. B. Eerdmans Publishing Co.

McQuilkin, J. R. (1993). An Evangelical assessment of mission theology of the kingdom of God. In C. Van Engen, D. S. Gilliland, & P. Pierson (Eds.), *The good news of the kingdom: Mission theology for the third millennium* (pp. 172-178). Maryknoll, NY: Orbis Books.

Myers, B. (1999, July). In response: Another look at "holistic mission." *Evangelical Missions Quarterly, 35*, pp. 285-287.

Neff, D. (1999, December 6). Market-driven missions? *Christianity Today, 43*(14), p. 28.

Nelson, M. L. (1976). *The how and why of Third World missions: An Asian case study.* South Pasadena, CA: William Carey Library.

Nelson, M. L. (Ed.). (1976). *Readings in Third World missions: A collection of essential documents.* South Pasadena, CA: William Carey Library.

Netland, H. A. (1994, Spring). Theology and missions: Some reflections on an ambivalent relationship. *Trinity World Forum*, *19*(3), pp. 1-4.

Noll, M. A. (1996, January). The challenges of contemporary church history, the dilemmas of modern history, and missiology to the rescue. *Missiology*, p. 50.

Padilla, R. C. (Ed.). (1976). *An international symposium on the Lausanne Covenant*. Minneapolis, MN: World Wide Books.

Pate, L. D. (1989). *From every people: A handbook of Two-Thirds World missions with directory, history, analysis*. Monrovia, CA: MARC.

———. (1991, April). The changing balance in global mission. *International Bulletin of Missionary Research*, *15*(2), pp. 56, 58-61.

Pittman, D. A., Habito, R. L. F., & Muck, T. C. (Eds.). (1996). *Ministry and theology in global perspective: Contemporary challenges for the church*. Grand Rapids, MI: Wm. B. Eerdmans Publishing Co.

Rommen, E. (1987, Winter). American missiology: Which way? *Trinity World Forum*, *12*(2), pp. 1-3.

———. (1991). *Missiology's place in the academy*. Deerfield, IL: Trinity Evangelical Divinity School. Also appears in *Trinity World Forum* (1992, Spring), *17*(3), pp. 1-4.

———. (1993, Fall). The de-theologizing of missiology. *Trinity World Forum*, *19*(1), pp. 1-4.

Scherer, J. A. (1987). *Gospel, church, and kingdom: Comparative studies in world mission theology*. Minneapolis, MN: Augsburg Press.

———. (1987, October). Missiology as a discipline and what it includes. *Missiology: An International Review*, *15*, pp. 507-528.

———. (1999). Key issues to be considered in global mission today: Crucial questions about mission theology, context, and expectations. In P. V. Martinson (Ed.), *Mission at the dawn of the 21st century: A vision for the church* (pp. 10-18). Minneapolis, MN: Kirk House Publishers.

Scherer, J. A., & Bevans, S. B. (Eds.). (1992). *New directions in mission and evangelization 1: Basic statements, 1974-1991*. Maryknoll, NY: Orbis Books.

———. (1994). *New directions in mission and evangelization 2: Theological foundations*. Maryknoll, NY: Orbis Books.

———. (1999). *New directions in mission and evangelization 3: Faith and culture*. Maryknoll, NY: Orbis Books.

Shenk, W. R. (1996, January). The role of theory in mission studies. *Missiology: An International Review*, *24*, pp. 31-45.

Stafford, T. (1986, February 21). The father of church growth. *Christianity Today*, *30*(3), pp. 19-23.

Stott, J. R. W. (1975). *Christian mission in the modern world*. Downers Grove, IL: Inter-Varsity Press.

Taylor, W. D. (Ed.). (1991). *Internationalising missionary training*. Grand Rapids, MI: Baker Book House.

———. (1997). *Too valuable to lose: Exploring the causes and cures of missionary attrition*. Pasadena, CA: William Carey Library.

Thomas, N. E. (1989, July). From missions to globalization: Teaching missiology in North American seminaries. *International Bulletin of Missionary Research*, *13*(3), pp. 103-107.

Thomas, N. E. (Ed.). (1995). *Classic texts in mission and world Christianity*. Maryknoll, NY: Orbis Books.

Tippett, A. R. (1974). Missiology: A new discipline. In A. Martin (Ed.), *The means of world evangelization: Missiological education at the Fuller School of World Mission*. South Pasadena, CA: William Carey Library.

———. (1987). *Introduction to missiology*. Pasadena, CA: William Carey Library.

Utuk, E. (1994). From Wheaton to Lausanne. In J. A. Scherer & S. B. Bevans (Eds.), *New directions in mission and evangelization 2: Theological foundations* (pp. 99-112). Maryknoll, NY: Orbis Books.

Van Engen, C. E. (1991). *God's missionary people: Rethinking the purpose of the local church*. Grand Rapids, MI: Baker Book House.

Verkuyl, J. (1978). The history of missiology during the 19th and 20th centuries. In D. Cooper (Ed. and Trans.), *Contemporary missiology: An introduction* (pp. 26-88). Grand Rapids, MI: Wm. B. Eerdmans Publishing Co.

Verstraelen, F. J., et al. (Eds.). (1995). *Missiology: An ecumenical introduction: text and contexts of global Christianity*. Grand Rapids, MI: Wm. B. Eerdmans Publishing Co.

Wagner, C. P. (1986, Spring). Power encounter in Christian mission. *Trinity World Forum, 11*(3), pp. 1-4.

Warner, T. (1985, Winter). Critical issues for evangelism today. *Trinity World Forum, 10*(2), pp. 1-3.

Winter, R. D. (1976). The highest priority: Cross-cultural evangelism. In M. L. Nelson (Ed.), *Readings in Third World missions: A collection of essential documents* (pp. 159-170). South Pasadena, CA: William Carey Library.

Wong, J., Pentecost, E., & Larson, P. (1976). Missions from the Third World. In A. F. Glasser, P. G. Hiebert, C. P. Wagner, & R. D. Winter (Eds.), *Crucial dimensions in world evangelization* (pp. 345-396). Pasadena, CA: William Carey Library.

David Tai-Woong Lee is the chairman of the WEF Missions Commission. Together with his wife Hun-Bock Lee and their two sons, Young-Min (Sam) and Kyoung-Min (Ben), he resides in Seoul, Korea. He has been actively involved in training Korean missionaries for the past 14 years as the director of Global Missionary Training Center. He has also served as the chairman of Global Missionary Fellowship, which is one of the largest indigenous interdenominational missionary sending organizations in Korea since its founding in 1987. He has received both M.Div. and D.Miss. degrees from Trinity International University in Deerfield, Illinois. His publications include Korean Missions: Theory and Practice (Joy publisher in Korea) and A Philosophy of Training Disciples (Hall of Tyrannus, publisher).

10

The Scriptures, the church, and humanity: who should do mission and why?

ANTONIA
LEONORA
VAN DER MEER

IT IS VERY SAD THAT missiology has not yet received its due appreciation from many Evangelical churches and theological colleges. It still seems to be a kind of hobby for those who really like it and for people who perhaps aren't capable of more serious theological discussions or who are unable to be successful in a more normal career. In reality, mission is the main reason the Christian church exists. I believe strongly that the most relevant theological thinking is directly related to mission, and it requires those who engage in it to seek answers in the Scriptures to the pain, questions, and needs of specific people in specific contexts. Mission practice is very important and must flow from serious missiological thinking based on a scriptural perspective. The Scriptures are our model, for the deep theological truths found therein were written in a missionary context, as evidenced in Paul's epistles.

To many of us as Brazilian and Latin American Evangelicals, mission has become a very important issue. We are still very excited in discovering that *we* are called to be involved in mission; that God chooses *us*, enables *us*, and supports *us*; and that he can use *our lives* for his glory and to be a blessing to others. Our calling doesn't mean that we don't have problems or that all churches share this perspective. We are still learning, and we make many mistakes, often with painful consequences for the missionaries and even for the people we want to bless on the mission fields. Some of these mistakes are the fruit of this taste of something new and exciting. For example, missionaries are often sent out with little training and still more often with no missiological training whatsoever. Instruction at a good Bible institute is often considered more than sufficient to go and work with "primitive people." Just a few years ago, a team of over 100 Brazilian missionaries was sent out. A number of them had no more than two weeks of training. The churches on that specific mission field felt offended. "Do you think we are children?" they asked reproachfully.

Most missionaries do not receive any pastoral care either. The churches generally expect missionaries to be God's specially chosen and enabled people, some sort of heroes, and they expect great stories of accomplishments. One missionary came back from the field with a medical recommendation for rest, as his health was poor. What did his agency do with him? They said, "All right, you can rest three or four days a week and speak at conferences all over Brazil for only three or four days a week." Soon the missionary's health was much worse. Other missionaries have come back depressed by painful experiences on the field, by problems within the team, or by confrontation with war, death, and evil. Nobody even asks if they need any help. People just expect them to be well and to go out on their preaching tours. Some workers are learning to say, "Hey, I'm human. I need some holiday first, and I need medical care." But it is hard to make demands when you depend on what most of the churches still see as special gifts. When there are other projects (such as a new church building), quite often the first item to be cut from the budget is support for the missionaries.

God, Scripture, and Mission

How does revealed Scripture help us to understand the role of the church in our world of multiple polarizations? I agree wholeheartedly with A. W. Tozer that it is tragic when "in an effort to get the work of the Lord done, we often lose contact with the Lord of the work." I have seen this happen not just with mission theo-rists, but even in the lives of missionaries on the field, who then dry out and no longer have a transforming message of hope for others. We can only offer our own poor goodwill or our well or not so well organized good works, which often create dependence and new problems. More important than what we do for God as missionaries is our own continuing relationship with him. He is not the manager of a successful mission business. He is the God who loved us so much that he gave us his only Son. He is our Father.

I believe that God has to be the subject and the object of mission. Mission flows from God—from his nature, his love, and his sovereign rule over the whole universe. If we lose this perspective, we become just another non-governmental organization trying to help people. We may possibly do a lot of good and hard work, but often we tend to be very paternalistic, not seeing the people we want to serve as people of equal value who need respect, understanding, and real partnership as much as or even more than they need any practical service.

I believe that the entire canon is about God's mission and that it is very clear that God's purpose has always been to reach and to bless all nations. This is affirmed by the fact that the Bible starts with the creation and fall of humanity as a whole. Then, starting in Genesis 3, there is the promise of restoration of a relationship with God through the seed of the woman. Genesis teaches the unity of the human race—in creation, in being formed in God's image and likeness, in the fall, and in God's purpose of redemption (see also Acts 17:26-27). When Abraham was called, he was called to be a blessing to all families on the earth (Gen. 12:3). He was called as a means to achieve God's end, the salvation of humanity. Sometimes Abraham was a blessing, as when he liberated the people of Sodom and Gomorrah and prayed for them (Gen. 14:12-24; 18:22-33). At other times he became a stumbling block due to his lack of faith, as when he denied that Sarah was his wife (Gen. 12:10-20; 20:1-18).

This position of being chosen as an instrument of God's grace to humanity clearly applies to Israel as well (Ex. 19:4-5; Deut. 28:9-10). The Jews knew this, but either they followed the evil ways of the Gentiles, or they developed strong prejudices and barriers against the Gentiles instead of being a blessing to them. When Solomon prayed at the consecration of the temple, he recognized that the temple was not only the house where Israel could meet God, but also the place where God wanted to bless the Gentiles (1 Kings 8:22-53; 2 Chron. 6:12-42).

The Psalms clearly reveal God's purpose to reach and bless all nations. Psalm 96 is a totally and surprisingly missionary psalm, inviting Gentiles to worship God and to "come into his courts" (with no dividing wall). Psalms 2:7-11, 22:27, 68:31, 72:8-19, 86:9, 87:3-7, and many others clearly show that the Gentiles are among the people whom God loves and whose worship he desires to receive. In the prophets, God's love and interest for the nations are evident, as are his judgments on those who commit evil, be they Israelites or Gentiles. Jonah is the story of Israel's resistance against their missionary role and of God's breaking through this resistance to save the Ninevites (who were real and powerful enemies of Israel). Isaiah has many references to God's love for the nations and for all peoples (Isa. 2:2-4; 11:9; 18:7; 19:16-25; 25:6-9). He speaks about the ministry of God's servant in taking light and salvation to the Gentiles (Isa. 42:1-6; 49:6), and he affirms that God will choose his messengers from the Gentile nations as well (Isa. 66:19-23).

During Jesus' life and ministry in Israel, we clearly see that his love was for all nations and that he was working to break through the disciples' prejudices and to prepare them for a worldwide ministry. He showed special care for Gentiles and Samaritans, and he referred to them frequently and respectfully in his personal contacts, teaching, and parables. Before Jesus left his disciples, his command to reach all the nations was unmistakably clear. The book of Acts shows us how the Holy Spirit came with the specific purpose of enabling the church and individual Christians to witness to all the nations, how he broke through the prejudice that was still present (Acts 1:8; 10; 11; 15), and how he started to incorporate Gentiles into God's kingdom. Acts also shows how God uses ordinary human beings powerfully to accomplish his purposes. The epistles and Revelation are written out of a missionary practice to churches on the "mission field." Thus it can be seen that the whole Bible clearly and consistently reveals the same message.

Christian Response to Human Needs

For many centuries, starting with Constantine and extending through the eras of more modern colonialism (regardless of the continent), there was the idea that Christendom was called to conquer the pagan world. Today there is no longer a "Christian" and a "non-Christian" world. Because of the de-christianization of the West and the multiple migrations of people from many faiths, the West has become very pluralistic, while the church is growing stronger in other regions (also in daily confrontation with other religions).

Another issue is the fact that devotees of other faiths have proven to be more active missionaries than the Christian churches. People from the West have become tired and have lost faith in humanism and rationalism. They have started to seek new spiritual answers and truths—as long as all are free to decide for themselves what truth they prefer. Also, more than ever now, the world is divided between the rich and the poor, with the rich getting richer and the poor getting poorer. Seemingly all-powerful economic forces control the world and are controlled by the rich. For a time, Christianity and Christian mission were identified with the "rich world." Thank God that the church has grown strong among the poor and that they are becoming a tremendous missionary force. But how are we going to relate our missionary challenge and responsibility to these realities? How can we respond to the tremendous needs and pains of our own time?

David Bosch (1991, pp. 1, 8-11) defines Christian mission this way: "The Christian faith sees 'all generations of the earth' as objects of God's plan of salvation or, in New Testament terms, it regards the 'reign of God' which has come in Jesus Christ as intended for all humanity.... Christianity is missionary by its very nature, or it denies its very *raison d'être*. Christian mission gives expression to the dynamic relationship between God and the world ... supremely, in the birth, life, death, resurrection, and exaltation of Jesus of Nazareth."

So we reinforce the biblical emphasis on God's plan of salvation intended for all peoples of all times. God knows and cares for people of each generation and each culture and has great love, understanding, and compassion for them. Paul's strategy to "become all things to all men" (1 Cor. 9:22) is clearly inspired by the Holy Spirit. If God had not been a missionary God, all of us would have been lost. But God was willing to pay the price to bring about reconciliation with mankind, which includes people of all tribes, tongues,

peoples, and nations, until he comes again.

Bosch (1991) continues, "Foreign mission is not a separate entity; its foundation lies in the universality of salvation and the indivisibility of the reign of Christ. The church has often defined mission in terms of its addressees, not in terms of its nature. *Mission (missio Dei)* is God's self-revelation as the One who loves the world. *Missions* refers to particular forms—related to specific times, places, or needs—of participation in the *missio Dei*.

Today some churches become so "mission minded" that they feel the only valid work is in the 10/40 window. Others refuse to think of foreign countries at all, as long as the work at home (which may be either one's country or one's neighborhood) has not yet been finished. We must recover the understanding of *mission* according to its nature. I know serious young people who are willing to give their lives to serve the Lord, yet they have a guilt complex because they haven't discovered *where* they should go (the problem of the church defining mission according to its addressees).

Bosch (1991) says further, "In our time, God's yes to the world reveals itself, to a large extent, in the church's missionary engagement in respect of the realities of injustice, oppression, poverty, discrimination, and violence. Mission includes evangelism as one of its essential dimensions. Evangelism is the proclamation of salvation in Christ to those who do not believe in him, calling to repentance and conversion, announcing forgiveness of sin, and inviting them to become living members of Christ's earthly community and to begin a life of service to others in the power of the Holy Spirit."

Bosch's definition is very broad and biblical. It shows that the Christian church can never leave mission as a secondary item on its agenda, because a truly Christian and biblical church is missionary by its very nature. The whole Bible clearly reveals God's saving love for all humanity, as we have seen. Mission is basically a statement of God's relationship of love with his creatures and an expression of our calling and privilege as his partners and ambassadors. Bosch also maintains a healthy balance between the fundamental importance of evangelism and our service to whole human beings in all aspects of their fallen and suffering humanity. He clearly defines mission as holistic.

As recently as Lausanne I in 1974, through the clear and bold biblical teaching of Latin American theologians like René Padilla and Samuel Escobar, it became evident and was agreed that social action and evangelism are both essential aspects of the church's mission, i.e., that the proclamation of the gospel cannot be separated from concrete manifestations of God's love. Hundreds of Evangelical leaders from all continents signed the Lausanne Covenant, which affirms that God is concerned with justice and reconciliation in the whole of human society and with the liberation of human beings from all sorts of oppression. Further, the message of salvation also includes a message of judgment against all forms of alienation, oppression, and discrimination (Padilla, 1989, p. 4). Since Lausanne, John Stott has expressed this same view in many books, courses, and Bible expositions.

This new emphasis was not accepted quietly by many theologians from the West, and even now a number of them are still writing and preaching to show that mission has to do with saving from sin and not with all aspects of human life. The Lausanne II conference seems to have been an effort to get back to the more traditional vision of proclaiming the simple gospel to all peoples. Perhaps intentionally, Latin Americans were all but absent among the speakers, with the exception of a few long-term residents in the U.S.—Luis Palau, Carmelo Terranova, and Luis Bush. But theologians from other continents—Caesar Molebatsi from South Africa, Peter Kuzmic from Yugoslavia, and Vinay Samuel from India—clearly continued to present the need for the unity between evangelism and social action (Padilla, 1989, p. 5).

It may be difficult for countries that have evangelized the rest of the world with great effort and high cost—especially a cost in human lives—to accept the fact that their daughter churches have grown up. The mother churches need to stop doing all the teaching and must learn to be real partners. They must trust that the development of more contextualized theologies in other continents does not necessarily mean that these theologies are deviating from the biblical truth.

Mission is the fruit of the love of God, who so loved the world that he gave his only Son in order to redeem human beings from their blindness, oppression, captivity, and poverty, so they can experience a new life of fullness given by his grace. As Evangelical churches, we sin when we are too busy with our Christian activities and with making our Christian systems function smoothly and successfully, while thousands of people groups and billions of people still have no hope or knowledge of the God who loves them and who offers them new life as his beloved children. People need to hear the gospel in a way that they can understand and that it is relevant to their needs. It needs to be something that they can relate to, not something abstract, such as teaching a tribal people about the dichotomy or trichotomy of human nature, when they haven't yet learned how to face witchcraft or how to deal with the fear of evil spirits.

As mentioned above, mission means more than preaching the gospel. It means caring for whole human beings with God's compassionate love and becoming engaged in the whole context of their lives and suffering. When we look at Jesus' life as our model (John 20:21) and at his call to take up our cross, deny ourselves, and follow him, it becomes very clear that our missionary call is to reach out to people in a holistic way. Jesus spent a lot of time responding to all kinds of human suffering in addition to teaching and preaching. He saw these activities as an integral part of his ministry (Luke 4:16-18). This means that responding in Jesus' way to suffering caused by hunger, economic exploitation, war situations, floods, earthquakes, and droughts also is mission—if we do it as followers of Jesus, because of his love and his calling.

This emphasis was proclaimed in the Curitiba Covenant, which was drawn up in 1976 during the first-ever Latin American missions conference. The conference was attended by more than 500 students from Brazil and other Latin countries, as well as by representatives of mission organizations and churches. The Curitiba Covenant states: "In the past, the call of Jesus Christ and his mission required the crossing of geographical barriers; today the Lord calls us to cross the barriers of inequality, of injustice, and of ideological idolatry. We are called to take the presence of Jesus Christ, proclaiming his redeeming gospel, serving the world and changing it by his love, patient in the hope of a new creation that he will bring, because of which we are groaning" (Covenant, 1978, p. 125).

Until recently, Africa, Asia, and Latin America were always considered mission fields—dark continents dominated by "heathenism and evil practices." The Western churches were the mission-sending churches, because they had a history of many years of Christianity. They also had theologians, books, know-how, and financial resources. But the churches in these other continents have now grown strong and become mature. More and more, churches have become partners in mission to the whole world, while the mother churches are having to struggle to keep alive in a secular or pluralistic society.

It has been hard for Western churches to allow the development of authentic local Christianity, as this can seem dangerous and open to all sorts of heresies. But living Christianity is always local in its expression, related to human experience in historical categories, with its own cultural colors. A uniform and abstract "universal" expression of the Christian faith which does not become real in a human context does not really exist and does not bring forth any real fruit in changed lives and changed society. Missionary experience must always be marked by an attitude of dialogue, in such a way that the gospel will become relevant and contextualized in each area where it is shared (Steuernagel, 1993, p. 21).

If Western churches offer a service to human needs in the poorer countries—a service born out of real Christian love and offered with respect—I believe this service is right and necessary. But when Christians and even missiologists call Africa "the cursed continent," call African culture "demonic," and look down upon our African brothers and sisters, I become very angry. The same is true when European or American missionaries share about their work in Latin America or Asia in a way that is humiliating to the national people, making unhealthy jokes and showing contempt for the lack of hygiene and the inefficiency of the people's habits.

We must understand that poverty, epidemics, and war are not the only great evils of our time. They are very evil indeed, but they often serve to open many hearts and lives to Christ, although this fact certainly cannot be used as a justification to let injustice and oppression continue to rule. But in the midst of poverty, there are still many human values in Africa, Asia, and Latin America—values of solidarity and amazing generosity and hospitality. (My omission of the Pacific area, about which I know very little, shows my ignorance, not criticism.) At the same time, consumerism and capitalism control our world more and more. They are dominated by evils such as idol-worship of the god Mammon and exclusion of the "have nots," and they make people more isolated, defensive, competitive, and egotistic. It is more than obvious that excessive wealth and material prosperity in some parts of the world can continue to grow only at the cost of poverty in other regions. In the wealthy West, post-modernism and pluralism make it more difficult to speak about Christ, because it is not politically correct to respect the exclusive claims of Christ. I would say that these Western systems are no less demonic than the evils of Africa, Asia, and Latin America.

I faced a lot of extreme poverty and suffering during my ministry in war-torn Angola. I became close to people who had lost most of their family members, who had been raped in very cruel ways, who were hurting inside and outside, and who had very little comfort—no sheets, no soap, very little and poor-quality food, often no medical supplies for broken bones, no relatives to visit them, no hope for the future. Sometimes the situation made me physically ill and unable to sleep. But I knew I had to do my little bit, sharing God's love with them, praying and reading God's Word, and listening to their very sad tales. I would take a little soap to one, a towel to another, a bit of oats to a third—like a cup of water in a desert. But the people were willing to listen; they were willing to respond to God's love.

It was important that they knew that I was willing to listen and that I cared. They didn't demand that I solve all their problems. But in response to my caring, many believed—orphan children, young men who had served as soldiers against their will, and women—and their faces would be transformed. A joyful smile would replace the dead stare of hopelessness. Many recovered a deep joy and hope and meaning for their lives when they understood God's love for them. They understood that they were still able to serve others and were not just social parasites. I know that war is a great evil indeed, but I know that God's super-abundant grace can manifest itself in each and every context.

There are more recent trends that are also cause for concern, as Alex Araujo (1998, p. 158) states: "In recent years we seem to have shifted our paradigm of how we see ourselves in relation to the world from Christian belief to Christendom, from the call to repentance and a life of faith and obedience to Christ to a concern with the visible, collective, organized Christian presence, a sociological force to be seen and reckoned with by the non-Christian world.... Our popular terminology is that of a clash of religious cultures, and seems excessively preoccupied with great numbers and comparative statistics, with territorial mapping and war room strategies."

It took the church a long time to free itself from imperialism and worldly powers, first of Constantine, later the Papacy, then the colonial powers. Are we now returning to our original "square one," leaving behind us once again the model of mission according to Christ, which is characterized by humble service? Are we once again speaking and thinking in terms of warfare, of large numbers and great structures, of the human greatness of our institutions? Is it possible to be successful according to worldly standards and continue to be humble servants of our Lord? Not "great servants of Christ," but servants of a great but humble Christ. May God have mercy.

Enabling Local Churches and Christians to Do the Work

As a missionary to Angola and Mozambique, my main ministry was not so much to bring new people into the kingdom, although by God's grace and with great joy I have been involved in that as well. My main ministry was enabling national Christians to do the ministry, and they are doing it much better than I ever could have done. Some examples:

1. I had a young Angolan friend who was a journalist and radio reporter. He was also a staunch Communist. For some months, we had weekly dialogues, with abundant questionings on his part, until he decided to believe and to follow Christ. I then continued to help him along on this new way. About two years after his conversion, the Angolan government opened up politically, in preparation for their first-ever elections. Desiring to become more friendly to the Evangelical churches, they offered a two-hour program free of charge on Sunday mornings on the state radio (there were no other radio stations). This young man became the capable leader of this program, which preached the gospel to millions.

2. A young male nurse suffered a serious spinal injury while he was traveling about, serving the government in fighting sleeping sickness. He was thrown onto the road, where he lay for hours, unable to move, until a truck finally came by and stopped. The occupants, having no knowledge of healthcare, simply heaved the young man onto the back of the truck. After two hours on a bumpy road, he reached a hospital. He suffered intensely, but he became a Christian through our visits. Now he operates a small clinic, and since there was no church in his neigh-

borhood, we started meetings in his back yard. Now 150 people, most of them new converts, are meeting regularly, and they are struggling to build their own church. This man has become an able evangelist from his wheelchair, and many of his family, friends, and patients have become Christians.

3. A young Angolan couple whom I taught at a YWAM course went to serve in a tribe in the mountains, where nobody had ever taken the gospel. They started with a translator and learned the language, and now people are becoming Christians. There is still no Bible translation available, but this isolated Angolan tribe is already sending its own evangelists to neighboring tribes.

4. My sister works in a tribe in the north of Brazil. For more than 15 years, she and some missionary friends had preached and were translating the gospel and serving the community. People were not completely against the message, but very few believed. Then some of the leaders of the community became Christians. One of them wanted to travel around the villages with my sister to help "sow the seed." He had a gift of singing the gospel stories in the people's own traditional way. In about five years, 80% of the Suruí people had become Christians and were active members of the church.

These vignettes show how the national or local Christians often serve much better than foreign missionaries do—and with less training and support. But this does not mean that they don't need any training or teaching. After living for about three years in Angola, I began to discover how deep an influence the people's own traditions still had on them in times of crisis such as serious mental or physical illness, sterility, fear of witchcraft, etc. The people had never learned to face these crises from a biblical point of view. They knew that white people did not agree with their solutions ("because they do not understand our traditional problems"), so they wouldn't talk about the situations with the missionaries. But they had not been offered alternative solutions or relevant biblical teaching. So they went back to their diviners and traditional healers, with their roots, leaves, and spiritual/magical solutions.[1] I did some reading and started to question some young people and mature African Christians. I then prepared a lecture with questions for discussion on the subject. I received dozens of invitations from many churches. Many people came to listen, and it was amazing how open the people became during these discussions. Often they asked, "Why did no one speak to us about these questions before?" They really wanted to learn but had not had the opportunity.

So I see one very important aspect of our missionary endeavor as enabling national Christians to do the work. Some of my missionary friends accepted the challenge to serve some African Independent Churches in Angola and Mozambique. These churches had much syncretism in their religious practices, but their spiritual understanding was limited because they did not have the Bible available in their own language. My friends started teaching them the Bible. Whole churches became Evangelical, and the pastors, elders, and members all wanted to follow the teaching of the Bible according to their new understanding. Often as Evangelicals we tend to reject some groups as heretics. If only we could see them as sinners for whom Jesus died on the cross, just as he did for us! We need to treat all groups as people who have the right to learn and to understand all things that Jesus has commanded us (Matt. 28:20).

Who Should Do Mission?

Mission is entrusted to the church, which is the multi-ethnic body of Christ. The unity of the church is not only a deep theological truth (John 17); it is also a strategic need. Sadly, it is something that is difficult to live out in our daily lives. There is no way that the world will believe our message or see God's glory in us while we are divided and fighting inner wars over small differences in understanding, jealousy, prejudice, a desire for power, and other negative things which Satan rejoices to sow and to see flourish among God's people. These conflicts weaken our witness and strengthen the influence of other religions, sects, and cults, which are as missionary minded as the church of Christ.

I believe that the ultimate goal of mission is to give God the glory due to his wonderful name. This glory is related to the universal spread of the gospel, for the gospel is the light of Christ shining upon all men and overcoming darkness (2 Cor. 4:1-6). In John 17, it is clear that God's name is glorified when Christ offers eternal life to all the people that God has given him. The true unity of the church is based upon and results in the glory of Christ. It convinces sinners powerfully of the truth of our message of hope and love.

Christ clearly revealed that the main goal of the church was to reach all peoples. The Holy Spirit was given for this specific purpose. But there has been a resistant blindness among God's people. It took a long time for the Reformation and Evangelical churches of Europe to understand their missionary responsibility. When they finally went out into the world, they formed daughter churches, but they usually did so without sharing the vision and

---

[1] African traditional religions will always condemn witchcraft (the use of evil powers to harm others secretly for the witch's benefit), but they see diviners and traditional healers as a way out of the influence of evil powers.

the privilege of being involved in obeying the Great Commission. It took many years for these daughter churches to begin to understand that the responsibility of reaching all nations was theirs as well. Today, we still need to learn to plant missionary-minded churches. It is very encouraging to hear about tribal people in India saving a handful of rice at each meal to raise support for their missionaries. The mission enterprise can start in some simple ways as soon as there is a living community. The important thing is to remain teachable, not to think we have all the answers and the know-how.

I have already mentioned why I believe that African, Latin American, and Asian Third World countries can still be considered mission fields, but at the same time they are developing more and more mission-sending churches. Praise God! It is a great privilege to be a missionary who does not come from a country with a powerful economy, whose country does not represent any threat whatsoever, and who cannot be expected to solve all financial problems that arise. Often, with the best of intentions, mission agencies and missionaries have created a great deal of dependence. But if our home church has difficulty in supporting us as their missionary, and we live a simple lifestyle, people will not put such high economic expectations on us (though in some ways we will continue to reap what others have sown in terms of expectations). Thus, we are freer to serve as partners, as equals, as it was in the beginning when the apostles went out from one of the least significant countries of the Roman Empire.

Sadly, some Brazilian missionaries have begun to relate to people of other Latin American countries or to Africans as if they are now the wise and powerful masters of knowledge, with the right to behave toward others in a condescending way. Human sinfulness, ignorance, and perhaps

wrong lessons learned from some Western missionaries cause this behavior. I believe that the richer countries are more and more in need of missionaries from other continents—missionaries who can show that the gospel is not an old, outdated, and insignificant message, but the greatest and most incredible news anybody could ever tell. It demonstrates that people who feel dry, empty, and tired can overflow with joy and life and make a meaningful contribution.

I was pleased to read that the Wycliffe Bible Translators have come to the conclusion that the only possible way to finish the great task of offering the Word of God to people of all languages is by training more and more local translators. These local translators can do the work better and more rapidly, although they still need foreign missionaries to train them, as well as to serve as consultants until there are more experienced local translators who can take over these roles as well. This is an important strategy, and I hope more mission agencies will follow suit.

Two important prerequisites for the church to reach out in mission are humility and unity. We certainly need to start by humbling ourselves, recognizing our weakness and our sin. In an effort to foster unity in Brazil, we have created a number of Evangelical national associations of mutual cooperation. We have AMTB, an association of mission agencies; APMB, an association of mission teachers; and ACMI, and association of mission departments in churches, alongside the broad Latin American COMIBAM. All of these organizations are serving well. We are learning to support and encourage each other and to listen to each other instead of developing a spirit of competition.

But on the other hand, there are more and more Brazilian denominations and self-sufficient local churches who insist on their own training program and their own agency and who see no need to work together with others. In some churches, there is such an identification between the values of the church and the values of the global society that churches feel good when they can construct great palaces for worship costing millions of dollars or when they can invite a famous preacher to speak or an expensive gospel group to sing. They feel great, successful, and important. Some pastors live and look more like successful, powerful businessmen or managers. But how can we discover our weakness, guilt, and sin in such a false environment? May God be gracious, and may his Holy Spirit help us to see our true identity. Maybe we are becoming like the church of Laodicea, believing we are rich and prosperous while we are really very poor. Sadly, the poorer churches often try to follow this kind of example and feel less blessed and less spiritual because they don't have the same financial prosperity. But praise God that most missionaries still come from the poorer churches who invest costly gifts in them.

It is encouraging that a growing number of Christian leaders are showing heightened concern to reach other peoples with the gospel. In Angola and Mozambique, most of the churches are still very poor and are struggling to survive, but they recognize that they have something to share with others. They are like the church in Smyrna, to whom Jesus says: "I know your afflictions and your poverty—yet you are rich!" (Rev. 2:9). Some of our former students (from seminaries where I used to teach in Angola) are doing a splendid job, taking the gospel to as yet unreached areas. They are training young leaders under extremely difficult conditions and with very little support. One Mozambican pastor walked long distances in one of the provinces that was most affected by the war. In five years he planted 40 churches in unreached villages.

Women missionaries are helping too. I know how difficult it is, at least in Angola and Mozambique, for single women to receive any respect in society. Women are more respected as unmarried mothers than if they remain totally alone. But I praise God for some Angolan and Mozambican sisters who have heard God's call, are serving him wholeheartedly as single women, and by God's grace have the support of their families. I know that Nigeria, Kenya, Ghana, and South Africa have missionary sending and supporting churches. And I trust many more will be added to this number. The same is happening in more and more Latin American countries, as well as in Asia. Praise God!

Why Do Mission?

Mission has existed since the very beginning of the Christian church, and for a few centuries the Evangelical church has been involved. For a long time, mission was motivated not only by the scriptural basis, the Great Commission (Matt. 28:18-20), but also by more ambiguous convictions, such as those mentioned by Bosch (1991, p. 5): "(a) the absoluteness and superiority of Christian religion when compared with others; (b) the acceptability and adaptability of Christianity to all peoples and conditions; (c) the superior achievements of the Christian mission on the mission fields; (d) the fact that Christianity has shown itself to be stronger than all other religions."

Other motives were theologically more adequate but also ambiguous in their practical manifestations: "(a) the motive of conversion, which emphasizes the value of personal decision and commitment, but tends to narrow the reign of God spiritualistically and individualistically to the sum total of saved souls; (b) the eschatological motive, which fixes people's eyes on the reign of God as a future reality but ... has no interest in the exigencies of this life; (c) the motive of *plantatio ecclesiae* (church planting), which stresses the need for the gathering of a community of the committed but is inclined to identify the church with the kingdom of God; (d) the philanthropic motive, through which the church is challenged to seek justice in the world but which easily equates God's reign with an improved society" (Bosch, 1991, p. 5).

Bosch shows that often the success of Christian missions became the foundation for mission. Some missiologists of the 19th century trusted in a continuing, growing success of Christian mission, which would have meant that before the end of the 20th century the whole world would have been won for the Christian faith while "heathenism was dying" (Bosch, 1991, p. 6).

Without diminishing the work of our missionary brothers and sisters of the 18th and 19th centuries, we have to recognize that they were very much children of their times, born in a Western world that was very confident of its moral, intellectual, and spiritual superiority. Their ministry was very much marked by these attitudes of superiority, and their success was very strongly tied to the whole colonial enterprise—the spread of Western domination, culture, and technology to other continents. They were so convinced about the baseness and evil of other cultures that most did not take time to try to really understand them. Those who did were criticized by their mission boards because they were spending time learning about heathen religions and cultures, instead of teaching the truth of the gospel and the light of Western culture (Neill, 1979, p. 230).

Today we need to listen to God's Word again. We need to pray and think about our motivation for mission and about the purpose of mission. Our motivation is not primarily to look at the world with com-

passion, though that is a necessary attitude if we follow Christ as our missionary model and are true children of a loving God (1 John 4:7-11). Our main motivations must be our obedience to God and our concern for the glory of God. God who has paid such a precious price for our salvation is Lord of all—a just and merciful Lord who should and shall receive glory through people from every nation, tribe, and tongue coming to worship him. My former Angolan leader, Pastor Octavio Fernando, the General Secretary of the Evangelical Alliance of Angola, was angry when he discovered that the main motivation of some Brazilian missionaries was to help the Angolan people. He said: "That is not right. Your main motivation must be your obedience to God." Thank God we can learn such truth from national leaders.

The goal of mission is not only to save individual human beings, but also to establish communities that worship the Lord and have a missionary responsibility. These quality communities will develop with a vision of the values of the kingdom of God and of their responsibility to serve Christ and their fellow human beings in all fields of human action.

Why should we do mission? Because God still loves this world that groans in pain. Because he has a marvelous project for the restoration of the whole of creation, and he wants people to be saved and to have the great privilege of belonging to his international family. Because without this gospel we really are lost, without hope and without God. Because God's grace is so rich and abundantly sufficient to reach any and every sinner— of all generations and cultures. And because of the joy of seeing people who have lost all hope and meaning rediscover life, joy, and a new calling to serve when they hear and understand the gospel. What a great privilege to be called to be involved in such a marvelous and meaningful project! May God give wisdom and guidance each step of the way to all of us, whatever our nationality, race, mission agency, or denomination.

References

Araujo, A. (1998). What is our message? *Evangelical Missions Quarterly, 34*(2), p. 158.

Bosch, D. J. (1991). *Transforming mission: Paradigm shifts in theology of mission.* Maryknoll, NY: Orbis Books.

Covenant of the missionary conference in Curitiba. (1978). In *Jesus Cristo: Senhorio, propósito e missão.* São Paulo, Brazil: ABU Editora.

Neill, S. (1979). *A history of Christian missions.* Baltimore, MD: Penguin Books.

Padilla, R. C. (1989). Misión y compromiso social. *Misión* (Buenos Aires), *8*(4), pp. 4-5.

Steuernagel, V. (1993). *Obediência missionária e prática histórica.* São Paulo, Brazil: ABU Editora.

Antonia Leonora (Tonica) van der Meer is Brazilian, daughter of Dutch immigrants. She studied languages and then engaged in student ministry as a staff worker in Brazil. She studied at All Nations Christian College in the U.K. and then worked with IFES to pioneer student work in Angola for 10 years. She served the Evangelical Alliance of Angola and taught at different seminaries in that nation. She completed her master's degree in theology at the Baptist Theological Faculty in São Paulo. For the last four years, she has been Dean at the Evangelical Center for Missions in Vicosa, Brazil, and is on the board of the Association of Brazilian Mission Teachers.

Spiritual warfare and worldview

PAUL HIEBERT

IN RECENT YEARS, there has been a renewed interest in the gospel as power in the lives of people and in spiritual warfare between God and Satan (Anderson, 1990; Arnold, 1997; Kraft, 1992; Moreau, 1997; Powlison, 1995; Wagner, 1991, to name a few). This comes as an important corrective in many Western churches to the earlier emphasis on the gospel as merely truth and on evil as primarily human weakness. Both truth and power are central themes in the gospel and should be central in the lives of God's people as well.

Much literature on spiritual warfare has been written by missionaries who are forced to question their Western denial of the spirit realities of this world through encounters with witchcraft, spiritism, and demon possession, and who base their studies on experience and look for biblical texts to justify their views. These studies generally lack solid, comprehensive, theological reflection on the subject. A second viewpoint is set forth by biblical scholars who seek to formulate a theological framework for understanding spiritual warfare but who lack a deep understanding of the bewildering array of beliefs in spirit realities found in religions around the world. Consequently, it is hard to apply their findings in the specific contexts in which ministry occurs.

We need a way to build bridges between the biblical teaching and the particularity of different cultures. We hold that Scripture is divine revelation and the source of definitive understandings of truth. We take for granted here that Satan and his hosts are very real and that there is a spiritual battle going on. We also affirm that the battle has already been won and that Christ is establishing his reign on earth through his angels, the church, and his followers.

Doing Theology

How can we reflect theologically on spiritual warfare? Before answering this, we need to clarify what we mean by theology. I am assuming here that Scripture is divine revelation given to us by God, not our human search for God. Theology, then, is our attempt to understand that revelation in our historical and cultural contexts (Figure 1). It is important, therefore, that we study Scripture carefully so that our theologies are biblically informed. We must remember, however, that all our theologies are shaped by the times and cultures in which we live. Even the languages we use are shaped by our worldviews. We must remember, too, that there are great gulfs between biblical times and our times, between universal theories and the particulars of everyday life, and between synchronic theologies

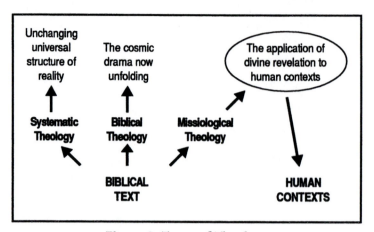

Figure 2: Types of Theology

which examine the unchanging structure of reality and diachronic theologies that study cosmic history. It is important in any theological reflection to work to bridge these differences.

There are several ways to do theology, each of which has its strengths and weaknesses (Figure 2). We will examine some of these types briefly.

Systematic theology

In the West, by theology we traditionally mean systematic theology. This form of theology emerged in the 12th century with the reintroduction of Greek algorithmic logic through the universities of the Middle East and Spain (Finger, 1985, pp. 18-21).[1] At first, systematic theology was seen as the "queen of the science," but over time it became one discipline among others in theological education—alongside biblical exegesis, hermeneutics, history, missions, and other disciplines (Young, 1998, pp. 78-79). The central question systematic theology seeks to an-

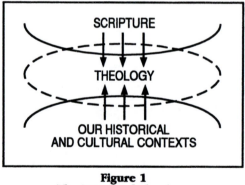

Figure 1
The Nature of Theology

---

[1] Peter Lombard founded systematic theology when he sought to disengage key theological questions from their original biblical contexts and to arrange them in a logical sequence of their own that would provide a comprehensive, coherent, and synthetically consistent account of all the major issues of Christian faith and that would demonstrate the rational credibility of Christian faith (Finger, 1985, p. 19). Lombard's *Scentences*, written in the 1140s, provided the form of much of later Medieval and Reformation theology. For an historical summary of its emergence, see Fuller (1997) and Evans, McGrath, & Galloway (1986, particularly pp. 62-173).

	SYSTEMATIC THEOLOGY	BIBLICAL THEOLOGY	MISSIOLOGICAL THEOLOGY
SOURCE	The Bible is divine revelation.	The Bible is divine revelation.	The Bible is divine revelation.
KEY QUESTION	What are the eternal, unchanging, cosmic realities?	What is the cosmic story?	What does Scripture say to this particular human situation?
METHOD	Abstract analogical logic	Historiography	Precedent teachings and cases
RESULTS	Helps develop the synchronic understandings of a biblical worldview	Helps develop the diachronic understandings of a biblical worldview	Helps develop missional vision and motivation based on a biblical worldview
LIMITATIONS	Difficulty in bridging from: —structure to story —universal to particular —explanation to mystery Not missiological in nature	Difficulty in bridging from: —story to structure —universal to particular Not missiological in nature	Difficulty in bridging from: — today to cosmic structure — now to cosmic time and story

Figure 3: A Comparison of Evangelical Systematic, Biblical, and Missiological Theologies

swer is, "What are the unchanging universals of reality?" It assumes that there are basic, unchanging realities, and if these are known, we can understand the nature of reality (Figure 3). Systematic theology also assumes that truth is non-historical and non-cultural and that it is true for everyone everywhere. This type of theology uses the algorithmic logic and rhetoric of Greek philosophy, which are propositional in nature, rejecting all internal contradictions and fuzziness in categories and thought.[2] Its goal is to construct a single systematic understanding of universal truth that is comprehensive, logically consistent, and conceptually coherent. To arrive at objective truth, systematic theol-

ogy, like the modern sciences, separates cognition from feelings and values, because the latter are thought to introduce subjectivity into the process.

The strength of systematic theology is its examination of the fundamental categories and structure implicit in Scripture. It gives us a standard against which to judge our own beliefs, and it helps us develop a biblical worldview, both of which are essential for any contemporary reflection on spiritual warfare.

Systematic theology also has its limitations. Because it sees ultimate reality in structural, synchronic terms, it cannot adequately deal with change and the cosmic story revealed in Scripture. Because

---

[2] An algorithm is a formal logical process which, if carried out correctly, produces the right answer. Algorithmic logic is sometimes called "machine" logic, because it is the basis upon which calculators and computers work, and calculations can be done faster and more accurately by these instruments than by humans. For an introduction to fuzzy categories and fuzzy logic, see Hiebert (1994, pp. 107-136).

it focuses on universals, it does not tell us how to deal with the particular beliefs and practices found in different cultures.[3] Because it seeks to be exhaustive, it leaves little room for mystery in our understanding of reality. Finally, because it is based on precise algorithmic logic, it has little place for wisdom, ambiguity, or paradox.[4]

Systematic theology plays a vital role in helping us develop a biblical worldview, but it has not been the motivating force driving people and churches into missions.

Biblical theology

A second approach to the study of Scripture is biblical theology (see Figure 3). Reacting to the scholasticism of post-Reformation theologians, Johann Gabler advocated a new way of doing theology. He saw theology as a practical science, and he stressed experience, the illumination of the Spirit, and a return to the study of the Bible as text (Evans, McGrath, & Galloway, 1986, pp. 170-171). His central question was, "What did the biblical passages mean at the time to those writing them, and what lessons can we learn from them for today?"

Biblical theology examines the narrative nature of Scripture. It assumes that the heart of revelation is historical in character—that there is a real world with a real history of change over time, which is "go-

ing somewhere" and which has meaning because it has a beginning, it has a plot, and it culminates in God's eternal reign. Biblical theology argues that this view of truth as cosmic story is fundamental to the Hebrew worldview and to an understanding of Scripture.

Biblical theology uses the methods of historiography. It uses the temporal logic of antecedent and consequent causality, and it accepts teleological explanations in which God and humans act on the basis of intentions. Biblical theology is important, because it gives meaning to life by helping us see the cosmic story in which human history and our own biographies are embedded. It helps us understand the cosmic battle between God and Satan—between righteousness and evil.

But biblical theology also has its limits. It focuses on diachronic meaning, leaving the unchanging structure of reality in our peripheral vision. It focuses on past biblical history, not on present events. It also looks at the universal story, not the particular lives of individuals and communities outside the biblical narrative. Consequently, it does not directly offer us applications of biblical truth to the problems we face in specific cultures and persons today. Biblical theology is important because it too helps us develop a biblical worldview, but like systematic theology,

---

[3] Today non-Western theologians are developing theologies based on other systems of logic. For example, in many African philosophies, meaning is not gained by understanding a logical progression, but by grasping the dynamic relationship of the parts to the whole. Indian philosophies are based on fuzzy sets and fuzzy logic—terms used for precise logic based on non-Cantorian sets.

[4] The discovery of different systems of logic, such as non-Euclidian geometries, non-Cantorian (fuzzy) algebra, and concrete-functional logic, raises the question whether systematic theologies can be constructed on these as well. The problem is not new. Origen and others used allegory, analogy, and other tropological methods in developing their theological frameworks. Tropological methods are essential in studying poetical, wisdom, parabolic, and apocalyptic passages in Scripture. An excessive trust in algorithmic logic also overlooks the fact that all human reasoning is touched by our fallen state and that Paul warns us against putting too much trust in it (1 Cor. 1:20-25).

it has not been the motivating force driving people and churches into missions.

Missiological theology

To deal with the contemporary, particular problems we face in missions, we need a third way of doing theology—a way of thinking biblically about our lives here and now.[5] Martin Kähler wrote almost a century ago that mission is the "mother of theology." Missionaries, by the very nature of their task, must do theological reflection to make the message of Scripture understood and relevant to people in the particularities of their lives. David Bosch (1991, p. 124) notes, "Paul was the first Christian theologian precisely because he was the first Christian missionary."

What is missiological theology? Clearly, it draws on systematic and biblical theologies to understand Scripture, but it must build the bridge that brings these truths into the socio-cultural and historical contexts in which the missionary serves (see Figure 3). Its central question is, "What does God's Word say to humans in this particular situation?" Evangelical mission theologians affirm that the gospel is universal truth for all. They also recognize that all humans live in different historical and socio-cultural settings and that the gospel must be made known to them in the particularity of these contexts. Eugene Peterson (1997, p. 185) writes: "This is the gospel focus: *you* are the man; *you* are the woman. The gospel is never about everybody else; it is always about you, about me. The gospel is never truth in general; it's always a truth in specific. The gospel is never a commentary on ideas or culture or conditions; it's always about actual persons, actual pains, actual troubles, actual sin; you, me; who you are and what you've done; who I am and what I've done." The task of the mission theologian is to communicate and apply the gospel to people living today, so that it transforms them and their cultures into what God wants them to be. Missiological theology seeks to bridge the gulf between biblical revelation given millennia ago and human contexts today.[6]

The method of analysis used in missiological theology is to use the biblical

---

[5] We can also speak of tropological theology. Tropological theology is done in the context of worship and stresses the mystical, sacramental, and iconic nature of truth. The central question is, "How can we comprehend complex, transcendent truths about God and reality that lie beyond words, logic, and human reason?" Theologies of this nature use tropes such as metaphors, types, myths, parables, and icons to communicate transcendent truth, and they are able to deal with the fuzziness and ambiguities of concrete human life. They use the logic of analogy which recognizes that (1) in some ways two entities, A and B, are alike, (2) in some ways A and B are different (areas in which the analogy does not hold), and (3) there are areas in which it is not clear whether there is a similarity or not. It is this area of uncertainty that generates new insights as the mind explores the power and limits of the analogy.

Tropological theology is doxological. It is not an abstract reflection on the nature of truth for the sake of truth itself. It sees theological reflection as an essential element of worship. Christopher Hall (1998, p. 67) writes, "For the [early church] fathers, the Bible was to be studied, pondered, and exegeted within the context of prayer, worship, reverence, and holiness." Tropological theology is also tied to the character of the exegete. For example, among the Russian Orthodox, the spiritual leader must be "knowledgeable in the Holy Scriptures, just, capable of teaching his pupils, full of truly unhypocritical love for all, meek, humble, patient, and free from anger and all other passions—greed, vainglory, glutton... (Oleksa, 1987, p. 14). In other words, one cannot trust a brilliant scholar if he or she is arrogant, unfaithful, impatient, or deceitful.

[6] The process of "critical contextualization" is discussed in more detail in Hiebert (1994, pp. 75-92).

worldview developed through systematic and biblical theologies and to apply the findings through the method of precedent cases, the method used in the British and American legal systems.[7] For example, in dealing with polygamy, mission theologians examine cases of marriage in the Bible, such as Adam, Abraham, and David, and they draw on the instructions given by Moses and Paul to develop biblical principles of marriage. They then study the contemporary case they are addressing and seek to apply the biblical principles to the situation, taking into account the present context and the many principles that may apply to the case.

Missiological theology involves four steps. The first is *phenomenology*—the study of current ministry cases and biblical parallels to find precedents in Scripture. Mission theologians must seek to understand the cultural context as the people they serve understand it.[8] They must also examine their own worldviews—the assumptions and logic which they bring with them—to see how these color their analysis. Here the methods developed by the social sciences to exegete human realities can be of help.

The second step in missiological theology is *ontology*—the examination of both the people's and the theologian's understandings of the particular situation in the light of biblical revelation. This is closely tied to the third step, namely, an *evaluation* of the present situation in the light of biblical teachings and a decision on what should be done.

The final step in missiological theology is *missiology*—helping people move from where they are to where God wants them to be. Missiology recognizes that humans all live in and are shaped by particular cultural and historical contexts, and they can only begin an ongoing process of transformation by starting with their existing systems of thought. We cannot expect people simply to abandon their old ways and adopt new ones. This transformation must also involve whole communities as well as individuals.

Complementarity

Systematic, biblical, and missiological theologies are complementary. Just as an architect makes different blueprints for the same building—structural, electrical, and plumbing—so theologians need to look at reality from different perspectives and through different lenses. We need systematic theology to help us understand the questions, assumptions, categories, and logic found in Scripture regarding the structure of reality. We need biblical theology to help us understand the cosmic story unfolding in Scripture, the "mystery" now revealed to us. We need missiological theology to communicate the transforming gospel into the particular contexts in which humans find themselves.

Human Understandings of Spiritual Warfare

Applying this model of missiological theology to the current debates regarding spiritual warfare, we must begin by examining what the people we serve believe about spirits and spiritual battles. Stories of battles between good and evil and of power encounters between good gods

---

[7] This stands in contrast to the French system of law that examines cases in the light of the Napoleonic Code and not in terms of precedent cases that help to interpret and nuance the application of law in the present setting.

[8] This is referred to as an "emic" analysis. It stands in contrast to "etic" analysis, which uses the categories and logic of the analyst, which are based on a comparative study of many cultures and societies.

and evil demons are found in all religions. In Hinduism, Rama battles Ravana; in Buddhism, Buddha fights Mara; in Islam, Allah wars against Shaitan; and in traditional religions, tribal gods fight one another for conquest. It is not possible here to examine the specific views of spiritual warfare found in the many cultures around the world.[9] That is the task of each missionary as he/she ministers in specific human contexts. Our task, rather, is to examine our own worldviews to see how these shape our reading of Scripture. If we are not aware of our own worldviews, we are in danger of reading the understandings of war and warfare of our culture into Scripture and of distorting its message. We will briefly examine three worldviews underlying the current debate in the West regarding the nature of spiritual warfare, to see how they have shaped this debate.

Modern supernatural/ natural dualism

The worldview of the West has been shaped since the 16th century by the Cartesian dualism that divides the cosmos into two realities—the supernatural world of God, angels, and demons and the natural material world of humans, animals, plants, and matter. This division has led to two views of spiritual warfare. First, as secularism spread, the reality of the supernatural world was denied. In this materialist worldview, the only reality is the natural world, which can best be studied by science. For modern secular people, there is no spiritual warfare because there are no gods, angels, or demons. There is only war in nature between humans, communities, and nations. Some Christians accept this denial of spiritual realities, and they de-

mythologize the Scriptures to make them fit modern secular scientific beliefs. Angels, demons, miracles, and other supernatural realities are explained away in scientific terms. The battle, it is claimed, is between good and evil in human social systems. The church is called to fight against poverty, injustice, oppression, and other evils which are due to oppressive, exploitative human systems of government, business, and religion.

The second view of spiritual warfare emerging out of this dualism is that God, angels, and demons are involved in a cosmic battle in the heavens, but the everyday events on earth are best explained and controlled by science and technology (Figure 4). People pray to God for their salvation, but they turn to modern medicine for healing and to psychology for deliverance from so-called demon possession, because demons, if they exist, exist in the heavens, not on earth. Western missionaries influenced by this dualism deny the realities of witchcraft, spirit possession, evil eye, and magic in the cultures where they serve. Consequently, they fail to provide biblical answers to the people's fears

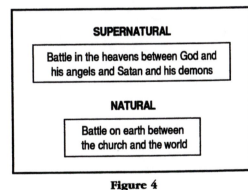

Figure 4
Modern View of Spiritual Warfare

---

[9] For example, in a village in India, missionaries must be aware of the battles of the Hindu gods such as Krishna, Rama, and Narasimha. They must also examine the nature and activities of *raksbasas, dayams, bhutams, ammas, gboshams,* and other earth-bound spirit beings that the people believe inhabit the village, which are not a part of formal Hinduism.

of earthly spirits and powers and fail to deal with the reality of Satan's work on earth.

Tribal religions

For most tribal peoples, ancestors, earthly spirits, witchcraft, and magic are very real. The people see the earth and sky as full of beings (gods, earthly divinities, ancestors, ghosts, evil shades, humans, animals, and nature spirits) that relate, deceive, bully, and battle one another for power and personal gain. These beings are neither totally good nor totally evil. They help those who serve or placate them. They harm those who oppose their wishes or who neglect them or refuse to honor them. Humans must placate them to avoid terrible disasters.

Spiritual warfare in animistic societies is seen as an ongoing battle between different alliances of beings (Figure 5). For the most part, these alliances are based on ethnicity and territory. The battle is not primarily between "good" and "evil," but between "us" and "them." The gods, spirits, ancestors, and people of one village or tribe are in constant battle with those of surrounding villages and tribes. When the men of one group defeat those of another, they attribute their success to the power of their gods and spirits. When they are defeated, they blame this on the weak-

ness of their gods and spirits. We see this worldview in the Old Testament in the way the Arameans viewed their battles with the Israelites (1 Kings 20:23-30).

Land plays an important role in tribal views of spiritual warfare. Gods, spirits, and ancestors reside in specific territories or objects and protect their people who reside on their lands. Their powers do not extend to other areas. When people go on distant trips, they are no longer under the protection of their gods. When a community is defeated, the people are expected to change their allegiance to the stronger god and serve him. Conversions to new gods often follow dramatic power encounters.

Some Christians interpret the biblical data on spiritual warfare using the traditional tribal themes of territory and power encounter (Peretti, 1988; Wagner, 1991). Satan is viewed as having authority over the earth—an authority which he exercises through delegation to his demonic hierarchy. As Chuck Lowe (1998) points out, this view of territorial spirits has little biblical justification. The belief in spirits who rule territories and control people implies that these people are hapless victims of the cosmic battles of the gods and that once they are delivered they will be ready to convert to Christ in mass. This sells human sinfulness short. Even if demons are driven out, humans call them back and renew their individual and corporate rebellion against God. Belief in evil spirits now ruling geographic territories also denies the work of the cross. Whatever delegated authority Satan had at the time of creation was taken away after the resurrection, when Christ declared, "All authority in heaven and on earth has been given to me" (Matt. 28:18). Satan now has no authority over the earth, except the authority given him by his demonic and human followers.

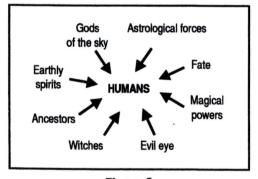

Figure 5
Tribal View of Spiritual Encounters

Cosmic dualism

A third worldview of spiritual warfare is based on a cosmic dualism (Figure 6). This is found in Zoroastrianism, Manicheism, Hinduism, and cultures shaped by the Indo-European worldview, including those in the West. In it, mighty gods battle for control of the universe: one seeking to establish a kingdom of righteousness and order and the other an evil empire. The outcome is uncertain, for both sides are equally strong. Further, the battle is unending, for when either good or evil is defeated, it rises to fight again. All reality is divided into two camps: good gods and bad ones, good nations and evil ones. Ultimately the division is not between cosmic good and evil, for good gods and nations often do evil in order to win the battle, and evil gods and nations do good. The real division is between "our side" and "the enemy." If we win, we can establish the kingdom, and by definition it will be good. If the others win, they will establish what we see as an evil empire.

Central to this worldview is the myth of redemptive violence. Order can be established only when one side defeats the other in spiritual warfare. In other words, violence is necessary to bring about a better society (Larson, 1974; Lincoln, 1986; Puhvel, 1970; Wink, 1992). To win, therefore, is everything. The focus is on the

battle. The myths tell of the battles between the gods and of their effect on humans. Conflicts and competition are intrinsic to the world and lead to evolution (biology), progress (civilization), development (economics), and prowess (sports).

Morality in the Indo-European battle is based on notions of "fairness" and "equal opportunity," not on some moral absolutes. To be fair, the conflict must be between those thought to be more or less equal in might. The outcome must be uncertain. It is "unfair" to pit a professional ball team against a team of amateurs. Equal opportunity means that both sides must be able to use the same means to gain victory. If the evil side uses illegal and wicked means, the good side is justified in using them. In movies, the police officer cannot shoot first. When the criminal draws his gun, however, the police officer can shoot him without a trial. In the end, both the good and the bad sides use violence, deceit, and intimidation to win the battle. In this worldview, chaos is the greatest evil, and violence can be used to restore order.

Indo-European religious beliefs have largely died in the West, but as Walter Wink (1992) points out, the Indo-European worldview continues to dominate modern Western thought. It is the basis for the theories of evolution and capitalism and is the dominant theme in Western entertainment and sports. People pay to see the football battle, and they go home at the end claiming victory or making excuses for the loss. The story ends when the detective unmasks the villain, the cowboys defeat the Indians, Luke Skywalker and Princess Leah thwart the Evil Empire, and Superman destroys the enemies of humankind. Victory in the

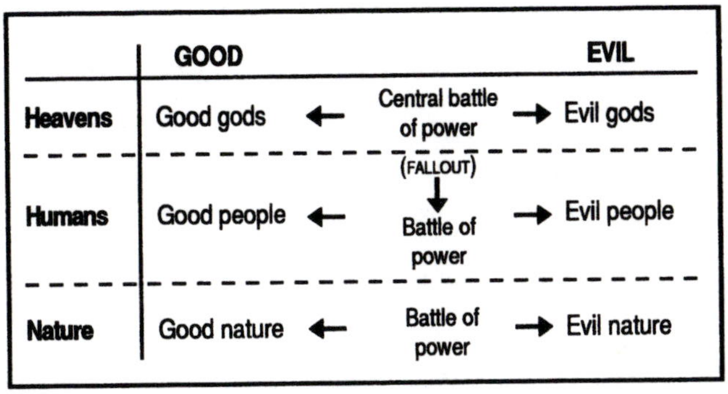

Figure 6
The Myth of Cosmic Dualism

Indo-European myth is never final, however, nor is evil fully defeated. Every week Bluto grabs Olive Oyl. Every week Popeye tries to rescue her. Every week Bluto beats up Popeye. Every week Popeye gets his spinach and defeats Bluto. Bluto never learns to leave Olive Oyl alone. Popeye never learns to take his spinach before he attacks Bluto. Evil always rises again to challenge the good, so good must constantly be on guard against future attacks.

Many current Christian interpretations of spiritual warfare are based on an Indo-European worldview, which sees such warfare as a cosmic battle between God and his angels and Satan and his demons for the control of people and lands. The battle is fought in the heavens, but it ranges over sky and earth. The central question is one of power: Can God defeat Satan? Because the outcome is in doubt, intense prayer is necessary to enable God and his angels to gain victory over the demonic powers. Humans are victims of this struggle. Even those who turn to Christ are subject to bodily attacks by Satan.

Biblical Views of Spiritual Warfare

Warfare is an important metaphor in Scripture, and we must take it seriously. Eugene Peterson (1997, pp. 122-123) writes: "There is a spiritual war in progress, an all-out moral battle. There is evil and cruelty, unhappiness and illness. There is superstition and ignorance, brutality and pain. God is in continuous and energetic battle against all of it. God is for life and against death. God is for love and against hate. God is for hope and against despair. God is for heaven and against hell. There is no neutral ground in the universe. Every square foot of space is contested."

The question is, what is the nature of this battle in biblical terms? One thing is clear: the biblical images of spiritual warfare are radically different from those in the materialistic, dualistic, animistic, and Indo-European myths (Figure 7). For example, in the Old Testament the surrounding nations saw Israel's defeats as evidence that their gods were more powerful, but the Old Testament writers are clear—Israel's defeats are not at the hand of pagan gods, but the judgment of Yahweh for their sins (Judg. 4:1-2; 6:1; 10:7; 1 Sam. 28:17-19; 1 Kings 16:2-3; 2 Kings 17:7-23). Similarly, the battle between God and Satan is not one of power (Job 1:1-12; Judg. 9:23-24). The whole world belongs to God. The gods of the pagans are, in fact, no gods. They are merely human-made images fashioned from wood and stone (Isa. 44–46). Satan is a fallen angel created by God.

In the New Testament, the focus shifts to a more spiritual view of battle. The Gospels clearly demonstrate the existence of demons, or unclean spirits, who oppress people. The exorcists of Jesus' day used techniques such as shoving a smelly root up the possessed person's nose to drive the spirit away or invoking a higher

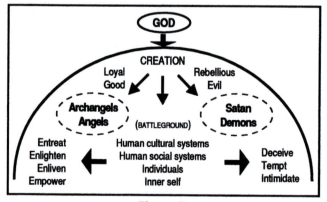

Figure 7
Biblical View of Spiritual Warfare

spirit through magical incantations (Keener, 1993). Jesus, in contrast, simply drove the demons out on the basis of his own authority (Mark 1:21-27; 9:14-29). He was not simply some mighty sorcerer who learned to manipulate the spirits through more powerful magic. He is the sovereign God of the universe exerting his will and authority over Satan and his helpers.

The nature of the battle

The Bible is clear: there is a cosmic battle between God and Satan (Eph. 6:12). There is, however, no doubt about its outcome. The dualism of God and Satan, good and evil, is not eternal and coexistent. In the beginning was God, eternal, righteous, loving, and good. Satan, sin, and sinners appear in creation. Moreover, God's creation is an ongoing process. The very existence of Satan and sinners, and the power they use in their rebellion, is given them by God and is a testimony to his mercy and love. Finally, whatever the battle, it was won at Calvary.

If the cosmic struggle between God and Satan is not one of power, what is it about? It is the establishment of God's reign on earth as it is in heaven. It is for human hearts and godly societies. God in his mercy is inviting sinners to repent and turn to him.

Two parables help us understand the nature of the warfare we face. The first is the parable of the wayward son (Bailey, 1998). The father lavishes his love on his son, but the son rebels and turns against his father. The father is not interested in punishing his son but in winning him back, so the father reaches out in unconditional love. The son wants to provoke the father into hating him, thereby justifying his rebellion, but the father takes all the evil his son heaps on him and continues to love. When the son repents, he is restored back fully into the family (Luke 15:21-24). Similarly, God loves his rebel-

lious creations and longs to save them. If he were to do less, he would be less than perfect love. In this battle for human allegiances, humans are not passive victims. They are active co-conspirators with Satan and his host in rebellion against God, and God urges them to turn to him for salvation.

The second parable concerns the rebellious vassals or stewards (Matt. 21:33-44). At first, the stewards are faithful, and their appointment gives them legitimate authority over part of the kingdom. Later they rebel and persecute the righteous. In Indo-European mythology, the king simply defeats the rebels by might and destroys them. In the biblical worldview, the king first seeks reconciliation, so he sends his servants. When they are mistreated, he sends his son. Even then the king does not remove the rebellious servants arbitrarily. He shows their unfitness to rule by sending his son, who is found guilty and put to death by the servants. The case is appealed to the king, who finds the lower court evil and removes the rebellious servants from power. The central question in Scripture is not power but authority.

The weapons of warfare

Scripture makes it clear that the weapons of spiritual warfare are different for God and for Satan. Satan blinds the minds of humans to the truth through lies and deception. He tempts them with the pleasures of sin by appealing to their old nature. He intimidates them with fear by sending misfortunes. He accuses them of their sins. Above all, he invites them to worship themselves as gods (Gen. 3:1-7; 2 Tim. 3:2). God uses the weapon of truth to enlighten the mind, the weapon of righteousness to combat sin, and the weapon of peace and *shalom* to counter temptation. Above all, he invites all into the kingdom of God, in which Christ reigns in perfect love and justice. Satan and his followers (demonic and human) devise cultures and societies of rebellion that blind human minds. They seek to control those who turn themselves over to the rebellion, to keep sinners from converting, and to cause the saved to fall. Human rebellion is both individual and corporate. God and his followers (angelic and human) create the church as a counter-cultural community where Christ is recognized and worshiped as Lord and where truth, love, and righteousness reign. In the battle, God, his angels, and his saints minister to protect and guide his people (2 Kings 6:17; Gen. 24:7; 31:11-12; Dan. 8:15-16; 9:20-23; Matt. 1:20).

Power encounters

At the heart of much of the current debate regarding spiritual warfare is the concept of "power encounter." Often this is seen in Indo-European terms (Figure 8). Proponents see such encounters as opportunities to demonstrate the might of God through dramatic healings, casting out of demons, and divine protection, and they assume that when people see God's miraculous interventions, they will believe. Scripture and church history show that demonstrations of God's power often lead some to believe, but they also excite the enemy to greater opposition, leading to persecution and death. We see this in the book of Acts, where victories are followed

POWER ENCOUNTERS IN ACTS	
Acts 2:	Pentecost; power of the Holy Spirit; apostles are ridiculed; some believe.
Acts 3:	Peter heals a crippled man; Peter is put in jail; some believe.
Acts 5:	Ananias and Sapphira die from God's judgment; great fear seizes the church. (God judges evil in believers and in the church, as well as the evil of Satan.)
Acts 5:	The apostles heal many; they are put in prison.
Acts 6:	Stephen performs signs and wonders; he is killed; persecution spreads.
Acts 11:	Growth of the church; persecution; death of James.
Acts 13:	Paul confronts Elymas; proconsul believes.
Acts 14:	Paul and Barnabas do signs and wonders; some believe; Paul is stoned.
Acts 16:	Paul and Silas cast out a demon; they are beaten and put in jail.
Acts 17:	Paul preaches the gospel; some scoff; others believe.
Acts 21:	Paul preaches and defends himself; he is jailed and sent to Rome.

Figure 9

by persecution, imprisonment, and death (Figure 9). Above all, we see this pattern in the Gospel of John, where Jesus confronts the religious and political establishments and is crucified (Figure 10). In biblical spiritual warfare, the cross is the ultimate and final victory (1 Cor. 1:18-25). If our understanding of spiritual warfare cannot explain this, we need to reexamine it. On the cross, Satan used his full might to destroy Christ or to provoke him to use his divinity wrongly. Either would have meant defeat for Christ—the first because Satan would have overcome him

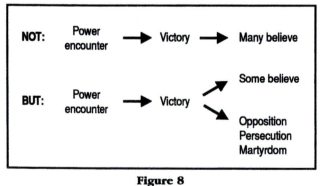

Figure 8
Power Encounters in Scripture

POWER ENCOUNTERS IN JOHN
(Jesus Confronts the Powers
of Jerusalem and Rome)

John 1:	Birth — Jesus' birth as a king challenges Herod and earthly kingdoms.
John 2:	Overturns the tables — Jesus challenges the corrupt religious order which turned the court of evangelism into a marketplace.
John 3:	Nicodemus — Jesus challenges the ignorance of a leader of the religious establishment.
John 4:	Samaritan woman — Jesus violates Jewish religious exclusivism.
John 5:	Heals on the Sabbath — Jesus confronts the legalism of the establishment.
John 6:	Feeds the five thousand — Jesus shows up the failure of the establishment to care for the people.
John 7:	Feast of Booths — Jesus confronts the religious leaders and their unbelief.
John 8:	Preaches — Jesus challenges the merciless interpretation of the law.
John 9:	Heals — Jesus shows the powerlessness of the religious establishment.
John 10:	Confronts the Pharisees — Jesus challenges their teachings.
John 11:	Raises the dead — Jesus shows the powerlessness of the religious leaders.
John 12:	Triumphal entry — Jesus challenges the leaders' understanding of God's kingdom.
John 13—19:	Jewish and Roman leaders conspire and kill Jesus.
John 20—21:	Rises from the dead — Jesus defeats Satan and the political/ religious establishments and establishes his kingdom.

Figure 10

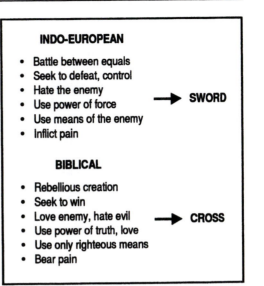

Figure 11
**Indo-European and Biblical
Views of Warfare**

and the second because it would have destroyed God's plan of salvation through the use of unrighteous means.

The cross as victory makes no sense in the Indo-European and tribal worldviews. In the Indo-European worldview (Figure 11), Christ should have taken up the challenge of his tormentors, called down his angelic hosts waiting ready in heaven, and come down from the cross in triumph to establish his kingdom. In Scripture, the cross is the demonstration of victory through weakness. At the cross, Satan stands judged because he put Christ, God incarnate as perfect man, to death. On the cross, Jesus bore the sins of the world and triumphed over all the powers of evil. His obedience unto death was "so that by his death he might destroy him who holds the power of death—that is, the devil" (Heb. 2:14). The cross was Satan's undoing (Col. 2:15), but Satan's defeat was not an end in itself. Rather it removes the obstacles to God's purpose of creating people fit for his kingdom (Gen. 12:1; Ex. 19:3ff; 1 Peter 2:9). The cross is the victory of righteousness over evil, of love over hate, of

God's way over Satan's way. If our understanding of spiritual warfare does not see the cross as the final triumph, it is wrong.

The biblical heroes in spiritual warfare are given in the hall of fame in Hebrews. Some overthrew kingdoms, escaped death by the sword, put whole armies to flight, and received their loved ones back from death (Heb. 11:33-35). Even greater are the victors who were tortured, mocked, whipped, chained, oppressed, mistreated, and martyred (Heb. 11:36-38). They were "too good for this world." In all these cases, victory lies not in defeating the enemy, but in standing firm in faith and bearing witness to Christ, no matter the outcome.

Christians and churches are in desperate need of showing God's power in transformed lives and in a Christlike confrontation of evil wherever they find it, whether demonic, systemic, or personal. Here we face two dangers. On the one hand, we may avoid bold demonstrations of power for fear these may become magic. The church then is poor in the manifestations of God's might. On the other hand, in our zeal to demonstrate God's power, we can run after the sensational and be tempted to use power for our own glory. Neither miracles nor the cross can be taken out of the gospel without distorting it.

The coming kingdom

Finally, a biblical view of spiritual warfare points to the final establishment of the kingdom of God throughout the whole universe. When we focus too much on the current battle, we lose sight of the cosmic picture in which the real story is not the battle, but the eternal reign of Christ. That vision transformed the early church, and it should be our focus in ministry today.

References

Anderson, N. T. (1990). *Victory over the darkness: Realizing the power of your identity in Christ*. Ventura, CA: Regal Books.

Arnold, C. E. (1997). *Three crucial questions about spiritual warfare*. Grand Rapids, MI: Baker Book House.

Bailey, K. E. (1998, October 26). The pursuing father. *Christianity Today, 42*(12), pp. 33-40.

Bosch, D. J. (1991). *Transforming mission: Paradigm shifts in theology of mission*. Maryknoll, NY: Orbis Books.

Evans, G. R., McGrath, A. E., & Galloway, A. D. (1986). *The science of theology*. Grand Rapids, MI: Wm. B. Eerdmans Publishing Co.

Finger, T. N. (1985). *Christian theology: An eschatological approach* (Vol. 1). Scottdale, PA: Herald Press.

Fuller, D. P. (1997). Biblical theology and the analogy of faith. *International Journal of Frontier Missions, 14*, pp. 65-74.

Hall, C. A. (1998, May 18). "Augustine who?" A window on the Greek Christian world. [Book review of *The Bible in Greek Christian antiquity*]. *Christianity Today, 42*(6), pp. 66-67.

Hiebert, P. G. (1994). *Anthropological reflections on missiological issues*. Grand Rapids, MI: Baker Book House.

Keener, C. S. (1993). *The IVP Bible background commentary: New Testament*. Downers Grove, IL: InterVarsity Press.

Kraft, C. H. (1992). *Defeating dark angels: Breaking demonic oppression in the believer's life*. Ann Arbor, MI: Vine Books/ Servant Publications.

Larson, G. J. (Ed.). (1974). *Myth in Indo-European antiquity*. Berkeley, CA: University of California Press.

Lincoln, B. (1986). *Myth, cosmos, and society: Indo-European themes of creation and destruction*. Cambridge, MA: Harvard University Press.

Lowe, C. (1998). *Territorial spirits and world evangelization?* Borough Green, Kent, UK: OMF International.

Moreau, A. S. (1997). *Essentials of spiritual warfare: Equipped to win the battle.* Wheaton, IL: Harold Shaw Publishers.

Oleksa, M. (Ed.). (1987). *Alaskan missionary spirituality.* New York: Paulist Press.

Peretti, F. E. (1988). *This present darkness.* Westchester, IL: Crossway Books.

Peterson, E. H. (1997). *Leap over a wall: Earthy spirituality for everyday Christians.* New York: HarperCollins.

Powlison, D. (1995). *Power encounters: Reclaiming spiritual warfare.* Grand Rapids, MI: Baker Book House.

Puhvel, J. (Ed.) (1970). *Myth and law among the Indo-Europeans: Indo-European comparative mythology.* Berkeley, CA: University of California Press.

Wagner, C. P. (1991). *Engaging the enemy: How to fight and defeat territorial spirits.* Ventura, CA: Regal Books.

Wink, W. (1992). *Engaging the powers: Discernment and resistance in a world of domination.* Minneapolis, MN: Fortress Press.

Young, M. (1998). Theological approaches to some perpetual problems in theological education. *Christian Education Journal,* 2(Spring), pp. 75-87.

Paul Hiebert completed a seminary degree in missions and a doctoral degree in anthropology at the University of Minnesota. He and his wife, Frances, served as missionaries in India with the Mennonite Brethren Church for six years. Paul taught in the Department of Anthropology at Kansas State University and the University of Washington, Seattle, and in the School of Mission at Fuller Theologial Seminary and Trinity Evangelical Divinity School. He has published many books and articles in missions and anthropology, including **Anthropological Insights for Missionaries; Anthropological Reflections on Missiological Issues; Incarnational Ministries** *(church planting in tribal, peasant, and urban societies); and* **Understanding Folk Religions: A Christian Response to Popular Beliefs and Practices** *(deals with the problem of split-level Christianity and folk religions: why do many Christians go to church on Sunday and to the diviner and spiritist on Monday?). Paul and Fran are parents of three adult children.*

12

Rethinking trinitarian missiology

ALAN
ROXBURGH

THIS CHAPTER MUST BEGIN with an acknowledgment that locates the writer. In a post-modern world, we must not assume a position that speaks on behalf of all humanity or all Christian understanding in all places. I write from the perspective of a Western, Canadian, North American Christian whose life is shaped by the context and history of this continent. As Miriam Adeney (see chapter 26) pointed out in her paper presented at the 1999 Iguassu Consultation, this description holds within it a way of seeing and responding to the world that is particular and perspectival. It is neither a neutral nor a universal perspective, though the latter has often been assumed in many mission strategies.

The following discussion comes from my particular perspective. The challenge for the church in North America is missional, as the North American church shows little or no ability to engage its own culture with the gospel. Christopher Coker (1998; cited in *Context*, 1999, p. 3) in his book *Twilight of the West* comments: "The two dominant strands that defined the West, gave it animating vigor and a sense of purpose, were religion and Enlightenment exceptionalism. Both are in tatters." The North American church has to address its own loss of missional identity in this culture. In the words of Canadian theologian Douglas John Hall (1997, p. 1): "... the winding down of a process that was inaugurated in the fourth century ... to the great shift that began to occur in the character of the Christian movement under ... Constantine, there now corresponds a shift of reverse proportions. What was born in that distant century, namely, the imperial church, now comes to an end. That beginning and this ending are the two great social transitions in the course of Christianity in the world."

Commenting on the current state of Christian meaning in North America, sociologists suggest that the place of the church in American society is changing at a rapid pace. They state that the realities of pluralism and privatism have undermined the old religious and cultural control that the church once enjoyed. Three critical elements now characterize religious life in North America: the erosion of a public faith, the polarization of American life, and the heightened religious individualism of our time (see Roof & McKinney, 1987).

As much as anywhere else, the church on the North American continent is in desperate need of a new missional framework, and it must become anchored deeply in a trinitarian theology if it is to be redeemed from its cultural reductionisms. The embracing of technique, success, and functional models of growth has blinded us to our captivity to modern culture. The North American church has too often designed a reductionistic gospel customized for expressive individualists desiring spiritual life *a la carte* (see Guder, 2000). In the words of Harold Bloom (1992), Christianity in America is far more gnostic than anything else. This brief paper addresses issues confronting mission and suggests ways in which the controlling motif of the Trinity might inform our thinking.

Careful Attention As We Engage the Subject

Mission is the people of God giving witness to the reality of God through the church as the sign, foretaste, and presence of the kingdom. Mission must, therefore, be preoccupied with the nature of the One to whom it witnesses. We must speak of, announce, and witness to the God who is revealed as Father, Son, and Spirit. This revelation is only known in and through Jesus Christ. The mission of Jesus, the gospel of Jesus Christ, is the mission of the trinitarian God who is at the heart of Jesus' revelation. Therefore, a trinitarian framework must inform our missiology. This is the distinctive nature of Christian proclamation. This trinitarian basis of missiology is not an abstract doctrine, but the essence of the gospel's witness and power. In a globalized, post-modern context, we urgently need to recover the Trinity as the central interpretive framework for missiology.

Missiology in the West now engages a new, pluralist world of cultures as a result of the transformations that reshaped our world in the 20th century. How does the church's encounter with God as Trinity inform and shape this new context? How does the church respond to the questions of authority and knowledge underlying much of the current ferment around the world? Even within the Christian world, pluralism and post-modernism raise significant questions about the nature of Jesus and the exclusive claims of the gospel.

A current best-seller (Borg & Wright, 1999) features debates on the identity of Jesus. What are the most basic convictions from which Christians respond to this question today? Are there ways of engaging such profoundly missional questions that enable us to question the very principles used to deconstruct Christian belief? Will our theologies of mission (which must involve critical questions of how we know something) remain tied to the methodologies of modern foundationalist objectivism, or can we free ourselves from this Western perspective? What are the options in a post-modern context?

These are critical questions for an emerging missiology. They take us back to the trinitarian nature of God. If God is the three-person Trinity revealed in Jesus Christ, then our methodologies and frameworks must articulate and practice a missiology that corresponds with and is derived from the nature of God known only in and through Jesus Christ.

Perspectives for Trinitarian Missiology: Rooted in Confession

Christians begin with confession. In the language of Augustine, we are those who from faith are seeking understanding. This framework results from the encounter of Jesus Christ with the early disciples. It arises from the formation of a disciple community that witnesses to Jesus as the One sent from God in the fullness of time with the good news of salvation. From this point of beginning, the church is compelled to confess that there is no other God of whom we can speak, except the God revealed in Jesus Christ. The early church fathers were compelled to this confession through their encounters with the Gospels. For Christians there is no other way of confessing the reality of God except as Trinity.

The doctrine of the Trinity is not an abstract dogma created by the church out of some social need to convert pagans or to argue with Greek philosophers. The confession of God as Trinity was a response to the love of the Father, the historical reality of Jesus Christ, and the experience of the Holy Spirit. The early Christians were compelled toward this confession by their encounter with Jesus. It is critical to understand that this revelatory compulsion to understand God as Trinity was utterly central to the ability of the early apologists to engage their contexts. Out of this confession, they created a new basis for understanding how we think about reality. As it was with them, so it will need to be for us today. The genius of the early fathers was precisely their recognition of the God whom Jesus revealed to the world.

The Trinity, so clearly central to Christian self-understanding, is crucial for the church's mission in this new millennium. This may seem both an obvious and a strange way to state the case. After all, the Trinity functions like a bedrock conviction that has guided the church from its beginnings. It is at the heart of Evangelical conviction. No one present at the Iguassu Consultation would waver from this tenet of our faith. We are, in doctrine, if perhaps not in practice, Trinitarians. This we believe, and for this conviction we would die. But the obviousness of it all isn't really all that obvious, nor are its critical missiological implications. Perhaps this accounts for the disjunctive way in which we believe, for that belief is neither informing nor shaping our missiology, as it should.

As the differing formulations of Nicea (325 A.D.) and Chalcedon (451 A.D.) reveal, the doctrine of the Trinity was not immediately obvious to the early church. It did not emerge fully shaped; rather, it had to grow and emerge with its own profile and reality, as the early church fathers struggled with a variety of challenges from within their own community concerning the nature of Jesus. It must have been a fascinating, familiar discussion! The Council of Nicea was focused almost entirely on the Christological framework of Christian meaning. The two-person nature of Christ in both the incarnation and the form of God was a huge intellectual battle to be engaged by the early fathers against heresies that reduced the revelation of God into Greek thought categories.

This is an important point to make. One of the crucial struggles in this period was over the basis for knowing—in other words, epistemology. The question of the two natures of Jesus had to be addressed in the context of a Greek framework whose commitment to an unmoved, universal Idea could not tolerate a notion like the incarnation. The debate was, again, not that of academics abstractly defining the nature of Jesus in a context removed from the missional realities of their setting. It was a vigorous struggle to articulate the meaning of the incarnation in the midst of a potent, pluralist, philosophical and religious culture. It was the categories of this philosophical culture that were coming to be seen as the normative way of interpreting the incarnation from within the church.

Beneath these debates were basic questions about God's nature, the meaning of Christian witness, the nature of the world, and the intention of salvation. A response to the last three was dependent on the first. These were missional debates that have important lessons for us as we engage a post-modern world with the gospel.

By the time of Chalcedon (451 A.D.), the focus of debate had shifted. There is now a far stronger and more extended statement of God's trinitarian nature. What we, quite properly, take to be a non-negotiable foundation of the church was being discerned and unfolded. The church was being compelled to understand the nature of God as trinitarian through its encounter with Jesus Christ and its engagement with the currents of religious and philosophical perspectives. In its encounters with diverse cultural and philosophical perspectives, each claiming the ascendant interpretive position in the world, the church engaged this context by working through the fuller implications of the incarnation for the meaning of God's nature. These men resisted allowing the revelation of Jesus to be placed within the categories of the world of ideas that surrounded them. The key to this process lay in their articulation of God revealed in Jesus as Trinity. What the early fathers accomplished was to articulate a new basis for knowing and interpreting the meaning of the world.

The Trinity was this new basis, and it had profound implications for the communication of the gospel.

This is precisely the challenge with which a missiology for a new millennium is confronted today. The source of our response can be no different from that of the early fathers. There was now a different starting point from which to read the world. This trinitarian starting point was critical for the missional energy that lay behind the expansion of the early church. Lesslie Newbigin (1995, pp. 25-27) has described with great eloquence the worldview against which the early fathers had to struggle: "Within such a worldview there is room for, and in fact necessity for, a whole range of intermediate entities to bridge the gap between the pure being, which is essentially unknowable and unapproachable, and the ordinary world of things and events.... The story of the first three centuries of the Christian era furnishes a rich variety of variations on these themes. What they have in common is that they leave intact the classical thought-world. They leave unhealed its dichotomies. Above all they leave it with a God finally uninvolved in human history ... new way of understanding was embodied in the doctrine of the Trinity ... it became a new way of making sense of the world."

Unfortunately, in many ways, in part resulting from our amnesia about church history, our contemporary missiological encounters in our globalized, post-modern world have lost the powerful trinitarian framing of the early fathers with Scripture and Jesus Christ.

A Focal Basis in the Early Fathers

In the pressing questions that the church must address in a globalized world about how we know anything at all and about the nature of reality, the trinitarian affirmation is the starting point for a new missiology.

As indicated, the doctrine of the Trinity was something the early church was compelled to confess out of their encounter with Jesus Christ. The church emerged from a Jewish context in which God is One. Further, in the Greek world of the first century, Platonizing influences emphasized the fundamental unity and oneness of all things through an ascending hierarchy of being. It was not natural for the notion of the Trinity to emerge as a readily acceptable category of meaning. But the doctrine was not developed simply as a philosophical argument. It emerged from the church's own encounter with Jesus Christ as its Lord. Christology compels the doctrine of the Trinity on the church.

For the early Christians, Jesus was the hinge around which all of reality was now to be understood and interpreted. Jesus was the basis of both describing reality and explaining how we know. Questions about the fundamental nature of reality, the meaning of human life, the purpose of the world, and how we know anything at all were no longer decided on the basis of speculative theology or philosophy but by the revelation of Jesus Christ. At the heart of that revelation is the communication of God's nature and, therefore, of the nature of reality. If it was the case that God had, finally and completely, been revealed in Jesus (see John 1:1-14, Philippians 2, and 1 John 1), then questions about the meaning of reality and our source of knowledge are determined by this revelation of God's nature. All other explanations and philosophies are relativized. As the doctrine of the Trinity was impressed upon the church, the church came to recognize a fundamentally new basis for knowing that was distinct from that of either the Greek or Hebrew world. The Trinity became the hinge through which to engage the missional challenges of their time.

Church fathers like Athanasius and the Cappadocians engaged the most creative minds of the ancient world. They were forced to confront the most fundamental questions about the meaning, purpose, and direction of the cosmos. How they responded was critical to the future direction of the gospel. Again, the Trinity was foundational to their mission.

What were the questions that had to be dealt with in these early centuries of the church's life, as the church encountered a sophisticated Greek and Roman world outside the womb of Palestine? There were questions on the nature of being: What actually comprised reality? Where was a notion of God within that worldview? Also, what is the nature of the meaning of the cosmos? Is there really a distinction between the cosmos and the notion of a creator, or are they essentially one and the same?

Trinitarian Missiology in a New Millennium

These questions may sound distant and abstract to us. But they are as alive today as they were in the second and third centuries of the Christian era. From modern developments in physics, biology, and cosmology through to the re-emergence of spiritualities from both the East and the more ancient West, the same questions about the nature of the cosmos and the meaning of God are back on the front page of engagement. A trinitarian missiology is foundational to engaging the cultures of a pluralized, post-modern world.

A new set of challenges also confronts mission, and not only in the West, with the emergence of a post-modern world and the end of an imperial Christianity. We must not simply engage these movements on their own terms. This is what happened to so much of modern apologetics, as they were reshaped into the categories of modernity. We must approach our world from the new starting point in Jesus Christ. We are a community formed by a particular story and context of worship and life. If we engage our world from this other perspective, we shall find ourselves asking different questions to the pluralized world of post-modernity.

Our starting point is the question of who is the God who has entered into relationship with us through Jesus Christ. Note the meaning of this question. We do not automatically assume that we know the answer. We must not assume that this question has been answered and that we can go directly on to proclaim and deal with Jesus Christ. This would fail to engage the radicality of the revelation of God's nature. If we assume we have worked out the questions of God's nature, we will move quickly to strategic questions of how to bring the message of Jesus into the new post-modern, pluralist context. Most of us in the West are unconsciously shaped by the views of the Enlightenment. (To varying degrees, this includes most of the international Christian scholars who have studied in European or North American educational institutions, whether Christian or secular.) Our understanding of Jesus and of the gospel is deeply entwined with modernity. While we might embrace a personal Jesus, we are also shaped by a world of an abstractionist God, the autonomous self, the disembodied soul, and a created world that is essentially a secondary, non-essential holding place that will pass away. We cannot ask the question of the gospel of Jesus Christ for our time without returning to the prior and more fundamental question about the God who has entered into relationship with us in and through Jesus Christ.

The question of God's nature is foundational to the related questions of how we know anything is true. Newbigin's earlier observations are critical. The early church fathers developed their confession of God as Trinity into a new way of understanding all of reality and the nature of truth. Reality could no longer be understood as a "timeless, passionless monad beyond all human knowing, but as a trinity of Father, Son, and Spirit ... it becomes the basis of a new way of understanding the world" (Newbigin, 1995, p. 26).

What would it mean today for Evangelical missiology to engage this new post-modern context from a similar starting point? How would this starting point inform our theologies of creation and redemption? In what ways would the interpenetrating dynamic of God's relationality affect our notions of the kingdom of God and the eschatological future that has come in Jesus Christ through the Holy Spirit? Some of the most basic challenges confronting a gospel-shaped encounter with a post-modern world and its diverse cultures emerge as we articulate our own understanding of what it means to know. We cannot afford to engage these issues on a field of discourse already set out by those now writing their post-modern agenda in our newly globalized world. We must recover the fundamental revelation of the trinitarian God in Jesus Christ.

If Christians now know the world through their faith in Jesus Christ, then they also know it as the material world that has been created and is being redeemed by God the Father, God the Son, and God the Spirit. Questions about the nature of ultimate reality and human life are at the core of the human quest for meaning around the globe today. They lie at the basis of the massive changes and shifts reframing our period of history. Unless we understand what is at stake in these questions and how to respond to them as Christians, our missiologies will fail to penetrate in transformative and redeeming ways into the core issues of our time. These are not frustrating, academic, abstract questions that interfere with the "pure" and "simple" gospel. They are the foundations for any faithful engagement of the gospel with the world in which we live.

There is another side to this conviction. While trinitarian confession seems obvious and we are deeply committed to an Evangelical faith in God as three persons, the Trinity is generally relegated to the level of a theological doctrine. It is left to the realm of academic theologians to explain rather than seen as an essential shaper of an Evangelical missiology. For too many of us, the Trinity is a dense, complex, theological conundrum best left to the few who can make sense of its meaning. It's not that we disbelieve the Trinity. On the contrary, it is an essential confession. But beyond confession, it has little bearing on our missiology except as a concept that needs to be explained and defended. There are reasons for this. Explanations of God's threeness feel so dense and complex that they escape ordinary Christians.

Operating out of categories that belong more to the Greeks and especially to the Platonists, Evangelicals are often still guided by frameworks in Western thought which hold that the fundamental basis of all reality is monadic—singular in nature and form. This is not simply a Platonic influence. It has remained one of the core beliefs of modernity. Contemporary Evangelicalism was formed in the womb of this modernity. The idea of God as Trinity is, therefore, viewed as one of those difficult conundrums. It doesn't fit easily into our monadic, singular worldview. How does one explain the three modes of God in ways that make sense within a logic that defines the basis of all being as singular-

ity? This is one of the sticking points in mission to Islamic peoples. That God, first and foremost, is One seems to be the correct, normative way of understanding the basis of reality. This notion of oneness is our starting point. We have been trained to think in a world of universals and objective singularities. The problem is to make a trinitarian understanding fit this perspective of singularity.

In Western culture, the mathematical sense of singularity functions as the dominant metaphor explaining the meaning of God's oneness. Alongside this is the neo-Platonic philosophy of an ascending order of reality in which all the plurality of the cosmos finds completion in a singular whole. These views influence the frameworks Christians use to think about God. Within these mathematical and Platonic metaphors, it is difficult to reconcile, in any rational manner, the meaning of God as Trinity. Consequently, most Christians begin with an understanding of God as One and then seek alternating images and metaphors to make sense of the three within the oneness.

This becomes such a process of descriptive abstraction that trinitarian thinking is, consequently, left in the realm of the abstract and is perceived to have little practical or functional application for the outworking of ecclesiology or missiology. This illustrates how central Christian convictions get filtered through frameworks that transform their meaning. Missiology must rethink these frameworks through a fresh engagement with the doctrine of the Trinity.

Calling Forth the Trinity in Missiology

The neglect of the Trinity has had profound effects on our missiologies. There are several implications of how this absence of a trinitarian center shapes our missiologies, making it difficult to see how we might appropriately encounter our world with the gospel.

In the West, mission theology has tended to locate the meaning of reconciliation and salvation within a relatively narrow framework. The locus of God's activity is seen as primarily that of the individual person. It is a prevalent Evangelical view that the central mission God has given to the church is the salvation of individual souls. This perspective moved through Pietism in Europe into contemporary evangelism. It is a retreat from the full sense of community and relationality of God's salvation in Jesus Christ.

Further, following early Platonic reshaping of Christian understanding, an almost gnostic division has developed in Evangelical thinking and in missiology. This is seen as we juxtapose the existence of a spiritual reality in the world that is essential and eternal over against the physical reality that is secondary and passing. The physical and material are perceived as of relatively small importance in the scheme of salvation and reconciliation. These two forces—the gnostic and the individualistic—are alien to the revelation of God in Jesus Christ. The gospel's meaning has tended toward a primary focus on the individual, spiritual soul.

This fact suggests the extent to which we have ceased to engage the gospel and, hence, our missiology from the perspective of the Trinity. The Trinity speaks of a quite different understanding of human life from that of the autonomous individual. For God, to be means to be in communion, in relationship. This communion-relationship is the most basic fact about reality, because creation has come from the Trinity. For the creation to be healed, for salvation to come into the world that God so loved, creation must be drawn back into communion across all its systems. All its distinct and separate

agencies and parts (samples of more Newtonian, modern language) are to be drawn into relationship out of their separateness. Relationship is far more than contracts and covenants defining what we do or do not participate in together.

In our own time, the closest image for understanding the communion of God is that of systems theory. Here the rich network of the world and its organisms interpenetrate each other even while having separate identities. So much of the 20th century was an unfolding of these discoveries in physics and biology. We have come to understand the deep levels of connectivity within all creation. Surely this reflects our creator, redeemer, and sustainer God! In the revelation of the Trinity, we are given, as Christian witness, the key to articulating and reflecting the glory of God in the world. A missiology for the new millennium is one that must recognize that creation is not comprised of material things, in the modern sense of *nature*. Human beings are not, fundamentally, unconnected individual *souls*. We are all, human and nonhuman, part of the vast web of life—an interrelated communion. The gospel message must be addressed into this emerging understanding of our globalized world, but we must do this from the basis of our own confession of faith: our encounter with the God of Jesus Christ, who is Trinity. The Western-based church has lived for so many centuries in an abstractionist, objectivist worldview. Now one of our greatest challenges in the years ahead is to discover again a way of thinking that allowed the early church fathers to engage their cultures with the gospel. And this way of thinking was profoundly trinitarian.

The social nature of the Trinity opens for us a perspective of human life radically at odds with the social forms of life and church that emerged in modernity. The ideas of the kingdom of God and the people of God take on very different social forms when they are read from the perspective of the Trinity. If missiology is about our contextual witness to the revelation of this God in Jesus, then the old Evangelical dichotomies and battles between personal salvation and social action are deconstructed. They are seen for what they actually are—reductionistic expressions of a gospel below the true gospel, that miss the profoundly social nature of the God who enters and redeems all of creation. The biblical imagery of the table, especially at the Last Supper and at the Great Feast in Revelation, underlines this foundational gospel reality.

We must address this unbalanced focus on the individual, spiritual soul as the essence of the gospel's focus. It reflects how we have continued to view fundamental reality through the mathematical categories of singularity. The excessive focus on the singular, the one, is reflected in the way that missions tend to direct their primary focus to the salvation of the discrete, autonomous individual. These comments are not meant to deny the fact that in biblical revelation God is clearly at work in Christ to save and reconcile persons. Persons are incredibly important to God. This is not the dispute. The point is that this perspective, understanding the person in terms of the individual, has become the central locus of our modern gospel. Our missiology reveals our failure to develop a communal missiology from a trinitarian foundation.

This tendency continues to see activities like caring for the social and material needs of others or concern for the state of the earth as secondary elements that aid the primary task of saving individual souls and reconciling individuals to God. This form of modernity Christianity cannot be sustained in the days ahead. It is not simply because the human community is rapidly coming to see the empti-

ness of this way of thinking. More importantly, it is so deeply antithetical to the trinitarian God who has been revealed to us in Jesus Christ. If a trinitarian theology of mission is allowed to become the generative center for our conversation, then Evangelical missiology would be helped immensely in these difficult conversations that divide and create suspicions across the global church family.

Drawing to a Close

The Trinity compels us to confess that God is actually made flesh in Jesus the Son. God is involved in history. Therefore, this material and physical and historical world is not just a pale reflection of some universal essence beyond time. It is a part of God's great salvation and eschatological future. Consequently, a whole new vision of the world has been opened before us. It was to such a vision that the historic living and preaching of the gospel drew the poor, the widow, the dying, and the outcast. Salvation was far more than the evacuation of souls from this planet or their escape from hell. The new social reality of God's kingdom and the language of a new creation proclaimed that a new world had begun. So much of our Evangelicalism and its ecclesiologies have managed to turn this all upside down by recreating the very dichotomies the early church was compelled to deny because God is Trinity. The dichotomies between the sensible and intelligible, the material and spiritual, the particular and the relational can be healed with this new vision. The confession of God as Trinity is good news to be heralded in a post-modern world that has increasingly had enough of how these very dichotomies have embedded themselves into the economic, social, and political systems of modernity.

Through the Father and the Son, the creation has been re-established on a whole new basis. Through the Spirit, human beings are invited to participate in the new creation as sons and daughters through faith in Christ. The relational interpenetration of the cosmos means that through the revelation of the new community, the rest of creation waits, groaning as in the labors of childbirth, for the final revelation of what is promised in Ephesians 1:9-10 for the bringing together again of the whole creation.

Only through the empowering presence of the trinitarian God can the barriers of race, gender, ethnicity, and human/nonhuman in creation break down. And this is happening! It is the Spirit who brings us into this new social reality of the church, the *ecclesia* of Jesus, the Son. As members of this eschatological society, we become the Father's priests in and between the trinitarian God and all the rest of creation. It is this Spirit who now impels the called-out people of God into a broken cosmos to live as incarnated witnesses. By its life as a new society, the church proclaims that the life of the world resides in the love of God the Father, the grace of God made incarnate in Christ the Son, and the indwelling power of the Holy Spirit. We can only imagine the power of such an incarnational proclamation and lifestyle in cultures and religious systems where the communal/familial/clan structure is natural and all-inclusive. It is no wonder that our personalized and reduced gospel has had such little effect in the world.

This trinitarian missiology becomes a radically missional assertion of faith based upon the revelation of God in Jesus Christ. May God grant us the joy of seeing some of its implications worked out in the true-life situations of our broken world. And all of this is to the glorious praise of our God. Maranatha!

References

Bloom, H. (1992). *The American religion: The emergence of the post-Christian nation.* New York: Simon & Schuster.

Borg, M. J., & Wright, N. T. (1999). *The meaning of Jesus: Two visions.* San Francisco: HarperSanFrancisco.

Coker, C. (1998). *Twilight of the West.* Boulder, CO: Westview Press.

Context. (1999, February 15). (Available from Claretian Publications, 205 West Monroe Street, Chicago, IL 60606).

Guder, D. (2000). *The continuing conversion of the church.* Grand Rapids, MI: Wm. B. Eerdmans Publishing Co.

Hall, D. J. (1997). *The end of Christendom and the future of Christianity.* Valley Forge, PA: Trinity International Press.

Newbigin, L. (1995). *The open secret: An introduction to the theology of mission.* Grand Rapids, MI: Wm. B. Eerdmans Publishing Co.

Roof, W. C., & McKinney, W. (1987). *American mainline religion: Its changing shape and future.* New Brunswick, NJ: Rutgers University Press.

Alan Roxburgh was born and grew up in Liverpool, England. He emigrated to Canada as a young man, where he now lives in Vancouver with his wife, Jane. They have three grown children. Alan has earned graduate degrees from the Toronto School of Theology, McMaster Divinity College, and Northern Baptist Theological Seminary. He is ordained Baptist and has pastored and planted churches in Canada. He has taught full time in seminary and directed an urban training program. Alan is a Coordinator of the Gospel and Our Culture Network and a member of the writing team which produced Missional Church: A Vision for the Sending of the Church in North America. He has authored three other books dealing with the mission of the church in North America. Alan currently works as a consultant with the Precept Group in Costa Mesa, California.

Part 3

Grounding our reflections in Scripture: biblical trinitarianism and mission

AS FURTHER DEVELOPED elsewhere in this book, trinitarian missiology has at least a triple focus. Perhaps the best known alternative is the exegetical, theological, and missiological study that identifies the specific role in mission played by each Person of the Trinity. Each member has a distinct and yet overlapping role in creating, revealing, and redeeming.

A second dimension looks at the Trinity in the context of community. The Trinity is our primal first community, an eternal one, self-revealing in creation, history, and the life of the church. In this light, new questions would emerge. For example, what is the communal role of the Trinity in creating, revealing, redeeming, and building communities of faith? In what ways do the three Persons operate together and not separately? What does it mean that each member of the Three in One cedes to, honours, and enhances the others, releasing each other to his specific role in divine realities?

The missiological implications of this second approach challenge much of current church life and mission. In what ways has our Christian concept of community come primarily from pragmatic human organizational models? In what way would this trinitarian communal model impact our pre-

sentation and living out of the gospel, with the epic Story centered in the shared values of divine community?

The invitation to Fernando was to present his exegetical work in a way that identifies the unique contribution of Father, Son, and Spirit to mission, and then the church as the trinitarian community. We therefore experienced the result of careful exegesis over 11 months of study, presented by a colleague from the Two-Thirds World, inviting us into his personal study, and pointing us in the direction of further understanding and application. Fernando's study of God was rooted in the Pauline corpus; that of Christ in the Gospels and Epistles; the Holy Spirit material came primarily from the Epistles but also dipped into the Gospels and Acts; the church study was rooted in the teaching of Jesus and Paul.

But additional themes emerged from Fernando's foundational messages: servanthood, suffering, martyrdom, and holiness. These concerns resonated with convicting power, and they shaped the Consultation participants through the empowering presence of the Spirit.

13

God: the source, the originator, and the end of mission

DURING THE 20TH CENTURY, there have been many different emphases in the church's attempt to define its mission. Usually each emphasis has focussed on some important aspects of the calling of the church, and often other important aspects have been neglected as a result. If we were to look at mission from a trinitarian basis, many of the pitfalls of these earlier formulations on mission could be avoided. A trinitarian viewpoint helps us to capture some of the richness of the nature of the Godhead. Through that, we can see some of the richness of the way God works through the church. The last study in this series will present the church as the mirror of the Trinity.

The Approach Adopted in These Studies

These studies began out of a concern for the churches in nations like Sri Lanka, where there has been significant growth through the conversion of non-Christians but where the quality of the Christian life among the converts leaves much to be desired. We are seeing serious integrity problems and frequent divisions that give evidence of much that is lacking in our churches. I have been asking the question whether there is something that is lacking in our preaching and teaching that may be contributing to the lack of growth in godliness among our people. The invitation to give four Bible studies on a biblical trinitarianism and mission at the WEF Missiological Consultation afforded me with a good opportunity to pursue this question.

Over a period of about 11 months, I went through all of Paul's Epistles and listed what he taught on God the Father, on some aspects of the life and work of Jesus, on the Holy Spirit, on the church, and on godly living. Thereafter I subdivided these references (except those on godliness, which

AJITH
FERNANDO

will be done at a later time) according to topics and subtopics. I ended up with about 2,975 entries covering 72 topics and 431 subtopics. The present four Bible studies will glean some of the fruit of that study of Paul's Epistles. It would help the reader to know that Paul's Epistles cover a total of 2,005 verses.

The aim of my study was to look for trends and emphases in Paul's writings. The statistics were compiled to look for the recurrence of themes. My assumption was that if a theme recurs many times, it could be important to Paul. This is not, of course, an infallible guide to levels of importance of the themes covered. But such a study does, I believe, have some limited value, in helping us get a feel of what Paul thought about God and what he wanted the church to think about God.

So our purpose is not to develop accurate statistics of the occurrence of themes. In fact, this is not a systematic study of Paul's theology. I wanted to see trends and emphases by looking at the frequency of their occurrence. The figures given in these studies are based on my reading and observation. They are obviously fallible, because I may have missed some references to a topic and even perhaps missed some topics too. Sometimes, as in this study, I have gone beyond Paul's Epistles as was considered significant for the particular study. These studies may lack the enrichment that comes from frequent references to other missiological works. But they have the advantage of discovering missiological emphases directly from Scripture, without being coloured by the opinions of what others regard as being important emphases.

God as Source, Originator, and End

When we think of God the Father and mission, the theme that emerges is that he is the source, the originator, and the end of all things, including mission. His will determines the creation of the world, the revelation of truth to humanity, the nature of the gospel, the course of history, and the election of individuals to salvation. He prescribes the way in which saved individuals are to live. It is he who in love initiates a relationship with us and comes after us wooing us until we respond to him. He will wrap up history so that in the end he will be "all in all" (1 Cor. 15:28). In this study, we examine how God is presented in the evangelism and teaching of the early church, and we explore the implication of that to the church today.

Acts: God in the Evangelism of the Early Church

To look at the way God is presented in the evangelism of the church, we will need to go to the book of Acts.

Attraction through power

The first thing we see is that a primary means used to attract people to the gospel was the power of God.

• In Acts 2, God sends the Spirit to give the disciples miraculous utterance and to arouse the people's attention, resulting in the preaching of the gospel.

• In chapter 3, God heals a lame man with the same result.

• In chapter 4, the praying church is comforted (just after evangelism has been outlawed) by the shaking of the place where they were gathered.

• In chapter 5, God strikes Ananias and Sapphira down, and fear of God spreads within and without the church.

• In chapter 6, God gives Stephen the power to perform mighty miracles and thus opens the door for his eloquent apologetic ministry.

- In chapter 7, Stephen is given a vision of the exalted Lord as he faces death by stoning.
- In chapter 8, the Samaritans are open to the gospel through Philip's ministry in the miraculous.
- In chapter 9, through a vision, God arrests the man who was on his way to Damascus to arrest Christian believers.
- In chapter 10, God opens the door to Gentile evangelism through visions to Cornelius the Gentile and Peter the apostle to the Jews.
- In chapter 11, the occurrence of the miraculous phenomena of the Holy Spirit in Cornelius' home is presented as evidence that God has granted salvation to Gentiles.
- In chapter 12, God gives comfort and strength to the church through Peter's miraculous escape from prison and the miraculous judgement resulting in Herod's death.
- In chapter 13, the sorcerer Elymas is struck blind, and when the proconsul Sergius Paulus "saw what had happened, he believed, for he was amazed at the teaching about the Lord" (v. 12).
- In chapter 14, the people of Lystra pay attention to the message after a lame man walks for the first time in his life.

These examples show that an important, God-appointed way to arouse people is to give them a demonstration of God's power. And this has been a most effective means of arresting unreached people in the exciting growth of the church in the second half of the 20th century. Fear is a dominant emotion determining the actions of people in both poorer and richer countries. The poor live in terror of poverty and demonic forces. The rich live in terror of economic reversals and the harsh realities of the hostile business environment that has evolved, with its fierce competition and lack of commitment to the welfare of individuals. To both the rich and the poor, then, the power of God is a vitally relevant truth to drive home.

Previously the Evangelical Movement, possibly influenced by the rational bent of the modern era, focussed so much on the content of the gospel in terms of the atoning work of Christ that it may have ignored this aspect of the power of the gospel. This was clearly an inadequate presentation of the gospel. When the Charismatic Movement burst into the scene in the 20th century, that situation changed quite dramatically.

The evangelistic message

When we look at the evangelistic preaching of the early church, however, another picture of God emerges. What we see is a God who is fuller and greater than one who simply responds to individual situations with a display of power. Interestingly, there isn't much about God's love—though that figures a lot in our preaching. The fuller picture of God is a persistent theme in the Epistles, and I believe that we can use it in evangelism, as it is an essential feature of the gospel and as it is (like miracles) an effective means of winning the attention of unbelievers.

The fuller picture of God emerges especially in the emphasis on the sovereignty of God in the speeches of Acts. God's sovereignty over history recurs often in these speeches. Special attention is given to proclaiming God's sovereignty in the death of Christ and in the raising of Christ from the dead. Five purely evangelistic speeches in Acts are given to Jews and God-fearers.[1] Of these five, four contain references to

[1] Two were given in Jerusalem (Acts 2 and 3), one in Antioch of Pisidia (Acts 13), and one each to the Ethiopian eunuch (Acts 8) and those assembled at Cornelius' house (Acts 10). We are not including the legal defences of Paul and Stephen here.

the fact that the death of Christ was a fulfilment of God's purpose or of prophecy (2:23; 3:18; 8:32-35; 13:27, 29). Four of these and the only full message to a purely Gentile audience (in Athens) mention that God raised Jesus from the dead (2:24; 3:15; 10:40; 17:31). Three times it is stated that the resurrection or reign of Christ was predicted in prophecy (2:25-31; 3:21-26; 13:32-37).

God's sovereignty in Israel's history is presented twice when Jews are being addressed (3:22-25; 13:14-42). In both messages to Gentile audiences (in Lystra and Athens), God is presented as the sovereign creator and Lord of the universe and of history (14:15-17; 17:24-27). The coming judgement by God or Christ is also proclaimed in five of the seven evangelistic messages of Acts (2:40; 3:23; 10:42; 13:40-41; 17:31).

The sovereignty of God is presented in various other ways too: for example, in the election of Jesus (2:34), the appointing and sending of Jesus (3:20, 26), and the call to audiences to repent, which appears in four talks (2:38; 3:19, 26; 14:15; 17:30). The last of these references is an all-inclusive command to "all people everywhere to repent" (17:30). In his two evangelistic talks to purely Gentile audiences, Paul attempts to give a full introduction to who God is (14:15-17; 17:23-31).

All these references show that though the thing that attracted people to listen to the message was the demonstration of power in a personal and individual way, when the apostles proclaimed the gospel they gave a much fuller picture of who God is. When I was working on a commentary of Acts a few years ago, one of the things that struck me forcefully was the fact that in Acts the three great miracle workers—Peter, Stephen, and Paul—were also great apologists. Though they performed many miracles, their message was primarily not about miracles. It was about the enduring truths of God and the gospel. It is very rarely that we see this combination in today's evangelism, where the emphasis is often on the temporal blessings which God gives us.

God in the Teaching of Paul's Epistles

We will turn to Paul's Epistles to see how God is presented in the teaching of the early church. My study of God in Paul's Epistles dealt with about 600 references to God,[2] which yielded almost 1,000 entries in my topical listing. Here I took into consideration all the references to "God" or to the "Father," and other references that clearly imply that the Father was being referred to. A limitation of such a study is that I may have left out some references to God which may not specifically mention God. The huge picture of God that emerges from Paul's references to him is that of his greatness. Let's look at some of the statistics I found:

He is sovereign

There are nine references to God as living and eternal, covering 11 verses. Seven references covering nine verses present him as the only God. 3/4 [3] state that he is the ultimate reality. In 3/3 he is said to be beyond our comprehension. 15/19 refer to God as the creator, sustainer, and end of creation. 15/20 affirm that God is sovereign over history, and this truth implies some other truths.

---

[2] Leon Morris (1986, p. 25) puts the figure at 548 in Paul, out of 1,314 references to God in the New Testament.

[3] In these studies, the figures like 3/4 present first the number of references to a theme (three here) and secondly the number of verses covered by those references (four here).

He is glorious

The glory of God is a very important theme, appearing 65 times covering 87 verses. 45/60 of these state that God deserves to be praised, glorified, and/or thanked. 8/10 state that the honour of his name must be shared and upheld and will be upheld in the end.

He is righteous

The wrath and/or judgement of God is another major theme, appearing 67 times and covering 86 verses. Paul also has 28 references to the righteousness of God covering 29 verses.

He is the source of revelation and salvation

There is a pronounced emphasis on God being the originator and source of revelation and the gospel (77/92). Of these, in 20/22 the gospel is the wisdom, mystery, or word of God. In 28/33 God is the cause of the gospel events, which encompass Christ's life and work. In 13/13 the gospel and salvation work through God's power. In 8/10 God is the one who acts to bring people to himself.

Salvation is God's gift

Not only is God the source of salvation; salvation is his gift (116/137). Of these, in 4/5 God is described as our Saviour. 5/6 speak of God's patience and forbearance. 33/40 deal with the election and call of God to salvation. 11/14 state that salvation is a result of mercy. In 23/26 salvation is a result of grace. In 5/6 salvation is a result of love or kindness. In 16/19 God imputes righteousness and justifies us. In 8/9 as a result of salvation, we are accepted by God and have peace with him.

God has a will for our lives

Often Paul says that, as the sovereign God, God has a will for our lives (31/33). Yet when we think of God's will, we usually think of it for things like daily guidance and decisions we have to make. These are indeed important aspects of his will. But such references are very few in Paul, and usually they have to do with submission to the will of God. Twice Paul refers to his submitting his desire to come to Rome to God's will on the matter (Rom. 1:10; 15:32). Three times he refers to the need to submit to God's will for the individual regarding marriage and singleness (1 Cor. 7:7, 17, 24). Eleven times he refers to his call to ministry. The remaining 15 references have to do with God's will for our salvation, holiness, and spiritual life.

Under a separate heading, I listed all the texts which talk of the way God gives us gifts and the ability to minister through the Holy Spirit (43/49). These references are not relevant to this study on God the Father.

God's post-salvation blessings to us

Paul mentions many blessings which are available to Christians apart from the basic blessing of salvation. This is a major theme in Paul with at least 266 references covering 305 verses, that is, over 15% of the verses in Paul. Here, of course, is an area in keeping with today's preaching and teaching. Yet the particular blessings mentioned may be different from those we usually mention in our preaching. In other words, there may be a difference in emphasis between Paul's treatment of God's post-salvation blessings and ours. Here are some statistics:

There are 10/14 on our great riches in Christ. Of these references, eight are about spiritual riches, while two are on earthly riches. But of these two, one is about the need for the rich to be generous (1 Tim. 6:17), and the other one is about God's supplying Paul's needs while Paul is in prison (Phil. 4:19).

The theme of God's love, grace, mercy, and peace in daily life appears often (31/33). Of these, 1/1 concerns healing (Phil. 2:27), 1/1 deals with the ministry we have been given because of God's mercy (2 Cor. 4:1), and 1/2 is a long list of things that cannot separate us from the love of God (Rom. 8:38-39). The rest are general references to these blessings being given to us.

Paul refers to the fact that God is committed to our welfare (7/8). Five of these describe God's commitment to us amidst difficulty (Rom. 8:28, 31, 32, 33; Phil. 1:28). The other two refer more to our salvation than to the life that follows (Rom. 9:25-26; 11:28). The fact that God is our Father and we are his children is a common theme (23/26). So is the truth that we are God's people who belong to him (14/27). Nine times Paul says that God is with us (9/9).

God's provision for daily life together with his strength and comfort is another common theme (34/47). Almost all the references are to strength to live the Christian life, i.e., the power to be godly. Exceptions are two references to rescue from trouble, two to comfort in trouble, and three to the strength we have through God's armour for spiritual warfare (Eph. 6:10, 11, 13). I did not find many references to spiritual warfare, as it is spoken of today. Paul does talk of the gospel coming with power, which implies spiritual warfare (Rom. 5:19; 1 Thess. 1:5). 2 Corinthians 10:3-5, which talks of the breaking down of strongholds, seems to refer more to an intellectual battle rather than what is today typically referred to as spiritual warfare. I may have missed something here, but I do not think this is a key theme in the Epistles. Acts, of course, has many descriptions about the way spiritual warfare as it is understood today was used in evangelism.

Paul speaks of God revealing truth personally to individuals (10/9). But each time it is a spiritual revelation that will help edify us and bring us closer to God and to knowing and doing his will. (1 Corinthians 12 and 14 refer to this often. But in this study I have included only the verses where God is specifically mentioned.)

It is thrilling to read four times that God praises or commends us. Eschatological blessings are also mentioned (20/25). Another of God's blessings is the giving of the Holy Spirit to us (10/12). We will cover this area in our third study.

We can see that many of the blessings that are emphasised in today's proclamation are either missing or not given much prominence in Paul.

Our response to God

I found 236 recommended responses to God covering 270 verses in Paul's Epistles. That represents 13.5% of the verses in the Epistles.

Belief in God

Belief is our basic response to God (47/57), and that is described in various ways: 20/27 are on believing God or on not trusting in works or idols. 5/5 deal with hoping in God. 1/1 is about seeking God. 3/7 are on confidence before God. 4/5 speak of loving God. 7/5 refer to knowing God. 3/2 are on relying on God during troubles. 4/5 address fear and reverence before God.

Worship (54/66)

If belief is the basic response to God, possibly the noblest response is worship. And Paul describes worship in different ways: 5/7 are about worshiping God, 14/17 are on praying to God, 2/2 are on rejoicing in God, and 33/40 are on thanksgiving and praise to God.

Commitment and obedience (66/75)

Not only do we worship God; we commit ourselves totally to him and seek to please him in all we do. 10/10 deal with honouring God or living lives that are worthy of him. 42/50 are on obeying him, pleasing him, or accepting his will. 7/8 are on living for God. 2/2 are on exclusive loyalty to God. Two important metaphors describe this commitment in terms of slavery or servanthood to God (5/5). We will discuss this image in the next study.

Godliness

Closely related to commitment and obedience is holiness, godliness, or Christian character, which we will encompass under the term godliness. This is presented as a response to God 28 times covering 30 verses. 18/19 describe Christians as consecrated or holy to God. 4/4 express this as honesty and sincerity before God. 6/7 refer to reflecting or bearing God's glory or image or honour.

Godliness is possibly the biggest theme of the Epistles in terms of frequency of occurrence, though it does not always appear along with some reference to God. I found that about 1,400 of the 2,005 verses in Paul's Epistles deal in some way with the issue of godliness—that is, about 70% of the verses. Different scholars have focussed on different features that they regard as the key emphasis in Paul. Justification by faith, redemption through Christ (Longnecker, 1971, p. 90), reconciliation (Martin, 1981), freedom (Bruce, 1977), mystical union with Christ (Schweitzer, 1931), being in Christ (Stewart, 1935), the coming of the new age (Ladd, 1993, pp. 412-413), and the doctrine of God (Ryrie, 1982, pp. 167, 203) have been suggested as the key to understanding Paul's thought. I think in addition to these, the idea of Paul being a preacher of godliness needs fresh consideration.

Accountability to God

The awesome truth that we are accountable to God also appears often (33/37). Before making a solemn statement, Paul often presents God as his witness, or he sometimes takes oaths by God's name (13/15). He alerts us to the prospect of having to give an account to God either now or at the second coming or judgement (20/22). Wrong relationships with God are described 53 times in Paul covering 57 verses.

The statistics given above show that the response to God recommended by Paul primarily has to do with spiritual things. There is almost nothing on how to do ministry, though Paul has a lot of advice on leadership. Acts, of course, gives us models of how ministry was done in the early church. I think there is a striking difference between the emphases of Paul and of those of the church today.

Challenges for Today

The above study demonstrates that the doctrine of God is a very important theme in the evangelistic preaching in Acts and in Paul's teaching to the young churches. In Paul's basic introduction to the gospel (Romans), for example, he uses the word "God" 153 times, an average of once in every 46 words (Morris, 1986, p. 25). If we are to have a healthy church, then, we must certainly capture the essence of the New Testament teaching about God.

The Evangelical church has been experiencing remarkable growth in many parts of the world. Some of the growth has taken place in so-called Christian countries through the renewal of nominals. But also there has been growth through the conversion of non-Christians. In both of these evangelistic ministries, people have been attracted to the gospel through the demonstration of some of the subjective blessings that come from trusting in God. This is a valid method and, as we have seen, was an important means of making contact with non-Christians in Acts. But that experience of God's power in meeting individual needs may have caused the church to neglect emphasising other important aspects of God's nature, as is seen in the preaching of Acts and the Epistles.

We have seen that the sovereignty of God, his righteousness, and judgement are important themes in Paul. We have seen how important it is for us to view God as the one who gives us the great gift of eternal salvation. We have seen that the theme of godliness figures heavily when Paul talks about God's will for us, about God's post-salvation blessings, and about our response to God. These factors pose significant challenges to the church today, and their neglect could result in our missing some important features of biblical Christianity. Below I will discuss just a few features in the New Testament portrayal of God that present a challenge to today's church.

God's sovereignty and our involvement in the world

We saw above that both in the preaching of Acts and in the Epistles of Paul, God is presented as the creator of the world who is the sovereign Lord of history. Paul even asserts that the "secular" governing authorities in society have been established by God (Rom. 13:1). The book of Revelation looks forward to the day when "the kingdom of the world has become the kingdom of our Lord and of his Christ, and he will reign for ever and ever" (Rev. 11:15). "The image suggests the transference of the world empire, once dominated by a usurping power, that has now at

length passed into the hands of its true owner and king" (Johnson, 1981, citing H. B. Swete).

If the world is so much the arena of God's activity, then Christians must think of this world as a key arena of their service. Trinitarian mission would include involvement in the world, whereby Christians seek to uphold God's values (some would say "kingdom values"), so that the various structures of society are brought into conformity with God's will. Some would not include such activity under the word "mission." The church will debate on the nature of the relationship between this activity, evangelism, the church, and the kingdom of God.[4] While these necessary debates will continue and hopefully will help us to clarify the nature of our mission, we can affirm that our belief in God as creator of the world and sovereign Lord of history drives us to active involvement in this world.

Jesus asked us to be "the salt of the earth" (Matt. 5:13). That means, "What is good in society his followers keep wholesome. What is corrupt they oppose; they penetrate society for good and act as a kind of moral antiseptic" (Morris, 1992, p. 104). I am mentioning this aspect of Christian responsibility only in passing, for the sake of completeness in expounding on a trinitarian basis of mission.

The crisis of holiness in the church today

A magical view of God

Many non-Christians who have come to Christ recently have come from backgrounds where the relationship with and understanding of God were somewhat magical. In their earlier faiths, there wasn't the idea of a love relationship with a holy

---

[4] For a brief and helpful summary of approaches used on the issue of how the church should influence the structures of the world, see Bosch (1993). For a helpful attempt to harmonise the different biblical emphases, see Hiebert (1993).

God to whom they are accountable. Instead, the gods were viewed as powerful beings to whom they could go for favours. There was no idea of being accountable to God in daily life. Instead, there were some rules that had to be followed, if they were to receive the blessing. The rules might be something like abstaining from meat or making regular offerings at the temple. This conception of God has been associated in the minds of some with Christianity too. Often in Sri Lanka when I talk to non-Christians, they tell me that they also believe in Christianity. When I probe the matter further, I find that what they mean is they believe in the power of St. Anthony and go to St. Anthony's Church in Colombo in order to receive some favours.

Today many are attracted to the God of the Bible through the demonstration of power. They see God meeting some need in their lives, and that prompts them to accept the Christian gospel that is presented to them. But often they come to him as if they were coming to any of the other gods, though they have come to believe that this God is more powerful than these other gods. So they shift their allegiance to the Christian God. They will try to follow the rules prescribed by this God. They will attend church. They will pay their tithes. (Today's teaching about tithing has such a high emphasis on the blessings promised to tithers that it can become like a magical formula for blessing.) The idea that they are accountable to a holy God who demands their total allegiance and who hates their unholiness is not very strong in the thinking of many new Christians. Most did not come to God to be saved from the terrible consequences of sin. They came for things like healing from a sickness or deliverance from a demon or a financial crisis.

Consequently, some recent converts are reverting to old practices when they do not seem to receive positive answers to their requests. They do not seem to sense the horror with which the Bible views such a reversal to past practices. There is a great need, then, to ensure that converts to Christianity understand that the heart of the gospel has to do with eternal salvation and that the greatest blessing of becoming a Christian is the rescue from eternal damnation and the gift of everlasting life. Then converts would stay along the Christian path, even if some temporal blessings they wanted are not granted, not wanting to forfeit the greatest blessing—eternal salvation.

Most of the people in the church I attend are converts from Buddhism. Most of them were first brought to church by another member who said that God could meet some specific need in their life. They kept coming after their first visit and gradually came to understand the gospel. They subsequently accepted Christ as their Saviour, took baptism, and joined the membership of the church. Most of these people could explain the gospel quite clearly. But when they think of God, I believe that most often their focus is on the temporal blessings he provides.

This is seen in the testimony time that we have every Sunday. Most of the testimonies are on God's provision of temporal blessings, such as healing from sickness and the provision of a job or sufficient funds to meet a need. I was thinking about this a few Sundays ago, when one person got up and gave thanks for the riches of God's grace in salvation. He is paralysed from his waist down, but he has been used mightily by God, through his powerful and radiant personal witness, to introduce many to Christ. I wondered whether the negative answer to thousands of prayers for his healing had nourished in his soul a fuller appreciation for the riches of God's saving grace, which are far richer than the temporal blessings often mentioned.

When Philipp Nicolai was pastor at Unna, Germany, a plague hit the town resulting in hundreds of deaths. His window overlooked the cemetery, and sometimes there were as many as 30 burials in a single day. The following words he wrote describe how he got through this difficult period in his life: "There seemed to me nothing more sweet, delightful, and agreeable than the contemplation of the noble, sublime doctrine of eternal life obtained through the blood of Christ. This I allowed to dwell in my heart day and night" (Peterson & Peterson, 1995, Nov. 11). The focus on eternal salvation has been a hallmark of the Evangelical Movement over the years. There may be a need for fresh emphasis on this in this era when many are coming to Christ by first being attracted to his ability to meet their felt needs.

The crisis of godliness

One of the sad consequences of the scenario I have described above is the lack of godliness among Christians. This has reached epidemic proportions in many countries, as in Sri Lanka. Though thousands have come to Christ, many of them still continue to lie, are dishonest with money, or are unchristian in the way they relate to their spouses, neighbours, employers, or employees. The incidence of serious sexual immorality among Christian workers is alarming.

This lack of godliness is a problem in all societies that do not take into account the reality of a supreme and holy God to whom people are morally accountable. So in spite of the high moral ethic of Buddhism, Sri Lanka's national religion, we are crippled by corruption, and the level of sexual immorality in our supposedly conservative villages is shocking. The same could be said of Hinduism in India. The veteran theologian/missionary to India, Dr. Bruce Nicholls, once told me that he feels that one of the primary causes for the rise of Hindu fundamentalism in India is the moral vacuum that exists there and the havoc it is causing.

This has become a problem in the West also. Many of the social structures of the West are built upon the foundation that we are accountable to a holy God. Therefore, there is a high place given to trust in the way society functions. People are expected to be honest at supermarkets, to be pure when dating a member of the opposite sex, and to be truthful when exercising their freedom of expression in the media. The freedom and democracy, which the West jealously guards, were originally founded upon the fact that the supreme God to whom we are accountable is just and holy. I shudder to think of the final consequences of people jettisoning that idea for a more pluralistic or pantheistic idea of the divine.

Communism worked relatively smoothly as people were restrained through the totalitarian authority of the state. But now that the people have won their political "freedom," many former Communist countries have become enslaved to corruption and the Mafia. Recent polls taken in some of these countries suggest that large numbers of the population prefer the situation they had under Communism. There isn't the restraining influence of a belief in a holy God, which enables them to handle their freedom responsibly.

Biblical Christians are afraid of sinning, partly because they know that God hates sin and punishes it. Much of the teaching about judgement in the New Testament is given to Christians. The prospect of reaping what we sow is a serious one for biblical Christians. So when they are tempted to do the sinful acts that are commonplace in society, there is a check in their spirit that warns them of the awful consequences of sin. Jesus put it bluntly when he said that it would be better to gouge out the eye and cut off the hand that cause us to sin rather than keep them and be cast into hell (Matt. 5:29-30). But the church today, reflecting the post-modern mood of the day, has focussed more on the subjective blessings that come from God than on the important implications of the holiness of God. Therefore, as statistics are showing, there is an alarming incidence of moral lapses among Christians. While moral lapses have always accompanied the life of the church, what is new today is the lack of moral criteria—Christians don't seem to feel that sin is all that serious (see Veith, 1994, p. 18).

So we are faced with a huge crisis in the church. There are Christians who could describe the way of salvation but whose behaviour is not influenced by the Christian worldview: people who could lie without batting an eyelid, pastors who could speak abusively to their wives on Sunday morning and preach a little later from the pulpit. We are in danger of losing the blessings that have come as a result of the recent church growth. If we do not urgently take remedial action, we are in danger of entering another dark age of nominalism.

Towards an Answer

What is the answer to this problem? I believe a key is for the church to be presenting a fuller (biblical) picture of God in its various activities. This way Christians could imbibe the biblical worldview, because it is a natural part of the Christian environment in which they grow. This should be reflected in the church's programmes of evangelism, nurture, and worship.

Evangelism

I have heard some powerful healing evangelists, such as Reinhard Bonke, who give good emphasis to the gospel facts in their preaching. But I know that there are many others whose evangelistic preaching focusses primarily on the power of God to help overcome temporal problems and whose invitation to the people is to come to God in order to have these problems solved. I think there is a subtle temptation here. Needs-oriented preaching is so attractive to people that it is easy to ignore the other aspects of the gospel. Yet, as we saw earlier, the preaching to the unreached in Acts emphasised such things as God as creator and as the sovereign and holy One who will judge all people. The first preachers confronted people about their accountability to him and about the need to repent and turn from sin and idols to God. We too must learn the art of moving from felt needs to the gospel, from the appetiser to the main meal.

Some exciting new programmes have been developed recently to introduce the unreached to the Christian worldview. For example, the "Chronological Approach" developed by New Tribes Mission introduces people to the Old Testament understanding of God before presenting the story of Jesus. The result is that by the time missionaries present the story of Jesus' sacrifice for sin, the people are ready to receive it.[5]

Christian nurture

Even if many do not fully understand the gospel when they first trust in God for salvation, the basic gospel facts should constantly recur in the teaching and preaching to believers in the church. We must show that God hates and judges

---

[5] This approach is vividly presented in two videos entitled "It Is True" and "Now We See Clearly" and the series of books entitled *Building on Firm Foundations*, all produced by New Tribes Mission.

unbelief, sin, and falsehood and that in our natural state we would be headed for an eternity in hell. This will give a good background for presenting the marvels of grace, which caused the gospel events and enabled such a holy God to grant us eternal salvation. I have heard of missions that are using the book of Ephesians as a basic follow-up book for new Christians because of its emphasis on grace and its implications for daily life.

Reflection on God's holiness and sovereignty will also serve as an incentive to holiness. This will provide us with a good background for presenting the strong ethical teaching that appears in the Epistles. The strong ethic of Buddhism in Sri Lanka includes a regular pledge to abstain from lying as one of its most basic features. But that has not helped reduce the lying which seems to be a characteristic feature of our people. We have found that, despite teaching on the Christian ethic in the church, converts from Buddhism still continue to lie. We need a worldview to back ethical teaching if we are to expect people to have the strength and the will to conform to it. For the Christian, such a worldview comes from the doctrine of God.

A Western Christian leader who had served in Asia for several years recently told me that we should not define integrity for Asian Christians in the same way that those in the West do it, because our understanding of right and wrong is different from that in the West. I have thought about that a lot recently. The thought that came to me is that we do not need to look at the West for a definition of integrity. Rather, let us look at the Bible, which sets a very high standard and challenges every culture in every generation. Besides, what havoc the practical understanding of integrity in our nations has caused in Asia! Surely Christianity should be judging the culture rather than conforming to it when it comes to moral issues like integrity.

Over the past few years, I have been preaching the message of scriptural holiness a great deal in different Evangelical churches in Sri Lanka. What people keep telling me is that this is a message they rarely hear in the church today. Recently, I taught at a pastor's conference in the east of Sri Lanka. As the people there were Tamil-speaking, I had to speak through interpretation. My interpreter remarked that what I taught was the other side of what they are usually taught. He agreed fully with what I said, but it was a message that had been taught only very rarely. I don't think the problem with our churches is one of heresy. Rather, it is one of a lopsided emphasis. The message of God meeting our temporal needs and the message of God's power over evil forces are so relevant to people's needs that we are focussing primarily on these areas and are neglecting other important truths.

During the prayer request time in our church, as with the testimony time, most of the requests are about temporal needs. And this is very valid, for God cares about our personal, temporal needs. One Sunday a godly leader, whose life is an example to all of us, got up to ask for prayer that he will listen to his wife and consider her opinions more carefully. A jarring shift of gears seemed to have taken place. It placed before all of us the need to seek the most important things in life.

The contemporary approach to truth will be a major obstacle in our efforts to present the Christian ethic in the church. Words have lost their value in this postmodern generation. This is a fairly new phenomenon in the West, but we have lived with such a state of affairs for a longer time in the East. Often a person, when asked to come to do a repair job in a home, will say something like, "I'll come tomorrow," without any intention of coming on that day.

Because of this mindset, many Christians find it difficult to believe that the Word is powerful to effect a change in people's lives. Yet the Bible is clear about the sanctifying power of the Word. Jesus said, "Sanctify them by the truth; your word is truth" (John 17:17). Hebrews 4:12 says, "For the word of God is living and active. Sharper than any double-edged sword, it penetrates even to dividing soul and spirit, joints and marrow; it judges the thoughts and attitudes of the heart." Evangelicals subscribe to the doctrine of Scripture's inspiration as presented in 2 Timothy 3:16a: "All Scripture is God-breathed." But in practice we act as if we don't believe in the rest of that sentence: "... and is useful for teaching, rebuking, correcting, and training in righteousness, so that the man of God may be thoroughly equipped for every good work."

One of our greatest challenges today is to restore confidence in the power of the Word among Christians in a generation that has lost its belief in the power of words. Surely one of the keys to this is giving sufficient time to prepare biblical messages which demonstrate that the Bible is relevant to the issues of the day. This is a discipline to cultivate in this activist generation. I believe the primary cause for the drop in popularity of expository sermons in the church today is that such messages take much longer to prepare than other types of sermons.

Another key is for church leaders to demonstrate the power of the Word by putting into practice what it teaches, thus living loving and holy lives. Because of our pragmatic orientation, we might permit talented but unholy people to represent the church publicly in its programmes. We may end up having good programmes and large crowds who are attracted because of their quality. But these unholy but talented people will, in the long run, communicate the message that the biblical ethic is neither practical nor essential for Christian living.

Worship

It seems that the focus of our worship also has moved away from a focus on the fullness of God's nature and its implications to the Christian. We have already talked about how testimonies today focus almost entirely on God's provision of temporal needs. The praise of God in the Epistles is primarily based on grace. This is evidenced by the number of times the grace of God and related themes appear. Five of Paul's great doxologies in his Epistles spring from his contemplating the marvels of grace (Rom. 11:33-36; 16:27; Gal. 1:5; Eph. 3:21; 1 Tim. 1:17). 46 times Paul says that God deserves to be praised, thanked, and glorified. An analysis of the cause for such praises yielded the following results: Several times the praise or thanks is over faithful Christians. A few times it is over the ministry that God has given Paul, over missionary giving, and over things like food. The rest of the occurrences either say simply that God himself must be praised and glorified or that he is praised for the gospel or for salvation.

A key to worship is the church's hymnody. It is also a key to the churches' educating of Christians. It used to be said that Charles Wesley's hymns were the means by which the early Methodist Movement taught its people doctrine. Therefore, our hymns can take a major role in teaching Christians the biblical worldview. The current revival of interest in worship is a promising sign, with great possibility for enriching the church. The "song leader" coming from days of the evangelistic rallies has been replaced by the "worship leader."

It is well known that worship songs have by and large replaced the great hymns of the faith and gospel songs, which were the two previous forms of song in the Evangelical church (see Hamilton, 1999; Noll, 1999). The hymns of the faith came primarily from the 18th and 19th centuries. They emphasised God's nature and the glory of his salvation. There was a high emphasis on praise and adoration. The gospel songs came from the late 19th to mid-20th centuries. These focussed more on testifying about the marvels of grace. Unlike the hymns, the emphasis was more on testimony (people to people) than worship (people to God), in keeping with the emphasis on evangelism and personal salvation in the Evangelical Movement of that era. These emphases are keys to the rich heritage of Evangelicalism.

We can be thankful that the worship songs have helped the Evangelical church to rediscover biblical worship. We would hope that the emphases conveyed by the hymns and the gospel songs would now be conveyed through this medium to enrich worship and teach Christians the basic features of the Christian worldview. I believe that this is happening in the English-speaking world through the works of songwriters like Graham Kendrick. But I believe a great deal of work remains to be done in this area in the churches in other cultures.

Conclusion

The burden of this study is that the church needs to be giving fresh emphasis to the biblical doctrine of God. There are concepts in the Bible that are strange to the world around us, and the church may not have emphasised them as much as she should. In order to remedy this situation, we will need to communicate "the whole counsel of God" carefully and effectively in our evangelism, nurture, and worship. We will need to model Christianity by conscientiously putting into practise in our lives the truths implied by God's nature.

We will need to engage, with a reasoned critique, those features of the culture which are hostile to the biblical understanding of God and show why the Christian gospel has provided "a new and living way" that surpasses by far all other ways. This is going to be more urgent in the 21st century than before, as ideas hostile to the Christian worldview are growing rapidly all over the world.

References

Bosch, D. J. (1993). God's reign and the rulers of this world. In C. Van Engen, D. S. Gilliland, & P. Pierson (Eds.), *The good news of the kingdom* (pp. 89-95). Maryknoll, NY: Orbis Books.

Bruce, F. F. (1977). *Paul: Apostle of the heart set free*. Grand Rapids, MI: Wm. B. Eerdmans Publishing Co.

Hamilton, M. S. (1999, July 12). The triumph of praise songs: How guitars beat out the organ in the worship wars. *Christianity Today, 43*, pp. 29-35.

Hiebert, P. G. (1993). Evangelism, church, and kingdom. In C. Van Engen, D. S. Gilliland, & P. Pierson (Eds.), *The good news of the kingdom* (pp. 153-161). Maryknoll, NY: Orbis Books.

Johnson, A. F. (1981). Revelation. In F. E. Gaebelein (Ed.), *Expositor's Bible commentary* (pp. 397-603). Grand Rapids, MI: Zondervan Publishing House.

Ladd, G. E. (1993). In D. A. Hagner (Ed.), *A theology of the New Testament* (rev. ed.) (pp. 412-413). Grand Rapids, MI: Wm. B. Eerdmans Publishing Co.

Longnecker, R. N. (1971). *The ministry and message of Paul*. Grand Rapids, MI: Zondervan Publishing House.

Martin, R. P. (1981). *Reconciliation: A study of Paul's theology*. Atlanta, GA: John Knox Press.

Morris, L. (1986). *New Testament theology*. Grand Rapids, MI: Zondervan Publishing House.

———. (1992). *The gospel according to Matthew*. Grand Rapids, MI: Wm. B. Eerdmans Publishing Co.

Noll, M. A. (1999, July 12). We are what we sing: Our classic hymns reveal evangelicalism at its best. *Christianity Today, 43*, pp. 37-41.

Peterson, W. J., & Peterson, R. (1995). *One year book of hymns.* Wheaton, IL: Tyndale House Publishers.

Ryrie, C. C. (1982). *Biblical theology of the New Testament.* Chicago: Moody Press.

Schweitzer, A. (1931). *The mysticism of Paul the apostle.* London: A. & C. Black, Ltd.

Stewart, J. S. (1935). *A man in Christ.* London: Hodder & Stoughton.

Veith, G. E., Jr. (1994). *Postmodern times: A Christian guide to contemporary thought and culture.* Wheaton, IL: Crossway Books.

Ajith Fernando has led Sri Lanka Youth for Christ since 1976. Convinced of a call to theologise from the grassroots, he has always led a small division in YFC and presently leads the work with drug dependents. His YFC responsibilities include teaching and pastoral care of staff. Ajith and his wife Nelun are active in the leadership of a Methodist church, most of whose members are converts from other religions. He has a Th.M. in New Testament from Fuller Theological Seminary. His nine books have been in the area of either Bible exposition, such as the NIV Application Commentary: Acts (Zondervan, 1998), or mission theology, such as The Supremacy of Christ (Crossway, 1995).

WHEN WE LOOK at the Second Person of the Trinity in our trinitarian approach to mission, our study could take two directions. The first and most basic direction would be to look at Jesus as the message of mission, that is, at the person and work of Christ. The second would be to look at him as the model for mission, that is, to focus on his life and ministry. Perhaps because I have written four books relating to Jesus as the message of mission (Fernando, 1983, 1989, 1994, 1995), I decided to focus on Jesus as the model in this study.

Jesus: the message and model of mission

AJITH
FERNANDO

Jesus: The Message of Mission

For the sake of completeness, we will briefly list what we would mean by Jesus being the message of mission. Essentially we would say that Jesus is the way, the truth, and the life,[1] and that no one comes to the Father but by him (John 14:6). Salvation is from God, and it is made real in our lives by the work of the Holy Spirit, but it is made available to us through the work of Christ. His work, consisting of incarnation, life on earth, death, resurrection, exaltation, and consummation at the end of time, makes him the way to salvation. The idea of the work of Christ resulting in saving grace upon unworthy sinners goes contrary to much of the thinking of the New Age Movement and world religions that give more weight to the place of human ability in earning salvation. This is a challenge calling for fresh thinking by Evangelical thinkers.[2]

---

[1] My book *The Supremacy of Christ* (Fernando, 1995) follows the outline of Jesus as the truth, the way, and the life and deals with various challenges arising today to these affirmations.

[2] I have tried to do this in Fernando (1995, chaps. 9-11).

There are challenges today from within the church too to the affirmation that the work of Christ is the way of salvation for humankind. It is customary to refer to three approaches to this issue: pluralism, inclusivism, and exclusivism. But within these three viewpoints, there is a wide spectrum of variation and shades of emphases.[3] Pluralists will not confine the means of salvation to the work of one saviour, keeping all proposed ways to salvation as more or less equals in the universe of faiths.[4] The inclusivists include all possible ways of salvation under the work of Christ, affirming that all who are saved are saved by Christ. But they do not confine salvation only to those who have heard and responded to the gospel of Christ. On one extreme there are inclusivists who speak of salvation through (the "sacraments" of) other faiths.[5] On the other extreme are inclusivists who say that only those who respond in repentance and faith to what they know of the supreme God, in a way similar to what is described in the Bible, can be saved (Anderson, 1984). There are other inclusivists who are found at different positions between these two extremes.[6] The exclusivists or particularists confine salvation to those who hear and respond to the gospel of Christ.[7] There are some today who would have previously been described as inclusivists, who prefer to call themselves exclusivists because they only leave the door open to salvation according to the second group of inclusivists described above, but they place their emphasis on the saving work of Christ and its efficacy (Wright, 1997, p. 51). There are others who prefer to remain agnostic on the issue of whether those who have not heard the gospel could be saved (Newbigin, 1978, pp. 88, 196; Shenk, 1997; Stott, 1988).

Then there is the huge issue of universalism, the view that in the end all will be saved. Those in the church who hold this view generally leave room for repentance and a sort of purgatory or even reincarnation after life on earth (Bonda, 1998; Hick, 1976, 1979; Robinson, 1968). Annihilationism, the view that those who remain impenitent to the end will be annihilated through the destructive fires of hell, has been gaining ground among Christians of different traditions in recent years (Froom, 1965; Fudge, 1982; Pinnock, 1990; Wenham, 1992).

The dual nature of Jesus as divine and human expressed during his life, ministry, and teaching on earth makes us confident to affirm that he is the truth (John 1:1-14; 14:6-11). By that we mean that he is the ultimate reality—not just the bearer of truth, but absolute truth personified. This affirmation runs counter to the religious pluralism that is a popular approach to truth in intellectual circles today. It needs to be defended, and one of the keys to this defence is demonstrating that the

---

[3] There is such an enormous amount of literature that has been published representing the different views in recent times that I have decided to mention only names of representatives of the different views. Four different views are presented in Okholm & Phillips (1995). John Hick argues for a pluralistic view, Clark H. Pinnock argues for an inclusivistic view, and Alister McGrath, Douglas Geivett, and Gary Phillips argue for two particularist varieties of views. See also Crockett & Sigountos (1991), which gives a variety of Evangelical positions.

[4] See the writings of John Hick, Paul Knitter, and Wesley Ariarajah.

[5] See the writings of Raymundo Pannikkar, Karl Rahner, Hans Küng, and S. J. Samartha.

[6] See the writings of Clark Pinnock and John Sanders.

[7] See the writings of Dick Dowsett, Ajith Fernando, Hywel Jones, Erwin Lutzer, Ronald Nash, and Ramesh Richard.

Gospels contain objective and true statements of Jesus which present his absolute Lordship and deity. If these points can be demonstrated, then the Jesus of history is the same as the Christ of faith. Demonstrating the historical validity, the objective reality, and the enduring importance of the statements attributed to Christ in the Gospels is therefore a key challenge facing Evangelicals in today's pluralistic environment.[8]

The result of experiencing salvation is that Jesus opens the door to what the Bible calls eternal life (John 3:16; 5:24). Jesus said that he came to enable us to enjoy a completely fulfilling life (John 10:10). Therefore, we can refer to Jesus as "the life" (John 14:6). At its essence, this life consists of a relationship with God (John 17:3), who is both loving and holy. I have argued elsewhere[9] that this relationship opens the door for biblical spirituality, which provides an experience surpassing, by virtue of its completeness, the fulfilment claimed by the many other spiritual systems vying for the allegiance of people today.

Jesus as Example in the New Testament

The rest of this study will look at Jesus as the model for mission, together with some of the implications for today. Jesus is directly presented as the missionary model in John 17:18 ("As you sent me into the world, I have sent them into the world") and John 20:21 ("As the Father has sent me, I am sending you"). In preparing this study, I looked for ways in which Jesus was presented as a model in the New Testament. I may have missed locating some important passages, but those I found yielded some surprising discoveries.

Non-Pauline passages

I considered 13 (14 with repetition) non-Pauline passages which present Jesus as a model. Three make general statements of the principle. These are the two passages just referred to (John 17:18 and 20:21) and 1 John 2:5-6, "But if anyone obeys his word, God's love is truly made complete in him. This is how we know we are in him: Whoever claims to live in him must walk as Jesus did." All the others deal with either servanthood, humility, suffering, or deprivation.

There are three passages on servanthood and humility. When Jesus explained that he came to serve and to give his life as a ransom for many, he presented that as our model for greatness (Mark 10:43-45; also repeated in Matt. 20:25-28). When a dispute arose about which of the disciples was the greatest, Jesus said that the greatest is the one who serves. He then said, "I am among you as one who serves" (Luke 22:24-27). After Jesus washed the feet of the disciples, he presented that action as something his disciples were to emulate (John 13:14-17).

The remaining seven passages present Jesus as a model of suffering and deprivation. This number would climb to nine if we considered the two times already discussed of Jesus giving his life as a ransom for many (Mark 10:43-45; Matt. 20:25-28). I will simply list some of these passages below:

- "My command is this: Love each other as I have loved you. Greater love has no one than this, that he lay down his life for his friends" (John 15:12-13).

---

[8] On the topic of Jesus as the truth and related issues, see Fernando (1995, chaps. 1-8).

[9] See Fernando (1995, chaps. 12-16) and especially Fernando (2000).

- "Let us fix our eyes on Jesus, the author and perfecter of our faith, who for the joy set before him endured the cross, scorning its shame, and sat down at the right hand of the throne of God. Consider him who endured such opposition from sinful men, so that you will not grow weary and lose heart" (Heb. 12:2-3).

- "And so Jesus also suffered outside the city gate to make the people holy through his own blood. Let us, then, go to him outside the camp, bearing the disgrace he bore" (Heb. 13:12-13).

- "This is how we know what love is: Jesus Christ laid down his life for us. And we ought to lay down our lives for our brothers. If anyone has material possessions and sees his brother in need but has no pity on him, how can the love of God be in him?" (1 John 3:16-17).

The passages I left out are 1 Peter 2:19-24, 1 Peter 3:17-18, and 1 Peter 4:1-2.

Paul's Epistles

I was able to find 15 references to Jesus as a model in the Epistles of Paul, and a similar pattern was found here as in the non-Pauline sections of the New Testament. I found one general reference to Christ as our model: "Follow my example, as I follow the example of Christ" (1 Cor. 11:1). Two references are about forgiving as Christ forgave (Eph. 4:32; Col. 3:13), and two are about meekness and gentleness (2 Cor. 10:1; 11:17).

Two passages about servanthood are worth noting. The first is given in a passage that is describing Christian behaviour, Romans 15:7-9: "Accept one another, then, just as Christ accepted you, in order to bring praise to God. For I tell you that Christ has become a servant of the Jews on behalf of God's truth, to confirm the promises made to the patriarchs so that the Gentiles may glorify God for his mercy."

The other is the famous Christological hymn given in the context of striving for unity: "Your attitude should be the same as that of Christ Jesus: Who, being in very nature God, did not consider equality with God something to be grasped, but made himself nothing, taking the very nature of a servant, being made in human likeness. And being found in appearance as a man, he humbled himself and became obedient to death—even death on a cross!" (Phil. 2:5-8).

This passage carries the idea of suffering also. It and eight other passages present Jesus as a model of suffering and deprivation. Consider the following:

- "I am not commanding you, but I want to test the sincerity of your love by comparing it with the earnestness of others. For you know the grace of our Lord Jesus Christ, that though he was rich, yet for your sakes he became poor, so that you through his poverty might become rich" (2 Cor. 8:8-9).

- "Be imitators of God, therefore, as dearly loved children and live a life of love, just as Christ loved us and gave himself up for us as a fragrant offering and sacrifice to God" (Eph. 5:1-2).

- "Husbands, love your wives, just as Christ loved the church and gave himself up for her" (Eph. 5:25).

- "May the Lord direct your hearts into God's love and Christ's perseverance" (2 Thess. 3:5).

The passages I left out are Romans 15:2-4, Ephesians 5:28-29, 1 Thessalonians 1:5-6, and 2 Timothy 2:8.

These are not the only ways in which Christ is an example to Christians. But the evidence presented above suggests that these exhortations should be particularly significant when considering Christ as a model, for they are the features that are specifically mentioned in the New Testament. When we think of Jesus as the missionary model, therefore, the main themes that should come to mind, on the one hand, are meekness, humility, servanthood, and forgiving others, and on the other hand, suffering and deprivation.

The Sufferings of Christian Leaders in Paul

Paul presents Christian leaders as examples 13 times covering 23 verses. But only four of these references present leaders as models of suffering (1 Thess. 1:5-6; 2:14-15; 2 Thess. 1:5; 2 Tim. 3:10-11). However, in eight places covering 23 verses Paul presents suffering as a source of credibility for ministry. This is implied in many more passages too. Here are three key passages:

• "But I have not used any of these rights. And I am not writing this in the hope that you will do such things for me. I would rather die than have anyone deprive me of this boast" (1 Cor. 9:15).
• "Let no one cause me trouble, for I bear on my body the marks of Jesus" (Gal. 6:17).
• "As a prisoner for the Lord, then, I urge you to live a life worthy of the calling you have received" (Eph. 4:1).

The Epistles of Paul vividly present different ways in which he and other Christians suffered:

• 17 times covering 24 verses we have what we may call general listings of suffering.
• 6(times)/6(verses) he mentions weakness.
  • 5/6 danger
  • 6/12 enemies and hostility
  • 1/1 being unsettled
  • 5/8 false accusations and slander
  • 6/8 humiliation
  • 2/3 loneliness
  • 8/15 voluntary deprivation
  • 16/20 imprisonment
  • 1/1 martyrdom

  • 3/4 being deserted by friends and/or other Christians
  • 6/8 physical harm and deprivation
  • 7/7 hard work
  • 3/5 groaning
  • 8/11 anguish and distress
  • 1/1 pressure

Interestingly, not all of these forms of suffering have to do with persecution. Often I hear Christians in affluent countries comment that Christians who live in poorer countries where they are a minority suffer a lot. The implication is that Christians in the West don't have to suffer much. Most of the types of suffering in the above list cannot be confined to poorer nations where Christians are a minority. Of the 17 points listed, only three or four are not applicable to those in richer Western cultures. The rest are experiences that Christians anywhere who are committed to the gospel and to people will face. Christian leaders who are committed to people will suffer wherever they are. The problem is that this type of suffering can be avoided by avoiding some of the implications of being committed to people. As commitment to people seems to be a lost art today, I think we are seeing a lot of avoidance of suffering by Christian leaders.

Thus far we have come up with a few conclusions in our quest for what it means to follow Christ's model in mission. Firstly, the predominant themes presented to us to model from the life of Jesus are meekness, humility, and servanthood on the one hand and suffering and deprivation on the other. Then we looked at what Paul presented about the suffering of leaders and concluded that suffering is a key to the credibility of leaders and that leaders even today do suffer a lot in various ways, wherever they may be living. Now let us turn to look at what Paul has to say about the servanthood of leaders.

Servanthood in the New Testament

There are two word groups commonly used for the idea of servant in the New Testament. The *diakonos* word group carries the idea of servant or minister and the *doulos* word group the idea of slave. Both these words are used for Jesus and for Christians. For this study, I did not consider the *oikonomos* word group, which has the stewardship idea, as it is not used for Jesus in the New Testament.

The *diakonos* word group

Words belonging to the *diakonos* group are used three times for Jesus (four with repetition). Jesus said of himself that he "did not come to be served (*diakonëthënai*), but to serve (*diakonësai*), and to give his life as a ransom for many" (Mark 10:45; also Matt. 20:28). He said, "For who is greater, the one who is at the table or the one who serves? Is it not the one who is at the table? But I am among you as one who serves" (Luke 22:27). Paul said, "For I tell you that Christ has become a servant of the Jews on behalf of God's truth, to confirm the promises made to the patriarchs so that the Gentiles may glorify God for his mercy" (Rom. 15:8-9).

This word group is used of Christians in different ways. Looking only at Paul's Epistles, we find it used in the following ways:

- 14 times, as servants/ministers in a general sense.
- 15 times, as servants of fellow Christians or the church.
- 9 times, as servants of the gospel, evangelism, or the New Covenant.
- 4 times, referring to the office of deacon in the church.

The frequency of occurrence of these words suggests that the idea of servant is very important when constructing a biblical idea of leadership and mission, especially as this word is used of Jesus, our model for mission.

The *doulos* word group

The *doulos* word group, which carries the idea of slave, is used twice for Jesus (three, with repetition). Its use for Jesus is implied in Mark 10:43-45, where Jesus says, "Whoever wants to become great among you must be your servant (*diakonos*), and whoever wants to be first must be slave (*doulos*) of all. For even the Son of Man did not come to be served (*diakonëthënai*), but to serve (*diakonësai*), and to give his life as a ransom for many" (also Matt. 20:27). After saying that we must be slaves of all, Jesus presents himself as the example of such slavery. The connection between Jesus and slavery is clearer in Philippians 2:7, which says that he "made himself nothing, taking the very nature of a servant (*doulou*), being made in human likeness."

This word group is used often for Christians too. Looking again only at Paul's Epistles, we find *doulos*-related words used of Christians in the following manner:

- 15 times, we are slaves of Christ or of God.
- Twice, the slavery principle is outlined as a neutral value.
- 13 times, people are slaves to sin, law, demonic powers, fear, and wine.
- 5 times, we are slaves to righteousness.
- One verse refers to subduing our body and making it our slave.
- There are 18 references to slavery as one's job in society.
- Once, creation is a slave to decay.

The above instances are not of much significance to our study, though we must note that the idea of our being slaves of Christ or of God is basic to Christian living and thus to mission. The following uses of *doulos*-related words, however, are very significant for our study. Once Paul describes Timothy as a slave of the gospel: "But you know that Timothy has proved himself, because as a son with his father he has served (*edouleusen*) with me in the work of the gospel" (Phil. 2:22). Three times in Paul we see the idea of Christians being slaves of people to whom they are called to minister. 1 Corinthians 9:19 says, "Though I am free and belong to no man, I make myself a slave (*edoulōsa*) to everyone, to win as many as possible." In 2 Corinthians 4:5 Paul describes himself as the slave of the incorrigible Corinthians! "For we do not preach ourselves, but Jesus Christ as Lord, and ourselves as your servants (*doulous*) for Jesus' sake." In Galatians 5:13 he advises Christians, "You, my brothers, were called to be free. But do not use your freedom to indulge the sinful nature; rather, serve (*douleuete*) one another in love."

There is an interesting translation practice followed by most English translations, and in translations in other languages too. When the slavery metaphor is used for slavery to forces like sin, law, and demonic powers (e.g., Rom. 6-7; Gal. 4-5), the translators used words such as "slave" and "slavery." But in most of the references where Christians are presented as slaves of Christ, of God, of the gospel, or of the people they serve, the translators used the words "servant" or "serve." This strange phenomenon was found from the time of the earliest English translations. Experts in biblical Greek are now telling us that this is an inadequate way to translate these *doulos*-group words, i.e., they should carry the idea of slave rather than servant.

Murray Harris (1999) has recently written a monograph, *Slave of Christ: A New Testament Metaphor for Total Devotion*

to Christ, where he does a thorough study of the use of the *doulos* words and shows that they should be translated with the slave idea rather than the servant idea. He looks for reasons for this strange phenomenon that *doulos* was not translated as slave. He suggests that modern slavery was so terrible that the translators would not have wanted to bring that idea to our biblical thinking. First century slavery was much more humane:

"In the first century, slaves were not distinguishable from free persons by race, by speech, or by clothing; they were sometimes more highly educated than their owners and held responsible professional positions; some persons sold themselves into slavery for economic or social advantage; they could reasonably hope to be emancipated after 10 to 20 years of service or by their 30s at the latest; they were not denied the right to public assembly and were not socially segregated (at least in the cities); they could accumulate savings to buy their freedom; their natural inferiority was not assumed" (Harris, 1999, p. 44).

I think that if Paul encountered slavery of the type found in modern times, he would have attacked it more vehemently.[10] Anyway, we have missed an important biblical emphasis by replacing "slave" with "servant."

What, then, does the term *doulos* imply when it is used in the New Testament of our relationship with God, Christ, and the people we serve? After a long discussion, Harris (1999, pp. 104-105) concludes, "The term *doulos* expresses both a vertical and a horizontal relationship of the Christian, who is both a willing vassal of the heavenly Master and the submissive servant of fellow believers." He says, "The

---

[10] Yet Paul proclaimed the breaking of social distinctions through Christ (Gal. 3:28; Philemon). Harris (1999, p. 68) says, "... in undermining the discriminatory hierarchy of social relations that is at the heart of slavery, Christianity sounded the death-knell of slavery."

term epitomises the Christian's dual obligation: *unquestioning devotion* to Christ and to his people" [emphasis added].

I believe that by not using the slavery idea where it should be used, we have missed some key features of the nature of the Christian life and of Christian ministry. Christian leaders are servants of the people. It is unfortunate that the most popularly used Sinhala word for pastor in recent times has the idea of "ruler of the church"—an idea so distant from the idea of slavery!

We will now look at some of the challenges the church faces when it considers the missionary model as presented by Jesus as involving servanthood, slavery, meekness, suffering, and deprivation.

Servanthood/Meekness and the Warfare Mentality

As we look at the growth of the church amongst the unreached today, we would see that at the forefront of it are bold pioneers who have trusted God and gone to the unreached with a fiery sense of vocation. They have resisted persecution and overcome numerous obstacles. They have doggedly stuck to their task amidst much to discourage them. And they have reaped a great harvest for the kingdom. Most of them are unknown outside their immediate ecclesiastical circles, but I believe they are the real heroes of this era in the history of the church.

Recently these pioneers have been influenced by the fresh emphasis on spiritual warfare that has come from the West. This has been an integral part of ministry in the Third World all along, as encounter with the demonic is a very common experience in day-to-day life. However, in recent years Christian workers have seen an emphasis on breaking down strongholds, which has further sensitised them to the battle before them. There is much that is healthy here. With the breakdown of the rationalist stranglehold of modernism in the West, there is now a greater openness to the supernatural among Christians too. But sometimes it is not easy for these rugged pioneers, now influenced by this fresh emphasis on victory over opposing forces, to harmonise their battle emphasis with the emphasis on the meekness and gentleness of Christ and servanthood. There is a sense that they must win, in a worldly way, every battle they encounter with forces (human and supernatural) that oppose their work.

Some Sri Lankan Christian leaders were invited to a television dialogue with some Buddhist leaders on inter-religious relationships and conversion. Some came with a desire to use the opportunity to witness to the power of the gospel. They went outside the accepted norms for such programmes, debating on behalf of the supremacy of Christ. This could have been an opportunity to allay some of the unfounded fears of the Buddhist leaders who are strongly opposing Christian evangelism in Sri Lanka. It served instead to confirm those fears and increase their resolve to stamp out all Christian evangelistic efforts. This was an opportunity to gently present an apologetic for Christian evangelism to those who oppose it, in keeping with the advice presented in 1 Peter 3:15, "Always be prepared to give an answer to everyone who asks you to give the reason for the hope that you have. But do this with gentleness and respect." It turned into an occasion when the opponents of Christ got more entrenched in their false conviction that Christians are a dangerous threat to the harmony of our nation.

Sometimes when faced with opposition by human forces, we are finding Christians acting with the same attitude that they would if they were fighting demonic forces. They may attack people when they should love them. Sadhu

Sundar Singh was once proclaiming the gospel on the banks of the Ganges at a place called Rishi Kesh. Several Hindu Sadhus and other devotees were in his audience. One of them lifted up a handful of sand and threw it in his eyes. Others in the audience, however, were enraged by the act and handed the man to a policeman while Sundar Singh was washing the sand from his eyes. When he returned and found that the man had been handed over to the police, he begged for his release and, having secured it, proceeded with his preaching. The man, Vijayanada, was so surprised that he fell at Sundar Singh's feet, begging his forgiveness and declaring his desire to know more about what he was saying. Later this man joined Sundar Singh on his travels (Parker, 1918, pp. 25-26).

Hudson Taylor refused to take the compensation the Chinese government had agreed to pay after his missionaries and their property had been badly affected in the Boxer uprising. This decision resulted in the Chinese leaders extolling the virtues of Christ and his principles of tolerance (Glasser, 1975, p. 171). Taylor refused to win the battle for compensation. We are fighting a great war on behalf of the eternal kingdom of God. Therefore, we do not need to come out victors in all the relatively minor encounters we face along the path to victory. The meekness and gentleness of Christ may sometimes lead Christians to respond to battles in such a loving way that the world would consider it a defeat, a loss of face. Jesus said, "Do not resist an evil person. If someone strikes you on the right cheek, turn to him the other also. And if someone wants to sue you and take your tunic, let him have your cloak as well. If someone forces you to go one mile, go with him two miles" (Matt. 5:39-41). Many today would view these courses of action recommended by Jesus as personal defeats

involving a loss of face. But Christians are too big and their battle is too great for them to be bothered by these minor cases of a loss of face.

Sometimes Christians, convinced that the sovereign Lord of the universe has given them authority to worship him freely, may shout so loudly while praying that they disturb their neighbours. This has become a major problem in many poorer parts of the world, where church buildings are not air conditioned. Unnecessary opposition to the gospel has resulted.

The law of love operates alongside the laws of spiritual warfare. While Acts describes for us the way spiritual warfare was done, the Epistles describe for us how we should live responsible lives of love. Both these emphases are needed, and they are not mutually exclusive. In our emphasising the message of Acts in recent times, we may have neglected the message of the Epistles. Following Christ along the path of meekness and gentleness will require fresh reflection on how we should be sensitive to the concerns of our non-Christian neighbours. When we think of spiritual warfare, we must not only think of immediate victories and immediate answers to problems. We must not forget that the warfare passages in the Epistles usually imply hardship and strain. Paul said, "Endure hardship with us like a good soldier of Christ Jesus" (2 Tim. 2:3). This seems to be missing in some of the attitudes of triumph that we see today. I think these attitudes are getting dangerously close to triumphalism.

Servanthood and the Challenge From Pluralism and Fundamentalism

Today we are facing two great threats to evangelism in the form of pluralism and what is probably incorrectly called "fundamentalism."[11] Pluralism claims that all religions are more or less equals in the universe of faiths. Fundamentalism presents exclusive claims, which cannot tolerate the idea of others trying to convert their own. They are strange bedfellows, as they seem to hold opposite views. But both share a common distaste for conversion.

Pluralism

Religious pluralism is found inside and outside the church both in the West and in so-called Third World countries, especially where there is a memory of a colonial past. Pluralists associate claims to the uniqueness of a faith with arrogance. Those who preach the exclusive claims of Christ are considered blind or insensitive to the rich religious heritage found outside the church. Pluralists say such an attitude is similar to the old colonialism, which had the underlying conviction that the culture of the colonial rulers was superior to that of the colonies. In this way, the colonial rulers justified their rule and the imposition of their customs and culture in the colonies.

When pluralists make this charge of arrogance against those who evangelise non-Christians, they are making the same mistake that opponents of Christ made in the first century. The first century Jews wanted a king, not a servant. Jesus was both. When they saw him as a servant, they rejected him, saying he could not be their king. Today in the post-colonial era, servanthood is "in," and kingship and authority are "out of fashion." So when we preach Christ as Lord, we are accused of

arrogance. We counter that biblical evangelism has the ideal balance of affirming the Lordship of Christ while adopting a servant lifestyle. Paul said, "For we do not preach ourselves, but Jesus Christ as Lord, and ourselves as your servants for Jesus' sake" (2 Cor. 4:5).

If we present ourselves as servants among those we evangelise, then it will be difficult for them to oppose us. I have often wondered why Billy Graham is invited so often to the highly pluralist programme "Larry King Live," which hosts psychic counsellors, those who talk to the dead, etc. It is clear from the way King talks to Graham that he is very fond of him. What I have seen from the times that I have seen Graham on this programme is that he gives the impression of being both humble and gentle in the way he speaks, even when he is talking about such difficult topics as heaven and hell.

Fundamentalism

If pluralism is embarrassed by the colonial past, fundamentalism is fearful of a repetition of the colonial past. In Sri Lanka we often hear statements like, "Earlier they came with the Bible in one hand and the gun in the other. Now they are coming with the Bible in one hand and dollars in the other. They are buying up the poor with their aid." There is a lot of talk about "unethical conversion." This is a very complex issue and is a huge challenge to the church. I think there is a desire to protect the authority of the religious establishment over their own people, an authority that is getting eroded through the conversion of some.

---

[11] Many of the distinctives of "fundamentalist" movements are not basic to the fundamental beliefs of these religions. For example, the intolerance of Buddhist fundamentalists is very contrary to the Buddhist ideal of tolerance. Therefore, it is argued that it is wrong to use the term fundamentalism for such movements (see Ramachandra, 1999, pp. 29-30). Ramachandra opts for words like Islamists and Hindutva to describe what we will call fundamentalists in this paper. We use the term "fundamentalist" because of what the word has come to connote to most people today, even though it may be improperly used.

I believe servanthood is a great anti-dote to these problems. If they see us as humble, unpretentious people, their hostility toward us is usually greatly reduced. I believe this is one reason why so many in India considered Mother Teresa a hero. She publicly expressed her opposition to the anti-conversion bill which fundamentalists were trying to introduce. She even joined in public processions protesting it. Yet she presented herself as a servant of the people.

The strong embarrassment among so many Hindus in India over the murder of the Australian missionary Graham Staines and his two sons was surely fuelled by the fact that the Staineses were servants of the people, working sacrificially among lepers. To add to that, there were the amazing expressions of Christ-like forgiveness by Mrs. Staines, which further commended the family to sincere people.

Even our big shows such as large evangelistic crusades can be a huge threat to non-Christians. They reason, "We don't have the money to organise that kind of programme. What chances have we against such power? We must stop them before they defeat us." I am not saying that we should not have big programmes, but that in some situations this type of programme may not be wise. But, more importantly, let our lives be simple and gentle. Let them see us as servants.[12]

Strength for servanthood

We must not forget that the strength to be servants comes from our understanding of the Lordship of Christ. We go with his authority. This is why just before giving the Great Commission he said, "All authority in heaven and on earth has been given to me" (Matt. 28:18). The next verse starts (in the English translations) with

"therefore" (*oun*), and what follows is the Great Commission. Our freedom to go into the world with the gospel comes from the authority of Christ. This is also what gives us the strength to be servants of the people. Just before the record of Jesus washing the feet of the disciples, John makes a comment about Jesus' identity, which gave him the motivation to perform this lowly deed. He says, "Jesus, knowing that the Father had given all things into his hands, and that he had come from God and was going to God, got up from the table, took off his outer robe, and tied a towel around himself" (John 13:3-4, NRSV).

Without our prior identity and security coming from the Lordship of Christ who sends us out in mission, we would be misfits in mission. We may get our identity from our work, resulting in numerous unhealthy patterns of ministry. We may feel angry and exploited by people as servanthood brings us down in society, and such descent needs a prior exaltation by Christ. We may be so insecure that we will act like "fundamentalists," overreacting to the obstacles that come our way. Therefore, in order to be servants of the people, we must first know the joy, the authority, and the security of being children and ambassadors of the king. This is what gives us strength for servanthood.

Fulfilment in Ministry

Dying for your people

We saw that an important aspect of Jesus' model of ministry is suffering. He died for his people, and he asks us to do the same. He said, "My command is this: Love each other as I have loved you" (John 15:12). He then went to on to explain what that love means: "Greater love has no one

---

[12] On the issue of servanthood as a response to pluralism and fundamentalism, see Fernando (2000).

than this, that he lay down his life for his friends" (v. 13). Then he drives the message home by saying, "You are my friends if you do what I command" (v. 14). John 10 has an interesting sequence: Jesus said, "I am the good shepherd. The good shepherd lays down his life for the sheep" (v. 11). Then he said, "The hired hand is not the shepherd who owns the sheep. So when he sees the wolf coming, he abandons the sheep and runs away. Then the wolf attacks the flock and scatters it. The man runs away because he is a hired hand and cares nothing for the sheep" (vv. 12-13). Those who, unwilling to die for their flock, run away in times of crisis are like hired hands: they care nothing for the sheep.

Many of today's reflections on ministerial fulfilment in the West have been taking ideas of job satisfaction and fulfilment from the world. According to these ideas, people should have ample opportunity to use gifts and to specialise in what they are good at. A good earthly remuneration in keeping with educational qualifications should be given. We deserve to be comfortable and to have the most efficient systems, so we can get our work done as quickly as possible. There is, however, not much reflection on the call to die.

This approach is causing havoc in many poorer countries. People are coming back after several years of study in the West and are expecting to have job satisfaction and rewards using measures from richer nations. The result is that many are living a life that is distant from the people. They don't really identify with them. Consequently, they cannot have a deep impact through their ministries. Given the lack of integrity that plagues our cultures, they are often taken for a ride by people who latch onto them with impure motives. Some are disillusioned because they seem to be so unfulfilled and underused. There-

fore they remain unhappy while serving, lacking the joy of the Lord that commends the way of Christ to the world. Many leave after a few years, feeling that they cannot really use their gifts properly in this setting. We desperately need ministerial reflection that bears in mind the dual truth that both Jesus and Paul were very joyous people while they also experienced deep suffering for their people.

Emotional pain and stress

Jesus and Paul were not only willing to die for the people; they also experienced much emotional pain because of their love for others and their call. When Jesus approached Jerusalem, he wept (Luke 19:41). In the garden he experienced tremendous anguish as he took the cup of the sins of the world—something which in his purity he hated with absolute hatred (Mark 14:33-34; Luke 22:42). While we would love to know the content of Jesus' prayers described in Hebrews 5:7, we cannot miss the sense of pain in his prayer life described there: "During the days of Jesus' life on earth, he offered up prayers and petitions with loud cries and tears to the one who could save him from death, and he was heard because of his reverent submission."

Paul vividly describes the intensity of his emotions as he agonised over the lostness of the Jews: "I speak the truth in Christ—I am not lying, my conscience confirms it in the Holy Spirit—I have great sorrow and unceasing anguish in my heart. For I could wish that I myself were cursed and cut off from Christ for the sake of my brothers, those of my own race" (Rom. 9:1-3). His description of his pain over the Galatians is even more vivid: "My dear children, for whom I am again in the pains of childbirth until Christ is formed in you, how I wish I could be with you now and change my tone, because I am perplexed about you!" (Gal. 4:19-20). He lived with this type of thing daily. He says, "Besides everything else, I face daily the pressure of my concern for all the churches. Who is weak, and I do not feel weak? Who is led into sin, and I do not inwardly burn?" (2 Cor. 11:28-29).

In society in general in affluent nations, there has been a strong quest for comfort and convenience, and people have tried to eliminate stress and strain. Those suffering from stress and strain because of their work are asked to consider a change. They are told that perhaps they are in the wrong place or are doing something wrong. The result is that we have a generation of emotionally weak people who break their commitments like hired hands. When stress comes, they run away. They leave their spouses far too soon when serious problems arise. They leave difficult churches. They hop from organisation to organisation. They don't have a theology of commitment and suffering which helps them face this challenge. They are too weak to practice the Christian ethic of commitment to people and tasks!

Society in general has redefined commitment into something that does not need to withstand stress and strain and cost. But the church is supposed to be different from the world, especially because we follow the Lord who showed such unswerving and costly commitment to us. But the same trends relating to the lack of commitment seem to be plaguing us too. Actually there isn't much difference between the divorce statistics in the church and outside the church in some places.

Young people in the West often ask me what advice I have for them about how to prepare for missionary service. My answer to them is to stick to the group to which they belong, however difficult that may be! I tell them that when they go to the mission field, they are going to face great frustration, and if they cannot face frustration at home properly, it is unlikely that they will face frustration in the field properly. They would likely move to some easier work which will take them away from their original call. I have a great fear that the West may be disqualifying itself from being a missionary sending region, because the Christians have gotten too soft. They have lost the art of sticking to their commitments.

Open-hearted ministry

Jesus and Paul hurt while ministering, because they adopted an open-hearted approach to ministry. Paul describes this type of ministry saying, "We loved you so much that we were delighted to share with you not only the gospel of God but our lives as well, because you had become so dear to us" (1 Thess. 2:8). The verb translated "loved you" (*homeiromai*) is a rare word meaning "to long for" or "yearn for." Some older translations rendered it as "being affectionately desirous" (ASV). Paul goes on to say that they shared "not only the gospel of God but our lives as well." The word translated "lives" (*psyche*) has the idea of "soul" or "inner being." Paul yearned for people so much that he opened his inner being to them. He crossed from professionalism into yearning. Today we are warned not to get too close to our people, because we will hurt ourselves if we do. But to Jesus and Paul, hurt was an indispensable ingredient of ministry.

If we realise the indispensability of suffering to ministry, we will suffer less when we face suffering. Those who haven't included this in their understanding of ministry will suffer more than they should when they encounter suffering. They will be regarding something normal as something wrong. They will be ashamed of something they should be proud of.

Lifestyle Issues

Choosing deprivation

It is well known that Jesus deprived himself of riches in order to bring us salvation. Paul says, "For you know the grace of our Lord Jesus Christ, that though he was rich, yet for your sakes he became poor, so that you through his poverty might become rich" (2 Cor. 8:9). He "made himself nothing, taking the very nature of a servant, being made in human likeness. And being found in appearance as a man, he humbled himself and became obedient to death—even death on a cross!" (Phil. 2:7-8).

Today those who propagate prosperity theology state that Jesus took on the curse of poverty upon himself so that we do not need to take it on now. Therefore, some would even say that it is wrong for Christians to be poor. They say passages like those we quoted above do not apply to us. But both these passages present Jesus as an example for us to follow. Though Christ became a curse for us, we take up a cross when we follow him. His death does not exempt us from the cross. In fact, to be close to him we will need to suffer. Paul said, "Now I rejoice in what was suffered for you, and I fill up in my flesh what is still lacking in regard to Christ's afflictions, for the sake of his body, which is the church" (Col. 1:24). And this suffering is not something to be ashamed of. Paul rejoiced in it. Paul often boasted about his deprivation. Talking about things like not taking remuneration for his ministry, he said, "But I have not used any of these rights. And I am not writing this in the hope that you will do such things for me. I would rather die than have anyone deprive me of this boast" (1 Cor. 9:15). Recently in Sri Lanka a prosperity preacher from the West ridiculed Job,

claiming that he should not be regarded as a model for us today! That is clearly wrong!

Still a huge portion of the world's population is poor and deprived. Recently the World Bank President, James Wolfensohn, stated that by 2025 about 4 billion people would live in poverty, that is, on less than $2 a day. And of that group, 2 billion would live in absolute poverty.[13] Those who live and work among the poor will also need to see what deprivation they need to take on in order to identify with the poor. Did not Paul say, "To the weak I became weak, to win the weak"? (1 Cor. 9:22a). We certainly cannot legislate here for anybody, but our passion for the gospel will cause us to make sacrifices. After talking about becoming weak, Paul goes on to say, "I have become all things to all men so that by all possible means I might save some. I do all this for the sake of the gospel, that I may share in its blessings" (vv. 22b-23).

I believe this matter of poverty is very pertinent in this era where free enterprise and the market economy have brought prosperity into the open for all to see. This is taking place especially through advertising that is available to all in this media generation. Yet the percentage of poor people continues to grow and with it the level of discontent among a large mass of our people. I fear that many of our nations are heading for a Communist-type revolution by these disgruntled masses. At such times, a life of voluntary deprivation by Christian ministers could be a great asset in winning credibility. As the poor see the rich getting richer while they get poorer, and as their anger grows against the rich, it will be refreshing for them to see some people who could be better off who choose to deprive themselves in order to serve the poor.

---

[13] From an AFP news report, September 1999.

Caution with partnerships

We should be careful about the lifestyle issue when we enter into partnerships between Christians from rich and poor nations. Partnership is certainly a good and necessary thing, and it is one of the heartening areas of growth in missions today. Many churches in richer nations honestly want equality with other Christians, and this is a key missionary motivation for partnership. Paul said, "Our desire is not that others might be relieved while you are hard pressed, but that there might be equality" (2 Cor. 8:13). Richer Christians feel bad that there is such a difference between their lifestyle and that of Christians from poorer nations. But when they come to our nations, they live in luxury hotels where a day's cost is about the monthly salary of a Christian worker. Unconsciously, the local leaders also get sucked into this lifestyle. And the guilty rich visitors feed this desire by suggesting that the locals need more conveniences. This is a powerful temptation, because we all like comfort and efficiency, and the simple lifestyle may be quite inefficient. If we succumb to this pressure, we will soon become distant from the people we are called to serve.

My father is a layman who has been active in the Evangelical Movement for a long time. He once told me that often a young evangelist goes to an unreached area and begins a good work of pioneering evangelism. This goes on for a time, until he comes in touch with a foreign sponsor who takes him on as "Our man in Sri Lanka." From that point on, the ministry goes downhill. The worldwide missionary movement, therefore, needs to do a lot of thinking about the whole issue of lifestyle and how that affects the way missionary partnerships work.

I will close this discussion of Jesus as a missionary model with the words of Hebrews 13:12-13: "And so Jesus also suffered outside the city gate to make the people holy through his own blood. Let us, then, go to him outside the camp, bearing the disgrace he bore."

References

Anderson, J. N. D. (1984). *Christianity and the world religions: The challenge of pluralism*. Downers Grove, IL: InterVarsity Press.

Bonda, J. (1998). *The one purpose of God: An answer to the doctrine of eternal punishment*. (R. Bruinsma, Trans.). Grand Rapids, MI: Wm. B. Eerdmans Publishing Co.

Crockett, W. E., & Sigountos, J. G. (Eds.). (1991). *Through no fault of their own: The fate of those who have never heard*. Grand Rapids, MI: Baker Book House.

Fernando, A. (1983). *A universal homecoming?* Bombay: Gospel Literature Service.

———. (1989). *The Christian's attitude toward world religions*. Wheaton, IL: Tyndale House Publishers.

———. (1994). *Crucial questions about hell*. Wheaton, IL: Crossway Books.

———. (1995). *The supremacy of Christ*. Wheaton, IL: Crossway Books.

———. (2000). The uniqueness of Christ. In D. A. Carson (Ed.), *Telling the truth: Evangelizing postmoderns*. Grand Rapids, MI: Zondervan Publishing House.

Froom, L. E. (1965-1966). *The conditionalist faith of our fathers*. (Vols. 1-2). Washington, DC: Herald & Review Publishing Association.

Fudge, E. (1982). *The fire that consumes: A biblical and historical study of final punishment*. Houston, TX: Providential Press.

Glasser, A. F. (1975). China. In D. E. Hoke (Ed.), *The church in Asia*. Chicago: Moody Press.

Harris, M. (1999). *Slave of Christ: A New Testament metaphor for total devotion to Christ*. Leicester, England: Apollos.

Hick, J. (1976). *Death and eternal life*. London: Collins.

———. (1979). *Evil and the God of love*. Glasgow, Scotland: Collins, Fount Paperbacks.

Newbigin, L. (1978). *The open secret: Sketches for a missionary theology*. Grand Rapids, MI: Wm. B. Eerdmans Publishing Co.

Okholm, D. L., & Phillips, T. R. (Eds.). (1995). *More than one way? Four views of salvation in a pluralistic world*. Grand Rapids, MI: Zondervan Publishing House.

Parker, Mrs. A. (1918). *Sadhu Sundar Singh: Called of God*. Madras, India: The Christian Literature Society.

Pinnock, C. H. (1990). In C. H. Pinnock & D. Brown (Eds.), *Theological crossfire: An evangelical/liberal dialogue* (pp. 226-231). Grand Rapids, MI: Zondervan Publishing House.

Ramachandra, V. (1999). *Faiths in conflict? Christian integrity in a multicultural world*. Leicester, England: InterVarsity Press.

Robinson, J. A. T. (1968). *In the end God*. New York: Harper & Row.

Shenk, C. (1997). *Who do you say that I am? Christians encounter other religions*. Scottdale, PA: Herald Press.

Stott, J. R. W. (1988). In D. L. Edwards & J. R. W. Stott (Eds.), *Essentials: A liberal-evangelical dialogue* (pp. 327-329). London: Hodder & Stoughton.

Wenham, J. W. (1992). The case for conditional immortality. In N. M. de S. Cameron (Ed.), *Universalism and the doctrine of hell* (pp. 161-191). Grand Rapids, MI: Baker Book House.

Wright, C. (1997). *Thinking clearly about the uniqueness of Christ*. East Sussex, UK: Monarch.

Ajith Fernando has led Sri Lanka Youth for Christ since 1976. Convinced of a call to theologise from the grassroots, he has always led a small division in YFC and presently leads the work with drug dependents. His YFC responsibilities include teaching and pastoral care of staff. Ajith and his wife Nelun are active in the leadership of a Methodist church, most of whose members are converts from other religions. He has a Th.M. in New Testament from Fuller Theological Seminary. His nine books have been in the area of either Bible exposition, such as the NIV Application Commentary: Acts (Zondervan, 1998), or mission theology, such as The Supremacy of Christ (Crossway, 1995).

The Holy Spirit: the divine implementer of mission

AJITH FERNANDO

WHEN WE THINK of the Holy Spirit, we usually think of him as the implementer on earth of the divine will. If so, when it comes to mission, the Holy Spirit would be the implementer of mission. The work of the Holy Spirit is as diverse as the work of the Trinity. So it will not be easy for us to summarise this in one study. Some elimination will have to take place as we look for emphases that are relevant for mission today. At the risk of oversimplification, we could say that the Gospels focus on the promise of the Spirit, Acts on the power of the Spirit in mission, and the Epistles of Paul on life in the Spirit. Owing to the limitations of this single study, I have decided to focus primarily on the Epistles of Paul. This is in keeping with my aim of looking to the teaching given in the Bible to the first century churches as a source of material for instructing today's young churches.

We can be thankful that the church has rediscovered the importance of the power of the Spirit for mission. She always believed it, but often in history she restricted the work of the Spirit to a limited number of activities. The phenomenal growth of the Charismatic Movement in the 20th century changed all of that. In fact, with the re-emphasis on previously neglected factors by the Charismatic Movement, she took on the designation of being "full gospel." Yet every movement in the history of the church has usually been deficient in some areas. So strictly speaking, only the Bible can claim to contain the full gospel. We are all striving towards fullness and are often made aware along our pilgrimage on earth of how far we fall short.

Some Important Emphases in Paul on the Holy Spirit

Let us, then, look at the teaching of Paul about the Holy Spirit, especially as it impacts our thinking about the mission of the church.[1] We find that many important themes and three major themes (in terms of frequency of occurrence) appear. We will first look at the important themes.

His place in the Godhead (43/46[2])

The Holy Spirit's place in the Godhead is mentioned or implied 43 times covering 46 verses. 20 times he is referred to as the Spirit of God and three times as the Spirit of Christ. 15 times we are told that God gives the Spirit or works through him. Paul says that the Spirit knows the mind of God or God knows the mind of the Spirit (four times) and that the Spirit exalts Christ (five times).

The Spirit and truth (10/51)

In Jesus' farewell discourse in John, three times he refers to the Spirit as the Spirit of truth (John 14:17; 15:26; 16:13). Jesus promises that the Spirit will guide the disciples into all truth (16:13). The connection between the Spirit and truth is spelled out in Paul's Epistles 10 times covering a total of 51 verses (10/51). In 4/5 he is described as the agent of revelation (1 Cor. 2:13; Eph. 3:4-5; Eph. 6:17; 1 Tim. 4:1). 6/46 say that he shows or teaches us truth (1 Cor. 2:9-10, 12, 15, 16; 1 Cor. 12-14; Eph. 1:18). Included here are about 40 verses in 1 Corinthians 12–14 that describe gifts such as prophecy, words of wisdom and knowledge, and dis-

cerning between spirits.[3] Some people call these gifts illumination, though until recently, at least in the circles in which I have moved, the so-called charismatic gifts were not included under illumination.

The Spirit and salvation (15/16)

So important is the Holy Spirit to salvation that Jesus described the act of salvation as being "born of the Spirit" (John 3:8). Paul also shows this close link between salvation and the Holy Spirit (15/16). Here are some statistics: 2/2 list the Spirit's role in the central gospel events (Rom. 1:4; 1 Tim. 3:16). 2/2 speak of salvation or renewal through the Spirit (1 Cor. 6:11; Tit. 3:5). 1/1 refers to baptism (in a soteriological sense) by one Spirit (1 Cor. 12:13). 5/6 acknowledge the Spirit as first fruits or deposit (Rom. 8:23; 2 Cor. 1:22; 5:5; Eph. 1:13-14; 4:30). In 4/4 the Spirit is received by believing (Gal. 3:2, 5, 14; 5:5). In 1/1 the Spirit is given to us at salvation (Tit. 3:5-6).

The Spirit gives power for mission and ministry (5/6)

The connection between mission and the power of the Spirit is a major theme in Acts. But in Paul I could find only five references (six verses). Of these five occurrences, three are summary statements about Paul's ministry among his readers (Rom. 15:18-19; 1 Cor. 2:4; 1 Thess. 1:5). The other two refer to the work of the Spirit in pastoral situations: Those who have received the Spirit are to gently restore those caught in a sin (Gal. 6:1, NRSV). Timothy must guard the good deposit entrusted to him with the help of the Holy

---

[1] The definitive treatment on Paul and the Holy Spirit is Fee (1994).

[2] Here we are following the convention used throughout the series which presents the instances a theme occurs (43 in this case) and then the total number of verses covered, taking into account all these instances (46). So 43 instances and 46 verses will be represented as 43/46.

[3] We have not included the other passages in Paul about spiritual gifts (Rom. 12:3-8; Eph. 4:9-13), as they do not refer to the Holy Spirit in connection with the gifts.

Spirit (2 Tim. 1:14). In the economy of God's revelation to humankind, the role of the Spirit in empowering mission was covered in the book of Acts. Its relatively low occurrence in Paul should not cause us to neglect it, as an earlier generation of Evangelicals may have done. They looked mainly to Paul for their theology and neglected the Gospels and Acts as sources of theology. Thankfully this attitude is rapidly diminishing in the church.

The Charismatic Movement has focussed much attention on the abiding teachings that can come from Acts.[4] In the 20th century, biblical scholarship began to pay much more attention to the theology contained in the Gospels and Acts. This was emphasised more by non-Evangelical scholars of the church.[5] But recently Evangelicals have also found that looking for theological teaching is an important part of studying the Gospels and Acts.[6] They have, however, done so without sacrificing their belief in the historical reliability of these New Testament books, which is what many of the non-Evangelical scholars did. The result of this is that now we are looking more at the theology of Luke and therefore at the theology of the Holy Spirit. In this process, the church seems to have recovered the missionary character of the Holy Spirit.

Right at the start of Acts, Jesus showed the priority of the Spirit for missions when he commanded the apostles, "Do not leave Jerusalem, but wait for the gift my Father promised, which you have heard me speak about. For John baptized with water, but in a few days you will be baptized with the Holy Spirit" (Acts 1:4-5). In this first chapter, he also explained why the Holy Spirit is so important for mission. He gives us power for the work of witness (1:8). David Bosch (1991, p. 115) has shown how the relationship between the Holy Spirit and mission was a factor that was neglected in the history of the church. He says, "By the second century A.D. the emphasis shifted almost exclusively to the Spirit as the agent of sanctification or as the guarantor of apostolicity." Bosch says that the "Protestant Reformation of the 16th century tended to put the major emphasis on the work of the Spirit as bearing witness to and interpreting the Word of God." Bosch says that it was only in the 20th century that there was "a rediscovery of the intrinsic missionary character of the Holy Spirit." He says this came about "because of a renewed study of the writings of Luke." One of the pioneers here was Roland Allen, whose book, *Pentecost and the World: A Revelation of the Holy Spirit in the "Acts of the Apostles,"* appeared in 1917.[7]

Yet my focus is on Paul. And Paul does not say as much on the Holy Spirit as he does about God, Jesus, and the church. Gordon Fee (1994), through his magisterial book on the Holy Spirit in Paul, *God's Empowering Presence*, has shown that Paul does have a much more important

---

[4] See the scholarly study of Stronstad (1994).

[5] See, for example, Haenchen (1971). When the first edition of F. F. Bruce's commentary on the Greek text of Acts appeared in 1951 (Bruce, 1951), it was criticised by liberal scholars for its lack of theological content and described as the product of the humanity school of Aberdeen University. In the third edition of this book (Bruce, 1990, p. xvi), Bruce said that he esteemed this description as a high honour and expressed his debt to the great archaeologist and historian Sir William Ramsey.

[6] One of the earliest examples of this trend was Marshall (1970). More recent studies include Dollar (1996) and Keener (1997).

[7] This work is reprinted in Allen (1962, pp. 1-61).

theology of the Holy Spirit than Christians usually think.[8] However, I will not give as much emphasis to the power which the Holy Spirit gives for mission as it deserves,[9] owing to the need to be selective in the choice of subjects, given the limitations of this study. Besides, I feel that this is a doctrine that the church has rediscovered and that this has been well covered in several works[10] and in the practice of many churches.

There is, however, one issue related to the topic of the Holy Spirit empowering us for mission that I will address here because of its contemporary relevance. When the church appointed "relief workers" to distribute food to needy Christians, the two requirements for selection were the need to be filled with the Spirit and the need to be filled with wisdom (Acts 6:3). If we were to follow this pattern today, then we should be looking for the fullness of the Spirit and wisdom when appointing people to things like building committees, social service projects, and other tasks in the church. Usually we do not falter on the wisdom requirement, but on the spiritual requirement we often lower our standards because these are considered supposedly non-spiritual activities. Acts 6 shows that it is wrong, in the programme of the church, to distinguish between spiritual and non-spiritual activities in this way. All activities in the church's programme are spiritual and require spiritual people to be involved in their leadership.

This principle becomes very complex when Christian relief organisations are structured in a way that they must hire non-Christians on their staff because of government regulations. I have found that even when this is not a requirement, Christian relief organisations get very lax in the way they look for spiritual qualifications of those they hire. This is inexcusable! Often organisations that claim to be committed to holistic ministry do not hire holistic workers—those filled with both wisdom and the Spirit.

But sometimes government regulations require the hiring of non-Christians in Christian social agencies. This has happened in hospitals in countries like Nepal, where missionaries are not permitted to do evangelism and where there are strict policies about conversion of non-Christians. These organisations will need to do some really hard thinking to ensure that people filled with the Spirit influence the direction of the movement. This is an issue that Christian relief organisations need to constantly keep before them today. Perhaps something can be learned from mission groups in countries like Nepal, which have grappled with this issue for a long time. I fear that often it is tucked away into a safe place where it will not cause much discomfort to the pragmatically oriented hiring practices of many organisations.

While the subjects discussed above are important, they are not major emphases in Paul. When we consider the frequency of occurrence, we find three major emphases relating to the ministry of the Spirit in Paul: the Spirit as our companion and help, spiritual gifts, and holiness and the fruit of the Spirit.

---

[8] See also Turner (1996, pp. 103-135). Also, Carson (1987) is a superb study of one of the most important passages in Paul about the Holy Spirit.

[9] See Fernando (1998) for more complete treatment of this subject.

[10] In addition to the books cited so far, I have found the following books especially helpful: Deere (1993), Green (1975), Keener (1996), Kinlaw (1985), and Sargent (1994).

The Spirit as Our Companion and Help (32/38)

Jesus described the Holy Spirit as the *paraklētos* (John 14:16, 26; 15:26; 16:7), which has been translated as "counselor" (NIV), "helper" (NAS), or "advocate" (NRSV). Though Paul does not use the word *paraklētos* in the Epistles, his various descriptions about the Holy Spirit being our companion and helper provide a vivid commentary of this role.[11] Six times (covering seven verses) Paul simply says that we are given the Spirit. In 7/8 he says that the Holy Spirit lives in us and with us. Of these references, three times the word *oikeö*, meaning to come and take residence as in a house, is used of this activity of the Spirit (Rom. 8:9, 11; 1 Cor. 3:16). The beloved benediction at the end of 2 Corinthians refers to the fellowship (*koinönia*) of the Holy Spirit (13:14). His ministries of leading us and guiding our actions and speech particularly show his role as our helper (3/3; Rom. 8:14; 1 Cor. 12:3; Gal. 5:18). So is his ministry as the giver of life and of power to live the Christian life (7/9).[12]

The enabling of the Spirit to live the Christian life is one of the key arguments that we present for the uniqueness of Christ. We say that all religions teach us to do good, but that Christianity gives us the ability to live up to the principles of our religion. It does that by giving us the Holy Spirit as our helper so that, with his help, we can do what we otherwise could not do. The challenge for us today is to get our act together! People like Mahatma Gandhi accused Christianity, with its doctrine of unmerited forgiveness for sin, of opening the door to moral licence. He would point to examples of people who sinned boldly while claiming to be saved, because they were assured of forgiveness from God. We know that this is a distortion of the biblical doctrine of free grace, that those who have truly received Christ's salvation could not go on sinning in the way Gandhi said they did (1 John 2:1; 3:6, 9). Yet it is up to us to show a watching and sceptical world that Christianity does indeed work to change sinners into righteous people.[13]

The confidence we have as Christians is also through the ministry of the Spirit in our lives. Traditionally when speaking of the assurance of salvation, we have focussed almost exclusively on the passages of Scripture that say that those who have believed have been saved (John 1:12; 5:24; 6:37, etc.). This is indeed the basic means by which we can be assured of our standing in Christ. But the Bible also tells us that the Spirit has a direct ministry in our lives through which he gives us this assurance. Once we are told that the Spirit gives us hope (Rom. 15:13). The Spirit witnesses to us about our position in Christ (3/5; Rom. 8:15-16; 9:1-2; Gal. 5:5). Romans 8:15-16 is particularly clear about this: "For you did not receive a spirit that makes you a slave again to fear, but you received the Spirit of sonship. And by him we cry, '*Abba*, Father.' The Spirit himself testifies with our spirit that we are God's children." It is true that the primary way in which the Spirit does this is through the Scriptures. But there is a subjective element here too, where we could say that God has touched us and ministered to us individually through his Spirit.

---

[11] 1 John 2:1 uses this word for Jesus, referring to his ministry as our advocate when we sin.

[12] Rom. 8:6, 12-13; 15:13; 1 Cor. 12:13; Eph. 3:16-17; Phil. 1:19; 2 Tim. 1:14.

[13] For a fuller response to Gandhi's criticism, see Fernando (2000) and Fernando (1998, chap. 12).

This particular ministry of the Spirit is extremely relevant today for missions. I have often had the sad experience of meeting many Christian workers who are bitter and angry with the way that they have been treated by others, especially by the churches or institutions with which they have been associated and by the very people they have sacrificially served. We all know how hard rejection is to those who have made it their goal to love everyone they encounter and to be honourable in their dealings with them. This can make good people bitter. The best antidote to rejection on earth is acceptance in heaven. After G. Campbell Morgan learned that he was rejected as a candidate for the Methodist ministry, following a poor showing at his "trial sermon," he sent a telegram to his father with one word, "Rejected." The father promptly responded with a telegram that contained the words, "Rejected on earth. Accepted in heaven. Dad" (Morgan, 1972, p. 60).

Sometimes through the Holy Spirit God gives us a clear impression of the fact that we belong to him. Paul describes this as the witness of the Spirit to our spirit (Rom. 8:16). The joy of knowing that God has ministered to us in this way does so much to take away the bitterness of the rejection of people. The sorrow of it may remain, because we love the people who have rejected us, but the Spirit's ministry to us helps take away the despair and bitterness. Paul demonstrates this in 2 Corinthians, a book that exults in the glory of the ministry. It was written after some painful experiences, but the joy of God's ministry to him had helped replace the pain with joy. Here is how he describes God's ministry of comfort in the painful experience that he had: "Praise be to the God and Father of our Lord Jesus Christ, the Father of compassion and the God of all comfort, who comforts us in all our troubles, so that we can comfort those in

any trouble with the comfort we ourselves have received from God" (2 Cor. 1:3-4). Experiencing the joy of such experiences of the Spirit's witness is, I believe, essential for remaining happy in the work of the Lord.

Four times Paul describes the Spirit's involvement in our worship, prayers, and intercession (Rom. 8:26, 27; Eph. 6:18; Phil. 3:3). These verses show us how important it is to ensure that the Holy Spirit is given ample opportunity to influence and direct our worship activities. The first of these references has a beautiful wording: "In the same way, the Spirit helps us in our weakness. We do not know what we ought to pray for, but the Spirit himself intercedes for us with groans that words cannot express" (Rom. 8:26). That simple English word "helps" translates a double compound in the Greek, *sunantilambanetai*. It literally means, "to take share in." The idea is that the Holy Spirit fully identifies with us in our weakness by coming alongside us and taking his share of our burden. Here is another reason for rejoicing and confidence in ministry. Often our weaknesses become huge burdens to us. Sometimes we deny them and go through a complex process to hide them. This can hurt our effectiveness by hindering the closeness with which we relate to those among whom we minister. Once we know that the Holy Spirit is sharing the weakness with us, we do not need to set off on an elaborate process of denying the reality of our weaknesses. The result is that our effectiveness in ministry is increased.

We can be grateful that the church has rediscovered this ministry of the Holy Spirit that involves his constant, daily companionship with us. Around this fact is built the biblical understanding of spirituality. A strong rational bent seems to have restricted Protestant Christianity in the West to giving a relatively lower emphasis to spirituality. Earlier, to many

Evangelicals, Christianity was simply giving mental assent to facts about the work of Christ, followed by rugged obedience along the path of obedience. The personal, subjective experience of God through his Spirit was largely neglected. The rediscovery of tangible spiritual experiences came through various movements, such as the Wesleyan Holiness Movement, the Quakers, and more recently the Charismatic Movement. We are reminded of the reaction to a dry, rational approach to life, which caused the revolt against modernism, giving rise to post-modernism. A similar thing seems to be happening with the dry, rational attitude to truth that was found in many branches of Evangelicalism. People have taken a much greater interest in spirituality.

Recently Evangelicals have moved in different directions as they have looked for more vital experiences of spirituality. Firstly, some have moved to the more liturgical traditions, such as Anglicanism, Roman Catholicism, and Orthodoxy. Secondly, others have rediscovered the *charismata* afresh, and the Charismatic Movement has swept the globe with breathtaking force. While at one time the Charismatic Movement was considered by many to be a fringe group within Evangelicalism, today it is a vital part of mainstream Christianity, and its influence upon all segments of Christianity has been profound. Within this movement, spiritual gifts that illustrate the helping ministry of the Holy Spirit, such as prophecy and knowledge, are commonplace (see Deere, 1993, 1996).

The third direction that I will mention is from within traditional Evangelicalism, where there has been a new focus on the spiritual disciplines of meditation, prayer, and fasting. The popularity of the writings of James Houston (1989, 1990), Eugene Peterson (1996, pp. 107-111), Richard Foster (1989), Peter Toon (1987, 1991), and Dallas Willard (1988, 1998) is evidence of this encouraging trend in the Evangelical Movement. In an earlier generation, A. W. Tozer (1948, 1963, 1985) made the Evangelical Movement in the West aware of the need for fresh thinking about spirituality. Influencing this whole movement have been Catholic writers like Henri Nouwen and Thomas Merton. From a Reformed perspective, John Piper (1986, 1995, 1997a, 1997b) has been stressing the spiritual disciplines through his writings, which are rich in biblical, theological, and devotional content. Piper is following in the steps of his mentor, the great 18th century American theologian Jonathan Edwards, who was a great exponent of the experiential aspects of Christianity.[14] Another Reformed preacher/scholar to press home the importance of experiencing God in this way was D. Martyn Lloyd-Jones (1984, 1992; see also Eaton, 1989).

Perhaps the highly rational orientation of Western society may have hindered the growth of a vibrant experience of the Holy Spirit among Western Evangelicals in the modern era. But Asian Christianity has a noble tradition of spirituality during the same period. Sadhu Sundar Singh of India testified to what we would today call mystical experiences of God that directly and literally illustrate the promise that the Holy Spirit will lead and guide God's children (Appasamy, 1966; Sundar Singh, 1989). As a young man, Watchman Nee of China wrote a three-volume work on sanctification, *The Spiritual Man*, and he spent almost 20 of his mature years in prison.

---

[14] See his book, *A Treatise Concerning Religious Affections*, which is now available in various contemporary editions. This book and two other relevant books, *Narrative of Surprising Conversions* and *Thoughts on the Revival of Religion in New England*, are found in Edwards (1974).

He was a master of the spiritual life, as his numerous, still-popular books show. American missionary to India E. Stanley Jones (1968) made his unique brand of Indian spirituality known in the West through his writings and the Ashram Movement that he founded. While I am not too familiar with African, Caribbean, and Latin American Christianity, it is my understanding that they too have always had a place for the immediacy of the Spirit in Christian experience.

So we can say that there is a greater emphasis than before on experiencing the Spirit within the Evangelical Movement in the West. More and more people are talking about how he speaks to us and how he intervenes in our lives (sometimes miraculously), showing us his will for us, warning us of challenges we face, and promising us of his provision for needs that we face. Of course, there has been some abuse of this aspect, with people making outlandish claims of what God has said to them. We find situations of people who are claiming that God has promised them a thing that was a deep wish of theirs, without any real evidence that God has spoken to them. This is like the young man who told a girl that God had told him that he should marry her. She promptly replied that God had told her no such thing! But this tendency is to be expected with all types of special spiritual phenomena: excesses always accompany the genuine experience.

The significance for mission of this trend towards experiencing the reality of God is immense. Millions are coming to Christ, attracted by the possibility of experiencing the power and love of God in tangible ways in their personal lives.

Spiritual Gifts (37/140)

Spiritual gifts are mentioned several times in Paul's Epistles (37/140). The key passage I have considered is 1 Corinthians 12–14. The other two gifts passages (Rom. 12:6-8; Eph. 4:7-13) are not associated with the Holy Spirit and therefore, though significant, were not accounted for in my counting of verses. The Ephesians passage clearly states that it is Christ who gives the gifts (vv. 7-8), though we know that today Christ's blessings to us are given through the Holy Spirit.

In both the Romans and Corinthians passages on the gifts, the focus is on the unity of the body and how the gifts help preserve and establish that unity in practice. The Romans passage is prefaced with these words: "Just as each of us has one body with many members, and these members do not all have the same function, so in Christ we who are many form one body, and each member belongs to all the others" (Rom. 12:4-5). Then Paul says, "We have different gifts, according to the grace given us" (v. 6). After that is the listing of gifts (vv. 7-8). The Ephesians passage ends with the words, "… until we all reach unity in the faith and in the knowledge of the Son of God and become mature, attaining to the whole measure of the fullness of Christ" (Eph. 4:13). The connection to unity is clear.

The Corinthians passage (1 Cor. 12–14) was written in response to questions asked by the church there about the operation of the gifts in the church. Again we see that the focus was not on the gifts themselves but on how the gifts should operate in the body. Unlike the Romans and Ephesians passages, this passage clearly connects gifts with the Holy Spirit. Chapter 12 focuses on the fact that all are of equal importance despite having different gifts. Chapter 13 focuses on the fact that love is much more important than all the gifts. And chapter 14 gives instructions on how the gifts should operate when the body comes together. It has warnings about misuse and instructions about what is permissible when the community is together. The key to understanding this chapter is the *oikodomeō* word group, which carries the idea of building up. These words appear seven times in 1 Corinthians 14 and are translated as "strengthen," "edify," and "build up."[15] Paul is saying that when people exercise gifts in a gathering of the church, they must ensure that others are edified.

So the focus of the gifts passages is not purely on gifts but on how they should be regulated and on how they should mirror and foster Christian unity. This does not give us authority to downplay the importance of gifts, especially the so-called charismatic gifts, like tongues and prophecy. The Acts of the Apostles gives these gifts an important place and does not even hint that they were undesirable for the church's health. Acts was certainly written after Romans and 1 Corinthians and, most probably, after Ephesians too. Paul was Luke's close friend, and Luke would have known the mind of Paul about these gifts. Yet he presents them in a very positive light.

The oft-repeated statement that we must avoid the two extremes of charismania and charisphobia is appropriate here. These two extremes are expressed in two types of sermons that could be preached from 1 Corinthians 14. One type will take a statement like, "He who speaks in a tongue edifies himself" (v. 4), to argue that speaking in tongues is absolutely necessary for the edification of all Christians. In the context, of course, Paul is talking about how prophecy is more desirable than tongues in public worship. The verse goes on to say, "... but he who prophesies edifies the church." The thrust of the verse, then, is in a different direction. The sec-

ond extreme position is expressed in the type of sermon that focuses almost entirely on the wrong uses of tongues mentioned in this passage, leaving the hearer with a distinct sense that tongues is an undesirable gift that does more harm than good!

It would be instructive to mention two important verses in Paul on how we can stifle the work of the Spirit. 1 Thessalonians 5:19 says, "Do not put out the Spirit's fire." The next verse says, "Do not treat prophecies with contempt" (v. 20). So, according to this passage, the way to put out the Spirit's fire is to treat prophecies with contempt. This is a sobering verse that should cause us to be cautious about unguarded criticism about the prophecies that are being made these days. Of course, the next verse says, "Test everything" (v. 21). If a statement that purports to be a prophecy contradicts what is clearly taught in the Scriptures, it must be shown to be wrong. But we must be careful about treating prophecies with contempt, a thing that we often find sophisticated Evangelicals doing.

The other verse about stifling the Spirit has another emphasis. Ephesians 4:30 says, "And do not grieve the Holy Spirit of God, with whom you were sealed for the day of redemption." The context shows that the way we can grieve the Holy Spirit is by unholy living. Verse 31 asks us to turn from unholy living: "Get rid of all bitterness, rage and anger, brawling and slander, along with every form of malice." Verse 32 presents the positive side of holiness: "Be kind and compassionate to one another, forgiving each other, just as in Christ God forgave you." So we can stifle the Spirit by stifling gifts or by living unholy lives. This brings us to the third major emphasis of Paul regarding the Holy Spirit.

---

[15] 1 Cor. 14:3, 4, 5, 12, 17, 26.

Holiness and the Fruit of the Spirit (59/81)

When we look at the frequency of occurrence of the theme of holiness/godliness and its relation to the work of the Holy Spirit, it becomes clear that this is the function of the Holy Spirit that Paul wants to highlight most in his Epistles. I am using the words "holiness" and "godliness" here in a broad sense to refer to what we might call Christian character or Christ-likeness.

The ability to be holy

Paul stresses some key ideas relating to the role of the Holy Spirit in the life of holiness. He summarises the Christian life as living in or according to the Spirit (6/6; Rom. 8:4, 5, 6, 9, Gal. 5:16, 25). 11 times (covering 14 verses) he refers to the inner work the Spirit does in us in contrast to the law. Romans 2:29 is representative: "No, a man is a Jew if he is one inwardly; and circumcision is circumcision of the heart, by the Spirit, not by the written code."

Even more frequent are Paul's affirmations that the Spirit helps release the hold of sin or the flesh over us and helps make us godly (17/25). Paul's classic statement in Romans 8:2 summarises this teaching well: "... through Christ Jesus the law of the Spirit of life set me free from the law of sin and death."[16] The next two verses show that this is something we cannot do in our natural state: "For what the law was powerless to do in that it was weakened by the sinful nature, God did by sending his own Son in the likeness of sinful man to be a sin offering. And so he condemned sin in sinful man, in order that the righteous requirements of the law might be fully met in us, who do not live according to the sinful nature but according to the Spirit" (vv. 3-4).

Considering the crisis of godliness in the church today, this group of texts should be regarded as being of vital importance to us. We must show Christians that holiness is a work of the Spirit, who does in us what we in our natural state cannot do. I believe the church should bring this truth to the forefront of Christian conversation and teaching. If Christians believe that it is possible for them to be holy, then half the battle for holiness is won. They will not give up this quest for godliness as futile; neither will they neglect it as unimportant. Instead, believing in God's ability to change them, they would aspire to godliness and use whatever means God gives towards helping them achieve this goal.

Another major theme is that the Spirit is the giver of love and the other fruit of the Spirit (17/27).[17] A key text here is Romans 5:5, "... God has poured out his love into our hearts by the Holy Spirit, whom he has given us."[18] Though the Spirit is not mentioned in 1 Corinthians 13, we have included it in our study of the Spirit for the following reasons: First, the chapter is sandwiched between two parts of Paul's treatment of the gifts of the Spirit. Second, verses 1-3 are describing the insufficiency of what Paul has described as gifts of the Spirit in chapter 12. Third, the Spirit is described several times in Paul as the giver of love.[19] And fourth, love is mentioned first in the listing of the fruit

---

[16] Other key references here include Rom. 8:12-13; 2 Cor. 3:3; Gal. 5:5, 16, 24.

[17] Included in this list is 1 Cor. 12:31–14:1, the 15 verses of which I have divided into 6 references.

[18] Other key references here include Rom. 8:6; 15:13, 30; 1 Cor. 12:21–14:1; 2 Cor. 6:6; Gal. 5:22; 1 Thess. 1:6.

[19] Rom. 5:5; 15:30; 2 Cor. 6:6; Gal. 5:22; Col. 1:8.

of the Spirit in Galatians 5:22. So when we think of the Spirit, we must think of love and the other fruit of the Spirit. This emphasis is summarised well in a verse from Samuel Longfellow's hymn, "Holy Spirit, Truth Divine":

> Holy Spirit, love divine,
> Glow within this heart of mine;
> Kindle every high desire;
> Perish self in thy pure fire.

The need for a fresh emphasis

If our statistical survey is to guide us in what we should emphasise today when talking about the Holy Spirit, then holiness and the fruit of the Spirit should be given a very high place. In the study on God, I mentioned that 1,400 of Paul's 2,005 verses are connected with the call to be holy/godly. This is about 70% of the verses in his Epistles. I suggested that this could be the most important theme in the Epistles.

Yet I believe I am right in saying that today, when we talk about the Holy Spirit, it is generally not in connection with godliness. The focus is on power for ministry and for the exercise of gifts. As we saw, this is not a key emphasis in Paul's teaching. There is a conspicuous absence of emphasis on power for ministry and technique in ministry in Paul. It is conspicuous because there is so much teaching on these aspects today. Because of this and because of the crisis of godliness in the church today, I have decided to include an extended discussion on this here.

We repeat that Acts has given us ample evidence on how important the exercise of the miraculous gifts is for evangelism. God used tongues, signs, and wonders to open the door for the preaching of the gos-

pel. Yet Paul is writing to people who have responded to the evangelistic message and who belong to the church. Like today, many of them were attracted to Christ through the exercise of power—a fact which Paul mentions in the Epistles (Rom. 15:18-19; 1 Cor. 2:4; 1 Thess. 1:5). For such people, there should be a high emphasis on the Holy Spirit as the One who enables godly living. To this we add what we discussed in the study on God about the need to supplement the almost magical view of God which people have with the emphasis on the sovereignty and holiness of God.

Throughout the modern era, God raised up reform or revival movements in the history of the church to give greater emphasis to holiness. In the 16th and 17th centuries, the Puritans played a big part in renewing the church in the English-speaking world, and their writings continue to influence the church.[20] The works of John Bunyan (1628–1688), Richard Baxter (1615–1691), and John Owen (1616–1683), for example, still remain very popular. In the 18th century, Pietism, which gave a high place to holy living, played an influential role in Continental Europe. John Wesley (1703–1791) was greatly influenced by the Pietists, especially by the Moravians and their founder Count Nikolaus Von Zinzendorf (1700–1760). Wesley emphasised the sanctifying work of the Holy Spirit with a focus on holiness and love, and he used words like "perfect love" or "full sanctification" to describe what he regarded as the desired standard of holiness for Christians (Wesley, 1998 reprint). Because of this emphasis, a segment of the Wesleyan Movement in America was called the Holiness Movement.[21] The so-called "Keswick

---

[20] See Packer (1990) and Ryken (1986).

[21] For a brief introduction to Wesley's theology of sanctification, see Coleman (1990, pp. 79-97) and Dieter (1987). For a more comprehensive study, see Wynkoop (1972), Greenlee (1994), and Wood (1980).

Theology" also placed emphasis on holiness, focusing more on the victorious Christian life and urging people to completely abandon their lives to the rule of God.[22] These two movements influenced many leading 19th and 20th century Evangelical leaders in the English-speaking West, including D. L. Moody, F. B. Meyer, Andrew Murray, and W. H. Griffith Thomas, who gave emphasis to the fullness of the Spirit and to the fact that this results in holiness and service.[23] The American Holiness Movement is said to be the parent of the modern Pentecostal Movement.[24] They took the Wesleyan emphasis on the Holy Spirit and on a second definite work of grace after initial salvation, but they focussed more on the so-called charismatic gifts.

In the book *Five Views on Sanctification* (Dieter, 1987), Melvin E. Dieter describes the Wesleyan position, Anthony A. Hoekema the Reformed position, Stanley M. Horton the Pentecostal position, J. Robertson McQuilkin the Keswick position, and John F. Walvoord the Augustinian-Dispensational position. Commenting on this book, Robert E. Coleman (1990, p. 96, n. 13) says, "While the distinctives of each position are defended, it is interesting how these major schools of thought coalesce around the necessity of Christians living a holy life." Permit me to express a heart cry that once more God would raise movements in the church that will focus on the priority of holiness.

Sensuality in ministry

Recently we have seen a sensuality that has become part of what is now being called "power ministry." There is a lot of touching and laying hands on people. Yet we know how easy it is for this to get out of hand. This area is posing such a big problem to the cause of mission in our part of the world that I thought that it would be good to consider it as part of our discussion on holiness and the Holy Spirit.

We have recently had far too many instances of male ministers laying hands on women in the wrong places. Besides, powerful male ministers are becoming like the Gurus of Hinduism. They are looked up to with awe by female disciples. The minister can enjoy this position of power too much. Often—in church and society—strong leaders are insecure people whose insecurity has made them driven and ambitious people. These qualities have brought them to the top of the leadership of the church. This position can be a great testimony to the grace of God. But it can also be very dangerous, because it makes them vulnerable to temptations that they will find difficult to handle. One such temptation is the adoration of female disciples. The leaders may enjoy too much the power they have over these disciples. They may begin to do things that extend their control over these disciples. As they get bolder and bolder, they begin to cross more frontiers of control. Usually the last frontier to be crossed is the sexual one. A friendly touch or hug from the father figure is accepted with gratitude by the female disciple. But soon the expressions of concern get more physical, and great damage is done as trust is betrayed and the disciple is violated.

Churches that emphasise the ministry of the Spirit too are not immune to this problem. Yet, one of the key answers to victory over this temptation is Paul's doctrine of sanctification by the Spirit. We put

---

[22] See the treatment of the Keswick View in Dieter (1987).

[23] See Clouse, Pierard, & Yamauchi (1993, p. 527).

[24] See Dayton (1987) and Clouse, Pierard, & Yamauchi (1993, pp. 527-528).

to death the deeds of the body by the power of the Spirit. Paul explains this in Romans 8:12-13. First he presents the problem: "Therefore, brothers, we have an obligation—but it is not to the sinful nature, to live according to it. For if you live according to the sinful nature, you will die...." Then he presents the answer: "... but if by the Spirit you put to death the misdeeds of the body, you will live."

This passage shows that there are two keys to victory. First, Christians must be skilled in the principle of daily crucifying of the flesh; daily we are saying "No" to the prompting of our sinful nature. Second, we do this by the power of the Spirit. This point gives us the assurance of victory. The first point, however, shows us that we also have a part to play along the path to victory. The spiritual muscles that enable us to "put to death the misdeeds of the body" must be kept trim and fit for the big temptations. And the only way we can do this is by constant practice.

Leaders sometimes don't get an opportunity to keep spiritually fit in this way. They get everything they want. They came to the top through rugged discipline and endurance against great odds. If we were to look at this climb to the top in another way, we could say that they were determined people who were able somehow to achieve the things they wanted to achieve. People admire them for their courage and determination. But even they have to learn the discipline of crucifying the flesh. This explains the strange phenomenon of leaders who are determined and disciplined falling into sexual sin. Their determination got them to the top of the ecclesiastical ladder. But when they experienced temptation to sinful sexual gratification, they were not skilled in resisting. The temptation became desire,

and they used their skills in achieving what they wanted to achieve, in order to win the sexual prize they desired.

The Christian community may need to help leaders by confronting them when the uncrucified self is manifested. Hebrews 10:24 describes this action: "And let us consider how we may spur one another on toward love and good deeds." The best people to do this are close colleagues and family members, especially spouses. Leaders should be spiritually accountable to such people. Unfortunately, often leaders have ascended so high in the ecclesiastical ladder that they are not accountable to anyone. Colleagues are reluctant to confront them because they are God's chosen leaders with miraculous gifts and spiritual power and authority. They are placed precariously on top of the ladder, with no one to help them avoid moral lapses. Our point is that a frank and open community life will help leaders stay spiritually trim so that they can handle the big temptations victoriously.

How then can we account for the common phenomenon of powerful preachers who continue to minister in the miraculous while their life is stained by serious immorality? Their ministries give evidence of the power of the Spirit, but their personal lives do not give evidence of the holiness of the Spirit. It seems as if the power of Acts can exist independently even when the holiness of the Epistles is missing, though it is one and the same Spirit who is responsible for both.[25]

I can think of three things to say about this anomalous situation. First, the Bible accepts (without condoning it) that it is possible for miracle workers who are not holy to exist in the Christian community. Samson is a classic example of this. 1 Corinthians 13:1-3 has people exercis-

---

[25] Of course, Acts also does uphold holiness, as the story of Ananias and Sapphira makes clear.

ing some "powerful" gifts while still not having love—the most important feature of holiness. In Matthew 7:21-22 Jesus talks of people who did not do the will of God, who will say at the judgement: "Lord, Lord, did we not prophesy in your name, and in your name drive out demons and perform many miracles?" Jesus' answer to such is, "I never knew you. Away from me, you evildoers!"

Second, from the existence of people with this discrepancy between life and ministry, we can infer that while the holiness of some people may leave them owing to sin, their gifts may not leave them immediately. Is this because the gifts have become so much a part of them that it takes some time before the gifts leave them? Or are these sinful miracle workers performing miracles through the power of Satan, who looks forward with great relish to the day when this person will be exposed? These are questions that I find difficult to answer. But this we can say without a doubt: one day in this world or the next these people will be exposed for who they really are. As Moses said, "... you may be sure that your sin will find you out" (Num. 32:23). Perhaps they will be like Samson who "awoke from his sleep and thought, 'I'll go out as before and shake myself free.' But he did not know that the Lord had left him" (Judges 16:20). He had been living in sin for some time before the power of God left him.

Third, the Scriptures consider as deadly serious the situation of a discrepancy between personal life and public ministry. We have already seen how Jesus said these people will be punished (Matt. 7:21-22). Those who have a public role in the life of the church will be judged more severely if they do not practice what they preach. James says, "Not many of you should presume to be teachers, my brothers, because you know that we who teach will be judged more strictly" (James 3:1).

Those who live in this state may think that because it looks as if God is using them, things are all right. This way they do not have the motivation to turn from sin and subject themselves to the cleansing discipline of the church. But that is a misperception! They may be spared from judgement now, but a severe punishment awaits them someday! When Scripture was being written, God showed once for all how he felt about what Peter calls lying to the Holy Spirit (Acts 5:3). Ananias and Sapphira were killed on the spot! This Spirit is holy, and it is a fearful thing to violate his standards of holiness.

Conclusion

Let me summarise the thrust of this study. As we think of the Holy Spirit and mission, the first thing that comes to mind is the power to do ministry that the Spirit gives. We are grateful that the church has rediscovered this emphasis. Not only does the Spirit empower us for mission, but he also gives us gifts that we can use in mission, and he remains with us, banishing loneliness, ministering to our personal needs, and comforting us in times of crisis. Because of the Spirit's ministry, we can avoid the pitfalls of ministry, such as burn-out and bitterness.

But all the blessings of God's equipping and empowering us for ministry could be negated if the other aspect of the Spirit's work is neglected: he makes us holy. 1 Corinthians 13:1-3 gives us the boldness to affirm that while power is important, purity is more important. The force of the power exhibited in ministry could blind us from seeing the importance of purity, and this seems to be happening today.

Therefore, there is an urgent need to re-emphasise the purity aspect of the Spirit's work. This was something our spiritual forefathers knew a lot about, though some of them tended to restrict the power aspect. Therefore, we would do well to sit at the feet of our spiritual parents to rediscover their teaching on holiness. But more importantly, let us sit at the feet of Paul, that great miracle worker and apologist, who was also a preacher of holiness.

References

Allen, R. (1962). *The ministry of the Spirit* (D. M. Paton, Ed.). Grand Rapids, MI: Wm. B. Eerdmans Publishing Co.

Appasamy, A. J. (1966). *Sundar Singh: A biography*. Madras, India: Christian Literature Society.

Bosch, D. J. (1991). *Transforming mission: Paradigm shifts in theology of mission*. Maryknoll, NY: Orbis Books.

Bruce, F. F. (1951). *The Acts of the Apostles: The Greek text with introduction and commentary*. London: The Tyndale Press.

———. (1990). *The Acts of the Apostles: The Greek text with introduction and commentary* (3rd ed.). Grand Rapids, MI: Wm. B. Eerdmans Publishing Co.

Carson, D. A. (1987). *Showing the Spirit: A theological exposition of 1 Corinthians 12-14*. Grand Rapids, MI: Baker Book House.

Clouse, R. G., Pierard, R. W., & Yamauchi, E. M. (1993). *Two kingdoms: The church and culture through the ages*. Chicago: Moody Press.

Coleman, R. E. (1990). *"Nothing to do but save souls": John Wesley's charge to his preachers*. Grand Rapids, MI: Francis Asbury Press of Zondervan Publishing House.

Dayton, D. W. (1987). *Theological roots of Pentecostalism*. Metuchen, NJ: Scarecrow Press.

Deere, J. (1993). *Surprised by the power of the Spirit: Discovering how God speaks and heals today*. Grand Rapids, MI: Zondervan Publishing House.

———. (1996). *Surprised by the voice of God: How God speaks today through prophecies, dreams, and visions*. Grand Rapids, MI: Zondervan Publishing House.

Dieter, M. E. (1987). *Five views on sanctification*. Grand Rapids, MI: Zondervan Publishing House.

Dollar, H. (1996). *St. Luke's missiology: A cross cultural challenge*. Pasadena, CA: William Carey Library.

Eaton, M. A. (1989). *Baptism with the Spirit: The teaching of Martyn Lloyd-Jones*. Leicester, England: Inter-Varsity Press.

Edwards, J. (1974). *The works of Jonathan Edwards* (Vol. 1). Edinburgh, Scotland: Banner of Truth Trust.

Fee, G. D. (1994). *God's empowering Spirit: The Holy Spirit in the letters of Paul*. Peabody, MA: Hendrickson Publishers.

Fernando, A. (1995). *The supremacy of Christ*. Wheaton, IL: Crossway Books.

———. (1998). *NIV application commentary: Acts*. Grand Rapids, MI: Zondervan Publishing House.

———. (2000). Being a Christian: What difference does it make? In J. Woodbridge, J. Akers, & J. Armstrong (Eds.), *Good news!* Grand Rapids, MI: Zondervan Publishing House.

Foster, R. (1989). *Celebration of discipline* (2nd ed.). New York: Harper & Row.

Green, M. (1975). *I believe in the Holy Spirit*. Grand Rapids, MI: Wm. B. Eerdmans Publishing Co.

Greenlee, J. H. (1994). *What the New Testament says about holiness*. Salem, OH: Schmul Publishing Co.

Haenchen, E. (1971). *Acts of the Apostles: A commentary* (R. McL. Wilson, Trans.). Philadelphia, PA: Westminster Press.

Houston, J. (1989). *The transforming friendship: A guide to prayer*. Oxford, England: Lion Publishing.

———. (1990). *In search of happiness: A guide to personal contentment*. Oxford, England: Lion Publishing.

Jones, E. S. (1968). *A song of ascents: A spiritual autobiography*. Nashville, TN: Abingdon Press.

Keener, C. (1996). *Three crucial questions about the Holy Spirit*. Grand Rapids, MI: Baker Book House.

———. (1997). *The Spirit in the Gospel and Acts: Divine purity and power*. Peabody, MA: Hendrickson Publishers.

Kinlaw, D. F. (1985). *Preaching in the Spirit*. Grand Rapids, MI: Francis Asbury Press of Zondervan Publishing House.

Lloyd-Jones, D. M. (1984). *Joy unspeakable: Power and renewal in the Holy Spirit* (C. Catherwood, Ed.). Wheaton, IL: Harold Shaw Publishers.

———. (1992). *Enjoying the presence of God* (C. Catherwood, Ed.). Ann Arbor, MI: Servant Publications.

Marshall, I. H. (1970). *Luke: Historian and theologian*. Grand Rapids, MI: Zondervan Publishing House.

Morgan, J. (1972 reprint). *A man of the Word: Life of G. Campbell Morgan*. Grand Rapids, MI: Baker Book House.

Packer, J. I. (1990). *A quest for godliness: The Puritan vision of the Christian life*. Wheaton, IL: Crossway Books.

Peterson, E. (1996). *Take and read*. Grand Rapids, MI: Wm. B. Eerdmans Publishing Co.

Piper, J. (1986). *Desiring God: Meditations of a Christian hedonist*. Portland, OR: Multnomah Press.

———. (1995). *The purifying power of living by faith in future grace*. Sisters, OR: Multnomah Books.

———. (1997). *A Godward life: Savoring the supremacy of God in all of life*. Sisters, OR: Multnomah Publishers.

———. (1997). *A hunger for God*. Wheaton, IL: Crossway Books.

Ryken, L. (1986). *Worldly saints: The Puritans as they really were*. Grand Rapids, MI: Zondervan Publishing House.

Sargent, T. (1994). *The sacred anointing: The preaching of Dr. Martyn Lloyd Jones*. Wheaton, IL: Crossway Books.

Stronstad, R. (1994). *The charismatic theology of St. Luke*. Peabody, MA: Hendrickson Publishers.

Sundar Singh, S. (1989). *The Christian witness of Sadhu Sundar Singh: A collection of his writings* (T. Dayanandan Francis, Ed.). Madras, India: Christian Literature Society.

Toon, P. (1987). *From mind to heart: Christian meditation today*. Grand Rapids, MI: Baker Book House.

———. (1991). *Meditating as a Christian: Waiting upon God*. London: Collins.

Tozer, A. W. (1948). *The pursuit of God*. Harrisburg, PA: Christian Publications.

———. (1985). *Whatever happened to worship* (G. B. Smith, Ed.). Harrisburg, PA: Christian Publications.

Tozer, A. W. (Ed.). (1963). *The Christian book of mystical verse*. Harrisburg, PA: Christian Publications.

Turner, M. (1996). *The Holy Spirit and spiritual gifts in the New Testament church and today*. Peabody, MA: Hendrickson Publishers.

Wesley, J. (1998 reprint). A plain account of Christian perfection. In *The works of John Wesley* (3rd ed.) (Vol. 11, pp. 366-446). Grand Rapids, MI: Baker Book House.

Willard, D. (1988). *The Spirit of the disciplines: Understanding how God changes lives*. San Francisco: Harper & Row.

———. (1998). *The divine conspiracy: Rediscovering our hidden life in God*. San Francisco: HarperSanFrancisco.

Wood, L. W. (1980). *Pentecostal grace*. Wilmore, KY: Francis Asbury Publishing Co.

Wynkoop, M. B. (1972). *A theology of love: The dynamic of Wesleyanism*. Kansas City, MO: Beacon Hill Press of Kansas City.

Ajith Fernando has led Sri Lanka Youth for Christ since 1976. Convinced of a call to theologise from the grassroots, he has always led a small division in YFC and presently leads the work with drug dependents. His YFC responsibilities include teaching and pastoral care of staff. Ajith and his wife Nelun are active in the leadership of a Methodist church, most of whose members are converts from other religions. He has a Th.M. in New Testament from Fuller Theological Seminary. His nine books have been in the area of either Bible exposition, such as the NIV Application Commentary: Acts (Zondervan, 1998), or mission theology, such as The Supremacy of Christ (Crossway, 1995).

16

The church: the mirror of the Trinity

AJITH FERNANDO

WE HAVE SO FAR considered key features that should impact missionary thinking today by looking at the work of the three Persons of the Trinity. Now we will consider some important things that Paul has to say about the church, which could be described as the mirror of the Trinity. But first it would be good to summarise the main points of the previous three studies, which give us a trinitarian basis for mission.

The Trinitarian Basis of Mission

God

We saw that God is the source, the originator, and the end of mission. As such, it was he who conceived the gospel, who called people to himself for salvation and for mission. The gospel is an expression of his nature as being both loving and holy. This gospel shows how he saves us from eternal damnation and grants us eternal salvation, which is the greatest of his many blessings to humankind. The fact that he regards unholiness with so much seriousness implies that now we must live holy lives of obedience to him.

God is creator and sustainer of the world and sovereign Lord of history and, through the processes of history, he is working to fulfil his purposes for his creation. Therefore, we are also to think of the world as our arena of responsibility and are to go into the structures of the world in order to impact them with God's values. In this way, we become agents of seeing God's will done on earth. However, knowing the limitations of what can be achieved on earth, we await the end of time, when God will wrap up history according to his good purposes.

Jesus

Jesus is the message and the model of mission. As the message, he is the way to salvation, which he won for us through his life and work. He is also the truth, by which we mean that as God he personifies absolute truth. We can know this truth, because through his incarnation Jesus has made it known to us. Jesus is also the life, giving to us the only life that can be described as life to the full.

As the model of mission, Jesus presents us with a model of gentle lowliness and servanthood and of suffering and deprivation. But if we are to adopt such a sacrificial model successfully, we must first know the strength that comes from the fact that all authority in heaven and on earth has been given to Jesus and that this sovereign Lord is the one who commissions us to mission.

The Holy Spirit

The Holy Spirit is the one who gives us the power that enables us to carry out our mission. We are grateful that the church has rediscovered this emphasis. Not only does the Spirit empower us for mission, but he also gives us gifts that we can use in mission, and he remains with us, banishing our loneliness and ministering to our personal needs. Through the Spirit's ministry, we can avoid the pitfalls of ministry, such as burnout and bitterness.

But all the blessings of God's equipping and empowering for ministry could be negated if the other aspect of the Spirit's work is neglected: he makes us holy. 1 Corinthians 13 gives us the boldness to affirm that while the power and gifts of the Spirit are important for our life and ministry, the purity that the Spirit gives is even more important.

The Church Has a Trinitarian Experience

In the New Testament, there is a close relationship between the nature of the church and the Trinity. This is clear in some of the expressions of how the church functions. Paul says, "There are different kinds of gifts, but the same *Spirit*. There are different kinds of service, but the same *Lord*. There are different kinds of working, but the same *God* works all of them in all men" (1 Cor. 12:4-6). All three Persons of the Trinity are presented here as being involved in the operation of the gifts. It is almost implied here that our rich diversity amidst unity expresses the unity in diversity of the Trinity. Paul's popular benediction shows how the distinctive ministries of the three Persons of the Trinity are experienced. "May the grace of the Lord Jesus Christ, and the love of God, and the fellowship of the Holy Spirit be with you all" (2 Cor. 13:14). This trinitarian experience of the church is also described in Ephesians 2:18, "For through him [Christ] we both have access to the Father by one Spirit."

Paul also teaches that the unity Christians share has to do with the common tie we have with the three Persons of the Trinity. He says, "There is one body and one *Spirit*—just as you were called to one hope when you were called—one *Lord*, one faith, one baptism; one *God and Father* of all, who is over all and through all and in all" (Eph. 4:4-6).

The Church and the Trinity in John 17

Jesus in his high priestly prayer goes even deeper in expounding the relationship between Christian unity and the Trinity than the Pauline texts we just looked at. One of Jesus' key themes in John 17 is the unity of the church. The clause "that they may be one" (vv. 11, 21, 22, 23) appears four times in this prayer. Several times in this chapter, Jesus also makes a connection between the nature of the church and the nature of the Trinity, even describing the church as a mirror of the Trinity.

Five important affirmations about unity are made in this passage. The first of these comes from verses 11b-12a, where Jesus says, "Holy Father, protect them by the power of your name—the name you gave me—so that they may be one as we are one. While I was with them, I protected them and kept them safe by that name you gave me." Here Jesus is saying that our unity ensures our protection. The protection and preservation of the church would be an important concern in the mind of Christ as he prepares to leave his disciples. Verse 11 tells us that this protection takes place through the power of God's name. Then he describes what this protection involves: "that they may be one as we are one." So one of the ways in which the church is going to be preserved is by its unity.

Second, in this passage Jesus says that this unity reflects or mirrors the unity between Jesus and God. Three times in this prayer Jesus mentions that our unity with each other is like the unity between Christ and the Father (vv. 11, 21, 22).

The third great truth that this passage proclaims is that our unity with God is an essential part of our tie with God. Verse 21 says, "... that all of them may be one, Father, just as you are in me and I am in you. May they also be in us so that the world may believe that you have sent me." Note the sequence, "... that all of them may be one ... may they also be in us." There is a connection between our unity with each other and our unity with God. Verse 23 implies this too: "I in them and you in me. May they be brought to complete unity." Our unity with God cannot

be separated from our unity with each other.

The fourth truth to emerge from this passage is that part of Christ's glory that we are given is our unity, which is, of course, similar to the unity of the Trinity. "I have given them the glory that you gave me, that they may be one as we are one" (v. 22). While the exact meaning of this verse is disputed, we can say that glory in such contexts refers to "the manifestation of God's character or person in a revelatory context" (Carson, 1991, p. 569). This verse says that Jesus not only manifested the greatness of God's glory to us, but also gave (*didōmi*) it to us. A key aspect of this glory that we have been given is the oneness of the Godhead. So if we receive this glory, then we should be one. The next verse increases the impact of what Jesus has already said by repeating the truth of how the unity of the Trinity is related to our unity with Christ, and it adds force to the description of the unity by referring to it as "complete." "I in them and you in me. May they be brought to complete unity" (v. 23). So when we think of the glory of God, let us also think of how it is expressed when there is complete unity in the church.

Before we go to the fifth truth from this passage, we will point out some things about the importance of the unity proclaimed here. It is clear from this passage that the unity of the church is a basic feature of Christianity. Not only does Christian unity reflect the unity of the Trinity, but it also is part of our essential tie with God. So if we do not relate properly with other Christians, we do not relate properly with God.

The Evangelical Movement rediscovered the glorious truth that God is concerned for us and relates to us as individuals. This brought great joy to us and obviously became a key aspect of our thinking about Christianity. Naturally, if we rediscover such an amazing truth afresh, it would become our hallmark. But there is another important parallel truth in the Bible. While we relate to God personally, we also relate to him corporately. Salvation is individual, but it is not individualistic. Our being one with the rest of the church is connected to our relationship with God. So this passage teaches us that there is a three-fold unity in Christianity:

- God with Christ
- Christ with us
- Christians with each other

These then are foundational features of our being Christians: just as there is unity in the Godhead and unity between us and God, there must be unity among Christians. We can go so far as to say that our unity with each other is part of our essential unity with God and part of our essential identity as Christians. This is why John says, "If anyone says, 'I love God,' yet hates his brother, he is a liar. For anyone who does not love his brother, whom he has seen, cannot love God, whom he has not seen. And he has given us this command: Whoever loves God must also love his brother" (1 John 4:20-21). While we sometimes think that we can separate our relationship with God from our relationship with fellow Christians, the Bible does not give us a warrant to do that.

The fifth affirmation coming from John 17 is that unity is a means of evangelistic effectiveness. Jesus has said in verse 18, "As you sent me into the world, I have sent them into the world." Twice Jesus says that an important aspect of this missionary role of the Christians is for them to demonstrate the gospel through the unity of the church. In verse 21, he says that their unity with God and with each other demonstrates the fact that God has sent Jesus to the world. "... that all of them may be one, Father, just as you are in me and I am in you. May they also be in us so that the world may believe that you have sent me" (v. 21). In some way this tie shows the reality of the gospel. In verse 23, Jesus again says that the unity of the church demonstrates that God sent Jesus. But it adds the claim that unity also demonstrates that God loves the church. "I in them and you in me. May they be brought to complete unity to let the world know that you sent me and have loved them even as you have loved me" (v. 23). When we love each other, we show the world that God loves us.

John 13:34-35 gives a similar message: "A new command I give you: Love one another. As I have loved you, so you must love one another. By this all men will know that you are my disciples, if you love one another." I will not delve into how exactly this works. But let me say that the disunity of the church often crops up in my conversations with non-Christians. Once they feel the ice is broken and they can ask frank questions, they bring up this fact about the many divisions in the church. Their reasoning seems to be something like this: "How can this gospel be so great if it can't unite even the Christians?"

I believe that many Christians in the West, where there is a high emphasis on competition and individualism, cannot understand why Christian disunity is such a scandal. Competition is something that has an almost religious significance to some in the West. But in Sri Lanka, communities still have a strong emphasis on solidarity. This bonding is an almost religious aspect of this culture. Therefore, unbelievers find it difficult to see how competition can exist among Christians in the society.

There has been a remarkable turning to Christ among the tribal peoples of India in recent years through the ministries of missionaries who have gone to them, primarily from South India. But there was one sad instance of missionaries who went to a certain tribal people but were asked by the tribal leaders to leave after a period of time. The leaders said that the community had been united for many centuries. The Christians, however, were a divided community. So the leaders asked the Christians to leave because they did not want to see their people divided as the Christians were.

Paul's Theology of Unity

We now turn to Paul's exposition of Christian community. It would help to remind the reader that my study of Paul's Epistles focussed on the frequency of occurrence of certain themes. We considered themes that appeared often as being significant features of Paul's teachings to the early church. Our aim has been to see whether the church today is emphasising the things that Paul emphasised and to suggest remedial action in terms of emphases that should be found in our teaching of Christians today.

Clearly the church and how it functions is a very important theme in Paul. I want to highlight three features in Paul's teachings about the church: first, his theology of Christian unity; second, his exposition of how Christ breaks down barriers between humans; and third, his teaching on how Christians need each other.

Body of Christ theology and other metaphors

Paul presents an impressive array of theological points to show how Christians are united to each other. The most prominent of these is what we might call his body theology. I found 20 foundational statements covering 34 verses (20/34) which present the church as the body of Christ or a similar concept. Romans 12:4-5 is the first one I found, and it is repre-

sentative of the rest. Paul says, "Just as each of us has one body with many members, and these members do not all have the same function, so in Christ we who are many form one body, and each member belongs to all the others." The second reference I found is 1 Corinthians 10:16-17: "Is not the cup of thanksgiving for which we give thanks a participation in the blood of Christ? And is not the bread that we break a participation in the body of Christ? Because there is one loaf, we, who are many, are one body, for we all partake of the one loaf."

Paul talks about the unity we have in diversity (3/5; Rom. 12:4-5; 1 Cor. 12:12-13, 27), the fact that we belong to each other (3/7; Rom. 12:4-5; Eph. 2:19-20; 4:4-6). Five times he presents spiritual gifts as an illustration of body theology (5/19; Rom. 12:6-8; 1 Cor. 12:4-6, 7-11, 28-30; Eph. 4:7-13). He says that the working of individual ministries and gifts illustrates body theology (4/13; 1 Cor. 3:5-9, 10-11; Gal. 2:7-10; Eph. 4:6) and that all the gifts are of equal importance in the body (2/12; 1 Cor. 12:14-20, 21-25). In our study on the Holy Spirit, we stated that, in the passages about gifts in the Epistles, the emphasis is not on the gifts per se but on the unity in diversity that is expressed through the gifts. In 1 Corinthians 14, Paul was trying to remedy the disorder resulting from the improper use of gifts within the body.

There are several other metaphors, apart from the body metaphor, that describe the nature of the church.[1] Here is a listing:
- 13/21 – Household/building/family of God (1 Cor. 3:9, 10-11; 2 Cor. 6:18; Gal. 4:4-7; 6:10; Eph. 2:19-22; 3:14-15; 4:6, etc.).
- 3/5 – Temple of God (1 Cor. 3:16-17; 2 Cor. 6:16; Eph. 2:21-22).

---

[1] For a complete listing, see Minear (1960).

- 1/4 – God's nation (Eph. 2:19-22).
- 3/9 – The new humanity (Rom. 5:17-21; 1 Cor. 15:21-22; Eph. 2:15-16).
- 2/5 – The bride of Christ (2 Cor. 11:1-2; Eph. 5:25-27).
- 6/25 – The new Israel or children of Abraham (Rom. 9:8, 23-26; 11:17-21; Gal. 3:7-9, 26-29; 4:24-31).

Other theological bases for unity

There are other ways in which Paul affirms our unity in Christ. The "in Christ" motif is very common in Paul, and that is important in understanding Paul's conception of the nature of the church. I counted about 150 occurrences of expressions like "in Christ," "in Jesus," and "in the Lord." Many of these describe our personal experience of Christ. For example, Paul often uses expressions such as "faith in Christ" and "saved in Christ." But some of these "in Christ" expressions clearly have to do with the unity we have as a Christian community (e.g., "my brother in Christ"). Sometimes it is difficult to sense whether a community connotation is included, but I was able to count about 65 occurrences of this community related use of the "in Christ" phrases. Paul viewed all Christians everywhere to be joined to each other because of their union with Christ.

Five times covering eight verses he talks of unity in the truth. An example is Ephesians 4:13, "... until we all reach unity in the faith and in the knowledge of the Son of God and become mature, attaining to the whole measure of the fullness of Christ." Paul often emphasises the fact that all Christians have a common experience of Christ or of God or of the faith (11/21). The trinitarian verse Ephesians 2:18 says, "For through him [Christ] we both have access to the Father by one Spirit." In this verse, "both" refers to Jewish and Gentile Christians, implying that despite big cultural and racial differences, we are one because of our common expe-

rience of the Trinity. Paul's appeal to unity in Philippians uses, among other arguments, their common experience of God. Philippians 2:1-2 says, "If you have any encouragement from being united with Christ, if any comfort from his love, if any fellowship with the Spirit, if any tenderness and compassion, then make my joy complete by being like-minded, having the same love, being one in spirit and purpose."

Paul also highlights the spiritual unity that Christians enjoy across the miles (4/5). In 1 Corinthians 5:3-4 he says, "Even though I am not physically present, I am with you in spirit. And I have already passed judgement on the one who did this, just as if I were present. When you are assembled in the name of our Lord Jesus and I am with you in spirit, and the power of our Lord Jesus is present...."

Practical implications

A strong theology of the church is the basis from which our body life operates. When we realise that we have so much in common, such important things to unite us, those aggravating things that divide us pale into insignificance. Indeed, things that break the harmony of the church will upset us. But because of our strong body theology, we will do all we can to bring back unity. We have the determination to persevere without giving up until unity is restored.

Ephesians 4 is a good example of this. A strong theological base for unity is presented here. In chapter 2, Paul had already appealed to the fact that Christ has broken the dividing wall of hostility between Jews and Gentiles, creating one new person in place of two. Ephesians 4 is an extended description of the unity of the church. Paul begins the chapter by stating that he is going to show us how to live a life that is worthy of our call. He says, "As a prisoner for the Lord, then, I urge you to live a life worthy of the calling you have received" (v. 1). What follows is a description of how to live a life worthy of our calling. The main verb is in verse 1 and is about living this life worthy of the call. Verses 2 and 3 have participles that illustrate how to live such a life.

In verse 2, Paul describes how our attitude to others in the body will help foster unity. "Be completely humble and gentle; be patient, bearing with one another in love." To be united, we must have Christian character (humility and gentleness), and we must be willing to put up with the weaknesses of people (being "patient bearing with one another in love"). The word translated "patient" is *makrothumia*, which the older translations rendered as "longsuffering." When there are things we don't like in our church or group, we don't leave the group. We suffer long, bearing with these weaknesses in love. So the first way we live a life worthy of our call is through exhibiting Christian character in community relationships.

The second way is described in verse 3, which also begins with a participle (see NRSV, NAS, etc.). Here Paul describes the urgency of striving for unity: "... making every effort to maintain the unity of the Spirit in the bond of peace." This is a strong statement. The word *spoudazō* means to do one's best, to spare no effort, to work hard. Markus Barth (1974, p. 428), who translates this word as "take pains," says, "It is hardly possible to render exactly the urgency contained in the underlying Greek verb. Not only haste and passion, but full effort of the whole man is meant, involving his will, sentiment, reason, physical strength, and total attitude." An application of this idea is Christ's words about leaving our offering in front of the altar and getting reconciled with a brother who has something against us before making the offering (Matt. 5:23-24).

This action is for situations when others have problems with us.

The early church illustrates the urgency of peacemaking well. In Acts 6, when there is murmuring among the Grecians, there is an immediate meeting of the church, and a new structure is developed with leaders appointed to help meet the needs of the poor. In Acts 15, when a divisive teaching comes to Antioch from Jerusalem, Paul and Barnabas immediately make the long trip to Jerusalem to confront the issue. The result is a conference where a peacemaking theological statement was produced. It contains those wonderful words, "... it seemed good to us, having become of one mind.... For it seemed good to the Holy Spirit and to us ..." (Acts 15:25, 28, NAS). The urgency to solve the problem had resulted in a groundbreaking statement that not only avoided a split in the church, but also took the church forward to a great step of theological clarification.

Paul vehemently attacks disunity in his Epistles. There are 54 appeals to unity and direct confrontations of disunity covering 108 verses. There are 24 instances (covering 49 verses) of practical keys to dealing with disputable issues. That is a sizeable portion of the Epistles. Clearly, striving for unity is a priority in church life. To be committed to Christ and to holiness includes a commitment to the unity of the body of Christ.

Yet this is hard work that is very painful and stressful. In my 23 years of leading Youth for Christ in Sri Lanka, I believe this has been the most absorbing and toughest challenge I have faced. It is so stressful and so painful that I am often tempted to ignore the problem or postpone the confrontation of it. Yet when I have done that, the movement has always suffered. I believe that the biggest incentive to me to pursue unity has been the theology of unity found in the Bible. If I take the Bible seriously, I must grapple for unity. Yet the Bible tells us that we have so much in common by virtue of our union with Christ that we can grapple for unity with much hope. We don't have to create a non-existent unity; we have to "maintain" what is there by divine appointment and action (Eph. 4:3) but which may have been temporarily clouded through human sin and weakness. We leaders have a huge role to play here in facilitating activities that restore unity.[2] As we see the way people are hopping from church to church and the way churches are splitting today, we sense that this teaching of Scripture is being neglected and violated on a large scale. This has become a serious scandal as far as the gospel is concerned.

Why is this happening? I think many growing churches are so practically oriented in their teaching and programme that they have not imbibed the biblical theology of community. If they had, they would realise that disunity is really serious business. Of course, theology is scorned today, so that people don't think it is such an important feature in determining behaviour. If we are to produce biblical Christians, we have a lot of repair work to do in this post-modern generation, which is a generation that downplays the importance of things like theology. We have to teach theology from the Word attractively and demonstrate how it is our standard not only for faith but also for practice—for day-to-day life.

Paul's appeal, "... making every effort to maintain the unity of the Spirit in the bond of peace" (Eph. 4:3), is steeped in a rich theology of community. First, we note his expression "the unity of the Spirit." The Spirit is the one who joins us together. And because he lives with us, we have been made one by virtue of our unity with Christ. Our unity is a theological and actual fact. This is why Paul says that we are to "maintain" this unity, not create it. Second, we note Paul's vigorous description of the theological ground for unity in verses 4-6: "There is one body and one Spirit—just as you were called to one hope when you were called—one Lord, one faith, one baptism; one God and Father of all, who is over all and through all and in all." Our oneness is an established fact, and our job is to express what already exists. Third, verses 7-13 tell us that the operation of gifts given to each individual in the church also helps foster unity. After his description about how the gifts operate in the church (vv. 7-12), Paul says, "until we all reach unity in the faith and in the knowledge of the Son of God and become mature, attaining to the whole measure of the fullness of Christ" (v. 13). The end results are unity and maturity.

What if these theological truths were burned into our hearts? When confronted by a problem and tempted to give up, our theology would challenge this tendency to lose hope about a resolution. Our theology would tell us that the problem is minute in comparison to the strength of what unites us. This theology will also give us the courage to persevere till a solution is found. In the darkest night, when we are hurt and tired and everything in us says, "Just drop it!" our theology will tell us, "What unites us is bigger than what divides." And we have the courage to persevere till there is a resolution. Perhaps, like Paul, we will be hurt and express our pain, as Paul did in his Epistles. But we will be agents of peace in the church.

Now this teaching about unity should not be confined to internal relationships within local churches only. Our body the-

---

[2] For a helpful guide to peacemaking in the church, see Sande (1997). Sande is an attorney who heads Peacemaker Ministries, a ministry devoted to conflict resolution.

ology tells us that all local Christian groups should relate to each other in unity, because they all belong to the same body of Christ. This theology of unity would cause us not to hurt other Christians in our quest for success and growth. How amazing it is that Christians are not afraid or ashamed to try to persuade people to leave one church or group and join another, even though they know that such a move will really hurt the group being left. How amazing that people will have discussions and make plans without mentioning anything to the other group.

I think this type of behaviour is related to the ethics of a market-oriented society that is sweeping the world today. In such a system, many people have no qualms about hurting a competitor in their march towards success. In the kingdom of heaven, we are not competitors. We all belong to the same body, and therefore we should not hurt others. Rather, we should be hurt when other Christians and groups hurt. Speaking at the North American Urbana Student Missionary Conference, Dr. Sam Kamaleson (1971, pp. 158-159) complained that we "reduce" the church by calling her "an international institution." He said, "She is not an organization but a supernatural organism: She feels, she throbs with vitality. In other words, when the church in the United States is pinched, the church in India must say, 'Ah, that hurts!'"

If we hurt another group in our march towards success, our little personal kingdom may expand a bit (perhaps it is like people becoming overweight with growth in the wrong places), but the kingdom of God will not ultimately grow. Eternity will show us that such work will be burnt up at the judgement. The church needs to rediscover the horror of sinning against the body of Christ by expanding in a way that hurts another member of the body. I have observed some groups that adopt an "us" versus "them" mentality that causes them to compete against other Christian groups whom they regard as rivals. I have seen that often this divisive spirit ultimately affects the internal life of the group too. Factions form within the group, and often one of these factions ends up leaving the group. These groups do not have an adequate body theology to sustain them when conflicts hit them.

I was so heartened to hear that in a pastors fellowship in one of our cities in Sri Lanka, there is an agreement that when a member of one church goes to another, the pastors of the two churches will talk about the move and come to some agreement. I pray that they will persevere along this straight and narrow path, without getting distracted by the lure of quick success.

Christ Breaks Human Barriers [3]

A key feature of a biblical theology of the church is the truth that the gospel breaks human barriers, unifying believers into one people in Christ. Jesus showed how this is an essential feature of the gospel in his discourse on the Good Shepherd. After stating that he will give his life for the sheep (John 10:11-15), he says, "I have other sheep that are not of this sheep pen. I must bring them also. They too will listen to my voice, and there shall be one flock and one shepherd" (v. 16). The Jews who heard him would have understood what he meant by this statement. He was saying that his death would result in a new flock where the Jew-Gentile barrier would be broken. And one new people would be raised up who would be under one shepherd, Jesus Christ.

---

[3] For a fuller description of this theme, see chap. 13, "The New Humanity," in Fernando (1995).

This theme appears prominently in Paul too. 12 times covering 31 verses Paul expounds the truth that the gospel breaks human barriers. This includes 10/25 basic statements of this truth and 2/6 statements where Paul describes his call to be a herald of this great message of the new humanity where barriers are broken. Let's look at two of these passages.

The first passage is 2 Corinthians 5:14-17. Verses 14 and 15 describe the work of Christ: "For Christ's love compels us, because we are convinced that one died for all, and therefore all died. And he died for all, that those who live should no longer live for themselves but for him who died for them and was raised again." Then Paul goes on to describe the consequences of this work of Christ. "So from now on we regard no one from a worldly point of view. Though we once regarded Christ in this way, we do so no longer" (v. 16). This verse begins with the word *hōste*, meaning "so" or "therefore." There is a clear connection, then, between the work of Christ and the renunciation of the practice of regarding people from a worldly point of view (literally, "according to the flesh," *kata sarka*). What the world considers important about people is not what Paul considers important. Race, class, caste, and education are all insignificant in the light of the amazing thing that God has done, the light of which is so strong that other human factors pale into insignificance. Now we look at people from the perspective of verse 17: "Therefore, if anyone is in Christ, he is a new creation; the old has gone, the new has come!" The blessing of this new life is so great that earlier differences are so small in comparison.

I like to describe this situation as the difference between two people, one of whom had 10 cents and the other had 20 cents. Now both are given a million dollars. Can the second tell the first, "I am richer than you are"? Earlier differences are insignificant. We are all hell-bent sinners with no hope, who have now been given the wonderful grace of eternal life. Those who feel inferior or superior to others because of earthly distinctions have not understood the horror of sins or the marvels of grace.

This same theme is repeated in Ephesians 2. After talking about how grace saves us (2:1-10), Paul goes on, through a vivid, rich, and sustained statement, to mention how the cross broke the Jew-Gentile barrier. He first describes our miserable pre-Christian state (vv. 11-12). Then he says, "But now in Christ Jesus you who once were far away have been brought near through the blood of Christ" (v. 13). Next he proceeds to present the work of Jesus on the cross as the work of peacemaking (vv. 14-18). This is such a rich passage I will simply quote it in full: "For he himself is our peace, who has made the two one and has destroyed the barrier, the dividing wall of hostility, by abolishing in his flesh the law with its commandments and regulations. His purpose was to create in himself one new man out of the two, thus making peace, and in this one body to reconcile both of them to God through the cross, by which he put to death their hostility. He came and preached peace to you who were far away and peace to those who were near. For through him we both have access to the Father by one Spirit."

In light of this strong emphasis on the breaking of human differences through the cross, we should be very careful about overemphasising the homogenous unit principle that is very popular in Evangelical missiological circles today. The church is characterised by the unifying of different peoples and not by the segregation of peoples according to their own kind. Indeed, with cultural contextualisation, it is necessary to gear our evangelism bearing cultural distinctives in mind. But that truth must be balanced by the other truth that Christ joins different groups of people into a united community. This is not easy in practice. But we must patiently grapple to find a biblical balance without going headlong into unprincipled church growth.

For example, it is inevitable that worship services have to be separated according to language when people speaking two different languages worship in the same church building. But there must be times when the two groups could get together in order to affirm their oneness in Christ, despite the cultural diversity. One such way to do this is to have an occasional bilingual service. Having been involved in organising such, I must say that this is an extremely difficult thing to do. If we slavishly have everything in both languages, the service could drag on and be extremely boring. Often the dominant group has a service which is reasonably comfortable for them but which in the meantime infuriates those in the other group, thus increasing the alienation. Immense creativity and hard work are needed to have a meaningful service. And even after all the creativity and hard work, it will probably be not be as "exciting" or "entertaining" as the usual service. Most people, therefore, just choose to not have any combined events, as it is simply too difficult to do. But our theology of the body should drive us to strive to do such things, in order to affirm our unity in this fragmented society.

Anyway, this is a basic Christian principle. We work at differences in order to affirm our unity in Christ in practice. This is how two diverse people can forge a happy marriage despite their differences. It calls for hard work at unity. Unfortunately, these days, people seem to be willing to work hard for growth but not for unity.

While overemphasis of the homogenous unit principle may produce short-term evangelistic gain, it may result in long-term evangelistic loss. Christians would get the reputation of perpetuating unjust class structures. There have been several instances of so-called "low caste" Hindus or "untouchables" or *Dalits*, as they prefer to call themselves, turning to Buddhism or Islam, when they wanted to reject the Hinduism that bred the terrible caste system of which they are victims. The most famous of these instances was under Dr. B. R. Ambedkar (1891-1956), the principal framer of the Indian Constitution, who led a mass movement of his fellow "untouchables" to Buddhism (see Bechert, 1984, pp. 277-278). The Hindus rejected Christianity because they felt Christianity perpetuated the caste system. They would cite instances of churches that were constituted (unofficially, of course) along caste lines.

How important this message is in a world torn by national, racial, ethnic, and social strife. We can affirm that in Christ we are one, and through the church we can present a model of integration and harmony. This becomes a point of hope in a gloomy situation of mistrust and strife. It could show that people of different races could indeed live together without separating nations according to ethnic divides. This is my great hope for the church in my nation of Sri Lanka that is torn by ethnic strife. I hope that by looking at Sinhala and Tamil Christians living in harmony with each other, our fellow citizens would develop hope to believe that it is indeed possible for people of the two races to live together in harmony and trust.

But if the church is to do this, it must first proclaim this message. I believe this is one of the most urgent messages to proclaim in a world that is destroying itself through social strife. But in keeping with our marketing orientation, we are so committed to giving people what they want to hear that we could be neglecting to tell them some of the things that God wants them to hear. We can focus so much on felt needs that we ignore real and urgent needs, which remain unacknowledged by people, such as the need to repent of prejudice. The result is that Christians do not think of unity as a basic feature of Christianity. They still have the class, caste, and race prejudices of the society around them. This accounts for the terrible history of prejudice among supposedly conservative Christians. We have a lot of work to do here because of the sad history of Christians. Sometimes rulers used the Bible to justify their belief in the superiority of one race over another. Some suggested that they belonged to the people who have entered a new Promised Land. By doing so, they justified their crushing of the original dwellers in this land to submission.

This theme, then, must come into the forefront of the preaching of the church. Paul made a radical statement in his evangelistic preaching in Athens when he said, "From one man he made every nation of men" (Acts 17:26). On this, F. F. Bruce (1990, p. 382) comments, "The Athenians prided themselves on being *autochthones,* sprung from the soil of their native Attica…. The Greeks in general considered themselves superior to non-Greeks, whom they called barbarians. Against such claims to racial superiority, Paul asserts the unity of all mankind, a unity derived *ex enos,* i.e., from Adam." By making this statement, Paul risked losing his audience. But it was a truth so basic to Christianity that he needed to proclaim it. In today's context, when we challenge people to repent and come to Christ, we may need to challenge them to repent of the sins of racism and prejudice. People should know that when they become Christians, they cease to be racists.

If we hold back things like this, we will pay a heavy price in the end. People would be comfortable with the idea of being racist and Christian at the same time, though these are two mutually exclusive ideas. They should know that when they come to Christ they turn from, among other things, fornication, greed, idols, and racism. Let the message that Christ breaks human barriers, then, come to the forefront of Christian proclamation.

Christians Need Each Other

The idea that Christians are very much a part of a community and not individuals operating independently of others is another of the very forcefully presented teachings in the Epistles of Paul. This is the implication in all the passages on body theology that we mentioned before. It is implied in most of the other metaphors used for the church by Paul, such as household, building, or family of God. The passages discussed above that present the theological base for unity also imply this. But there are many other factors that push us to this idea that we are not independent of others. Let me list some of these, giving the number of references and the number of verses covered, followed by one representative reference.

- 8/15 – We have a common destiny and inheritance: "This mystery is that through the gospel the Gentiles are heirs together with Israel, members together of one body, and sharers together in the promise in Christ Jesus" (Eph. 3:6).
- 26/55 – Love in the community: "Be devoted to one another in brotherly love" (Rom. 12:10).
- 25/34 – Generosity, helping each other: "Share with God's people who are in need" (Rom. 12:13).
- 15/21 – Accepting/bearing with/ helping those who are weak or different: "Accept one another, then, just as Christ accepted you, in order to bring praise to God" (Rom. 15:7).

- 3/7 – Seeking to please others rather than ourselves: "Each of you should look not only to your own interests, but also to the interests of others" (Phil. 2:4).
- 3/6 – Believing each other: "Love always trusts" (1 Cor. 13:7).
- 5/7 – Sharing joy: "Rejoice with those who rejoice" (Rom. 12:15).
- 10/10 – Hospitality: "Share with God's people who are in need. Practice hospitality" (Rom. 12:13).
- 15/25 – No pride or superiority, rather humility and appreciating others: "Honour one another above yourselves" (Rom. 12:10).
- 5/3 – Sensitivity to etiquette and to others and their feelings: "Do not rebuke an older man harshly, but exhort him as if he were your father. Treat younger men as brothers" (1 Tim. 5:1).
- 1/1 – Accountability: "In the Lord, however, woman is not independent of man, nor is man independent of woman" (1 Cor. 11:11).
- 9/12 – Mutual edification: "I long to see you so that I may impart to you some spiritual gift to make you strong— that is, that you and I may be mutually encouraged by each other's faith" (Rom. 1:11-12).
- 21/37 – Intolerance for unholiness: "Do not let any unwholesome talk come out of your mouths, but only what is helpful for building others up according to their needs, that it may benefit those who listen" (Eph. 4:29).
- 4/5 – Intolerance for dishonesty and untruthfulness: "Therefore each of you must put off falsehood and speak truthfully to his neighbour, for we are all members of one body" (Eph. 4:25).
- 14/26 – Church discipline: "Hand this man over to Satan, so that the sinful nature may be destroyed and his spirit saved on the day of the Lord" (1 Cor. 5:5).
- 3/6 – Judgement for impurity in the church: "For anyone who eats and drinks without recognising the body of the Lord eats and drinks judgement on himself. That is why many among you are weak and sick, and a number of you have fallen asleep. But if we judged ourselves, we would not come under judgement. When we are judged by the Lord, we are being disciplined so that we will not be condemned with the world" (1 Cor. 11:29-32).
- 7/8 – Fellowship of suffering among Christians: "So do not be ashamed to testify about our Lord, or ashamed of me his prisoner. But join with me in suffering for the gospel, by the power of God" (2 Tim. 1:8).
- 11/18 – Suffering out of concern when Christians have problems: "Besides everything else, I face daily the pressure of my concern for all the churches. Who is weak, and I do not feel weak? Who is led into sin, and I do not inwardly burn?" (2 Cor. 11:28-29).
- 13/14 – Sharing in comfort and suffering: "If one part suffers, every part suffers with it" (1 Cor. 12:26).
- 4/7 – Enjoying fellowship: "Recalling your tears, I long to see you, so that I may be filled with joy" (2 Tim. 1:4).
- 10/16 – Refreshment through fellowship: "… so that by God's will I may come to you with joy and together with you be refreshed" (Rom. 15:32).
- 26/37 – Joy and pride over others and their actions: "Therefore, my brothers, you whom I love and long for, my joy and crown, that is how you should stand firm in the Lord, dear friends!" (Phil. 4:1).
- 16/36 – Paul prays for his readers: "I thank God, whom I serve, as my forefathers did, with a clear conscience, as night and day I constantly remember you in my prayers" (2 Tim. 1:3).
- 8/13 – Paul requests prayer for himself: "Pray also for me, that whenever I open my mouth, words may be given me so that I will fearlessly make known the mystery of the gospel, for which I am an ambassa-

dor in chains. Pray that I may declare it fearlessly, as I should" (Eph. 6:19-20).

• 37/110 – On community worship: "Let the word of Christ dwell in you richly as you teach and admonish one another with all wisdom, and as you sing psalms, hymns, and spiritual songs with gratitude in your hearts to God" (Col. 3:16).

What a huge list this is! It includes 25 topics. To this we could add the so-called *sun* compounds which Paul is fond of using. This name is given when the Greek prefix *sun*, which means "co-" or "fellow," is added to a word. Scholars tell us that such compounds are not as significant in Hellenistic Greek as they are in classical Greek.[4] But there are a few somewhat significant occurrences of *sun* compounds that refer to relations within the body. I found 18 such occurrences of nouns and 27 of verbs. An important noun is *sun-ergos*, meaning "fellow worker," which is found nine times.

It is clear that, according to Paul, Christians cannot grow alone. John Wesley said, "The Bible knows nothing of solitary religion." Miroslav Volf (1998, p. 162) says, "No one can come to faith alone, and no one can live in faith alone." Volf (1998, pp. 11-18) shows how it is the free churches that are growing today, but that these churches have a very individualistic ecclesiology. Perhaps we have overreacted to the Roman Catholic understanding of salvation. The Catholic slogan *extra ecclesiam, nulla salus*, which means, "Outside the church, no salvation," shows how they view the church's role in salvation. They give salvific value to the means of grace, such as the sacraments of baptism and the Eucharist, and thus view salvation as being mediated through the church. The Protestant Reformation rediscovered the glorious truth of individual salvation. But we may have gone to the other extreme and neglected the fact that the context in which this salvation occurs is the church.

Charles Van Engen argues that the individualism of the church is an example of the church taking on the features of modernism. He gives an extended quotation from a description of American society by Norman Kraus (1993, pp. 31-32; cited in Van Engen, 1996, p. 211):

"In American society today, the unquestioned assumption is that the individual takes precedence over the group. Freedom means individual independence. Civil rights means the individual's right to 'life, liberty, and the pursuit of happiness' ....

"The concept of organic community has been heavily eroded by technology, urbanisation, political ideology, and legal definition. Even marriage and family are increasingly accepted as matters of individual contract and convenience. The group has become for us a collection of individuals created *by* individuals for their own individual advantages."

When we contrast this description with the many times Christians are described as those who die for others, we realise how different the Christian ethic is from that of the society around us. This ethos has certainly influenced the church in the West, and it is trickling to churches in other lands too. The extreme form of this is the electronic church, where people don't even need to go to church on Sunday.

To many people, the purpose of fellowship is to get a blessing. Accountability and commitment are not serious considerations. When someone sins, we may simply ignore it because it is "none of our business." Yet a life without accountability is a lonely life. Society has tried so many things to get over this lone-

---

[4] D. A. Carson in a personal conversation.

liness. Small groups are flourishing in the church once again. This is an encouraging sign. But often the small groups consist of people who have entered into an artificial grouping, where they don't live or work closely to each other. So there is isn't much opportunity to develop deep ties and honest and open accountability. Often the groups meet only for a short period of time. They break up before real trust and openness have developed. Accountability is a body function, something that people who work close to each other develop. The type of group that I have just described will certainly help those who are involved in them. But a longer time and closer ties are needed to develop the type of fellowship that we can call spiritual accountability, where people walk in the light with each other (1 John 1:7).

Internet chatting is helping many. But here too one does not need to be accountable. Can people find security in anonymous conversations with people to whom they are not even willing to disclose their identities? Counsellors and psychotherapists are being used by many to fill this void caused by the individualisation of society. Thomas Szaz, himself a psychotherapist, has said, "Psychotherapy is the purchase of friendship." So a deep void remains in the lives of many people today.

And what can we say about our pursuit of holiness? In Paul, much of the pursuit of holiness is to be done in community. 2 Timothy 2:22 is a great holiness verse: "Flee the evil desires of youth, and pursue righteousness, faith, love, and peace...." I preached on this text in my homiletics class in seminary. During the evaluation of the sermon, my professor, Dr. Jerry Mercer, gently reminded me that I left out the last part of that verse, which may be the most important part of it. It says, "... along with those who call on the Lord out of a pure heart." I think that by not noticing such an important feature of this verse, I was reflecting the individualism that is so typical of Evangelicalism.

So many Christian leaders today have no one to whom they are spiritually accountable. Many have Boards to help them to be accountable with their schedules, programmes, and finances. But they don't have people to check them on things that challenge them in their Christian life. How helpful it would be to have people to check on how our devotional life is going or on how we are faring with a bad habit like losing our tempers at home. So many stories are circulating about how adult television is being watched in hotels by Christian leaders at conferences that it is a thing that should be causing a lot of concern. This is especially so with the moral fall of many travelling Christian leaders recently. All of us have areas of vulnerability to sin in our lives, and the biblical pattern is for us to get help from other Christians. Hebrews 10:24 says, "And let us consider how we may spur one another on toward love and good deeds."

The biblical pattern is for all ministry to be done in community. Travelling preachers, for example, should never consider themselves as lone persons who perform in their area of expertise and then go on to their next assignment. In the Gospels and Acts, you almost never find a preacher travelling alone. They did their ministry in community. Today, for many, travelling with another is not economically viable, though it should be encouraged whenever possible. George Müller had an amazing travel schedule for 17 years after retiring from his orphanages at age 70. But he travelled with his wife Susannah on most of these trips (Steer, 1975, p. 236). Paul pointed out that several apostles took their wives along with them on their travels, though he did not have that luxury

(1 Cor. 9:5). But he always had others travelling with him.

Even when travelling preachers travel alone, they can do their ministry in community. Journeys today do not take too long, unlike in the New Testament era. A car or train or bus or plane gets them to their destination fairly soon. They could have friends in their home base support them with prayer and concern. These same people could receive the report of how they fared in ministry and in personal behaviour during the trip. When John Stott retired from being Rector at All Soul's Church in London to launch into an itinerant ministry, he remained on the staff team there as Rector Emeritus, living in a flat owned by the church. Now, after retiring from the staff team, he still has what he calls his Accountability Group of Elders, which helps him decide what assignments to take and generally monitors his ministry. While travelling ministers are ministering in a place, their hosts could be the community that supports them. This ministry to the travelling minister would be greatly enhanced if they live in homes from this community. In this way, the tie with the church is deepened, and the minister can identify with the people much better by being among them in this closer way. Besides, just as in New Testament times, when hospitality for travelling Christians was strongly encouraged,[5] hotels today are not very clean places in terms of morality.[6]

We are facing a new phenomenon in many of our nations, where foreign groups appoint "their representative" in a given country. They help this person, whose ministry they now consider as an extension of their own ministry. Unfortunately, the accountability that they can offer is a long-distance one which is confined to occasional visits to the country and regular written reports. The pioneer is not blessed with a community that will help him or her. Often major problems emerge after a time, as unhealthy patterns are allowed to grow with no one to help check them. Is it any wonder that so many Christian leaders are falling into serious sin today? Such falls are never sudden. If these leaders had been accountable to others, the problems would have surfaced much earlier, and remedial steps could have been taken before the problems went so deep.

We repeat the major point in this section: Christianity is a community religion, and all Christians, both new and mature, are expected to live their Christian lives and carry out their ministries with help from fellow Christians.

Conclusion: A Prophetic Community Life

Biblical community is an area in which the church will have to present a prophetic alternative in today's society. Yet I fear that this is an area in which we have conformed greatly to the pattern of the world. I fear that cultural blinds, which cause us to ig-

---

[5] Rom. 12:13; 16:23; 1 Tim. 3:2; 5:10; Tit. 1:8; Heb. 13:2; 1 Pet. 4:9; 2 John 10; 3 John 5-8. Hospitality is a key theme in the Lukan writings. Acts often mentions the names of hosts who opened their homes for missionaries to live in and/or stay at for meals or meetings (9:43; 10:23, 48; 12:12; 16:15, 34; 17:5-7; 18:2-3, 7, 26; 21:8, 16; 28:7). On this subject, see Koenig (1985, pp. 85-123). On hospitality for travelling preachers, see Fernando (1998, pp. 312-315, 438, 444, 448, 452-453, 491, 552).

[6] On the moral impurity of inns in New Testament times, see Ferguson (1993, p. 82) and Fernando (1998, p. 312).

nore important principles of biblical community, often hamper us.[7] I fear that many of our structures of community life are derived more from the business world than from the Bible. Success is measured by numerical growth, and we can achieve such growth by using the best principles of marketing. When Christian leaders hear the biblical teaching about community expounded, they say "Amen" and heartily agree. But often, because of the passion to grow, they will ignore or break these biblical principles in practice.

We will use an unholy but talented pianist for a big programme because we cannot find someone to replace him or her at the last moment. We will start new programmes without ensuring that the workers there are well looked after in terms of accountability and pastoral care. We will lower our standards of community solidarity. We have small groups that don't demand long-term commitment from people. The content of the gospel message is so powerful and relevant to human need that the church will grow if we proclaim it. But people will join us as they join the group of people who drink Coca-Cola. They are not committed to the church. So the moment they find another church that will meet their needs better, or the moment they have problems in their church, they will switch churches—just as they switch to lemonade when they decide that they do not like Coke.

We have to be prophetic in the way we practice biblical community, because biblical community is so different from what we see in the world. This may seem evangelistically problematic, because it may look as if we are not meeting people's acknowledged needs. But, though biblical community may seem not to meet acknowledged needs, it certainly meets real needs that cause an ache deep in the heart. Among these needs are the need for accountability and correction, the need for an authority to which to submit, the need to be holy, and the need to have the security of knowing that people will stick with us no matter what happens to us. How many people today live with deep, unarticulated hurt because they have been dumped by the group to which they belonged! The prophetic way may seem at first to be irrelevant and unpopular. But because it meets these deep needs, it could ultimately prove to be very relevant.

By practising Christian community, we could help foster holy, secure, and loving people. And the world will look at us and notice the difference. They will see that this is what they are really looking for, even though they did not acknowledge this need at first. Actually we are seeing that post-modernism is placing a new emphasis on the need for community life, which was undervalued in the strongly individualistic modern era. I am convinced that when the world recognises the awful loneliness and unfulfilment of the independent and private lifestyles that are rampant today, Christian community could be one of the most powerful forces for people coming to Christ (see Storkey, 1994).[8] Then Jesus' claim that the world would believe when the church is one, as the Father and Jesus are one (John 17:21, 23), would prove to be true. Being a prophetic presence through radical biblical community life may be one of the biggest challenges facing the church in the 21st century.

---

[7] For an attempt at remedying this situation, see Fernando (1991).

[8] This was confirmed to me in a conversation with the eminent British Christian sociologist Alan Storkey.

References

Barth, M. (1974). *Ephesians: Introduction, translation, and commentary.* The Anchor Bible. Garden City, NY: Doubleday & Co.

Bechert, H. (1984). Buddhist revival in East and West. In H. Bechert & R. Gombrich (Eds.), *The world of Buddhism.* London: Thames & Hudson Ltd.

Bruce, F. F. (1990). *The Acts of the Apostles: The Greek text with introduction and commentary* (3rd ed.). Grand Rapids, MI: Wm. B. Eerdmans Publishing Co.

Carson, D. A. (1991). *The Gospel according to John.* Grand Rapids, MI: Wm. B. Eerdmans Publishing Co.

Ferguson, E. (1993). *Backgrounds of early Christianity* (2nd ed.). Grand Rapids, MI: Wm. B. Eerdmans Publishing Co.

Fernando, A. (1991). *Reclaiming friendship: Relating to each other in a fallen world.* Leicester, England: Inter-Varsity Press.

————. (1995). *The supremacy of Christ.* Wheaton, IL: Crossway Books.

————. (1998). *NIV application commentary: Acts.* Grand Rapids, MI: Zondervan Publishing House.

Kamaleson, S. (1971). The local church and world evangelism. In J. R. W. Stott et al. (Eds.), *Christ the liberator.* Downers Grove, IL: InterVarsity Press.

Koenig, J. (1985). *New Testament hospitality: Partnership with strangers as promise and mission.* Philadelphia, PA: Fortress Press.

Kraus, C. N. (1993). *The community of the Spirit: How the church is in the world.* Scottdale, PA: Herald Press.

Minear, P. S. (1960). *Images of the church in the New Testament.* Philadelphia, PA: Westminster Press.

Sande, K. (1997). *The peacemaker: A biblical guide to resolving personal conflict* (2nd ed.). Grand Rapids, MI: Baker Book House.

Steer, R. (1975). *George Müller: Delighted in God!* Wheaton, IL: Harold Shaw Publishers.

Storkey, A. (1994). *The meanings of love.* Leicester, England: Inter-Varsity Press.

Van Engen, C. (1996). *Mission on the way: Issues in mission theology.* Grand Rapids, MI: Baker Book House.

Volf, M. (1998). *After our likeness: The church as the image of the Trinity.* Grand Rapids, MI: Wm. B. Eerdmans Publishing Co.

Ajith Fernando has led Sri Lanka Youth for Christ since 1976. Convinced of a call to theologise from the grassroots, he has always led a small division in YFC and presently leads the work with drug dependents. His YFC responsibilities include teaching and pastoral care of staff. Ajith and his wife Nelun are active in the leadership of a Methodist church, most of whose members are converts from other religions. He has a Th.M. in New Testament from Fuller Theological Seminary. His nine books have been in the area of either Bible exposition, such as the NIV Application Commentary: Acts (Zondervan, 1998), or mission theology, such as The Supremacy of Christ (Crossway, 1995).

Part 4

Addressing issues
of globalized
Evangelical missiology

ONE OF THE MAJOR PURPOSES of the Iguassu Consultation was to offer models of biblical and globalized missiology. We sought a theology of mission that was true to Scripture, sensitive to the world's cultures, and relevant for the entire family of God in mission. We are convinced that this international perspective has become one of the unique contributions of this book. In this spirit, we offer the diverse metaphors of the feast—the refracted diamond and the tapestry—rich, diverse, light-giving, variegated, relevant, beautiful. There was also a sense of releasing a new "architecture of contextualization," with open space for new designs and ways of doing theology and missiology, with a "round table" that allows equal sitting space for all participants.

The anchor came in Adeyemo's presentation, followed by the flow from the major regions of the church around the world—Turaki of Africa, Daimoi from the South Pacific, Tan from East Asia, Rajendran from India, Greenlee from North Africa, Masih of the Middle East, Saracco from Latin America, McAlister presenting the younger Western generations, and Adeney from North America. This material was initially presented in regional break-out sessions, and therefore it is not

until the release of this book that we are able to enjoy the nourishment that comes from this globalized table.

It has been encouraging to read these chapters, crafted with integrity, confession, and courage, and certainly with creativity. The diverse styles reflect the writers' giftings as well as their approach to the subject. The authors speak for themselves, and these are their serious reflections. Now these chapters become foundations for further study and contextualization of missiology for the church.

17

Profiling a globalized and Evangelical missiology

TOKUNBOH ADEYEMO

"**A**S THE TURN OF THIS century approaches with its challenges and opportunities, we, the Evangelicals of Africa, see the need for an invigorated, compassionate, and uncompromising Evangelical response to the contemporary social, political, economic, and religious realities of our day....

"We reaffirm our commitment to the Lordship of Christ and our obedience to the great command of loving God and our neighbours and the Great Commission of discipling all nations....

"In the light of the tremendous social, political, and religious burdens Africa bears today, the call of winning Africa for Jesus is urgent and requires all Christians of Africa to respond in order to impact their continent for the kingdom of God.

"We therefore resolve to win Africa for Jesus...!"[1]

This is the united voice of a movement, the Association of Evangelicals in Africa (AEA). Representing over 60 million Evangelicals in 44 duly organized national Evangelical alliances, the AEA is determined to reach all of Africa with the gospel by planting churches and establishing Evangelical networks in all of the 56 nations of Africa by the year 2000. When the call was made in November 1993, there were only 27 such national networks. As we meet at Iguassu, in

---

[1] Taken from *Declaration: The Resolution of the Association of Evangelicals in Africa (AEA)*, made at the end of its Sixth General Assembly held in Lagos, Nigeria, October 31 – November 9, 1993, under the theme, "Africa for Jesus." It was attended by over 500 delegates from 46 nations.

October 1999, there are 44 of them, leaving 12 nations to go.[2] This is a partial story of a continent that was dubbed "dark" in the middle of the 19th century by its explorers. Then her coasts were hazardous, her jungles impregnable, her pests deadly, and her people full of savagery. Many were the explorers and missionaries who died and were buried on her soil. In spite of their shortcomings—and there were many of them—and though Africa still has other problems, she can no longer be called a "dark continent," because the entrance of God's words has brought light to her (Psalm 119:130). We are indelibly grateful to God and thankful to those who brought the gospel to us. Nothing could stop them—hostile chiefs, fierce lions, unfriendly climate, nothing; the King's job must be done even at the expense of their lives. By faith and courage, the men and women who brought us the good news dared to step out into what appeared as a void. Sweat and tears characterized their endeavours.

Take, for example, the SIM International (then Sudan Interior Mission) founding fathers. Within the first year of their arrival in my country, Nigeria (December 1893), Tom Kent and Walter Gowans took ill and died, leaving Rowland Bingham to the vision of reaching the interior part of black Africa, then known as the Soudan. This was not exceptional. The graveyards of missionaries at Kijabe, Kenya, bear a silent testimony to the commitment and sacrificial love of these great forebears. My colleague, Canon Bayo Famonure (1994), writes, "While one tombstone reads 'Satisfied,' another one says, 'He has done all things well.' In fact, the west coast of Africa claimed so many lives that it became known as the 'white man's grave.'" The superintendent of the Methodist Mission for West Africa based at the coastal city of Lagos in Nigeria was reported to have said to Kent, Gowans, and Bingham upon their arrival in 1893, "Young men (they were aged 20, 23, and 25), you will never see the Soudan; your children will never see the Soudan; your grandchildren may" (SIM *NOW*, p. 4).

He was wrong, for the three men did see the Soudan. Though the death of Kent and Gowans brought temporary setback, Bingham remained tenacious to the original passion and vision. Today, the national church that was founded through their efforts, the Evangelical Church of West Africa (ECWA), is not only one of the largest denominations in Nigeria but also has the largest missionary society in the country.[3]

This heroic, laudable, missionary heritage became the cradle for the birth of the church in Africa during the 19th century. Alongside their European and American counterparts, African missionaries blazed the dark forests of their motherland to spread the gospel and plant churches in different cultures. They laboured together in beautiful biblical partnership. What are

---

[2] Each national Evangelical network serves as a light-bearer to the nation. Its primary purpose is to rally together and mobilize member churches, mission agencies, and individual believers to reach the unreached people groups within its national boundary. Five of the remaining 12 nations are Islamic (Libya, Mauritania, Morocco, Western Sahara, and Tunisia); four are small islands (Cape Verde, São Tomé/Príncipe, St. Helena, and Reunion); and the remaining three are Equatorial Guinea, Congo Brazaville, and Gabon. Plans are afoot to reach at least seven of these nations by A.D. 2000.

[3] In 1998, the Evangelical Missionary Society of ECWA reported a missionary force of 1,200 missionaries (including spouses and children) serving in 13 different fields (8 within Nigeria and 5 in other nations).

the foundations of their (and of our) Evangelical missiology, that also reflect the unique contextualizing contributions of the globalized church?

Foundations of Evangelical Missiology

The Christ-event

The first and foremost foundation is the Christ-event. By the Christ-event, Evangelical missiologists speak of the six major "salvific events" portrayed in the New Testament. David Bosch (1991, pp. 512-518) identifies this sixfold event as "the incarnation of Christ, his death on the cross, his resurrection on the third day, his ascension, the outpouring of the Holy Spirit at Pentecost, and the parousia."

By his incarnation, Jesus, our supreme missionary model, fully identified with those he came to seek and save. "Since the children have flesh and blood, he too shared in their humanity..." (Heb. 2:14). Jesus of Nazareth left his glory in heaven, wearily trod the dusty roads of Palestine, and poured out compassion on the social outcasts of his day. "In this model," writes Bosch (1991, p. 513), "one is not interested in a Christ who offers only eternal salvation, but in a Christ who agonizes and sweats and bleeds with the victims of oppression." No Evangelical theology (of the West or of the Two-Thirds World) will ever deny the kenosis of Jesus. Yet it is the rise of liberation theology in Latin America that has given the incarnation of Jesus the missiological prominence that it deserves (see Núñez & Taylor, 1989, p. 255). Commenting on the birth of Jesus and its implication for missions, John Stott (1978, p. 451) states, "Jesus could not have served human need by remaining aloof in the safe isolation of his heaven; he had to enter our world. And his entry was not a superficial visit like a tip-and-run raid, or like the arrival of an immigrant who refuses to

become acculturated to the land of his adoption, or like a spaceship touchdown in which the astronaut protects himself from exposure in a spacesuit. No. He laid aside his immunity to pain, weakness, sorrow, suffering, and temptation. He became flesh and lived among us. He made himself vulnerable when he made himself one with us."

Next to the incarnation in the continuum of the Christ-event is the cross. Having made himself one with us in our humanity and sorrows, now Jesus also identified himself with our sins, our guilt, and our death. The Apostle Paul says, "God made him who had no sin to be sin for us, so that in him we might become the righteousness of God" (2 Cor. 5:21). According to Moltmann (1975, p. 4), the cross of Jesus is, uniquely, the badge of distinction of the Christian faith. Without the cross, Christianity would be a religion of cheap grace.

John Stott (1986) has clearly summarized the fourfold theological significance of the cross—namely, propitiation, redemption, justification, and reconciliation. But it was Shutz (quoted in Bosch, 1991, p. 514) who aptly drew out the missionary significance of the cross saying, "Suffering is the divine mode of activity in history.... The church's mission in the world, too, is suffering ... is participation in God's existence in the world."

In the traditional non-Christian religious milieu, the cross with its rituals and symbolism is most appealing. The ultimate sacrifice has been made by God himself in the death of his Son, the "Peace Child," so that through the cross humanity may be reconciled not only to God but also one to another. "For he himself is our peace, who has made the two one and has destroyed the barrier, the dividing wall of hostility.... His purpose was to create in himself one new man out of the two, thus making peace" (Eph. 2:14-15). Therefore, our missionary message is that in Christ there is no Hutu or Tutsi, no white or black, no rich or poor, and no male or female. The late Bishop Festo Kivengere stated powerfully, "At the foot of the cross the ground is level, and there is no raised platform."

Great as the doctrine of the cross is, it will be meaningless without the resurrection. Early Christians viewed the Easter event as the vindication of Jesus. Peter could boldly declare on the day of Pentecost, "God has raised this Jesus to life" (Acts 2:32). To Paul, if Jesus wasn't raised, everything was vain—both the apostolic preaching and the disciples' faith (1 Cor. 15:14). According to Berkhof (1966, p. 180), the cross and the resurrection are not in balance with each other. Rather, the resurrection has the ascendancy and victory over the cross. The resurrection is a message of joy, hope, and victory—the first fruits of God's ultimate triumph over the enemy. Bosch (1991, p. 515) declares, "Missiologically this means, first, that the central theme of our missionary message is that Christ is risen, and that, secondly and consequently, the church is called to live the resurrection life in the here and now and to be a sign of contradiction against the forces of death and destruction—that it is called to unmask modern idols and false absolutes."

Christ's commission to his church to make disciples of all nations is predicated upon the reality of his resurrection and consequent Lordship (see Matt. 28:18-19; John 20:19-21). As Lord, he commands—not suggests nor advises—his church to make disciples.

Following the resurrection is the ascension. The ascension is the symbol of the enthronement of the crucified and risen Christ, who now reigns as King. Paul by the Spirit declares, "Therefore God exalted him to the highest place and gave him the name that is above every name, that at the name of Jesus every knee should bow, in heaven and on earth and under the earth, and every tongue confess that Jesus Christ is Lord, to the glory of God the Father" (Phil. 2:9-11).

By this declaration, both the scope and the essence of Christ's reign are underscored. No one is excluded from submission to his Lordship—whether a socialist French, a secularist English, a religious Indian, a Communist Chinese, or a superstitious African. As Lord, Jesus Christ has both power and authority to control and shape human destiny.

Confessing Jesus as Lord has untold missiological implications. It means complete surrender of our will to his and total, unequivocal obedience to his commands. Under Communist regimes, confessing Jesus as Lord has meant coming into conflict against the powers-that-be, with consequent imprisonment or death. In many a totalitarian regime, it could mean civil disobedience of unjust rules and corrupt structures. And in post-modern secularist society, it means a radical examination of our lifestyle and values and an unequivocal denunciation of all atheistic humanist tendencies and theories. Bosch (1991, p. 516) states, "Mission from this perspective means that it should be natural for Christians to be committed to justice and peace in the social realm. God's reign is real, though as yet incomplete." To assist and empower the church to bear its witness to Christ effectively, the Holy Spirit was poured out on the day of Pentecost. The apostles were not to go out on their mission alone, without the abiding presence and power of the Holy Spirit. To do otherwise would have been tantamount to abysmal failure. The Holy Spirit with them, who would reside in them from Pentecost on, would among other things:

- Testify about Jesus Christ.
- Prepare the hearts of unbelievers before the arrival of evangelists.

- Convict unbelievers of sin, righteousness, and judgment.
- Lead them to repentance.
- Quicken faith in them to believe in Jesus Christ.
- Bring about the new birth through Christ (John 15:26-27; 16:8-11; 7:37-39).

It is inconceivable, therefore, to think of Christian mission without a central place being given to the Holy Spirit. "We cannot win souls to Christ merely by advertizing or by preaching, or by witnessing, or by arguing," writes John Stott (1978, p. 454). He goes on to say, "I do not say that these methods of evangelism are unnecessary, for the Holy Spirit can and does use them all. What I am saying is that they are insufficient without the work of the Holy Spirit in and through them." The Manila Manifesto (1989, par. 5) puts it succinctly: "The Scriptures declare that God himself is the chief evangelist. For the Spirit of God is the Spirit of truth, love, holiness, and power, and evangelism is impossible without him. It is he who anoints the messenger, confirms the word, prepares the hearer, convicts the sinful, enlightens the blind, gives life to the dead, enables us to repent and believe, unites us to the Body of Christ, assures us that we are God's children, leads us into Christlike character and service, and sends us out in our turn to be Christ's witnesses. In all this the Holy Spirit's main preoccupation is to glorify Jesus Christ by showing him to us and forming him in us."

It can be stated categorically, therefore, that our mission is God's mission: the Son supplies the model, and the Holy Spirit supplies the power.

Between ascension and parousia, the disappearance and the reappearance of Jesus, the church is to engage in worldwide witness in the power of the Holy Spirit. The parousia will terminate the mission period, which began with Pentecost. Since the parousia could be any moment, the eager eschatological expectation gave the early church a sense of urgency. Admonishing the believers at Rome to live soberly, Paul writes, "The hour has come for you to wake up from your slumber, because our salvation is nearer now than when we first believed. The night is nearly over; the day is almost here" (Rom. 13:11-12). In the light of this, Paul could not afford the extravagance of mission duplication and competition that often marks contemporary missionary enterprise. He made it his ambition to preach the gospel where Christ was not yet known (Rom. 15:20).

The return of the Lord also communicates a time of stewardship accountability with attending reward or punishment. "We must all appear before the judgment seat of Christ," Paul writes, "that each one may receive what is due him" (2 Cor. 5:10). Stott (1992, p. 373) adds, "The reason why we seek to persuade people of the truth of the gospel is that we stand in awe of the Lord Jesus and his tribunal, before which we will one day have to give an account."

The foregoing sixfold christological salvific event constitutes the primary foundation of our Evangelical missiology. We proclaim the incarnate, crucified, resurrected, and ascended Christ, who is present among us in the Spirit and who is taking us into his future as "captives in his triumphal procession" (2 Cor. 2:14, NEB).

The commission of Christ

True discipleship is obedience to Christ. He himself says, "Why do you call me, 'Lord, Lord,' and do not do what I say?" (Luke 6:46). With regard to mission, Jesus simply says, "As the Father has sent me, I am sending you" (John 20:21). His commission, therefore, and loving obedience to the same, becomes the second foundation for Evangelical mission. As mission was central in the mind of Jesus, so it was in the minds of the apostles. The next verse (John 20:22) makes it abundantly clear that the granting of the Holy Spirit is primarily to enable the disciples to fulfill their mission in the world, just as Jesus was enabled to fulfill his. Michael Green (1970, p. 72) comments, "The apostolic church were quite clear that God's gift of his Spirit was intended not to make them comfortable but to make them witnesses."

So compelling was the charge that Paul said, "Woe to me if I do not preach the gospel!" (1 Cor. 9:16). Yet Paul's obligation depends not upon a legal command as such, but upon his love for Jesus and in keeping with Christ's example. In 2 Corinthians 5:14-15 he writes, "For Christ's love compels us, because we are convinced that one died for all, and therefore all died. And he died for all, that those who live should no longer live for themselves but for him who died for them and was raised again."

Ajayi Crowther was a slave boy from Nigeria who was rescued from a slave ship by a British boat in Sierra Leone. He became a Christian and immediately started missionary work in that country. In 1842, through the help of the Church Missionary Society of the Church of England, he received theological education in England, was ordained and consecrated a bishop in the Anglican church, and later returned to Nigeria, where he served as a church leader and missionary statesman. It was he who single-handedly translated the Bible into the Yoruba language in 1864. Crowther would always sign his episcopal letters with the phrase, "In loving obedience to the Master."

If Jesus is inexplicable apart from his mission, his church is equally inexplicable apart from its mission. If God the Father was to Jesus, "He who sent me," then Jesus

is to his church, "He who sent us." If any were to ask us why we proclaim the gospel to the poor, freedom to the captives, recovery of sight to the blind, and release to the oppressed, our response should be simple: because we are sent. Stott (1978, p. 450) rightly states: "An introverted church, pre-occupied with its own survival, has virtually forfeited the right to be a church, for it is denying a major part of its own being. As a planet which ceases to be in orbit is no longer a planet, so a church which ceases to be in mission is no longer a church."

The composition and character of the Triune God

Evangelicals are in general agreement that mission arises primarily out of the nature not of the church but of God himself. The Reformer John Calvin referred to John 3:16 as the whole gospel in a capsule. In this verse we see God the Father, who by nature is love, taking the initiative in mission vis-à-vis sending his one and only Son as a missionary to redeem lost humanity. Implied also in the verse is the activity of the Holy Spirit, the executive officer of the Godhead, who alone brings conviction upon sinners and causes faith to be born in them, resulting in salvation. It can be said in the words of Richard Bowie (1993, p. 61), "Evangelism is theocentric." George Peters (1972, p. 57), the late Professor of World Missions at Dallas Theological Seminary, used to say, "A rethinking of our missionary premises is imperative. Not the welfare and glory of man, not the growth and expansion of the church, but the glory of God forms the highest goal of missions—for of him and through him and to him are all things, to whom be glory forever."

In this concept of mission arising primarily from the nature and character of God, John Stott (1975, pp. 15-34) sees room for a biblical synthesis of mission: a marriage of the evangelistic and social responsibilities of the people of God. In another volume, after extensive treatment of biblical texts dealing with the calling and sending forth of the patriarchs, the prophets, and the apostles (not to talk of the mission of the Messiah), Stott (1978, p. 445) makes his characteristic passionate call for global Christians. He says, "I pray that these words 'all the families of the earth' may be written on our hearts. It is this expression more than any other which reveals the living God of the Bible to be a missionary God. It is this expression too which condemns all our petty parochialism and narrow nationalism, our racial pride (whether white or black), our condescending paternalism and arrogant imperialism. How dare we adopt a hostile or scornful or even indifferent attitude to any person of another colour or culture if our God is the God of 'all the families of the earth'? We need to become global Christians with a global vision, for we have a global God."

In his book, *The Kingdom of God in Africa*, Dr. Mark Shaw has examined the history of Christian witness in Africa through an understanding of the Triune God. Borrowing from H. R. Niebuhr's threefold kingdom of God principle,[4] Shaw (1996, pp. 292-295) divides the last 2,000 years of church/mission history in Africa as follows:

"1. The kingdom as the sovereign reign of God. In the first 1,500 years of African Christianity, the dominant witness to the kingdom was through theocratic institutions of church and state. The assump-
tion of the theocratic model is that the presence of God's rule is experienced through the institutionalizing of divine law.... In more recent years, the civil religion of Afrikanerdom reflected this witness to the kingdom.... Modern-day prophets in Africa such as Isaiah Shembe have done the same.

"2. The kingdom as the redemptive rule of Christ. Three primary models to the redeeming power of the kingdom can be seen in the African past:

"a. The transformational model witnesses through the building of Christianized societies.

"b. The inner model ... such as the Revival Movement of Uganda and the Charismatic Christianity of W. F. Kumuyi's Deeper Life Bible Church of Nigeria.

"c. The 'heavenly' model, which emphasizes not the individual piety of the soul, but the spiritual communion of the church on earth with the church in heaven through prayer and the sacraments.

"3. The kingdom as a coming utopia of justice. Common to each variant is the emphasis on the kingdom as bringing about human liberation and human fulfillment within time.

"a. The subversive model ... e.g., Alice Lenshina's Lumpa church in Zambia and a host of liberation movements.

"b. The utopian model ... advocates are more optimistic about a new world order being established through the efforts of sincere and committed Christians, e.g., Beyers Naude and Desmond Tutu.

"c. A third group emphasizes the future character of the coming kingdom. Tertullian, conservative Evangelical groups

---

[4] H. R. Niebuhr (1937) advocates three elements in the kingdom of God. The first is confidence in the divine sovereignty which, though hidden, is still the reality behind and in all realities. Second, in Christ the hidden is now revealed and is affecting the lives of believers. Third, all life is directed to the coming of the kingdom in power.

associated with Lausanne, and older Pentecostal theology.[5]

That there is a fervency in indigenous missionary movements in Africa within the past 30 years cannot be denied. Numerous evangelistic operations have been launched in different parts of Africa. Calculated to reach Africa for Christ, these efforts include New Life for All (Nigeria), Operation Good News (Nigeria), Here Is Life (Kenya), Operation Joshua (Kenya), Operation Samson's Fox Fire (Zimbabwe), and GO Festivals (Zambia and Nigeria), to name a few. Side by side with these efforts have arisen hundreds of indigenous missionary societies, such as Calvary Ministries or CAPRO (Nigeria), Christian Missionary Foundation (Nigeria), and The Sheepfold Ministries (Kenya). There seems to be a serious spiritual awakening sweeping across college and university campuses throughout Africa (thanks to various student ministries). Thousands of young graduates are moving out for Christ, following the path of the "Cambridge Seven." We can learn from these young missionaries what it means to live by faith, to live simply, to labour in adversity, to carry the cross, and to persevere. With an estimated force of over 25,000 African missionaries today, both in Africa and in the rest of the world, it can be rightly said that missions in Africa is approaching an epidemic level to the glory of God.

In addition to the three fundamental foundations for Evangelical missiology discussed above—the Christ-event, the commission of Christ, and the character of God—three other motivations for mission among Evangelicals are the human crisis, compassion for the lost, and vision.

Time and space do not permit their discussion here.

Global Realities Facing Christian Missions

Decline of Christianity in the West

The most striking reality facing Christian missions in the world today is the decline of Christianity in the West, largely caused by a deadening, anti-Christian, humanistic, secularist philosophy. It is disheartening to see church buildings being converted into cinema houses and entertainment centres in Europe. More and more young people in the West are committing themselves to Eastern mystery religions and cults such as Transcendental Meditation, Hare Krishna, Yoga, and New Age. In his *World Christian Encyclopedia*, David Barrett (1982, p. 7) states that the massive gains Christianity made across the Third World throughout the 20th century are being sadly offset by an average loss of 7,600 Christians leaving the church daily in the West. After extensive research, George Peters (1972, p. 57) said, "I do believe that Europe, to a great extent, is an unevangelized continent." In the West, people now speak of a post-Christian era. The implication of this situation for Christian mission is that it makes Western missionary enterprise open to suspicion in the non-Western world.

Religious plurality

While religious plurality has been part of sociological ordering for the church in Africa and Asia for centuries, the phenomenon is comparatively new in the West. It can be said that the church in Africa has

---

[5] It is interesting to note that Shaw did not include the classical mainstream Evangelicals under the auspices of the Association of Evangelicals in Africa (AEA) in his classification. Their position is the typical dialectics of "now and not yet." They advocate bringing justice to the nations together with soul winning, without the utopia of establishing a new world order.

lived and borne its witness in the midst of vigorous rivalry and opposition of Islam and African traditional religion. More than that, the church in Egypt and Ethiopia has survived for the past 2,000 years. Equally, the church in Africa south of the Sahara continues to grow numerically (though admitting some syncretistic tendencies).

The point here, however, is the rapid spread of Islam in Europe and America today. It is reported that France has more Muslims than Protestant Christians. Supported by petrol dollars, Islamic organizations are undertaking massive major projects all over Europe and America. All this should be of missiological concern for the church as a whole. One implication is learning from the church in Africa and Asia and partnering with their missionaries who have been raised in the context of religious plurality.

Global hostility

There is an air of global hostility against the West in general and the United States in particular. The feeling extends to Western eco-political systems and institutions and comes in various garbs. Sometimes it is strictly religious, as in the case of Iran under the late Ayatollah. Sometimes it is ideological, as in the case of Libya and the pre-Glasnost Russia. Sometimes it is economic, as in the case of the former colonies who are clamouring for debt relief. In many of these nations, visas and work permits are not readily granted to Westerners, especially those serving as traditional church-planting missionaries.

One can add to the above sketch such issues as economic recession, international terrorism, and general moral decadence. Rather than becoming easier, Christian mission enterprises in our day are becoming more difficult, risky, precarious, and expensive. The only way forward as we cross over into a new millennium is to engage in partnership. Before we conclude this essay with a call for global partnership, let us take a quick look at some of the advantages and handicaps for African missionaries.

African Missionaries

Advantages

Prime among the advantages for African missionaries is the lack of a record of cultural imperialism. Africa has no history of socio-political and cultural expansionism. On the contrary, we were colonized. Our application for visas and work permits in any country of the world cannot be denied on the basis of our historical record of political ambition. In fact, African nations are wooed by both East and West. Chances are that black African Christians applying to live and work in any country of the Islamic bloc, for example, may be denied on the basis of lack of economic support rather than because of political grouping.

Equally, the history of Africans in diaspora (in North America, Europe, West Indies, etc.) has demonstrated the high degree of cultural adaptability which is one of the chief pre-requisites of cross-cultural missions. Africans do not break easily under adversities. They have outlived the sugarcane plantations of America and have made homes out of a "wilderness." I have no reason to think that African missionaries will not thrive in other lands. Wherever one goes, be it the extremely cold country of Greenland or the isolated islands of New Zealand, one finds Africans in pursuit of education or hunting for treasures. Such energy can and must be used for missions.

On the labour market, it is still cheaper to employ Asians and Africans than Westerners. This is true in the Christian ministry in Africa. One of the Kenya daily newspapers, *Daily Nation*, carried a feature article on the missionary involvement of the church in Africa in its July 28, 1985 issue. In what the reporter described as the "church come of age," the article narrated a tripartite arrangement between the Anglican Church in Zaire (now Congo) and the Church of the Province of Kenya (Anglican) on the one hand; and the Anglican Church in Zaire and the Episcopal Church of North America (also Anglican) on the other. A need for pastors/teachers exists in the Kiswahili-speaking Anglican Church in eastern Zaire. A request for missionaries was sent to the Anglican Church in Kenya, while a request for the support of these missionaries was sent to the Episcopal Church of North America. All three parties agreed, and the contract was concluded. Thus the first set of four Kenya missionaries supported by a North American church went to work in Zaire. It was stated that the support for the four was equivalent to what is needed to support only one American missionary family working in the same setting. Added to this is the cultural/linguistic advantage of these Kenyans.

This doesn't mean that Africans can finish the task alone. Neither does it mean a call for moratorium on Western missionaries. What it does mean is "togetherness in world missions!" African missionaries working hand in hand with their counterparts from other parts of the world will not only demonstrate the oneness of the church—thus enhancing the credibility of the gospel—but will also correct some of the traditional misconceptions that identified Christianity with the West and saw missions only in one direction. The mission field is the world, and missions flows in the direction of needs.

Handicaps

In spite of the advantages, there are also handicaps for African missionaries. The Christian Missionary Foundation (Ni-

geria) is currently supporting a Kenyan missionary family in Uganda and two nationals in Malawi. The greatest handicap they have faced is getting foreign exchange for funds raised in Nigeria. This problem of foreign exchange is common to almost all African countries.

Equally limiting is the inadequate cross-cultural training available to would-be African missionaries. Most of our existing missionary force are graduates of government universities; Bible colleges and seminaries offering courses in cross-cultural missions have not received adequate attention. It is fitting to create missions departments in our existing institutions, where funds are available to establish schools of missions, such as the African Inland Church Missionary College in Eldoret, Kenya. The West has had rich experience in all these areas and can be an asset to their brethren in Christ.

Matters of logistics, such as travel arrangements, medical needs, children's education, correspondence, and maintaining contacts with home churches constitute another set of handicaps. In the case of career missionaries, questions of old age and retirement will come into the picture as well.

Global Partnership

The church in Africa needs to work shoulder to shoulder with the church in North America, in Europe, in Asia, and in other parts of the world. No single one of us—regardless of how skilled, gifted, experienced, or rich we may be—can finish the task of world evangelization alone. It will take all of the true Christian church and para-church organizations all over the world working together in obedience to Christ. The size of the task before us demands cooperation. The first man ever to be in space was Major (later Colonel) Yuri Gagarin, who was launched on April

12, 1961. He made a complete circuit of the Earth, landing safely near the pre-arranged position. It wasn't a solo but a team effort. Ever since, the colossal size and intricacies of the space program have demanded and received due cooperation. World evangelization demands more. With about 12,000 people groups numbering over 2 billion people still unreached, no price is too high for world-wide cooperation for evangelism. We salute the pattern of cooperation being forged by the World Evangelical Fellowship, especially its Missions Commission.

Next to size is the seriousness of the sickness of our world. We must not allow science and computer technology to deceive us. Our world is more sick, confused, and paralysed today than ever! Ethical and moral abuses of our day defy numeration. American military General Omar Bradley lamented, "We know more about war than peace today, more about killing than living. Knowledge of science outstrips capacity for control. We have too many men of science but too few men of God. Our world has achieved brilliance without wisdom, power without conscience. Ours is a world of nuclear giants but ethical infants."[6]

When AIDS epidemics struck, scientists across ideological divides abandoned their differences to seek a common solution. We must wake up to the fact that a more deadly disease than AIDS has struck: the lostness of millions dying and going to a Christless eternity. This situation was so serious that it brought God down to earth, stripped him of all, and sent him to Calvary.

Once we agree on solid biblical theological parameters, we should not allow anyone or anything to prevent us from working together to reach the world. Someone has said that the vision Christians need to prompt them for world evangelization is not of heaven but of hell.

As the sickness is serious, so the barriers are severe. In place after place, religious persecution (e.g., in the Islamic states), political hostility, and cultural intolerance are on the increase. Barriers are placed in the way of missions—sometimes by individuals, sometimes by whole societies, sometimes by our own excuses, but ultimately by Satan. Yet there has not been any other time in history when the church has enjoyed the blessing of human and material resources, together with the waves of spiritual renewal to get the job done, as it does today.

The 700 ways to evangelise the world, as suggested by Barrett and Reapsome (1988), are good and will be effective only after we have gotten rid of what Os Guinness described as the demons of privatisation and individualism. We must become what David Bryant called "World Christians." The commission from above, the cry from beneath, the call from the world (Macedonia), and the compulsion from within all speak one language: *unite for world evangelization!*

The diversity of the world we are sent to reach will require the diversity of our cultural backgrounds and expertise. When in unity of purpose and for the glory of God we marshal together our various diverse gifts, we not only demonstrate the oneness of the body of Christ, thus enhancing the credibility of the gospel, but as the Lord said, the world shall see and believe that Jesus is the Messiah.

---

[6] Quoted in *Time* Magazine (1999, Millennium ed., p. 29).

References

Barrett, D. B. (Ed.). (1982). *World Christian encyclopedia: A comparative study of churches and religions in the modern world, A.D. 1900-2000*. Oxford, England: Oxford University Press.

Barrett, D. B., & Reapsome, J. W. (1988). *Seven hundred plans to evangelize the world: The rise of a global evangelization movement*. Birmingham, AL: New Hope.

Berkhof, H. (1966). *Christ the meaning of history* (L. Buurman, Trans.). London: SCM Press.

Bosch, D. J. (1991). *Transforming mission: Paradigm shifts in theology of mission*. Maryknoll, NY: Orbis Books.

Bowie, R. W. (1993). *Light for the nations* (2nd ed.). Singapore: Haggai Centre for Leadership Studies.

Famonure, B. (1994, January–June). Reaching Africa for Jesus. *Vision, 2*(1).

Green, M. (1970). *Evangelism in the early church*. Grand Rapids, MI: Wm. B. Eerdmans Publishing Co.

The Manila Manifesto: An elaboration of the Lausanne Covenant 15 years later. (1989). Lausanne Committee for World Evangelization.

Moltmann, J. (1975). *The experiment hope* (M. D. Meeks, Ed. & Trans.). London: SCM Press.

Niebuhr, H. R. (1937). *The kingdom of God in America*. New York: Harper & Row.

Núñez, E. A., & Taylor, W. D. (1989). *Crisis in Latin America*. Chicago: Moody Press.

Peters, G. W. (1972). *A biblical theology of missions*. Chicago: Moody Press.

Shaw, M. (1996). *The kingdom of God in Africa: A short history of African Christianity*. Grand Rapids, MI: Baker Book House.

SIM *NOW*. (1992, Winter).

Stott, J. R. W. (1975). *Christian mission in the modern world*. Downers Grove, IL: Inter-Varsity Press.

———. (1978). The living Christ is a missionary Christ. In M. Cassidy & L. Verlinden (Eds.), *Facing the new challenges: The message of PACLA*. Nairobi, Kenya: Evangel Publishing House. [This volume is a compilation of addresses presented at a continental leadership conference called the Pan African Christian Leadership Assembly (PACLA) held in Nairobi, Kenya, December 9-19, 1976.]

———. (1986). *The cross of Christ*. Leicester, England: Inter-Varsity Press.

———. (1992). *The contemporary Christian: Applying God's word to today's world*. Leicester, England: Inter-Varsity Press.

Tokunboh Adeyemo was born to a wealthy Muslim family in Nigeria. Following his miraculous conversion in 1966, he abandoned his partisan political ambition in order to train for Christian ministry in particular and service for humanity in general. Following his undergraduate studies in Nigeria, Dr. Adeyemo proceeded to the U.S., where he did his master's at Talbot Theological Seminary and his doctorate at Dallas Theological Seminary. He later did post-doctoral research at Aberdeen University in Scotland. In 1994, he was awarded an honorary doctorate degree in theology in recognition of his contribution to Christian higher education, scholarship, and leadership by the Potchefstroom University in South Africa. He has written a number of books, including Salvation in African Tradition (1978), The Making of a Servant of God (1994), and Is Africa Cursed? (1997). Since 1978, he has served as the General Secretary of the Association of Evangelicals in Africa (AEA), as well as the Chairman of the International Council of the World Evangelical Fellowship since 1980. He is married to Ireti, and they are blessed with two sons. The family lives in Nairobi, Kenya.

18

Evangelical missiology from Africa: strengths and weaknesses

MATTHEW 9:35-38 lays a foundation for the major missionary activities that have taken place in Africa during the 19th and 20th centuries: (1) the ministry of teaching, (2) the ministry of preaching, (3) the ministry of healing, (4) the ministry of prayer, and (5) the ministry of recruiting and sending missionaries. The theory and practice of Christian missions in Africa has revolved mainly around these five major areas.

Response or criticism to the theory and practice of Christian missions in Africa usually addresses the methods, models, theologies, and assumptions about Africa and Africans. Some people dwell on the human weaknesses of the missionaries. Others focus on the socio-political forces that entrapped the missionaries. Still others emphasise the socio-political benefits of the work of Christian missions. The weaknesses and benefits of mission work in Africa must not obscure the *reason* for mission. Any criticism or praise that does not strengthen the divine reason for mission as established by Christ and the apostles does a disservice to the cause of mission in Africa. Criticism, if it is to have value, must be constructive and not vindictive. There is no place for a critical spirit against missionaries and the gospel of Christ.

I confess that I harbored a critical spirit against missionaries for many years. I was a product of African nationalism. I grew up at the time when Africans were fighting for their political independence from their colonial masters. I interpreted the work of Western missionaries from a nationalistic perspective. But I thank God that I was converted and delivered from such a mindset.

Yusufu Turaki

My conversion to mission took place in 1981 in the basement of the SIM archives in Scarborough, Ontario, Canada. I had gone there to do doctoral research on the question of British colonial policy, administrative practices, and attitudes towards the Muslim and non-Muslim groups of the northern region of Nigeria. I wanted to know how the British Administration treated Christian missions in northern Nigeria. I found that they did very little in terms of educational and social development of non-Muslim groups. Christian missions did far more than the colonial administration in establishing schools, medical work, dispensaries, health clinics, hospitals, leprosy work, literature work, and translation work in the middle belt of Nigeria.

The massive archival records of missionary activities in the areas of education, medical work, literature work, translation work, and the general development of the people overwhelmed me. There had been over 100 mission stations in Nigeria, and I read the archival records of each. One day in the basement of the archives, I was overwhelmed by the thought of what Christian missions had done for my people, in contrast to what the colonial masters had done. Tears rolled down my face as I was gripped by the anguish and guilt of having had a critical spirit against missionaries and also of not being thankful for what the missionaries had done. I confessed my sin to God in that basement room. I also confessed to some SIM missionaries in a small gathering. The SIM leader turned the occasion into a time of mutual confession. This experience greatly changed my view, my approach, and my relations with Western missionaries and with mission itself. I made a promise to God that one day I would commit what I had found in the archives into writing. I thank God that in 1994, I was able to complete my studies of the work of SIM in Nigeria. The title of the resulting work is *A Century of SIM/ECWA History in Nigeria, 1893-1993: A Theory and Practice of Christian Missions in Africa*. Most of the ideas developed in this paper are drawn from this and related works.

Biblical and Historical Foundations and Principles

Mission work in Africa has both biblical and historical foundations and principles. We must constantly go back to these for inspiration and motivation.

1. God's will and agenda for the nations. The entire Bible is the unfolding drama of God's will and agenda for evangelising the peoples of the world (John 3:16). If we study the Bible from this perspective, we will be able to draw much inspiration and motivation for mission.

2. Christ's commission to the church. Our Lord Jesus Christ came as the divine fulfillment of God's will and agenda for the salvation of the nations. After laying a solid foundation for mission through the cross, Jesus then commissioned his church to accomplish God's purpose among the peoples of the world (Matt. 28:18-20; John 17:18; 20:21; 21:15-17; Acts 1:6-8).

3. The apostolic example and model. God has revealed models of doing mission work through the activities of the apostles as recorded in the book of Acts. The Pastoral Epistles of Paul give further insight into these patterns of mission. The universal gospel of Christ is to be presented to all peoples as the only means of salvation. New believers are to be established through baptism and discipleship and are to be formed into fellowships. The established churches are to have trained leaders who will multiply the work of mission (2 Tim. 2:1-2; 4:1-5).

The apostles set an example of total obedience to Christ and his commission.

Now the church must act in obedience as the apostles did:

- We must go in total obedience.
- We must witness by our testimony.
- We must make disciples through baptism and teaching.
- We must feed, tend, and nurture through discipleship and teaching.
- We must pass on both the vision and the burden of mission by training leaders for the church.

This last point is especially important. The missionary pioneers were driven into mission work by both a *vision* and a *burden*. We regret to say that some aspects of mission work in Africa today lack both of these qualities. Para-church organisations and mission agencies have done well in keeping the vision and burden of mission alive, but the church, upon which the responsibility of mission ultimately rests, must recapture her first commitment to her Lord. She must be found faithful to her Lord in keeping his commission of mission for the whole world.

Theory and Practice of Christian Missions in Africa

The history of Christian missions has always been an outgrowth of the church acting in obedience to the biblical and historical foundations listed above. The biographies of faithful missionaries over the centuries have always revealed their commitment to these principles. Pioneering missionaries in Africa frequently testified to anchoring their vision and burden for mission in Africa in these truths. Our understanding of the work of Christian missions in Africa must therefore begin from this base.

There were Christian missions that predated the Evangelical missions of the 19th and 20th centuries in Africa. The following periods should be noted in passing:

- Apostolic era
- Patristic era
- Medieval era
- Muslim conquest of North Africa
- Portuguese Catholic missions in Africa
- Modern Christian missions, 19th and 20th centuries
- Pentecostal movements, late 1970s–1999

Christian missions played a significant role in the transformation of African societies in modern history. Humanitarian ministries included the planting of mission stations and churches; the establishment of educational programmes and institutions; medical work, services, and institutions; literature work, programmes, and institutions; and other forms of spiritual, moral, and social development of peoples and societies. These activities had a profound influence on the nature of church structures, on theology and philosophy, and on the patterns of relationships and approaches to African tradition and culture, Islam, colonial policies, and other socio-political issues.

Planting of mission stations, churches, and institutions

Christian missions used the strategy of founding mission stations, out-stations, churches, and institutions as a means of occupying and entrenching their presence in the vast continent of Africa. Mission stations were the centre of missionary and church activities, and they significantly shaped the emergent church structures. Mission agencies administered churches, institutions, and general missionary activities from the mission stations, and the patterns of church administration, structures, policies, and practices were passed on to the Africans.

The politics of creating dioceses (districts and their headquarters), church offices and officers, and titles of clergy drew extensively from the missionary legacy. The African church today spends much time, energy, and resources on these matters. Schisms, crises, conflicts, and tensions caused by these issues have in one way or another affected most churches in Africa. This phenomenon is part of the legacy which Christian missions left in Africa.

Education ministry

Christian missions established Western education in Africa. Their education programmes included literacy, classes for religious instruction, Sunday school and catechism, elementary and primary education, teacher training and secondary education, and theological education and training. The bulk of educated civil servants and professionals in Africa today had their humble beginnings in mission education programmes. Christian missions pioneered education where the colonial governments could not provide such benefits for their subjects.

The major contributions of Christian missions in the area of education include literacy; social, moral, and spiritual upbringing; and general development of the peoples and societies. Education was the most powerful tool for the transformation of African societies and also the most effective tool for evangelism. Research reveals that more people became Christians through the mission ministry of education than by any other means.

Although Christian missions undertook Western education programmes, most did so very reluctantly. Theological or Christian education was more favoured than general (secular) education. Most missionaries during the pioneering periods were against intellectualism and modernity. This stance affected the quality and policies of mission education. Education for

some mission societies was narrowed down to the popular three R's (reading, 'riting, and 'rithmetic) together with Bible knowledge; anything beyond these was considered worldly. The fear of too much education, of modernity, and of worldliness dominated mission education policies and adversely affected the concept of education and its administration by the missionary church in Africa.

The government take-over of mission and church schools in many African countries after independence was motivated by the assumption that a mission or church cannot provide "neutral" education; missionary education was thought to be nothing but Christian "propaganda." This dualistic concept of education as both "secular" and "spiritual" affected both state and church policies towards education across Africa. After the state take-over of schools, many churches turned their focus to theological education.

A holistic Christian approach to all aspects and disciplines of education must be developed—and not only theological or spiritual. This is a great task that awaits the African church in the 21st century.

Medical ministry and services

Christian missions began medical ministries where colonial governments had no adequate medical services or institutions for their subjects, especially in the remote rural areas. They built health clinics, dispensaries, maternity homes, and hospitals. They also developed leprosy services and built eye clinics and hospitals. Just as in the field of education, the colonial governments needed the help of Christian missions in this area. The missions contributed immensely to the state of health and the social well-being of the peoples of Africa in general.

Both medical and education activities were regarded by Christian missions as secondary to the gospel of Christ. They were simply tools for evangelisation and church planting and were never viewed as an integral part of the gospel. This led to the dichotomy between "word" and "deed," "spiritual" and "social." This dualism affected the holistic gospel approach to the total man and woman.

As in the area of education, the government in some African countries took over the medical work and services from the missions and churches. This reflected the belief that the church should limit its activities to what is "spiritual"; what touches on politics, economics, social concerns, etc., should fall under the purview of the state.

Today, the government medical sector in most African countries is struggling, as is the education sector. If the church is to meet the needs of Africa's people in the 21st century, it must go beyond a dualistic worldview and the impediments of the missionary legacy.

Literature ministry

Christian missions established literature and translation work in many parts of Africa. They reduced African languages to writing and analysed their structure. They then printed, sold, and distributed Christian and general literature through their translation work and bookshops. They also introduced Christian journalism. By developing social critics, they greatly influenced nationalist movements.

The preoccupation of Christian missions with what is "sacred" as opposed to what is "secular" led to their ambivalent approach to social, cultural, political, and economic issues. These areas were seen as "off limits" for any literature being produced. Anyone who wanted to get involved with these issues had to do so outside of the church. The contributions

of missions to these areas were mainly indirect in nature or consequential to mission policies.

The bulk of Christian literature pertained to spiritual needs. Very little was written on how the church, Christianity, Christians, and the Bible addressed or should address other issues. Serious biblical and theological reflections on these subjects were lacking. A Christian worldview of culture, religion, politics, economics, ethnicity/race, etc., still needs to be fully developed by the African church.

General social formations and transformations

Christian missions have done more to bring about social, religious, and human development and change than any other human agent in Africa south of the Sahara. As with educational and medical ministries, from the beginning, social and human services were viewed as auxiliary to the gospel of Christ. They were only a means to share the gospel and were not ends in themselves. In spite of any limitations or weaknesses on the part of Christian missions in their theory and practice of missions, as pioneers they made substantial contributions to nation-state building and to modernising African societies.

Christian missions had clear goals and objectives, which made them pioneers and social reformers. This pioneering and reforming spirit is lacking in the African church today. We may ask what agenda the church in Africa today has for society. If the church is to be relevant in the 21st century, this area must be addressed.

Overall, the work of Christian missions achieved the following in Africa:

- Rapid growth of Christianity.
- Firm establishment of the church.
- Educational development.
- Spiritual, social, political, and material uplift.

Emerging Issues of the Western Missionary Model in Africa

Western cultural baggage

European expansionism and colonialism can be seen as a gradual historical process from the Age of Discovery (explorers), to the Age of Mercantilism (merchants and traders), to the Age of Missions (missionaries), to the Age of Empire Building (colonialists). Colonialism is quite distinct from missions, even though both were products of the same society and shared the same socio-political roots, worldview, and ethos. They differed from each other in their primary motif, goals, objectives, and interests.

We must distinguish between emigrant or European cultural Christianity and Evangelical missions. Emigrant Christianity was a by-product of the European spirit of expansion and colonisation of the world. In essence, it was merely an exportation of emigrant culture, religion, and civilisation. Missions, on the other hand, were primarily driven by the spirit of Christ's Great Commission and by other religious forces such as revivals. The contrast must be kept in focus; otherwise it is easy to fall into the fallacy of lumping together both missions and emigrant Christianity as having been propelled by the spirit of colonialism.

We must admit here that it is not always clear as to where, when, and how a line of differentiation can be drawn between colonialism and some missions. With most Evangelical missions, the motif of missions was quite distinct, but sometimes it may have come under the influence of the prevailing cultural and colonial milieu. Also, for most mission agencies, the Lord Jesus Christ and his gospel were the ends of Evangelical mission, but this was not always the case.

The prevailing Christian and social worldviews of the European and North American societies shaped the type of Christianity and also the church structures which missionaries planted in Africa. Because of this influence, we must examine these worldviews as we search for an authentic, relevant, and effective Christianity and church structure for modern Africa. It is also important that we adequately assess the instruments of both social and religious change. The impact of such changes in Africa can be properly evaluated only in light of the philosophy and methods that were used.

There are many missionary practices, beliefs, assumptions, and models of change in Africa which are no longer relevant today. The earlier general negation of African culture and personality has robbed African Christianity of some basic and valuable African foundations, which African Christians want to recover but which are somewhat lost to history. Some basic features of African societies such as the family unit, marriage, kinship, social and communal morality, ethics, and justice have been lost to modern secular forces which are hostile to African society and Christianity. Christianity in modern Africa is facing many crises, and it seems unable to cope with them because certain African features were not utilised in establishing Christianity in African soil.

Western culture has introduced dualism and individualism as ways of seeing and interpreting life, as opposed to the traditional African and biblical holistic view of life. The biblical and African concepts of community and communal life must be recovered and developed by the African church. In addition, the quest for authentic Christianity in Africa must examine all aspects of missions in an African setting. This approach should lead to a reconstruction of a Christian worldview which is relevant and effective in Africa.

Authoritarian and bureaucratic church structures

African Christianity inherited hierarchical, authoritarian, and bureaucratic church structures from the missionaries. These structures tended to undermine the African communal way of life. The recent Pentecostal and charismatic emphasis on loose church structures and spontaneous religious expression is now creating powerful, authoritarian church personalities. The search for relevant church structures must cut across both the older churches and the newer Pentecostal and charismatic churches.

Capital intensive missions

The first Evangelical missions in Africa were industrial missions. They believed in both the gospel and commerce. This concept was later dropped as a result of the debates between "social gospel" and "pure gospel," that is, "deed" versus "word."

Christian missions raised funds and personnel from their home mission office and gradually became more and more dependent on the home mission. As a result, the economic and personnel potential of the field missions was not fully developed. The powerful personalities of some of the new Pentecostal and charismatic movements have not addressed this issue, nor have they provided an alternative. Instead, they have tended to rely more heavily upon Western capital and monetary philosophy. Internal resource generation and personnel development must be given priority attention in Africa if change is to occur.

Indigenisation policies and mission/church relations

The indigenisation policy of some Christian missions led to the founding of national churches in the 1950s in some African countries. This phenomenon occurred mostly among non-denominational Christian missions. These independent faith missions did two important things. First, they developed new church structures and organisations, and second, they trained Africans to take over their mission work. They emphasised building churches that were self-governing, self-supporting, and self-propagating, in accordance with the "three-self" formula espoused by Rufus Anderson, Henry Venn, and Roland Allen. Denominational missions, on the other hand, such as the Baptists, Presbyterians, Methodists, Anglicans (CMS), and Catholics, merely trained Africans to take the places of missionaries and subsequently incorporated the African mission churches into their world denominational church structures.

Indigenisation principles had a profound influence upon Christian missions. These policies defined in general terms the nature of the church, its quality, structures, etc. The preparation of Africans to take over the mission work depended very much upon what missions understood by these indigenous policies and also what models they used in implementing them. The following techniques were used:

Evangelism and church planting

Principles of evangelism were taught to early converts, who became itinerant evangelists alongside the missionaries. Church planting resulted from a variety of missionary activities, including evangelism, itineration, education, medical work, literature work, etc. Organised evangelism and church planting based upon indigenisation principles were quite evident even during the pioneering stages of the mission work.

Theological training

Christian missions founded many vernacular Bible training schools with the primary purpose of developing indigenous Bible teachers, evangelists, and pastors who would later provide church leadership.

Teacher training

Teacher training centres were also built by Christian missions with the primary purpose of developing indigenous teachers. Similar advanced schools were established with the view of preparing indigenous leadership within the African church.

Pastoral training

Pastoral training was the least developed by Christian missions. Theological institutions were mainly centres of training evangelists and Bible teachers. Pastoral training and church administration were less emphasised. The missionaries felt that these two areas should not be introduced to the Africans too soon. Unfortunately, this simple preference became doctrinaire over the years. Licensing and ordination of Africans for pastoral duties and church leadership were most difficult to come by, so the number of national church leaders was very limited.

Training of African evangelists

African evangelists were trained as an auxiliary work force to that of the missionaries in the mission field. For the most part, indigenous missionary agencies similar to those of Western societies were not formed. One exception was SIM in Nigeria, which developed an indigenous organisation, the African Missionary Society/ Evangelical Missionary Society in the late 1940s.

Church autonomy

The issues of church control and church autonomy plagued the indigenisation policies of Christian missions in Africa. Relinquishing control and granting autonomy to Africans was the most difficult aspect and created the greatest source of conflict between Western missionaries and African church leaders. The major cause of this conflict was the missionary ecclesiology, which was incompatible with African expectations and their simple biblical understanding of the church.

Transfer of mission vision

Two simple truths failed to be realised when it came time for Western missionaries to transfer the vision of mission to Africans. These truths were, "Like father, like son" and "Like begets like." By and large, the African church has failed to grasp the mission vision and burden of Western missionaries. This is our greatest puzzle, and it is the greatest indictment of mission work in Africa. How could a missionary not transfer his vision and burden of mission to Africans? And how could Africans not catch the vision and burden of mission from the missionary who brought them the gospel of Christ? The most serious weakness of the African church lies in this area. This aspect needs to be re-introduced to the African church today.

Contributions of the African Church to the Global Church

The place of the African church within the global church needs to be clarified. Discussions and issues arising from partnership consultations reflect the problem. We must recognise that the indices used to measure the contributions of the African church may not necessarily be the same as those that are being used to measure global success, strength, and influence. Judged by the contemporary issues facing it, the African church may be said to occupy a very weak position within the global church. We must look elsewhere to find a standard that gives the African church a position within the global church. 1 Corinthians 1:18-31 provides a theological basis in this case. The position of the African church can be judged not only from a human perspective, but also from God's divine wisdom. If we look at the African church from this perspective, its contribution will become more apparent. The church can be strengthened if its contribution is appreciated.

Numerical size

With over 230 million adherents, the African church is bound to shape the global church by its size alone. Andrew Walls has noted that the center of Christianity has shifted from the North to the South. This is an astonishing change. Kwame Bediako asserts that the vibrant life and size of the African church demand that a serious study be made so as to ascertain the church's place, role, and contribution to global Christianity.

The non-Christian world has recognised the size of Africa in world affairs, and this fact has influenced the appointments of Boutrous Boutrous Ghali of Egypt and Kofi Anang of Ghana as Secretaries General of the United Nations and Chief Emeka Anyoku of Nigeria as Secretary of the Commonwealth. The World Evangelical Fellowship has done the same, with Tokunboh Adeyemo of Nigeria as its Chairman. The World Council of Churches has made similar appointments. But we must go beyond just having a "black face." True representation must be based upon equality and upon respect for the dignity and worth of persons. It also means understanding the views and needs of the person being represented. It requires hearing and not just listening. Representation means allowing the other person to be a participant and not just a spectator. A spiritual understanding of representation will definitely make the African church the centrepiece of global strategies of mission.

General weaknesses

The weaknesses of the African church in terms of biblical theology,

resources, and leadership all serve to manifest God's strength and wisdom in raising up his church in Africa. The Bible is clear on how a weaker brother should be treated. The weaknesses of the African church should not translate into paternalism, a dependency syndrome, dominance, or lack of respect for human dignity and worth. Critics of mission work in Africa usually give up on mission when they come across the manifest display of human weakness. But this is a gross failure to understand that God uses the weak things of this earth to manifest his glory. A lot has been done by weak missionaries to establish the church of Christ in Africa.

The church in Africa is still struggling with human weaknesses in its short missiological history, resulting in crises of mission/church relations in Africa. In global Christianity, weakness will become a virtue in a biblical sense if we correct some of the problems of mission ecclesiology in Africa by recognising and assigning to the African church its proper place and role in global Christianity.

Potentials and possibilities

The African church is numerically strong and has great potential. Africans have some general characteristics which can be utilised in the global strategy of mission. They generally possess vitality of life, with the ability and the perseverance to live in very harsh and difficult conditions. Furthermore, Africans generally understand the language of the spirit world. Can Africans be recruited as missionaries by Western mission agencies? We are all aware of the fact that Western sporting clubs recruit African stars to play for their clubs. Westerners should likewise tap into the potentials and possibilities that abound within the African church.

Indigenous missions

We do not have adequate information about indigenous missionary movements in Africa. Serious research is needed in this area. We have identified the following models. There could be more of which we are not aware.

1. The pioneering missionaries trained itinerant evangelists who helped to evangelise Africa along with the missionaries.

2. Some Africans received prophetic messages and visions and went out to evangelise Africa quite independent of Western missionaries and mission churches.

3. African missionary societies were founded by Western missions for Africans to run parallel to the Western mission agencies. Only a handful of Western missions did this experiment.

4. Christian youth movements of the 1970s gave birth to independent mission agencies. Leaders of such agencies were usually young university graduates.

5. Migrations and movements of peoples contributed to the spread of Christianity across Africa.

New expressions of Christianity

Either by reacting against Western mission models and methods or by spontaneous development, Africans have sought ways of affirming their culture and values. The result is that there are many new ways of expressing Christianity through theology, liturgy, worship, and cultural expressions. These theological forms and expressions of Christianity in Africa must be subjected to critical biblical scrutiny so as to ascertain their biblical authenticity.

Global migrations of African peoples

As noted above, migrations of African peoples to other parts of the world have significantly aided in the spread of Christianity. Such migrations should help the church in Africa to define its position in the global church today. Both Africans and Western missionaries must go beyond the mission legacy by overcoming the shortcomings of the past and must move towards creating a new mutuality and a new spirit of working together to evangelise the whole world.

Current Problems and Challenges

Problems

Following is a summary presentation of the current problems facing the African church. Space does not permit elaboration.

1. The African church has a weak biblical and theological base. In other words, there is inadequate biblical teaching in the churches and Christian communities. This area does not refer to the spirituality of the people or theological reflections and expressions of Christianity. Rather, there is inadequate ecclesiology/theology of the church to handle issues such as church life, missions, spirituality, morality, social matters, and ethnic/tribal conflict.

2. The African church has a weak vision for mission. Quite a lot is happening in the area of missions, but there is still general weakness in this area. The vision and burden of mission were not properly transferred by the missionaries, nor were they properly received by the African church leaders. The African church needs to make this aspect its highest priority.

3. The African church has weak leadership, especially in its modes of training and development.

4. The African church has inadequate financial resources and trained personnel.

5. The African church faces numerous crises, such as poverty (both internally and externally induced); external debts; ethnicity, tribalism, and social conflict; bad

politicians and governments; and militarism and corruption.

Challenges

The African church faces some serious challenges worth mentioning.

Strength and power of traditional religions and worldview

The church in Africa seems not to have a good knowledge of the traditional African religious beliefs, religious practices, general religious and cultural life, and traditional theological reasons for adhering to the traditional religions and cultures. Many African theologians and scholars were trained in the West. Unfortunately, Western theology does not address adequately the theological questions and issues arising from the Christian study of African traditional religions and cultures. The traditional religious beliefs and practices are in great measure different from those of Christianity. There may be similarities in some areas, but there are differences in terms of religious purposes, religious meanings, religious motivations, religious beliefs, religious practices, and theological foundations.

This background is essential if we are going to formulate a biblical theology that can address adequately the African traditional religions and cultures. Furthermore, this background is necessary to help African Christians sort out traditional religious beliefs, practices, and behaviour that are in conflict with their Christian faith. Many African Christians have serious problems understanding how the Bible and the Christian faith should address their traditional African religious system. There are those who still hold to some of the "precious" traditional religious beliefs, practices, and behaviour, even after becoming Christians.

The manifestations of dual religious beliefs and practices among African Christians are abundant. Many professing Christians go back to their traditional religious practices, because these are thought to meet certain needs. For example, they consult traditional diviners, sorcerers, medicine men/women, and other specialists. We have observed that this is indeed a pervasive religious phenomenon in African Christianity. The most crucial theological issue at hand is that most African Christians lack sufficient knowledge of the Bible and its teachings on African traditional religions and cultures. It is very important for African Christians to know how the Bible addresses these matters.

Even though the influence of the African traditional religions and cultures is profound in modern Africa, most African Christians have little knowledge of how this influence is exerted. They live under its influence every day but still exhibit much ignorance of it. The religious life of a traditional African can be better understood if the nature and functions of the traditional religion and culture can be well defined. For this reason, a working definition of African traditional religion is essential, first of all, to our understanding of the impact of Christianity in Africa and, second, to developing a theological method to address the challenge of traditional religions to Christianity.

Nominalism of second generation Christians

Nominalism among second generation Christians is on the increase in Africa. Children born to Christian parents show a lack of interest in Christianity. However, nominal second generation Christians are the major target of the Pentecostal and charismatic movements. Credit must be given to these groups for their work in this area.

Growth and influence of new religions and cults

The decline of living standards and spiritual standards in many African countries, especially in the educational, medical, economic, and social sectors, has given impetus to the rise of new religions and cults.

Growth and strength of Islam in Africa

Post-independent Africa has witnessed an increase in the growth and strength of Islam in Africa. If the conquest of North Africa by Islam in the 8th century is a lesson for the church, then the challenge of Islam in Africa today cannot be ignored.

Influence of global culture and values

The influence of global culture and values cannot be taken lightly, since any negative effects could entrench Africa in its traditional dependency role. If globalisation leads to the liberation of the global man or woman, then the enslavement of any man or women is to be dreaded. The challenge for global Christianity is how to use globalisation as a liberating tool for the church in Africa.

The greater proportion of the problems confronting Africa today have been externally induced. Similarly, solutions to some of these issues need to be external. Global Christianity has a great role to play in helping the African church face some of these formidable forces.

Overcoming Barriers and Working Together

The emergent problems and issues resulting from the history of missions in Africa require that an effective collective effort be instituted. It is only by working together that we can successfully overcome some of the barriers. Below is a list of strategies to consider in the new millennium.

1. Promote and strengthen African indigenous missions.
2. Identify and prioritise areas of needs in mission.
3. Identify and prioritise areas of cooperation.
4. Suggested projects:
   - Find out which mission agencies or societies are doing missions in Africa.
   - Formulate new strategies of mobilising African churches for missions.
   - Formulate a new philosophy and curriculum of mission.
   - Embark upon leadership training for practical mission.
   - Network and facilitate mission.
   - Find mission partners outside of Africa.

Conclusion: Some Guiding Questions

We conclude this paper by stating some guiding questions.

1. What lessons can the African church learn from historical missions, especially Western missions of the 19th and 20th centuries?
2. In what ways can the African church be helped and strengthened in its mission strategy for the 21st century?
3. Given the weak position of Africa in the global community, does God have any need and use for the church in Africa for his strategy of global evangelisation?
4. What are the most serious challenges for the church in Africa, and how can they be addressed?
5. Historically, Africa has been a mission field. How can the global church move from being a sender of missionaries *to* Africa to being a partner *with* Africans in global mission?

6. What has the African church done to further the cause of mission? What models of mission were developed from the African church? What can Christians from other continents learn from African missions? What are the obstacles that hinder African missions, and how can we overcome them?

References

Turaki, Y. (1999). *A century of SIM/ECWA history in Nigeria, 1893-1993: A theory and practice of Christian missions in Africa.* Jos, Nigeria: ECWA Book Trust.

————. (1999). *Christianity and African gods: A theological method.* Potchefstroom, South Africa: IRS, Potchefstroom University.

Turaki, Y., & Galadima, B. (1988, June). The church in the African state towards the 21st century: The Nigerian experience. *Journal of African Christian Thought, 1*(1), pp. 43-51.

Yusufu Turaki and his wife, Deborah, have four children. Yusufu is a Professor of Theology and Social Ethics. He obtained theological training in Nigeria and the U.S. He studied theology and ethics at Gordon-Conwell Seminary and got a Ph.D. in social ethics at Boston University. He is a founding member of Jos ECWA Theological Seminary in Nigeria and served as Provost of the seminary. He has also served as ECWA General Secretary; ECWA Director of Education; Executive Secretary of the Ethics, Peace, and Justice Commission of the Association of Evangelicals in Africa; a member of the WEF Religious Liberty Commission and the WEF Theological Commission; and National Vice-President of the Christian Association of Nigeria. He has done extensive research on ethics, missions, politics, ethnicity, church administration, church leadership, theology, and religion. He has published a number of books, including The British Colonial Legacy in Northern Nigeria; Tribal Gods of Africa: Tribalism, Ethnicity, Racism, and the Gospel of Christ; Christianity and African Gods; A Method in Theology; and A Century of SIM/ECWA History in Nigeria, 1893-1993: A Theory and Practice of Christian Missions in Africa. He is currently the Regional Director of International Bible Society Nigeria.

Missiological challenges from the South Pacific region

THE SOUTH PACIFIC REGION is the home of three racial groups: Melanesians, Micronesians, and Polynesians. The area encompasses 11 sovereign nations scattered over the mighty Pacific Ocean, with an approximate total population of 6.5 million. These island nations were brought under the power of the gospel in the 19th century. Like other regions, this one has its own missiological challenges and concerns to face. At the same time, the people of the South Pacific are ready to move out to the unreached areas with the gospel. This paper seeks to highlight these challenges and concerns, as well as the joy of reaching out to others. The paper is in three parts:

1. Light *to* the South Pacific, which sets out the coming of the gospel to the South Pacific and the response of the Islanders to the gospel.

2. Light *for* the South Pacific, which highlights the needs and the concerns of the church in the South Pacific.

3. Light *from* the South Pacific, which outlines the desire of the Pacific Islanders to take the gospel into the world.

JOSHUA
DAIMOI

Light to the South Pacific

When Matthew the evangelist reflected on the appearance of Jesus the Saviour in Galilee, he saw it as the fulfilment of the Old Testament missiological expectation. He saw in the Lord the light that would penetrate the dark world of the Gentiles, bringing hope to those living in the shadow of death (Matt. 4:12-17). Light is a missiological symbol which evokes pleasant home memories among Pacific Islanders. John Williams, one of the early LMS missionaries to the South Pacific, saw light as one of his three guiding principles for the expansion of the missionary movement from the Eastern to the Western Pacific (Hitchen, 1984, p. 576). The South Pacific nations have always seen themselves as people of the womb of the new dawn and the going down of the sun. Tonga is the first nation in the world to welcome the sun every day, and Samoa is the last country to bid farewell to it. Light starts in the South Pacific and finishes in the South Pacific.

The nations of the South Pacific are forever grateful for the light of the gospel that was brought to them. Even though the sun ascended and descended over our heads, our lives were as dark as the deepest part of the Pacific Ocean, impenetrable by the sunlight. When the light of the gospel beamed on us, it found us busy killing and eating each other. A missionary vividly captured the Pacific way of life in a stanza of a song he wrote: "Dark were the days when men lived in fear, / Fear of the arrow, stone-club, and spear, / Fighting and hatred filled every hand, / That was my country, that was my land" (Basket, 1971, p. 198).

Nothing but the power of the gospel could conquer cannibals for the kingdom of light. The light received is light to share. The gospel not only removed the arrows, stone-clubs, and spears from our hands, but also transformed our warring deep sea canoes into bearers of the good news— the message of freedom, love, and peace. Our enemies, once the targets for our weapons, became targets for the gospel of peace, friendship, and fellowship. Instead of carrying destructive spears by our side in the canoes, we carried the sword of the Spirit, God's healing and renewing power for the transformation of the peoples of the islands of the South Pacific. Conversion for us was our call to take the gospel from island to island. In the history of world mission, the Pacific Islanders became the first non-Western people to be involved in cross-cultural missionary work. The Fijian and the Tongan deep

sea canoes, formerly used for war, carried these missionaries from island to island until they reached the dark continent of New Guinea. The Pacific Islanders, in company with John Williams, James Chalmers, and many others, went out without looking back. Many never returned to their homeland. John Williams was killed and eaten by Ni Vanuatuans (New Hebridisians). James Chalmers was killed and eaten by Papua New Guineans. Many Pacific Islanders went home into the presence of their Lord at the hands of cannibals; others died from black water fever, malaria, and other sicknesses.

Fiji suffered a great measles epidemic in the late 19th century, which claimed 40,000 Fijians, including 200 pastor-teachers. Dr. Brown, head of the Methodist Mission Board from Australia, arrived in Fiji by ship in 1899. His intention was to take Fijian evangelists to commence mission in New Guinea. After what the church had gone through, Dr. Brown felt reluctant to ask them to release the few teachers and pastors they had. He therefore decided to go to the theological institution to recruit some of the students for New Guinea. After he spoke to them, the students were given time to think about his request overnight. The next morning, when the principal asked those who wanted to go to stand up, the entire student body of 84 stood. They had made their decision with their wives and children. Neither the principal nor the British administrator could persuade them to remain home. They went. Most of them died, but the church was planted on the soil of New Guinea (Tippett, 1977, pp. 42-44).

The saying is ancient, but its missiological content is fresh and refreshingly worth repeating: "The blood of the martyrs is the seed of the church." The seed of the gospel planted on the islands of the South Pacific has borne 100-fold and more. Today, the most prominent building in every village is the church, the centre of the community life and activity. It stands as an eternal testimony to the commitment and sacrifice made by the missionaries of the cross—white, brown, and black—who side by side fought for the faith of the gospel. Charles Forman (1982, p. 90) captures this phenomenal change: "As the old religion has provided the framework and rationale for the traditional way of life, so Christianity was seen as a new framework within which there could be a rationale for the new way of life that was appearing." When the Methodist Mission handed over its work and responsibility to the Fijians, at the installation of the first president of the church, the official presidential stole carried "two symbols of faith, the cross which is a reminder of the power of the gospel, and a deep sea canoe, a cultural symbol of the commission to go forth beyond the reef" (Tippett, 1977, p. xi). The present-day mission of what is known as the Deep Sea Canoe Missionary Movement will be taken up in part three of this paper.

Light for the South Pacific

The church in the South Pacific region has grown by leaps and bounds. I was reminded of this growth when I heard an African brother at a conference in Oxford, England, describing the phenomenal growth of the church on the continent of Africa. He said, "The church in Africa is one mile wide but only one inch deep." This African brother could well have been describing the church in the South Pacific. The countries of the South Pacific are the most missionised countries in the world. Today, South Pacific Islands nations consider themselves Christian nations. Figures from the 1980 census show that 95% of Papua New Guinea citizens described themselves as belonging to a Christian church (Synders, 1986). David Barrett's (1982, p. 552) figures in the *World Christian Encyclopedia* show that in the 10-year period 1970–1980, the number of nominal Christians stood at 23.5%, which is about a quarter of those who claimed to belong to a Christian church. For the same 10-year period, Barrett presents the yearly rates of conversion (2.74%) as almost equal to the percentage becoming nominal (1.91%).

Nominalism is a missiological phenomenon the South Pacific churches cannot ignore. Nominals are real handicaps to the progress of mission in the world. Neither God nor the church can use nominals in mission around the globe or in the locality to which the church belongs. Nominals are like excess luggage the deep sea canoe cannot afford to take on board. On the other hand, nominal Christians are potentials for the mission of the church. Nominals are there because the church has failed in her mission towards them. The presence of the nominals testifies to the fact that the church has no vision or mission to recover the untapped resources within her reach for her mission to the world.

Factors contributing to nominalism

The factors contributing to nominalism are many. The gap between conversion and nominality reflected in the figures given above suggests that the church has no follow-up programme for new Christians. In missiological terms, the church has failed and is failing to bring new converts to full maturation in their faith or to incorporate them effectively into the membership of the church. My experience of the Papua New Guinea situation tells me that our keenness to evangelise sadly lacks effective follow-up programmes.

The second factor leading to nominalism in our churches is "people stealing" or name-making programmes. In 1972, I was involved in coordinating a Ralph Bell Evangelistic Crusade in Papua New Guinea. In our pre-crusade preparations, the two areas we had great difficulties agreeing on were counselling and follow-up. In short, we did not have faith in each other to allow people from other churches to counsel and follow up the people who belonged to our churches. We did not want people to use counselling and follow-up sessions to take our people away, in order to increase their church membership and thus make a name for themselves. Missiologically expressed, we lacked the courage and the faith to trust in the sovereign ministry of the Holy Spirit to use God's people to encourage and nurture new Christians.

This brings us to the third factor contributing to nominalism: conversion that is not reflected at a worldview level. Our Lord sent the Holy Spirit into the world to lead those who come to him by faith to live under his Lordship. Missiologically understood, to believe in Jesus Christ is to denounce all previous loyalties and to embrace Jesus Christ as Lord without turning back. Those whose entire lives have been dominated by the power and influence of magic, sorcery, and witchcraft would not readily exchange the faith of their forefathers for a new faith, without power encounter and culturally relevant teaching.

The fourth factor for nominalism grows out of the need for relevant teaching and culturally relevant evangelism. The Christian Leaders Training College (CLTC) is an interdenominational, Evangelical Bible and theological institute established in 1964 to train students from Evangelical churches in Papua New Guinea, Solomon Islands, and other South Pacific nations. For many years, the staff and students used to go out every weekend to carry out open air evangelistic meetings at nearby plantations and market places. We went there

to announce the King's message about life and death, following the pattern of open air evangelism done in Australia, New Zealand, America, and Europe. We followed this pattern of evangelism and still do it, with some slight modifications, because missiologically we felt that whatever worked in the West must work in the non-Western world, because it appeared to be a sacred and God-ordained method. We believed blessings were bound to flow in if we followed the set procedures.

Reaching communities

We are slowly beginning to realise that in community-conscious societies, the most effective way to present the King's life-giving message is to do it in the context of the community. In the language of the Church Growth Movement, reaching the people in their homogeneous groups is far better than reaching them as isolated individuals. The Holy Spirit moved the early church out for evangelism at a worldview level—meeting the people where they were, as they were, walking with them step by step, and sitting and talking with them about the deep realities of the world they lived in.

The Bible endorses the importance of the family in relation to the community to which each family belongs and in relation to world mission. In the South Pacific, a nuclear family exists within the circle of the extended family. The existence of family within the family demonstrates community solidarity and mutuality. A converted and committed nuclear family is an effective tool for evangelism to reach out to the extended family. As far as world evangelism is concerned, families are keys for effective evangelism among Muslims. Christian families with a deep commitment to the principles of marriage and to the Lord of all human families have much to offer to the Muslim world, lifting up the dignity of women and demonstrating the sacred bond of marriage, which nothing but death can separate.

Challenges and concerns

Not only is a culturally relevant evangelistic method important, but culturally relevant teaching is also vital. Unless the biblical teaching is related meaningfully to the culture of the people, Christians will remain babes in their faith.

The use of name-making programmes mentioned above is of deep concern to many South Pacific church leaders. From our perspective, missionaries came and continue to come to us preaching two gospels—a Bible-centred gospel and a church-centred gospel. The Bible-centred gospel, rooted in the person and work of Jesus Christ, is a message to which South Pacific Islanders have no problem subscribing. What concerns us most is the church-centred gospel or denominational distinctiveness that is also preached. My observation shows that missionaries appear to be much more concerned about converting us to their particular denominational doctrines rather than helping us grow in our Christian faith. In the 1960s and '70s, Evangelical missions in Papua New Guinea, as members of the Evangelical Alliance of the South Pacific, agreed to respect each other's areas of work and witness. Today, that agreement is no longer honoured. Some members deliberately enter other Evangelical mission/church areas to establish their denominational names. This kind of activity splits villages and families into different groups, thus destroying the family units which are important keys for evangelism.

A further weak link in the chain of world mission in our part of the world is "drifting" Christians. These are Christians who get carried away by the different teachings they hear. They are like dry coconuts swept across the Pacific Ocean, following the direction of the current.

These people float around on the sea of emotionalism. They want a Christianity that is full of excitement with very little cross-bearing. They want healing without a faith commitment to the Healer. This group also is an untapped potential for world evangelism.

Contextualising the gospel

What the South Pacific churches need today is for God's Word to be a lamp to their feet and a light for their path (Ps. 119:105). Light for the South Pacific in this case calls for clear and meaningful teaching of God's Word. There is a real need for the contextualization of the gospel. Many people still think that Christianity is a white people's religion and that Jesus Christ is a white person who does not understand Melanesians, Micronesians, and Polynesians and is therefore irrelevant to them (Gaqurae, 1985, p. 211).

The task of contextualising the gospel can best be done by nationals who know the Word of God and the culture of their people. The Evangelical churches in the South Pacific need well-equipped leaders at master's and doctoral levels who can theologise and contextualise the gospel for their people. At present in the Evangelical churches belonging to the Evangelical Alliance Fellowship, we have one or two people with master's degrees but none with a doctoral degree in Christian ministry. In comparison to other non-Western countries, the Evangelical family in the South Pacific lacks top-level academics and other leaders. This is understandable, because the Evangelical body of the South Pacific region is for the most part a forgotten part of the world. Evangelicals have poured a great amount of their resources into Africa, Asia, and Latin America, because these are the areas where the great populations of the world live. It is important that we continue to give priority to these regions, but we should not neglect smaller regions with less population, such as the South Pacific.

As far as I can recall, the gathering at Iguassu was the very first world Evangelical gathering in which an Evangelical from the South Pacific region was asked to make a presentation. I am grateful to Dr. William D. Taylor for this insight and confidence in his Evangelical brothers and sisters in the South Pacific region. I trust that in the years to come, the world Evangelical leaders will endeavour to correct this weakness in our Evangelical body. One word of caution: Do not lump us together with Australia or New Zealand or Asia. We are Melanesians, Micronesians, and Polynesians, with our own identity and destiny under the same Almighty God.

Meeting the shortfalls

Now let me address what we are doing to meet the shortfalls we see in our Evangelical work and witness in the South Pacific. At this point, I will concentrate on the work of the Christian Leaders Training College (CLTC), an interdenominational, Evangelical Bible and theological college based in the Western Highlands Province of Papua New Guinea. The college was set up by the Evangelical missions in 1964 to offer training in English to upper-level church and community workers. In order to assist the young Evangelical churches financially, the college's founding principal, the late Dr. Gilbert McArthur, decided to set up a business programme alongside the Bible and theological programme. Today the business programme of the college subsidises the tuition fees of all the students by meeting in full the salaries of all the national staff and 50% of most of its overseas staff. In the college's 35 years of ministry, some 2,000 students have graduated and are serving the Lord in many parts of the South Pacific.

To meet the shortfall in suitable Bible teaching and Bible study material in the churches, in 1972 CLTC set up a theological education by extension (TEE) department within its ongoing teaching programme, at the request of Evangelical Bible schools. The department has developed many sound Evangelical Bible study courses which are very popular. Some of the material has been adapted in Australia, New Zealand, other Pacific nations, and around the world. Some 300 students in Switzerland are doing the "Come Follow Me" course translated into German. At present, a total of 5,200 students are enrolled in TEE courses in English and Pidgin English (the trade language) in Papua New Guinea. Our goal is to have 1,000 TEE students in other parts of the South Pacific by the year 2000. To promote world mission in our churches, two courses on mission are available: "Launch Out" studies in missions and the "Deep Sea Canoe" based on Alan Tippett's book by that title. TEE tutors for the programme are trained using the TEE method through a short course called "Take the Teaching." In the past two years, 700 students have enrolled in this course. Following the concept of "Discipling the Whole Nation," discipleship courses have been written, including "Go and Make Disciples," a new course emphasising discipling others.

Realising that it is very expensive to send students overseas for post-graduate studies, CLTC has decided to offer a master's course at home, drawing on lecturers from Australia and New Zealand at present. We will be glad to welcome lecturers from other parts of the world. Seeing the need to equip church and community leaders in urban areas effectively, CLTC has established two Extension Centres, one in the nation's capital, Port Moresby, and the other one in the city of Lae. To meet the rapid growth of the Port

Moresby Extension Centre programme, CLTC is erecting a three-story building on its Port Moresby property in 1999. As a follow-up to the first South Pacific Consultation on World Mission in Suva, Fiji in 1989, CLTC has conducted Missions Week and Launch Out programmes annually on its main campus since 1990 to promote mission in the churches. To cater to the growing interest in the churches to send missionaries, CLTC has commenced offering a Diploma in Mission and is working on setting up a Centre for World Mission.

At the regional level, Evangelicals in the South Pacific region need to develop theologically and biblically based materials to address such issues as cargo and its relationship to the spirit world; the ongoing challenge of nominalism; land and its relation to the ancestors; the role of the ancestors in the community; a theological apologetic for saying farewell to the dead; the inadequacy of our systematic theology in the areas of death, heaven, and afterlife (especially the ancestors); the ongoing challenge of animism; commitment and transformation in the lives of the people; the significance of Acts 26:18; the problem of sin in relation to Romans 7:7; meaningful Bible teaching after power demonstration; group and individualistic approach to conversion; repentance and deliverance from the fallen structures of the culture; the historical use of the prayers of renunciation; the ongoing teaching that accompanies the discipling process; and developing and equipping top-level leadership.

While these areas need to be addressed, what is stirring the hearts of the Christians in the South Pacific is the challenge to re-launch the Deep Sea Canoe Missionary Movement. This introduces us to the third part of this paper.

Light From the South Pacific

For over 200 years, Christians in the South Pacific lived on "milk and honey," enjoying the goodness of the gospel with no thought of sharing it with the rest of the world. However, in the last 20 years we have been witnessing the rise of a mighty wave about to roll over from the Pacific Ocean into the Indian and the Atlantic Oceans. From the womb of the dawn, a new missionary wave is about to burst forth. The youth of the Pacific are on the rise. They want to take their place among the missionaries of the cross. We want to take the light from the East back to the West. However small we are in number, we want to have a share in God's purposes for the world. Already we have our spies out, driving the stakes into the ground, ready to move in and claim territory for the Lord. We hear Africans and Asians saying, "Send us more Papua New Guineans!"

Once Papua New Guineans discovered the power of the gospel over the forces of sorcery, magic, and witchcraft, they immediately joined the Eastern Pacific Islanders in preaching the same gospel they had previously sought to wipe out, experiencing the same sufferings they had previously brought on the Pacific Islanders. Those from the seaboard areas began to penetrate into the hinterland with the gospel. Many went to people who were their enemies or people with whom they had had no dealings in the past. When the highlanders received the gospel, they were transformed by its power and soon joined the missionary force, taking the gospel to those beyond their own ranges of mountains. So the gospel spread from the coast to the highlands, from valley to valley, from mountain to mountain. In 1964, as a student of the Baptist Theological College in Sydney, Australia, I visited the Baptist work in Papua New Guinea. I was quite amazed to witness the Baptist church, after 15 years of receiving the gospel, commissioning some of its senior pastors as missionaries to a new area. As these men were sent forth, others promised to stand with them in prayer.

A burst of missions

Prayer has played a very important role in the lives of the South Pacific Islanders. Every time our forefathers crossed the Pacific Ocean from one side to another, they did so on the wings of prayer and faith. They prayed to their ancestral spirits, in whose power their faith rested, to take them safely over the great ocean. Today we still follow their example, except that our prayers are directed to the Lord of the ocean, the anchor of our faith.

In the last 20 years, prayer and faith continue to be the basis of the drama that unfolds. In 1982, Marilyn Robertson Rowsome, a faculty member at CLTC, wrote a paper for her course with the Fuller School of World Mission entitled, "Can History Repeat Itself for a Burst of Missions From Melanesia?" She became so excited by the concept of a burst of mission from Papua New Guinea that she started praying for it. That year God brought Walo Ali and his family to be students at the college. God had already placed a similar burden and interest for world mission on Walo's heart. Marilyn and Walo shared their burdens together and decided to meet every Tuesday during lunch hour to pray for a burst of mission from Papua New Guinea. Soon they were joined by some more students. This prayer meeting turned into the Global Prayer Warrior (GPW) Movement, whose aim was to mobilise the Melanesian churches to pray for the birth of the Melanesian Missionary Movement.

In December 1989, the first-ever South Pacific Consultation on World Mission was held on the campus of the University of the South Pacific in Suva, Fiji. The two major concerns of the consultation were the formation of the Evangelical Fellowship of the South Pacific (EFSP) and the formation of the Deep Sea Canoe (a vehicle to move South Pacific missionaries across the world). Halfway through the consultation, a divinely directed drama took everyone by surprise (God moves in mysterious ways, his wonders to perform). What took place that morning, none of us had ever dreamed of or thought about. The drama? After a fine devotional exposition of Scripture brought by Dr. Theodore Williams of India, Michael Maeliau of Solomon Islands took the microphone. On behalf of the Melanesians, he thanked all who had had a part to play in bringing the light of the gospel to us, the Melanesian people. Then he continued, "I want to say I am sorry to you, our Polynesian brothers and sisters, our brothers and sisters from Australia, New Zealand, Europe, and America, for killing and eating the missionaries you sent to us. We didn't know who they were. We didn't know what they had come to do. We didn't know that they were messengers of the cross. We your Melanesian brothers and sisters sincerely ask you to forgive us for what we did to the missionaries you sent us."

Continuing on, Michael said, "We want to ask you, why didn't you tell us that we too have the same responsibility to take the gospel to the world? Why did you treat us like children? Did you think we were only good at receiving but not good enough to give? Well, let me tell you, we are coming. We are coming to you. We are coming, whether you like it or not. You can kill us and eat us, but we are coming. We did that to your missionaries. We are not afraid to die."

Before Michael could place the microphone back on its stand, the entire Australian delegation, both men and women, walked up to the platform, handkerchiefs in their hands, eyes wet. Their spokesman,

Rev. Ray Overend, said, "We want to say *we* are sorry to you our Melanesian, Micronesian, and Polynesian brothers and sisters for the paternalistic attitudes we have shown to you. We are sorry for treating you like children. Please accept our apologies." In God's timing, the entire morning turned into a time of reconciliation between the nations, apologising and accepting apologies from each other. Tongans apologised to the Samoans, Fijians to the Indians. An English man apologised to the Pacific Islanders. An American missionary said, "I want to say I am sorry to you, our Pacific Islands brothers and sisters, on behalf of us Americans, for the damage we brought to you during the Second World War."

Before that morning of divine encounter with God and with each other had ended, the whole gathering was on the platform, crying and hugging each other. Michael called me as chairman of the consultation to the microphone. I stated, "This is the Lord's doing, and it is marvellous in our eyes. Today I declare the Deep Sea Canoe launched. It is not in its final shape. We will take the Deep Sea Canoe home to our individual countries to work on it to give it its final shape." I then called on the late Dr. J. Oswald Sanders, a great missionary statesman and Bible teacher, to close the morning's programme in prayer. On the evening of that same day, the Evangelical Fellowship of the South Pacific was established.

Ongoing results

Four specific things have come out of the Fiji consultation:

1. The Evangelical Fellowship of the South Pacific (EFSP). Part of its responsibility is to coordinate and direct the Deep Sea Canoe Movement.

2. The South Pacific Prayer Assembly. This group was established in 1991 and has met on a yearly basis in different South

Pacific nations. It is a prayer movement for reconciliation amongst the Pacific nations and the mobilisation of the South Pacific churches for world mission through prayer. The Melanesian churches, in initiating the prayer movement, believed that they cannot move into the world with the message of reconciliation without being reconciled to their Polynesian brothers and sisters for killing and eating the missionaries they sent to the Melanesian nations. Cleaning our own back yard is the prerequisite for going forward with the message of reconciliation.

3. The establishment of the Launch Out Missions Movement through CLTC in the past 10 years to mobilise Papua New Guinean churches for mission beyond their shores.

4. The commencement in 1999 of a Diploma in Mission at CLTC to prepare Papua New Guineans for cross-cultural missionary service and the setting up of the Centre for World Mission.

In the South Pacific, Papua New Guinea is the largest island and has more population than the other islands. More than this, Papua New Guinea is rich in mineral resources. It also owes a great debt to the rest of the world, because it has singularly enjoyed a greater number of missionaries per capita than any other country. It is important for Papua New Guinea to recognise that the resources God has given her must be used for God's purposes. To whom much is given much will be required. The arrows of mission from East and West, North and South have ended up in Papua New Guinea. The time is right for Papua New Guinea and other South Pacific nations to rise up and be involved in God's mission around the world.

At the ninth Prayer Assembly held in Port Moresby in 1999, two regional movements for youth and women emerged. These two initiatives were born out of two conferences that were held prior to the

Prayer Assembly itself. These movements recognise that both youth and women have a significant part to play in what God is doing, both in the region and beyond, through this new missionary movement.

Conclusion

The nations of the South Pacific are forever grateful for the light of the gospel brought to them. They are in need of well-trained leaders who can meaningfully contextualise the gospel to their people, making clear the relevance of Jesus Christ in their daily living. The nations of the South Pacific believe that the time has come for them to join hands with fellow Christians around the world to bring the gospel to the nations of the world.

Here are some questions to consider in conclusion:

1. How can we turn nominal Christians into a productive missionary force?

2. What is our missionary message? Is it denominationalism or Jesus Christ? How can we cooperate in places with established Evangelical witness to overcome the problem?

3. How can we cooperate internationally in sending out missionaries? How can we prepare missionaries to work internationally?

4. How can we participate in leadership development for the South Pacific churches?

5. How can we help the "drifting" Christians?

References

Barrett, D. B. (Ed.). (1982). *World Christian encyclopedia: A comparative study of churches and religions in the modern world, A.D. 1900-2000.* Oxford, England: Oxford University Press.

Basket, G. F. H. (1971). *Sing his praise.* Wewak, Papua New Guinea: Christian Books Melanesia.

Forman, C. W. (1982). *The island churches of the South Pacific: Emergence in the 20th century.* Maryknoll, NY: Orbis Books.

Gaqurae, J. (1985). Indigenisation as incarnation: The concept of a Melanesian Christ. In May (Ed.), *Living theology in Melanesia: A reader.* Goroka, Papua New Guinea: Melanesian Institute.

Hitchen, J. M. (1984). *Training "tamate": Formation of the 19th century missionary worldview: The case of James Chalmers.* Unpublished doctoral dissertation, University of Aberdeen, Scotland.

Synders, J. (1986). Towards a religious map of Papua New Guinea. *Melanesian Journal of Theology, 2*(2), p. 210.

Tippett, A. R. (1977). *The deep sea canoe: The story of Third World missionaries in the South Pacific.* Pasadena, CA: William Carey Library.

Joshua Daimoi is the Executive President of the Christian Leaders Training College of Papua New Guinea after 17 years of serving as Principal of the College. Joshua and his wife Mone did church planting work in Port Moresby before joining the Bible Society of Papua New Guinea, where Joshua became the first national to serve as the Executive Secretary. He is the only national who has served as the President of the Evangelical Alliance of Papua New Guinea and the Papua New Guinea National Council of Churches. Joshua was born in the Indonesian Province of West Papua, where he received his primary and secondary education. Joshua and Mone and their two children, Mason and Evelyn, live in Papua New Guinea. Joshua holds the degrees of B.A. (Hon.) from the University of Papua New Guinea and Th.M. in mission from the Fuller School of World Mission at Pasadena, California. Joshua received his theological training at the Morling (Baptist) College in Sydney, Australia.

Evangelical missiology from an East Asian perspective: a study on Christian encounter with people of other faiths

THIS PAPER SEEKS to present some missiological contributions that come from the church in East Asia, through a study on Christian encounter with people of other faiths. The immediate context of the paper is Malaysia, a multicultural and multi-religious country of 23 million people; the broader context is Asia as a whole, particularly East Asia. Asia is undergoing tremendous challenges: the challenge of economic and social interdependence that comes with globalization; the challenge of religious resurgence among Asian traditional religions such as Hinduism, Buddhism, and Chinese and Japanese religions; the growth of Islam and Islamization in Southeast Asia; the challenge of increasing restrictions for missionary entry; and the challenge of the maturing churches in Indonesia, China, Korea, and the Philippines.

Surely Asia defies any sweeping generalizations, given its diversity and vastness. And there are no easy answers to the challenges facing Evangelical missions. Therefore, I am painfully conscious that this paper is merely one attempt to reflect on the challenges facing Evangelical missiology from a Malaysian perspective, rather than a synthesis of other Asian Evangelical writings. I look forward to learning from and interacting with Western, African, Latin American, and particularly Asian colleagues. Note: The term "Evangelical" is used in this paper to refer to conservative Evangelicals who identify themselves, at least informally, with the Lausanne Covenant (Covell, 1993, p. 163).

KANG SAN TAN

Christian Encounter With Other Religions

In *Transforming Mission*, David Bosch (1991, p. 477) highlights two crucial theological issues facing the church. They are (1) Christianity's relationship to secular worldviews and (2) Christianity's relationship to other religions. For some missiologists, the theology of religions is the theological issue for Christian mission in the 21st century (Sharpe, 1974, pp. 77-95; Anderson, 1993, pp. 200-208). Anderson (1993, p. 200) states, "No issue in missiology is more important, more difficult, more controversial, and more divisive for the days ahead than the theology of religions."

In addition to the theological issue, there is also a contextual dimension to the problem. While the problem of non-Christian religions is heightened in the West in recent times (1950s onward) due to the rise of pluralism as a celebrated virtue, the problem of religious plurality has been a fact of life in Asia since the first millennium. How Christians relate to people of other faiths is a long-standing issue in Asia. Today, the problem is heightened as the church in Asia witnesses the revitalization of other religions, the ethnic violence that is often divided along religious lines, and the growing theological relativism within the church.

Modernization, ethnicity, and the religious encounter

The study of Christian encounter with people of other faiths must now grapple with the processes of multi-ethnicity, modernization, and globalization in Asia. Modernity refers to the increasingly global culture produced by (1) the processes and institutions of modernization and (2) the intellectual developments of the past 250 years in the West. According to Berger (1973, p. 9), modernization is "the insti-

tutional concomitants of technologically induced economic growth.... Modernization consists of the growth and diffusion of a set of institutions rooted in the transformation of the economy by means of technology."

Harold Netland, Professor of Mission at Trinity International University, in an unpublished article highlights two implications when modernity is seen in terms of modernization. First, modernity is not simply a Western phenomenon; it is a global phenomenon. Second, as a worldview, modernity is not something a particular culture either has or does not have in completed form. Rather, we should think in terms of a continuum of modernization, with different societies being at various stages on the continuum.

Malaysia, as is true of most Asian countries, is undergoing a rapid process of modernization. How does modernization affect Christian encounter with people of other faiths? Peter Berger (1973, pp. 79-80) highlights the effect of modernization on religion: "Through most of empirically available human history, religion has played a vital role in providing the overarching canopy of symbols for the meaningful integration of society.... This age-old function of religion is seriously threatened by pluralization. Different sectors of social life now come to be governed by widely discrepant meanings and meaning-systems. Not only does it become increasingly difficult for religious traditions, and for the institutions that embody these, to integrate this plurality of social life-worlds in one overarching and comprehensive worldview, but even more basically, the plausibility of religious definitions of reality is threatened from within, that is, within the subjective consciousness of the individual."

According to Berger's secularization thesis, modernization will eventually result in the relativizing of all perspectives, especially religious perspectives. There will be privatization of religious beliefs and a pluralization of ideologies and world-views. In addition, Netland (1994, p. 94) highlights that modernity poses a direct challenge to the biblical perspective on two points: "First, the notion that one particular religious figure and one religious perspective can be universally valid, normative, and binding upon peoples in all cultures.... And second, even if in principle it is granted that one religion is superior to the rest, and that one religious figure might be universally normative, why should we assume Christianity and Jesus Christ are in this privileged position?"

If Berger's and Netland's observations are correct, one can expect a greater openness for dialogue among the religions. At present, Malaysia has not witnessed the type of cultural pluralism that takes place in the West. Urbanization and the bringing of all races together have not resulted in the type of pluralism espoused by Western liberals such as John Hick and Paul Knitter, where all religions are homogenized. On the contrary, due to the "extreme pluralism" where race and religion coincide, modernity and religious plurality sparked religious revivalism (Ackerman & Lee, 1988) and in some cases resulted in increased intolerance. At the time of writing, East Timor has yet to recover from the ravages of ethnic violence along religious lines. Therefore, despite the process of modernization, Christianity still enters into missionary encounter with other religions in a highly sensitive atmosphere of religious intolerance.

Ethnicity and religious relations in contemporary Malaysia

The following section seeks to illustrate the complex realities of Christian encounter with people of other faiths in Malaysia. In presenting a study on race relations in Malaysia, I hope to illustrate the complexities facing the church in East Asia whenever religions coincide with ethnicity. The same study can be done for each country of East Asia, exploring the dynamics of ethnicity and its varied implications for Christian mission.

The racial composition in West Malaysia is as follows: 54% Malays, 34% Chinese, 8% Indians, and 4% other minority races such as Sikhs, Siamese, Eurasians, and aboriginal peoples. In the same census, the religious composition was as follows: 56% Muslims, 19% Buddhist, 15% Chinese religionists, 8% Hindus, and 2% Christians.

Most Chinese in Malaysia practice a mixture of Taoism, Confucianism, and Buddhism. They borrow from and freely integrate their folk religious practices with the three Chinese religions to fulfill the practical needs of family, finances, and business. It is common for Chinese homes to have a kitchen god, a family-ancestor altar, and a Buddhist or Confucius deity. Most Chinese in Malaysia are adherents of the Mahayana tradition (Ackerman & Lee, 1988, p. 47). Many Mahayana religious groups are affiliated with the Malaysian Buddhist Association. Apart from many small temples scattered throughout the country, a few Mahayana temples such as Kek Lok Si (a Pure Land Sect temple) bring symbolic unity to Buddhists. Increasingly, as more Mahayana monks are being trained (mostly in Taiwan), these temples may appoint a resident monk.

Theravada Buddhism in Malaysia received its influence and funding mostly from Thailand and Sri Lanka. Through the Buddhist Missionary Society, there was a resurgence of missionary interest among university students during the early 1970s. There were other groups, such as the Japan based Nichiren Daishonin Buddhist Movement and the non-sectarian Dhamafarers' Movement, that emerged during this period of Buddhist revivalism.

The Hindu religious system in Malaysia can be broadly arranged around three categories: family shrines in villages, large temples dedicated to well-known deities such as the Sri Maha Mariyamman Temple, and newer non-sectarian movements such as the Ramakrishna Mission (Ackerman & Lee, 1988, pp. 46-47). 80% of Indians in West Malaysia are Hindus, mostly of the Saivite tradition. Most of the smaller village temples rely on the *pandaram* or ritual specialists who do not have formal priestly training, while the larger urban temples may employ some initiated priests (*kurukkal*) from India. Similar to their Muslim and Buddhist counterparts, many Indians turned to their religions for ethnic identity during the religious revival of the 1970s. As more than 80% of the Indians in Malaysia are of Tamil origin, Ackerman and Lee (1988, p. 97) note that the Tamil influence is strong: "Tamilization of Hinduism became the order of the day as various urban religious movements took to organizing classes and religious gatherings using Tamil as the principal medium of communication. Religious experts from Tamilnadu were invited to deliver lectures and instruct Malaysian Hindus on Saivite philosophy."

Christianity draws its adherents mostly from Chinese, Indians, and indigenous peoples. The 1990 census revealed that Christians constitute 7% of the population in Malaysia as a whole. As stated earlier, Christians constitute only 2% of the population in West Malaysia, while in the East Malaysian states of Sabah and Sarawak, they are 27% and 29% respectively. The Christian population is largely middle-class and is concentrated in urban areas. Slightly more than 51% of the Christian population are Chinese, 35% are Indian, and the remaining are mostly indigenous peoples of East Malaysia. About 4% of the Chinese and 8% of the Indians profess Christianity as their religion.

Analysing Malay and Non-Malay Relations

Because religion largely coincides with ethnicity, interreligious relations are greatly affected by individual racial perceptions of the other ethnic groups. This sharp division is most pronounced when it comes to the relationship between the Malays and non-Malays in Malaysia. Relations among the races become more complicated when they function not only as a sociological or religious category, but also as "a tool of the state for resource allocation and political control" (Ackerman & Lee, 1988, p. 4). Within such a framework, the Malaysian government implemented the New Economic Policy (NEP), a social engineering program that was enacted to achieve the twin goals of eradicating poverty and restructuring society. More specifically, the NEP set a goal that Malays would control 30% of the commercial and industrial sectors by 1990; non-Malays (i.e., Chinese and Indian) would control 40%; and foreign investments would be limited to 30%. In other words, the Malay-Muslim identity was "materially reinforced" (Ackerman & Lee, 1988, p. 4).

In addition, political parties draw their support along ethnic constituents, making communalism a key political issue since the independence of the country. Though the Chinese and Indians are part of a political alliance in the government, the Malays are in control of the political process. The conjunction of ethnicity and political power (from which economic interests are inevitably linked) deeply polarized not only the issue of race, but also the religious commitments of the people in Malaysia. If a Malay decided to convert to another religion, that person would lose not only his or her ethnic identity, but also his or her social, political, and economic privileges.

The complex relationship outlined above, where ethnicity functions as a tool for resource allocation and political alliances, was further complicated when Islam was enshrined as the state religion in the Malayan Constitution of 1957. In return for the recognition of Malays' special rights and Islam's special position, the immigrant communities were accepted as citizens with equal rights. Furthermore, two legal strictures that have been used to restrict the freedom of religion are the federal law and the state law. Many state laws clearly restrict the freedom to propagate religion. For example, section 156 (2) of the Malaccan legislation states: "Any person, whether or not he professes the Muslim religion, who propagates any religious doctrine or belief other than the religious doctrine or belief of the Muslim religion among persons professing the Muslim religion shall be guilty of an offense cognizable by a Civil Court and punishable with imprisonment for a term not exceeding one year or a fine not exceeding Three Thousand dollars" (quoted in Koh, 1987, p. 17).

Muslim sensitivities are now legalized in such a way that any attempt to proselytize Muslims can result in imprisonment without trial. Various legislation was introduced not only to define the Muslim's religious responsibility, but also to curtail directly any activity among non-Muslims perceived as challenging the superior position of Islam vis-à-vis other religions. It was in this context that in the Twelfth Schedule of the Federal Constitution, a Malay came to be defined as someone who (1) habitually speaks the Malay language, (2) professes the Muslim religion, and (3) conforms to Malay customs (Kaur, 1993, p. 91).

In conclusion, Malay ethnic identity becomes inseparable with its social, religious, material, and legal categories, there-by creating an extreme polarization between the Malays and non-Malays in the country. That division also unites the non-Malays as a category, with Christianity strongly associated with the non-Malay grouping. In a society of extreme pluralism and polarization, the Malaysian church, as a reconciling community, has the responsibility to seek creative ways to bring about spiritual renewal and racial reconciliation.

I have thus far argued for the need to place Christianity's relations with other religions within the context of the historical and complex forces of nationalism, religious resurgence, and modernization. In particular, I tried to illustrate that there is no such thing as a purely religious conversation in Asia. For example, Christians need to understand that ethnicity and religion in Malaysia are complicated by the way that they have become markers not only for communal and religious identity, but also as tools for resource allocation, political affiliation, and constitutional restrictions.

Future Developments for Asian Missiology

Missiology is the study of the expansion of Christianity through the critical examinations of biblical and systematic theologies on the one hand and cultural anthropology, church history, sociology, and the study of religions on the other. As we look into the future, there are developments within Evangelicalism that should contribute positively toward new directions in Evangelical missiology in Asia.

Doctrinal developments

Evangelicals are increasingly aware that new situations require fresh theological categories. Alister McGrath (1992, p. 492) in his seminal study on the origins of doctrines, noted how significant doctrinal developments during the history of the Christian church arose in response to religious encounters with those outside the Christian faith: "Dialogue is one pressure to ensuring that this process of continual self-examination and reformation continues. It is a bulwark against complacency and laziness and a stimulus to the source of faith rather than resting content in some currently acceptable interpretation of them."

In fact, McGrath (1990) identifies evangelism and mission as the keys to the future development of Christian doctrine. Until recently, most creative theological engagements with other religions have been in the field of missiology rather than in the arenas of biblical or systematic theology. Today, fresh attempts are being made by systematic and biblical theologians (Beyerhaus, 1996; Pannenberg, 1988; Pinnock, 1992; McGrath, 1990) to formulate theological perspectives on other religions. Wolfhart Pannenberg, for example, provides a fresh model for engaging non-Christian religions within a context of commitment to Christianity (Grenz, 1989). Pannenberg's understanding of theology as the quest for the eschatological truth of God means that all religious truth claims are provisional and result in a more positive evaluation of all religious traditions (Pannenberg, 1988, pp. 297-299). Peter Beyerhaus (1996, pp. 14-16) proposes a tripolar view of religions where the three sources of the origin of religions are taken seriously. These sources are the human, the divine, and the demonic.

In general, the Evangelical community's perspectives on Christianity's relations with non-Christian religions have gradually shifted from Barth's model of total discontinuity (Christ against religions), to Kraemer's model of radical discontinuity (Christ above religions), to a post-Lausanne II dialectic model of "continuity and discontinuity" (Christ in creative tension with the religions). This dialectic model is to be differentiated from the Catholic's inclusive model (Christ as the fulfillment of religions) and the pluralist's model (Christ in the midst of religions).

As we think of the future, these developments within Evangelicalism provide some building blocks for Asians doing theology cross-culturally and will give rise to disciplines such as cross-cultural apologetics, cross-textual readings of religious texts, and the critique of Asian philosophies from Evangelical perspectives. Traditionally, Christian reflection on God, Christ, and the gospel is done primarily within Christendom. However, within the dynamics of sharing the gospel across racial and religious lines, missiological reflections must be done in conversations with other religions and presuppositions.

Shift in epistemological framework

In order to foster a genuine development in Asian missiology, Evangelicals need to break away from the traditional framework of doing theologies (Bosch, 1991, pp. 422-425). Among the implications of the new epistemology highlighted by Bosch that are relevant to Asians seeking missiological reflection are (1) profound suspicion that Western theology was designed to serve the interest of the West, (2) refusal to endorse the idea of the world as a static object which only has to be explained, (3) emphasis on commitment as the "first act of theology," and (4) emphasis on doing theology in context (Bosch, 1991, pp. 424-425).

Paul Hiebert (1994, pp. 19-34) argues that the epistemological shift in the philosophy of science, from idealism and naive realism to critical realism, presents valuable insights for missionary encounter. Thomas Wright (1992, p. 35) explains critical realism as follows: "This is a way of describing the process of 'knowing' that acknowledges the reality of the thing known, as something other than the knower (hence 'realism'), while also fully acknowledging that the only access we have to this reality lies along the spiraling path of appropriate dialogue or conversation between the knower and the thing known (hence 'critical'). This path leads to critical reflections about 'reality,' so that our assertions about 'reality' acknowledge their own provisionality."

According to Hiebert (1994, p. 25), the critical realist "makes a distinction between reality and our knowledge of it, but like naive realism, it claims that knowledge can be true. Theories are not regarded as photographs of reality, but as maps or blueprints. Just as it takes many blueprints to understand a building, so it takes many theories to comprehend reality."

This shift in epistemological foundations for science affects the epistemological foundation of systematic theology. In particular, the critical realist acknowledges the objectivity of Scripture without insisting that there is only one way of interpreting and knowing truths (Hiebert, 1994, pp. 31-34). According to Hiebert, one implication of critical realism is a deeper interest in translating the gospel into culturally appropriate forms. This requires deep knowledge of other cultures and religions. As Hiebert (1994, p. 49) states, "Missionaries, therefore, must study other religions and dialogue with their leaders, not to create a new synthesis between Christianity and other religions, but to build bridges of understanding so that people may hear the call of the gospel in ways they comprehend, without compromising the truth of the gospel."

Biblical Interpretations

Any Evangelical theologies need biblical studies. But Asian Evangelicalism has inherited ways of reading the Bible from Enlightenment thinking and ways that are strangely similar to post-modernism (Wright, 1992, p. 60). Biblical scholars such as N. T. Wright (1992, 1996), Bar-Efrat (1989), and Robert Alter (1981), through their emphases on narrative and historical studies, have brought fresh approaches to biblical interpretations. These are exciting developments for Asian theologies. In *Jesus and the Victory of God*, Wright (1996) develops the use of stories as Jesus' tools to transform the prevailing Jewish worldviews. Walter Brueggemann's works (1993a, 1993b) are another example of the type of developments in biblical studies that will fund imaginative proclamation of the gospel for Asian missiological thinking.

Given alternative faith commitments among non-Christians, God's starting revelation begins with the present experience and action of people. People (in the context of our discussion, unbelievers) can be encouraged to reflect on their daily life experiences in the light of the Christian Bible, the Christian story, and the Christian vision of the kingdom of God. The community's story and vision serve as a critique of the unbeliever's present experience and as a guide to future action. At the same time, the present experience of the unbeliever serves as a critique of the community's tradition and may lead to its revision.

Some Implications for Encountering Religions

In this final section, I seek to explore some implications for an Evangelical encounter with religions, taking into consideration the doctrinal, biblical, and epistemological developments highlighted above.

The study of other religions

The resurgence of religions and of post-modern interests in spirituality have contributed to the popularity of various disciplines such as comparative religion, philosophy of religions, and history of religions. Such new interest accorded to the study of other religions produced a new generation of scholars of religions throughout Asian institutions of higher learning. Most of these scholarly studies are in Asian languages and focus on specific contextual interests of each region. Evangelicals within each country need to identify these centres of religious studies, promote in-depth studies on various religions, and engage in meaningful dialogues with these writings. Two excellent examples of what I mean by such studies are *Christianity Through Non-Christian Eyes* by Paul Griffiths (1994) and *Majesty and Meekness: A Comparative Study of Contrast and Harmony in the Concept of God* by John Carman (1994). Most of us (Christians are not exempt) do not like to hear criticisms from others about what's wrong with our religions, and even fewer are able to withstand the temptation of telling others what is wrong with their religions. In particular, there are many things about life and God that can be learned from non-believers and other religions. The key missiological contribution of such an approach with non-believers is it enables believers to learn more about others and how they perceive themselves, and about ourselves and how others perceive us.

Interreligious dialogue

Interreligious dialogue has been a controversial issue among Evangelicals. Fundamentalists and conservative Evangelicals are generally wary of the idea of dialogue. Part of the problem is the fact that "dia-

logue" means different things to different people. Dialogue in this paper refers to "a conversation in which each party is serious in his approach both to the subject and to the other person, and desires to listen and learn as well as to speak and instruct" (Stott, 1975, p. 61).

With the collapse of Enlightenment thinking and positivism, Evangelicals increasingly realized that one-sided proclamation could not function by itself in a relativistic culture. This understanding gave rise to receptor-oriented, person-centered, and dialogical approaches (Bosch, 1991, pp. 477-480; Clark, 1993, pp. 102-126). Vinay Samuel and Christopher Sugden are both actively involved in theological education in Asia. At the First Conference of Evangelical Mission Theologians, held in Bangkok in 1982, these men called for "a praxiological approach" that "go[es] into a context with deep convictions shaped by the gospel" (Samuel & Sugden, 1984, p. 129). They highlight the fear of syncretism as the key reason Evangelicals have not entered into dialogue. They explain that some of the false assumptions beneath this fear are (1) the belief that both Christianity and pagan religions are closed systems; (2) the stress on the uniqueness of Christ rather than on the universality of God at work in history; and (3) the judging of other religions based on an Evangelical's abstract belief system (Samuel & Sugden, 1984, pp. 132-133).

In Malaysia and in most parts of Asia where Christianity is a minority religion and Christians suffer various kinds of political, social, or religious restrictions, the maintenance of traditional approaches to evangelism that focus merely on proclamation is problematic. Due to various legal and cultural restrictions, churches tend to retreat into a form of ghettoism. As Lesslie Newbigin (1964, p. 28) states:

"Ghettoism—a practical withdrawal into the position of a tolerated minority, a cultural and religious enclave within the majority community. Correspondingly, the great need is to find ways of breaking out of this isolation and entering into real dialogue with men of other faiths."

The question is whether Asian Christianity can discover forms that can be useful in communicating the gospel and yet do not violate the basic tenets of faiths. And the issue is not just how the non-Christian will hear; equally important is how the Christian will listen. For how shall they hear if we do not listen?

The contribution from anthropological insights

Anthropologists such as Paul Hiebert (1985, 1994), Jacob Loewen (1975), and William Smalley (1978) have brought anthropological insights into the mainstream of Evangelical missiology. In his book *Anthropological Insights for Missionaries*, Hiebert (1985) points to the importance of (1) understanding people in their cultural and historical contexts, (2) understanding the effects that cultural differences have on missionaries and their message, and (3) building cultural bridges in bicultural communities. We thank God for the growth of indigenous missions from within Asia. It is no secret that Asian missionaries, without critical reflection, have repeated the same mistakes of cultural imperialism and domination practised by their 19th century Western colleagues.

Local cultural style of conflict management

At the end of the day, whether informally or through scholarly exchanges, Christian encounters with other religions need to address the problem of criteria for evaluating truth claims across cultures and religions. Without some form of evalu-

ation, the distinctive characteristic of our Evangelicalism is lost.

By way of illustration, there is a style of conflict management among the Malays in Malaysia that is commonly termed the "The Malay Way." Diane Mauzy (1986, p. 213) describes The Malay Way as follows: "[It is] a method of problem solving and conflict avoidance that has helped to soothe political tempers. It emphasizes traditional courtesy and good manners, wide consultation, compromise, avoidance of direct confrontation when possible (but leaving a role for innuendo), and a striving for consensus rather than imposing the will of a (sometimes narrow) majority."

Despite the decline of The Malay Way in the political arena, traditional courtesy and consensus building are still highly valued virtues in the Malay community. In many Asian societies—the Thais and the Japanese in particular—there is a high value placed on a cultured non-confrontational conflict-management style.

As I have tried to demonstrate, the evaluation of truth claims is problematic when one considers the interrelations between historical prejudices, ethnic identities, and the relativistic cultures we live in today. Many of the Evangelical writings in the West on the subject of pluralism and dialogue have been given to the conceptual role of truth, as ought to be the case. But too much emphasis can be placed here, as though it is the only criterion of truth. For Christians in Asia, living in the midst of other religions, a more functional concept of truth can also be helpful. In Asia, the way one communicates truth cannot be divorced from the truth one communicates.

If Christianity's truth claims are to be taken seriously by other religions, then Christians in Asia need to master social graces, not only in behavioural patterns but also in communicational styles and attitudinal changes.

Encountering the Triune God in Creative Tension With the Religions

Christian encounter with other religions that is firmly rooted in God's sovereign character must hold in creative tension the aspects of both God's righteous judgement and his loving kindness. Without such "biblical realism," Christianity's approach to other religions is bound to fall into reductionism.

Commitment to the God revealed in Scripture means Christ becomes the model for approaching people of other faiths. More specifically, a distinctive Evangelical theology of Christian encounter holds a high Christology that does not compromise the truth of the finality of Christ over world religions. If Jesus is central, religious encounter will follow Jesus' total mission: the challenge of discipleship, the confrontation with demonic powers and religious authorities, a compassion for the lost, and the creation of a new society. The implications are profound, because Christians are not merely to be interested in sharing the gospel, but also to be seeking the total transformation of the person and societies. In the Asian context, for example, Evangelicals should be willing to work with other religious groups on common concerns, such as constitutional freedom of religions, human rights issues, the role of religion in society, racial polarization, and the general decline in morality. Such engagements with structural evils are not to be considered as "second class" involvement within the mission of the church.

Within a trinitarian perspective, one needs to take into account the role of the Holy Spirit in the world and in the church. Christian encounter is possible because the Holy Spirit is the one who reveals the mystery of the kingdom, has been active before Christ's earthly ministry, and continues to reveal God's truths to all people, unbelievers included. Evidences of the hidden work of the Spirit include revealing truths about Christ in dreams to unbelievers, planting in the minds of unbelievers an irresistible desire to worship the Creator, and convicting unbelievers of their sins through their conscience that was created in the image of God.

The Holy Spirit points to the place of prayer and spiritual discernment in Christian encounter. Recognizing the hiddenness of God's working in people's minds and hearts, the role of the Christian is to explain truth in intelligible fashion and to help unbelievers discern God's work in their lives. God's part is to make the truth effective. The real enemy is Satan, who blinds the eyes of unbelievers, not unbelievers themselves. Therefore, believers approach non-believers with an attitude of dependence upon the Lord, as well as an attitude of humility and compassion in relation to people of other faiths.

References

Ackerman, S., & Lee, R. (1988). *Heaven in transition: Non-Muslim religious innovation and ethnic identity in Malaysia*. Honolulu, HI: University of Hawaii Press.

Alter, R. (1981). *The art of biblical narrative*. New York: Basic Books.

Anderson, G. H. (1993). Theology of religions and missiology. In C. Van Engen, D. S. Gilliland, & P. Pierson (Eds.), *The good news of the kingdom: Mission theology for the third millennium* (pp. 200-208). Maryknoll, NY: Orbis Books.

Bar-Efrat, S. (1989). *Narrative art in the Bible*. Sheffield, England: Almond Press.

Berger, P. L., Berger, B., & Kellner, H. (1973). *The homeless mind: Modernization and consciousness*. New York: Random House.

Beyerhaus, P. J. (1996, June 13). *The authority of the Gospels and interreligious dialogue*. Address given at a colloquium sponsored by the School of World Mission and Evangelism at Trinity Evangelical Divinity School, Deerfield, IL.

Bosch, D. J. (1991). *Transforming mission: Paradigm shifts in theology of mission*. Maryknoll, NY: Orbis Books.

Brueggemann, W. (1993). *Biblical perspectives on evangelism: Living in a three-storied universe*. Nashville, TN: Abingdon Press.

———. (1993). *Texts under negotiation: The Bible and postmodern imagination*. Minneapolis, MN: Fortress Press.

Carman, J. B. (1994). *Majesty and meekness: A comparative study of contrast and harmony in the concept of God*. Grand Rapids, MI: Wm. B. Eerdmans Publishing Co.

Clark, D. K. (1993). *Dialogical apologetics: A person centered approach to Christian defense*. Grand Rapids, MI: Baker Book House.

Covell, R. (1993). Jesus Christ and world religions. In C. Van Engen, D. S. Gilliland, & P. Pierson (Eds.), *The good news of the kingdom: Mission theology for the third millennium* (pp. 162-171). Maryknoll, NY: Orbis Books.

Cragg, K. (1968). *Christianity in world perspectives*. New York: Oxford University Press.

Grenz, S. J. (1989). Commitment and dialogue: Pannenberg on Christianity and the religions. *Journal of Ecumenical Studies*, *26*(1), pp. 196-210.

Griffiths, P. J. (1994). *Christianity through non-Christian eyes*. Maryknoll, NY: Orbis Books.

Hick, J., & Hebblethwaite, B. (Eds.). (1980). *Christianity and other religions: Selected readings*. Glasgow, Scotland: Fount Paperbacks.

Hiebert, P. G. (1985). *Anthropological insights for missionaries*. Grand Rapids, MI: Baker Book House.

———. (1994). *Anthropological reflections on missiological issues*. Grand Rapids, MI: Baker Book House.

Kaur, A. (1993). *Historical dictionary of Malaysia*. Asian Historical Dictionaries, No. 13. Metuchen, NJ: Scarecrow Press.

Knitter, P. (1985). *No other name?* Maryknoll, NY: Orbis Books.

Koh, P. T. N. (1987). *Freedom of religion in Malaysia: The legal dimension*. Petaling Jaya, Malaysia: Graduate Christian Fellowship of Malaysia.

Loewen, J. A. (1975). *Culture and human values: Christian intervention in anthropological perspective*. South Pasadena, CA: William Carey Library.

Malaysia. (1992). Department of Statistics. *Preliminary count report for urban and rural areas*. Kuala Lumpur, Malaysia: Government Printing Press.

Mauzy, D. K., & Milne, R. S. (1986). *Malaysia: Tradition, modernity and Islam*. Boulder, CO: Westview Press.

———. (1988). Malaysia in 1987: Decline of "The Malay Way." *Asian Survey*, *28*(2), pp. 213-222.

McGrath, A. E. (1990). *The genesis of doctrine: A study in the foundation of doctrinal criticism*. Oxford, England: Blackwell.

———. (1992). The challenge of pluralism. *Journal of Evangelical and Theological Society*, *35*(3), pp. 361-373.

Netland, H. A. (1991). *Dissonant voices: Religious pluralism and the question of truth*. Grand Rapids, MI: Wm. B. Eerdmans Publishing Co.

———. (1994). Truth, authority, and modernity: Shopping for truth in a supermarket of worldviews. In P. Sampson, V. Samuel, & C. Sugden (Eds.), *Faith and modernity* (pp. 89-115). Oxford, England: Regnum Books.

Newbigin, L. (1964). *Trinitarian faith and today's mission*. Richmond, VA: John Knox Press.

Pannenberg, W. (1988). *Systematic theology: Vol. 1*. Grand Rapids, MI: Wm. B. Eerdmans Publishing Co.

Pinnock, C. (1992). *A wideness in God's mercy: The finality of Jesus Christ in a world of religions*. Grand Rapids, MI: Zondervan Publishing House.

Samuel, V., & Sugden, C. (1984). Dialogue with other religions: An Evangelical view. In V. Samuel & C. Sugden (Eds.), *Sharing Christ in the two-thirds world* (pp. 122-140). Grand Rapids, MI: Wm. B. Eerdmans Publishing Co.

Sharpe, E. J. (1974). The goals of inter-religious dialogue. In J. Hick (Ed.), *Truth and dialogue in world religions: Conflicting truth claims* (pp. 77-95). Philadelphia, PA: Westminster Press.

Smalley, W. A. (Ed.). (1978). *Readings in missionary anthropology II*. South Pasadena, CA: William Carey Library.

Stott, J. R. W. (1975). *Christian mission in the modern world*. Downers Grove, IL: Inter-Varsity Press.

Wright, N. T. (1992). *The New Testament and the people of God*. Minneapolis, MN: Fortress Press.

———. (1996). *Jesus and the victory of God*. Minneapolis, MN: Fortress Press.

Kang San TAN studied business management and worked as a hospital administrator in his home country, Malaysia. He has a master's degree in Christian studies (Old Testament) from Regent College, Vancouver, Canada, and a D.Min. in missiology from Trinity International University, Illinois. He is married to Lee Loun-Ling, a Singaporean lawyer by training, and they are currently serving as missions mobilizers in Malaysia. Kang San is Home Director of OMF International in Malaysia and teaches missions at a number of Malaysian seminaries.

Evangelical missiology from India

K. Rajendran

INDIA IS A NATION of dichotomies. It is extremely difficult to explain India as rich or poor, educated or uneducated, Hindu or secular, progressive or regressive, Aryan or Dravidian, high caste or low caste, North Indian or South Indian, majority or minority—the list is endless.

Since its independence in 1947, India as a nation has progressed in many ways. It has now arrived at a crossroad—the crossroad of intolerance and communalism. The political parties are bent on cashing in on the feelings of the various religions in the country. In the process, they are setting one religion up against another to win the favour of the major vote banks. The major Indian political secular congress has been replaced by the communalist BJP (Barathiya Jantha Party), instigating the feelings of Hindus against the minority groups of Muslims, Christians, and others. There is an attempt to rewrite history as the history of triumphalistic Hindu contributions to India, rather than acknowledging the contributions of all people to build the nation. In the midst of all these triumphalistic statements, the poor continue to be poor, the landless continue to be landless, women continue to be treated as inferior to men, and the poor and the untouchables continue to be harassed as a part of the Hindu ethos/theology.

Most of these attributes apply to Christians also, whether Evangelical or ecumenical, inclusivist or exclusivist, Methodist or Mennonite or Anglican. In this very divisive situation, everything that is said or done has two sides and is often justified, whatever the case may be. Against this backdrop, we need to consider the contribution of Evangelical missiology.

The Impact of Christianity in India

The pioneering European missionaries were brave and sacrificed much for the sake of bringing the gospel to India. About the spread of the gospel, C. B. Firth (1961, p. 127) observes, "It was early in the 18th century, while the Jesuits were still carrying on their work in Tamilnadu, the Protestant missionaries first appeared in India." The early Protestant missionaries, starting from Bartholomaeus Ziegenbalg, Heinrich Plutschau, Christian Friedrich Schwartz, William Carey, Alexander Duff, Ida Scudder, Isabella Thoburn, John P. Jones, William Goudie, Stanley Jones, Waskom Pickett, and many others who followed them, accomplished much. They revolutionised India by preaching the gospel, winning people for Christ, discipling, establishing churches, igniting social changes, and even influencing the Freedom Movement.

These missionaries had much to do with building modern India and with developing a new ethos in the country through their many social endeavours. Isaac Taylor Headland (1912, p. 4) wrote that the products of missions are regenerated human beings. All other things are simply by-products, consciously or unconsciously, directly or indirectly, the result of mission work. Khushwant Singh (1992, p. 76), a secular journalist, states, "More far-reaching than the number of converts it made was the influence of Protestantism on Hinduism. Protestants took active part in suppression of *sati*,[1] ending female

infanticide, and suppressing the thugs [rowdies and ruffians]; alleviating the condition of Hindu widows and temple prostitutes; raising the marriage [sic], etc. It was the Christian missionaries ... [who] roused the admiration of Hindu reformers like Ram Mohun Roy, whose *Brahmo Samaj*, set up in 1829, drew a great deal of its inspiration from Christianity. So also did the *Prarthana Samaj*."

These missionaries impacted India in the areas of politics (Singh, 1992, p. 76), education (especially uplifting education for women and thus elevating their pitiful status), and journalism (thus influencing the mass thinking) (Beaver, 1981, p. 199). They also brought peace between warring European colonialists and the Indian kings (Firth, 1961, p. 137)[2] and discipled many Christians in India.

In 1969, Dr. Radha Krishnan, the President of India, hosting Bishop and Mrs. Pickett, fervently wished that Christians in all parts of India were far more numerous, because significant peace and law and order prevailed in the areas where there were more Christians (Firth, 1961, pp. 31-32). Swami John Dharma Theerthan (p. 17) summarised the situation in these words: "The direct results of Christian missionary activity are but a small fraction of what Christ has accomplished in numerous ways in all the varied departments of thought and behaviour of many millions in this continent. The transformation that has been effected in the inner and outer life of the nation is one of the profoundest phenomena of human history."

---

[1] *Sati* was a Hindu custom in which widows were burned with their dead husbands. Although *sati* was not practised by all Hindus, the gruesome practice was perpetuated by many as religious fanaticism. *Sati* was outlawed in 1829 by the British Viceroy to India, William Bentinct, through the efforts of William Carey and Raja Ram Mohun Roy.

[2] Even Hyder Ali, a Muslim ruler, had a high regard for Schwartz. When the English found out that Hyder Ali had allied himself with the French, they wanted to negotiate with him. For this task, none could reach him except Schwartz, for Hyder Ali had said, "Let them send me the Christian [Schwartz]; he will not deceive me."

Thus the success of the missionaries is measured not just by words but by the fruits of their labour. There is ample evidence of lasting impact by the pioneering missionaries as a result of their labour of love and their commitment to the Lord Jesus Christ.

Indian Missionary Movements

Foreign missions

Before the independence of India in 1947, foreign mission organisations were affiliated with church denominations, including Baptists, Presbyterians, Anglicans, Mennonites, Methodists, and others. The churches established by these missions consolidated their members at the time of independence, and for a time there were no foreign missionary movements doing pioneer work in the country. Thus there was a definite discontinuity in pioneering missions.

International affiliated missions such as CCC, OM, YWAM, BGEA, IEHC, AFC, YFC, SU, UESI (IVF), ECC, and others carried on their ministries without much interruption. Their success was due to Indian personnel and funds coming partly from India. Thus the work to fulfil the Great Commission was carried on, even in the absence of classical missionaries.

Indian indigenous missions

The number of Indian missions has increased from only three or four prior to Indian independence to over 125 that are affiliated with the India Missions Association (IMA) today. Outside IMA, there are scores of other mission agencies, including several denominational agencies (Jayaprakash, 1987, pp. 22-68). Patrick Johnstone (1993, p. 276) quoted 198 mission agencies in India in 1993. A. Gnanadasan (1998), a minister of the ECI, listed 300 mission organisations in 1992. These mis-

sion societies have achieved much in sharing the gospel with millions. Yet there is more—much more—to be done. Rev. Vasantharaj Albert (1995, p. 36) points to the following progression in the number of Indian missionaries:

1972 – 543
1980 – 2,208
1983 – 3,369
1988 – 10,243
1994 – 12,000
1997 – 15,000

There could actually be 20,000 missionaries including 5,000 church workers involved cross-culturally in E2 and E3 evangelism. This is an approximate figure (Sunder Raj, 1997, June). Thus, India has become the largest cross-cultural missionary sending country in the Two-Thirds World (Pate, 1991, p. 32).

Evangelicalism in the Light of Evangelisation

Evangelical Fellowships: EFI, FECI, and PFI

The Evangelical Fellowship of India (EFI) was born in 1951 as an overarching fellowship and a catalyst for many of the Evangelical churches, associations, and networks in India. Its goal is to promote unified action directed towards spiritual renewal in the church, active evangelism, effective witness, and a safeguarding of the Evangelical faith in the church (Arles, pp. 32-34). J. C. Thiessen (1955, p. 39) remarks that the EFI "gives priority consideration to the recovery of spiritual life in all the churches of India."

EFI has done much to awaken Evangelical vision and to promote a renewed focus for mission in India. Das (p. 34) notes, "In the first two decades of its existence, the various activities of EFI served to strengthen the Evangelicals. For example, Union Biblical Seminary was established in 1953 for Evangelical theological education, All Christian Book Club in 1953, and the Evangelical Radio Fellowship of India in 1957, to name just a few."

EFI achieved much by a gathering of Evangelicals in several congresses: the All India Congress on Mission and Evangelism at Devlali in 1977; the All India Christian Communication Seminar at Nagpur in 1978; the All India Christian Education Seminar and All India Church Growth Seminar, both at Hyderabad, in 1978; the All India Conference on Evangelical Social Action at Madras in 1979; and the All India Evangelical Women's Conference at Pune in 1979. These conferences contributed positively to the growth of Evangelical movements in India (Arles, p. 33).

EFI gave birth to many associations and networks, including IMA, EFICOR, CEFI, EMFI, ENFI, and others. It was the Evangelical counterpart of the National Council of Churches in India (NCCI). EFI specifically came into being to counter liberal influences of the ecumenical church (Sunder Raj, 1997, July). It is still pressing on to contribute to the Evangelical churches and missions in India. New leadership has provided it with a new lease on life.

An EFI pamphlet (1991, p. 39) states, "In 1974, the position of neutrality towards the ecumenical movement adopted by EFI began to find disfavour with some members of EFI who wished for a more authentic Evangelical structure." As a result, the Federation of Evangelical Churches in India (FECI) was born at Akola, Maharastra, with eight different church denominations joining as members (McMahon, 1971, p. 8). Daniel Abraham (quoted in Harris, 1997, p. 115), the president of FECI, said in his presidential speech during the 20th anniversary of FECI, "The FECI came as a result of a long felt need

in the Evangelical churches in India to stand united in upholding the fundamental biblical truths against the attacks of liberalism and other similar destructive forces that are actively at work in the church today."

Because EFI seemed to lack theological clarity, in 1979 the FECI Theological Commission started an Association for Evangelical Theological Education in India, which with the Asia Theological Association started promoting Evangelical separatism, thus destabilising the Serampore accreditation for theological studies (Harris, 1997, p. 39).

While EFI is an overarching body of Evangelical missions and churches, FECI defends primarily the Evangelical churches, and thus it is a church-oriented association (Sunder Raj, 1997, July). However, at present FECI is docile.

Another organisation is the Pentecostal Fellowship of India (PFI). This group has many active works, including a large number of women workers.

Other groups to enhance evangelisation

The increase in the number of missions and missionaries necessitated setting up associations and networks for better organisation of efforts. The prominent associations are EFI, IMA, FECI, PFI, EHA, ETANI/ETASI/ETAI, EMFI, and a few others. The prominent networks are CGAI, AD 2000 Movement, NIHNW, CONS, DAWN, National Forum for Measuring the Results of Indian Evangelisation,[3] Tentmaker Centre, ELFI, GRCP, MI 2000, and others. Some support groups are GFA, MUT/MUF, and others. The social action agencies which worked through the churches and missions are EFICOR, CASA, World Vision, Inter Mission, and others.

---

[3] This group was pioneered by IMA through the National Consultation on Missions and Evangelism at Hyderabad in 1996.

All these associations and networks have a mandate to support missions in India.

Apart from the above associations and federations, the following national federations also have unique functions. The names themselves suggest some of their functions: National Council of Churches in India (NCCI); Christian Medical Association of India (CMAI); Indian Christian Media Association (ICMA); National Association for Christian Social Concerns (NACSC); India Association of (Itinerant) Evangelists (IAE); Evangelical Literature Fellowship of India (ELFI); and All India Association for Christian Higher Education (AIACHE). Each federation has scores (some hundreds) of organisations in its federation, representing thousands of staff workers spread all over India (Sunder Raj & Team, 1992, p. 136).

Ten Mega-Confusions in Missions and Churches

In carrying out the Great Commission of the Lord Jesus Christ, Indian missions and churches have become confused. This confusion has resulted in a polarisation in theology, which in turn has affected the philosophy and methods of evangelisation, as well as the training of theologians, missiologists, and others. It partly explains why India has not been evangelised as a whole and why the percentage of Christians, on the average, remains at only 3-4% of the population. Bookish and twisted theological thinking lacks intensity for an overall strategy for India. It will eventually result in pluralism and extreme inclusivism, resulting in the stagnation and diminishing of the church of Christ.

Confusion #1: Ambiguous terms and meanings

In the midst of growth, a need has been recognised to consolidate the terms and meanings of all that is being done in relation to evangelism. There are many definitions of evangelism, mission, holistic outreach, and other terms. These terms need to be defined according to a general consensus of understanding before the missions grow further. Otherwise, there will be a very high probability of divisions and further confusion. The suggestion is for a core group to compile consensus definitions of each concept and term used in mission work. This is top priority.

Confusion #2: Social work and evangelism

Joshi Jayaprakash (1987, p. 20b), in his survey of missions in 1987, said that 57.17% of the missionaries were involved in church planting, and only 7.17% were doing development work. Today, among the 125 IMA missions with 20,000 missionaries, the majority are equally involved in church planting and social work. This means that since 1987 the amount of social work performed by missions has increased dramatically. It also implies that in the future, social work might grow more than direct evangelism. This change in focus is related to the holistic approach in evangelism. The increase in social work needs to be watched and a balance maintained, or else missions could become merely social organisations. Thus there is a need for missions to keep reiterating their goals, visions, and ethos of the end result—leading people to Christ—both to themselves and to their workers.[4]

---

[4] Reiteration of the ultimate goal of the mission can be done by repeating vision statements, printing them in all mission publications, gathering workers periodically and informing them where the mission is heading, etc. Doing these things will keep the missions on track. The leadership must be thoroughly convinced where they want to take their mission. If the leadership is weak, it could confuse the agency and weaken it, with disastrous results.

Confusion #3: Neglecting major unreached people groups

Muslims, middle and upper class people of the cities and towns, the handicapped, and the non-animistic Hindus of India are yet to be reached with the gospel. Very few missions train people for reaching specific people groups. They are also unprepared to pay adequate allowances for the missionaries who work with such peoples (Daniel, 1997b, p. 8).[5]

Confusion #4: Strong tribal and "win the winnable" emphasis

Undue emphasis has been given to tribals, who comprise only about 8% of the total population of India. This is connected to the fact that these people are generally open to the gospel, and it is economically easier to support missionaries who live among them. It also comes from a "win the winnable" philosophy. This strategy needs to be consciously revised.

Confusion #5: Homogeneous unit principle emphasis

There is much stress on reaching people according to the homogeneous unit principle (HUP) concept of "one people at a time." Regarding this concept, Indian missions are divided into two strong camps, for and against. Although HUP has worked in some people groups, many missions sing a song of oneness in Christ, but they are not really convinced that it will work.[6] Many mission leaders and missionaries feel that theologically HUP is not right, in light of the "one body/one in Christ" concept. Some feel that HUP will not work in cities where people are not divided along caste lines. HUP proponents counter this objection by classifying working groups as part of the people groups in the cities. However, many of the other backward castes and the forward castes will never come to Christ unless they are brought to him as communities.[7] Once a realisation dawns on them that they will be divided in their communities if they accept Christ, they shun Christianity even if they believe that Christ is the way of salvation.

---

[5] For additional information, refer to the appendix at the end of this chapter.

[6] Except among mature Christians, oneness is often merely a lip service rather than reality. Inability to celebrate oneness is more of a cultural problem than anything else. Accepting others with different cultural, language, and habitual behaviours is difficult. Christian oneness must be consciously cultivated. Unity is often put to the test in situations such as a marriage between people from different backgrounds. Even Christians continue to marry and relate in a mono-caste framework. Although Christians are better at relating to others in the church, there are still many discrepancies and divisions which affect missions. Is this a theological problem or a missiological problem? There is a long way to go in accepting others as brothers and sisters in Christ.

[7] There are three forward castes (FCs) of Indians (priests, warriors, and the business class). After them are the other backward castes (OBCs), the scheduled castes (SCs), and the scheduled tribes (STs). The tribals constitute only 8-10% of the Indian population. About 30% of the population is included in the SCs and OBCs. 60-70% of all Indian missionaries work among the 10% of tribal Indians. The remaining 90% of the population has only about 30% of the missionaries. Most of these work among the SCs and OBCs and not among the rest. Just the Muslims of India (14%) are much more numerous than the tribal population. There is definitely a lopsided approach in thinking about and strategising for Indian evangelism.

Sensitivity and innovation are needed in Indian missions. Multiplication of philosophies must be encouraged to win many communities to Christ. Although Christians may agree on the "one in Christ" concept, initially some people groups may have to be brought to Christ in their own communities. Sadly, though, some groups who came to Christ 100 years ago still cling to their own communities. Where is their spiritual maturity? Is this a theological problem or a missiological one?

The issues of numerical church growth versus spiritual growth and of personal conversion versus group conversion are related topics in the discussion of HUP emphasis. Peter Wagner (1981, p. 181) takes a middle-of-the-road position, saying, "The homogeneous unit principle, though it is a penultimate not an ultimate characteristic of the kingdom of God, does provide a useful tool not only for the effective implementation of the evangelistic mandate, but also for helping people of differing human groups to live together in greater love and harmony." A balanced and pragmatic approach must be designed according to the receptivity of people.

Confusion #6:
Contextualisation

For many Christians and missionaries, the cathedral is synonymous with Christianity. Stanley Soltau (p. 120) cautions, "There is sometimes a tendency to forget the wide difference between the two and to think that to introduce Christianity means also introducing Western ways of life." When Christians are diverted from the finality of Christ, they became sidetracked with their goals and purposes, and evangelism is neglected (Rajendran, 1996).

Francis Xavier, the famous Jesuit who served in India from 1506 to 1552, followed the thinking of the medieval missionary church that everything in non-Christian life and systems should be abolished before Christianity is introduced. Of course, he changed his mind when he reached Japan, where he saw a culture superior to that of the West (Fuller, 1980, p. 13). Frederick Norris (1984, pp. 55-56) called this abolishing act a "radical displacement," in which Christianity with all its Western (or whatever the national culture of the missionaries) cultural baggage was transplanted whole, and ethnic religion was brushed aside as valueless. Such an iconoclastic mindset seemed to have deterred the contextualisation of Christ's teachings to the cultures in India.

To the question of why Christianity did not take root in India, Khushwant Singh (1992, p. 76) explains, "Christianity did not make strong impact on India. The chief reason for this was that Christianity was never able to erase the taint of being alien to the soil of India. Efforts made to Indianise Christianity had a limited success. India did not produce a Christian saint of its own.... Sadhu Sunder Singh came close to it.... Other [Indian Christian] leaders ... were good men but without the charisma of sainthood ... were hardly known outside of Christian circles. What Indian Christianity needed in the Indian setting was a *Mahatma*; all it produced were men and women, good scouts, girl guides, directors, YMCA and YWCA."

In this Indian context, it has become inevitable to contextualise the teachings of Christ in multiple ways of service, worship, and proclamation. Neill Anderson (1993, p. December 13), president of Freedom in Christ Ministries, says, "The world is changing at an alarming rate.... The ecclesiastical challenge is to give anxious people the timeless message of Christ and present it in a contemporary way that relates to a changing culture." Vishal Mangalwadi (Richard & Mangalwadi, 1997) sees the need for an inward change in Christians and not just an outward one. When there is an inward change, he notes, there is less fear and less worry about syncretism when contextualising to Indian culture.

The issue of contextualisation has no clear solutions either in the churches or in the missions. Many agree that there is a need for change, but what changes to make and how to go about making them are unclear. Very little has been done to change the scene and swim against the current of Christian traditionalism. Once people are entrenched in their tradition, it is hard to change them.

Bruce Nicholls (p. 386) differentiates indigenisation and contextualisation as follows: "An earlier generation used the word indigenisation, which meant relating the gospel to the traditional cultures of the people. Contextualisation includes all that is right in indigenisation but in a wider context including contemporary and changing cultural patterns of life. Increasingly Christians worldwide are recognising that the gospel must be contextualised from one culture to another if God's kingdom has to be established on earth."

S. D. Ponraj (pp. 37-38) explains, "Contextualisation means to translate or interpret the gospel and its implications in terms of the needs of the whole man and society. Contextualisation was not another word for indigenisation, but includes the concept. Both words have important meanings in the context of planting churches in India."

Doug Priest, Jr. (1984, p. 200) suggests that in a cross-cultural church-planting situation, the church should maintain as many of the indigenous forms as possible. It should explore the need for functional substitutes but remain alert in order to safeguard the faith against the incorpora-

tion of pagan beliefs. This is where the tension exists.

O. M. Rao (p. 110) reflects, "It is necessary that the Christian faith should be interpreted in the context of its environment and culture. It involves risk, as all interpretations of the Christian faith face in terms of the communication process in different places and times. The Indian Christian thinker should engage himself in this task and thereby be exposed to the risk involved. But in interpreting the Christian faith in the context ... one has to watch.... No interpretation is valid if the core of the Christian faith is sacrificed on the altar of adoption to the Indian situation."

Frederick Norris (1984, pp. 56-57) outlines six ways to contextualise. First, there is *radical displacement* of the culture, in which the old host culture is completely shelved. Second is the *discontinuity theory*, in which Christianity feels superior and feels no comparison with the local culture, but it still seeks to adapt itself to the cultural forms of the people. Third, there is the *uniqueness theory*, in which both religions are recognised as unique, but Christianity is assumed to be superior. Fourth is the *legitimate borrowing theory*, in which the commonality from both religions is accepted and borrowed so as to be truly indigenous. Fifth is the *fulfilment theory*, in which the gospel of Christ is accepted as the fulfilment of people's quest in that culture. Lastly is the theory of *relativistic syncretism*. In this it is accepted that all religions contain different truths that lead to the ultimate Truth.

Indigenisation, contextualisation, and the term de-Westernisation are all interrelated themes. Rajaiah Paul (1952, p. 106) heatedly called for de-Westernisation nearly a half century ago: "The fact is that after 200 years of [Protestant] Christianity, the Christian message is still being presented in a language unintelligible for the most part to the people of the country. For two centuries or more we have been studying Christian theology as presented by the Western minds and in Western books, and we have trained ourselves to think only along those lines. Indian Christians have not yet begun to think for themselves and re-think ... and re-define the Christian message in thought forms and in language that our countrymen will understand."

Ralph Winter, in his speech at the GCOWE conference in South Africa in August 1997, challenged people to de-Westernise Christianity to accommodate the coming of mass movements to Christ, without any hangover of imperial Westernism attached to the message of Christ. Ebenezer Sunder Raj (1997, September), responded that the concept of de-Westernisation is not something that the church in India should worry about. This problem is a hangover from the past. Now all that the missions and the churches need to do is to think and act in responsible ways which would accommodate mass movements to Christ. Thus, it is not a question of de-Westernisation, but instead one of developing strategies to present Christ without compromising the message. For this, the church and missions do not need to be either inclusivists or exclusivists. Rather, they need to present the gospel and change the forms of Christian traditions to make them palatable to the majority of the people in the country.

The above men all agree that there is a great need to change our approach to the evangelisation of India. Stanley Soltau (p. 120), a missionary to Japan, emphasises the fact that the introduction of Christ will inevitably bring changes: "As the gospel enters the lives of the people, it will naturally change many of their customs, but it must be understood that it is the gospel that is making the change and not the Western [or any] missionaries."

O. M. Rao (p. 2) points out that missionaries do not need to infuse other cultures into the community to "make" them Christians. "The present task of indigenisation is to apply some surgery, separating the Christian message from Western culture, then translate that same message into the context of Eastern culture."

S. D. Ponraj (pp. 37-38) suggests three broad areas to consider in contextualising. These are contextualisation of the theology of the gospel interpretation, contextualisation of forms of the gospel expression, and contextualisation of the church in its leadership, finance, and witness. He goes on to say that there should be more detailed focus on witness, evangelistic methods, leadership, church government, finance, worship (including seating, reading, and posture), church buildings, and lifestyles.

Rao (pp. 2-9) cautions about the danger of going to extremes with contextualisation and indigenisation. For one thing, indigenisation is not being more Indian than Western. Second, there is a great temptation for the Ashramites to compromise with the Hindus in the extremity of identification. Third, Western culture must be separated from the message of Christ. Fourth, there is a need to identify the essential and non-essential elements in Christianity. These non-essentials, in St. Paul's terminology, were truly permissible, yet for the higher purposes they were not beneficial (1 Cor. 10:23). Thus, when sacrificing non-essentials, it is for the effective retention of essential truth. Lastly, some react to the term indigenisation, as they feel the common man would equate the indigenised forms to Hindu forms. Some feel also that these efforts are not successful and thus should not be attempted. This mentality must be overcome.

According to Soltau (pp. 122-126), the distinguishing features of the indigenised churches or missions are their strength, their rapid growth, a more wholesome relationship between the missionaries and the locals, a more effective presentation of the gospel, and a wider outreach.

S. Pillai (1997), a first-generation follower of Christ, queried, "Why could the churches not be kept open for people to visit at any time of the day or night?" This is a question that is relevant to the culture. More innovative ways for contextualisation must be found. However, these will need to be made in the midst of the traditionalists within the church itself.

Confusion #7:
People group adoptions

Some feel that peoples should be reached not on caste lines but on language lines. They say that each group must be reached by the spoken languages of the people. However, some language groups are too large for this approach to be effective. Among them are the Bhojpuri in UP and Bihar and the Maithili in Eastern Bihar and Bengal. These language groups must be further divided into dialects and caste groups.

With IMA leading the PIN code research, NIHNW, GRCP, GFA, GEMS, and a few other supporters of this concept are trying to get missions to concentrate on placing missionaries in each PIN code area. Thus it would be easier to measure the results of mission work. In each PIN code area, missionaries would be free to adopt any HUP or language division in their work. Whatever the method, peoples *must* be reached.

Whatever the strategy may be, the confusion lies in the adoption of people groups. Some in the U.S. and many in India claim to be people group clearinghouses. This causes much confusion and must be worked on.

Confusion #8:
Neglect of missionary welfare and short-sightedness in future recruiting

Many Indians joined mission organisations in the wake of the departure of Western missionaries after India gained independence, and also as a better understanding of missions dawned in the churches. As a commitment to the Lord and to the Great Commission, many left lucrative jobs in which they could have flourished. Most workers served in the tribal areas. As they sought to carry out the Great Commission, their wives and children were forced to bear the brunt of many hardships.

In the current Indian missionary scene, workers suffer from deficient medical care, insufficient salary, inadequate schooling facilities for children, meagre retirement benefits, lack of retirement housing, and inadequate insurance coverage.

Pastoral care

There is also a great need for missionary pastoral care as the missionary force expands. Workers face mounting personal pressures and the strain of sharing Christ with those who do not understand. Many missionaries face pressures from their own organisations in the form of difficult relationships with co-workers, poor leadership, clan-ruled authority structures, unorganised plans, and inadequate training for accomplishing the task. In the organisational structure, too much accountability is expected of some missionaries, while others go scot-free due to favouritism.

The lack of adequate teams for pastoral care, the absence of able administrators, and incompetent leadership in some missions are issues that must be addressed in order for missionaries to work effectively. More training in missionary pastoral care has to be planned in the future.

In addition, those providing pastoral care need encouragement. Unfortunately, even if some recognise the need for pastoral care for missionaries, they are often discouraged as wasting time.

Medical needs

When missionaries fall ill, they are often faced with inadequate medical facilities, and they frequently have no medical insurance. Also, most missions do not settle the affairs of the family members of workers who die on the field.

Children's care

Children of missionaries often study in hostels which may be 1,000 kilometres away. Most families are able to be together only once a year during holidays. They have to separate again just when the children and parents are getting adjusted to each other. Some missions have been insensitive and have laid undue burdens on families by requiring the children and parents to be separated by great distances, just because it is cheaper for missions to support the children in certain prescribed schools. Missionaries have been unable to bear the expenses for the children to study in schools within 100 kilometres, where the parents could meet them frequently. This situation has angered both parents and children.

Ironically, much money has been contributed towards scholarships for non-Christian children, and much social work is being done for others, but when it comes to meeting the expenses of the missionaries, missions and donors shy away as though the missionary is destined to suffer! This abrasive short-sightedness will result in the missions not reaching peoples effectively with the gospel of Christ. Many potential missionary candidates today prefer various kinds of social work through the mission, where the pressure to share the gospel is less and the

salary is better. The progress of future mission work is dependent on how missionaries are being cared for. This area is being carefully watched by the new generation and by other concerned people.

Inadequate salary to meet genuine needs

Modern Indian indigenous missions do not have sufficient money to do the best for their missionaries (Winston, 1997, August). Publications urge readers, "Pray for financial support and more workers for all the Indian missions" (IMA, 1996, p. 3). Individual missionaries struggle for survival. One former missionary to the Muslims in Assam said that his mission, 10 years back, paid him a monthly salary of 400 rupees. After 10 years, he received around 1,000 rupees a month. The mission insisted that both husband and wife work in the same mission. This meant the man's wife could not pursue her career. This worker felt that even if his salary was doubled, financially he could not survive. Therefore, he resigned and left the mission.

Lesslie Newbigin (1977, p. 54) asks, "How has it come that we use the name 'evangelist' for the lowest category of church workers—half trained, half paid, and half starved? How does it come that respectable Christians feel uncomfortable with the very idea of evangelism?" One particular mission was reported as having 87 workers, but it did not have a regular pay structure for the missionaries. Each missionary was paid 200–300 rupees a month. The missionaries struggled to survive. According to Roy Daniel (1997a, p. 6), living in a one-bedroom house in North India cost a missionary, his wife, and two school-age children Rs. 4,000 a month in 1991. Today it would cost Rs. 4,000–6,000 in large cities and Rs. 6,000–10,000 in cosmopolitan cities and commercial townships, excluding house rent (Daniel, 1997b, p. 8).

Missionaries have as many material needs and aspirations as anyone else. Just because they have committed themselves to the cause of evangelism, people expect them not to entangle themselves in so-called "worldly" things. Shyam Winston (p. 21) notes, "The missionary is not above material needs but has intentionally ceased to give priority to his material welfare in the presence of a call to evangelise. His material needs still exist, and they must be met by those sending him."

Several missionaries who were interviewed agreed that missionaries and Christian workers did not have much savings, nor any health insurance, nor retirement benefits, nor death relief schemes. The consensus was that this state of affairs resulted from the false theology called "faith," until some disaster such as a heart attack struck them. One missionary's wife became mentally ill, and the mission could not treat her because of lack of funds. Eventually the missionary died, and his wife was left mad and homeless on the streets (Winston, 1997, September).

Many Indian missionaries are reluctant to speak about their financial needs for fear of being branded as "unspiritual." Instead, they quietly suffer insecurities (Shunmugam & Shunmugam, 1997). Missionaries have endured much in the name of "true spirituality" and "faith." With this line of reasoning, many missionaries have entered upon mission work without adequate physical preparation, and some have needlessly suffered. These situations lead to problems when the missionary faces a crisis, or when he retires and has no place to go, or when he dies and his family is left stranded in the streets with no sustenance.

These warped "faith elements" have come from many sources. Some are from the convictions of the missionary himself. Some missionaries believe that having insurance means dependence upon men and is therefore unspiritual. Some plainly do not want to pay the insurance premiums, and so they take chances, mainly because of a lack of funds. Others feel that money should not be tied down to insurance premiums when it could be used to support missionaries and buy the tools for evangelism. Some of these ideas have also come from the inflated life-stories of famous missionaries such as William Carey and Hudson Taylor. It was Hudson Taylor who said, "God's work done in God's way will not lack God's supply."[8] These kinds of thoughts have been taken to extremes.

Some convictions have come from the missions. Most missions project the convictions of their leader(s) in their policies. Some policies are indistinguishable as to whether they are derived from biblical ethos or situational convictions. One such conviction is appealing for funds. Men like Hudson Taylor applied the principle of looking solely to God for their needs, and they seemed to have done well. At times the principle was applied to extreme degrees by subsequent followers. Others who did not repeat such practices were judged "unspiritual" by some so-called "spiritual giants."

Some agencies have held onto convictions which are obsolete and irrelevant for the present era, as carryovers from the past. Some convictions have come from the nations from which a particular mission originally emerged. Each mission carries its special culture and thus develops its own convictions and work ethos. Some are biblical, and some are cultural and interpretive.

---

[8] Hudson Taylor's quote is inscribed in the stone at the entrance of SAIACS, Bangalore, India.

These convictions and faith elements have a bearing on the lifestyle of missionaries. Because missionaries' salaries are low, the only place they can survive is among the tribal people. They cannot survive economically in other situations or work strategically to win India for Christ. Thus the cities, the Muslims, the women, the educated, and others are neglected in India. Reaching people groups is partially connected to meeting the actual needs of the missionary, as secular companies do. Are missionaries less than normal human beings? Are missionaries' expenses in any way less than those of others?

Many promotional workers do not present the whole need of missionaries but only parts to donors. The actual expenses have to be appealed from donors instead of partial funds.

Pension and retirement housing

The missionary's self-worth must be strengthened by planning for housing and a pension after retirement. A missionary who has given his life for the service of the Lord Jesus Christ, in the front lines, is worthy of his own house and a respectable life when he retires. Even secular companies have recognised this. The missions must be very careful of false teaching that the things of this world will not last, and so missionaries do not need a house when they retire. Some mission leaders make missionaries feel guilty by messages of a lost world and Jesus' imminent return. This automatically makes a missionary feel that even thinking of a house and pension after retirement is sinful. This attitude perpetuates insecurity both in the missionary and in his family members.

All the above issues have weakened the efforts of missionaries and have become factors for missionary attrition and future recruitment. Recruiting quality missionaries will very much depend on how missions will tackle the situation of missionary welfare. Lack of attention to missionary welfare will cause missionaries to abandon missionary work. It will also result in some missionaries moving to other missions where the facilities are better, causing missions to lose their experienced leaders and church planters. This also will affect future new missionaries who watch how the missionaries are being treated. More and more, missionary appeals must have more than emotional appeal. If the needs of the missionaries are not looked after, the missions in India will diminish. Is this a theological or a missiological problem?

Confusion #9: Foreign funds, Indian funds, and partnership

There has been much discussion about indigenous funds and local funds. Some people, especially foreigners, would like to know when the Indian church is going to assume total responsibility for the evangelisation of India in terms of utilising local finances. The answer is not simple, in light of the vastness of the need in the entire nation. The church is young, as far as its missionary endeavour is concerned. While these factors are present, some assume that the church in India is weak and irresponsible and that it does not see the necessity of giving for missionary work.[9]

---

[9] In an interview with Mr. Ebenezer Sunder Raj, the question was posed, "Why are Indian churches not giving money for evangelisation of this nation?" This question assumed that the Indian churches were irresponsible and were not giving enough to reach the nation. Knowing that this assumption was not true, Mr. Ebenezer declined to comment. The churches need education and need to be coached.

Although there might be some truth in this, several factors need to be kept in mind:

1. The church in India has progressively given much towards meeting the need for their own evangelism in the past 50 years (Dozo, 1984, p. 23).

2. The church in India is small compared to the vast task of Indian evangelism.

3. The vast majority of the church is from the lower, Dalit strata of society, which is unable to bear the whole burden of the huge task. Christians are from 14 scheduled castes, according to Roger Hedlund (1986, p. 154). Ashish Massey (1992, p. 89), a Christian sociologist and journalist, reflects, "The Christians are simply poor. They get little opportunity to seek employment outside church institutions. They have very little role in business." Within mission organisations, missionaries are paid meagrely, and missions have focused only on the poor and the tribals. The major parts of Indian society have not been touched.

4. The Evangelical church, which has been responsible for most of the evangelisation efforts, has been very small and is still emerging. "The task is too big without partnership," concludes George Ninan.

5. The church is still being educated in the area of giving, especially giving for mission needs. Rajaiah Paul (1952, p. 110) observed, "The Indian Christian community ... has not yet learnt the importance of Christian giving." Although this statement was made nearly 50 years ago, the struggle of teaching Christians still exists.

"Our church members need to be informed of the unreached people of the world who have to be reached with the gospel of the Lord Jesus Christ, and remind them of their responsibility and privilege to share the gospel with those who have never heard. We have also to educate our members to pray for unreached people and ask God to send more labourers to gather them" (Massey, 1992, p. 89).

Some missions claimed that they were indigenised, and thus there was a great applause for their efforts. Unfortunately, most of these missions are barely able to meet the needs of their missionaries. Lawrence Keyes (1983, p. 74) reports that according to a study made in 1980, an average of 35% of Third World missionaries did not receive their promised full salary. Lack of finances is one of the main reasons that missionaries have chosen to work among the tribals and villagers. Of course, the tribals and villagers are also unreached. But more than that, with the kind of salary the missionaries receive, they cannot afford to live in the growing cities and towns. This also affects the education of missionaries' children. In addition, most missions provide no pension, no medical insurance, no life insurance, no savings, and no plans for retirement housing.

These deficiencies are basically due to the inability to manage with the paucity of funds. Although the vision of reaching India is big, the means to meet the need are inadequate. Often the money which should be spent on missionary welfare is spent on the social needs of those who do not know Christ. The salary of the missionary is comparable to that of the poor of India. Some missions take advantage of the situation and try to recruit more people for less money. Number games among these indigenised missions are performed at the cost of missionaries' welfare. Instead of looking after two missionaries with the funds available, agencies employ 10 missionaries to make the numbers look better. Some missions may not consciously play the numbers game, yet their burden for unreached people makes them lose sight of counting the cost of maintaining missionaries (Winston, 1997, August).

Missions which claim indigenised funding explain that their missionaries are supported by the church in India. There are also funds raised from non-resident Indians (NRI). Many of the larger indigenous missions employ foreign funds through their sister organisations for social activities. These funds sometimes support the evangelistic and holistic activities on the mission field. Thus, some large indigenised missions have one agency for Indian funds and another for foreign funds. Lawrence Keyes (1983, p. 75) says that it is a good idea to separate missionary salaries from projects. He suggests, "Perhaps the best policy, in the light of world nationalisation and missionary indigenisation, is to support special missionary projects, but allow the national churches to pay personal salaries." Thus, indigenisation of funds is somewhat of a myth, providing only a partial perspective.[10]

Ashish Massey (1992, p. 89) claims, "Foreign sources are sizably curtailed, and the indigenised resources have not developed so far to fill the gap." Therefore, financially the Indian church is not able to bear all that is demanded to meet the great needs of all the missions in India, in all their evangelistic and social activities. However, the Indian church does have the manpower which could be trained and which could contribute to the evangelisation of India and in neighbouring countries.

The church must be educated regarding the priorities of giving. Many in the church do not know the difference between giving to a glamorous crusade speaker and giving to missions like FMPB. Most of the giving has been based on returns and non-returns. Because of lack of education in missions and in giving among the Christians, the best and most worthy appeals have not raised all the needed funds. Some groups do not know how to appeal for the credible work of missions. Thus, the wrong people have received much money from the Christians, while the credible missions have suffered. Giving should be based on understanding and enlightenment, not on excitement. It should be based on objective information, rather than just inspiration towards the wrong cause. Christians in India need to be taught to give. This is nearly as great a task as reaching an unreached people for Christ.

Overall, in the growing Indian missions, much is done indigenously. Notable amounts of money, manpower, leadership, and strategies are acquired from within India itself. However, the proportion of funds from within India and from abroad is hard to pinpoint. The Indian church has also grown in maturity in the last 50 years, to the extent of upholding much of the mission work. A great deal of Indian missionaries' salaries (though not adequate) and some projects are paid by the churches in India. For training and for large capital expenses, many overseas partners are involved in one way or other. We praise God for these meaningful partnerships.

Confusion #10: Preparation of leadership for the future

The Indian missions have come of age in their first generation. Most of the leaders in the Evangelical mission organisations are in their 50s. One issue which is slowly affecting the missions is the issue of the next set of leaders. Across India there is going to be a time of leadership

---

[10] The names of the partially indigenised agencies are not given here for security reasons.

322 ADDRESSING ISSUES OF GLOBALIZED EVANGELICAL MISSIOLOGY

change in missions. It has been noticed that a number of missions are ill prepared for this inevitable occurrence. Many of the past and contemporary charismatic leaders, consciously or unconsciously, have not prepared new leaders to take over upon their retirement or in any other eventuality. Many see themselves as indisposable, or they are insecure about letting go of their power in a position. There is a reluctance to let go of the power of an office, as occurs with many secular politicians. Those in a position tend to view it as a life-long "post." There is a great respect for the "post-position" but not for the person himself for the contributions made.

The existing old leadership style in the Indian missions scene is generally either patriarchal with dictatorial tendencies or else family oriented, where the parents pass on the leadership to their next of kin. Often a mission is passed on to the family, the way a private company is passed on to the sons and daughters and other family members. Even though secular companies have changed to corporate leadership, the pattern of leadership transfer is still felt on the Indian scene. Not giving leadership to the next generation early enough is going to be the greatest single challenge of Indian missions in the near future.[11]

The office of Christian leadership must change in the ethos of discipling, mentoring, and passing on the mantle while the original leaders are still present. The experienced leaders could always function as consultants and advisers. Often the excuse for not mentoring and installing new leaders is that "the right person is not available" or that everyone is "too young" or "too immature"—as though some of the older leaders were and are "very mature"

for the job. However, a balance has to be maintained to identify and place potential leaders as they are being tested in a growth-producing environment and are fulfilling the responsibilities given to them. Discernment must be exercised to distinguish the talkers from faithful people. Conscious search and a sense of mentoring multiple candidates over a period of time should lead missions to find and install the next generation of leadership.

The proliferation of missions is attributed in some cases to the fact that the non-relatives in missions have felt that they have no chance of leadership if they continue with certain existing missions. When the leadership issue explodes, there is much politicking without the matter being dealt with at the leadership level. Often matters have been taken to the grassroots level for a political campaign. Culturally, there is very little direct talk in private. Matters are reduced to clichés, or the confrontation is postponed until the issue blows up in the faces of the ones involved.

This problem has to be recognised and tackled immediately by the present leaders. Executive boards, especially the "Yes Boss" ones, must start asking pertinent questions to the existing directors on this issue without threatening the leadership. The boards need to become a positive influence in placing the leaders of the future. Often the boards themselves get used to certain leaders and become complacent. They complain when the team breaks down because the leadership is in a rut and is nonproductive. Instead, the boards need to become proactive and guiding groups.

This is again a matter of biblical ethos being exercised. Openness, honesty, brokenness, confronting issues as soon as possible, and believing the best in each

---

[11] Already several cases of this problem have been reported around the country.

other, especially at the leadership level, must take place, or else the missions will inevitably break down. Evangelicalism without the practice of the above ethos will be worse than secular political leadership. May God save the missions from such disaster. May God help each of the leaders to be serious in the responsibilities toward the men and women God has placed in their hands. May the leaders be the stewards of the ministry and pass it on to good, growing leadership. May they cause the talents of their people to proliferate and let many ministries blossom to tackle the issue of unreached India. Pray!

Conclusion

In the 53 years since Indian independence, missions have sprouted, and the churches have matured. Many associations, networks, and support groups have emerged. In spite of the progress, there are dichotomies in ethos, a lack of consensus, and a lack of comprehensive strategies. There is a sense of fragmentation in missions which needs to be mended. This is seen in the ambiguity of concepts and duplication of efforts. Missions in general are heading off on a slight tangent in terms of where they ought to target. There has to be more application of biblical principles to keep missions close to God's intention for the fulfilment of the Great Commission of the Lord Jesus Christ. This is necessary for a true Evangelical missiology which will help Indian evangelisation move in the direction it should go.

All the mentioned confusions in Indian missions today have to be vigorously worked out, even the ones that come from outside India. Each issue must be thought through, and both local and international flaws must be dealt with. To impact all of India, more appreciation, trust, cooperation, and supportiveness of each other are needed to keep missions moving forward

in unison. The future of mission recruiting efforts depends heavily on how existing missionaries are treated. The future missions leadership will depend on how new leaders are groomed and mentored over a long period of time. Waiting until the present leadership can no longer serve before transferring the reins of leadership will cause missions to suffer and become ineffective in their missionary vision and movement.

Evangelical Christianity and missions basically flow from the experience of the Lordship of Christ in the daily lives of individuals. If the Lordship of Christ is ignored, then self will take over and destroy the missions. Indian missions need many models of leadership and not just talkers. Thus the contribution of Evangelical missiology needs to be seen in each of the above areas in order to impact the nation for Christ.

Appendix:
The Realities of
Actual Indian Challenges
in Presenting the Gospel

1. Massive population growth

India's population has burgeoned since its independence:

    1947 – 400 million
    1987 – 800 million
    1997 – 950 million

The percentage of Christians ranges from 2.6% to 4% across the nation (Johnstone, 1993, p. 274). The unfinished task of reaching all peoples, including the population that is added every year, is daunting. While many are coming to Christ, the evangelistic efforts are not keeping up with the population growth. Thus the percentage of Christians will remain the same or will decline.

As the population grows, there is a need for innovative multiple means, methods, and mission partnerships to present

Christ to the masses. Harvesting missions must humbly acknowledge the grace of God in using other agencies and methods to bring people groups to Christ. Such an understanding increases the mutual respect of Indian missions with empathy and appreciation.

2. The status of women

According to the 1991 census, India has 437,597,929 males and 406,332,932 females. Andrea Singh (1983, p. 103) observes, "India is one of the few countries in the world where males outnumber the females in the population as a whole, and the gap is steadily increasing." The sex ratio in India has always been in favour of males (Matthew, 1995, p. 462).

"The teachings of the Bible will help people with renewed minds to understand the equality of men and women as the equal creation of God. Till then, dowry deaths and perpetuators of gender violence will go unpunished" ("5,000," 1997, p. 7).

"Women have a very important place in influencing their family to certain religious, cultural, and social values" (Pramila, *Urban*, p. 17). "In the Indian society, generally women have been the custodians of religious faith" (Hedlund, 1992, p. xi). "The condition of women is the truest test of a people's civilisation. Her status is her country's barometer" (Azariah, 1915, p. 18). Traditionally, non-Christian Indian women can be reached only by Christian women. Men cannot influence them as much as women (Athyal, 1995, p. 108). "Women are more receptive to the gospel in most instances than men, and they are easily reached by the women missionaries" (Abraham, 1992, p. 104).[12] Thus there is a great need to plan creatively to help the women of India to understand Christ.

Most women in mission are prepared to be assistants and prospective wives. Very little emphasis has been given to the need for women to win the women of India (Pramila, 1997). Often it is automatically assumed that missionary wives will do this. However, this is not the case, as many wives struggle to survive in the mission field looking after the needs of their husbands and children and offering hospitality to the cascading crowds. Most wives trained for mission have ended up assisting their husbands in their ministry, which has had a very positive effect. This configuration of a husband and wife team is good and has some influence among the women. However, could there be more ways to reach half of the population of India apart from reaching them incidentally as a by-product?

Historically, since there is no alternative, the male missionaries have taken this challenge on themselves as a general strategy, without any specific plan. This muddles the mission trainers, as they are unable to train women for anything specific. "What God intended for the Christian woman was partnership with men in the ministry and mission of the church. However, those in charge of training programmes for women and full-time workers found the obstacles to partnership so many and so formidable that they kept wondering out loud what specifically they were training the women for" (Wigan, 1948; cited in Webster & Webster, 1985, p. 38).

Most women missionaries who have been recruited for missions serve either in Christian schools, hostels, or mission offices. Very few end up directly influencing non-Christian women for Christ (Annathai, 1995). Apart from these indirect

---

[12] It has also been noticed that some Christian women influence their neighbours especially through the children. This needs to be explored more in the future.

ventures, there has not been any specific emphasis on reaching the women of India on a mass scale. Operation Mobilisation's Gospel in Action Fellowship and Blessing Youth Mission have extremely effective women's ministries. According to the latest research (Pothen, 1990, p. 255), 72% of the national women missionaries are working with Pentecostal-Charismatic Missions (PCM) (P. T. Abraham, 1992, p. 104). In spite of the above efforts, very little is being done by Christian women to reach out to other women, compared to the outreach by men missionaries to other men.

There has been much talk and very little action on a large scale to affect Indian women. Even if there were training centres available, missions usually have not known the proper way to employ trained women missionaries, especially if they were single. Hedlund (1992, p. xi) aptly summarises the situation by saying, "The role of women in ministry has been a neglected theme among Indians.[13] Significant conversion movements to Christ in Andra Pradesh and other areas are led by women." Graham Houghton in his research found that the Muslim *Zenana*[14] and the upper class Hindu women are out of reach of evangelism by male members. Thus it becomes apparent that it is necessary to establish special work among these women who live behind *Pardah*.[15] In light of this, Houghton (pp. 79-80) notes, "It was deemed necessary to employ a special female agency, known as Bible

women, to reach them and enlighten them in their homes."

If Indian women are touched with the gospel, they will influence their families more than many men (Pramila, *Urban*, p. 47). Thus, it is imperative to reach women with the gospel by innovative means, in order to influence the society through them. Ironically, oblivious to this situation, with very few exceptions, the majority of mission workers are men, even though nearly 50% of the population of India consists of women. What will the implications of this oversight be?

3. Cities and the urbanites

Almost 30% of India's population—300 million—live in cities. There are six megacities having more than 8 million people each and 303 cities with more than 100,000 people each (IMA, 1996, p. 4). Many from the rural population have been moving to urban areas in search of better income and education, even though the living conditions in the cities for these new migrants are deplorable (Abraham, 1992, p. 9). The urban poor and the middle class must be targeted and reached with the gospel. Kevin Murphy, a business executive, reminds us, "There is more to India than Mother Teresa and her poor charges" (Matthew, 1995, p. 547).

The urban worldview is shaped, first of all, by the environment and associations. Secondly, it is shaped by education and enlightened minds. Thirdly, industrialisation, automation, and modern tech-

---

[13] In Christian circles, the topic of women in ministry centres around whether women are to be ordained in the church as the pastors or not. The equal partnership of women in the mission field is a subject largely bypassed, knowingly at times!

[14] *Zenana* means "women" in the Urdu language. Thus the term "zenana work," that is, the work among women, came into being.

[15] *Pardah* means "veil, curtain." Even today in most villages, women live behind the curtains. Without covering their faces, they do not venture into an open area. Even if they are emancipated from covering their heads, they do not sit with visitors in the sitting room with the men. This scene is slowly changing in the city areas.

nology have caused city dwellers to be more efficient and competitive in their jobs (Misra, pp. 5-6). Further, materialism and consumerism have changed people's lives. The mass media—radio, television, cinema, newspapers, and magazines—have swayed people for both good and bad with their appeals. Lastly, the process of internationalisation and globalisation has opened people's minds to new worlds. Brand new worldviews and ethos have emerged. New values have blended with old perceptions, beliefs, and lifestyles. Thus, cities today offer many opportunities and are composed of a new class of people for whom the missions in India are hardly prepared!

The church and missions need to plan strategies to reach the powerful, growing, urban middle class while these people are open, before they settle down in their new society and become complacent to the gospel of Christ.

Urban church planting among the middle class is a pioneering effort in most cities. This situation will not change unless there is a new perspective, in contrast to the old one in which missions means targeting tribals, the down-trodden, and the rejected poor. Thus the scope of missions must become broader. Would that the church and missions become like Abraham praying for the salvation of Sodom and Gomorrah!

4. The educated

India's literacy rate has risen from 5.1% in 1901 to 52.21% in 1991 (Sachdeva, 1995, p. 712). The reading appetite of the educated has grown enormously. The newspaper industry illustrates this point. "At the end of 1991, the number of newspapers [dailies, tri/biweeklies, and other periodicals] stood at 30,214 compared to 28,491 in 1990, showing an increase of 6% during the year" (Sachdeva, 1995, p. 773).

While the missions have sat back and have not produced a single Christian magazine, the secular press has presented the public with an astonishing array of innovative literature. Most of the books produced for the non-Christian masses are not well understood by the public. Many Indians read Christian devotional literature along with other religious books, but a punch line to help them decide to follow Christ is often missing!

In this present challenge, very little effort has been made to place quality Christian literature in the hands of the educated. Most evangelistic books translated from non-Indian writers come with funds for printing, but they are often culturally irrelevant. Very little has been done to encourage Indian writers of evangelistic literature. One exception is the Centre for Communication Skills (CCS),[16] which has worked hard to encourage Christian journalism. More encouragement is needed for Christian Indian writers, and funds need to be made available to print their works. There are a few professional Christian journalists in the press. They also need to be encouraged and need to have their skills tapped. The reading, globalising, information-hunting, educated masses certainly need to be targeted in communication. This is a challenge for both the missions and the churches.

5. The illiterates

Despite 50 years of reforms, approximately 50% of the total population in India is still illiterate. Of this group who can neither read nor write, 35% are men and 65% are women. Half of the 200 million

---

[16] Contact information: Mrs. and Mr. Pamela and George Ninan, Centre for Communication Skills: Equipping and Empowering Witnesses in the Market Place, 9, Ashoka Road, Ashville Apts., St. Thomas Town, Bangalore, India 560084. Phone: 5476998.

children in India do not attend school (Prayer Concerns, 1997). Paul J. Koola (1979, p. 104) maintains, "Illiteracy accounts for many a superstitious belief that makes man nothing more than a two-legged beast.... Intellectual poverty is more dreadful than the economic poverty." Taking the gospel meaningfully to the illiterates still lingers as a challenge.

6. The expansive geography: PIN codes

Because India is so vast geographically, the country is officially divided into small sections designated Postal Index Numbers (PIN) code areas, each having about 30,000 people. Out of 28,000 PIN code areas, nearly 20,000 do not have a single pastor, evangelist, missionary, or Christian development worker residing among them (Prayer Resources, 1997, p. 24).

7. People groups

There are about 920 people groups in India, each with a population of over 10,000. At present, only about 300 of these groups have any Christian witness or congregation. An IMA report (IMA, 1997) indicates that 204 peoples with populations of over 50,000 are yet to be reached. These groups have no known witnesses among them.

8. Multiplicity of languages

There are 219 language groups in India, each with more than 10,000 speakers. Eighty-five of these language groups do not have even a single verse of Scripture in their language. The Bible is available in only 46 of the Indian languages, and the *Jesus* film has been dubbed into only 47 languages (*Indian Missions*, 1997, p. 24). Jacob George (1997), coordinator of the Indian Institute of Cross-Cultural Communications (IICCC),[17] reports that 170 Bible translators have been trained, and translation of Scripture is being attempted in 34 languages. Much more needs to be done to get the Word into the local languages of the people.

9. Islam

There are 140 million Muslims in India. This is one of the world's largest and most accessible Muslim communities (AD 2000 & Beyond, 1997, p. 11). Based on the size of the Muslim population, at least 14% of India's missionary force should be working among this group. Ironically, only about 80 Christian workers are serving here. The missions have not been making any concerted efforts to strengthen this force. Among the 125 member missions of IMA, only two or three agencies have had anything exclusively to do with Muslims.

The reasons cited for this lack of ministry among Muslims are that the mainstream missions and the churches do not understand the work among the Muslims, nor are they burdened to work among them (Abubakker, 1996). In addition, the missions have felt that the Muslims are hard to reach and are unresponsive to the gospel. Thus, missions bypass the Muslims to "win the winnables" who are ready to respond.[18] Many missions and churches do not even recognise the various Muslim groups existing in different parts of India (*Reaching*, p. 1).

---

[17] The IICCC is the Bible translation wing of the India Missions Association. It sponsors translation work through the missionaries who work among people who do not have the Scriptures in their languages. The number of Indian missionaries thus trained is slowly increasing. These translators are starting to bear the fruit of Scripture portions in the languages where they work.

[18] The usual debate by many missions is, "Why work among the hard peoples while there are many 'winnables' among whom much has to be done?"

There is a need for creative approaches to reach Muslims. One such effort is a new English New Testament that is being published for a Muslim audience. *Pulse* (News, 1996) reported, "Missionaries are nearing completion of an English-language New Testament for Muslims. The volume uses familiar names such as Ibrahim for Abraham and Yakub for Jacob. It will have a culturally appropriate cover and illustrations. An estimated 5% to 25% of Muslims worldwide speak English." Such attempts have been made in Urdu, Hindi, and other languages, but this is one of the first attempts to produce an English Bible to fill the need.

There is a need not only to reach Muslims with the gospel, but also to acknowledge those who work with Muslims. We need to encourage these Christian workers, train them, stand with them, and send more people to reach out into the neighbourhoods of Muslims with the gospel. Abubakker (1996) points out, "Even in the Bible seminaries, studying comparative religions should result in leading at least one or two Muslims to Christ."

The fault of not reaching out to Muslims must be taken seriously and must be remedied in the future, or else unreached Muslims will continue to be the foremost failure of missions in India.

10. Marginalised Dalits and tribals

In the Indian population, 20% are Dalits, and 8% are scheduled tribes (IMA, 1996, p. 3). Henry Thiagaraj (1997, based on 1981 statistics) comments, "The Dalits have a very low literacy. For instance, the Dalit women have only about 11% literacy, whereas women from the other communities have about 20% literacy." With some

controversy, Dalits have been classified as Hindus. Many Dalits struggle to accept themselves as Hindus, because of the kind of treatment they encounter from the upper caste Hindus. Tribals are not Hindus, since they are actually animists (spirit worshippers).

As Dalits and tribals become Christians, they are discriminated against and are denied government scholarships and reservations given to other Dalits and tribals. More than anything else, bringing justice from the oppression of the caste system will free the nation to enjoy greater economic and spiritual growth. Dalits and tribals have actually not realised the true independence which is supposedly enjoyed by all Indians.

11. The neglect of the handicapped

According to the 1981 census, there were 9 million visually handicapped individuals in India. Every seventh Indian was a blind person.[19] Apart from the blind, 10% of all Indians are handicapped in other ways (Prabhu Rayan, 1999). Chinnasamy Sekar (1997), the director of Living Light, has adamantly refused to move to any other ministry and has committed himself to work among the handicapped. He and his wife strongly feel that God has kept them among these people to serve them. They are involved in leading many to Christ. Sekar reasons that there are very few churches in Bangalore which are able to receive and accommodate handicapped people. He runs a hostel for the blind and personally looks after them and feeds them for a small cost. He feels that running a hostel and feeding the blind keep him close to the reality of his call, so it is not just theory for him.

---

[19] A person is classified as blind if his visual acuity is 20/200. This means that what he sees with difficulty at a distance of 20 feet can be seen clearly from a distance of 200 feet by someone with normal vision.

R. Z. Prabhu Rayan (1990, p. 30) feels that two main hindrances for this ministry are the ignorance and the attitude of Christians. Christians have to be made aware of this need. Prabhu Rayan suggests that in the future every church and mission could plan to work among the blind and could also integrate them into church life. Sam Danaseelan (1999) of Mission to the Blind continues to work with all the blind. He is especially concerned for over 400 blind individuals working in various jobs in Chennai, as they need ongoing help in other areas of life to continue working.

Sue Stillman (1990), from the *Nambikkai* Foundation and working among the deaf, shares that it takes a lot of patience, perseverance, love, and encouragement to reach out to the deaf. To communicate the gospel, all types of tools and methods have to be employed. Stillman indicates that it would be better to train Christians who are deaf themselves so they can share Christ with others. She says that the deaf have a very low self-image. Sekar (1997) says that this is true of most handicapped persons. Thus he himself spends much time counselling and encouraging these people. Special efforts must be made to impact the 10% of the Indian population who are handicapped.

12. Global Indian missionaries

Secular Indians have felt the need to stick together in spite of their diaspora to other countries around the world. Ramyata Limbu (1997) notes, "At Katmandu more than 400 people of Indian origin gathered ... to discuss and deliberate on the challenges faced in their respective countries of adoption and in the world."

In fulfilling the Great Commission of the Lord Jesus Christ, Indian Christians have two responsibilities. One is to reach their own diaspora fellow Indians. Second,

they need to reach others for Christ around the world. In the efforts to send Indian missionaries to other countries, money has been a deterring and limiting factor, especially when sending missionaries to countries that are economically well off, where the cost of living is higher. The North African countries, the newly opened CIS countries, and South Asia have become the focus in recent years.

"Indian missionaries abroad? Will it work? Why not? If Indian textile businessmen can flourish in Central Asia, if MARUTI and TATA can run in Central Asian roads, why can't we send missionaries there?" (OM India News, 1997). Many missions such as CCC, SISWA, OM, IEHC, GFA, KEF, BCM, EUSI, IEM, and others are already progressing in this direction.

Conclusion

Even though the numbers of missions and missionaries have spiralled upward, they are only a drop in the bucket in meeting the ocean of Indian challenges. The unchanging gospel has to be presented to the people of India against this backdrop. Whether the churches and missions are up to these new challenges or not will only be known in the future as they respond. Over 60% of India's missionaries are still concentrated among about 20% of India's population. Missions executives need to plan afresh with a new perspective if the gospel is to affect the whole of India. Unless a new strategy is administered, India will continue to be the greatest challenge for the gospel. The work can only be done with a core belief that the gospel is the only way to bring about a change for the better of human behaviours and to create an improved society. Only then will missions echo the Apostle Paul, saying, "I am not ashamed of the gospel, because it is the power of God for the salvation of everyone who believes" (Rom. 1:16).

References

Abraham, P. T. (1992). Pentecostal-charismatic missionary outreach. In S. Lazarus (Ed.), *Proclaiming Christ*. Madras, India: Church Growth Association of India.

Abraham, V. (1992, June). The call of Indian cities. *Aim, 23*(16), p. 9.

Abubakker. (1996, August 31). FFNI. Interview in Vellore, India.

AD 2000 & Beyond. (1997). *To the uttermost part: The call to North India*. Colorado Springs, CO: AD 2000 & Beyond & Joshua Project.

Albert, S. V. (1995). *A portrait of India III*. Madras, India: Church Growth Association of India.

Anderson, N., with Anderson, J. (1993). *Daily in Christ: A devotional*. Eugene, OR: Harvest House Publishers.

Annathai. (1995, October). Former missionary with FMPB and OM. Personal interview.

Arles, S. Evangelical movement in India: An evaluation. In Arles & Benwati (Eds.), *Pilgrimage 2100* (pp. 32-34).

Athyal, S. M. (1995). *Indian women in mission*. Bihar, India: Mission Educational Books.

Azariah, V. S. (1915). *India and missions*. Madras, India: CLS.

Beaver, R. P. (1981). The history of mission strategy. In R. D. Winter & S. C. Hawthorne (Eds.), *Perspectives on the world Christian movement: A reader*. Pasadena, CA: William Carey Library.

Danaseelan, S. (1999, May 2). Director of Mission to the Blind. Interview in Chennai, India.

Daniel, R. T. (1997, April–June). Evangelists need more. *Insight India: Assembly testimony journal*.

———. (1997, April–June). Missionary's cost index. *Insight India: Assembly testimony journal*.

Das. *The Evangelical roots: 1793-1966*.

Dozo, P. (1984, April–June). Awakening resulting in church growth in the hills. *ICGQ*, p. 23.

EFI. (1991). *To God be the glory 1951–1991: 40 years of the EFI*.

Firth, C. B. (1961). *An introduction to Indian church history*. Madras, India: CLS.

5,000 dowry deaths a year. (1997, August 15). *The Asian Age*, p. 7.

Fuller, W. H. (1980). *Mission-church dynamics: How to change bicultural tensions into dynamic missionary outreach*. Pasadena, CA: William Carey Library.

George, J. (1997, June 18). IICCC Coordinator. Fax.

Gnanadasan, A. (1998). Mission mandate. In L. D. Pate (Ed.), *From every people: A handbook of Two-Thirds World missions, with directory, histories, analysis* (pp. 461-492). Monrovia, CA: MARC.

Harris, J. J. (1997). *The theological pilgrimage of the Indian church: A study of contrast – The futility of polarisation*. Doctoral dissertation, SAIACS.

Headland, I. T. (1912). *Some by-products of missions*. New York: The Methodist Book Concern.

Hedlund, R. E. (1986, April–June). Christianity in India. *ICGQ*, p. 154.

———. (1992). Introduction. In S. Lazarus (Ed.), *Proclaiming Christ*. Madras, India: Church Growth Association of India.

Houghton, G. *Dependency*.

IMA. (1996). *My prayer guide*. Madras, India: IMA.

———. (1997, November 13). Letter to the CEOs of member missions.

Indian Missions. (1997, January–March).

Jayaprakash, L. J. (1987). *Evaluation of indigenous missions in India*. Madras, India: CGRC.

Johnstone, P. J. (1993). *Operation world: The day-by-day guide to praying for the world*. Carlisle, England: OM Books.

Keyes, L. E. (1983). The new age of cooperation. In T. Williams (Ed.). *Together in missions*. Bangalore, India: WEF.

Koola, P. J. (1979). *Population and manipulation*. Bangalore, India: Asian Trading Corporation.

Limbu, R. (1997, August 24). People of Indian origin abroad meet in Nepal. *The Asian Age*, p. 4.

Massey, A. K. (1992). Challenges to mission in North India. In S. Lazarus (Ed.), *Proclaiming Christ*. Madras, India: Church Growth Association of India.

Matthew, K. M. (Ed.). (1995). *Manorama year book 1995*. Kotayam, India: Manorama Publications.

McMahon, R. J. (1971). *To God be the glory: The EFI of India 1951–1971*. New Delhi: MSS.

Misra, B. B. *The Indian middle classes*.

Newbigin, L. (1977). *The good shepherd: Meditations on Christian ministry in today's world*. Grand Rapids, MI: Wm. B. Eerdmans Publishing Co.

News. (1996, September 6). *Pulse*.

Nicholls, B. The gospel in Indian culture. In M. E. Sargunam (Ed.), *Mandate*.

Ninan, G. *Partnership*.

Norris, F. W. (1984). God and the gods: Expect footprints. In D. Priest, Jr. (Ed.), *Unto the uttermost: Missions in the Christian churches/churches of Christ*. Pasadena, CA: William Carey Library.

OM India news. (1997, July). *India Area Communiqué*.

Pate, L. D. (1991). Two-Thirds World missions. In W. D. Taylor (Ed.), *Internationalizing missionary training: A global perspective*. Grand Rapids, MI: Baker Book House.

Paul, R. D. (1952). *The cross over India*. London: SCM Press.

Pillai, S. (1997, September 10). Interview in Chennai, India.

Ponraj, S. D. *Church growth studies in mission*.

Pothen, A. (1990). *Indigenous cross-cultural missions in India and their contributions to church growth*. Doctoral dissertation. Pasadena, CA: Fuller Theological Seminary.

Prabhu Rayan, R. Z. (1990). Ministry among the visually handicapped people. In R. Z. Prabhu Rayan (Ed.), *Changing world*. Madras, India: UESI.

———. (1999, June 25). Executive Director of India Fellowship for Visually Handicapped. Interview in Chennai, India.

Pramila, R. (1997, November). Former women's leader of OM India. Personal interview.

———. *The urban Christian wife*.

Prayer concerns. (1997, August–September). *O.M. Arpana prayer letter*.

Prayer resources based on research done by IMA. (1997, January–March). *Indian Missions*.

Priest, D., Jr. (1984). A Maasai purification ceremony. In D. Priest, Jr. (Ed.), *Unto the uttermost: Missions in the Christian churches/churches of Christ*. Pasadena, CA: William Carey Library.

Rajendran, K. (1996). *Understanding the finality of Christ and its effect in the mission field*. Bangalore, India: Unpublished paper written for SAIACS.

———. (1998). *Which way forward India missions?* Bangalore, India: SAIACS.

Rao, O. M. *Some concerns of the Indian church*.

Reaching Bombay's Muslims.

Richard, H. L., & Mangalwadi, V. (1997, August). A review dialogue. *To All Men All Things, 7*(1), p. 8.

Sachdeva (Ed.). (1995). *Competition 1995*.

Sekar, C. (1997, March 12). Interview in Bangalore, India.

Shunmugam, D., & Shunmugam, G. (1997, July). Ex-missionaries to North India. Interview in Chennai, India.

Singh, A. M. (1983). Rural-urban migration of women: Some implications for urban planning. In A. de Souza (Ed.), *Urban growth and urban planning*. New Delhi: Indian Social Institute.

Singh, K. (1992). *India: An introduction*. New Delhi: Vision Books.

Soltau, S. *Mission at the cross roads*.

Stillman, S. (1990). Ministry to the handicapped (deaf). In R. Z. Prabhu Rayan (Ed.), *Changing world* (pp. 33-38). Madras, India: UESI.

Sunder Raj, E. (1997, June 16). Interview in Chennai, India.

———. (1997, July 17). Interview in Chennai, India.

———. (1997, September 12). Interview in Chennai, India, for the magazine *Mission Frontiers*.

Sunder Raj, E., & Team (Eds.). (1992). *Management of Indian missions*. Chennai, India: India Missions Association.

Theerthan, J. D. *Choice before India*.

Thiagaraj, H. (1997, June 9). Managing Trustee of Dalit Liberation Education Trust and the Convenor of Human Rights Education Movement of India. Open letter to all concerned following the presentation of the paper, *Statement of the Dalit Liberation*

Education Trust in the Working Group on Minorities of the United Nations Human Rights Commission: Geneva. Paper presented in the UN Working Group on Minorities, Third Session (26-30 May, 1997), Geneva, Switzerland.

Thiessen, J. C. (1955). *A survey of world missions.* Chicago: Inter-Varsity Press.

Wagner, C. P. (1981). *Church growth and the whole gospel: A biblical mandate.* San Francisco: Harper & Row.

Webster, J. C. B., & Webster, E. L. (Eds.). (1985). *The church and women in the Third World.* Philadelphia, PA: Westminster Press.

Wigan, M. H. (1948, October). Educated Christian women and missionary vocation. *NCCR,* pp. 408-413.

Winston, S. Life savers. In Rathnakumar & Krupa (Eds.), *Mission and vision.*

————. (1997, August). IMA Management Consultant. Interview in Chennai, India.

————. (1997, September). IMA Management Consultant. Interview in Chennai, India.

K. Rajendran, a pioneer missionary and a missionary trainer, has been in Christian leadership both in India and abroad. Originally from Tamil Nadu, be has nearly 30 years of experience in missions with over 25 years in Operation Mobilisation. Now be is the General Secretary of India Missions Association, one of the largest mission associations in the world with over 125 mission agencies representing 20,000 missionaries. Rajendran lives with his wife Pramila, daughter Preeti and son Pradeep. He earned his doctorate in missiology from South Asian Institute of Advanced Studies (SAIACS) at Bangalore. He is an Executive Committee member of the WEF Missions Commission.

F LYING HIGH OVER the Sahara, I could see only a stark landscape, with rocks emerging from the sand and up-start hills giving way to the rugged mountains farther north. Later, driving in the same region with my family in our trusty Peugeot 505, we discovered many surprises. To the delight of my children, the rocky ground was littered with fossils indicating a long-disappeared but once verdant region. Then we spotted the little flowers, tiny dots of beauty responding to the recent sprinkling of rain. Driving further, we were overwhelmed by a rich band of green. Date trees and other fruits flourished, their roots digging deep to find the ancient underground springs, and the oasis dwellers and their camels were refreshed by the water bubbling to the surface.

Reflecting on Middle East missiology has reminded me of that oasis. The first, but false, impression as an Evangelical looking in from the outside may be that there is little to be found except a few fossils from the ancient past. The second impression, giving yet another partial view, is that there are only a few flowers, beautiful but very fragile. The fullness, though, is that in a hostile environment, sweet fruit springs to life, nourishing those who live there and providing delight to the fortunate ones who, though living far away, are yet privileged to eat these dates of the desert.

An Overview of the Current Setting

The Middle East provides a rich diversity of peoples, geography, and religious expression. Stretching from Mauritania and Morocco on the Atlantic to Iran on the Caspian Sea, the region is inhabited by some 414 million people. Perhaps 17 million Middle Easterners are part of one of the many Christian communities of the region, with about 1.5

22

Ancient springs and sweet fruit: missiological contributions from the Middle East

DAVID
GREENLEE

million who identify themselves as Protestant or Anglican (Wasiim, 1993.)

Ethnicity and economics

Arabic, of course, is the principal language of the region, binding together the diverse ethnic groups collectively known as the Arabs. But Arabic, in its many dialects, is not the only language, and Arabs are not the only ethnic groups of the Middle East.[1] Millions of North Africans prefer to speak one of a number of Berber languages, tracing their ethnic heritage to a time long before the Arab Muslim armies advanced. Persian Iranians speak Farsi, and Turks speak Turkish, but in these countries large but minority ethnic groups speak Kurdish, Azeri, Armenian, and other languages. And, of course, Jews speak Hebrew.

Economically we can divide the region into three strata (Myers, 1998). A privileged few, including those with Gulf oil wealth, other business elite, and royalty, make up the rich. Some countries, such as Tunisia, have done well at producing an economic middle class, people who are able to live above the level of basic necessities. But throughout this region, there are large numbers of the very poor. Unemployment and underemployment are at a critical stage in many countries of the Middle East.

Christian presence in the Middle East

Another important division of the Middle East is in terms of Christian presence. We can somewhat loosely consider three regions:

Region 1: Egypt, Sudan, Jordan, Israel, Iraq, Lebanon, Syria, Turkey, and Iran. In these countries, there is an existing Christian presence made up of communities and churches that trace their roots back to pre-Islamic times. These churches are recognized by the government, although newer churches and especially converts from Islam may not have legal recognition.

Region 2: Kuwait, Qatar, the United Arab Emirates, Oman, Saudi Arabia, Bahrain, Yemen, and Libya. The ancient Christian communities have disappeared in these countries. There are very few, if any, national Christians today, but there are large numbers of expatriate Christians.

Region 3: Mauritania, Morocco, Algeria, and Tunisia. The ancient Christian communities have disappeared. There are very few national Christians and only small numbers of expatriate Christians.

The differences in these regions should not be underestimated in reflecting on Christian presence and witness. In Region 1, even if Arab Christians are viewed as a distinct community, there is at least a recognition of the existence of this group. But in Morocco, secondary school students of several major cities in 1989 perceived no distinction between Arabs and Muslims, nor did they even give recognition to another possibility, since "Arabic-speaking people are, *ipso facto*, viewed as Muslims" (Suleiman, 1989, p. 20). While Jordan's king includes senior church leaders among his circle of advisors, Morocco's King Hassan II told the representative of Pope John Paul II, *"Monseigneur, il n'exist pas de population marocaine chrétienne"* ("Monseigneur, there are no Moroccan Christians") (Laurent, 1993, p. 235)—even while his police had frequently detained and at times abused those who had turned to Christ.

Christians in the Middle East can be broadly grouped into four categories. For a fuller review of the subject, consider, on

---

[1] Unless otherwise noted, I will use "Middle East" hereafter to refer to the broader region including North Africa, Sudan, Iran, and Turkey.

an introductory level, Myers (1998). Napper (1992) provides a more complete treatment by an Evangelical missionary, and for a detailed treatment of the subject, read Horner (1989) or the excellent overview of the Middle East Council of Churches (1986).

In Region 1 we find the ancient churches which trace a continuous presence over hundreds of years. These churches can be grouped into four categories (Napper, 1992, pp. 15-16):

• The Assyrian Church of the East, sometimes called the Nestorians, separated from others in the 5th century over the doctrine of the nature of Christ.

• The Oriental Orthodox churches, including the Armenian, Ethiopian, Syrian, and Coptic (Egyptian), separated from Constantinople by the year 500 in disagreement with the conclusions of the Council of Chalcedon.

• The Eastern Orthodox churches include those with patriarchs in Alexandria, Cyprus, Jerusalem, Antioch, and Constantinople (now Istanbul).

• The Uniate churches, or Eastern Catholic, include the Armenian Catholics, Coptic Catholics, Syrian Catholics, Chaldeans, and Maronites. In large part, these churches were formed from those who turned in theology and allegiance from their traditional head to Rome.

A second group, also principally in Region 1, are those Protestant[2] churches which trace their roots to missions from America and Europe which began in the 1800s. Most of their members came from the ancient churches.

A third group are the Muslim background believers (MBBs), "people from Muslim families who have turned to Christ. They are found in Orthodox, Catholic, and Protestant churches, and in none" (Myers, 1998). And, of course, they are found in churches and cell groups made up entirely of MBBs.

Finally, a fourth group are the expatriate Christians.[3] Their presence is of particular significance in Region 2. The national origin of these expatriates is global, from India to the Philippines to North America, across Europe and including several countries of Region 1. Their various host country governments often allow a degree of freedom for public worship within the confines of the expatriate, non-Islamic community.

Muslim attitudes toward Christians

Finally, we must briefly consider the Muslim attitude toward Christians in their midst. Bishop Kenneth Cragg (1979, p. 274), respected by Muslims and Christians alike for his intimate knowledge of Islam and Islamic culture, reminds us: "Here we need to remember that Islam is far other than a religious option of opinions, freely chosen or freely abandoned. It is a totality which includes a dimension very like nationality, as well as belief. There is no more tenacious community than Islam. The traditional concept of apostasy is the negative side of this. Islam, at least in Arab and most Asian lands, is hardly yet a faith one is free to leave. Its tolerance, historically, has meant a freedom of continuing what one may have been, if born outside it, e.g., Jewish or Christian. Or it meant a freedom to migrate into Islam. There was no liberty for the born Muslim to migrate

---

[2] Although "Evangelical" is often used to describe these churches, since they do not all adhere to "Evangelical theology" in WEF terminology, I will refer to these churches as "Protestant."

[3] Here I refer to the general expatriate population, not to those small numbers who have intentionally gone as missionaries to a number of Middle Eastern countries.

out of it. It was never supposed that a Muslim would desire to become anything else, and were he to do so it would be indicative of the utmost perversity.... The role of minorities is notoriously difficult in many cultures. Islam has a better record than some, in letting 'others' be. But they have to be 'others.' ... It does not envisage that minorities can, should, or may expect to recruit from its own ranks. They may persist by dint of their own natal fertility and their spiritual survival power."

This comment about survival leads us into a consideration of the missiological contribution of the Middle East by looking to the region's rich past.

Missiological Contributions From the Past

The Bible is a Middle Eastern book. Until Acts 16, the human events recorded took place on Middle Eastern soil. Drawing on a childhood and career rooted in Middle Eastern lands, Kenneth Bailey (1983, 1992) aptly illustrates that the Bible is best understood when we also understand its original setting. Although we recognize that God speaks to all humanity through the Bible and that even Middle Eastern culture does not alone unlock all its truth, insights from the historical past as well as the modern Middle Eastern milieu will aid us in our missiology, wherever we are.

Where did missiology begin? Andrew Walls (1999) suggests that Origen, born about 185 A.D. in Alexandria, deserves the title "Father of Mission Studies." "He saw the need for Egyptian gold and Egyptian cloth to furnish the tabernacle in the wilderness, and he turned the learning of the Greek world to the worship and glorification of God." But Origen also saw that

"spoiling the Egyptians" was no easy matter. Far more followed the paths of Jeroboam, who brought from Egypt the idea of the golden calves set up at Bethel and Dan, than those who took what is useful to make objects for divine worship (Walls, 1999, p. 104).

Space allows us to touch on only a few of the significant missiological insights from this era. Issues such as persecution, the priesthood of all believers, the link between social action and evangelism, and the Christian's public role and apologetics in a hostile society are not merely 20th century issues.

Tertullian, born about 160 A.D. to a Roman centurion, observed from Carthage (modern Tunis) that "the blood of the martyrs," blood which he had too often seen spilled before and after his conversion, "is the seed of the church." Among his many writings are his later views maintaining the priesthood of all believers. "He maintained the right of any Christian man, if far from an existing church, to baptize, administer the Lord's Supper, and undertake any task normally reserved to the recognized leaders" (Daniel, 1992, pp. 190-191).

As the plague brought death to Carthage, Cyprian urged the Christians not to leave the city, but to care for the sick and bury the dead. Although he himself was martyred short years later, these acts of love did much to win the hearts of the people (Daniel, 1992, pp. 174-179).

Although the Islamic armies quickly took political power throughout much of the Middle East, religious conversion tended to spread over many decades, even centuries.[4] Born some 30 years after Muhammad, John of Damascus was the son of a government official in the Umayyad capital. After becoming the victim of

---

[4] See Ira Lapidus' (1988) comprehensive history for a readable but detailed study, especially pp. 242ff.

political intrigues, he became a monk. The miraculous restoration of his hand, severed by order of the caliph, was a sign of his innocence. The caliph, seeking to make amends, offered John great wealth and honors, but John refused everything (University of Balamand, n.d.). Known for his systematic formulation of Orthodox doctrines, he was also active in responding to Islamic theology during the middle of the 8th century. He referred to Islam as a Christian heresy. Some of his arguments, such as using Quranic titles for Jesus to argue for his divinity, are still used by Christians (Chapman, 1995, pp. 205-206; Nazir-Ali, 1983, p. 145).

Timothy, the Nestorian patriarch in Baghdad, had a similar level of dialogue with the Abassid court late in the 8th century. The anonymous correspondence between al-Hashimi and al-Kindi, written about 820 A.D., provides over 200 pages of Christian response to Islam, apologetic arguments which are still valid (Chapman, 1995, pp. 207-208; Nazir-Ali, 1983, p. 145).

In Cordoba, at the far end of the Arab world of the day, early in the 9th century a different approach was taken. In contrast to the accommodation of Islam afforded by many Christians, St. Eulogius' eschatology linked the Antichrist to Islam. His writings openly challenged the bases of Islamic faith. A martyrs' movement arose with at least 50 Christians beheaded over a decade. Only the Emir's threat that all Christians would be put to death caused moderate Christians to pressure the more radical to silence (Wolf, 1996).

The Crusades severely damaged the ancient churches of the East, contributing to the ascendancy of Islam and the eventual capture of Constantinople. Muslim minds were poisoned against Christianity. In the ensuing years, rather than creating initiatives to reach out to Islam, the ancient churches settled into something of a steady state in relationship with the po-litical rulers, whose attitudes toward the minority Christians varied over time. Attempts were made to minimize defections not only to Islam but also to missionary efforts from Rome. As Napper (1992, p. 12) observes, "Innovation was out. Community solidarity, religious and social, was all important." But Nazir-Ali (1983, p. 145) insists that "their tremendously important achievement in coming to terms with Islam and maintaining a Christian presence (however emasculated) in Muslim countries is often ignored when Muslim-Christian dialogue is discussed."

Western Protestant missionaries of the 1800s entered a setting dominated by Islam, in which the Orthodox patriarchates were weakend by the political power of the Ottoman rulers, although the Maronite and other Catholic churches displayed more vitality (Sabra, 1998). No simple explanation describes the motivations and strategies of these dedicated workers and the various agencies which sent them. One desired result, the conversion of numerous Muslims, was not achieved. However, two other results do affect mission in the Middle East today. Most obvious is the formation of the new Protestant churches, made up in large part of converts from the ancient churches. Less tangible yet significant are the challenges to trust and mutual understanding between the Protestants (including those who arrived in recent years) and other churches.

Contemporary Missiological Contributions of the Middle East Churches

Missiological contributions from the Middle East come in various forms. One contribution is found, and at times unfortunately lost, in the rich history of the region. More questions than answers are available concerning the early missionary successes of the Nestorians and Egyptian

Christians, the interaction of Christians with Muhammad in Arabia, and the failure of North African Christians to extend further south.

Today, freedom exists for public discussion of issues of importance to the legally established Christian communities. The websites of the Middle East Council of Churches (MECC), http://www.mecchurches.org/, and the Orthodox University of Balamand, http://www.balamand.edu.lb/ (including a link to their Center for Christian-Muslim Studies), demonstrate this freedom and provide a sampling of some of their missiological contributions.

However, once the focus switches from theology or internal affairs of the Christian community and from coexistence with the majority Muslims to intentional evangelistic outreach among Muslims and integration of Muslim converts into the churches, then, if anything is being said or done, there is no freedom for discussion in public forums. Some Middle Easterners do write on these themes, ranging from evangelistic websites and radio broadcasts to books and doctoral dissertations. But these expressions tend to be made only by those who live outside the region. Indeed, the very real security constraints which limit our brothers and sisters from openly disseminating their thoughts also limit the scope of this paper, lest we harm others through our incessant desire to know details which perhaps we do not need to know.

Having said this, among those involved in outreach among Muslims in the Middle East, there is a very significant missiology. Unlike what we might call the "formal missiology" associated with centers of formal education, I suggest that it is a "nonformal missiology" which fits in with the nonformal mode of training so vital to the growth of the church beyond its current perimeters.

Frieda Haddad (1987), from Lebanon, helps us see the importance of such a nonformal missiology in the Middle Eastern setting: "It has too often been forgotten in the past that for the Arab Middle East, the spoken word, not the written one, is the main cultural carrier.... Moreover, while speaking about the future of mission in such a culture, we have to bear in mind that the Arab culture, having been born in the desert, bears its stamp. In a desert the landscape is not cluttered with too many objects and therefore the eye is able to encompass vast expanses with great clarity. An object stands silhouetted against the barren land as well as the sky and is distinguishable from other objects so that the eye is able to take it in at one time in its entirety. It thus is in the habit of looking at the totality of the object rather than becoming entangled with details. The mind develops an approach to knowledge that has a tendency to emphasize the whole, not the part, of direct life experience rather than discursive knowledge, and therefore stresses faith-as-experience rather than as propagation of a body of doctrine. To the importance of what is 'heard,' we would also therefore stress what is 'seen.'"

What, then, are some of the issues of importance and key contributions from the Middle East?

Christian unity

Several streams have come together in the move toward formal unity among the churches of the Middle East (Middle East Council of Churches, 1998). As early as 1902, the Ecumenical (Orthodox) Patriarch of Constantinople issued an encyclical regarding relationships with Catholics and Protestants, while even before the 1910 Edinburgh conference Protestants had been seeking ways to work together.

Writing in 1955, the Iranian Anglican (now retired bishop) H. B. Dehqani-Taft (1955, p. 322) declared: "Inter-church cooperation and friendship are good, but they are not enough for a country like Iran. If the missionaries were certain to stay in the country indefinitely, and if there were no sense of urgency, church union might not have seemed so pressing. Things being as they are in the world today, at least the younger churches in Iran must unite in one organized church or, if one may dare to say so, face the possibility of extinction when the darkness comes."

Spiritual life, not formal unity, has doubtless been the key factor in preserving the Iranian churches since 1979. But such pressures on the churches helped lead to the formation of the Near East Christian Council in 1956 and, by 1974, the formation of the Middle East Council of Churches. With the inclusion approved in 1995 of the Ancient (Assyrian) Church of the East, all of the major conciliar churches of the region were linked.

Relationships between several Evangelical churches—and especially those scattered congregations of MBBs—and the churches of the MECC, however, have not reached such a degree of formal unity. Gabriel Habib, an Orthodox theologian and then Executive Secretary of the MECC, wrote an open letter to Evangelicals worldwide as they prepared for the 1989 Lausanne II congress (Habib, 1990). The theme of the congress, "Proclaim Christ Until He Comes: The Whole Church Taking the Whole Gospel to the Whole World," expressed an aim which, Habib stated, "Middle Eastern churches would support." Decrying the lack of knowledge and effort among expatriate missionaries to learn about Middle Eastern Christianity, Habib highlighted a need for the recognition of the work of the Holy Spirit in all the church—Orthodox, Catholic, and Protestant.

Some Evangelicals have attempted to overcome the divisions. The group Evangelicals for Middle East Understanding provides one avenue, in particular linking Western Evangelicals with the ancient Middle Eastern churches. An Iranian Evangelical leader affirmed to me the importance of relating to the historic churches and of recognizing what God is doing among them. But he also stressed the importance of unity within the Evangelical churches themselves. He noted that publication of some arrangements between the churches, especially regarding outreach among Muslims, could prove harmful.

One of the major obstacles to unity in the Middle East is the issue of proselytism. David Kerr, with the commendation of Gabriel Habib (1996), deals with proselytism from a Middle Eastern perspective. Kerr (1996, p. 13) refers to a 1989 MECC study document which looks at proselytism in terms of the historical approach of the Catholic missions of medieval times and later Protestants, as well as contemporary "sects" (MECC's word), by which "... the MECC means millenarian or messianic groups, independent 'neo-missionary' groups of fundamentalist persuasions, groups that represent syncretistic forms of religious universalism, charismatic renewal movements within established churches, and new religious movements that claim to draw upon Asian forms of religious spirituality. While proselytism in West Asia/North Africa occurs unconsciously as well as consciously, its underlying presupposition is that a missionary 'vacuum' exists throughout the region, where indigenous churches are considered to be lacking missionary motivation and resources."

It is evident that, even with good intentions, a great gap of understanding remains. What one group might define as seeking spiritual renewal, another group calls proselytism. As Cecil Robeck (1996, p. 7) points out, "Those who use the term [proselytism] have defined it *for* Evangelicals rather than *with* Evangelicals." George Sabra (1998), a Lebanese Protestant theologian, provides a challenge which may help point the way ahead:

"To bring about a change, Evangelicals must learn not only to respect their Orthodox sisters and brothers in their different traditions, but also to work with them in witnessing to the gospel and speaking the truth to the world. Evangelicals must come to recognize that not all non-Evangelicals are 'nominal' Christians. For their part, the Orthodox must make a place for non-Eastern Christianity, i.e., Evangelical Christianity, as an expression of world-wide Christianity, and not simply as a foreign transplant in their 'territories.' Some Orthodox in positions of intellectual and ecclesiastical leadership should abandon the notion that individuals born in a certain religious community are the exclusive property of that community."

These concepts of formal unity meet their test in the crucible of opposition and isolation. I have followed with great interest the missiological struggles of a North African colleague as he has appreciated the warm friendship and hospitality of a Catholic priest, now martyred, yet has wanted to maintain a protective distance between the church which meets in his home and the theological failings he perceives in the Roman confession. This man trusted his martyred Catholic friend; trusting the Catholic Church is another thing.

Dialogue and relating to other religions

Middle Eastern church history is a vital source in developing a theology of religions. Perhaps only southern India provides a setting of equal length of interaction between Christianity and other faiths.

In the contemporary setting, dialogue with Islam in the Middle East is principally carried out, on a formal level, by the legally established churches. The MECC has engaged in various conferences, such as the 1998 "Abrahamic Heritage" gathering of Muslims and Christians, which was favorably described as "an illustration of how civil society in the Arab world is a viable option" (Makari, 1998).

Darius Panaphour (1996) is not so optimistic about such gatherings: "There is a tendency to become cynical about the possibility of any good coming out of formal dialogues on Muslim-Christian relations. They are usually attended by those who are eager to see differences eliminated or at least discarded as far as possible. Indeed, for the World Council of Churches, the mission is not the conversion of non-believers but dialogue itself."

Dialogue between Muslims and Evangelicals, including MBBs, does take place but normally in the sphere of private witness. One MBB who has found a public arena in the streetside coffee shop is Hasan al-Ghazali (1989): "Following initial discussions, we invite people to our home for deeper talks. But it is very important to speak the kernel of our message in the coffee shop. We must have the same language in private as in public."

Another MBB who has dared to venture into the public sphere wrote a letter published anonymously in a North African newspaper some two or three years ago. Responding to an editorial attack on those who had turned to Christ from Islam, the writer declared that he and his friends had not betrayed their homeland nor broken any civil laws. His appeal was that they could be recognized for what they were and granted at least the rights normally allotted in Islamic culture to Christians and Jews.

Reconciliation, justice, and peacemaking

There is an increasing awareness that God's people must be involved in issues of reconciliation, justice, and peacemaking. Elias Chacour's widely circulated biography (Chacour & Hazard, 1987) passionately demonstrates one response from a Palestinian Christian perspective to issues of injustice and ethnic divisions. Another Palestinian, the Anglican Naem Ateek (1986) of Jerusalem, commends the numerous schools, hospitals, and programs to care for the aged and handicapped—services provided by Christians. But he argues that we must move beyond service to peacemaking.

A program run by Palestinian Evangelicals takes Arab and Jewish youth on trips into the desert. There they find unity in the hardship of the desert and their common Christian faith, the program itself stressing the centrality of Christ's atonement in any effort for reconciliation.

Tuvya Zaretsky (1995) gives another vital Middle Eastern perspective on these themes. A Jewish Christian (his term), he rejects both the extreme which "takes the form of Christian Zionism and ... a 'Christianized' version of human rights." Avoiding what he considers a low view of eschatology, Zaretsky looks to the day when political strife will be ended, when Jesus sets up his throne on earth. In the meantime, though, "he brings peace ... to the Middle East and wherever he reigns as Lord and Savior in the hearts of individuals."

Suffering, persecution, and perseverance

One cannot think of the Middle East without thinking of the suffering of Christians. The 20th century began with the massacre of over one million Armenian Christians at the hands of the Turks; it ended with the ongoing murder of tens of thousands of Sudanese Christians.

One response to suffering is conversion. Far too many Christians, over the centuries, succumbed to the many pressures they faced and converted to Islam.

Another response to suffering is emigration. Speaking of the Middle Eastern churches, David Zeidan (1996) states: "Once large, relatively powerful and missionary minded, [the Middle Eastern churches] have gradually dwindled due to devastating wars, massacres, conversion to Islam under long-term Muslim pressure, second rate status, expulsion, emigration, and ever lower birth rates compared to their Muslim neighbours."

Only the Coptic Church, Zeidan says, has bucked this trend, whereas, "Evangelicals, because of their good contacts to the West, have been in the forefront of emigration in this century. Whilst their numbers in the Middle East have been constantly replenished by conversion from the older churches, their emigration accelerated the general tendency to an ever smaller percentage of Christians in the total population."

Sudanese Christians have set an example for the world in their response to suffering. Many northern Sudanese believers have paid a great personal price for their bold witness, while God has blessed them with a vibrant, growing church. Sudan bears the reputation as a hotbed for Islamic fundamentalism. Perhaps it will not be long until it is also known as a source of great Evangelical missionary passion.

How should we respond to persecution? An Iranian Christian leader believes that: "We need to stand for our brothers who are being persecuted, we need more prayer for them. But the church needs to realize that when Paul could have appealed to his Roman citizenship in Philippi in the first instance he didn't do it. There are times when God uses persecution for his purposes.... We want the Christian church to be safe, but safety is not the only goal. The goal is to preach the gospel at the cost of death if necessary. If our only approach is to bail out the Christian church at the cost of not leaving a witness in the area, then something is wrong."

Churches around the world should learn from the Middle East important lessons in perseverance, not just through one lifetime but across long generations.

Contextualization

Two years ago I was asking my leader and mentor, a Sudanese Arab, for advice on an issue involving Christian family life and witness in an Islamic setting. One family was facing incredible pressures due to the incessant stream of visitors at their door. "What," I asked, "was the culturally appropriate response to these visitors?"

"Sometimes our culture tells us to do one thing," he replied, "but if the Bible tells us to do something else, we have to do what the Bible says." This godly Sudanese man, deeply committed to personal relationships, would not hide behind "culture" to support an unbiblical practice.

Frieda Haddad (1987, pp. 73-74) refers to a "print-made split between head and heart that never quite made its way into the Arab world." Mission strategy will fail, she says, if it fails to see the Bible not just as a book for private devotion but as "a word to be heard and interpreted in community." Commending the increased use by Christians of electronic media, she points out that Muslim teachers never distribute "copies of the Koran and other educational printed material ... without cassettes and video-recordings of celebrations and major feasts, thus underlining and strengthening the global village's collective unconscious so necessary to the spread of the faith."

Middle Eastern Christians do make a significant contribution to the way the Christian message is presented. Several of the major Christian radio and television broadcasting agencies are staffed by Middle Easterners, not just in the "on camera" roles but in positions where content and production decisions are made.

In terms of Christian lifestyle, Middle Easterners are increasingly taking a significant role in coaching missionaries from other regions. One example of this is the insightful book of Christine Mallouhi (1994), long-term resident of the Middle East and wife of an Arab. She helps see many cultural issues, at least partially, through Middle Eastern eyes. As Elias Chacour says in the foreword, "... reading the mentality, tradition, and rules of decency ... is far more important than the hopeless attempt to learn Arabic or any other African or Asian language. The language that communicates the best is the one that needs no words, but regards attitudes and inspires respect of one's own self and of the host country."

Another very positive insight from the Middle East is in the contextual understanding of the Scriptures. Kenneth Bailey (1983, 1992), who has spent much of his life in the Middle East, draws from the parables of Jesus rich meaning on a popular level and deep theological insights which would be hidden to those who do not understand the Middle Eastern cultural setting.

Sobhi Malek (1989, pp. 212-213) presents the case that we must meet Muslims "at their level in two major areas: theology and culture." Regarding theology, in his witness Malek first presents Christianity as an encounter with Christ, not as theological dogma. Regarding culture, the gospel must be presented "in a form that appeals to them culturally and attracts their attention.... Muslims can ... become authentically Christian and yet retain their Islamic culture."

However, several Middle Eastern Evangelical leaders are concerned that some issues of contextualization are being pushed too far (e.g., Madany, 1997, and related papers linked to that web page).

A Lebanese missions leader, intimately involved with the *Jesus* film project, told me that in one major Middle Eastern country Muslims are beginning to accept the name "Yesua" for Jesus rather than the Quranic "Isa." His source, a respected national leader in the country, believes this is due to the use of "Yesua" in the *Jesus* film translation. By comparison, there has been some difficulty in relationship to church leaders in two North African countries. There, the missions leader told me, "Messiah of God" was used rather than "Son of God" in the local Arabic dialect version. Evidently the North Africans had, all along, preferred to use "Son of God," but expatriate workers, on the grounds of contextualization, had argued for the less confrontational but also less biblical phrase.

Elsewhere, some expatriates would suggest that MBBs refer to themselves in Islamic terms as people who are "submitted to God" and who style their worship and community around a "Jesus mosque." Although some MBBs have doubtless gone along with this, many others reject it completely. Kabyle Christians of Algeria and the Turkish believers who have legally registered their churches want to be known as Christians, not in the pejorative sense linked with Western culture but, as at Antioch, as true followers of Christ.

Summarizing this position, an Iranian leader told me: "When it comes to Islam, the issue of contextualization is sometimes taken too far. What is important is that we need to share the love of Christ openly, and the Word of God says, 'You shall know the truth and the truth shall liberate.'

There is so much deceit in Islam that you don't want to keep somebody in that situation. People would go to the extent to say, 'Let them stay in an Islamic setting, Islamic churches.' That is out of the question for us, because historically the way the church has approached Islam has not been a successful one. In the beginning we fought with them, then we ignored them, and now there is a tendency to appease them.... In evangelism we contextualize to the point you want to understand the culture, become a 'Jew to the Jew and Greek to Greeks.' Yes. But you don't want to compromise to the extent that there is continuity and discontinuity."

Ethnicity

An understanding of ethnicity in the Middle East unlocks not all but at least several important doors in understanding church history as well as the contemporary challenge to the churches.

The church of ancient Carthage (Tunis) was strong. Why did it die out? One contributing factor lies along ethnic lines. Church leadership structures tended to be Roman, as was the language of the Scriptures (Daniel, 1992, p. 231). Only in these days are the Scriptures being provided in the language of the native Berber populations. Studies of the Councils of Nicea and Chalcedon and of controversies involving groups such as the Donatists and Montanists are often limited to the theological content alone. What more can be learned when we also consider the possible ethnic divisions between the various camps, difficulties for those who did not speak Latin or Greek fluently, or perhaps had "visa problems" and could not attend the great councils due to national origin?

In the Arab world today, Arabization is a major threat to minority populations, including Christian groups. In the Middle East this opens new challenges in helping the youth avoid succumbing to the dominant culture. Kabyle Berbers of Algeria resent the imposition of Arabic by the national government and proudly, at times defiantly, insist on using their own tongue. Many Kabyle Christians share these feelings of ethnic identity, and when they are with Algerian Arab Christians they may settle for French as a common language of worship.

On the other hand, in another North African country, a Christian leader of a Berber ethnic group leads worship in Arabic and insists that there should be no division based on ethnicity. His preoccupation is for the formation and maintenance of a united national church. An Iranian Christian leader recognizes that there should be evangelistic witness in the various languages of his country. But he fears that too much emphasis in the church on ethnic origins will create "a division that is not there."

Ethnic issues also compound the problems of incorporating MBBs into churches of openly Christian communities. In a limited number of churches, it appears to be working. But the long-term test perhaps lies not in whether the existing churches say such converts are welcome, but whether those MBBs actually feel welcome.

Missionary outreach

There was tremendous missionary vitality in the first centuries of the church. The Church of the East followed the Silk Road to China, Egyptians sailed far down the Nile, and Mediterranean Christians marched—and witnessed—in the Roman legions occupying Britain.

Little can be freely said about contemporary missionary outreach by Middle Eastern Christians, especially when it deals with Muslims and the other religious groups of the region. New signs of vitality and missionary zeal, however, are a cause for rejoicing and encouragement to God's people worldwide.

Conclusion

Recently, a brother in Christ brought me dates from the desert of Algeria. If you were to sit at my kitchen table we could share some of this sweet fruit. Far better, though, would be to travel together to the desert and, with the warm evening wind in our faces and a cup of sweet tea in one hand, enjoy the fruit in its natural environment.

My writing has been a feeble attempt, from an outsider who is very much still a learner, to share some of the fruit of Middle Eastern missiology. To enjoy its full savor, we must go together to a place where springs gush forth in the desert, where our Christian brothers and sisters of the Middle East work out in daily life a missiology whose flavor can only be captured in part when print and cyberspace separate it from daily life.

References

Ateek, N. (1986). Christ's mission in the Middle East: "And having done all to stand." *International Review of Mission*, 75, pp. 393-396.

Bailey, K. E. (1983). *Poet and peasant through peasant eyes.* Grand Rapids, MI: Wm. B. Eerdmans Publishing Co. ISBN: 0-80281-947-8.

———. (1992). *Finding the lost: Cultural keys to Luke 15.* St. Louis, MO: Concordia Publishing House. ISBN: 0-57004-563-0.

Chacour, E., & Hazard, D. (1987). *Blood brothers* (reprint ed.). Grand Rapids, MI: Chosen Books. ISBN: 0-80079-096-0.

Chapman, C. (1995). *Cross and crescent: Responding to the challenge of Islam.* Leicester, England: InterVarsity Press. ISBN: 0-85110-992-6.

Cities.com. (1999). Internet: http://www.world-population.com/. Accessed September 30, 1999.

Cragg, K. (1979). Conversion and convertibility—with special reference to Muslims. In J. Stott & R. Coote (Eds.), *Gospel and culture: The papers of a consultation on the gospel and culture convened by the Lausanne Committee's Theology and Education Group* (pp. 263-282). Pasadena, CA: William Carey Library.

Daniel, R. (1992). *This holy seed*. Harpenden, Herts., England: Tamarisk.

Dehqani-Taft, H. B. (1955). Prospects for the church in Iran. *International Review of Mission, 44*, pp. 316-322.

al-Ghazali, H. (1989). Here is how I share in coffee houses. In J. D. Woodberry (Ed.), *Christians and Muslims on the Emmaus Road* (pp. 198-199). Monrovia, CA: MARC. ISBN: 0-912552-65-4.

Habib, G. (1990, July). Renewal, unity, and witness in the Middle East: An open letter to Evangelicals. *Evangelical Missions Quarterly*, pp. 256-260.

———. (1996). Response to David A. Kerr. *International Bulletin of Missionary Research, 20*(1), p. 22.

Haddad, F. (1987). Reflections on perspectives of mission in the Arab Middle East. *International Review of Mission, 76*, pp. 72-77.

Horner, N. (1989). *Guide to Christian churches in the Middle East: Present-day Christianity in the Middle East and North Africa*. Elkhart, IN: Mission Focus Press.

Kerr, D. A. (1996). Mission and proselytism: A Middle East perspective. *International Bulletin of Missionary Research, 20*(1), pp. 12-22.

Lapidus, I. (1988). *A history of Islamic societies*. Cambridge, England: Cambridge University Press.

Laurent, E. (1993). *Hassan II: la mémoire d'un roi*. Paris: Plon.

Madany, B. M. (1997). *Missions to Muslims in the 21st century*. Convocation address delivered to Westminster Seminary, Escondido, CA. Internet: http://www.safeplace.net/members/mer/MER_INTR.htm. Accessed September 21, 1999.

Makari, P. E. (1998). Abrahamic heritage. *MECC News Report, 10*(2&3). Internet: http://www.mecchurches.org/newsreport/vol10/abrahmicheritage.htm. Accessed September 21, 1999.

Malek, S. (1989). Here is how I share through contextualized forms. In J. D. Woodberry (Ed.), *Christians and Muslims on the Emmaus Road* (pp. 211-213). Monrovia, CA: MARC. ISBN: 0-912552-65-4.

Mallouhi, C. (1994). *Mini-skirts, mothers, and Muslims: Modelling spiritual values in Muslim culture*. Hemel Hempstead, UK: Firm Foundations. ISBN: 0-990401-29-4.

Middle East Council of Churches. (1986). *Who are the Christians of the Middle East? MECC Perspectives*. Reprint ed., June 1987.

———. (1989). *Proselytism, sects, and pastoral challenges: A study document*. Quoted in Kerr, D. A. (1996). Mission and proselytism: A Middle East perspective. *International Bulletin of Missionary Research, 20*(1), pp. 12-22.

———. (1998). *The Middle East Council of Churches: History and mission*. Internet: http://www.mecchurches.org/history.htm. Accessed September 21, 1999.

Myers, G. (1998). *The Arab world*. Carlisle, UK: OM Publishing. ISBN 1-85078-287-3.

Napper, J. (1992). *Christianity in the Middle East*. Larnaca, Cyprus: MECO.

Nazir-Ali, M. (1983). *Islam, a Christian perspective*. Philadelphia, PA: Westminster Press. ISBN 0-664-24527-7.

Panaphour, D. Y. (1996). Islam and Christianity: Approaches and difficulties. *Premise, 3*(4). Internet: http://capo.org/premise/96/april/p960407.html. Accessed September 22, 1999.

Robeck, C. M., Jr. (1996). Mission and the issue of proselytism. *International Bulletin of Missionary Research, 20*(1), pp. 2-7.

Sabra, G. (1998). Orthodox-Evangelical dialogue: An MECC perspective. *MECC News Report, 10*(2&3). Internet: http://www.mecchurches.org/newsreport/vol10/oedialogue.htm. Accessed September 21, 1999.

Suleiman, M. W. (1989). Morocco in the Arab and Muslim world: Attitudes of Moroccan youth. *The Maghreb Review, 14*(1-2), pp. 16-27.

University of Balamand. (n.d.). *Righteous Saint John of Damascus*. Internet: http://www.balamand.edu.lb/uob/theology/live_of_saint_john_of_damascus.htm. Accessed September 21, 1999.

Walls, A. F. (1999, July). In quest of the father of mission studies. *International Bulletin of Missionary Research, 23*(3), pp. 98-105.

Wasiim, A. (1993). *Christian mission in the Arab world.* Cooperative Strategy Group.

Wolf, K. B. (1996). Christian view of Islam in early medieval Spain. In J. V. Tolan (Ed.), *Medieval Christian perceptions of Islam.* London and New York: Garland.

Zaretsky, T. (1995). Peace in the Middle East. *Jews for Jesus "Newsletter."* Internet: http://jewsforjesus.org/topics/newsletters/5755-09Aug95/peace.htm. Accessed September 14, 1999.

Zeidan, D. (1996). *The decline of Christianity in the Middle East.* Internet: http://www.angelfire.com/az/rescon/DECLCHRCH.html. Accessed September 28, 1999.

David Greenlee's years in Colombia (where his parents were missionaries) and at high school in Ecuador helped to shape his perspective on missions. After training in electrical engineering, David joined Operation Mobilization, serving first in a technical capacity on the ship "Logos" and then in various leadership roles for the "Logos," "Doulos," and "Logos II." After 14 years serving around the world with OM's ship ministry, David obtained his Ph.D. in intercultural studies from Trinity Evangelical Divinity School, Illinois. Several years leading OM's teams in one part of the Muslim world led into his current role for the mission as International Research and Strategy Associate. David met his wife Vreni, from Switzerland, on the "Logos." Their daughter Rebekka was 16 months old at the time they experienced the shipwreck of that vessel. Shortly after that experience, Jonathan was born in the U.S., and three years later, while the ship "Logos II" toured West Africa, Sarah was born in Côte d'Ivoire.

TWO **THOUSAND YEARS** after the establishment of the church, at the threshold of a new era and the beginning of a new millennium, we notice that the church worldwide is still facing many challenges in the area of missions. Nevertheless, many contributions have been made to the area of missiology, as better methods of reaching out to others in their different social and cultural living conditions are found.

After 2,000 years of preaching and mission work, the number of Christians today is only 33% of the total world population. Moslems number about 18%. This means that Christians and Moslems together comprise more than half of humanity. Moreover, these two religions are the most widespread geographically of all the world's religions.

Islam,[1] the only major faith younger than Christianity, has rapidly become a world religion. It is second only to Christianity in its missionary zeal and worldwide outreach. In some parts of the world (both East and West), it is making converts faster than is Christianity.

What kind of relations do Moslems and Christians want in the 21st century? What are some of the obstacles and challenges to be reckoned with? What steps can be taken to overcome the obstacles and meet the challenges? How can the church better reach out to the Moslem world?

The book of Acts and the Epistles document the missionary enterprises of the church of the first century. The history of the church can be viewed as a history of its expansion by missionary work. In the 19th and 20th centuries, this has become a vast Christian enterprise, the size of which is

Further contributions to missiology from an Arab perspective

RAED
ABDUL MASIH

---

[1] The term "Islam," as Jamal Badawi (1989, p. 187) talks about his faith, "is derived from the word that means *peace* or *submission ... to Allah*."

not easily perceived because it is so scattered. Almost every European nation has its missionary patron who brought the faith to the region—Augustine of England, Patrick of Ireland, Boniface of Germany, and many others. The church has always been conscious of the mandate to make disciples of all nations (Matt. 28:19), and both Catholic and Protestant churches have undertaken extensive missionary operations.

The sudden rise and rapid spread of Islam in the 7th century marked a turning point in history and created a particular challenge to Christianity that is still noticed today. Will Durant (1950, p. 155; quoted in Kane, 1971, p. 49) observed, "The explosion of the Arabian Peninsula into the conquest and conversion of half the Mediterranean world is the most extraordinary phenomenon in medieval history." With lightning speed, the Arabs conquered Damascus (635 A.D.), Antioch (636 A.D.), Jerusalem (638 A.D.), Caesarea (640 A.D.), and Alexandria (642 A.D.). To consolidate their power, they established the Umayyad Caliphate in Damascus (661–750 A.D.) and the Abbasid Caliphate in Baghdad (750–1058 A.D.).

A second tide of Moslem invasion took place in the 13th and 14th centuries. The Ottoman Turks and the Mongols of Central Asia became fierce and fanatical followers of the prophet Muhammad and went on the rampage, pillaging and destroying everything in their path. Seljuk Turks, who had earlier been evangelized by the Nestorians, became Muslims and occupied large areas of Asia Minor. It was against these intruders that the Crusades were launched. Certain areas of Syria and the Holy Land were regained, but on the whole the Crusades were a failure.

By the 15th century, the Ottoman Turks had invaded Greece and the Balkans. Constantinople fell in 1453 A.D. At this time, the Arabs were retreating in Spain, giving up Alhambra (Granada), their last stronghold, in 1492 (Kane, 1971, pp. 49-52).

The Meaning of Missions

When we talk about missions and missionaries, the first thing that comes to mind is something *foreign*, something that comes from *outside* one's own country. As a matter of fact, the work of missions is not the work of the West or the East or any specific nation. Rather, it is God's plan to reach out to humanity (John 3:16).

Missions[2] means the ministry of the gospel, and all evangelists[3] are bringers of good news. Since for our purposes the Bible is the source of these words, it would be good to make a quick summary of the biblical background of evangelism and missions.[4] This study is closely connected to the theological basis of evangelism.[5]

---

[2] The word "mission" is derived from the Latin word *mitto* ("send"), denoting a task that a person or group has been assigned and sent out to perform. The New Testament uses the word in a specific way, denoting the ministry of the gospel in both word and deed. The Greek word *diakonia* is also translated "mission" in Acts 12:25. *Apostello* is used to denote sending on service or with a commission, and *apostolos* ("apostle") is one sent forth.

[3] Greek *euangelistes* ("a bringer of good news") (Acts 21:8; Eph. 4:11; 2 Tim. 4:5). Also *euangelizomai* ("to announce good news").

[4] There are many good books on the biblical background and basis for missions, such as Senior & Stuhlmueller (1983). (This book is written from a Catholic perspective.)

[5] Many books have been written on the theology of Christian missions, such as Anderson (1961) and Bosch (1991).

Theological Basis of Evangelism

Theology and evangelism are relevant. The heart of the gospel is theological. Sadly, some theologians look with suspicion upon evangelism, considering it shallow and overly emotional, and many evangelists avoid theology. The time may come when many will study theology without evangelism, but there can be no effective and permanent evangelism without theology.

Evangelism and theology complement each other

The leading evangelists of each generation have considered theology a help rather than a hindrance. There are many examples, including the Apostle Paul, Augustine, Jonathan Edwards, and Charles Finney. These men were all mighty theologians as well as great evangelists.

Theology often produces revival, and revival greatly strengthens theology (see Finney, 1964). Historically, an overlooked or otherwise dormant theological truth has been used to give biblical weight and drive to every great revival. In the Reformation, it was "salvation by grace." In the Wesleyan revival, it was the "new birth." In the Western revival, the conscience was awakened to the great theological truth that all men are accountable before God and are responsible to co-operate with God in repentance and faith to receive salvation.

Evangelism depends upon theology

The evangelist confronts the lost world with Evangelical truth and urges this truth upon those who hear. Evangelism is the living expression of doctrinal theology. It is founded upon the total meaning of the Christian faith. It must draw upon the very truth by which the church lives and moves and has its being

(Kantonen, 1954, p. 3). Theology is to evangelism what the skeleton is to the body. The great system of theological truths forms the skeleton which enables our revealed religion to stand. But what theology—whether Protestant, Orthodox, or Catholic—that is another question altogether!

We need to keep in mind that inadequate theology curbs evangelism. For example, an inadequate theology based on humanism and naturalistic psychology undermines the main thrust of evangelism. Humanistic theology is inadequate because it neglects the evidence of God's self-revelation. Humanism depersonalized God and robbed us of the power of God. And naturalistic psychology has subtly poisoned the currents of theological thought by explaining all human action in psychological terms. It distorts the modern conception of conversion.

A vital theology of evangelism

Two of theology's most vital points are the issues of sin and salvation and repentance and faith.

Regarding the former, Fisher (1951, p. 53) states, "Salvation is not a matter of laws and regulations, ceremonies and institutions ... it is a redemptive fellowship between a personal God and a personal man." Salvation is God's answer to the sin problem. Through the cross, God provides forgiveness, which has to be through a personal contact with God.

Hebrews 11:1 reminds us that faith is confidence in God. Fisher (1951, p. 55) observes, "The necessary response may be described as a complete change of allegiance on man's part from sin to God and a trusting committal of self to God." Repentance, like faith, is a work of grace. Man responds to the goodness of God (Rom. 2:4). When the goodness of God leads to repentance, then God forgives sins.

Biblical Background

In the New Testament, we find that Jesus used both mass evangelism and personal evangelism.

What evangelism is

Evangelism is bearing witness to the gospel with soul aflame and teaching and preaching with the express purpose of making disciples of those who hear. The inner drive which we call *passion* is basic in evangelism (Whitesell, 1949, p. 22). Jesus was moved with compassion towards the crowds (Matt. 9:36).

Since evangelism includes a confrontation, there can be no adequate definition of evangelism apart from the Evangel, the directions given the sinner when he is confronted with Christ. The proclamation calls the sinner to repent—to turn back to God, salvation, and eternal life.

A positive spirit in evangelism is also important (Phil. 4:13). One important underlying principle that is deep-seated in the spirit of evangelism is sacrifice. And we need to remember that the spirit of evangelism which is basic in soul-winning cannot endure apart from the presence and power of the Holy Spirit.

What evangelism is not

Some people think that evangelism is everything we do (Sweazey, 1953, p. 19). But many times we do everything except evangelism. So evangelism is *not* everything we do. Evangelism is *not* leading people to unite with the church. On the other hand, a healthy New Testament evangelism will add great numbers to our churches. Evangelism is *not* merely enlisting people in a new kind of activity. And evangelism is *not* syncretism. Syncretism would ignore the very heart of the gospel of Christ.

Inculturation and Syncretism

It is worth saying a word on syncretism here in relation to the Christian faith and evangelism. In the Bangkok Assembly of 1973, which had the theme "Culture and Identity," the World Council of Churches affirmed that "culture shapes the human voice that answers the voice of Christ." In 1983, the Vancouver Assembly reminded us that "culture is what holds a community together." In 1991, the Canberra Assembly, reflecting on the theme "Spirit of Unity – Reconcile Your People," stated, "The diversity of cultures is of immediate relevance ... for it affects both the relationships within churches and also the relationship with people of other faiths." Today we face the challenge of bringing the gospel into the Arabic culture, which is influenced and dominated by the Muslim religion.

The church, being aware of the cultural challenges relating to faith and syncretism, has developed methods of dealing with the various cultures in a way most suited to the cultural context. We are facing a global culture, and we talk about a "global village," but it is still important to apply evangelism and mission work in a way that adapts to the geographical, ethnic, and religious identities.

Christianity has been present in the Middle East and the Arab world since the first century A.D. The Bible is one source of information regarding the way of life, cultural identity, social life, and traditions of ancient Israel. Roland de Vaux (1997, p. 3) notes that other sources include "texts about the Arabs in pre-Islamic times and ethnographical studies about the Arabs of today. These nomad Arabs, by race and country, are closely related to the Israelites, and what we know of pre-Islamic, modern, and contemporary Arab life can help us to understand more clearly the primitive organization of Israel."

The fact that the Arab culture is very close to the culture of biblical times in many ways is both an advantage and a challenge for missionaries. Workers must get to know the language, culture, and history of the Arabs in a way that makes a clear presentation of the gospel possible. But in spite of the common ground, there may still be a barrier to the gospel message, due to the existence of the Muslim faith in the region from the 7th century on.

Contribution to Missiology From the Middle East/ Arab World Perspective

From the experiences of the church in the Middle East/Arab world, many lessons have been learned about how to evangelize the Arab world today. Some of the lessons have been positive, while others have been negative. In both cases, the experiences have contributed much to the field of missions and to missiology in general.

It is good to remember that this region of the world has supplied many missionaries to many parts of the world, as well as martyrs. We need to keep in mind also that Christianity reached the Arabs on the day of Pentecost (Acts 2:11). Arab Christians have a history and heritage, according to the following timeline:

- Pre-Islamic era (1st – 7th centuries)
- Islamic rule (7th century on), which can be divided into three periods:

- 7th century until the 15th century
- Ottoman rule (15th century to the beginning of the 20th century)
- Modern era

Arab Christians contributed in many ways to the culture and community in the pre-Islamic era. They also made a contribution to the Islamic state when it came to power in the 7th century and during its golden era in the 9th – 13th centuries. Many Arab Christian poets, scientists, architects, physicians, and theologians were famous in their works and contributions to the community and the church. The Arabic worldview is seen in the many manuscripts that exist today from monasteries in the Middle East. These writings by Arab Christians fit the culture of the Middle East in all its aspects and forms.[6]

Being under Islamic rule, Middle East theologians presented mostly issues such as the cross, the Word of God, the Trinity, the Virgin Mary, the deity of Christ, and the icons in an effort to defend the Christian faith from the attacks of Islam.[7] They approached mission work in a very clear, apologetic manner.

Today, many people are praying for the Arab Christians, for the local church, and for the work of missions in the Middle East. The term "10/40 window" has been given to the region from 10° to 40° north of the equator, stretching from West Africa to Japan (see Otis, 1995; Johnstone, 1993). The area of the Arab lands of North

---

[6] One manuscript that has received some attention is found in the British Library in London under the number *Or 4950*. It goes back to the year 877 A.D. and contains writings to an Arab theologian called Abu Qurrah, defending the crucifixion of Christ.

[7] See, for example, *Entretien d'Elie de Nisibe avec le vizir Ibn 'Ali al-Magribi, sur l'Unité et la Trinité*. Introduction, édition critique du texte arabe et traducion annotée (Rome, 1979). Also *Une correspondance islamo-chrétienne entre Ibn al-Munaggim, Hunayn Ibn Ishaq et Qusta Ibn Luqa*. Introduction, édition, divisions, notes et index par Khalil Samir, traducion et notes par Paul Nwyia, in *Patrologia Orientalis*, N° 185 (Turnhout, 1981).

Africa (as the region is sometimes defined)[8] is 15,654,000 sq.km. Only 5% of the land in the Middle East has sufficient water to support cultivation. Johnstone (1993, pp. 69-70) speculated in 1993 that in the year 2000, the total population of the region would be 430,057,000. He estimated that Christians would constitute 5.2% of the population (17.1 million), with a growth rate of 2.4%. Protestants would comprise 0.77% (2.5 million), Catholics 1.7% (5.6 million), and Orthodox 2.7% (9 million).

Unknown minority

There are two important contributions that can be made to mission work among Arabs. One is to take away the many stereotypes that affect the work of missions. The other is to spread the news that there are Arab Christians and that they go back to the first century A.D. When I tell people I meet in the U.S. and Europe that I am a Christian, I always face the question, "And when did you convert from Islam?" Lack of knowledge of the Arabic language keeps people from recognizing that my family name "Abdul Masih" means "Servant of the Messiah," which is a typical Christian name that reflects the faith of a person.

It is true that the Christian presence dwindled to a minority due to the spread of Islam. Yet this minority has accomplished great deeds among the community at all levels. One significant example of the work of Christians in a Muslim surrounding is the ministry of the Bethlehem Bible College among the Palestinian people. Indeed, the local church is lifting up its voice to make it clear to the body of Christ around the world that it is still witnessing for Christ and doing its mission as the Lord commanded.

Minority in a Muslim majority

During the period of Ottoman rule (which was ushered in by the fall of Constantinople to the conquering Turks in 1453 and lasted until the end of World War I), all Christians were regarded as forming a single nation and were treated differently from the Moslems. Later, at the end of the 19th century, great massacres took place. Many Christians, lay people as well as religious, were slaughtered, and many monasteries were destroyed. Many people fled from their home towns, leaving everything behind. Such actions minimized the Christian presence in the region and greatly affected evangelization and the spread of the gospel.

Despite all that the Middle East has gone through and all that has happened to Christians in the region, the Christian presence of faith and prayer is still significant. However, as a minority group living among a Muslim majority, Christians are still treated differently in many ways. For example, they are viewed as infidels because some Christians drink alchohol, which is forbidden in the Quran. Christians are believed to have changed and twisted the words of the real Gospels. According to Islamic teaching, it is lawful to steal from a Christian. Moslems are also taught that they should do acts of mercy and charity only to other Moslems and never to Christians.

Arab Christians: Bridges to the Moslem world

Because Arab Christians existed long before the coming of Islam, they welcomed Islam as part of Middle East culture and history. Today, they share the traditions and cultural heritage of the

---

[8] The countries included here are Algeria, Bahrain, Egypt, Iran, Israel, Jordan, Kuwait, Lebanon, Libya, Mauritania, Morocco, Oman, Palestine (West Bank and Gaza), Qatar, Sahara, Saudi Arabia, Sudan, Syria, Tunisia, Turkey, United Arab Emirates, and Yemen.

Moslem Arabs. But a far more important element is the Arabic language.

Alber Hourani (1991, pp. 54, 57) writes, "By the 3rd and 4th Islamic centuries (9th or 10th century A.D.), something which was recognizably an 'Islamic world' had emerged.... Men and women in the Near East and the Magrib lived in a universe which was defined in terms of Islam." The defining terms were the Arabic verses of the Quran, which by the 8th century were to be found not only in the pages of the Quran and in the hearts of men, but also on the road signs of Palestine (Sharon, 1966) and on the caliph's coinage (Walker, 1956; Bates, 1988). They were also publicly proclaimed from minarets across the land and were artfully displayed for all to see on monuments of incomparable beauty, such as the Dome of the Rock in Jerusalem, which is a supreme monument of Arabicization (Grabar, 1973).

Such Arabicization (the spread of Arabic as the public language of business in the caliphate) brought about the circumstance by the end of the first Islamic century that members of the Christian community living within the *dar al-Islam* ("house of Islam") adopted Arabic not only as their daily language but as their ecclesiastical language as well. This move happened first in the Melkite communities, whose patristic and liturgical tradition was Greek. It is not surprising that members of the monastic communities in the Holy Land took the lead in this enterprise, for the most active centre of Greek culture in the 8th century lay in Palestine, notably in Jerusalem and the neighbouring monasteries. Beginning well into the Greek period and coming into its own in the 9th century, there was a determined undertaking on the part of monastic scholars to present the Christian tradition in the Arabic language, which was the primary bearer of religious culture in the world of Islam

(Griffith, 1988). Surprisingly, some modern writers view this phenomenon as the major stumbling block for Christianity in the Arab world. Bishop Kenneth Cragg (1991, p. 31) writes, "The crux of Arab Christianity might be linguistically expressed; it is bound over to a language that is bound over to Islam." But the new circumstances also provided a new context for Christian theology, as the monks of Palestine were quick to grasp. They seized the opportunity to inculturate their faith into the Islamic, Arabic milieu of the caliphate and to express it in the language of the Quran.

Major efforts were expended in the 9th century to translate the Scriptures and numerous liturgical books into Arabic (Griffith, 1985). In addition, translations were made of patristic and monastic classics that the communities of monks in the Holy Land required in order to function as the intellectual centres of Melkite life in the caliphate (Griffith, 1989). In fact, the majority of the Christian Arabic manuscripts which have survived from this period are just such texts: translations of church books required for religious services or versions of spiritual classics which monks and others might have used for spiritual reading. Nevertheless, among these texts there is a small percentage which are original compositions in Arabic. The writers are the first ones known to us who took advantage of the new opportunity to compose Christian theology in the Palestinian context of the late Umayyad and early Abbasid eras.

Today, many writings are made by Arab Christians on many similar issues, as at the dawn of Islam and during the early centuries of its establishment. The Arab Christian church and Arab Christians are truly the bridges to reach to the Muslim heart. Because they have shared in the language, culture, common history, tradition, and heritage of the Arabs, Arab Christians have in many ways developed better strategies to reach out to Moslems than Western missionaries have. One example is a greater sensitivity on the part of Arab Christians to the political issues of the Middle East.

Presence of faith and prayer

Mention should be made of some of the characteristics of our faith and mission as Arab Christians. The word "presence" has been chosen as a fact of faith which accompanies our reflection, gives unity to its different aspects, and defines its overall orientation. Presence means that in the midst of the society in which we live, we are a sign of God's presence in our world. That presence invites us to be with, in, and for, and not against, outside, or on the margin of the society in which we live. This is an essential demand of our faith, our vocation, and our mission.

Presence is situated between two opposing pitfalls: marginalization and dissolution. Marginalization nullifies our mission, and dissolution produces the same effect as regards our identity. Authentic presence is a guarantee of both mission and identity. Presence deepens our faithfulness as a local church to God, to ourselves, and to the society God has given us as the theatre of our earthly progress.

As churches in the Arab world, our Christian presence is not a presence for our own sake alone. Christ did not found his church to serve itself, but that it might be a confessing church with a mission— the same mission as that of the founder and Master.

In the past, Christian communities in the East turned in on themselves because of the constraints of the historical conditions. They lost their sense of mission and witness, content merely with the effort to survive. Today, they are called to free themselves from the after-effects of the past. They are called to incorporate a sense

of mission into their lives, to open themselves up to the world which surrounds them, and to bear witness to the buried treasure that brings joy to their hearts, as it brings joy to the heart of every person (cf. Matt. 13:44-46).

Incarnation in Arab civilization

Christians in the Middle East do not limit themselves to using the Arabic language as a means of expression for their rites, their particular culture, and their daily relations. They have gone beyond this to concern themselves with the future of the whole of culture and civilization. Christians have played an active part through the work of translation and the production of original works. They have thus created an outstanding means of cooperation among Muslims, Jews, and various Christian denominations; it is a model of coexistence. Mutual assistance and cohesion among these three groups have thus become a reality engraved on the fidelity of each side to its own faith and beliefs. We invite Christians, Muslims, and Jews to a creative dialogue in our countries—a dialogue which thay can pursue in the new historic conditions which are opening up to the future.

Presence and service

Christ served the disciples and the people around him. He also called his disciples to follow in his footsteps and to be a sign of his presence among men by their service to one another (John 13:13-15). The church has always seen in the example of Christ an urgent call to serve all people, whoever they might be, particularly those who suffer the different forms of human wretchedness. The church is called to serve the whole person, both body and soul.

There are different fields of service— education, health, and many others—and through these fields the good news is also presented. In serving every person in need, our churches are not acting out of self-interest, and most certainly have no hidden agenda.

Continuing challenges

Due to the political and economic conditions of the Middle East region, the contribution by Arab Christians to the field of missions has been limited. Middle East churches are very limited in both funds and leadership. Nevertheless, many changes have taken place in the last decade or so. A few churches and some individuals are taking the initiative and are pioneering short-term missions. These endeavors are influenced by Western approaches and are ruled by Western methodologies, but they are a beginning. We anticipate further contributions in the future.

References

Anderson, G. H. (Ed.). (1961). *The theology of the Christian mission*. New York: McGraw-Hill.

Badawi, J. (1989). Islam: A brief look. In J. Hick & E. S. Meltzer (Eds.), *Three faiths—one God: A Jewish, Christian, Muslim encounter*. Albany, NY: State University of New York Press.

Bates, M. (1988). Coinage of Syria under the Umayyads, 692–750. *1987 Bilad al-Sham Proceedings, II*, pp. 195-228. Amman, Jordan.

Bosch, D. J. (1991). *Transforming mission: Paradigm shifts in theology of mission*. Maryknoll, NY: Orbis Books.

Cragg, K. (1991). *The Arab Christian: A history in the Middle East*. Louisville, KY: John Knox Press.

De Vaux, R. (1997). *Ancient Israel*. Grand Rapids, MI: Wm. B. Eerdmans Publishing Co.

Durant, W. (1950). *The age of faith: A history of medieval civilization—Christian, Islamic, and Judaic—from Constantine to Dante, A.D. 325–1300*. New York: Simon & Schuster.

Finney, C. G. (1964). *Revivals of religion*. Old Tappan, NJ: Fleming H. Revell.

Fisher, F. L. (1951). *Christianity is personal*. Nashville, TN: Broadman Press.

Grabar, O. (1973). *The formation of Islamic art*. New Haven, CT: Yale University Press.

Griffith, S. (1985). The gospel in Arabic: An inquiry into its appearance in the first Abbasid century. *Oriens Christianus, 69*, pp. 126-167.

———. (1988). The monks of Palestine and the growth of Christian literature in Arabic. *The Muslim World, 78*, pp. 1-28.

———. (1989). Anthony David of Baghdad, scribe and monk of Mar Sabas: Arabic in the monasteries of Palestine. *Church History, 58*, pp. 7-19.

Hourani, A. (1991). *A history of the Arab peoples*. London: Faber & Faber.

Johnstone, P. J. (1993). *Operation world: The day-by-day guide to praying for the world*. Grand Rapids, MI: Zondervan Publishing House.

Kane, J. H. (1971). *A global view of Christian missions from Pentecost to the present*. Grand Rapids, MI: Baker Book House.

Kantonen, T. A. (1954). *The theology of evangelism*. Philadelphia, PA: Muhlenburg Press.

Otis, G. (Ed.). (1995). *Strongholds of the 10/40 window*. Seattle, WA: YWAM Publishing.

Senior, D., & Stuhlmueller, C. (1983). *The biblical foundations for mission*. Maryknoll, NY: Orbis Books.

Sharon, M. (1966). An Arabic inscription from the time of the Caliph 'Abd al-Malik. *Bulletin of the School of Oriental and African Studies, 29*, pp. 367-372.

Sweazey, G. E. (1953). *Effective evangelism: The greatest work in the world*. New York: Harper & Brothers.

Walker, J. (1956). *A catalogue of the Arab-Byzantine and Post-Reform Umaiyad coins*. London.

Whitesell, F. D. (1949). *Basic New Testament evangelism*. Grand Rapids, MI: Zondervan Publishing House.

Raed Abdul Masih completed his B.A. and M.T.S. studies in the U.S. He returned to Jerusalem with his wife and child in 1996 after finishing his doctorate studies in Spain. Since then, he has been working with the Bethlehem Bible College as a teacher and in Al-Aman counseling center that belongs to the college. He is on the Shepherd's Society board and is a member of the Gideons International. Raed has participated in many local and international conferences related to the church and missions in the Middle East in general and in Palestine in particular. He knows nine languages besides the other skills that God has given him.

24

"**M**ISSION IS INTRINSIC** to the very life of the church. There is no other church than a missionary church. To be the church is, therefore, to live in a crossroads situation; to be constantly encountering the world; to be challenged by it and to be impelled by the Spirit of Christ to witness in and to it of the gospel of the kingdom of God" (Costas, 1976, p. 7).

Both the fulfilment of the divine commandment (mission) and the critical reflection on this praxis (missiology) take place in the midst of the ideological, political, economic, social, and religious tensions of a given time. This "external context" (Costas, 1976, p. 7) of missions affects the missionary practice at the same time that it helps shape a certain mission profile.

In this brief presentation, we will approach what are, for us, the distinctive elements, though not the only ones, of mission in and from Latin America. Our interest will focus mainly on the Protestant/Evangelical field; however, we cannot ignore the Catholic side in a continent where this persuasion reaches almost 85% of the population.

Mission in a Context of Christianity

More than 500 years ago (1492 A.D.), Christianity reached Latin America through Spanish Catholicism. The discovery of the American continent was both a political and a religious undertaking. For more than seven centuries (718–1492), Spain had been occupied by the Muslims, until the Moor kingdom fell in April, 1492. The *Reconquista* was for Spain not only a military and political victory, but also the victory of Christianity over Islam, in that the identity of the Spanish nation was intimately linked to the Catholic persua-

Mission and missiology from Latin America

NORBERTO
SARACCO

sion. The monarchs of Spain were for the Catholic Church the missionary tool for the conservation and expansion of the Christian faith both in Europe and overseas. Columbus' discovery of the American continent (October, 1492) was not only an epic enterprise naturally resulting from the Spanish predominance in that period, but also a missionary undertaking.

The presence of priests in expeditions was customary as with Columbus' second trip to the American continent. At the same time, the Spanish *Conquistadores* (conquerors) saw themselves as Christian crusaders. There was a unanimous conviction that both conquerors and priests were responsible for the conversion of the natives of these lands. They sought to submit the natives of the American continent as they had done with Muslims and Jews in Spain. The New World offered them the possibility of a land where Catholic hegemony could be practised without competition from Jews, Muslims, or Reformers.

This concept of missionary work made use of both the sword and the cross to achieve its goal. Massive killings of natives took place at the same time as truly humanitarian and civilising practices. Compulsive and massive baptism of natives and the forced exclusion from society of anything that was not Catholic were some of the predominant evangelising methodologies that made the New World a Christian and Catholic land. The religious practices of the natives were not taken as objects of evangelisation. Mostly they were ignored or integrated into a syncretism that had no scruples in mixing the sacred and the profane. A people's religiousness was born full of syncretism. Forced evangelisation of natives destroyed their sanctuaries but could not wipe out their faith. Native religious symbols were re-placed by Christian symbols, but in the minds and hearts of the people, the same old gods were still being worshipped.

The Catholic Church has not only failed in the evangelisation of the ancient gods, but also in the confrontation with the new non-Christian cults. In a survey taken in 1996 at a Catholic church, 38% of the members had visited a quack doctor or a fortune teller and were, at the same time, devoted to a saint; another 35% had seen a quack doctor or a fortune teller and were not devoted to a saint. This means that 73% of the people who attended that church were seeing quack doctors or fortune tellers regularly (Carozzi & Frigerio, 1992).

From this perspective of Christianity, it was thought that the evangelisation of Latin America had already taken place. At the beginning of the 20th century, Catholics did not see the need for evangelising Latin America. But as time passed, they realised that they had been mistaken.

At Puebla, Mexico, in February 1979, the Third General Conference of the Latin American Episcopate met under the theme, "Evangelisation in the Present and the Future of Latin America." The second part of the final document includes a summary of the contents of evangelisation. It then focuses on the evangelisation work in Latin America, the missionary dimension of the church, and the church's preferential option for the poor. This last aspect had already been emphasised at the previous Episcopate Conference in Medellín, Colombia (1968), and it was one of the significant contributions made from Latin America to the understanding of mission.

We must also note that one of the contributions of Catholic missiology is the special interest in culture evangelisation. The Puebla document says about this, "The church thus calls for a new conversion on the level of cultural values, so that the structures of societal life may then be imbued with the spirit of the gospel. For by their very nature, these structures are supposed to exert a restraining influence on the evil that arises in the human heart and manifests itself socially..." (Document, p. 438).

Now, and in spite of still considering Latin America as a Christian continent, the Catholic Church has made evangelisation a priority in its mission. Whether as a result of the uneasiness caused by the flow of members to Evangelical churches or because of a conviction that many Catholics are living a Christianity that is only nominal, this church is adapting its message and methodology in search of a more effective evangelistic work.

Mission as Incarnation

Only in the 19th century did Protestantism start to take roots in Latin America. Beyond some isolated cases, it was at the end of the second decade that the first congregations settled. In the beginning, the priority was spiritually assisting the European immigrants who had come to these lands, so much so that the first services were held in English. The traditional Protestant churches shared the vision that the American continent had already been evangelised, and they did not want to create an area of conflict with the Catholic Church in this respect. Diego Thompson's (1822) and Penzotti's (1890 and following) pioneer work was evangelisation through Scripture distribution, but it did not ultimately modify the general concept. This situation started to change only with the start of faith missions and the rise of denominations with a missionary outlook. It is important to note here that the lack of evangelistic emphasis in Protestant missions prompted the insertion and development of these communities and their priorities in mission.

In July, 1969, the III CELA (Third Latin American Congress on Evangelisation) was held in Buenos Aires, Argentina. The conference was marked by the social and political effervescence of the '60s, and although it tried to reach the whole Evangelical spectrum, its dynamics and subjects were influenced by traditional Protestantism. The III CELA is important because it shows us how this segment of the church understood mission at the time. The congress theme was suggestive: "Debtors to the World." Part of the "debt" was the way in which the church had inserted itself into the lives of Latin American peoples. They said, "We as churches are responsible for having tolerated oppressive systems that have exerted control and power over the life of our societies" (CELA, 1969, p. 23). Within this context, they considered that the mission of the church includes:

"a. To proclaim God's sovereignty over all human life and relationships....

"b. To point out the precariousness and relativity of all human institutions.

"c. To offer an interpretation of the historical moment the continent is living.

"d. To act as spokesperson and defender of all victims of social injustice, pointing out the causes and those who are responsible for that injustice" (CELA, 1969, p. 25).

Thus, the three main lines of thought of the III CELA were established: the recognition of a conflictive and revolutionary situation, an affirmation that the redeeming work of God affects more than personal life, and the acceptance of the possibility of political involvement for Christians.

The basic concept behind this model of mission is incarnation. This was an inescapable point of reference in the missiology of the 1960s and '70s. In the report of one of the III CELA commissions, we read: "Christ in the Incarnation identifies with humanity in its misery in order to reconcile all with God through his sacrifice on the cross and to give them ... the power and the hope of a new life" (CELA, 1969, p. 22). As Orlando Costas (1976, p. 94) said, "The evangelisation, identification, committed efficacious service and a paradigmatic witness—this is the mission which, modelled on the life and work of Christ, Protestants owe to the continent."

We must note here that the contribution to missiology was related to a concept of incarnation that included ideological and political components. It was not incarnation as commonly understood in missionary circles, where the emphasis is on understanding the culture of those whom we want to evangelise and being willing to renounce our own culture to reach our goal. Here, incarnation was to take an option—to take sides with the ones that suffer most. Naturally, not all those who attended the III CELA supported this view, to the point that there is a report in the official documents of a minority group that expressed their disagreement.[1] But the challenge had been given, and over time, many Evangelical groups, in one way or another, incorporated this understanding of incarnation as they developed a concept of holistic evangelisation.

The Inescapable Call: Evangelisation in Depth

In the spring of 1964, Dr. Kenneth Strachan gave a series of lectures on missions at the Fuller Seminary, under the title, "The Inescapable Call: Missionary Work of the Church in the Light of the Urgent Needs and Opportunities of Today's World." These addresses were to be his legacy, since he died the next year. The content of the speeches was not a theoretical proposal of work, nor some abstract reflection on the mission of the church. The lectures were a summary of the experience and the theological foundation of the Evangelism in Depth Movement, which arose in the midst of the Latin American Mission under Dr. Strachan. Evangelism in Depth's basic postulates were applied almost universally and were decades ahead of what is now commonly accepted by churches around the earth.

The extraordinary population growth, the post-war social and technological revolution, and some successful experiences in massive evangelisation spoke to the church of a time of opportunities. But these opportunities turned to frustration as Evangelical churches were only an imperceptible minority that had not yet found the key to growth. In Strachan's (1969, pp. 126-128) view, there were several reasons for this. On one side, "a sense of discontent with the structure of foreign missionary societies. Some years of participation in evangelistic enterprises that were inspired, financed, and carried out by foreigners had produced the sensation that such campaigns ... did not represent the true solution." Secondly, it seemed that church life was an important cause of the failure of its witness. It was a static, self-centred structure depending upon professionals for ministry. Another side of the problem was the great number of Protestant organisations working unconnected and with no sense of co-operation or fellowship.

From this reality, and after observing the factors that influenced the expansion and growth of certain movements in Latin America, the research reached a basic postulate: *"The expansion of a movement is*

---

[1] C. Peter Wagner, *Confidential Report*, p. 4, quoted in Costas (1978).

in direct proportion to its success in mobilising all of its members in a constant propagation of their beliefs."

Based on this postulate and aiming at modifying the inertia of evangelisation failure, Evangelism in Depth developed four statements that proved their worth in practice:

1. An abundant harvest depends on abundant sowing.

2. Christians can and must work together.

3. When Christians share their resources, God multiplies them.

4. A consecrated minority may make a strong impact on a whole nation (Strachan, 1969, p. 10).

The contribution of Strachan and Evangelism in Depth was revolutionary for its time and may be summarised in three main emphases:

1. Total mobilisation for total evangelisation. This concept opposed evangelisation "only by evangelists" and gave each member a share in the responsibility.

2. The role of the local congregation in evangelisation. It took the priority of the evangelisation work out of the hands of structures and missionary organisations, to put it back in the congregation's hands.

3. The essential quality of unity in mission. Thus, it attempted to counter fragmentation and division caused by the very missionary structures.

Evangelism in Depth's ideology was a new dimension in evangelisation, born in Latin America but with a world reach. Arthur Glasser (1961) said about it, "I see nothing comparable to its vision and dynamic force in present missionary thinking.... This marks an encouraging breakthrough in the sinful confusion that has stopped for so long the progress of the gospel both here and overseas."

Evangelisation and Mobilisation

The I Latin American Congress on Evangelisation (CLADE I) was held in Bogotá, Colombia, at the same time that the III CELA was meeting (1969). CLADE I gathered a significant number of delegates (920), mostly representing the Evangelical wing of Latin American Protestantism. CLADE I was strongly conditioned by missionary structures; however, some prophetic voices could be heard through it, and there was an attempt for a national leadership that, from the evangelistic militancy, tried to be sensitive to fast social changes. CLADE I had a fundamentally evangelistic orientation, imbued with the mobilising drive of Evangelism in Depth. We could say there was an internal tension between activism and reflection there. The theme of the congress is significant: "Action in Christ for a Continent in Crisis." It clearly summarises the two main concerns: what actions should be taken for evangelisation and how to evangelise in a continent in crisis. The final document of this congress shows that:

1. Evangelisation is the church's supreme task.

2. It is important to mobilise the whole church for the evangelistic task.

3. The process of evangelisation takes place in concrete human situations. Social structures influence the church and those who receive the gospel.

4. The time has come for us Evangelicals to be aware of our social responsibilities.

5. Men will not build God's kingdom on earth, but Evangelical social work will contribute to the creation of a better world.

In this declaration, we may see a first attempt to go beyond the traditional model of evangelisation, but still the remnants can be seen of an Evangelical mindset that considered social work as a "manifestation of evangelisation" and not a companion to it (Stott, 1977, p. 34).

An interesting aspect to mention is the fact that a plan was presented here for the evangelisation of Latin America. Both the author of this plan, Carlos Lastra, and the final document of the congress admit that a proposal of such magnitude, considering the autonomous character of Evangelical churches, may only serve as a thought-provoking motivation on lines of action. The objective of this plan was "to evangelise, proclaim the word of the gospel, convert Latin American people to the gospel, and make disciples of huge multitudes" (CLADE I, 1970, p. 73). Seven objectives were proposed in order to accomplish the task:

1. Use the mass media.
2. Concentrate efforts on children, teenagers, and youth.
3. Give a new vitality to the local church.
4. Help train lay leaders.
5. Help reach classes that were left aside by the church: high class, intellectuals, government officials, university professors, union workers, etc.
6. Clearly define the social and economic responsibility of the church.
7. Work towards the unity of the church in a co-ordinated effort.

We must note here that both the reflections and the proposed lines of action were limited to Latin America. The central and excluding concern was how to evangelise in the context where the churches were. To say it in the language of the book of Acts, we would say that the mission was to Jerusalem and Judea. The idea of reaching the ends of the earth was totally absent.

One of the subjects dealt with at CLADE I was the relation with the Catholic Church. This area was addressed in a theological dissertation by Dr. Emilio A. Núñez and was later included in the final document. The space devoted to the subject and the seriousness of the approach would be unthinkable in an event of this magnitude in Latin America today. At that time, the emphasis was understandable, since the winds of the II Vatican Council were being felt in full strength. The subject was dealt with very seriously, showing the limits and possibilities of a relation with Catholicism. Section 9 of the CLADE I final document says: "In a continent with such a Catholic majority, we cannot close our eyes.... The connection presents us with both risk and opportunity. Our confidence in the Word of God, which is becoming more and more spread within Catholicism ... offers us an opportunity for dialogue at a personal level. This dialogue must be intelligent ... in order to avoid the risks of a naive, misunderstood ecumenism" (CLADE I, 1970, p. 135).

It was also within the context of CLADE I that a prophetic voice was heard through the Bible studies by Rubén Lores. He said then, "The moment has come for the Spirit to be poured on all flesh." Making his words those of Ernest Wright, he said, "Both leaders and people will be filled with the Spirit and filled with the Spirit's power to a level yet unknown" (CLADE I, 1970, p. 11).

The contribution made by CLADE I to mission was its emphasis on the importance of a church that is mobilised to evangelise, the attempt to include social and political tensions in the Evangelical missionary agenda, the need to start a serious and mature dialogue with the Catholic Church, and the fact that an outpouring of the Spirit on the South American continent was foreseen, which has been taking place since the mid-1980s.

Holistic Mission

The International Conference on World Evangelisation held in Lausanne, Switzerland, in 1974 was, in Leighton Ford's words, "the moment of history in which Evangelicals caught up with their time." The profound social changes that were taking place all around the world and the political tensions they generated opened to the church an agenda that could not be ignored. It was necessary to re-think mission to make it faithful to the gospel and relevant to the world. In order to do that, just as Jeremiah had to do, it was necessary to uproot and tear down, to destroy and overthrow, to be able to build and to plant. Latin American theologians had a central role to play in such a crucial task. They had forged their theology firmly rooted in the Word and facing the world. They had an understanding of the world and the role of Christians in it.

In his paper on the gospel and evangelisation, René Padilla (1986, p. 1) said, "The lack of appreciation of the wider dimensions of the gospel will lead, inevitably, to a distortion of the church's mission." From an eminently missionary concern, Padilla confronted the theological and ethical assumptions of the most accepted models for evangelisation and mission. His objections were included in the Lausanne Commitment, where it speaks about the "worldliness that can be detected in the adulteration of the message, the manipulation of the audience through pressure techniques, and an exaggerated concern for evangelisation statistics" (Padilla, 1986, p. ix).

This search for an evangelisation and a mission that fulfil its purpose (the redemption of persons and the transformation of the world), while at the same time taking care that the methodology is not worldly in itself, has been a constant concern for many Latin American theologians.

However, we must accept that even today in Latin America, faithfulness to the gospel is still being sacrificed on the altar of numbers. It is not a question of being "the faithful few," because God wants all to be saved; the matter is that "when the gospel is manipulated in order to make it easier for all to be Christians, the foundation is being laid from the very beginning to have an unfaithful church. Such as the seed is, the tree will be, and such as the tree is, the fruit will be. What really matters about church growth is not having a successful increase in numbers ... but faithfulness to the gospel, that will undoubtedly move us to pray and work so that more people will know Christ" (Padilla, 1986, p. 33).

Since Lausanne—and due to the development that the implications of the Lausanne Commitment had on Latin America through the Theological Fellowship—the concern for whole mission has been present in all reflections on missiology. Both at the Second Latin American Congress on Evangelisation (CLADE II) and the Third (CLADE III), reports, discussions, and proposals were made within this wide frame.

The theme of CLADE II (Lima, Peru, 1979) was, "Let Latin America Hear the Voice of God," and the introductory statement says clearly, "We reaffirm our allegiance to the CLADE I Affirmation and the Commitment of the World Congress on Evangelisation held in Lausanne, Switzerland, July 1974" (CLADE II, 1979, p. xix). An effort to relate the theology of mission to the context was both the greatest contribution of this congress and at the same time its greatest limitation. On speaking of sin, the subject was, "Sin and Salvation in Latin America." On speaking of hope, it was, "Hope and Hopelessness in the Continental Crisis." The congress was not merely an attempt to contextualise the message, but also a way to affirm the Latin

American churches' right to their identity and their model of mission. But in this emphasis, the global dimension of mission—the peoples beyond Latin America—was totally absent. The lack of mobilising proposals was also to be noted. It is very interesting to observe that in the Projections and Strategies Document, which churches were encouraged to implement, the segment on evangelisation and mission recommends, as lines of action:

"1. That churches and their leaders have a contextual and whole view of mission.

"2. Develop our own research tools.

"3. Encourage the exchange of personnel.

"4. Detect investigation candidates.

"5. Develop documentation centres" (CLADE II, 1979, p. 347).

The 1970s were, socially and religiously, a time of much ideological struggle. It was necessary to affirm beliefs, to clarify methodologies, to take a stand. CLADE II showed that from an Evangelical perspective, progress could be made in that direction. It also revealed that different Evangelical groups were struggling to articulate their own identity in church and mission.

Mission to the World

The social and political context changed completely in the 1980s. The Communist bloc disintegrated, Latin American dictatorships weakened and started to disappear, and the church in the continent was strengthened and growing with unusual energy. The time had come to lift our eyes and look to the world. In an anarchic way, lacking organisation but full of enthusiasm, churches started to send missionaries. Thus, the necessity appeared to have a continental meeting that would help churches in their missions development. In 1987, sponsored by CONELA and other organisations, COMI-BAM (Latin American Missionary Congress/Cooperation) was born. Its aim was to be a catalyst of missionary enthusiasm and a motivator for transcultural mission. Since COMIBAM, new indigenous missionary movements have been started, missionary training programs established, and initiatives promoted, such as "Adopt a People," whose goal is that Latin American churches take the responsibility of adopting 3,000 unreached peoples by the year 2000.

The Third Latin American Congress on Evangelisation (CLADE III, 1992) echoed this tendency, and its theme was, "All the Gospel, for All Peoples, from Latin America." The concept of holistic mission was present in theological and contextual reflection. Though the number of theological reports (8) doubled that of missiological reports (4), the final document stressed the sense of mission. On thinking about a gospel for "all peoples," it said:

"a. The universal character of the Christian faith and the confession of the Lordship of Christ give its missionary dimension to the church.

"b. All the church is responsible for evangelising all peoples, races, and tongues.

"c. The missionary vision, action, and reflection of the church must be founded on the gospel, which, when understood in its entirety, is proclaimed in word and deed and is directed to every human being.

"d. The Holy Spirit has developed a new missionary awareness in Latin America.

"e. Incarnation is the model for the mission of the church.... This demands the crossing of geographical, cultural, social, linguistic, and spiritual frontiers.

"f. The church in Latin America must assume its responsibility in world evangelisation fully and without delay" (CLADE III, p. 861).

The number of missionaries sent from Latin America increases day by day. Even small congregations strive to send a missionary. Comparing the relationship between income level and contribution for missions of Latin American churches with those of the U.S. and Europe, we might find that the former are giving, proportionally, more than the latter. However, in many of these missionary undertakings the important contributions made from Latin America to the theology of mission are not visible. In general, missions are undertaken with an alarmingly naive spirit. In many cases, Latin American missionaries are repeating mistakes that the missionary movement had in its beginnings, as if the experiences gathered over centuries were not of any use. It seems as if enthusiasm obliterated the fact that crossing a geographical frontier is not enough to do missions. As Samuel Escobar said in CLADE III (pp. 379-385), there are other frontiers to cross: cultural, social, urban, spiritual power, religious, etc., and it is not enough to show a passport to cross them.

Mission and Missiology: Concerns and Hopes

As in any pending task—and mission always is such a task—expectations in view of the future are a mixture of concern and hope. Each time and each context must re-elaborate their missionary agenda, not only in search of whom to reach, but how, and using which tools.

Thoughtless activism is one of the characteristics of the contemporary Latin American church. The search for success for success's sake has plunged the church into a frenzied race after experiences and activities that keep it always entertained. Our concern is that the answer to the missionary call may have the marks of a great movement that is in perpetual motion, without actually getting anywhere.

So many years of preaching against theological reflection as if it were, by itself, opposed to church growth, have left their mark. Today, we have a growing church that is, at the same time, quite hollow. It is a church that waits for the latest best-seller book to know what to believe. That is why we are living a contradiction: as the church grows, so do injustice, corruption, and immorality. It is no wonder when this happens in the world, but it is alarming when it happens within the church. That is just what mission is all about: making all persons live under the Lordship of Christ.

Prioritising unity is one of the most important contributions of the Latin American church. In spite of the flood of business models where church growth is mistaken for the success of "my own business," we still believe and defend the value of unity as something inherent to mission. We need to be one, so that the world may believe. However, our concern is that when it comes to mission, Latin American missionaries work under the spirit of free enterprise, duplicating efforts, wasting energy, and reproducing on the mission field a church model that denies one of the essential values of the kingdom: being one in Christ.

Incarnation and contextualisation, not only cultural but also social and political, have been ongoing subjects in missiological discussion in Latin America for the last 30 years. But the world has changed so much that the reality of globalisation forces us to redefine these terms. Our concern is that missiological thinking in Latin America be trapped in a localism that no longer makes any sense.

In summary, our concerns have to do with sharing a relevant message, being faithful to the gospel, and understanding the world. But at the same time, there is also hope. The strength and forward push of the Latin American church are among the most visible manifestations of the move of the Spirit. It is a church that has learned to depend on the Lord's grace and his resources for mission.

There is hope, because this church is alive and seeking. We believe that the new generations of Christians will be able to take advantage of such a rich legacy of experience and reflection.

There is hope, because in spite of multiple limitations, this is a church that has lifted its eyes to see the fields that are white, and it wants to work sacrificially in the harvest.

Finally, there is hope, because beyond all else we still believe that the One who is building up his church all around the world will help us, equip us, and use us.

References

Carozzi, M. J., & Frigerio, A. (1992). Mamae Oxum y la Madre María: santos y religiones afro-brasileñas en Argentina. *Afro-Asia*, CEAO/UFBA, *15*, pp. 71-85.

CELA (III Conferencia Evangélica Latino-americana). (1969). *Deudores al mundo*. Montevideo, Uruguay: UNELAM.

CLADE I. (1970). *Acción en Cristo para un continente en crisis*. San José, Costa Rica & Miami, FL: Caribe.

CLADE II. (1979). *América Latina y la evangelización en los años '80*.

CLADE III. (n.d.). *Todo el evangelio para todos los pueblos desde América Latina*. FTL.

Costas, O. (1976). *Theology of the crossroads in contemporary Latin America*. Amsterdam, Netherlands: Rodopi.

———. (1978). Una nueva conciencia protestante. *Pastoralia*, *1*(2), p. 66.

Document of the third general conference of the Latin American Episcopate at Puebla.

Glasser, A. (1961, noviembre-diciembre). Evangelismo a Fondo. *The Evangelist*.

Padilla, C. R. (1986). *Misión integral*. Grand Rapids, MI & Buenos Aires, Argentina.

Stott, J. (1977). *La misión cristiana hoy*. Buenos Aires, Argentina: Certeza.

Strachan, K. (1969). El llamado ineludible. San José, Costa Rica & Miami, FL: Caribe.

Norberto Saracco and his wife, Carmen, have three children. Born in Argentina, Saracco was ordained as a Pentecostal pastor at the age of 21. During his theological studies (1972–1976), he was pastor of an AIBC church in Costa Rica. Saracco founded the International Faculty of Theological Education (FIET) and was General Secretary of the Association of Seminaries and Theological Institutions in Latin America (1982–1986). He has been a member of the International Council of WEF since 1983. He has a Ph.D. in Pentecostal studies from the University of Birmingham, England. Saracco lives in Buenos Aires, where he is currently Director of FIET and pastor of the Good News Church.

25

Younger generations and the gospel in Western culture

STUART McALISTER

ROMANS 1:16-17 has always been an inspiring part of Scripture to me, and I firmly believe in its contemporary relevance. As a young convert, I quickly took to the streets to share my encounter with the gospel, and within a year I was involved in taking literature and materials to the church in Communist Europe.

My vision was stirred as I saw the vast numbers of people who were unreached and, from what I could tell, were unlikely to be reached. As OM, we organized outreaches and various efforts to share the message, and we saw some degree of success. It wasn't long, however, before I encountered the entrenched beliefs that seemed to build walls of resistance to the gospel. The legacy of history, the two world wars, and the seeming irrelevance of the message all served to raise serious questions to any gospel presentation.

With many years of reflection on the European situation and context, and with some exposure to other Western nations, I began to see some patterns. I'd like to mention three to begin:

The Legacy and Effects of Christendom and Modernity

The assumption that Europe is Christian and evangelized has been and (for some) remains a stumbling block. The Parish system, with its territorial approach to identifying the people of an area as a part of the national church, is entrenched in European minds. To be Polish is to be Catholic, to be Greek or Russian is to be Orthodox, to be German or Danish is to be Lutheran, and so on, even though many people are rapidly departing from their heritage or never desired it in the first place. Christendom's apparent mission was to pastor the faithful, not reach the lost. A deep nominalism often resulted amongst those reared in the approach, which is quite resistant to evangelism.

Modernity's secularizing project was profoundly effective, as the beliefs in autonomous and good human beings using reason and science to build a better world by their own efforts captured imaginations. Progress was the goal, and rational means the way. The works of Darwin, Freud, Marx, and the prophets of the market came to expose old "myths" and offer a better, more satisfying vision. A new story had eclipsed the gospel and was spreading the news that happiness was the goal, money the means, and "stuff" the end.

The European context became quite gospel-resistant, and the general feeling was one of contentment and basic security. The developments in the economy and the overall sense of well-being in society have removed any sense of need or concern at one level, while generating new challenges in the process.

The challenge facing many of us today is double. First, how will we find an audience or access to one; and second, how can we demonstrate why the gospel is even an issue?

The dualistic inheritance

Much has been written on the subject of dualism, and we know its chief architects, but the fact versus value divide in society or the public versus private debate is compounded by an equally dualistic church that further divides everything into sacred and secular issues. The result has been that many well-trained believers do not know how to relate their faith to their everyday lives. They feel divided between private interests (church, spirituality, etc.) and public concerns (economics, politics, environment, etc.). This type of Christianity that is prevalent in the West is, in the words of Os Guinness, "privately engag-

ing but socially irrelevant." At root, I believe, is a misunderstanding of the nature and applicability of truth.

The growing consciousness of interdependence, of ecological balance, and of the spiritual and unseen dimensions of life—things which were ignored or repressed by the rationalism that dominated Western culture for many decades—have gained enormous ground and acceptance in Western culture. The more holistic view of life and experience raises a significant challenge to many Christians whose thought processes and more dualistic orientations increasingly serve to widen the gap between the church and the world.

Centuries of reflection on the nature of truth led to the Enlightenment and the quest for certainty. Within Western culture, a pervasive belief (often unexamined) shapes how we perceive reality and how we define what truth is. Paul Hiebert describes the approach that sees the individual's understanding of what is as "naive realism."

The Evangelical church has been deeply influenced not only by the impact of Scripture, but also by the particular philosophical views at various points in history which were often uncritically embraced and adopted, bringing with them their own set of problems.

The post-modern critique has challenged both the nature of truth and how we ground any belief. Increasingly, critical thinking and a de-constructive orientation are penetrating the life and work of the church with significant implications.

First, the very definition of truth itself and of who decides what is true seems to be up for grabs. Younger people are not willing to accept blindly views of truth or assertions simply because they are stated, but they feel compelled to check things out. Second, there are the issues of authority, power, and dominance. Truth has often been used as a justification for mistreatment, abuse, and many of the other problems of the 20th century, both in society and in the church. Red flags are raised when the word "truth" is used, unless the baggage that often comes with it is explicitly acknowledged and addressed. This leads to potential problems with generational differences within the church. The younger people could be perceived as asking illegitimate questions, challenging tradition and fixed realities, while often seeking a more faithful expression of what is meant by truth. Third, we must consider the centrality and primacy of truth as relational. The genuine and helpful insights raised by post-modern thought have revealed the inadequacy of many 19th and 20th century views of truth, yet they have also shown the depth of scriptural resources which can and do speak to our context, needs, and hopes. A theology and practice is needed that speaks to humanity in the totality of our experience and that is simultaneously lived as well as declared.

A conversation is urgently needed that will facilitate a rethinking about mission and recruiting, if many in the West are still to participate in the global task.

The privatization of faith

I shudder every time I read another of the popular Evangelical books that serve to reinforce individualism, privatism, and the inward life as if these are the sum and goal of the gospel. The reduction of faith to personal piety and privatistic belief is a tragedy of major proportion. The results for mission have been a loss of the scope of the gospel and the neutralizing of creative and imaginative energy for exploring fresh applications of God's Word in everyday situations.

In conversations with younger people about society and the future of mission, what often stands out is the breadth of concern and interest. Young people have grown up with a sense of interdependence. They see the relationship of one thing to another, and they are hungry for involvement in a diversity and range of areas all subsumed in the word "mission." The more holistic approach to theology and life is exposing many areas and arenas as potentials for mission—areas which all too often are neglected or rejected by traditional efforts. Environmental degradation, massive unemployment, racism, and ethnic cleansing are all seen as manifestations of sin and sinfulness. It is increasingly hoped that mission efforts will be broad enough to engage the existential crisis of our times.

The leaven of bad ideas and of cultural pressure has taken its toll on the churches of Europe and of the West. It is one thing to seek fresh inspiration for proclamation, but it is another to deal with the kind of churches needed to support a fresh communication of the gospel. We cannot think seriously about reaching afresh unless we give equal and adequate thought to discipleship and community. This throws us back to the message—its meaning and its application to daily life.

The message can only be authenticated by a people who truly and honestly seek to live it out and who struggle to embody it in every area of life. The church cannot simply be a place where we gather or which we visit. It must become a relational community which struggles together for faithfulness, love, and God's work in this world.

As we begin the 21st century, many of us have been seeking inspiration from the biblical vision of hope, which is articulated in Romans 15:13. The realities of globalization are only beginning to be felt, yet in Europe, the new realities of permanent unemployment and of old certainties being removed are raising questions. The post-modern prophets of despair are appealing to the collapse of certainty, the sense of fragmentation, and the desire to find "something" in the midst of it all. We hear multiple voices, all telling us that we simply need to find whatever is good for us, whatever works for us. Lost in a sea of relativism, where can one turn for coherence, harmony, peace, and making sense of it all?

Gurus, therapists, and counselors abound to offer diverse strategies or solutions to problems encountered. Some Evangelicals rush to join the latest trend in debunking modernism, only to end up embracing or adopting versions of postmodernism in a desire for relevance. Others retreat in fear and anxiety, building bigger walls of separation and issuing dark condemnations about the end times.

Times of transition are difficult, because old ways of doing things and of looking at things are seen to be inadequate or are up for examination. I have often experienced the tension, as sides are taken, lines are drawn, and positions defined. In my attempts to map the territory or frame the discussion, I have been described as a modernist or an analyst. I won't deny the likelihood that these labels are partially true; I only highlight that all views are situated somewhere. I have not consciously chosen a modern orientation; rather, I seek explanatory power wherever it can be found.

The danger at present is an unnecessary polarization, rather than a much-needed process of dialogue. As God's people, we all need to be willing to hear, to learn, to question, and to defer judgment as we are doing our thinking and reflecting.

The necessity of a clear vision

The Apostle Peter (1 Pet. 2:9-10) seems to grapple with two critical issues of our time: identity and mission. Globalization is being recognized as a major force in our modern world. In the West, the effect is fueling multiculturalism and all too often moral and ethical relativism, which is not a necessary outcome of the process, but which is propagated in the media and in the educational systems. Young people find themselves in the supermarket of multiple lifestyle choices. In terms of meaning, the message seems to be, "Define your own reality." The resulting frustration is compounded by the sheer range of choices and often leads to a feeling of being lost in the midst of so many options.

A culture of despair begins to arise, with deep expressions of suspicion, fear, cynicism, and anger, which can be seen inside the church as well as without. The need for vision is not simply for programs and activities, but for what kind of people we can be and how to live as God's people in this world under these conditions. Although many consultations have addressed key issues and needs, many at the grassroots level have never heard the results or substance of those discussions, and few strategies were employed to alert and equip local churches. We all believe that central to real change is a compelling vision; what vision is gripping hearts and minds in our churches? I appeal to hope, because it captures the imagination, can unleash creativity, and inspires courageous action, even in the face of severe difficulties.

Lesslie Newbigin did some excellent work in raising the issue of the church as the "plausibility structure" of the gospel. This is clearly defined in John 13:34-35. The embodiment of love is not seen as peripheral, but as central to being disciples. The way we live, the way we treat people, and the way we handle conflict or difficulties all speak to the vibrancy and reality of our message. The quality and substance of our lives and relationships are major components of the gospel and must be emphasized for fidelity to the truth and effectiveness in witness. However, a failure to take the message seriously or to consider it strategically has all too often led to sheer neglect. If missions in the Western context do not consciously shift to a more holistic theology and practice, then I cannot see how we can reach people. Practical models and demonstrated community are essentials in the post-modern era. The churches need help and resources to be able to move back and forth between Scripture and culture as they frame redemptive agendas. Few tools or models seem readily available to the Western church.

The Primacy of Scripture

At times, one feels that much of Evangelicalism is defined or shaped by reaction. Our reaction to liberalism led us to abandon serious societal engagement for a long time. Our reaction to the many trends appears to drive much of what is produced in popular Christian literature. Instead of reacting and copying models or ideas from the latest cultural analyst or "hot" critic, can we not be creatively imaginative in seeking metaphors, strategies, and innovations that derive from Scripture?

The same tendency to react may well limit us as we reflect on the modern/postmodern shift. It is real, and I believe it will not pass away, but we must avoid two extremes: first, hunkering down in bunkers and seeking to preserve the status quo at all costs or, second, throwing out centuries of insight, tradition, and wisdom as if everyone before us got it all wrong.

God's resources

A nuanced and careful approach is needed, one that is confident of the sovereignty of God, resting in the guidance of the Holy Spirit, yet open to honest evaluation and change. We can be deeply encouraged as we look at the Bible and the resources God has given as being more than adequate for our needs:

1. **The personalism and dynamic implications of the relational God in Trinity.** The work of writers such as Colin Gunton and Kevin VanHoozer is opening up untapped potential in the nature of relationships and the way things work in a created order. Much of this material can serve both to motivate and to mobilize the younger generation and to reach those outside the church.

2. **The implications for an ecologically concerned world from a good creation theology.** This generation is far more sensitive to the effects of unrestrained consumption and careless or nonexistent environmental policies. Sharing God's good news includes teaching others how to live in this world and helping them grasp the nature of stewardship.

3. **The tremendous resources for interpersonal relationships and reconciliation in the gospel and Scripture.** Within the church, the desire is for greater mutuality, openness, and dialogues. During our recent discussions in Brazil, the nature of relationships and the conditions surrounding healthy interaction were openly discussed. The issues of power, of being willing to listen, and of truly showing that we care were seen as essential and as having been severely neglected. A gospel that encourages us to be real and to live truthfully was seen as very compelling.

4. **The explanatory power and existential scope of the gospel narrative.** When the gospel is carefully unpacked and then sensitively applied, it speaks to the deepest needs of all cultures. The church must do more to teach believers what the message is in order to inspire a greater confidence in what God has given and in what will change lives.

The action orientation of many of our churches is one of our great strengths, yet I believe time spent in prayer and critical reflection should precede a rush to engage.

The church between gospel and culture

Lesslie Newbigin in the U.K. and George Hunsberger in the U.S. have been very helpful in framing vital issues for the contemporary church. As I have the privilege to travel constantly and have lived in continental Europe for 20 years and the U.S. for the last 1° years, I have had firsthand opportunity to observe several things:

First, there is an assumption that hermeneutics is largely unnecessary to a better understanding of Scripture. Here I do not refer to pastors per se. Rather, I refer to the experience of the average churchgoer, who operates according to what has been termed "naive realism" or "what I see is what is there." The general influence of post-modernism has been to highlight bias and to encourage uncritical acceptance of truth claims. A more discerning and dialogical approach is needed, both to foster confidence in God's Word and to address legitimate questions and concerns in a safe environment. The democratization of knowledge means that questions ignored or stifled in the church will be taken elsewhere and may end up with answers that bring more challenges in their wake.

Second, I have observed a blindness to the cultural and local beliefs that influence and shape what we see and how we see. Whether in the U.K. or Greece, India or the U.S., I have constantly run into a general lack of any concern or awareness as to how we may pollute interpretations through cultural preference, bias, or superiority. This I believe is a critical and urgent concern. We are all situated somewhere. Our cultures and traditions are not problems per se, but they require us to examine the accretions or subversions of

the gospel that are bound to occur as we seek to exegete God's Word and apply it. The tendency not ever to be aware of the possibility that we have adapted the gospel to our comfort zones is one that needs to be addressed.

Third, a concentration on information transfer versus transformation of values and lifestyle generates an absence of serious discipleship. The model being perpetuated is one that focuses almost entirely on correct beliefs and a general set of morals rather than on a personal relationship and spiritual formation. Little thought or effort is given to the actual means and methods of being a disciple. The issue of "how should we then live" is largely unaddressed, except by general moral exhortations. I cannot stress enough how much this issue lies at the heart of an inadequate approach to church and mission. The pressures of daily life, the constant bombardment by media and the market, and the saturation of time and space with images and demands compel us to find new ways to build the church and to facilitate the kind of character and qualities essential to life under post-modern conditions.

Agents of hope, images of exile, and the gospel of the kingdom

I believe we must give equal time to re-examining our message and re-envisioning what it means to be the church. The issue of strategy and means should flow from a deep engagement with the gospel, our context, and our moment. Faith must express itself in a faithful and faith-filled people. Hope must also be visible in those that model hope, offer hope, and work for hope. Love implies being loving, sacrificial, and compassionate. The need is to embody and demonstrate our theological and ethical commitments in everyday situations and contexts. Rather than withdrawing into end-times pessimism or its opposite, triumphalism, we need to explore the ongoing challenge of Christian subversion and the leavening of all cultures, tribes, and peoples with the good news and with good examples of God's new way of being. Rather than a "one size fits all" approach, we need multiple and diverse strategies that are situation specific, scripturally defined, and redemptively applied.

The following components should be present in our strategies:

• Listening carefully to Scripture to hear God's priorities and looking for specific "connections" that may bear particular relevance in this place and this time.

• Looking at our cultural context, interpreting its many voices and pursuits, and looking for the points of contact in it.

• Making a creative effort to cultivate people-friendly and situation-specific strategies that offer a real alternative and true contrast to what is.

These considerations are important when we attempt to motivate younger people to mission. Some of the suggestions given to me in this regard include the following: First, mission mobilizers need to move from need-driven or target-driven efforts to a focus on mission as an expression of our being as new creations. Second, there is a desire for greater flexibility and for less dependency on programs. Rapid response teams, serendipity, and more fluid approaches are called for. Third, a theology of creation is seen as essential to undergird the basic appeal, particularly seeing redemption in its restorative dimensions.

The only caution I express is the danger of repackaging mission strategies to meet consumer demands or to see mission as a means of existential validation, i.e., "I do this because it makes me feel good about myself." A church that takes seriously the message as well as the historical moment will give careful thought to what is needed to live faithfully in these circumstances.

The Challenge of Effective Communication

Living in an information age, we see the multiplication of data and voices, yet we struggle for understanding and comprehension. So much effort today goes into advertising strategies, slogans, and campaigns, and we get the message that large companies are serious about selling their products and communicating the value and relevance of what they have to offer. It strikes me that as Evangelicals we have too often been more interested in the "what" of the gospel (its content) rather than in its faithful communication. We cannot separate one from the other, and a clarity about the first concern should lead to improvements in the second.

John 1:14 and 1 Corinthians 9:19-23 are crucial passages for an incarnational approach, yet despite the many vital consultations dealing with this subject, they seem to be largely ignored in many congregations.

The lessons learned by effective pastors and missionaries around the world often boil down to the same general ingredients carefully and sensitively applied in the specifics of a local context. It is sad that many people continue to search for the latest technique or the newest strategy to somehow supply that "missing" component, where the basic elements seem to apply across time and cultures.

In conversations with friends who are pastors, I have often sensed that we would have a revolution in the church if many of our churchgoers simply knew how to be friendly to unbelievers. The distance and separation are such that little meaningful exchange takes place. A shift to a more relational versus a technique approach would be both more biblical and also more effective and true.

Can we learn from our contemporary approaches to communication? Can we invest effort, people, and time in understanding communication theories? Surely, for people with such a vital concern to share truth, this must be high on our agenda. The equal and opposite problem lies in placing relevance in such a high place that an indiscriminate or biblically shallow approach is employed to justify the use of the latest technique for reaching Gen-X or whatever. A serious dialogue needs to take place between biblical goals and means and the ends we seek.

The church in mission

The need for training, equipping, and ongoing dialogue and experiment should by now be clear. The twin issues are, first, our identity as we live out biblical holiness and consecration and, second, incarnational mission, where we live as effective communicators of the gospel in and to specific cultural contexts. Both of these need some serious time and effort. In every culture, we have issues relating to worldliness or compromise. In other words, how close can we come? How far is an essential distance? It seems to me that either the individual is left to decide, or a general conformity is required that is not grounded in good reasons. The issues of age, generations, and tastes are ignored or repressed with great cost. Styles and preferences do play a part in our decisions and choices, yet how do we find the common good in a "negotiated community" if there is little or no actual dialogue or conversation?

The massive changes in culture and society are not yet reflected in the mission community. Issues of style and approach take on new dimensions and importance for many of the younger generation. Words such as commitment, surrender,

and flexibility still count, but they may have a different sense when used by believers in their 20s versus those in their 50s. We cannot assume a particular understanding, nor should we ignore or simply declare the intent. Healthy discussion can take place, and learning can happen if we are all ready to listen, learn, and adjust.

I think we must reconsider how we do church and then remodel what we are doing. Allowing space for good exposition, we then need to wrestle with implications and application. The methods of Bible study must be such that the clear demands of the text are being grappled with. It is crucial that the Word be deeply explored, not only to grasp the basic meaning of the passages, but also to locate the necessary changes implied and any obstacles against them. We live in a time when authenticity is in high demand. Facing our weaknesses and failures honestly and openly is seen as essential by many younger people, and the feeling is that Scripture speaks clearly to this practice (see the Psalms, for example). As the life worlds of our churches are often diverse, we need to allow time and space for specific discussions relating to the different contexts, demands, and needs in order to facilitate effective applications. Should not World Evangelical Fellowship and the different Evangelical alliances be the catalyst to such essential dialogues? Again, the more effort that is made to produce resources and practical assistance, the better.

Relationships, networking, and information sharing

The top-down, leader-limited approach to addressing issues and challenges must change and be led by a vision of interdependence, strategic value, and practical outcomes. The abundance of analysis and reflections does not help if it never reaches those who can most benefit from it. It is essential, therefore, that for every missions consultation that takes place, serious time and effort are invested to insure the ideas, strategies, and resources are both widely distributed and carefully applied. As so many of us are seriously busy and often distracted, good consultations of the right kind are essential, but equally important is a serious effort to reduce the duplication, specialization, and fragmentation that mirror our time.

Considerations need to be made for financial limitations, as well as geographical and other hurdles. Many people need resources, yet for various reasons they do not have the technology, finances, or possibility of attending crucial events or of accessing them electronically. Getting resources to those who need them means demonstrating our shared relationships and commitment. The various networks can use their channels as vehicles of communication and connection. The rapidly changing world alerts us to the increasing levels of communication both by travel and by media such as the Internet. The free exchange of information, ideas, and influence has enormous potential for both good and ill. The church is a unique body and has both a universal element and a local face.

The insights gained from serious prayer, study, and effort can help others who are facing similar hurdles or challenges, if we can find the will and a way to express our common life and to explore our shared treasures. The dangers of the post-modern influence lie partly, I believe, in wrong attitudes. The world, cultures, and mission are all changing, and we must wrestle with the implications and learn to see both the possibilities and the threats. Our confidence must lie in the One who calls, who leads, and who will guide us safely to our final rest.

Conclusion

I have often longed for a series of books or materials that would integrate the various viewpoints and aspects essential to an effective missiology. These would include the role of Scripture, the need for good biblical and cultural hermeneutics, the role of the principalities and powers and how to address these entities, anthropological and sociological insights, philosophical and comparative religions, and how to critique the insights of others.

As with so many other things, leadership and vision are the key issues. Someone needs to sound the trumpet, expose the inadequacies of current ways of doing things, and offer a better direction and another way. I believe World Evangelical Fellowship is strategically placed to consider this need, but they will need to take some creative and courageous steps if they are to seriously offer what is so urgently needed. My prayer is that just such a resolution will be grasped and owned by the WEF leadership.

Some final questions

1. What role does the reflection of God as Trinity have in your thoughts regarding mission?

2. How do you present the gospel in your culture, and specifically what do you mean when you say it is the truth?

3. To what degree is the gospel proclamation limited by a failure of embodied discipleship in your context?

4. How do cultural realities, beliefs, or values influence or undermine the effective communication or living of the gospel?

5. To what resources would you like to have access to enhance your effectiveness in mission?

6. What aspect of the gospel message is most appealing in your geographical or cultural context? Why is this so?

Stuart McAlister was born in Glasgow, Scotland, and he met his American wife, Mary, while serving with OM in Eastern Europe. They have two children, Cameron and Katherine. Stuart served with OM 1978–1997. He spent time initially as a Bible courier during the Communist years, then developed the evangelistic and church ministry focus of OM in Eastern Europe. He was asked to lead the large effort "Love Europe." He then moved on to foster efforts at cooperation and unity through secondment to the European Evangelical Alliance 1992–1997. Stuart studied for a year at Precept Ministries, and in the last few years with Reformed Theological Seminary in Orlando, Florida. He is currently the international director for Ravi Zacharias International Ministries and is based in Atlanta, Georgia.

26

Telling stories: contextualization and American missiology

"**D**O YOU KNOW what it is like to work with you Americans? Let me tell you a story."

The speaker was Daniel Coulibaly. I was in Mali, West Africa, doing some consulting work for World Vision.

The elephant and the mouse were best friends, according to Daniel. One day Elephant said, "Mouse, let's have a party!" So they did. Animals came from far and near. They ate and drank and sang and danced. And no one partied more exuberantly than the elephant.

When it was over, Elephant exclaimed, "What a party, Mouse! Did you ever see a more wonderful celebration?" But there was silence. "Mouse?" Elephant called. "Where are you, Mouse?" Then to his horror Elephant discovered Mouse—crushed on the floor, stomped into the dirt, trampled to death by the enthusiasm of his friend the elephant.

"Sometimes that is what it is like to work with you Americans," said Daniel. "It is like dancing with an elephant."

MIRIAM
ADENEY

Why Listen to a Mouse?

In the face of great world need, dare American missiologists take time for mice? People are going to hell. People are perishing for lack of vision. For lack of teaching, Christianity in many places is "a mile wide and an inch deep." Physically, too, people are hungry. People need health care, schooling, and clean water. They need legal aid, title to land, job training, and secure child care. They need houses and churches built, marital counseling, drug and alcohol treatment, and special help for the marginalized. In some places, this is a *kairos* moment, a window of opportunity. If we have the resources and power to tackle such problems, why should we stop to listen to mice?

Why bother with diversity? Because—moving to another metaphor—each body part plays a crucial role. Ephesians speaks of God's great plan for unity in his universe, "the mystery of his will ... to bring *all* things in heaven and on earth together under one head, even Christ" (Eph. 1:9, 10). In chapter 4, this unity-in-diversity is applied to the church, capping a passage on Christian maturity: "From (Christ) the whole body, joined and held together by every supporting ligament, grows and builds itself up in love, as *each* part does its work" (Eph. 4:16). Every part has a role. A parallel passage, 1 Corinthians 12, says plainly that a hand must be a hand. An eye must be an eye. An ear must be an ear. Only then will a body be healthy.

Because such differences in the body of Christ are precious, we must—returning to our first metaphor—listen to the mouse and the hippo and the crocodile. A Brazilian church is not American. Brazilian evangelism, discipling, theologizing, teaching, administration, counseling, financial management, youth work, church discipline, leadership training, and publishing must be Brazilian. Thai ministry must be Thai. Nigerian ministry must be Nigerian.

Christian unity is prized throughout the book of Ephesians. Even in chapter 4, the word "one" is repeated seven times: one Spirit, one Lord, one God and Father of us all, one body, one hope, one faith, one baptism. Yet this unity is not colorless or uniform. Like a complex textile, it is woven of many hues. Like a dynamic ecosystem, it pulsates with amazing species.

American Missiology: Social Science

Although Americans often crash through the world like elephants, American missiologists have led the way in studying the crashes, applying anthropology, sociology, and psychology.

A pivotal figure in missiological anthropology is Eugene Nida of the American Bible Society (ABS). After World War II, many Christian ex-GIs wanted to go back overseas as missionaries. Preparing in college, they were drawn to the social sciences. These disciplines became recognized as training grounds for ministry. Both Jim Elliot and Billy Graham studied anthropology at Wheaton College, for example. An early textbook was Nida's (1954) *Customs and Cultures*.

As an ABS consultant, Nida worked closely with a relatively new mission, Wycliffe Bible Translators. This agency integrated linguistic theory with mission practice. Nida expanded that to anthropology. In the 1960s and 1970s, the American Bible Society published a journal, *Practical Anthropology*. Frequent contributors were Nida, William Smalley, William Reyburn, Jacob Loewen, and Louis Luzbetak, a Catholic.

In 1965, Donald McGavran became founding dean of the Fuller Theological Seminary School of World Mission. A former missionary to India, McGavran emphasized the study of church growth. Out of the Church Growth Movement, many book-length case studies applying the social sciences were written in the 1960s and 1970s.

In time, psychologists, too, began researching missionary care. "Psychology and Missions" is the topic of the Summer 1999 special issue of the *Journal of Psychology and Theology*.

Histories of American missiology will give a more complete picture.[1] One significant component is social science, the study of the encounter between "elephants and friends."

American Missiology: Foundations

"What a limited horizontal view!" some from other countries may protest. "Socially engineered success (church growth, cultural adaptation) isn't the goal of mission. Even the devil has successes. In all this emphasis on social science, where is theology? Where is the Holy Spirit? Where is suffering? Where is mystery?"

"It is not worth while to go round the world to count the cats in Zanzibar," observed Henry Thoreau, American essayist (1817–1862). Some would ask, "Is American missiological emphasis on social science unbalanced? Are Americans too busy 'counting cats'?" In the current volume, Samuel Escobar criticizes American "managerial missiology," for example.

Worship and piety

Throughout history, there have been many motives for mission in the U.S. and elsewhere. These include a personal call, obedience to scriptural command, rescuing the hell-bound, compassion for the hurting, eschatology, God's kingdom, civilization, the glory of God, the propulsion of God's love, a desire to be useful, and, for women (who constitute the majority of missionaries), empathy with women. We continue to be propelled into mission by a variety of motives. Yet in principle American missiologists would affirm the core of mission to be God's greatness over all the peoples, God's grace, and God's glory.

In this light, even "counting cats" may be done worshipfully. Management skill may be seen as a gift of God, just like medical skill. Management means stewardship and accountability, fulfilling the charge given in the "creation mandate" recorded in Genesis 1:26. Management is by no means the mother of mission, nor its base. It is subordinate to the Word and the Spirit. It is a tool. We must repent of the human tendency to idolize tools and of the tendency of some American missionaries to idolize management. But we need not see management as antithetical to the Holy Spirit, any more than we view medicine that way. We need not fear management. We need not call for muddling mediocrity in management. We call for excellence, as it is used in its own subordinate sphere.

Mission begins in worship. Therefore, American missiologists affirm the primacy of spiritual disciplines such as prayer, Bible study, fellowship, love, holiness, and perseverance. We admit a struggle with Christian workers' perpetual temptation to emphasize the kingdom more than the king. We resonate with the lines of T. S. Eliot's (1935, p. 45) play, *Murder in the Cathedral*:

> "Servant of God has chance of
>   greater sin
> And sorrow, than the man who
>   serves a king.
> For those who serve the greater
>   cause may make the cause
>   serve them,
> Still doing right; and striving with
>   political men
> May make that cause political, not
>   by what they do
> But by what they are."

---

[1] Two useful references are Shenk & Hunsberger (1998) and Shenk (1990).

We keep in mind also the words of a mission-minded American, A. W. Tozer (1969, p. 15), who said, "We are called to an everlasting preoccupation with God, to be worshippers first and workers only second. The work of a worshipper will have eternity in it."

Scholarship

Beyond worship, American missiologists are not satisfied merely with applied social science. We are also concerned for theory. What is the value of theory? In brief, theory adds historical depth, comparative breadth, ordered system, critical sharpening, and elegance. Theory protects people. Without theory, practitioners tend to shoot first and aim later. Sometimes they hit the target. Often they wound people. Always they waste bullets. Theoretical reflections help us avoid scandalous, laughingstock mission projects that dishonor the Lord.[2]

When doing scholarly work, we must also pay attention to research methods and resources. Pragmatic Americans excel here. "Tools of the Trade" is the theme of the January 1999 issue of *Missiology*. This detailed report of the 1998 American Society of Missiology annual meeting describes many impressive reference works-in-progress.

In sum, American missiology affirms the primacy of worship and scholarship, not just applied social science. Yet we struggle here. Some reasons for this will emerge in the next section.

Do Westerners Only Support Success? American Values Underlying Missiology

"Have you ever noticed that Westerners only support success?"

Two Asians at an international Christian conference were walking around a lake. One had supervised a highly praised socio-economic program. Western Christians had lionized him. Publications had described his work glowingly. But as he gazed across the lake, he mused to his friend—who reported it to me—"Have you ever noticed that Westerners only support successes? I wonder, would anybody be interested in me if I were to fail?"

Americans do expect success. And such expectations creep into missions. But who are Americans? There are striking differences between the G.I. generation, the Boomers, the Busters, and the Millennials. Economically, an abyss yawns between Bill Gates at Microsoft and an employee at McDonald's, and this gap is growing. Women and men value different things to some extent and respond differently to situations. Ethnicity intersects America: salsa now outsells catsup.

However, there are common concerns. Most Americans emphasize self-reliance, pragmatic problem-solving, and choice. Most have a strong sense of entitlement. Most have compartmentalized worldviews. And many are embarked on active spiritual journeys. To understand Americans in mission, it is worthwhile to explore these values.

Self-reliance

Americans admire active, assertive, ambitious achievers—self-starters. Many of us dream of leaving the big company and striking out on our own. A surprising number do so. Internet technology, in particular, has made it easier for one person to run an independent consulting business.

Whatever our jobs, we are raised to "do it my way." We are not antisocial. Far from it. Self-reliance doesn't mean ignoring people. What it means is that *I choose* my people. Often my choice will not be my

[2] See Hiebert (1999) for a helpful exploration of theoretical foundations.

kin. To compensate for weak kin ties, we are a "nation of joiners," forming all sorts of voluntary groupings. Some of these are essential for knitting the fabric of the community together, like the Parent Teachers' Association attached to every public school, the auxiliary assistants who help at hospitals, and the volunteer fire departments in small towns. It is easy to form new missions and ministries in America.

Many American individuals are philanthropic, giving money and time to causes ranging from ecology to the arts to Christian missions. Americans like to give, but they want to feel a sense of participation in deciding how the donation will be used.

Americans don't know much history or geography, and they have little appreciation for raconteurs who transmit the heritage orally. We live here and now. Although many of us cannot afford to buy a house or maintain health insurance, and although we are disillusioned with our national leaders, still we take charge of our own destinies where we can. For example, we take responsibility for our own emotional well-being. We seek counseling when necessary. To simply suffer our fate would be unthinkable. And on weekends we go to building supply stores or computer stores to buy materials so we can do our own home repairs or computer upgrades. That's the American way.

Problem-solving

Americans admire pragmatic, efficient problem-solving. We do not admire leisurely contemplation of the eternal mysteries. Even in theology, according to historian Mark Noll (1985), we have emphasized "methodological common sense," drawing on Scottish common sense philosophy. We value efficiency, statistics, and technology. We also value change. We expect new consumer goods, new amusements, new ways to get work done better. And we prefer frankness to nuanced courtesy and informality to hierarchy, because these enable us to get right down to business. In mission there is "a practical, activity-directed style of argument of American advocates of mission that runs through A. T. Pierson and John R. Mott to Ralph Winter" (Walls, 1990, p. 5).

We view much of life in measurable terms. Intelligence can be measured. Compatibility or adjustment can be measured. A girl's attractiveness can be measured on a scale of 1 to 10. Even faith: "If you do not commodify your religion yourself, someone else will do it for you," comments R. L. Moore (1994, p. 11) on the Amish.

Doing mission, we like to tackle pragmatic problems with quick, measurable solutions. Ten houses built. Ten dramas performed. Ten sermons preached. One hundred people won to Christ. We approach mission through systems management, diagramming strategy concepts such as tentmakers, nonresident missionaries, multi-individual decision-making units, or criteria to distinguish unreached peoples. Because we are goal oriented, we screen out imponderables that do not fit our planning procedures. Uncertainty and paradoxes are shoved aside. We avoid long discussions fraught with ambiguity, especially in another language. After all, we remind ourselves, our donors deserve results.

Money is valuable not only for its intrinsic usefulness, but also because it serves to measure intangibles. Can our ministry afford air conditioning? This year's software in all our computers? Travel budgets? Glossy paper in our promotional magazine? If so, we must be doing something right.

As a rule, Americans pay little attention to the rest of the world. Every so often, however, something propels us into the international arena. Then our pragmatic, problem-solving outlook shapes the way we connect. Looking at people in need, for example, Americans who care enough to get involved may ask, "What can we do to fix them?"

Choices

Americans expect choice. Supermarket aisles demonstrate this. Choosing starts early: Toddlers are urged to choose among breakfast cereals. In so doing, they are practicing assertiveness and self-reliance, which they will need as adults. Americans expect choices, from their doctors to their specialized magazines.

Ironically, the result is overchoice. It is exhausting to juggle all the options a well-balanced American considers necessary. With so many possibilities, Americans tend to work too hard and play too hard. There is little time left to think or simply to be.

Entitlement

Americans expect comfort, good health, happiness in marriage, and good grades in school. People have a right to these benefits, many feel. If things don't work out, they want to sue somebody. Youth, in particular, expect instant achievements and are impatient with time-consuming processes.

Even in the post-modern world, this sense of entitlement continues. A survey of U.S. high school seniors asked, "Do you think the world will be better or worse 10 years from now?"

"Worse," most answered.

Later in the survey, another question asked, "Do you think your own life will be better or worse 10 years from now?"

"Better," most answered.

The article reporting this was titled, "First Class on the Titanic." Wherever they may be, Americans feel entitled to good seats.

Fragmented worldviews

Paradoxically, in view of their sense of entitlement, many of the Buster generation lack hope for a coherent worldview. Politicians have betrayed them, they feel. Religious leaders have betrayed them. Families have betrayed them through divorce or busyness. They would like marriage, a vocation, a cause, but they are afraid to commit. They would like to end world hunger and promote world peace, but they don't see how. They don't see any overall purpose to history or pattern for the world.

Yes, they see technological progress. Some of them are Microsoft geniuses, after all. And they make existential discoveries. They fall in love. But these "truths" vibrate in separate worlds. They live split lives, half mechanist and half mystic.

The generation now coming of age is called the Millennials. Extensive consumer research on these young people born after 1983 finds that they respect authority; build large, strong friendship networks; accept diversity; live in an online global village; think iconically, learning through story and metaphor; are spiritually open, seeking the "whys" of life, not out of anger or alienation but out of curiosity; value their parents and siblings, although this is not always apparent; want to work for a better world and community; and want to *do* things that make a difference—mission trips, feeding the homeless, community service.[3] Some data suggest the Millennials also do drugs and sex earlier and more casually.

Increasingly, coherence and identity are constructed rather than organic. "The fragmentation of American identities and worldviews causes us to construct our personal identity, tribal 'community,' and

---

[3] Personal conversation with the Rev. Dr. Randy Rowland, generation researcher, Seattle, Washington, October 1999.

worldview," says Paula Harris, Urbana Convention coordinator. "We live in a constant and daily tension between the global (CNN, McDonald's, Target, GAP, Microsoft) and the local, between the image (grieving Kennedy's death, the TV sitcom groups we connect with, our Internet relationships) and the real. So we constantly construct identities, tell stories, and create new tribes." Other peoples face the same global/local tensions, but most have stronger ethnic heritages on which to draw. Many American ethnic foundations are flimsy.

Self-designed spirituality

On our mystic side, Americans recognize that spirituality is a legitimate area of need. So, for example, between the Starbucks coffee kiosk and the Thomas Cook money exchange in the Seattle airport, a shop space has been reserved for spirituality. Members of any religion may sign up to occupy part of this area. Here they offer spiritual counsel to travelers who ask for it.

This counsel need not be Christian. For many Americans, Christianity is suspect. They think it has contributed to patriarchal sexism, ecological rape of the earth's resources, racism, the fostering of low self-esteem because of an emphasis on people being sinners, and repression of emotions. Politically, they identify Christianity with right-wing extremists.

Young Americans prefer "designer religions." Individuals select the components that appeal to them, even if they draw from several religions. If they commit to one, they tend to emphasize those parts that they like. "I'm comfortable with that," is a common phrase. A conversion may be profoundly felt but transient. Since religion is individual, it is poor form to intrude one's religion on others unless they ask about it. A person may share

his story but should not push others to follow.

While statistics serve the mechanistic part of a person, they will not serve this spiritual side. The mystic wants stories—testimonies, experiences, and personal encounters. He wants songs and dance, drum-beating and incense, ritual and drama, tears and joy.

Like all human beings, Americans are limited, as this somewhat tongue-in-cheek survey of values has shown. Still, when practiced wisely and humbly, American qualities such as activism and sense of individual responsibility can be seen as gifts from God and potential blessings to the nations.

Born Again in the USA: Challenges to American Missiology

What, then, are the challenges facing American missiology today?

• One-third of the world's population is under the age of 15, often listening to the same music, watching the same videos, wearing the same clothes, and sharing many of the same fears as American teenagers.

• Catastrophic disasters slam the earth. Even without unusual crises, routine economic structures oppress millions. People whom God loves struggle to survive.

• Pastors and laity long for theological education. For some, interactive web-based courses might deliver these globally.

We would be foolish stewards if we ignored American organization and resources available to serve such populations. Americans bring to these needs "vigorous expansionism; readiness of invention; a willingness to make the fullest use of contemporary technology, finance, organization, and business methods ...; and an approach to theology, evangelism, and church life that emphasizes addressing problems and finding solutions," according to Scottish missiologist Andrew Walls (1990, p. 18).

Americans in mission today also bring a knowledge of the theory of contextualization. Knowledge is not enough, however. It takes time to learn a language, to adapt to a culture, and to be a friend. It requires openness to ambiguity and even to failure. This is true for individuals and for large projects. Yet because our activist values propel us, and because we have the resources to do so, we often jump into mission projects like elephants.

How we need to learn to dance lightly! How we need to learn to emulate the God who took on local form, talked the everyday language, and listened seriously to ordinary human neighbors.

In this context, let us consider four issues that challenge American missiology:

Compartmentalization

Often a missiologist is trained in a specific discipline: theology, Old or New Testament, a social science, management, pastoral ministry, communications, etc. He comes to the broad subject of missiology incomplete, struggling toward wholeness. Rarely do seminaries help. The major seminaries perpetuate deep cleavages between a "school of Bible and theology" and a "school of world mission." A student who enrolls in one division has little time to take courses in the other.

Admittedly, there are integrative networks that eddy against this fissioning stream. Missiological research journals include *Missiology*, *International Bulletin of Mission Research*, and *Evangelical Missions Quarterly*. Growing out of *Practical Anthropology*, the journal *Missiology* is published by the American Society of Missiology. This body cultivates equal representation from Catholics, conciliar Protestants, and independent Protestants.

The Evangelical Missiological Society, which meets concurrently with the Evangelical Theological Society, publishes an annual thematic compendium. These volumes have included *The Holy Spirit and Mission Dynamics*, *Reaching the Resistant*, *Missiology and the Social Sciences*, and *Christianity and the Religions*.

There are many parachurch movements which unite people of various denominations, such as the AD 2000 Movement, the InterVarsity Urbana Mission Convention, and mission agencies themselves. The "Perspectives" course, offered widely across North America, baptizes laity in mission theology, history, and strategy. This course is produced by the U.S. Center for World Mission, founded by Ralph and Roberta Winter.

In spite of these networks, American mission thinking suffers from compartmentalization. This happens even at the congregational level. Many Americans live in their own circle of friends, walled off from people who are different. This is called "cocooning." They don't want to think about the rest of the world. If they are Christians, they avoid thinking about mission. One hundred years ago mission may have been an adventure. Today it is often an annoyance. The masses of data pouring out of the media are overwhelming. An ordinary Christian feels he doesn't know enough to make intelligent decisions. He knows some missionaries have made mistakes in the past. Yes, sometimes he feels vaguely guilty. "But I know God doesn't want me to be upset. So I've decided not to think about that any more," one person told me. He has decided that mission is no longer his responsibility: "I have other priorities."

Most pastors graduate from seminary without being required to take a single world mission course. They have little breadth of missiological wisdom to offer their people. As a result, many church mission projects are done in spurts—uncontextualized, unsystematic, short term.

Since compartmentalization characterizes American life, it is not surprising that it also fractures missiology at every level. The challenge is to see the gaps, to plan for wholeness, and to build adequately comprehensive paradigms. This may be painful. Truly integrated thinking does not come naturally. It requires practice, energy, and time—the thing Americans lack most.

Uniqueness and unity

To cultivate both unity and diversity, in the spirit of Ephesians 4, is a prime challenge for missiology. This global issue appears in microcosm in the U.S.

How shall we reach Americans? Myriad books explore Americans' spiritual odysseys.[4] Most of these books focus on a certain segment of the population. Americans are not all the same. In worship, some belt out loud praise songs, while others praise more reflectively. Some lift up their hearts through country music. Others express heartfelt worship through traditional liturgy and Bach organ fugues. Some come to God in hymns. Often a large church will nurture two or three of these subcultures in different worship services.

Is this segmented worship to the glory of God? "No," says René Padilla (1983) in his classic essay, "The Unity of the Church and the Homogenous Unit Principle." Such segregation fosters classism and racism. It rips apart the unity for which Jesus prayed.

On the other hand, we may answer "Yes" if we see these subcultures as gifts of God, enriching his world, flowing out of his creative image which he has bestowed upon humans, providing local families, local worlds, where people can feel at home. The challenge, then, is to foster deep unity as well as particularity. This means teaching unity at every opportunity, developing exchange and interactive service programs, celebrating together, responding to crises together, doing mission together, empowering leaders from all congregations, and continually condemning racism and classism.

Today millions of Americans are Hispanic and Asian. Among them are spiritually vibrant, biblically knowledgeable believers. Repeatedly throughout history the American nation and church have been re-energized by immigrants. In the 21st century, the vitality of Hispanic and Asian believers could revitalize Anglo churches. Unfortunately, there is little traffic across the polite chasm that separates these family members.

The worldwide challenge to nurture unity in diversity is faced in microcosm in America.

Money and power

The first conference of Evangelical Mission Theologians From the Two-Thirds World subtitled their published papers, "Evangelical Christologies from the Contexts of Poverty, Powerlessness, and Religious Pluralism." How far removed from American missiology this is. While poverty and oppression are major realities for many peoples, these do not shape the categories and paradigms of white male theologians. Nor do missiological anthropologists offer better categories. Their preferred models (structural-functional, symbolic, cognitive, etc.) do not ade-

---

[4] Some recent works include Dyrness (1989), Schultze et al. (1991), Roozen & Hadaway (1993), Bell (1993), Barna (1998), Lippy (1994), Moore (1994), Guder et al. (1998), Roof (1999), and Housden (1999). Two books that continue to serve as baselines are Kelley (1972) and Hauerwas (1989).

quately accommodate painful power imbalances. Yet if conspicuous consumerism, poverty, economic and political injustice, and suffering are deep human realities, these cannot be peripheral in missiology.

A huge issue is how to transfer resources without fostering dependency or corruption. Andrew Walls (1990, pp. 22-23) paints one picture: "In some broken-backed nations, those marked out by poverty of resources, technological breakdown, political instability, or economic disaster, the missionary bodies, often working in concert (Missions Incorporated, as one may say), now have the most flexible, powerful, and efficient organization in the country. They can fly people around the country and in and out of it; they can bring in machinery and service ailing plants; they have radio telephones that work; they can arrange currency, get foreign exchange, and send an international message quickly. They can sometimes do things that the government itself cannot do. And the local church, however independent or indigenous, can do none of these things, except insofar as it can act as a link to an outside mission. In the end, what will be the implications of all this power held by Missions Incorporated?"

In the political dimension, American citizenship carries connotations which a relevant missiology must address. No matter how loudly we separate church and state, simply being an American in the world is a political statement that shapes the way our witness and service are received. Being white in multiracial America is a statement too.

The void of missiological attention in this area is not absolute. Jonathan Bonk (1991) has made a fine contribution, as have a number of urban missiologists (Conn, Greenway, Perkins, Tiersma, etc.). These perspectives need to leaven the whole loaf of missiology.

Post-modern Jesus

All scholarship today is affected by a post-modern ethos. We can no longer rest in the clear categories of the Enlightenment. Reality is seen to be much more multi-dimensional. Facts are not value-free. Objects are not known apart from the subjects who know them. Cause-effect explanations cannot answer the question, "Why?" Logic must be supplemented by metaphor. Western progress is not the only path. Optimism is chastened: Not all problems are solvable. The clear worldview of the Enlightenment no longer holds. Paradox and ambiguity loom large. We have lost our "metanarrative," academicians say. We live with fragments, compartments, bits and pieces of truth. There is no longer any single story that holds it all together.

The virtual realities of media abet this split. Media present us with fantasy worlds and "sound bites" where great tragedies and beer ads are juxtaposed. By contrast, in the world of nature and the world of society, there are sustained rhythms. Seed time and harvest. Friendship, courtship, marriage, parenting, aging, dying. Creation, use, maintenance, repair. Knowing these rhythms helps us know ourselves, our potential and our limits, and the sequences that support happy choices. But how many young adults know the grand rhythms of nature and community as well as they know the limited rhythms of their favorite computer games? They exist among *non sequiturs* rather than contextualized connections.

Here clear witness to Christ erodes. In his book on post-modernism and missiology, Paul Hiebert (1999) observes, "Most Western Christians have yet to develop epistemological foundations that enable them to affirm the uniqueness of Christ as the only way to salvation and life eternal, and to boldly witness to the truth in winsome ways.... Today Western Christians ride to work with Muslims and Hindus who are good people, often better than some Christians they know. How can they declare that these people are lost? The easy solution is to stress tolerance, to live our own lives and let others live theirs, and to hope that communities can somehow coexist in peace in the same nation and world. One of the greatest challenges to the Western church is to lay again the theological foundations of the uniqueness of Christ, and to train its members how to proclaim this with humility and love."

Hiebert recommends "critical realism" and "critical contextualization," drawing from both modern and post-modern reservoirs. While mystery, subjectivity, and symbol are essential parts of knowing, while "approximate knowledge may not be complete or exact, that does not make it relative or arbitrary.... Theology and science are not different ways of knowing. True, they ask different questions and use different methods of analysis.... But both begin with belief in premises, and draw on historical experiences to help them understand the order and meaning in reality. Both assume a real world characterized by an order that is continuous over time. Both assume the ability of human reason to understand the world, at least in part.... This has profound implications for us as Christians, for it means we must proclaim theological truth as public truth—true for everyone, not just those who believe it."

The Big Story

In the story of the mouse and the elephant, we have seen ourselves. Many postmodernists think that this is *all* we can know—single stories. We have lost our overarching metanarrative, our integrating story, they say.

But Christians share a metanarrative older than the Enlightenment. Ephesians outlines that story, in which God in Christ brings together all things in creation (chaps. 1 and 3), ethnic groups (ch. 2), members of the church (ch. 4), and members of the family (ch. 5). Here our American compartments, our diversities, our money and power, and our conflicting generations find their place in Christ and his kingdom.

We can tell that story, and surely the time for telling is now. When philosophers tinker with bits and pieces of the shattered edifice of truth, how blessed we are to be able to resonate the great themes of creation, stewardship of the earth, incarnation, substitutionary life-giving, resurrection, regeneration, spiritual empowering, community, heaven, and a God both powerful and personal. When evil is strong, it is time to tell about grace. When crucifixion takes place, it is time to tell about resurrection. Surely one of the resources most needed for the 21st century will be people of every nation—including Americans—who can tell the story.

References

Barna, G. (1998). *The second coming of the church*. Nashville, TN: Word Publishers.

Bell, J. L. (1993). *Bridge over troubled water: Ministry to baby boomers, a generation adrift*. Wheaton, IL: Victor Books.

Bonk, J. J. (1991). *Missions and money: Affluence as a Western missionary problem*. Maryknoll, NY: Orbis Books.

Dyrness, W. A. (1989). *How does America bear the gospel?* Grand Rapids, MI: Wm. B. Eerdmans Publishing Co.

Eliot, T. S. (1935). *Murder in the cathedral*. New York: Harcourt, Brace & World.

Guder, D. L., et al. (1998). *Missional church: A vision for the sending of the church in North America*. Grand Rapids, MI: Wm. B. Eerdmans Publishing Co.

Hauerwas, S. (1989). *Resident aliens: Life in the Christian colony*. Nashville, TN: Abingdon Press.

Hiebert, P. (1999). *The missiological implications of epistemological shifts: Affirming truth in a modern/post-modern world*. Harrisburg, PA: Trinity Press International.

Housden, R. (1999). *Sacred America: The emerging spirit of the people*. New York: Simon & Schuster.

Kelley, D. M. (1972). *Why conservative churches are growing: A study of sociology in religion*. New York: Harper & Row.

Lippy, C. H. (1994). *Being religious, American style: A history of popular religiosity in the United States*. Westport, CT: Greenwood Press.

Moore, R. L. (1994). *Selling God: American religion in the marketplace of culture*. New York: Oxford University Press.

Nida, E. A. (1954). *Customs and cultures: Anthropology for Christian missions*. New York: Harper.

Noll, M. (1985). Common sense traditions and American Evangelical thought. *American Quarterly, 37*.

Padilla, R. (1983). The unity of the church and the homogenous unit principle. In W. R. Shenk (Ed.), *Exploring church growth*. Grand Rapids, MI: Wm. B. Eerdmans Publishing Co.

Roof, W. C. (1999). *Spiritual marketplace: Baby boomers and the remaking of American religion*. Princeton, NJ: Princeton University Press.

Roozen, D. A., & Hadaway, C. K. (Eds.). (1993). *Church and denominational growth: What does (and does not) cause growth and decline*. Nashville, TN: Abingdon Press.

Schultze, Q. J., et al. (1991). *Dancing in the dark: Youth, popular culture, and the electronic media*. Grand Rapids, MI: Wm. B. Eerdmans Publishing Co.

Shenk, W. R. (1990). North American Evangelical missions since 1945: A bibliographic survey. In J. A. Carpenter & W. R. Shenk

(Eds.), *Earthen vessels: American Evangelicals and foreign missions 1880–1980* (pp. 317-334). Grand Rapids, MI: Wm. B. Eerdmans Publishing Co.

Shenk, W. R., & Hunsberger, G. R. (1998). *The American Society of Missiology: The first quarter century*. Decatur, GA: American Society of Missiology.

Tozer, A. W. (1969). *Gems from Tozer*. Bromley, Kent, England: Send the Light Trust.

Walls, A. (1990). The American dimension in the missionary movement. In J. A. Carpenter & W. R. Shenk (Eds.), *Earthen vessels: American Evangelicals and foreign missions 1880–1980* (pp. 1-25). Grand Rapids, MI: Wm. B. Eerdmans Publishing Co.

Miriam Adeney's grandfathers immigrated to the U.S. from Ireland and Germany. With an M.A. in journalism and a Ph.D. in anthropology, Miriam has served in Micronesia, Mali, Nepal, Russia, Brazil, and on a Canadian Indian reserve, as well as directing publications for the Philippine InterVarsity Christian Fellowship. Currently Miriam teaches at both Seattle Pacific University and Regent College, where she directs the program in Bookwriting for Asia, Africa, and Latin America. Miriam's own books apply Christian anthropology to economic development, women, writing skills, and Islam. She serves on the Board of Christianity Today and on the Editorial Board of the American Society of Missiology. Miriam and her husband Michael have three sons.

Part 5

Responding
to the challenges

IN THIS CENTURY, the challenge of world evangelization and full obedience to the Great Commission is vast and
will require all the creativity and resources of the global
church of Christ. All seven of these chapters were commissioned after Iguassu, though in a few cases they are partially
based on reports that came from regional discussions during the Consultation. But as we evaluated the future book,
there was need to release new and qualified writers to research, write, and speak from their heart and perspective.
Thus, this section parallels the previous one in that it comes
primarily from a regional perspective. We have two complementary analyses from vast India (D'Souza and Howell) and
one from East Asia (Prescott). A weakness on the Iguassu
program was the absence of any serious analysis of the Islamic reality around the world, and we are grateful to
Engqvist's careful chapter. Readers will discover a most creative approach on the re-evangelization of the West by
Dowsett and will be stimulated by Tiplady's piquant Generation X missiological voice.

The final chapter by Brynjolfson reports on nine working groups that met during the Consultation. The reader will
find recommendations related to sending (the church and
mission, national missionary movements, and missionary

training); recommendations related to strategy (partnership and strategic cooperation, intentional bi-vocational cross-cultural service, media and technology); recommendations related to "staying" in mission service (relief and development and member care); and concluding with recommendations related to global missiology.

Brynjolfson's nine topics emerged from the discussion and reflection of the 160 participants. The topics were then presented to the leadership of the WEF Missions Commission as suggestions and recommendations that would contribute to the process flowing out of the Iguassu Consultation. They also become substantive food for mission-minded churches, training programmes, missionary sending organizations, and reflective practitioners around the world.

27

The Indian church and missions face the saffronization* challenge

JOSEPH D'SOUZA

FOUR SETS OF MEDIA images have been forged into the Indian psyche in the last few years by current events. These images, in both electronic and print media, tell us the multifaceted story of India. It is the story of a nation in the midst of tumultuous changes—a nation of paradoxes that is churning at many levels. It is a story that does not fit the stereotype of the India of the British Raj or of an ancient nation where things are eternal.

Today's India is a turbulent place where globalization, religions, traditions, peoples, and politics have come to the fore and are in tension with each other. It is a place of turmoil which is rapidly developing into a culture of violence. Underneath the seeming calm on the exterior, you will find a society that is experiencing changes it has never known before.

The Indian church and missions are confronted with these changes along with everyone else, and they are bewildered at the fast developments. Until recently, the church and missions went about doing their good work with relative peace, and the number of indigenous Christian movements mushroomed in the era after independence.

India's church and mission leaders have been caught by surprise at the viciousness of the attacks of Hindutva forces against them. These attacks have both a religious and a political motive behind them, as a Human Rights Watch (1999b) report titled *Politics by Any Means* points out. The violent attacks have forced Christians to rally together to meet the challenge of the hostile Hindutva forces. It is a challenge that must be met with love, firmness, and courage, knowing

---

* Saffronization is the process of making India a Hindu nation, excluding Christians and Muslims from a core identity as Indians.

well the history of extremist movements in Europe. Future generations of Indians will judge us by our stand and actions in the present crisis.

The Hindutva movement by no means represents the majority of the Hindu population; nevertheless, their hold on social institutions and the institutions of democracy is growing stronger. Backed by the political party in the central government that supports this ideology, a major effort and movement are taking place to co-opt as many of the castes and religious groups as possible into the Hindutva movement, whose present targeted enemies are Christians and Muslims.

India well echoes the prophetic words of David Bosch (1991, pp. 188-189): "The point is simply that the Christian church in general and Christian mission in particular are today confronted with issues they have never even dreamt of and which are crying out for responses that are relevant to the times and in harmony with the essence of the Christian faith.... The new situation challenges us, across the board, to an appropriate response. No longer dare we, as we have often done, respond only piecemeal and ad hoc to single issues as they confront us. The contemporary world challenges us to practice a 'transformational hermeneutics' ..., a theological response which transforms us first before we involve ourselves in mission to the world."

Let us look at the four media images that capture the present realities of India and that affect the church and missions in the nation.

Growth of the New Middle Classes

The first image and the most recent took place during American President William Clinton's visit to India in March 2000. The media recorded the scene in the In-

dian House of Parliament of the President being swarmed by Indian MPs (many of them belonging to the ruling alliance), after Clinton's historic speech to both houses of Parliament. For once, a President of the United States had talked "with" Indian leaders and not just "to" them. He praised India and talked of a new vision for the relationship between the two nations. The ruling political leaders lapped it up.

The images that flickered on the TV screens showed members of Parliament scrambling over each other to shake the hand of the American President. India had come full circle. The nation had come to terms with the superpower of capitalism. She had come to acknowledge economic power and the accompanying deity of the modernized world—materialism. A land known for its spirituality and gurus had dramatically changed its image in the last few decades.

The Clinton visit to India was not primarily designed to bring peace to the sub-continent. In fact, the U.S. President achieved very little in this area. The visit was about economics. The U.S. had accepted the fact that India's middle class of over 250-300 million was set to become a major global economic bloc offering a new source of cutting-edge workers to the world in the field of information technology (IT). The President acknowledged that, along with the United States, India leads the world in global IT. India's large sector of educated professionals is thus a huge asset, and these workers are wanted in many places.

In the last two decades, the U.S. has become a happy hunting ground for Indian scientists, businessmen, and professionals. The sheer numerical strength of professionally trained Indians has given India an enormous advantage in the new economy built around knowledge and information. The present U.S./India economic alliance is the result of the massive globalization process that has swept over the Indian middle classes in the last decade or so. India's cities and towns, colleges and universities, cinemas and video parlors, hotels and restaurants, print media and television are in the throes of a huge cultural invasion by and interaction with the West. Future shock has hit India. It is too early, however, to predict the long-term consequences.

The upper middle classes, the rich, those who run the businesses, and those who manage the economy are not grumbling about the globalization process; after all, it is making them wealthy. The new middle class is not complaining either. Very happily, mammon is worshiped, and the new India is a rich and fertile ground for the great global god of the 21st century—materialism. The unabashed worship of materialism in the First World resonates and connects with the new middle class in India.

Members of this new Indian economic bloc of the largely literate middle classes are capable of conversing and doing work in English—over 150 million of them are reported to know English. This gives the Indian professionals a distinct advantage over other nationalities in the global marketplace. Despite harsh attacks on the English language by Indian politicians in the past, including those belonging to the present ruling party, English has now become a major asset and is an integral part of Indian culture. Notwithstanding their pronouncements, politicians who attack the English language have their children educated in English-medium schools and colleges. The poor masses now know this and are not fooled anymore. The knowledge of English is an economic asset in today's India.

This reality also opens up a huge new door of opportunity for India's English-speaking "global Christians" who want to share the love of Jesus wherever Indians are based in the global marketplace, whether in India or abroad. This witness, however, has to be done by first grasping the whole context of today's India.

Regionally, South India and the states of Maharashtra and Gujarat are experiencing a large percentage of the economic boom. The reason for the rise of the new middle classes is education. There are now huge numbers of business entrepreneurs and scientific research opportunities. Opportunities are also provided to many through reservation (affirmative action) policies, which have been incorporated into India's Constitution through the efforts of Dr. B. R. Ambedkar, the champion and hero of the backward castes. India has made immense progress in the post-independence period and has proved that the talent and enterprise of her people are second to none.

However, upper caste Hindus and the upper castes of other religious groups continue to own and control the economy. Here, nothing has really changed for thousands of years. The upper castes have been the first to cash in on the fruits of political freedom and economic liberalization, since they have had the prior social, economic, and educational advantages.

P. N. Chopra (1997, p. 130) states, "Despite modernisation, intellectual growth, and development, the Indian society still follows much of the old distinctions based on varna, i.e., caste and karma, the doctrine of accepting our distinctions as unalterable in our lifetime. It is on this basis that Brahminic leadership still functions in this country. Nowadays a leader is not necessarily a Brahmin, but the power he seeks is a Brahminical one with all the prerequisites that go with it, including, where necessary, being above the law."

The upper castes have become more powerful in the aftermath of globalization, with access to the media, travel, education, and vast assets. Paradoxically, many of these people who have migrated to the West and who enjoy the freedom and opportunities there are now supporting the extreme right wing forces in India. Their money, intelligence, politics, and diplomacy from abroad feed the Hindutva movement in India, which presses for a nation built on a monolithic ideology of one faith, one culture, and one people.

According to Kancha Ilaiah (1998, p. 131), "As of today, the non-resident Indians, NRIs [Indians who live abroad and with whom Westerners are most likely to come in contact] belong mostly to the upper castes. The post-capitalist markets into which these NRIs are integrated did not de-caste them. This is very clear from forces that financed Hindutva with dollars. The categorical shift of the Delhi 'intelligentsia' towards Hindutva, as against the Uttar Pradesh illiterate Dalitbahujan castes who preferred the Bahujan Samaj and the Samajwadi party, shows the direction of the future."

At the same time, globalization is eroding the religious values and traditions that have managed to hold Indian society together. The family structure is under attack. Sexual promiscuity, drugs, and the like are on the rise among the affluent.[1] Divorce among the middle classes is increasing, although the divorce rate is still much lower than in the West. Alienation, loneliness, and the breakdown of relationships—diseases bred by materialistic societies—are common in the major cities of India. Violence, rape, and crime have increased all over the country. New Delhi, the capital, has the distinction of being the most crime-prone city of India. Added to this is the rampant corruption that was prevalent even before globalization hit India.

The golden cow or Jesus?

Christian missions among the middle and upper classes have their work cut out—a complex work that will challenge both the attitudes and the lifestyle of the largely middle and upper class church in the urban areas. Sadly, this church is concerned primarily with getting on in life at the expense of costly devotion to Christ. It is marked by an ignorance of larger social developments and a lack of understanding of Indian culture. Often this sector is concerned only about itself. In this, Indian Christians are no different from other Indians.

What Chopra (1997, p. 124) says in a scathing criticism of certain Indians could be applied to a section of urban Christians as well, even though there are always many wonderful exceptions: "Indians ... are self-centered ... and inwardly. Self-aggrandisement and promotion of personal interests even at the cost of the community and the nation have marked their character.... They have not bothered if a neighbour's house is on fire or burgled as long as their home is safe. They have never been far-sighted enough to realise that a fire in the neighbour's house will engulf their own. The same attitude explains their total indifference to come to the rescue of a person involved in an accident; they would prefer to leave him alone."

The Indian leaders of both the church and missions will have to address several

---

[1] The *Deccan Chronicle* (1999) describes the scene in Mumbai: "Rave parties are generally characterised by carnal orgies. Techno music, drugs, and a heady atmosphere are usually followed by unabated sex at rave parties ... this seems to be another light on the ways of our rich and famous; the extent to which money can permit an individual to subvert all norms of decency and humanity and to pervert all social codes. This thrusts a question in the general direction of the Indian upper classes, a question about the limits of self-indulgence that money can buy."

issues in dealing with the new middle classes:

1. There needs to be a fresh critique of materialism as an ideology and way of life within the Indian context. How will the materialistic assumptions about the nature of man affect and further damage a wounded civilization? We know that materialism is no different from materialistic anthropologies which "absolutize the physical side of man while denying the reality of what we might call his or her 'mental' or spiritual side" (Hoekema, 1986, p. 3).

2. The gospel message will need to talk about the alienation, loneliness, broken relationships, and social destruction that materialism produces. It will state that the human race is made in the image of God, and therefore each individual is far more valuable than all material possessions. It will pronounce that man does not live by bread alone and that all of us need the Word of God to save and speak to our soul. All persons need the Holy Spirit to live in them. Thus the gospel will speak prophetically into a context and bring the good news of salvation in Christ.

3. Though there has been much writing and discussion in the past about a Christian counter-culture to deal with materialism and modernity, this has not come into being in the First World. Is it because the church there reacted too late to developments in society and had already lost the war against secularism and materialism? The Indian church is historically placed to counter this trend at the beginning stage. By and large, the church is still concentrated in the towns and villages and is comparatively poor. A biblical and balanced approach to legitimate prosperity needs to be articulated and taught in the churches. This instruction needs to be buttressed by teaching on stewardship in both the owning and sharing of wealth. In addition, the stewardship of God's creation must be taught. A stand against the wastage of resources and the culture of over-abundance will help build a counter-culture that can speak prophetically into the life of society.

4. The Indian Christian diaspora in North America, which is an affluent group even by U.S. standards, must consider their responsibility for bringing the love of Christ to their fellow Indians abroad. Indian Christians have tended to congregate abroad according to their community and denominational lines back home. The Indian Christian community abroad will need to deal with some of the issues raised in this paper for their own context. Indians are searching for the love of Christ in all locations. The larger Evangelical community in North America and Europe will need to address their responsibility towards Indian immigrants who are slowly becoming an influential and powerful economic bloc within these Western nations.

India's Poor Majority

The second set of images impressed on the Indian mind includes the images of poverty, illness, human suffering, and environmental waste. The recent cyclone in Orissa highlighted the plight of India's majority population, with millions of people rendered homeless (actually, the homes were not really homes, but merely places of shelter in extreme poverty). People wept openly in television interviews because they had lost all, even their human dignity. Soon urban Indians would hear tales of women and young girls being sold into prostitution in order to survive.

This tragedy is now compounded by the devastating drought that has hit over 50 million people in Gujarat, Rajasthan, and Orissa in the summer of 2000. *India Today* (2000) reports that, overall, close to 100 million people are affected in 12 states. The magazine notes, "As state after state falls prey to the great dry, government apathy only heightens the misery. It is a suffering so endless that it defies being catalogued." Environmentalists are pointing out that this is a man-made drought. Utter neglect and damage of the environment are the major causes. Government apathy in not taking action, despite warnings since last October, has resulted in a tragedy of immense proportions.

Some 300 million people learn to guzzle Coke, even as 700 million struggle to find clean drinking water. These are India's poor. Absolute poverty has grown in the midst of globalization and the emergence of the new middle class. Most of the poor belong to the lower castes. A large percentage of the Muslim population is also poor. Because of the pressure of economics and the age-old feudal systems that operate in the rural areas, most of the poor are illiterate. If India has over 25 million children involved in child labour and over 50 million people who live in dark and degrading holes called slums, it is because of grinding poverty. There is no respite for the poor in India.

Arundathi Roy (1999, pp. 11, 15), author of the award-winning best-seller, *The God of Small Things*, points out, "Thanks to us, Independence came (and went), elections come and go, but there has been no shuffling of the deck. On the contrary, the old order has been consecrated, the rift fortified. We, the Rulers, won't pause to look up from our heaving table. We don't seem to know that the resources we are feasting on are finite and rapidly depleting. There's cash in the bank, but soon there will be nothing left to buy with it. The food is running out in the kitchen. And the servants haven't eaten yet. Actually, the servants stopped eating a long time ago.

"It's like having an expense account. Someone else pays the bills. People from another country. Another world. India's poorest people are subsidising the lifestyles of the richest. Did I hear someone say something about the world's largest democracy?

"... India lives in her villages, we're told, in every other sanctimonious public speech. That's ... just another fig leaf from the government's bulging wardrobe. India doesn't live in her villages. It dies in her villages. India's villages live only to serve her cities. Her villagers are her citizens' vassals and for that reason must be controlled and kept alive, but only just."

The "trickle-down theory of economics" does not work in India. It may work in a more egalitarian society, where everyone has the same apparent opportunity regardless of where one is born. Political and social factors run Indian life, not what is guaranteed by the Constitution.

In his Republic Day speech on January 26, 2000, the President of India warned about full-scale rebellion from these masses if political and societal leaders did not take immediate action to alleviate the suffering of the poor masses. The President knows what he is talking about. Ominous signs are on the horizon. The violent Naxalite movements among the young and unemployed, which result in the destruction of lives and property, are causing havoc in different parts of the nation. Poverty and the inability to change one's condition in life drive these groups. Suicides among farmers because of poverty have become common in various states. Large-scale migration of the poor to the cities is giving rise to more and more slums. India's cities are already crumbling under the pressure of oversized populations and the lack of infrastructure to support the millions that are moving in. In the cities, underworld criminal gangs are prevalent, and blackmail and kidnapping of the rich are becoming increasingly common.

A violent revolution or the love of Jesus?

How do the Indian church and missions leaders now deal with this second major dimension of their Indian reality?

1. It is in this context that, first of all, the model of Mother Teresa's life and work towers above all. Her life said something to the Indian people about the love of Christ that motivated and drove her to the poorest of the poor. She did not do much about social structures, but she did what individual Christians can do, and she made a difference in the lives of the poor. The cry of India's poor goes out to God, and a Christian demonstration of holistic[2] mission of immense proportion is the need of the hour. The other person who has stood out as an example in this realm is the martyred Graham Staines, who touched the lives of lepers—outcasts of society. The sight of the poor and the lepers crying out at the funerals of Mother Teresa and Graham Staines will not be forgotten for a long time. More people have been drawn to Christ through the witness of these saints than we can imagine. The Indian church and missions need to give birth to more such individuals by the tens of thousands.

2. Indian missions need to be in the forefront in identifying, serving, and being involved with the poor because of the love of Christ. This is not the time to sit back and boast of our past efforts among the poor. Only the love of Christ can bring about the sacrificial service required at this time. Indian missions need not be embarrassed by the fact that the message and love of Jesus drive them in their holistic mission. Indian missions must not be intimidated by the propaganda of the Hindutva forces that constantly accuse them of being involved in compassionate work in order to convert people. There is a proper and bold defense against this accusation.

3. The Indian church must reject the notion that the poor and the illiterate do not have the capacity to decide on spiritual matters and matters of conscience. This idea goes against fundamental human dignity and denies basic individual freedom to people. The poor and the illiterate, in fact, have more capacity than the rest to imbibe faith and spiritual truths. The move to give the State legislative powers in deciding on matters of conscience is one of the worst forms of human rights abuse.[3]

4. Indian Christian leaders cannot escape from dealing with societal sin along with personal sin. The social conscience of the Indian Christian needs to be further awakened and activated. For too long the churches have talked only about personal sin. They need to talk about both personal and social sin. This will mean that in many places the church will itself have to go through transformation before she enters mission. Bringing the love and salvation that are in Christ to the poor will mean deep personal transformation (see Sider, 1984, pp. 120, 122). There are no shortcuts here. The gospel of Jesus will deal with sin in the church as much as sin in society. It will also confront issues of structural sin and will teach us not to participate in the fruits of unjust structures.

---

[2] Holistic is defined here as addressing the physical, emotional, mental, and spiritual needs of the people.

[3] The government of Orissa has further amended the anti-conversion bill, giving sweeping powers to the police to question and authenticate decisions in matters of conscience. This bill has now gone to the High Court as Christians and other minorities have challenged it.

Liberation of the Dalitbahujan Castes

The images of the 1990 caste riots and of students immolating themselves are still imprinted on Indian minds. India was then in the midst of caste turmoil, and the backward castes and the Dalits were forming strategic alliances.[4] The most significant social movement in present-day India was taking place—the churning among the so-called backward and Dalit castes, for which we shall use the term "Dalitbahujan," meaning the oppressed castes who make up the majority peoples. Together, they and the tribals make up over 70% of the Indian people.

If the forces of Hindutva do not have a stranglehold on the Indian State today, it is because of the major stirrings among these oppressed peoples all over the nation. The Dalitbahujan castes have seen Hindutva for what it is: "In fact post, postcolonial Hindutva is a Brahminical modernity which works strategically in the interests of Brahmin, Baniya, and neo-Kshatriya forces" (Ilaiah, 1998, p. 43).

The Dalitbahujan castes' social and political activism is keeping a religiously pluralistic democracy alive at the present time. Without their rejection of the Hindutva doctrine, the nation would be in trouble today, plagued by enormous religious conflicts. Joining the Dalitbahujan castes are many from the upper castes who are also not comfortable with the caste system.

In his seminal work, *Why I Am Not a Hindu*, Kancha Ilaiah, a Sudra by caste, a professor at Osmania University, and a Fellow at Nehru Memorial Museum and Library, tells us how Hindutva represents the Brahminization of India. It is the last-ditch, well-organized attempt by many of the upper castes and the neo-Kshatriyas to maintain their hegemony over Indian society and to co-opt those groups of people who have never been in their "Hindu" fold. Hindutva proponents are busy claiming that even Buddhists, Jains, and Sikhs are also Hindus. But the majority of the Dalitbahujan peoples have not agreed to this co-option and are asserting themselves more and more in every sphere of life. It is only a matter of time before the Dalitbahujan peoples increasingly take over the reigns of political and societal leadership in most parts of India, just as they have done in Tamil Nadu, Bihar, and other places.[5]

Is Indian society going through a process of fragmentation? By all the symptoms in society, it appears so. Is Hinduism as a religion vulnerable to fragmentation? Yes. It is not Christianity or some outside force

---

[4] The decision of the Indian Prime Minister V. P. Singh in 1990 to accept the recommendations of the Mandal Commission report of 1984 and grant 27% reservations in federal government and education for the 3,743 backward sub-castes throughout the nation was an historical event which changed the face of Indian society and politics. In 1993, the Supreme Court ruled in the Indra Sawhney vs. Union of India case that the Mandal scheme was constitutional. Earlier, the Constitution at its inception had provided reservations for the Dalits and tribals.

[5] See Ilaiah (1998) for an account of the stirrings in the Dalitbahujan communities. The fragmentation of the age-old, all-encompassing Hindu society is obvious. Dr. B. R. Ambedkar, according to Ilaiah, was the first thinker in 3,000 years from the lowly Mahar caste. Rejecting casteized slavery and influenced by the philosophy of Buddha, Dr. Ambedkar broke away from Hinduism and also decided not to join any political party led by a Brahmin, Baniya, or neo-Kshatriya. It would be appropriate to point out that Dalits venerate and adulate Dr. Ambedkar. His thinking and reformation were heavily influenced by liberal Western education. To the end, he remained a nationalist liberator of the Dalits.

that is causing this to happen. Rather, pushing the Hindutva doctrine on all Indians is producing this fragmentation.

Despite the best attempts of those who have defended the caste system and despite the motive originally behind the system, the fact remains that the caste system brought in racism.[6] What happens even in the present time to the Dalits of India is unbelievable in terms of atrocities, killings, rapes, and structured abuse of their human rights. These things are done despite the laws of the land and the Constitution that safeguards their rights (Human Rights Watch, 1999a). Racism must be the second original sin—man sinning against man—after man sinned against God. Racism has been found everywhere in India in one form or another.

The failure of Jesus or of Indian Christians?

The problem is that the Christianity that emerged through the missionary effort during the colonial rule ended up taking on a caste identity. Even though Indian social reformers like Ambedkar, Phule, and Periyar were rejecting both the caste system and the religion that perpetuated it, some sections of South Indian Christianity continued practicing the caste system and thus were not able to provide an alternative to this oppressive social system. These sections of the Indian church have been Brahminized. This stands as a major stumbling block for the Dalitbahujan commu-

nity in India and for a growing number of liberal upper caste people who reject the evil in the system.

Advocacy of the missiological "homogeneous unit principle" has not helped. Our reform-minded Dalitbahujan friends do not understand this emphasis. Why have the mass movements not had much impact on Indian society? How is it that so many of these movements have come to a dead-end and dissipated? Is it because the expected human dignity and reconciliation were never realized?

Christian communities from the Dalitbahujan castes have their own caste-driven prejudices among themselves. At a time when the nation needs an integrated Indian church model, there is very little to show. Missions too are seldom models of reconciled communities. This is an affront to the very gospel that is supposed to break down all barriers and provide for alternatives in fragmenting societies. Recently, when Naga Christians and Kuki Christians killed and slaughtered each other, one wondered what dimensions of the gospel have impacted our fellow Christians in the northeast?

Yet it is still not too late.

The church in India is being driven to the heart of the Dalitbahujan communities, who are proving to be the protectors of Christians under attack in a number of places. This is because, despite the caste system prevalent in the church, a lot of social work has been done by Christians

---

[6] Küng (1993, p. 151) comments, "One has to imagine the situation of the Aryan tribes in order to grasp what purity (caste) meant for them. The more some of them penetrated the Ganges plains and went east and south, the more distinctly they found themselves in the minority vis-à-vis the original population. If they wished to hold on to their special position, they had to maintain their racial and cultural identity. They had to avoid blending into subject peoples. This was possible only through isolation—an interesting example of apartheid in antiquity. (It led, by the way, to continually increasing tensions, even back then.) To the Aryans, 'purity' applied to race and, even more strictly, to religion. For this reason, non-Aryans were excluded from both active and passive participation in the Vedic religion. Simultaneously, their special religious position consolidated the Aryan upper castes."

among the lower castes, resulting in their education and knowledge of the broader world. Without doubt, this has empowered the lower castes to assert themselves as human beings in society. This is one of the reasons the Hindutva elements are bent on bringing a halt to Christian social involvement among the backward and low castes. They foresee a direct threat to their own power over these people. The Dalitbahujan castes see Christians as their natural allies. If only Christians would deal with the caste system within the churches themselves!

It is quite obvious that Indian missions will have to chart their own course and come out of the shadow of imported ideas and ways of working. We need to think for our own context, and we need to think long-term. We need to stay true to the foundational gospel principles of regeneration, reconciliation, and redemption. Our own Christian communities need transformation first. We must not be pressurized by the "hurry up" mentality of our day and go in for short-term results, statistics, and decisions, of which we have had many millions!

We now need to hold on for real, long-term change. We have a glorious gospel to share—a gospel of the kingdom that not only brings salvation, but one that also promises (a) an end to violence, (b)

complete social justice, (c) the reclaiming of social "wastes" in human lives, (d) that everything worthwhile in human lives will be tenderly fostered, and (e) that every legitimate interest of human life will receive its due (McClain, 1974, pp. 224-227). It is to this holistic gospel that we bear witness with greater boldness and integrity.

Missions as Both the Proclamation and Defense of the Gospel

Our last image comes from the lion-hearted Pope John Paul II, old and bent because of his years, wounds, and illnesses. Speaking to the Christian church and the Indian nation through the media on the uniqueness of Jesus Christ, he courageously called for open evangelization and the freedom of conscience in early December 1999, at the Asian Catholic Bishops Synod in New Delhi.[7] Those speeches cleared some of the fog around some of the accusations of the Hindutva brigade and compelled Christians to take a clear stand with regards to their faith in the uniqueness of Christ.[8] Indian Christians sitting on the pluralism fence were forced to make their stand known. The church becomes irrelevant in any land when it does not hold onto the salvation that is

---

[7] See *Ecclesia* (1999, pp. 39, 54). The Pope's visit was preceded by calls of protest from right wing Hindu groups who demanded that the Pope apologize for conversions to Christianity and state that Christ was equal to any other gods. The Pope did not oblige. He proclaimed the uniqueness of Christ as Saviour and Lord and pointed out that the church is called to evangelize. A few of the Catholic commentators felt that the Pope's position was a retrograde step in light of the liberal developments in the Catholic church since Vatican II.

[8] Communicating and holding to the uniqueness of Jesus Christ as Saviour and Lord are among the major challenges before Indian missions, which live and serve in the midst of many major world religions. An attitude of arrogance towards other people's faith is not the way forward, nor is ignorance about people's beliefs and traditions. Our message of salvation in Jesus Christ alone because of his finished work on the cross needs patient explanation. This will need to be done in the established context of friendly and long-term relationships. For further reading, see Gnanankan (1992).

available in Christ alone because of his finished work on the cross.

The attacks on Christians, churches, and their institutions have increased since the Pope left.[9] The cardinal doctrines of the Christian faith have been maligned. The Person of Jesus is targeted. Verbal abuse has been poured on our Lord (see Banerjee, 1998, p. 6). The miracles of Christ are ridiculed. Christian institutions and workers face more violence, and recent mission publications and reports have been ripped apart in the media. Christians are accused of engaging in fraudulent conversions. Further State legislation is being enacted which, if passed, which will force Christians to break the law in order to follow their conscience and the faith. After the demonizing of Muslims for decades, it is now the turn of the Christians to be demonized. The liberal and tolerant Indian society is being fed a daily quota of lies about the Christians. To their credit, many Hindus are not buying these lies.

It would be correct to say that the Indian church is where the early church was contextually, except that the Indian church has to contend with Christian history, a multiplicity of religions, the accompanying tensions, and a borderless world due to the impact of information technology in India. An insensitive statement or report in America can have overnight impact on Indian Christians, as demonstrated in the release of the prayer guide on India in October 1999 by the Southern Baptists in their U.S. congregations. Jerry Rankin tendered an apology to the Indian people, which was then released to the press and helped calm down the situation.

Regeneration in Jesus or proselytization to Christianity?

The Indian church now has the job of both proclaiming and defending the gospel in bewildering situations, and she has to contend with and evaluate major issues from various sides. Below are possible positions the Indian Christian leaders can take:

1. There needs to be an open admission of the sins and failures of the church through history, including the Crusades, the destruction of the native cultures of South America, the church's role in colonialism, the decline of faith in Europe and America, and anti-Semitism. The open state of confession must be followed by actual change of attitudes towards nations, peoples, cultures, and religions. A vigorous process of self-critique of the church is in order. This is the glory of the gospel. It teaches us to be broken and contrite and to pursue righteousness.

2. The church will have to repent of the caste system, of her inward-looking tendencies (which result in maintaining the status quo in society), and of her lack of involvement at the heart of Indian society. Repentance will need to be followed by giving the Dalitbahujan castes their due leadership and influence in the life of the church. After all, even within the churches, these castes represent the majority. They have an enormous amount to contribute to the growth and development of the churches. Their cultures, social experience, and insights can greatly strengthen the churches. Including these castes will enable the church to speak prophetically into the life of the nation, as well as to point people to Christ.

[9] See *The Statesman* (2000). Another series of attacks this time in the state of UP left a number of priests and nuns in several places wounded and badly injured after being beaten with iron rods. This was followed by physically attacking local evangelists in Agra and burning Bibles and Scripture portions. These attacks follow the familiar pattern: Hate literature and speeches result in violence against the peaceful community of Christians who are just trying to live out their faith.

3. Further, Christians will have to revisit and study India's vast and ancient philosophical ideas and learn from them wherever possible. The Christian captivity to Greek philosophical systems must end. In our opinion, it has gone on for too long. Indian philosophical thought has many strands that will shed further light and understanding under the guidance of the Holy Spirit on much truth in Scripture.

4. Now that Hindutva ideologues have attacked contextualization as a means that Christians employ in deceiving innocent Hindus, much care and thought must go into this whole area. For a start, there must be curbs on the use of Hindu religious symbols in the present atmosphere. Next, contextualization must stop when it transgresses in areas of social justice. Further, much work should go into understanding and developing a genuine Indian identity. This is the need for both the church and the larger society in the light of the Hindutva attempt to develop an extremist religious identity for the nation. The future for our great nation lies in the acceptance and development of a pan-Indian identity.

5. Indian mission workers need to develop a deep spiritual identity in Christ that is not afraid to draw on some of the spiritual traditions of India. Khushwant Singh, the well-known journalist, was right when he remarked that Indian Christianity has not produced enough saints; rather, it has produced bureaucrats, officers, managers, and the like. How can we expect to impact people who come out of traditions of intense spiritual quest and discipline if we follow shallow and instant spirituality?

6. Christ came to reconcile us to God and also to each other as humans—men and women. How does this reconciliation translate in a communal and caste-infested society that is being driven by evil forces to hate each other?[10] How can we affirm and appreciate the liberal upper caste Hindus who want to move away from the oppression of the caste system? How do we encourage and build up the Dalitbahujan caste people, many of whom are freely turning to faith in Christ all over the nation? Without any doubt, they see and experience Christ as the Saviour. Further, how do we, like Paul, challenge the forces that oppose equality before God and equality as humans? How do we witness for the gospel and get a listening, when people get into vicious conflict with each other because of religion?

7. How do we deal with the accusation that the Christian faith only makes slaves more docile under their oppressors and does not deal with the issue of basic human justice? How do we convince people that God is the God of justice, mercy, and compassion? How do we show people that at the human level Christ was nailed to the cross because he stood for justice, compassion, and mercy and that he was a real threat to the religious and political order of his day? How do we show that at the personal level he died for our sins and came to establish a new eternal kingdom with a new set of values and standards?

8. The forces of Hindutva ridicule the present power of Jesus to heal and deliver people from sin, sicknesses, and other problems. But the masses that are turning to Christ know that this power is true in their lives. Christ is meeting the majority of our people—the poor, the oppressed, the rich, and many in the upper castes—

---

[10] Marty (2000) notes, "If being reconciled to God is a finished work that the believer gets to experience, being reconciled to humans is never finished and hard to experience."

at the point of their need, and he responds to their simple, childlike faith. This does not mean he always answers all their prayers or that they see miracles all the time. It does mean that there is sufficient experience of the power of God in their daily lives and needs. This is a far cry from the health, wealth, prosperity, and instant victory fad in certain sections of the church. A proper articulation of the theology of forgiveness, healing, and deliverance that is balanced and real is essential for our times. Prayer for people in need has become a powerful catalyst in their turning to Christ.

9. Among all the issues for which Christians are attacked, conversion is the biggest. There are several reasons for this. Today, conversion is seen as a political activity and not just a religious decision. Then there is the lie that when people become Christians, they become anti-national. Most Indians do not believe this lie, as Christians are among the most patriotic and law-abiding communities in the nation. When people do turn to the Christian faith out of their own free will, they become what human beings are meant to be—the crown of God's creation.[11] Conversion is also seen as a means of social engineering—that is, a deliberate attempt to bring about change in the social structure. Social change for the good is a fruit of following Christ. Authentic Christian communities always threaten the powerful. The Christian ethos will mean educa-

tion and liberation for the people. To keep people illiterate is to deny them the use of their mind, an integral part of what it means to be made in the image of God. Education will also mean that every man and woman is able to realize his or her full potential.

10. Christians will have to work out and articulate a theology of tolerance and respect for the free will of individuals to choose the life and religion they want to follow. This is crucial as we seek to obey the Lord and communicate the uniqueness of Christ and how salvation is possible only in him because of the finished work on the cross. Our freedom to preach the gospel is limited by another person's free will in choosing not to the follow the gospel. There is a time for preaching, and there is a time for demonstrating the gospel through our lives when the audience has made the choice. The best witness to the gospel ultimately is the power of a Christ-like life.

11. To be ethically pure, Christian charity cannot have an ulterior motive, other than responding to people's need in compassion and love. This is what drives Christian love—the nature of Christ's love. It does not expect anything in return. It gives love freely. Christian missions do not hide the fact that Christ and his love drive them. Whether people accept or reject Christ is not in our hands. If in the past missionaries proselytized en masse for questionable motives, then we need to re-

---

[11] Hoekema (1986, p. 105) observes, "The fall resulted in two evil effects on our self-image. The first was pride. The second was the sense of utter worthlessness. These two problems have plagued the human race. Within the missions context, the tendency has always been to focus on the pride issue. The majority of India's oppressed have the reverse problem. Centuries of collective experience have damaged their sense of worth to unknown degrees. This leads to all kinds of personal and social malfunctioning and harmful behaviour. These people know too well the kind of life they live. The gospel of Jesus to them will be that he will not break a bruised reed, that he will forgive their sins and heal their wounds and strengthen and comfort them through their struggles and life. Instead, what they receive is an alien message designed for another audience where pride is the primary issue, etc. Churches that have brought the above message of the healing, love, goodness, and completeness in Christ are growing fast and strong."

pent of this practice. Proselytization is simply not acceptable in today's world. The emphasis today must be on the spiritual regeneration of people and not on numbers. Regeneration is divine and not in the hands of man. The other point is that many upper caste and rich Indians have turned to Christ all across India. They need to articulate the reason for their faith to their appropriate audiences to counter the accusation of proselytization.

12. Christian missions in the West must know that in the borderless world of the media and information technology, we have a wide-awake, watching world following our lives, words, actions, attitudes, and press releases, whether in print or on the Internet. Unless Western Christians learn to refer their mission concerns and intentions to the Indian church and missions, Christians in India will continue to face more problems. This does not mean that the Christians in India are not willing to face persecution. We are learning that, "However important programmes of formation and strategies of evangelization may be, in the end it is martyrdom which reveals to the world the very essence of the Christian message. The word itself, 'martyr,' means witness, and those who have shed their blood for Christ have borne the ultimate witness to the true value of the gospel" (*Ecclesia*, 1999).

Drawing to a Conclusion

I have attempted to present some of the challenges before us as Indian Christians and leaders. A religiously pluralistic nation watches us. A divided society watches us. Spiritually searching millions are examining us. The cry of the poor and oppressed reaches out to us. A developing nation looks for substantial spiritual realities that address the deep hungers that cannot be satisfied by any new materialism.

We are inheritors of an ancient civilization. Our strengths and weaknesses are unique. Our collective experience and consciousness are different from those of other societies. We take pride in our Indianness. On that basis, we want to forge ahead as Indians and as those who believe in Christ.

We Indian Christians are at a crucial and complex juncture in our history. Old categories of missiology and the latest fads from abroad won't do any good anymore. Any methodology that is one step removed from incarnational involvement in the life of our people just won't work. We will have to work through the loving and patient sharing of our faith in our complex context. We will need to focus on the prophetic dimensions of the gospel. We do not have the luxury of spending endless time in debates over definitions of mission. Rather, we are faced with hard realities. We have to carry on bearing witness to our faith and respond to the cry of our nation. In this we need the prayers and support of all God's people.

References

Banerjee, P. (1998). *In the belly of the beast*. Ajanta Books International.

Bosch, D. J. (1991). *Transforming mission: Paradigm shifts in theology of mission*. Maryknoll, NY: Orbis Books.

Chopra, P. N. (1997). *A nation flawed*. New Delhi, India: Vision Books.

Deccan Chronicle. (1999, June 18). Hyderabad, India.

Ecclesia in Asia. (1999). Vatican City, Italy: Libreria Editrice Vaticana.

Gnanankan, K. (1992). *The pluralistic predicament*. Bangalore, India: TBT.

Hoekema, A. A. (1986). *Created in God's image*. Grand Rapids, MI: Wm. B. Eerdmans Publishing Co.

Human Rights Watch. (1999). *Broken people*. New York.

———. (1999). *Politics by any means*. New York.

Ilaiah, K. I. (1998). *Why I am not a Hindu*. Calcutta, India: Samya.

India Today. (2000, May 8). New Delhi.

Küng, H. (1993). *Christianity and world religions: Paths of dialogue with Islam, Hinduism, and Buddhism* (P. Heinegg, Trans.). Maryknoll, NY: Orbis Books.

Marty, M. (2000, March 27). *Newsweek*.

McClain, A. J. (1974). *The greatness of the kingdom: An inductive study of the kingdom of God*. Winona Lake, IN: BMH Books.

Roy, A. R. (1999). *The greater common good*. Bombay, India: IBD.

Sider, R. J. (1984). *Rich Christians in an age of hunger: A biblical study*. Downers Grove, IL: Inter-Varsity Press.

The Statesman. (2000, April 25). New Delhi.

Joseph D'Souza lives in Hyderabad, India, with his wife, Mariam, where they both have been involved in church and missions for 30 years. Both of them served as cross-cultural workers in North India for nearly 15 years. Their ministry takes them across India, challenging the church for missions as well as training mission workers with various groups. Joseph has been overseeing OM's varied ministries run by nationals (over 800 alone with OM) in India and has been the Chairman of OM Books for the past 10 years. Under Joseph's leadership, a training programme for on-the-field mission workers was developed under the Asian College of Cultural Studies, Hyderabad, which now offers accredited bachelor's and master's degrees in missions and leadership. Since 1998, Joseph has been the Chairman of the All India Christian Council—a broad Christian front of over 2,000 groups, associations, churches, and denominations—that is proactively responding in many different ways to the persecution of Indian Christians and the attack on their fundamental liberties. He has a B.A. in chemistry from Karnataka University and an M.A. in Christian communication from Asia Theological Seminary, Manila. Joseph and Mariam have two children aged 21 years, Josh and Beryl.

28

The Hindu missionary movements and Christian missions in India

RICHARD
HOWELL

RELIGION TODAY PLAYS a crucial role in characterizing the nations of the world. The nationalist movements since the 1970s, based on the assertion that one majority ethnic or religious group defines a nation, have emerged with new force and creativity. Many countries have crumbled since Iran's 1978 Islamic Revolution. In 1992, the Soviet Union and Yugoslavia—two large, multi-ethnic states much like India—were torn into conflicting parts. In India, "communalism" does not refer to people getting together in warm community; to the contrary, the term is associated with hatred, hostility, and suspicion of the other party, and it is symptomatic of new trends emerging in the world order.

The centralized Indian State built on socialist lines by Jawaharlal Nehru is being vehemently challenged. Realizing the powers of the free market and religious nationalism, Indian businesses and some political parties are now confronting the weakening socialist state in India. Religion has become a natural populist force articulating people's cultural and national identities at a level of emotional meaning, more basic and fundamental than other kinds of political affiliations. Today "India" and "Hindu" are often equated when defining Indian culture. The core characteristics of the culture are taken to be Hindu. Indian Islam is thus portrayed as being foreign and derivative, alien to India. Christianity, in a similar strain, is depicted as the religion of the colonizers and is seen to be alien as well. In order to understand India today, it is important, first, to consider the Hindu missionary movements and, second, to give a brief account of the Christian missions so we can learn valuable lessons from history.

Hindu Missionary Movements

Some foundational issues

Aryanization

Hindu[1] mission is as old as ancient Aryanism. The missionary nature of Vedic and Brahmanical Hinduism may be summarized as "Aryanization." *Rig Veda*. 9:63:5 reads, *"Krinvanto visvamaryan,"* "Let us make the whole world Aryan." This verse apparently unfolds the missionary nature of ancient Hinduism. The political supremacy of Aryans and their culture played an important role in the expansion of Brahmanical religion. The Aryans attempted to accomplish this by establishing their supremacy over the dark-skinned *mlecchas* or the *dasyus* or barbarians.[2]

Absorption into caste infrastructure

Despite their political supremacy, the Aryans had to accept the reality of the continued presence of non-Aryans in their midst and elsewhere. This led to the Aryanization of the non-Aryans. This process meant bringing the *mlecchas* under the influence and acceptance of the Aryan customs and beliefs and absorbing the non-Aryans into the caste infrastructure. S. Radhakrishnan (n.d., p. 17) makes reference to the early Aryans' employment of caste infrastructure in the Aryanization of the natives. Bipin Chandra Pal states that Hinduism has always been a missionary religion. It differs from other missionary religions in its methodology. Pal (1913) explains, "Hinduism has propagated itself not through preaching a particular creed but through promulgating its special culture. Hinduism in its missionary work required the non-Hindus to subscribe to a set of Hindu psycho-physical disciplines and regulations, with special emphasis on particular food and drink. The outer orderings of life were first Hinduized, and this was followed by a natural mental and spiritual evolution. By adopting the mode of life peculiar to the Hindus, the non-Hindus became Hinduized." This "Hinduization" process through an altered psycho-physical life is the work of the caste system.

The *shuddhi* program, which was largely employed during the Muslim period in India and is now again employed for Christians under the name of *Ghar Vapasi*, "Returning Home," has the same goal of "purifying the defiled" and providing them with a place in the *dharma* or caste hierarchy. However, the Dalit liberation movements continue their fight against the caste system. Bhagwan Das (1994, p. 75) writes, "Upper caste Hindus have a vested interest in maintaining and perpetuating caste. If caste goes, Hinduism will die. With the Dalits, it is just the opposite. Caste is the greatest obstacle in the way of their unity and progress. If they do not destroy caste, caste will destroy them. They need them only to do the dirty work and to render them friendless by pitting them against Muslims one day, against the Sikhs the next day, and maybe against the Christians very soon. In the eradication of caste and adoption of the right code of conduct based on equality, compassion, loving kindness, and justice lies their salvation."

---

[1] The term "Hinduism" is a useful label for studying different indigenous religious expressions. However, Hinduism is made up of a diversity of religious sects. We have put all these sects together under a uniform name, even though the religious reference points of such groups might be quite distinct. Hindu identity is multiple by definition.

[2] See Matthew (1999); Tambimuttu (n.d.); Clemen (1930); Gray (1965).

Theory of accommodation and dharma

The Hindu missionary movement's "theory of accommodation" can only be understood against the backdrop of *dharma*, caste hierarchy. The disadvantaged communities in Indian society consented to their low status and the resulting exploitation, and they accepted their position as the *varnasamadharma*, order of things. Given the complexity of *dharma* understanding and the hierarchical society that *varnasamadharma* produced, the necessity arose to stress both the need for general accommodation as well as a degree of tolerance for local practices, specific demands, and proposals for change. These things were possible as long as the terms of upper caste *dharma* were not questioned. The Hindu understanding of toleration and accommodation must therefore be understood within the *varnasamadharma* context, which circumscribes and contains them, and not as independent qualities divorced from the context.

Indian society advocates toleration while maintaining an otherwise intolerant and cruel society. Who can leave the caste hierarchy and claim the benefits of toleration? Who can vertically challenge and aspire for the higher caste in the hierarchy and expect accommodation? The characteristics of "accommodation" to be found in a holistically conceived hierarchical society are not the same as those which will bring about a liberal egalitarian society (see Galanter, 1997).

British Raj and Brahmanism

A South Indian writer, S. D. Theeratha (1992, pp. 227, 235-236), maintains that Brahmanical Hindu leaders of the 19th century used the British Raj for their own advantage. Under British rule, in fact, Brahmanism acquired a constitutional status and the force of law. The colonial government failed to check inter-religious intolerance, hostility, caste, priestcraft, and increase of idolatry. At times, anarchy prevailed as two imperialisms, Brahmanical and British, placed one above the other, crushed freedom of the masses. "The Raj, as an imperial system of rule," writes Robert Frykenberg (1997), "was genuinely indigenous rather than a foreign [or colonial construct], ... in terms of religious institutions, indigenous elites and local forces of all kinds were able to receive recognition and protection, as well as special protection from the State.... It is in the sphere of religious establishments, however, that the Raj became especially 'Hindu.' It is in this sphere that, by yielding to special interests, the government of Madras itself became instrumental in facilitating the rise of a centralizing and modern and syndicated Hinduism."

Modern syndicated Hindu missionary movements

The modern, aggressive, syndicated[3] Hindu missionary movement is headed by the Hindutva forces of the Sangh Parivar, who define "nation" both ethnically and culturally. Their clear slogan is, "One nation, one culture, one people." This means that those who belong to the Hindu *dharma* are ethnically and culturally part of the nation. The "others" (Christians and Muslims) are to be hated and rejected, for they do not belong to the nation. As noted earlier, Christianity is viewed as the religion of the colonizers and Islam as the religion of the invaders; both are of alien

[3] Romila Thapar (1985) first used the term "syndicated" to describe Hindu missionary movements.

origin and therefore must be rejected. The move of the Sangh Parivar is to make India into a Hindu nation.

Syndicated Hinduism

Many who were attracted to neo-Hindu groups had at some point in their lives experienced Christian education and were thereafter familiar with Christian ideas. They attempted to defend, redefine, and create Hinduism on the model of Semitic religions. They sought for the equivalent of a monotheistic God, a Book, a Prophet or a founder, and congregational worship with an institutional organization supporting it (Thapar, 1997).

Missionary agencies and scheduled castes and tribes

Hindu missionary organizations, such as those attached to the Ramakrishna Mission, the Arya Samaj, the RSS,[4] and the Vishwa Hindu Parishad, are active among the *adivasis*, mainly scheduled castes and tribes. They are converting these latter groups to Hinduism as defined by the upper caste movements of the last two centuries. What is important for Hindu missionaries is that these communities declare their support for the *dharma* and are ready to be labeled as Hindu for the sake of either a census or support to a political party. That this conversion does little or nothing to change their actual status and that they continue to be looked down upon by upper caste Hindus is of little consequence. Thapar (1997, p. 76) comments, "The call to unite under Hinduism as a political identity is, if anything, anachronistic. Social and economic inequality, whether one disapproves of it or condones it, was foundational to Brahmanism."

Emergence of the middle class

A powerful middle class with urban moorings has emerged and is reaching to the rural rich of India. This group would find it useful to bring into politics a uniform, monolithic Hinduism. Under the guise of Hindutva, claiming to be a revival of an ancient, traditional form but in effect being a new creation, an effort is being made to draw a large following and to speak with the voice of numbers. This voice has been created to support the claims of majoritarianism based on a religious identity in the functioning of democracy. The appeal of such Hinduism to the middle class is obvious, since it becomes a mechanism for forging a new identity aimed at protecting the interests of the middle class. Those lower down in society would be attracted to upward mobility through a new religious movement. Such groups would have to accept the *dharma* of the powerful but remain subordinate.

Use of media

Equally important to Hindutva is the means of its propagation. It uses a variety of existing organizations, from the rather secretive RSS to the harsh-sounding Bajrang Dal. There is an impressive exploitation of modern communication media, both audio-visual and print, with a substantial dose of spectacle, drama, and hysteria. Information is power, and as Frykenberg (1997, p. 89) notes, "The Brahmans have always controlled information."

Hindu diaspora

Another factor of increasing importance for Hindutva is the Hindu diaspora—the dispersal of Hindus in various parts of the globe. The importance of this diaspora

---

[4] For a detailed study, see Andersen & Damle (1987).

is reflected not only in the social links between those in India and those abroad supporting Hindutva, but also in the growing frequency with which the Sanghs and Parishads hold their meetings abroad and seek the support and conversion of the affluent to their ideology. A convention was organized by Vishwa Hindu Parishad in Washington, DC, in 1993, to commemorate the anniversary of Vivekananda's visit to America. The commemoration was an intentional, aggressive drive for a religious identity with strong political aspirations.

Religious intolerance and violence

History bears witness to many religious conflicts in Indian society. "Religious intolerance is not alien to Hinduism," states Thapar (1997), "despite the 19th century myth that the Hindus are by instinct and religion a non-violent people. The genesis of this myth was partly in the romantic image of the Indian past projected, for example, by scholars such as Max Muller" (see Muller, 1892, p. 101ff.).

Thapar (1997; see also Thapar, n.d., p. 19ff.) continues, "Non-violence as a central tenet of behavior and morality was first enunciated and developed in the Sramanic tradition of Buddhism and Jainism. These were the religions which not only declined at various times in various regions in India, but also were persecuted in some parts of the sub-continent. Huan Tsang and Kalhana record the persecution of Buddhists by Saivas, and Karnataka witnessed the destruction of Jaina temples in a conflict with the Saivas. One is often struck by how different the message of the Gita would have been and how very much closer to non-violence if Gautama Buddha had been the charioteer of Arjuna instead of Krsna." Writing about "The Mahabharata Legacy and the Gita's Intent," Rajmohan Gandhi (1999, p. 34) says, "Proud as we are of the epic's codes of chivalry, we cannot be proud, I suggest in all humility, of the story, or history, it reveals. In particular, we cannot be proud of the epic's acquiescence in triumph of revenge over reconciliation. I suggest, further, that we cannot be glad that the epic is reproduced in varied forms in our history."

In 1984, Mrs. Indira Gandhi, the Prime Minister of India, was killed by some of her guards in revenge for "Operation Bluestar." To avenge Mrs. Gandhi's death, within days thousands of Sikhs were killed, in many cases burned alive.

On December 6, 1992, the Ayodhya's Babri Masjid mosque, built in 1528 by Mir Baqi under the authority of Babar, the first Mughal emperor of India, was demolished in revenge by a mob of more than 300,000 Hindus, most of whom wore the saffron color of Hindu nationalism. In the excitement of successful, even if long delayed revenge, a number of poor Muslims in Ayodhya were also killed. In the following weeks, hundreds perished in riots or in police firing in Mumbai; a large majority were Muslims. The serial bomb blasts set off in Mumbai in revenge also took the lives of several hundred, mostly Hindus. By this time, a number of Hindu temples in Pakistan and Bangladesh had been destroyed. The supporters of Ayodhya justify the action as the liberation of a Hindu sacred space to unify the Indian nation. Critics call it violence against Muslims—an attack on Indian civil society. David Ludden (1996, p. 2) writes, "Ayodhya symbolises Hindu-Muslim conflict in South Asia but also conjures the nightmare of nuclear war between India and Pakistan.... The men who destroyed the Babri mosque marched to a cultural movement whose ideas, images, media, organisations, and resources are transnational in form, scope, and influence. Ayodhya is a refraction of 'ethnic cleansing' in Serbia, the 'moral majority' in the United States, and other movements that define nations by ethnicity and religion."

Now Christians are being persecuted—their priests killed, churches burned, institutions attacked, nuns raped, and Bibles burned. Australian missionary Graham Staines and his two innocent children, Phillip and Timothy, were burned alive in the jeep they were sleeping in on the night of January 23, 1999. Mrs. Gladys Staines, the widow of Graham, and Esther, the couple's 13-year-old daughter, publicly forgave the perpetrators of the crime. Gladys' testimony, "I have no hatred; I forgive," was a living demonstration of the power of the gospel of Jesus Christ, who died to reconcile people to God and to one another. The mission of the church in India is to be a reconciling community.

Islam in India

Islam is as old in India as in Turkey. Indian Islam is older than European Protestantism or American Christianity. Islam found its entrance into India initially through Muslim Arab traders who had trade links with the kingdoms along the west coast of India. From A.D. 712 onwards, Muslims began to settle permanently in the Indus Valley and to make converts among low caste Hindus. R. C. Majumdar (1966, p. 478) highlights the significance of the reality of Islam in India: "The advent of Islam constituted the first great rift in the solidarity of the Indian community since the incorporation of the aboriginal peoples into the Aryan society." Indian society then came to be divided into two major communities—Hindu and Muslim. Islam wholeheartedly welcomed Hindus to its fold. Majumdar (1966, pp. 499-500) comments, "The position of the Hindus under the Muslim rule during the first two or three centuries was most unenviable, and the temptation to secure liberty, privilege, and higher sta-

tus by a change of creed proved irresistible to many. Through peaceful missionary propaganda and acts of terrorism and violence, Islam swelled its ranks at the expense of the Hindu community." The Muslims treated the Hindus with contempt as *kafirs*, infidels. Conversely, the Hindus with "injured pride" developed deep resentment against the *mlecchas*, the polluted people. Thapar (1997) observes, "The definition of the Hindu today has its roots more in the period of Muslim rule than in the earlier period, and many of the facets which are regarded today as essential to Hinduism belong to more recent times. The establishment of sects which accompanied these developments often derived from wealthy patronage, including that of both Hindu and Muslim rulers, which accounted for the prosperity of temples and institutions associated with these sects. The more innovative sects were in part the result of extensive dialogue between *gurus*, *sadhus*, *pirs*, and Sufis, a dialogue which was sometimes confrontational and sometimes conciliatory" (see Roy, 1983; Skyhawk, n.d.). In India's historical culture and civilization, Islam has very deep roots. Yet the idea that Islam is foreign in India is axiomatic among the Hindu nationalists. Ludden (1996, p. 5) points out, "Making Islam appear foreign to India is part of making India Hindu, pursued by the Hindu nationalist group."

Christian Missions in India

The church in India has a very ancient tradition and heritage, as it is believed that St. Thomas, one of the 12 disciples of Christ, came to South India and established a church around 52 A.D. But the church remained localized and did not engage in missions, reaching out to its neighbors with the gospel of Jesus Christ.

Robert de Nobili (1577–1656) and the Jesuit method of adaptation did not evoke a positive response from the Hindus. For de Nobili, the difference between Christianity and Hinduism was the difference between true and false religion. De Nobili (quoted in Chethimattam, 1969) asserts, "When we consider what is going on in these [Hindu] temples, the nude idols on the *gopurams*, and the dance, fun, and frivolity of the *devadasis*, and the many opportunities for the worshippers to sin with them, … we can say there is no chance of leaving sin and doing good."

With the coming of Western missionaries Bartolomaeus Ziegenbalg and Henry Pluetschau (sent by King Fredrick IV of Denmark, in 1706) and William Carey (of the Baptist Missionary Society, in 1793), the era of modern missions began. The Western colonial period saw a new era of Hindu-Christian relationship. The Christian mission under the Portuguese rule was extremely confrontational and insensitive. According to John Chethimattam (1969, p. 134), they employed "all kinds of rash and imprudent acts."

As Western colonial power increased, there was also an increase in missionary activity. Samuel Jayakumar (1999, p. xvi) maintains that Christian missions contributed to the awakening of the consciousness of the depressed classes, which resulted in their socio-economic transformation.[5]

Use of the vernacular

For the Protestant missionaries, the Bible was central to the Christian faith. Consequently, from the beginning they gave themselves to the translation of the Scriptures into the vernacular.

Tamil was the first Indian language into which the Bible was translated (Victor, 1984). As a result, the Protestant Christians

of Tirunelveli, who were predominantly from the outcastes, began to regard themselves as *Vethakaramga*, the people of the Scripture. It had always been the Brahmans and the caste Hindus who had possession of the Vedas, the Hindu scriptures, written in the Sanskrit language. For centuries, the outcastes were not only prohibited from possessing the Vedas, but also banned from hearing the Vedas being read. The Christian Scriptures thus gave these believers a particular identity.

Missionaries saw the practice of preaching in the vernacular as the means of awakening self-awareness. This often led to repentance and conversion as the people heard the gospel in their own language (Ragland, 1858; Hindu conversion, 1982).

Some Dalit liberation movements have rejected the Sanskrit language, which was used as a Brahmanical ideological tool to oppress the Dalits. The church must now play a conciliatory role. Many reformers who are involved in Brahman bashing are propagating a "spirituality" of caste hatred, which probably will not bring about much reform; rather, it may endanger the fragile unity of Indian society.

A dual mission

Early missionaries in India conducted a dual mission, going amongst the poor, the oppressed, and the outcastes and also amongst the caste Hindus (Seller, 1857). They found the former responsive to the gospel, while the latter group remained critical of Christianity (Caemmerer, 1855).

The American United Presbyterian Mission started its work in Sialkot in 1855 through Rev. Andrew Gordon. In 1857, two people were baptized—one a high caste Hindu and the other an elderly Dalit. The mission concentrated on working among high caste Hindus and Muslims. In the first 19 years of work, only 19 people

---

[5] We have made use of Jayakumar's research in this article.

turned to Christ. In 1870, a high caste Hindu named Nattu, who belonged to the landlord family and who was the son of a village head, decided to follow Christ. The missionaries had high expectations for him. They hoped he would succeed his father in becoming the next village head, but Nattu lost his right to that position. The missionaries considered him a "weak brother." But in 1873, Nattu came to the mission compound in Sialkot, along with a man named Ditt, who was short in stature, black, lame, and illiterate. Nattu asked Rev. S. Martin to baptize Ditt. That event marked the beginning of a mass movement to Christ among the Dalits in Punjab (Pickett, 1933, pp. 42-45).

The gospel of self-worth and dignity

The poor and the oppressed responded to the gospel, for it promised them self-worth and dignity (Hoole, 1996). The message that was communicated to them from the Scriptures was one of awakening and confidence. Texts such as the following were commonly used for preaching: "The night is nearly over; the day is almost here" (Rom. 13:12); "Come to me, all you who are weary and burdened, and I will give you rest" (Matt. 11:28); "Since, then, you have been raised with Christ, set your hearts on things above, where Christ is seated at the right hand of God" (Col. 3:1); "There is neither Jew nor Greek, slave nor free, male nor female, for you are all one in Christ Jesus" (Gal. 3:28); "It is impossible for those who have once been enlightened, who have tasted the heavenly gift, who have shared in the Holy Spirit, who have tasted the goodness of the word of God and the powers of the coming age, if they fall away, to be brought back to repentance, because to their loss they are crucifying the Son of God all over again and subjecting him to public disgrace" (Heb. 6:4-6).

The use of biblical images

The more recent imagery of spiritual warfare was not much in use during the 19th century missionary movement. Rather, the biblical images used were those of the wisdom of God, light, children of God, new creation, and members. These images symbolized the transformation that was taking place in the lives of the converted Dalits. Their use by the missionaries was an important strategy intended to quicken the converts' self-understanding. These images provided the Dalits with a self-worth and dignity which they had never had before.

Although the missionaries and their Indian priests did not use technical terms such as conscientization or awareness building, they did use other terms—enlightenment, awakening, spiritual formation, character formation, and disciplining—to denote the change they were promoting among the newly formed Christian communities. A new consciousness and identity were evident among the Dalits due to the Christian impact.

As we look to the future of the Christian church and missions in India, we must avoid any careless use of militant language that confuses and alienates non-Christians and that provokes persecution of believers. Terms that are military in nature include target, conquer, army, crusade, mobilize, beachhead, advance, enemy, and battle. We trust that our Christian colleagues around the world will refrain from using this language in reference to the church around the world as well.

Personal and social transformation of Dalits

The identity crisis and the aspirations for a new identity were obvious when the Dalits fully or partially revealed their motives at the time of their conversion. There is no question that the Dalits were influenced by a variety of reasons, such as spiritual, material, psychological, and social well-being. Awakening of consciousness was the singular reason behind the social transformation of the Dalits. Their conversion to Christ enlarged their thinking, sharpened their minds, and gave them self-respect.

While the Dalit liberation theologians have reduced the problems of the poor and the oppressed to socio-economic issues, the missionaries and the Indian priests maintained that the problems of the Dalits were not just economic or social but especially spiritual. Hence, the missionaries worked on the spiritual formation in the lives of the people, not merely on the change of customs and behavior. A biblical vision of society was and must be presented as the answer to the desperate communal tensions, economic disparity, and lack of human freedoms which continue to ravage the nation.

Cultural practice and the gospel

The missionaries did not intend to destroy the culture. They attempted to remove those cultural practices that they judged were incompatible and irreconcilable with the demands of the gospel, as also needed for the well-being of the community. As F. S. Downs (1993) contends, "From the time of their arrival on the scene, missionaries have called into question certain social practices of the indigenous culture on the ground that they were irreconcilable with the gospel." This included especially the ills such as child marriage, *Sati* (burning of widows), infanticide, and caste. Since social injustice was against God's will, the missionaries were called upon to fight it, irrespective of whether or not by so doing people would become Christians. Cultural sensitivity and contextualization of the gospel are of ut-

most importance as the gospel relates to the diverse cultures of India.

Enlightenment values: liberty, equality, and fraternity

Supported by the intellectual assumptions of the Enlightenment and influenced as they were by their Judeo-Christian background, the Anglicans serving in India were eager to achieve liberty, equality, and fraternity, which for centuries had been missing among the natives. According to James Alter (1974), these biblical and revolutionary principles were of fundamental importance to the British missionary movement in India. He writes, "Liberty, Equality, and Fraternity are, of course, not only political slogans. They are, first of all, religious terms deeply rooted in the biblical account of God's dealings with men."

Reasons for conversion

The reasons for conversion among the Indian people included an aversion to the "folly of idol worship," a desire to revenge the Hindu religion ("take our temples and dumb idols, which have ruined us thus far"), and a longing for a new life and change in social status (*SPG-MLR*, 1844, pp. 367-368). The converts were from the poor and oppressed community. It is important to note that the Nadars of Tamil Nadu converted not only to gain spiritual blessings, but also to enjoy the advantages that Christians had, including a church for worship and a school established in their own village for the advancement of their children.

Oneness in Christ

Both outcastes and upper-castes became Christians in groups. Thus Christian conversion to a great extent produced harmony between castes. At times, however, the converts to Christ also carried (and still carry) their caste baggage with them into the church. This highlights the need for in-depth discipleship. The Christian community must live out the biblical image of "one new man."

The Bible affirms, "For he himself is our peace, who has made the two one and has destroyed the barrier, the dividing wall of hostility, by abolishing in his flesh the law with its commandments and regulations. His purpose was to create in himself one new man out of the two, thus making peace, and in this one body to reconcile both of them to God through the cross, by which he put to death their hostility" (Eph. 2:14-16).

The power of the Christian gospel to break down the dividing wall of hostility between alien groups is amazing. The old man is the humanity in which divisions of race, sex, culture, citizenship, and class are important and cannot be forgotten or neglected. In the new man, these divisions cannot be primary. Fellowship of the local church must reflect the truth, which is highlighted by the corporate and relational image of the "one new man."

Persecution by the upper caste

Not all those who committed to the initial teaching of the Bible continued to the point of baptism. At times, a whole village withdrew because of the violent persecution by upper caste Hindu communities, in whose service the Dalits and other outcastes then worked. The reason behind the persecution was that the gospel of Christ came on the one hand as a message of liberation to the poor and the oppressed but on the other hand as a threat to the Brahmans and caste Hindus. During the 1820s, Brahmans and the Vellalas, frightened by the ever-increasing number of Christians, formed a society called *Vibhuti Sangham*, "Sacred Ash Society," in Tiruchendur to oppose the spread of the Christian gospel. Frykenberg (1997, p. 97) explains, "It advocated forc-

ible reconversions and subordination of radicalized Shanar Christians to the agrarian order from which they were seeking to extricate themselves." They resisted change with their rigid adherence to *varnasamadharma*. Later movements grew up in the north and west of India. Movements such as Arya Samaj, the Nagari Pracharini Sabha, the Hindu Mahasabha, and the RSS have been radical reactions to what were perceived as threats to the status quo.

The persecution of Christians continued for many decades. In 1891, native minister V. Abraham provided examples of persecution by the Brahmans and caste Hindus, which prevented other Dalit communities from becoming Christians. When some of the Edayers (shepherds) and Maravars of Thenthirupathi expressed their desire to become Christians, their Brahman landlords started persecuting them and refused to employ those who had converted, with the consequence that except for a few individual families, group conversions did not take place (Abraham, 1890). J. F. Kearns (1854, p. 639), who worked in different parts of the district, reports that persecution became a strong deterrent to the conversion of the low caste communities.

More recently, movements that seem to be even more extremist and revivalistic have arisen. Chief among these are such militant and revivalist *jagarans* as the Vishwa Hindu Parishad, with its Dharma Sansad and Bajarang Dal, or youth wing; the Virat Hindu Sammelan, Hindu Samajotsav; and the Shiv Sena, Hindu Jagaran Manch.

Commitment to mission
Dialogue with people

The church must engage in dialogue with people of other faiths or no faiths. In the spirit of Isaiah 1:18 ("Come now, let us reason together"), Christian leaders in

India sustained a formal dialogue with the BJP and RSS leaders in December 1998. Both Catholic and Protestant church leaders participated in this dialogue, in which I had the privilege of representing the Evangelical wing of the church in India. It was an open exchange, and we had a free and frank discussion which led to a greater understanding of each other's position. But the claims of Jesus Christ were the main issue, as we answered questions such as, "Why do you say Jesus is the only way?" and, "Why do you convert?"

To us, the central cause of and issue in the persecution of Christians is the essential gospel of Jesus Christ. How can a Bible-believing Christian ignore the offense of the gospel? This is not rhetoric but pure gospel. In some cases, persecution has helped the church take a stand for Jesus. In other instances, church leaders have indicated that we should not preach that Jesus is the only way. During the course of the 1998 dialogue, it was stated that Christians should adopt Indian culture, which is Hindu culture, and they should be called Hindu Christians. As noted earlier, this practice is an effort to define the nation of India ethnically and culturally; it may imply including Christianity under the *dharma* of the Hindu religion.

A newspaper article written by a Hindu clearly stated that even those churches which have adopted the Indian culture continue to bring in converts; hence, they must be opposed. The problem is not the Christian rhetoric; it is the Christian gospel which calls people to follow Jesus Christ that is opposed. The communal forces find ways to justify their persecution of Christians. On the other hand, we should be careful not to provide them with previously-listed warfare vocabulary which can be distorted by being interpreted out of context.

Proclamation of the gospel

The Christian church in India is the steward of the gospel of Jesus Christ. During his visit to India in November 1999, the Pope made a remarkable public declaration in New Delhi. In his Post-Synodal Apostolic Exhortation (2000, p. 10), he reflected, "This was not a celebration motivated by pride in human achievements, but one conscious of what the Almighty has done for the church in Asia (cf. Luke 1:49). In recalling the Catholic community's humble condition, as well as the weaknesses of its members, the Synod was also a call to conversion, so that the church in Asia might become ever more worthy of the graces continually being offered by God.... As well as a remembrance and a celebration, the Synod was an ardent affirmation of faith in Jesus Christ the Savior." Furthermore, the Pope affirmed, "The church went forth to make disciples of all nations (Matt. 28:19). With the church throughout the world, the church in Asia will cross the threshold of the Third Christian Millennium marveling at all that God has worked from those beginnings until now, and strong in the knowledge that just as in the first millennium the cross was planted on the soil of Europe, and in the second on that of the Americas and Africa, we can pray that in the Third Christian Millennium, a great harvest of faith will be reaped in this vast and vital continent" (Post-Synodal, 2000, p. 4).

We Indian Evangelicals are encouraged by this unashamed invitation to Christians to proclaim the gospel of Jesus Christ. God's saving revelation in Jesus Christ is unique and authoritative. In Christ, God has provided the only way for human salvation.

Embracing the alien

The mission of the church in India must also emphasize that God's people are to be the voice of the voiceless and the champion of the powerless. The equality of human beings is expressed in the Bible in familiar phrases, and we must show no partiality in our attitude to other people, nor give special deference to some because they are rich, famous, or influential. Moses declared, "For the Lord your God is God of gods and Lord of lords, the great God, mighty and awesome, who shows no partiality and accepts no bribes. He defends the cause of the fatherless and the widow, and loves the alien, giving him food and clothing. And you are to love those who are aliens, for you yourselves were aliens in Egypt" (Deut. 10:17-19). The love of God has been constantly displayed throughout history in his providential care for the widows, orphans, and aliens. He is especially concerned for those who are easily forgotten, the despised minorities.

The same emphasis occurs in the New Testament, for God is the impartial Judge. He does not regard external appearances or circumstances. He shows no favoritism, whatever our racial or social background may be. Peter speaks in Acts 10:34, "I now realize how true it is that God does not show favoritism." Note also Romans 2:11 and 1 Peter 1:17. The Pharisees said to Jesus once, "Teacher, we know you are a man of integrity. You aren't swayed by men, because you pay no attention to who they are; but you teach the way of God in accordance with the truth" (Mark 12:14). Our Lord neither deferred to the rich and powerful, nor despised the poor and weak, but gave equal respect to all, regardless of their social status. This biblical image of God defending the cause of the fatherless and the widow and loving the alien must be an integral part of the church's mission. The heart of the gospel is communicated by the loving Father embracing the prodigal and by the outstretched arms of the crucified Savior embracing and forgiving the ones who crucified him.

Drawing to a Close

These are the challenges before us in India:

First, the Indian Christian community must set an example to all other social and religious communities. The life of the local church is meant to be a sign of God's rule. The church should be the one community in the world in which human dignity and equality are invariably recognized; in which people's responsibility for one another is accepted; in which there is no partiality, favoritism, or discrimination; in which the poor and the weak are defended; and in which human beings are free to be human as God made them and meant them to be. These characteristics are brought about only through the Word of God, which makes us capable of perceiving ourselves as sinners and calls us to be God's partners in history. The spiritual formation of our congregations must take absolute priority, for we cannot survive with an over-simplified gospel and a minimalist Great Commission.

Second, the church in India has the duty of proclaiming the truth of Christ to all people everywhere, since that truth is of universal application. All human beings have the right to know of the One in whom the full salvation of humanity has been revealed. The local church is the primary place for the Great Commission to be realized. Our focus should be on equipping congregations for the task of holistic mission. By definition, mission involves moving beyond ourselves and telling others about our faith in Jesus Christ. We must equip congregations, theological institutions, and other Christian organizations to become centers of mission which can help broken people find wholeness in Jesus Christ. Christian witness must be borne with a deep regard for the feelings of those who have not accepted the Christian faith. There are men and women who in all sincerity and humility search for the ultimate light of God.

Third, the church in India can no longer remain fragmented. Neither can the church remain apathetic or distant from civil society. We must be alive to the reality of the day and must strengthen civil society, which in turn must defend the constitutional rights of Christians and speak against the persecution of Christians. Christians must participate more proactively in the life of the nation by engaging in the political process in order to develop national leadership. We must increase our social commitment with the poor and the marginalized. The church in India needs an entrepreneurial and a middle class, so that an indigenous church can sustain itself.

Finally, the church in India even in the midst of persecution must continue its God-given ministry of reconciliation. Compassion, not adversarial communalism, flows from the heart of the mission of the church. Compassion expresses an attitude of complete willingness to use all means, time, and strength to help others. It transcends all national, racial, and caste barriers. Compassion brought Jesus from heaven to the humble manger to be with his rebel creation and to love and care for them. The unclean he made clean; the defenseless he empowered; the exhausted he fed; for the human life he died. He is the exemplar of servanthood, the Lord divine. It is his mission we follow.

References

Abraham, V. (1890). Kadaiyanodai pastorate. *SPG-R*, p. 445.

Alter, J. (1974, September). Liberty, equality, and fraternity: Themes in Anglo-Saxon Protestant missions. *ICHR, 8*(1), p. 15.

Andersen, W. K., & Damle, S. D. (1987). *The brotherhood in saffron*. New Delhi, India: Vistaar Publications.

Caemmerer, A. F. (1855). *Extracts from journal*.

Chethimattam, J. (1969). *Dialogue in Indian tradition*. Bangalore, India: Dharmaran College.

Clemen, C. (1930, January). Missionary activity in the non-Christian religion. *JR, 10*(1), p. 126.

Das, B. (1994). Dalits and caste system. In J. Massey (Ed.), *Indigenous people: Dalits*. Delhi, India: ISPCK.

Downs, F. S. (1993, July). Reflections on the enculturation/social justice issue in contemporary mission. *ERT, 17*(3), p. 322.

Frykenberg, R. E. (1997). The emergence of modern Hinduism. In G. D. Sontheimer & H. Kulke (Eds.), *Hinduism reconsidered*. New Delhi, India: Manohar.

Galanter, M. (1997). *Law and society in modern India*. Delhi, India: Oxford University Press.

Gandhi, R. (1999). *Revenge and reconciliation*. Penguin Books.

Gray, C. S. F. (1965, July–September). Non-Christian missions. *CQR*, p. 350.

A Hindu conversion: How is it attained? (1982, November). *HF, 3*(4), pp. 265-269.

Hoole, C. (1996, June). An Anglican approach to church growth. *ICHR, 30*(1), p. 20.

Jayakumar, S. (1999). *Dalit consciousness and Christian conversion*. Delhi, India: Regnum International & Oxford ISPCK.

Kearns, J. F. (1854). *Muthalur mission*.

Ludden, D. (1996). Ayodhya: A window on the world. In D. Ludden (Ed.), *Making India Hindu*. Oxford University Press.

Majumdar, R. C. (Ed.). (1966). *The history and culture of the Indian people*. Vol. 5 (2nd ed.). Bombay, India: Bhartiya Vidya Bhavan.

Matthew, C. V. (1999). *The saffron mission*. ISPCK.

Muller, F. M. (1892). *India, What can it teach us? A course of lectures delivered before the University of Cambridge*. London: Longmans, Green.

Pal, B. C. (1913, January). Missionary Hinduism. *The Hindu Review, 1*, pp. 475-482.

Pickett, J. W. (1933). *Christian mass movements in India: A study with recommendations*. Cincinnati, OH: Abingdon Press.

Post-Synodal Apostolic Exhortation. (2000). *Ecclesia in Asia*. Pauline Publications.

Radhakrishnan, S. (n.d.). *The heart of Hinduism* (3rd ed.). Madras, India: G. A. Natesan & Co.

Ragland, T. G. (1858). On vernacular preaching. In *South India mission conference* (pp. 152-155). Madras, India: SPG Press.

Roy, A. (1983). *The Islamic syncretistic tradition in Bengal*. New Jersey.

Seller, J. (1857). Extracts from journal. *C/IND*. Madras, India.

Skyhawk, H. V. (n.d.). Vaishnava perceptions of Muslims in 18th century Maharashtra. In A. L. Dallapicola & S. Zingel-Avelallemant (Eds.), *Islam and Indian religions*. Stuttgart, Germany.

SPG-MLR. (1844).

Tambimuttu, E. L. (n.d.). *Dravida: A history of the Tamils from prehistoric times to AD 1800*. Colombo, Sri Lanka: General Publishers Ltd.

Thapar, R. (n.d.). *Cultural transaction and early India*.

———. (1985, September). Syndicated Moksha? *Seminar, 13*.

———. (1997). Syndicated Hinduism. In G. D. Sontheimer & H. Kulke (Eds.), *Hinduism reconsidered*. New Delhi, India: Manohar.

Theeratha, S. D. (1992). *History of Hindu imperialism*. Madras, India: DELT.

Victor, I. H. (1984, December). A brief history of the Bible. *ICHR*, 7(2), p. 106.

Richard Howell at the young age of 16 committed his life for full-time ministry. He has a post-graduation degree in English literature and earned his Bachelor in Divinity from Union Biblical Seminary, Pune, India. He married in 1982 and along with his wife, Sunita, served at the Allahabad Bible Seminary. They currently have three daughters. He and his wife spent two years in Vancouver, British Columbia, Canada, where Richard completed his Master in Theology from Regent College, Vancouver, and Sunita completed her Diploma in Christian Studies. They returned to the Allahabad Bible Seminary in 1986, serving as the first Indian principal to take over from Western missionaries (1990–1996). In May 1996, God led Richard to become the General Secretary of the Evangelical Fellowship of India, based in New Delhi. At present, Richard is working on his doctorate degree, registered under the Utrecht University. While in Allahabad in 1996, he authored a book, Mission, in the Hindi language.

29

The complex spiritual mosaic of East Asia

AT IGUASSU, 15 WOMEN and men, representing different parts of East Asia and different concerns for East Asia, met together to discuss the major issues we face in reaching East Asia for Christ as we enter the 21st century. This paper is built on that discussion, but it goes beyond what we could cover in our short time together, to try to paint a larger panorama of the challenges facing the church in mission in East Asia.

East Asia is an incredibly diverse place! But before we discuss it, we need to define it. The term "East Asia" is used here in the way that it is generally used in contemporary political and economic discussion, i.e., to describe collectively the countries of Northeast Asia (China including Hong Kong and Macao, Japan, North and South Korea, Mongolia, and Taiwan) and Southeast Asia (Brunei, Cambodia, East Timor, Indonesia, Laos, Malaysia, Myanmar/Burma, Philippines, Singapore, Thailand, and Vietnam). It needs to be noted that this politico-cultural definition—which is commonly used in East Asia today—differs significantly from the physiographic definitions traditionally used by Western geographers.[1]

Two billion people live in the 17 countries of East Asia, including significant groups of all the world's major religions, except Judaism. The region is not just one world but many worlds—sometimes intersecting, sometimes colliding, sometimes merging into each another.

IAN
PRESCOTT

---

[1] Geographers commonly use the term "East Asia" to refer to "the continental part of the Far East region of Siberia, the East Asian islands, Korea, and eastern and northeastern China" (Encyclopaedia Britannica, 1998).

421

A World of Whirlwind Economic Growth

East Asia caught the attention of the world in the 1980s and '90s for its remarkable economic growth: "The World Bank has pronounced that nowhere and at no time in human history has humanity achieved such economic progress" (Naisbitt, 1996, p. 10). With the Japanese economy in the lead and other Asian tigers close behind, it looked as though East Asia was set to overtake the West. Books about the East Asian Economic Miracle and talk of the coming Pacific Century abounded. "As we move toward the year 2000," wrote trend-watcher John Naisbitt in 1996 (p. 10), "Asia will become the dominant region of the world: economically, politically, and culturally."

Naisbitt's book, *Megatrends Asia*, probably marks the zenith of 1990s optimism about Asia's economies. The following year, the East Asian Economic Miracle was suddenly replaced by the East Asian Economic Crisis. The crash started in Thailand in July 1997 and rapidly spread to Korea, Indonesia, and Malaysia. Other East Asian economies didn't crash in the same way, but a sort of "economic guilt by association" sent their currencies tumbling and their economies into decline.

The crash, however, was followed in many countries by a remarkably fast recovery. Korea and Thailand (which followed the IMF prescription for recovery) and Malaysia (which rejected outside assistance and pursued an independent path) have all bounced back. Of the four that crashed, only in Indonesia, where the harsh IMF medicine unleashed a flood of unrest that unseated President Suharto and has gone on to inflame ethnic relations, does the economy continue to falter seriously. Much of East Asia appears to be back on a path of renewed economic growth. China, which proved to be an economic anchor during the crisis, is increasingly becoming the economic dynamo of the region, along with the vast network of 53 million overseas Chinese who control much of East Asia's economy.

The last 50 years have therefore been, for much of East Asia, a time of dramatic growth and massive modernization. In Asia as a whole, the incidence of poverty has been reduced from 400 million in 1945 to 180 million in 1995, while the population has grown by 400 million; Asia now has a middle class of almost half a billion (Naisbitt, 1996, pp. 10, 15). Modernization has brought urbanization: East Asia currently has nine mega-cities.[2] Moreover, while the cities of Japan have nearly stopped growing,[3] many of the others—particularly Jakarta, Bangkok, and Rangoon—are still growing uncontrollably,[4] overwhelming existing infrastructure and available resources.

Modernization and the dramatic economic growth have encouraged rampant materialism, epitomized by Deng Xiaoping's words, "To get rich is glorious."[5] In many places in East Asia, the old gods have been pushed aside, not in favor of a new ideology or a new religion, but in order to pursue success and prosperity.

Modernization and globalization have also created an enormous demand for

---

[2] Mega-cities are cities with a population of over 10 million.

[3] Tokyo has a growth rate of 0.23% and Osaka 0.00% (FEER, 1998, p. 63).

[4] Their growth rates are: Jakarta 2.60%, Bangkok 2.83%, Rangoon 3.19%, (FEER, 1998, p. 63).

[5] Deng Xiaoping said this in the early 1980s, and it rapidly became a defining aphorism for his economic reforms and China's new "socialist market economy."

English: from Mongolia, where English is now taught in schools instead of Russian; to Japan, where a recent paper suggested that English should be made the second language; to Phnom Penh, where students at the Institute of Technology burned French flags in protest when they were told they would have to learn French instead. It has even been suggested that within this century, English could replace the national language of some countries of East Asia.

Modernization, however, is not a single step but a continuum, and different Asian societies are at different points on that continuum. Even within one Asian society, different sectors can be at very different stages of modernization. In fact, even to talk of a continuum is too simplistic, as societies may adopt some parts of advanced modernity while retaining many pre-modern characteristics. This can be seen with modernity's external trappings: a tribal person may still live in primitive conditions while sporting a cellular telephone; the Mongolian living with his sheep and camels on the edge of the Gobi Desert may have a satellite dish outside his ger.

This patchwork adoption of the trappings of modernization has taken place not only on the level of material possessions, but also on the level of ideology and values. Consequently, the results of modernization—especially in the realm of religion—are often quite different from the results in the West. In particular, while it was often assumed in the West that the secularization of society and the privatization of religion were the inevitable byproducts of modernization, this has not always happened in Asia.

Malaysia, for example, was given independence in 1957 with a constitution that made it a secular state—though with Islam as the state religion. Since then, Malaysia has eagerly pursued modernization and very much desires to be a significant player in the modern world. For example, one of President Mahathir's grand projects is the Multimedia Super Corridor, which he hopes will place Malaysia in a place of leadership in the information age (MSC, 1999). In recent decades, however, the government, eager to prove that modernization and Islamization are not incompatible, has also pursued a vigorous program of Islamization.

At another level of Malaysian society, modernization and urbanization have brought Malays[6] out of their traditional *kampung* communities and exposed them to the wider world. One consequence of this, for many, has been a new emphasis on Islam, with its international stature, as key to defining their identity, rather than traditional Malay customs, which appear increasingly irrelevant (Muzaffar, 1985, pp. 358-359).

Challenges for the church

The economic growth, modernization, and rapid change pose many challenges for the church in mission in East Asia.

One challenge is not to be left behind by the pace of change. Churches are innately conservative, and they rapidly lose touch with their contemporary generation. They thus lose their ability to show the relevance of Christ to all peoples at all times, or in particular to their people at this time. The church in Korea is battling with this. Having enjoyed dramatic church growth up until recently, it is finding that

---

[6] "Malays" refers to the Muslim Malays who comprise about 55% of the population of Malaysia; not to be confused with "Malaysians," which refers to the entire population and includes Chinese, Indians, and some tribal peoples.

the methods and approaches that were so successful in reaching earlier generations are not effectively communicating the gospel to the new generation.

The new generation includes the "Net" generation, and with Internet access increasing exponentially, this "Net" generation is growing dramatically in urban East Asia. Although the number of Christian websites is also growing, few churches and Christian groups have done more than post the information that they normally give out in print. Much thought needs to be given to how to relate the gospel to the new generation. Christians also need to consider how to use the Internet for effective evangelism and discipleship among these young people and how to use it to reach and disciple those in restricted access communities.

Another challenge is to address the inequalities that rapid modernization has created or exacerbated. The flow of people into the cities has created a vast underclass of urban poor in cities like Manila and Jakarta, including a variety of groups who have been completely marginalized in the process. The recent economic crisis has exaggerated these inequalities, particularly in urban centers: World Bank figures suggest that the number below the poverty line in Indonesia increased from 11% in 1996 to 14-20% in 1999, while in Thailand, figures from the International Labor Organization suggest an increase from 8% to 14% in a similar period (Bhanu, 2000, p. 62). Rural East Asia was less immediately affected by the crisis, partly because it had gained less from the growth—many communities are still living as they have done for centuries—but also because its agricultural produce still had value.

Countries like Laos, where the population is largely rural and the per capita GDP is US$400, seemed immune at first, but the delayed impact of reduced foreign investment into the country and reduced export out of the country resulted in 100% inflation in 1998, making the poor poorer still (Freeman & Than, 2000, p. 74).

Finally, in the midst of success, one of the greatest dangers to spiritual vitality (which is the root of genuine mission) is materialism. Materialism has sapped the life out of much of the church in Europe more effectively than Communism's direct assaults ever succeeded in doing. One Christmas in Singapore, our local shopping mall boasted the biggest Santa Claus in the world, standing four stories high in front of the mall. Once Christmas was over, he was replaced by an even bigger, 17m high, god of fortune. This could easily be a parable of the church if its center is not Jesus Christ.

Thus far, I have spoken about modernization and the impact of the modern world, but we are now entering, if not already in, the post-modern world. Much has been written about post-modernism in the West, and we touched on it briefly in our East Asia group at Iguassu. We can certainly expect that Asia will be affected by the currents of post-modernism. It is, however, likely that the effect of post-modernism on East Asian societies will be significantly different from the effect on Western societies, if for no other reason than that significant elements of the post-modernist worldview are already present in Buddhism and other Asian religions.

World of Unreached Peoples

East Asia has roughly 2 billion people, less than 5% of whom know Christ. What knowledge of Christ there is is very unevenly distributed. For example, at one end of the spectrum are the South Koreans, among whom dramatic church growth has occurred and 27% are Protestants. At the other end of the spectrum, one of China's

Tibetan people groups has a population of over 1 million, yet we know of only nine Christians, only one of whom could be considered a mature believer. Even within ethnic groups, there can be huge disparities. For example, among the Han Chinese, Tony Lambert (1999, pp. 19, 29, 238) reports that in one area of China, 18% of the adults are registered Evangelical Christians (this does not include children or unregistered house-church believers). Yet in Sichuan province, there is only one church per million people, and in parts of the province less than 0.2% are Christians.

Except for Japan and Korea—both of which are ethnically highly homogeneous—the countries of East Asia are each home to a diversity of different ethnic groups.[7] In many of these countries, the church is strong and growing among one or more people groups, but it is nearly non-existent in others. Thus, in Malaysia and Singapore, the church is strong and growing among Chinese and Indians but tiny among Malays; in China, it has grown rapidly among the Han but not among the Muslims or Tibetans; in the Philippines, there has been vigorous church growth among nominal Roman Catholics but little among the Muslim tribes in the south; in Burma, the majority of the Karin and Chin are Christians but very few of the majority Bama people or the Buddhist Shan. This list could easily be continued.

Challenges for the church

One of the greatest challenges for the East Asian church in mission is to be a church engaged in cross-cultural mis-

sion—not just satisfied to continue the process of reaching their own people, but ready also to reach out in mission to other peoples.

There are many barriers to this. One is the natural tendency to gravitate to one's own kind—even (or particularly) when sent overseas. I remember listening to the national secretary of our mission in Taiwan lamenting that, although they had sent a number of missionaries to other East Asian countries, the workers had nearly all ended up as Chinese reaching other Chinese. The mission had found it very difficult to communicate a lasting vision for cross-cultural mission from the Chinese to non-Chinese. This would be true of much of the missionary movement from the overseas Chinese church throughout East Asia—most of it is directed toward other Chinese. The work is excellent and necessary, but it is not reaching cross-culturally to the unreached.

For the East Asian church, cross-cultural mission does not have to be overseas mission. It does not even have to cross national borders—the unreached of other cultures are there beside them. However, one of the biggest barriers to cross-cultural mission within countries is that of prejudice and hostility between neighboring but different groups. A Filipino brother, who regularly conducts awareness seminars about Islam among Filipino pastors and other Christians, finds that for many the immediate associations of the word "Muslim" are words like murderer, rapist, terrorist, and kidnapper. Not surprisingly, it has taken time to develop a vision among Filipino Christians for reaching out

[7] Johnstone (1993, p. 41) lists 1,859 national ethno-linguistic groups in the countries of East Asia, half of which he classifies as belonging to the unevangelized/unreached world. However, many of these groups are tiny. More recently, Joshua Project 2000 has brought together mission statisticians to produce a list of "least evangelized" peoples. These are people groups with a population of at least 10,000 who are less than 5% Christian of any sort and less than 2% Evangelical Christian. By March 1999, they had identified 429 such groups in East Asia.

to their Muslim neighbors. However, now that that has begun to happen, even in a small way, it means that the number of people concerned for Filipino Muslims is far greater than would ever have come as expatriate missionaries.

The barriers that divide ethnic groups can be very serious, and crossing them may be harder for someone from a geographically near but alienated ethnic group than for someone from a distant group. But crossing barriers is a sign of the gospel and must be done. Particularly in a world where ethnic division and fragmentation are on the increase, the church must be seen to be bridging those barriers rather than reinforcing them.

Creative Access World

Over half the countries of East Asia are closed to those identified as "missionaries," and they restrict or outlaw straightforward approaches to evangelism and church planting. But to talk of "half" is misleading; more than 80% of East Asians live in these "closed" or "restricted" countries—including many of East Asia's unreached peoples. Nor is it a simple case of "open" or "closed" countries. Rather, East Asia's countries lie on a continuum, with wide-open countries such as Japan and the Philippines on one end and tightly shut North Korea at the other. In the middle are countries like Indonesia and Singapore, which allow missionaries to enter for limited roles such as theological education but not for evangelism and church planting. Nearer the closed end are countries like China and Vietnam, which do not welcome missionaries but do welcome a wide variety of foreign experts, professionals, and business people.

"Creative access" is, of course, the view of the outsider trying to get in. In all of these countries, there is a church already inside. Countries that restrict the entry of outsiders often, but not always, also impose restrictions on national believers inside the country. Thus, there are repeated reports of pastors and believers who are imprisoned and fined in China, Vietnam, and Laos. This raises many questions of how best to tackle issues of religious freedom. Such believers are usually delighted to have the prayerful support of believers from outside the country, but they are often ambivalent about the value of political intervention by Western governments, particularly the United States. There are always the dangers that such intervention will reinforce the idea that Christianity is a Western religion relying on foreign support and that it will revive distorted memories of Christianity arriving in Asia on the coattails of Western imperialism.

Challenges for the church

These creative access countries present a number of challenges to the church in mission. One is to develop fresh approaches that will both win an entry into these countries as well as win a hearing. As Ted Ward (1999, p. 148) has pointed out, it is an "insidious colonial assumption" that missionaries should automatically be allowed to go anywhere they wish. "It is based on the presumed rights and actual power of people from a dominant society to enter wherever and whenever they choose within the empire." He notes further, "Resistance to outsiders and their agenda is an ordinary characteristic of a people's sense of dignity and purpose." Humanly speaking, we do not have a right of access to these countries but have to win our entry with the government, just as we will have to win our hearers once we have entered.

Though these countries exclude missionaries, they welcome those who can contribute to their development through sharing their professional expertise, developing businesses, or assisting in relief and development. It is the need for outside help that provides an open door. Don Hamilton (1987, p. 80) once noted, "From the perspective of the host government, the ideal 'foreign expert' has a Ph.D., 10 to 15 years of work experience in his field of expertise, and a willingness to work for a subsistence income." There are not too many people available on these terms. However, if Christians have the skills the governments are looking for and are ready to sacrifice their personal professional advancement and standard of living for the sake of the gospel, they can find open doors.

This approach requires a different kind of cross-cultural worker than many churches are used to sending. Asian churches need to develop their understanding of the calling and gifts needed for this kind of mission, particularly where the expectation of a missionary is that he will be an ordained man whose primary identity is that of a religious professional. Tentmakers, as they are often called, must be seen as more than just undercover missionaries—something that governments understandably react against. We must understand their distinct calling to contribute to the evangelization of a people through living a Christian life with integrity, serving in a professional job with excellence, and sharing the good news with sensitivity. Tentmakers need an integrated theology of their work as well as their evangelism. They are not simply missionaries in disguise, nor are they just professionals pursuing their professional vocation in another country and taking the opportunity to witness. They are individuals who have responded to a calling from God to contribute to the establishment and growth of the church in another country and culture—using their professional skills to enable them to do these things.

We also need to develop a deeper understanding of the process of evangelization in creative access contexts. Often a significant part of that process—and therefore an important contribution of those called to serve there—is winning the trust and confidence of both government officials and the target community, so as to increase the window of opportunity for Christian efforts now and in the future. It is also important to recognize that although these countries may be "politically resistant" because their governments oppose mission and make their people hard to reach (Tennent, 1998, p. 223), this says nothing about the receptivity of the people themselves to the gospel. Because of their culture or religion, they may also be highly resistant to the gospel. However, they may be very open, with a growing Christian movement among them. If the former is the case, a quiet witness may be the most appropriate contribution. However, if it is the latter, the creative access worker needs to be able to contribute to the work of harvesting among the people.

There is also a need for careful reflection on the platforms and approaches used. What does it mean for the gospel if we use teaching English, bringing in foreign expertise, or the victory of capitalist economics as the means to gain entry? We should not shrink back from taking the opportunities that God is giving. As missiologist Max Warren (1976, p. 92) once said, "For effective obedience to the Great Commission, the one thing supremely needed in every age is a lively response of Spirit-inspired opportunism, ever alert to the certainty that God will provide different opportunities in different circumstances." We do, however, need to reflect biblically and theologically on what we are doing and how we are doing it. This may be particularly important in this area, as professional, business, and entrepreneurial skills are needed in order to seize the opportunities. People with such skills may not have had much opportunity for training in the skills required for theological reflection.

China and the Communist World

Although the Soviet Union has disintegrated and Eastern Europe is no longer under its sway, Communism still lives on in East Asia in China, Vietnam, Laos, and North Korea. Mongolia is the only East Asian country that has moved from Communist government to democratic government.

In China, Vietnam, and Laos, Communism no longer represents an economic program or a program of social and cultural transformation. Marxist economics have been discredited and thrown out in favor of free-market economics. These countries are increasingly adopting free-market capitalism in their economic policies and in many of their social policies. "Free-market" implies increased freedom in the market. For this, they must be competitive, and it has therefore been imperative for these countries that they catch up with the rest of the world in skills, education, technology, etc.; thus, they have an urgent need for foreign expertise. Free-market has also meant opening their doors to foreign commerce, thus providing many business opportunities. Changing economic policy has been the main key to opening these countries up to the outside world.

Communism, however, remains as "a device of political rhetoric which proclaims, both externally and internally, that

the one-party state has no intention of allowing liberal-democratic reforms" (Evans, 1998, p. 2). One-party totalitarian rule remains and clearly plans to remain. What is called, for example, "socialism with Chinese characteristics" in fact appears to be "capitalism with totalitarian characteristics." These countries might be described as post-socialist, but they are not post-Communist.[8]

The truth is that of the two great Communist powers of the 1980s—the Soviet Union and China—China is doing much better. The Soviet Union, which put political reforms before economic reforms and has suffered national and social disintegration, is seen as a disaster—not as an example to follow. China, which has implemented extensive economic reforms while retaining tight political control, has seen significant and sustained economic growth. Vietnam and Laos now look to China as the example to follow. While many Western political commentators such as Chris Patten (1998), the last governor of Hong Kong, argue that a liberal political climate is essential for a free-market economy to flourish, these countries are determined to prove otherwise.

Their governments are also determined to remain in control. This was shown in China in the quick and decisive suppression of the Falun Gong in 1999. Founded only seven years earlier in 1992, Falun Gong (or Falun Dafa) combined Buddhism, Taoism, and qigong-traditional Chinese forms of meditation and exercise. However, it was not the beliefs or practices of this group that worried the government, but its dramatic growth as a

---

[8] Evans (1998, p. 1) calls these "post-socialist" regimes. "Why the term 'post-socialism'? For Laos I have argued that while it is economically and socially capitalist by almost any social scientific criteria, I prefer to use the term 'post-socialist' to describe the regime because of the political continuity between the revolutionary and post-socialist phases.... The parties that came to power are still in power, and the marks of radical ideological change—the names of the states and symbols such as their flags—remain unchanged."

highly organized mass movement, making sophisticated use of the Internet and claiming 100 million adherents, including many party cadres and military officials. Although this figure is probably optimistic, it still rivaled the Chinese Communist Party in size, which has 60 million members. Such a threat to the government could not be tolerated. Its leaders were arrested in April 1999, the movement was outlawed in July, and an anti-cult law was passed in October specifically to deal with this group.

The determination to control is also shown in the policy of these East Asian Communist countries toward Christians. There is some freedom to worship in the state-controlled religious bodies, but religious expression outside these bodies is often ruthlessly suppressed, including growth in new communities.

The church in many places has grown dramatically under Communism. The most well-known instance of this is in China: there Protestants numbered about 1 million when the country became the Peoples Republic of China in 1949, but now they number between 35 and 70 million. Today in China there are at least three distinct streams to the church: the official Three-Self Patriotic Movement churches, the unofficial house churches, and a growing number of Chinese intellectuals who have come to Christ but who are part of neither. In addition, there is a growing phenomenon that has been called "Culture Christians"—intellectuals who, finding Marxist-Leninism bankrupt, have turned to Christianity to provide a coherent worldview, but who have not made a personal commitment to Christ (Lambert, 1998; Liu, 1998; P. Lee, 1996).

North Korea, the hermit kingdom, has managed to stand apart from the dramatic changes transforming the rest of the Communist world. Despite the rapid economic decline that it has experienced since the end of Soviet subsidies in 1990, North Korea has remained as tightly shut as it can, firmly committed to the totalitarian rule that has passed from father to son in what has been called the world's only Communist monarchy. North Korea also remains committed to a socialist-style, centrally planned economy, although it is cautiously experimenting with Chinese-style Free Economic and Trade Zones. In recent years, the hermetic seal has been broken by the severe famine that has swept the country. As a result of this, a number of Christian aid agencies have been allowed very controlled access to parts of the country, and large numbers of North Koreans have crossed the northern border into Northeast China, where many South Korean missionaries are operating.

The situation also changed in 1998, when the South Korean government dropped its antagonism toward the North and adopted instead a "sunshine policy" of active engagement. The stated aim on both sides is reunification—it always has been. But it is difficult to see what shape the reunification will take. The North does not want to be simply absorbed into the South, the way East Germany was absorbed into West Germany, and the younger generation in the South is not sure that they want to pay the economic price for such absorption. North Korea watchers see a number of possible scenarios for the future.[9] The best is gradual reform leading in time to carefully planned reunification. The worst is war, which would be senseless, but some fear that the North Korean leadership could resort to it as a last desperate attempt to hold onto power. The other possibilities are that the

---

[9] See, for example, Foster-Carter (1998) and Noland (1998).

country may simply collapse or that somehow, defying the odds, it will manage to stumble on for some time, perpetuating the peculiar isolated state that it has created.

As I write, there are encouraging signs of a more open approach to the outside world. In January 2000, North Korea established formal relations with Italy, and in May it restored diplomatic relations with Australia. But the biggest breakthrough is a summit of the leaders of the North and South Korea leaders planned for June 12-14, 2000. This will be their first summit since the peninsula was divided in 1945. It also represents the first high-level talks for nine years. A meeting between the leaders of North and South Korea was due to take place six years ago, but North Korea leader Kim Il-Sung died of a heart attack just days before it was scheduled. We wait with prayerful but somewhat breathless anticipation to see whether this meeting will actually happen and what the outcome will be.

There is very little clear information about the church in North Korea. Many Christians fled to the South when the country was divided, and the 300,000 who remained suffered severe persecution. However, reports of a significant and growing underground church have been leaking out of the country. I have seen suggestions that there may be 30,000 or 100,000 Christians—even that there are 100,000 Christians imprisoned for their faith. In the circumstances, it is obviously impossible to get any accurate statistics, and so all such numbers must be treated with caution. However, there is clear evidence that the church has survived.

Challenges for the church

East Asia's Communist world poses numerous challenges to the church in mission. Some of these have already been mentioned: supporting our brothers and sisters who are suffering persecution and developing creative ways to reach both the resistant and the receptive who still live under Communism.

As the doors of these countries become more open, it is also vitally important that foreign mission groups and churches recognize that while they have been kept out, God has not. He has continued to work, raising up a people for himself. Initiatives from the outside must therefore be undertaken with respect for the church already on the inside. Cooperation and coordination are needed, so as to contribute effectively to the work God is already doing in these countries rather than hinder it. The mad rush that characterized post-Communist mission in Eastern Europe and Russia proved so destructive in many ways that Ralph Covell writes about "why I don't pray for China to open" (Covell, 1995). Even with today's levels of limited openness, the impact has not always been positive. For example, it is disappointing to see that in Vietnam, where the opening up of the country has allowed the involvement of all sorts of foreign groups in the lives of the churches, the result has been to halve the rate of growth of the church, fragment it into many different pieces, and introduce numerous complications through the generous but sometimes unwise use of foreign money. How can we avoid such outcomes?

There is also a broader challenge to the church, in the face of the bankruptcy of socialist economics and the wide acceptance of capitalism as the only viable economic system. Is there a Christian alternative? Do we share the belief that greed—carefully regulated with a light touch—will result in the best provision for all, particularly the poor and needy? Or does Christianity offer a perspective on economics that stands apart from both socialism and capitalism?

The Buddhist and Buddhist-Influenced World

Of East Asia's 2 billion people, about half are Buddhist or influenced by Buddhism. If that sounds a little vague, remember that vagueness is a Buddhist quality! Buddhism is inherently syncretistic and in many places has combined with other religions to form a new synthesis that you may or may not call Buddhism. As Patrick Johnstone (1993, p. 42) observes, "The boundary between Buddhism and China's Taoism or Japan's Shinto is hard to define"! And the Buddhist would probably ask, "Why do we need to define it?"

This confusion is particularly true of the Chinese, whose religion is a combination of Buddhism, Confucianism, and Taoism. Should they be called Buddhists? Often the religions are simply described as "Chinese religions"—which neatly avoids the question. The other difficulty with the Han Chinese in China is knowing how many should still be considered religious (never mind Buddhist) after 50 years of Communism. *Operation World* classifies 59% of the Chinese as "non-religious," though that figure is probably high, given the religious resurgence experienced in China in recent years.

If we set aside the Han Chinese but include the Japanese—whose Buddhism is blended with Shintoism—we still have a population of between 300 and 350 million strongly Buddhist peoples in East Asia. Though the kind of Buddhism varies—there being Theravada, Mahayana, and Lamaistic Buddhism—the reaction to the gospel is largely similar: polite indifference that is frustratingly hard to penetrate. Countries like Thailand and Japan have been open to missionaries for more than a century, but the church is still relatively small. The good news of Jesus still does not seem to have got under the skin of the culture in such a way and such a form as to bring about a spontaneously growing church movement.

Why is reaching Buddhists so difficult? One reason is that the Buddhist worldview is so completely different from the Christian one, making it very difficult to communicate the good news effectively. We speak about a God who loves the world and gave his Son for it, but Buddhists believe that the world is unreal and that love is a lower emotion from which the enlightened escape. What lowly kind of misinformed god is this—especially one that is so earthly as to have children!

Even when a Buddhist becomes a Christian, my colleagues say that it takes five to nine years for the "purification of the Buddhist mind" to take place, i.e., for the new believer to really understand and adopt the Christian view of the world.

In many parts of East Asia, it is very difficult for a Buddhist to conceive of following Jesus because of the prevalence of "extreme pluralism," in which ethnic identity determines religion. To be Thai is to be Buddhist; their religion is an integral part of their ethnic and communal identity. The same is true of the lowland Lao, the Burmans, and the Tibetans, as well as many others.

Related to this is the need for Christians to be able to offer seekers and new converts answers, not just to eternal questions, but also to very real practical questions that arise when becoming a Christian conflicts strongly with ethnic identity. These questions include: "Whom will I marry?" "Who will be my friends?" and "Where can I bury my dead?" Death and death rites are particularly serious issues for those from Buddhist and Chinese religious backgrounds. There are two major elements to this. One is the relationship with ancestors and finding adequate responses to ancestor worship, particularly when ancestor veneration and/or worship is often not just a religious activity but is also a critical element in the social hierarchy. The other problem is that of fulfilling filial responsibilities and determining appropriate Christian behavior at funerals.

Although indifference to the gospel leading to high levels of resistance is the hallmark of many of the purer Buddhist people of East Asia, this has not been as true where Buddhism has been blended with other beliefs. The most notable exception is the Han Chinese, among whom dramatic and spontaneous church growth occurred during the second half of the 20th century. This growth has continued and mushroomed without outside assistance. The church has also grown strongly among Koreans, where Buddhism was mixed with Shamanism and Christianity was strongly identified with nationalism. Among minority tribal peoples, where Buddhism is often mixed with animism, there generally has been more response the more animistic and less Buddhist the people have been.

But we are still praying for breakthrough among the purer Buddhist peoples who, as a whole, have been a very unresponsive group. However, there have been signs of such a breakthrough in two places in the last decade—places where the hegemony of Buddhism and ethnic/national identity has been broken or reduced.

The first is Mongolia, where for many years only a handful of known believers existed. Then, in 1990, after 65 years as a Russian satellite, the country suddenly became open and democratic. Today there are at least 40 Mongolian churches and between 5,000 and 10,000 Mongolian believers. In 1997, they formed the Mongolian Evangelical Fellowship. What is remarkable is that before the Communists came to power in 1921, Mongolia was an extremely Buddhist country with 700 monasteries and 110,000 lamas. (This number represented at least a third of the total male population.) Mongolia followed Lamaistic Buddhism, which was introduced by Tibetan lamas in the 16th century. There had been a number of attempts to reach the Mongolians over the centuries, and there were missionaries in Mongolia until the 1920s; however, when Mongolia became Communist, there was no indigenous Mongolian church.

Why the breakthrough now, we must ask? One effect of 65 years of Communist rule has been to break the identification of being Mongolian and being Buddhist. Although Buddhism is now enjoying a revival and is still seen as the natural religion of many Mongolians (mixed with Shamanism), it does not have the hold that it once had. Humanly speaking, this has given the gospel an opportunity that it did not have earlier in the 20th century.

The other place where we have seen a breakthrough is Cambodia. There the Khmer people have traditionally practiced a form of Theravada Buddhism that is very similar to the highly resistant Theravada Buddhism practiced in Thailand. Again, we have seen dramatic church growth in the last decade, with the number of Protestant Christians increasing from 1,000 in 1990 to 20,000[10] in 1997. This growth outstrips anything happening among Buddhists in Thailand. We have been sending Thai missionaries to Cambodia, but it may not be long before we start sending Cambodian missionaries to Thailand.

Again we must ask, why the breakthrough? In God's sovereignty, it may be that the terrible and traumatic incidents that took place under the Khmer Rouge have broken the Buddhist cultural hege-

---

[10] The figure of 20,000 is quoted by the Cambodian Ministry of Religion.

mony and opened hearts to the gospel. At the same time, we must recognize that the number of believers in both Mongolia and Cambodia is still less than 0.3% of the population. A church movement has begun, but there is still much to be done.

Challenges for the church

Buddhism still stands as an immense challenge to the church in mission. We surely cannot rest until there are spontaneously growing church movements among each of the Buddhist peoples of East Asia. How such movements will be achieved we do not know. There is no guaranteed church-planting formula for starting a movement among Buddhists. A lot of missionary effort will be required, along with a lot of prayer for the breakthrough that God alone can give.

The World of Islam

When we talk of Islam, people usually think of the Middle East and perhaps of Central Asia, but rarely of East Asia.[11] However, nearly a quarter of the world's Muslims live in East Asia, making it a critical part of the world for mission to Muslims.

In Southeast Asia, Muslims comprise 40% of the total population. In Malaysia, Indonesia, and Brunei, they are in the majority, with Indonesia having more Muslims than any other country in the world. Muslims form a significant minority in Myanmar, Southern Philippines, and South Thailand, where they have posed an armed challenge to the government. In Singapore, the existence of a significant Muslim minority is the main reason for a rigidly enforced policy of maintaining religious harmony.

Thirty million Muslims are to be found in China. Many of these are in ethnic groups such as the Khazak and Uygur, which straddle China's western borders with Central Asia. Nearly 9 million are Hui. These people are called Chinese Muslims because many of their customs and their architectural forms are as distinctly Chinese as they are Islamic. But there are reckoned to be only 50 Christians among the Hui and no Hui churches (Paterson, 1999, p. 150). There are also other smaller Muslim groups, such as the Salar of Qinghai, who migrated from Samarkhand in Uzbekistan in the 11th century. These people number only 100,000. There are no known believers among them, and as of January 2000, there were no known Christians trying to reach them.

In contrast to the Buddhists' smiling disinterest, the Muslims are fiercely antagonistic toward any attempts to evangelize them. Those who do attempt evangelization may face vehement opposition and even physical danger.

In Malaysia, the many barriers to sharing Christ with Muslims are reinforced with legal restrictions. Although the constitution allows freedom of religion, including the freedom to propagate one's religion, it also allows states to pass laws controlling and restricting the propagation of other beliefs among those professing the Muslim religion. Most states have therefore passed laws that effectively forbid the evangelization of Muslims (Lee Min Choon, 1998, pp. 92-98). In 1987, several Christians and believers from a Malay background were arrested and held under Malaysia's Internal Security Act for evangelizing Muslims (Ho, 1989). Although they were all eventually released and a

[11] This is not just an oversight in Christian mission. Robert Hefner (1997, pp. 8-18) laments and documents how Southeast Asian Islam has been consistently neglected in both Islamic studies and Southeast Asian studies.

successful legal challenge was made against arrest under the Internal Security Act for religious activities (Lee Min Choon, 1999, p. 88), this event had a chilling effect on Muslim evangelism.

Indonesia, despite its massive Muslim population, is not a Muslim country. Instead, it has an official ideology called Pancasila that recognizes five religions: Islam, Buddhism, Hinduism, Roman Catholicism, and Protestantism. However, there is a movement within Indonesia to make it an Islamic state, and the greening of Indonesia (similar in many ways to the saffronization of India) is already steadily underway. The country is currently in turmoil, and some see evidence to suggest that much of this turmoil has been orchestrated by those who would seek to make Indonesia much more strongly Islamic, as well as by those who support former President Suharto.

There has been an increasing campaign against Christians in Indonesia, which is exemplified in the dramatic increase in the number of attacks on churches. The figures speak for themselves: in the 10 years between 1945 and 1954, no churches were attacked; between 1955 and 1964, 2 were attacked; between 1965 and 1974, 46 were attacked; between 1975 and 1984, 89 were attacked; between 1985 and 1994, 104 were attacked; and between 1995 and 1999 (note that this is a five-year, not a 10-year period), 355 were attacked. A number of church leaders claim that Islamic troops, sometimes assisted by government troops, are waging a war of extermination on Christians in the Moluccan islands.

It is very difficult to know what is really happening or what the future will bring. The country is still in an economic mess and tottering on the brink of instability. The secession of East Timor has reignited other secessionist movements, particularly in Aceh, which threaten to fragment the country. At the same time, there are positive factors. There has been a strong movement for democracy that contributed to the downfall of President Suharto and led to the first authentically democratic elections in June 1999. As a result of those elections, Abdurrahman Wahid became President. He is a Muslim cleric and the head of a huge Muslim organization, but he is politically moderate, sensitive to Indonesia's diversity, and in the past has assisted Christians against persecution. However, his health is poor. At such a time; we certainly need to be very much in prayer for this nation and our Christian brothers and sisters there.

The international resurgence of Islam has also affected the region, encouraging greater assertiveness by Islamic groups generally, along with political movements for an Islamic state in Malaysia and Indonesia. The influence of Middle Eastern Islam has also been felt more strongly in recent decades. In South Thailand, wealthy Middle Easterners have become the model to emulate rather than the West. There are also reports of missions from the Middle East to Muslims in East Asia to strengthen and encourage their weaker brethren.

Challenges for the church

As we think about the church in mission to Muslims in East Asia, we can rejoice that in all of the East Asian countries where there are large numbers of Muslims (Indonesia, 180 million; China, 50 million; Malaysia, 11 million; Philippines, 5 million), there is also a strong and vigorous Christian church. In Indonesia, churches are established in a number of ethnic groups that are predominantly Muslim. In the other East Asian countries, the church's strength is in non-Muslim ethnic groups.

The barriers of language, ethnicity, fear, prejudice, and suspicion between Christians and Muslims are often high. The challenge to the churches in these countries is to cross these barriers in such a way as to share Jesus effectively. Those who are won to Christ must not be brought back across the divide as trophies. Rather, they need to remain in their communities and become the core of a growing movement to Christ among the Muslims of East Asia.

Many feel that to achieve this result, there will need to be significant contextualization of the form this movement takes. However, it often seems much more difficult for local churches to understand and endorse radical contextualization than for missionaries from outside, who are operating at a distance from their own church communities. Yet the missionaries from outside must also engage with the Christians inside in getting alongside the Muslims in these countries.

The Church in the Worlds of East Asia

The church in many parts of East Asia is well established and mature. It not only has its own well-qualified leadership, but also is increasingly contributing leadership to the church worldwide. In some countries of East Asia, the church is large, Evangelical, and vigorous. This is particularly true in Korea, the Philippines, and China. Even in countries where the church is numerically small, it is established and mature, as in Japan and Thailand. Mission to East Asia, even to unreached ethnic groups within East Asia, must come with respect for the church that the Lord has already established.

"Established, mature, and Evangelical" is not, however, an accurate description of all the church in East Asia. The problem of nominalism was raised in our discussion at Iguassu, with two different

issues being highlighted. The first is how we regard nominal Christians. The necessity of evangelizing nominal Christians was particularly stressed. It was noted that missions research that portrays nominal Christians as evangelized could be misleading, causing misunderstanding and undermining this important work. This is particularly an issue in the Philippines, where the majority of the population is nominally Roman Catholic.

The second issue is that of syncretistic Christianity. Many of those who would be identified as Christians, including Evangelical Christians, continue with pre-Christian practices and a worldview that is incompatible with the Christian faith. Thus, for example, some of the animistic Manobo tribal people in Southern Philippines, who responded to the gospel and now, at least in name, are Christians, still need to be evangelized (or re-evangelized) because their understanding is so shallow. In a different way, in Indonesia in the 1960s, everyone had to choose one of the five religions recognized by the government—Islam, Protestantism, Catholicism, Buddhism, or Hindu-Bali. Christianity proved attractive to many animists, because it appeared less restrictive than some of the others, since adherents could still eat pork. It was also attractive to a number of Communists, for whom becoming a Christian appeared to be a more progressive step than reverting to being Muslim. This forced choosing of a religious affiliation resulted in churches being filled with unconverted people.

The East Asian Church in Mission

One of the great encouragements in East Asia is the continuing growth in the number of missionaries being sent from East Asia to the other parts of East Asia and the world. The Japanese were some of the earliest pioneers; in the early 1990s, they had sent more cross-cultural missionaries per Evangelical Japanese Christian than any other country in East Asia. They were, however, overtaken by the Koreans, who had 6,000 Korean missionaries overseas in 1997. Today, the church in tiny Singapore, though it has not sent the largest number of missionaries, has sent more missionaries for every 1,000 Christians than any other national church in the world (Johnstone, 1998, p. 115).

The diverse nature of today's mission force is particularly evident in newly open countries like Cambodia and Mongolia, which have been allowing foreigners in for less than a decade. When I have visited these places, I have been struck by the way I do not see the same numerical dominance of Western missionaries from North America and Europe that I see in traditional fields. The Westerners are there, but so too are missionaries from Korea, Hong Kong, Japan, Singapore, the Philippines, and elsewhere—and they are clearly making a significant contribution.

The Asian missionary movement has had its difficulties and challenges, which it continues to wrestle with. Some were addressed at the Asian Missions Congresses held in Seoul, Korea, in 1990 and in Pattaya, Thailand in 1997. The first congress was a great celebration of the emergence of the Asian missions movement. The second, while continuing to celebrate, included more reflective evaluation of what needed to be done to ensure that movement's continued growth and effectiveness.

The Asian missionary movement also illustrates the strong relationship that often exists between overseas mission and economics: missionary sending has been strongest where both the church and the national economy have been strong, such as Korea and Singapore. Those who can pay can go. This was demonstrated in a negative way during the East Asian economic crisis: when the Korean won suddenly halved in value, many Korean missionaries suddenly had to return home or else make stringent economies in order to continue their ministries. But do wealth and overseas mission necessarily go together? There is an increasing interest in mission among the East Asian churches in countries with less developed economies. This includes the Philippines (which had the largest delegation at the second Asian Missions Congress), Indonesia, and East Malaysia. A major challenge for mission in East Asia is developing new models for mission that will break through the economic barriers and release this force into the harvest field.

The largest mission force, however, is yet to come. In the 21st century, the church in China, with its 35-70 million Christians, may become the largest sending church in the world. At the moment, it is very active in reaching other Han Chinese within China. There are signs of a very small but growing interest in reaching cross-culturally to China's minorities. The day will come when Chinese from China will be a significant part of the cross-cultural and overseas mission force around the world.

Conclusion

As I bring this brief survey to a close, it must be with apologies for all that has been missed. This has been an attempt to draw with the broad strokes of a Chinese brush-stroke painting rather than with the intricate details of Balinese art. I hope the survey has been helpful.

It is both exciting and daunting to look out over East Asia at the dawn of a new millennium. God has been mightily at work in this part of the world, and yet so many still do not know him or give him the glory he is due. Our commission remains. Our duty is faithfulness. We do not know all that God has in store. But our faith is in the Lord who can and will bring glory to his name throughout this part of the world.

References

Bhanu, S. (2000). The social impact of the Asian crisis. In *Regional Outlook: Southeast Asia 2000-2001* (pp. 62-63). Singapore: Institute of Southeast Asian Studies.

Covell, R. R. (1995, January). Why I don't pray for China to open. *Evangelical Missions Quarterly, 31*(1), pp. 14-19.

Encyclopaedia Britannica. (1998). Asia: Physical and human geography: The land: Relief: The regions of Asia. *Encyclopaedia Britannica CD 98.* CD-ROM.

Evans, G. (1998). *The politics of ritual and remembrance: Laos since 1975.* Chiang Mai, Thailand: Silkworm Books.

FEER: Far Eastern Economic Review. (1998). *Asia 1998 yearbook: A review of the events of 1997.* Hong Kong: Review Publishing Company.

Foster-Carter, A. (1998). *North Korea: Four scenarios.* Internet: http://www.megastories.com/nkorea/scenario/scenario.htm. Accessed December 20, 1999.

Freeman, N. J., & Than, M. (2000). Economic outlook: Indochina and Myanmar. In *Regional Outlook: Southeast Asia 2000-2001* (pp. 68-84). Singapore: Institute of Southeast Asian Studies.

Hamilton, D. (1987). *Tentmakers speak: Practical advice from over 400 missionary tentmakers.* Ventura, CA: Regal Books.

Hefner, R. W. (1997). Politics and religious renewal in Muslim Southeast Asia. In R. W. Hefner & P. Horvatich (Eds.), *Islam in an era of nation-states* (pp. 3-40). Honolulu, HI: University of Hawaii Press.

Ho, D. K. C. (1989). The church in the Islamic context: Malaysian Christian released. In Bong Rin Ro (Ed.), *Christian suffering in Asia* (pp. 101-103). Taichung, Taiwan: Asia Theological Association.

Johnstone, P. (1993). *Operation world: The day-by-day guide to praying for the world*

(5th ed.). Grand Rapids, MI: Zondervan Publishing House.

———. (1998). *The church is bigger than you think: The unfinished work of world evangelisation.* Fearn, Ross-shire, Scotland: Christian Focus Publications.

Lambert, T. (1998, November/December). "Culture Christians"—A new phenomenon. *China Insight*, p. 1.

———. (1999). *China's Christian millions: The costly revival.* London: Monarch Books.

Lee Min Choon. (1999). *Freedom of religion in Malaysia.* Kuala Lumpur, Malaysia: Kairos Research Centre.

Lee, P. K. H. (1996, December). The "Cultural Christians" phenomenon in China. *Ching Feng: A Journal on Christianity and Chinese Religion and Culture, 39*(4), pp. 307-321.

Liu Xiaofeng. (1998, November/December). The phenomenon of "Culture Christians" (T. Lambert, Trans.). *China Insight*, pp. 2-4. Originally published in *Tianzhujiao Yanjiu Ziliao* [Research Materials on Catholicism] in December 1996.

Marshall, P. (1998, January). Statistics, mission, and human rights. *International Bulletin of Missionary Research, 22*(1), pp. 2-8.

MSC. (1999). *What is the MSC?* Internet: http://www.mdc.com.my/msc/index.html. Accessed March 31, 2000.

Muzaffar, C. (1985). Malayism, Bumiputraism, and Islam. In I. Ahmad, S. Siddique, & Y. Hussain (Eds.), *Readings on Islam in Southeast Asia* (pp. 356-361). Singapore: Institute of Southeast Asian Studies. Excerpted from C. Muzaffar (Ed.). (1979). *Universalism of Islam.* Penang, Malaysia: Aliran.

Naisbitt, J. (1996). *Megatrends Asia: Eight Asian megatrends that are reshaping our world.* New York: Simon & Schuster.

Noland, M. (Ed.). (1998). *Economic integration of the Korean peninsula.* Papers presented at a conference of the same name, Arlie House, Washington, September 5-6, 1997. Institute for International Economics.

Paterson, R. (1999). *The continuing heartcry for China*. Tonbridge, England: Sovereign Word.

Patten, C. (1998). *East and West: The last governor of Hong Kong on power, freedom, and the future*. London: MacMillan Publishers Ltd.

Tennent, T. C. (1998). Equipping missionaries for the resistant. In *Reaching the resistant: Barriers and bridges for mission* (pp. 221-231). (Evangelical Missiological Society Series No. 6.) Pasadena, CA: William Carey Library.

Ward, T. (1999, October). Repositioning mission agencies for the 21st century. *International Bulletin of Missionary Research*, 23(4), pp. 146-153.

Warren, M. A. C. (1976). *I believe in the Great Commission*. Grand Rapids, MI: Wm. B. Eerdmans Publishing Co.

Ian Prescott was born in England and grew up in Argentina and Scotland. He studied engineering in Cambridge where he met Anne-Marie. Together they joined OMF International and served nine years in the Philippines, where they were involved in planting two churches and supervising a variety of other ministries. In 1996, Ian became OMF's International Director for Evangelization, based in Singapore and responsible for OMF's field work throughout East Asia. Ian and Anne-Marie have three children, all born in the Philippines and currently schooling in Malaysia and India.

30

THE MAN HAD WITHDRAWN from the worldly busyness of the market place. As all men seeking holiness, he desired revelation from beyond. Traveling with his uncle across the deserts as a young boy, he had come across the many religious expressions of the business centers of Western Asia. There he had met the Jews and Christians also. Could it be that his own many gods in the temple of Mecca were blasphemous?

His meditation was abruptly ended as a light appeared. In fear, the man tried to escape the angelic being from a world beyond. Wherever he looked, the vision could not be escaped. Silence was broken by a voice demanding, "Recite!"

Shaken by the experience, he made his way down the mountain to his home. He tried to describe the dreadful sight to his wife, Khadija. The former rather rich widow, slightly older than he was, lovingly shared that God would never allow an evil spirit to come to him. Destiny and calling came to Muhammad, and with them a new era dawned in the history of mankind, in the year 610.

A Vision for the World Beyond

A prominent leader of the Hizbollah party in Lebanon was asked if he wanted to see all of Lebanon become Muslim. He looked intensely at his questioner, then answered, "No." Quickly he added, "I want the world."

That has been the intention from the beginning of Islam. Perhaps we could question the motivation, but believing the best would be to understand that there was a genuine concern that people were not submitting to God and that it was time to establish the will of God among the peoples.

A vision from the world beyond: Islam

BERTIL
ENGQVIST

In Islamic teaching, there are only two groups of people: the House of God and the House of War (those that have rebelled or live in ignorance). Either you are in, or you are out. The struggle for souls has been one in which people should leave their way of unbelief. The mission of Islam is to call people back to their submitted place under God's sovereign rule.

This rule of God has not been limited to a geographical area. God is a God of all. Islam's rapid spread across the north of Africa, across European soil, and toward Asia was to establish God's rule over all people. However, there has always been room for the non-atheist and the monotheistic believer. In certain areas, it was seen as liberation. Indeed, there have even been circumstances in which the Christians and Jews were better off under Islamic rule than under the brutal hands of certain Byzantine rulers, who ruthlessly killed anyone opposing their power or doctrine!

A Vision of God

The call is a call back to the basics, to the One God who is sovereign and absolute. Man should not even think that he has freedom or power. No, God is sovereign. He is so sovereign that we cannot rightly accept anything but as from God. In the daily life, there are the "if God wills." It might be good or bad, but nothing can threaten the position of God. Man's relationship becomes, then, that of a slave to a master. God is God, and man exists to serve. God doesn't have any equal or son.

This is where we get into conflict. What about Jesus? Is he the Son of God? Our Muslim friends would oppose that statement strongly. Why? Because there is no God beside God. "You believe in three Gods!" they would say with dismay. "Me? No way!" Some of the more uneducated Muslims would gladly explain that we be-

lieve in God the Father, God the Mother, and God the Son! In amazement we would try to communicate that that is not what we believe. But many Muslims are convinced that this is indeed our belief.

The vision of God should be looked at again. In Matthew 16:16, Peter exclaims, "You are the Christ, the Son of the living God!" Jesus quickly points out that this was a spiritual revelation. "This was not revealed to you by man, but by my Father in heaven" (v. 17). Let us be careful with the mystery of our faith and not be too snappy with our Muslim friends who do not understand what Peter didn't understand, nor anyone else.

A Vision Given to Muhammad

"You Christians are funny!" the businessman from Saudi Arabia said. "You want the latest of everything, but not when it comes to religion. There you hold onto the things from the time before Muhammad received his revelation."

There is another name for Muhammad: the "Seal of the Prophets." Muslims declare him to be the last of the prophets. In Islam, previous revelations are superseded by the final. Muslims would even use John 16:7 to confirm the finality of the Prophet. Their argument is that *parakletos* ("the helper") should be *periklutos* ("the praised"), which is "Ahmed" or "Muhammad" in Arabic.

Muhammad's central place is seen in sayings such as, "No one will meet God that has not met Muhammad first." Compare this with Jesus' declaration, "No one comes to the Father except through me," in John 14:6. The basic creed of the Muslim is, "There is no God beside God, and Muhammad is the messenger of God." The messenger or apostle is there at the heart of the creed, the very testimony through which one becomes a Muslim.

Say it three times with intensity, and you are there!

A Vision of Renewal

All world powers experience periods of increase and of decline. Such is the case with Islamic rule as well.

As 18th century Europe grew in power, the Ottoman Empire was gradually partitioned, marking a general decline in Islamic power until political and economic developments of the late 20th century. At this time, as the post-Christian nations of the West fell more and more under the power of a materialistic view based on humanism and socialism, their own spiritual emphases diminished. Instead, welfare had taken the church's place, and Mammon grew fat again. The Industrial World was run on oil from mainly Islamic countries. When the taps were tightened, discussions could begin! Black gold became a valuable resource used to favor the cause of Islam.

Islam has not had this much success since their troops stormed across Europe in the 8th century (finally stopped in the Battle of Tours in modern-day central France) or since Islam was knocking at the gates of Vienna during the Ottoman Empire. Today the success is of a different kind. It is an issue of teaching and penetration through the movements of peoples due to wars, famines, or economic developments.

It is obvious that a political and economic bloc is created in areas where there is a dominance of Muslim lands. Organizations such as the Arab League, OAU, OPEC, and others have become global power factors. In the introduction to the 1970 Islamic Conference in Jeddah, the foreign ministers from about 25 Muslim nations agreed that their "common faith is a strong factor in drawing nearer and establishing an understanding between Muslim nations ... agreeing to protect spiritual, ethical, social, and economical Muslim values."

The Muslim World League, founded in 1961, declared during their conference held in Mecca in 1974 that they needed to cooperate not only in the realm of economics, but also in their mission activities which needed to increase. Sheikh Saleh al-Ghazzas emphasized the need to "develop a coordination plan for all Muslim activities in the whole world, to reach maximum result and a minimum of duplication and waste."

Let us look at one more statement. The Islamic World Festival was held in London in 1976, with the goal of letting Europe become familiar with Islam. At a related meeting, Prince Muhammad Ibn-Faisal stated, "Islam doesn't belong to East or West. It is God's message ... to each man whatever his background, nationality, color, race, or language might be.... The answer [to the challenge of this era] lies in a rediscovery of the controlling principles of human issues, shortly in the rediscovery of man's relationship with God. The Koran is inviting all those who belong to the Prophet Abraham to help each other to reach the goal that makes it possible for mankind to live in peace with God, through submitting to his will." It was also stated that, "Man is looking for a new future.... Islam is today offering mankind ... a new alternative as a foundation for the order of life and society."

As we enter the 21st century, that vision of the Muslims has not faded but developed in such a way that we today have over 15 satellites and hundreds of radio stations broadcasting Islamic teaching. Scores of publishing houses, university courses, and cultural centers around the world exist with the purpose of sharing their message. TV stations are focusing on the demands from an ever-increasing Muslim population as they claim their rightful say in the development of the nations. Through immigration, both voluntary and forced, we find that today some of the 1,200,000 Muslims live in each of the nations of the world.

A Sad Vision

The problems that the church is facing are multifaceted. We have a history of scars. From the old days of laughing at Muhammad in his search for truth, through the history with Crusades and wars, even into this new millennium, Russia's bombing of Chechnya is perceived by many as being the Christians bombing the Muslims. The vision of the ruins of Grozny is as sad as the ruins of the Crusaders' castles along the road to Jerusalem.

Apart from these political marks along the path of reconciliation, there are the scars that minorities from both sides bear. As the Bolsheviks crushed the Muslim tribes in Central Asia, so the Muslims in Indonesia treat the Chinese Christians. We can understand the effects of the broken Balkans, where Christian Serbs fight Muslim Albanians.

Then we have the prejudice of both sides. A Russian Christian believer who left Central Asia talks about *die Schwarze* ("the black ones"), referring to the majority people among whom he lived all his life, without learning either their language or culture. This is often a problem where minority groups of Christians live among the majority Muslims. The minority has been extremely protective, which is understandable in the light of potential persecution. "A poor status quo is better than losing all," goes the reasoning. However, it is also a matter of cultural preservation. In an attempt to protect traditions, one group keeps to itself even when it comes to questions of marriage. None of the groups wants to be diluted or, worse, defiled.

Even in our high-tech global village, there is segregation based on the differences of origin and religion. The great migrating groups are definitely harassed in many nations. Fear and separation become further ingrained. The migrants seek their identity deeper within themselves, in their culture, language, and religion.

A Vision of Today

As we look at the world today, we would see that the diversity among Muslims is as great as that among Christians. "Who is a Muslim?" is not as easy to answer today as it probably was in the 7th century. It is not only the fact that Islam is spread among all colors and races, but there are definite variations of Islam. Muslims are facing issues similar to those the church faces as splits and sects are formed. Islam also has a tendency to be eclectic and contextualized. Therefore, the Muslims of Central Asia will be different in many ways from the Muslims of Suriname, the American Black Muslim will be different from the Bedouin Muslims of Gaza, and the city-dwelling Muslims of Damascus will be different from the rural Muslims of Malaysia.

Christian missionary pioneers knew at the end of the 19th century what today the church worldwide is suddenly aware of. The breakdown of the former Soviet Union has opened the eyes of many to see that in that old bloc there were millions who counted themselves as Muslims, a thing made obvious as the new republics seek their identity. The trend in many countries in Africa seems likewise to be a stronger recognition of Islam, as some even introduce Sharia law (Islamic law which is not bound to any geographical region). Now we see it clearly: the Arabs are not the only Muslims. Actually, the great majority of Muslims are not Arabs!

A Muslim is a person like any other. The father is wondering where to get money to provide for his family. A mother is worrying about her sick child. A teenager is under pressure from her peers. Where do I get a job? Whom shall I marry? What is there to eat? What will my parents say? How can we buy a home of our own? What are these foreigners teaching?

The Muslims are not only the traditional blocs of peoples, but there is an increase in their numbers in nations that traditionally have another religion, such as Korea or Germany. These are Muslims who have migrated or through marriage or conversion have become Muslim. We must forget the camel-riding, sword-swinging image of old movies and The Arabian Nights, an image that anyway is so false. Instead, we must look at the technological wizards, professional soccer players, and scientists in Australia, Singapore, France, and elsewhere.

A Vision Unnoticed

Many of those early Asian missionary pioneers wrote about their experiences across the Silk Road, into the Asian subcontinent, and down the Arabian Peninsula. However, only a few wrote in English. This was and is a problem, as there has been an accepted tradition in modern mission that if it isn't done in English, it isn't done! This tradition is very unfortunate when it comes to mission. It could be particularly damaging as we look at the political involvement of nations easily identified as English speakers, particularly the United States and Great Britain. It is a reality that we have to consider.

This political identification or association can be difficult to avoid, but we must be aware of it. Either we communicate the view of our own governments, or people might attach that view to us. Once two American women were sitting in a shelter together with the local people during the fighting in Lebanon. They had a wonderful time of witnessing as they were sharing in the suffering of the people. Suddenly the battleship New Jersey launched its rocket attack on the hills above Beirut. The atmosphere changed in the shelter, and someone said, "That is your ship!"

Some years ago, I came back from a former Soviet republic where there was a struggle by the Islamic forces to take over the government. I cannot forget the look on the faces of my dear American colleagues as I asked them to pray that the Communists would remain in power! An unthinkable thought, it seemed.

Many long-term missionaries thought that the Gulf War could have been an answer to prayer, as it seemed to have the potential of opening up some of the least accessible nations for the gospel. But few ever considered that the oil-rich countries being attacked were also the powers behind the spread of Islam. Was it because the welfare of the West was threatened that those nations acted so harshly against Iraq?

An interesting twist on the political scene is the change of regime and system in South Africa. Suddenly there is a new-found eagerness on the part of many in the church. They are ready to get involved, feeling they want to do something, now that the isolation is broken. With the growth of the church in Latin America and in South Korea, two other major sectors of the church are on the scene. Neither of these areas is English speaking! It is good to know that the Holy Spirit demonstrates his skill in languages, as in Acts 2:4-12!

I am not pointing a finger at any certain nationality. However, we have to be aware of the reality. The problem would be similar for a Han Chinese to communicate with a Muslim Uighur in Xinjiang, or for a Serb to witness to a Kosovar, or for a Greek to witness to a Turk. These hostilities are based on historical political developments that might have nothing to do with the individual in question, but he or she is still subject to the circumstances and the history.

Unless we accept the fact that Christ is building his church (Matt. 16:18), we easily would come with our own models of what the church should be and look like. That could well be an Anglo-Saxon model. Never mind what nationality would try to realise it, but due to the common theological educational system, the model is likely to be Anglo-Saxon. This might be one of the great threats to the development of the church among the majority peoples. Our knowledge might become a hindrance, as we are rather set in our ways and in our understanding. Our knowledge actually creates detachment from the society and causes misunderstandings. For example, we may have a problem if the translated songs become a major element in the worship of the newly formed fellowships. In one Muslim country, I heard the missionary teach that the local instruments were of the devil and that their traditional way of singing was spiritistic.

A Vision of the Harvest

Having recognised that there are problems, we still have to move ahead. It is not my intention to discourage us, but rather to have us in all humility seek a solution to the issues at stake in the Muslim world. We all have a role to play. The thought of reaching the whole world is not one invented in a Bible college somewhere, but it is the desire of the God of love and compassion. It is his idea, and we have the privilege to work with him.

What bothers me is that we actually have the knowledge and the capacity to deliver the good news to the Muslim peoples, but we do not have the com-

passion to do it. We cannot say that we live in ignorance anymore. We know where the unreached live. We know their languages. We know how to get there. We have all knowledge—but if we do not have love, we are nothing. Love believes all things; therefore, we should press on by faith until all have heard.

In John 4, we see the Master go to Samaria. The Scripture states that he had to go there, although he was also tired. It is not by feelings that we do the will of God, but by obedience. The Jews had nothing to do with the Samaritans, but God did. He had a message for them. The disciples were puzzled by the Master who spoke to the Samaritan woman. They could only engage in commerce with the Samaritans. At times, we are like that too. We exclude the Muslims, although we don't mind envisioning the regions as tourist sites or doing business with them—particularly buying oil or using their fortune.

The disciples were told to lift their eyes to see the harvest, but it was nothing like what they expected. Beyond the muddy hills, they saw the commotion among the Samaritans. There was a movement among the ones whom the Jews considered untouchables. But the Master had touched the Samaritans through the testimony of an outcast. I think there is a movement among the people of Islam today. Who takes credit for it is in one way unimportant. What matters is that the Master is touching the Muslims today. There is a harvest already as thousands of Muslims are turning to Jesus—for instance, across Central Asia and among the Iranians both inside and outside their nation. There are surely still unreached peoples, but that should not stop us from following the Master's vision.

A Vision of the Bride

The final vision is one of the bride of Christ, the one that will make herself ready (Rev. 19:7). As we consider the unreached peoples of the world, we need to let knowledge express itself in action. The vision that God has shown us is an inclusive vision. All peoples. That includes the Muslims. To take it even further, if the Baluch or Qashqai or Lezgian people are not a part of the people reached, then the bride has not made herself ready. With the eyes of faith, we can take the facts as they are today and transform them into a vision of what will be tomorrow. The Lord's statement, "I will build my church," means exactly that.

Understanding the commitment of our Christian brothers and sisters in Muslim regions, particularly those coming from Islamic backgrounds, we need to listen respectfully to them. We need to support their ministry through prayer and resources in a wise, non-directive way. We must want them to succeed, even if that would mean less for others to report or take credit for. Their risk-taking is normally far beyond that of most followers of Christ. "You are my crown," Paul says of the believers in Thessalonica and Philippi. Would we say so too of the peoples that are said to be unreached at the beginning of the third millennium?

What does it take, then, to see the bride of the Lamb ready? Instead of a warfare mentality, we need the mentality of our self-sacrificing Master to display the love of God in all its beauty. This is the time for us to make an inventory of the way we use our time and finances. This goes for missions, churches, and individuals. The mental transformation is a change Paul writes of in Romans 12:1-2. We need to let Christ control our thoughts (2 Cor. 10:5-6). Would we aim to see the full gospel brought to every Muslim man and woman, even if it carried a high price tag on it (Col. 1:24-29)? Would we be determined to see these peoples as a part of our everyday life? It might be through prayer or giving to a particular purpose, e.g., Scriptures to the Pamyrians. Would we take it so seriously that we would actually talk about it, plan for it, and then do it?

In the first year of this millennium, an estimated two million Muslims went on the pilgrimage to Mecca. There has never been a Christian gathering of that size. Millions across the globe celebrate the Feast of the Sacrifice. This is one of the greatest feasts in Islam. It is a remembrance of Abraham's sacrifice, but they don't know that God's true sacrifice of the Lamb has been given for them. However, one day there will be a gathering that no one can count. The day will come when people from Libya, Turkmenistan, Bangladesh, and all other Muslim nations will together worship the Lamb. It is time to prepare for the wedding of the Lamb!

Bertil Engqvist, a Swedish artist, turned to Christ in 1965 at the age of 23 in the midst of a successful career. In 1968, he and his wife Gunnel moved to the Middle East with Operation Mobilization and remained in the region with their three children until 1992. After serving in the Arab world, he became OM's Area Coordinator for the Middle East in 1986 and later also for Central Asia. He is also the founder and International Director of Operation Mercy, an affiliated relief and development organization. The Engqvists have been missionaries with the Swedish agency InterAct since 1979, seconded to OM.

31

Dry bones in the West

ROSE
DOWSETT

"**M**Y NAME'S EZEKIEL, but you probably don't recognise me."

Some day, a film producer will make a blockbuster based on Ezekiel's prophecy. It has all the ingredients: colour, noise, drama, a tumbling succession of strong visual images, bizarre events, out-of-body experiences, riveting characters, intense emotion, even a heart-tugging love story.

The trouble is that no producer would know what to do with the real meaning of the story, if he even grasped it. How could he ever come to grips with God? He'd probably have to edit him out (just imagine, Ezekiel minus God!). He would have to cast the story as fiction (science fiction maybe) of a pre-scientific era (plenty of scope here for amazing vehicles, journeys through space, and special effects). Or maybe it could be classed as fantasy—fantasy on a par with a cross-fertilisation of The Hobbit with Mickey Mouse (though with a much weaker moral framework than either of those). A producer would need to be politically correct (tricky, with all those references to Israel, war, animal sacrifice, and women's "monthly uncleanness," to name but a few; quite a few potential lobby groups to keep a wary eye on, there, but nothing that some extensive editing couldn't handle). And he'd need to tone down the religion bits (though a good New Age spirituality spin would be fine).

But none of these obstacles need stand in the way. In the post-modern world, a producer would have no scruples, moral or intellectual, no restraints of reverence or commitment to truth, to prevent him from changing anything he wished or, for that matter, plagiarising anything that appealed to him. He'd simply do whatever he wanted, taking artistic (or any other) autonomy for granted. Likely to make a huge killing at the box office? Go for it! Just make sure you get the right screen idol to play the role of Ezekiel, and success is pretty much guaranteed. It wouldn't cross the producer's mind that the copyright for the story-line belongs to God—and anyway, who's going to sue on his behalf?

Perhaps this seems a far-fetched scenario. To be sure, a mere 40 years ago no mainstream film producer would have contemplated behaving in such a way, though the really avant garde, with their tiny audiences, might dare anything. Let imagination run riot in producing "Ben Hur," yes. But Ezekiel, gutted, freeze-dried, and reconstituted radically differently? No!

Yet today, most of the assumptions that would have kept "Ben Hur" in one category and Ezekiel in another have been swept away. Today, they're both just stories, imaginary stories about a past we cannot really know, and even if we could know it, would it really matter? We are disconnected from history. And with stories, you are entitled to tell them any way you wish, with or without the author's permission. The book, the film, and the book of the film of the book need have little in common, maybe not even a title. Fiction is there to be customised, like most other things, to suit yourself. Let the consumer reign supreme. The producer wants to do it his way. The trick is to persuade the audiences through carefully designed advertising that he is doing it their way too.

He probably is. That's why it's a blockbuster. And that's also why those in the audience go away with each having seen a subtly different story, and they are content that it is so. "This is what it means to me," they say, and they go home to party or to sleep. Tomorrow, there will be an-other experience to hold their attention. Briefly and only on the surface. So what? The producer made his money; the audience whiled away an hour or two pleasurably enough; life goes on.

Mind you, in heaven, Ezekiel doesn't recognise himself. It was a reinvented stranger on the screen in the cinema and on the screen of their minds. If they stopped to think about it at all, they didn't know that that was so. Come to think of it, by the time they stepped out of the cinema, they didn't even recall his name. The producer used a nickname "to resonate better with today's world." Ezekiel has a new identity, a million new identities, no identity at all. No matter. Life goes on. Maybe.

Short Circuits in Reality

The preceding scenario was intended to crank up your imagination a little and, especially if you are a Western Christian ostrich (with your head hidden in the sand), perhaps to rattle you a little. For the fact is that we in the West badly need to be rattled. Indeed, like the dry bones Ezekiel so famously saw in his vision in the valley, we desperately need God not only to rattle us back into shape, but also to re-clothe us in healthy flesh and then to pour new life into us by his Spirit. We, too, are very dry bones indeed.

The church in the West is in deep trouble. That is not to say that there are no signs of spiritual life at all. In the grace of God, there are evidences here and there of authentic, God-breathed vitality. Nonetheless, these are mostly few and far between in much of the West. Some former strongholds of Christendom are now spiritual wastelands. And even where the church is more visible, even very active, there may be very troubling questions about its health in terms of truth and faithfulness. More perhaps than we find comfortable, we need to face the fact: the church in the West is in deep trouble.

It is, of course, a mistake to think that being only a minority, sometimes a very tiny minority, is the trouble. Neither the Lord Jesus himself nor the early church regarded minority status as abnormal. It was only with the advent of Christendom that the church was seduced into believing that she should exercise majority control by force, not faith (in parts of Europe, we are still paying the price for that wrong turning). Nor is it even enough to point to the fact that that minority is shrinking to something smaller still, distressing though that should be. We may, in the mercy of God, be better able to see ourselves clearly and honestly for the first time in a long time, when our poverty and nakedness show up undisguised by nominal adherents. Alternatively, of course, it may be that the very size of some congregations, especially some of today's so-called mega-churches, is presumed to be evidence that all is well and that the church is successful, hiding deeper and less palatable realities. No, size and numbers are not an adequate measurement of health and life.

More fundamentally, the real trouble is that the church in the West, in very large measure, is indistinguishable from the world. We have lost our way and, with it, the integrity of new-creation-life. We have been taken captive, and we haven't even noticed. We are like dry-boned skeletons harmlessly, powerlessly clanking in our chains, while the world goes out to play. We think and act like the world, with the thinnest veneer of difference. There is a profound and widespread biblical illiteracy. Consequently, we are happy enough for the cosy psychological release of sins forgiven (vaguely understood) and the choice of club (the church) to meet with congenial people to pursue our hobby (Christianity) from time to time. We

may even (if we come from that sort of church) enjoy the adrenaline rush of upbeat events well orchestrated or the satisfaction of aesthetic pleasure. On the other hand, we may feel rather aggrieved, as if God hasn't treated us very nicely (even, we may think, fairly), if life is hard going. (Surely, he owes us something better in return for our efforts on his behalf?) Meanwhile, heads down, let's get on with the real business of life like everyone else: getting and spending, eating and drinking, raising families, avoiding sickness, staving off death.

All this is very far removed from the radical Christianity of the New Testament. There we find a template of lives lived entirely differently after conversion from those lived before. Not that the early Christians are to be idealised, as if they were perfect. They weren't. But both the Lord's teaching and that of the apostles point to a radical new life that is to be shown in the lives of Christian believers, at every level of the human personality. We are to be profoundly different from those around us in the way we think, in the way we behave, in our inter-relatedness with fellow believers, in our values and worldview, and in all our relationships with the world. Being men and women of faith involves having our lives shaped first and foremost not by what is seen (for that must pass away) but by what is unseen (for that is real and eternal reality). Truth, which must define the unseen (after all, animists and New Agers also live by the unseen), is not deduced by human reasoning but given sovereignly by divine revelation. We most urgently need to be deeply changed by God's Word.

To follow such a pattern, of course, has always required Christian people to live on something of a collision course with much of their culture. In the West, the dissonance between living the way of Christian faith and the way of the prevailing culture has steadily increased over recent centuries. But it was in the 20th century especially that the church in the West capitulated spectacularly but, paradoxically, without recognising that that was what she had done. In the 21st century, the crisis of falling numbers may, with hindsight, be seen to be the least of the church's problems. To focus primarily on numbers short-circuits reality. The bones are indeed numerous. They are also very dry.

The 20th Century:
Free Fall From Grace

For Europe, the 20th century began with a blaze of confidence—and the church basked in the glow. To be sure, for the church, there were some disquieting signs for those who cared to look. France, for example, with 100 years of aggressive rationalism and humanism behind it, already presaged what would happen elsewhere, with the church sidelined and held in contempt by more and more of the population and with Christian convictions largely excluded from public discourse. But if France was an embarrassment to the church, her gaiety, especially in Paris, her lively philosophers, and her scientific and artistic achievements ensured her popularity as a kind of loveable rascal. For those who wished to be so persuaded, the message from France was clear: shake off the shackles of the church and enjoy the freedom. Moreover, by and large, Europeans were supremely confident that their cultures were superior, that their empires were secure, and that progress and growing prosperity were inevitable. Human achievement, especially European human achievement, need know no limits.

The church shared that confidence, ironically supported the institutions and policies that seemed to be at the forefront of progress, and benefited from the prosperity. The 19th century missionary movements had extended the jurisdiction of the church alongside those of the Crown(s) and commerce. It was confidently expected that within a few years the heathen everywhere would have been gathered in, and every other religion would have quietly disappeared. In many European countries, the 19th century had also seen a massive church building programme in the expanding cities. Towering cathedrals and multiple churches appeared to testify to the approval of the God who was so signally (and, they felt, understandably) blessing them. But buildings are never the same as life.

The Trojan horse was already within the city walls, for much of the confidence was fixed firmly in the capacity of human beings to conquer and control the world and to do these things without divine assistance. Ironically, what had begun as an expression of faith became its undermining. The modern scientific enterprise grew precisely out of the belief that the God who had created the world had created it with coherence and dependability, with laws and order reflecting divine reliability. So it followed that the study of the natural world and of astronomy, physics, mathematics, and, later, every other branch of science would lead to more devout worship of God. As science disclosed hitherto undreamed-of intricacies, it would only serve to show how marvellous the Creator was.

But with all the tragic inevitability of fallenness, before long scientists were obsessed with their discoveries, not with the One to whom those discoveries pointed. Reverent exploration of God's world became proud explanation of man's world. The agricultural revolution, then the industrial revolution, and more recently the medical and technological revolutions have each in turn (alongside their many undisputed benefits) also reinforced human arrogance. Humankind, entrusted by God with dominion over the world on his behalf, instead usurped control and banished God.

Many Christians, in both the 19th and early 20th centuries, especially those with certain eschatological views, readily bought into the belief in progress. A growing number of people continued to attend church only as a matter of social correctness or as a cultural habit, rather than as a commitment of personal faith on which they had staked their lives. As science grew in confidence and supplied "expert" answers in ever expanding areas of human life, the Christian faith was regarded increasingly at best as a matter of private and personal conviction. Sadly, Christians ceded first intellectual ground (for example, miracles should be discarded because they are "superstitious," or they should be reinterpreted with scientific explanations), then moral ground. Religion had been privatised. Europe became more and more openly secular.

It is also hard to over-estimate the damage done to the Christian cause in Europe by two world wars. It is arguable that the spectacle of allegedly Christian nations tearing each other to shreds in barbaric manner undermined the credibility of the church in many people's minds. It also made possible the Russian Revolution and the tide of Marxism on the one hand and completely entrenched secular humanism through the rest of Europe on the other. While many people turned to the church in the dark days of war, in days of peace they left it again. They had regained control. God was unnecessary. Men returning home after surviving the unspeakable brutalities of war abandoned the church in disillusioned droves.

And even when events have shown how little faith deserves to be put in human nature, how double-edged "progress" is, and how incredibly precarious the con-trol over nature is, most Europeans—even those who discovered the emptiness of Marxism's promises—have not returned to the church. The dream has changed, but Christianity is not a part of the new dream either.

Christianity Discarded

Once the great cathedrals and abbeys of Europe towered over life below and pointed to the transcendent. Now the new cathedrals dedicated to commerce and frenetic human pride dwarf the ancient buildings and, Tower-of-Babel-like, scrape the sky. All over Europe, cathedrals and churches are tourist attractions—museums declaring the subliminal message, "Past but not present, quaint but irrelevant, art of a bygone age, empty house for rent"—while the shopping malls shout, "Come and worship! Here's life!" and buzz with purpose and participation.

In a visual age, architecture matters. But even more, the media, especially the visual media, shape minds and lives and overwhelm us in images and impressions and presuppositions we are not even aware of. The media sell us a dream, packaged as a promise. The media sell us opinion, packaged as truth; fantasy, packaged as fact. When it comes to Christianity, the media pounce gleefully on every church scandal, every internecine squabble, every whiff of heresy (or conviction), and they render not only the church but by association God as ridiculous, puerile, and absurd. In the ubiquitous TV soaps, watched by millions, Christians (and especially clergy) are portrayed as bigots or fools. No wonder that the world, relentlessly tutored by the media, is convinced that the church has nothing to say that's worth listening to. Christians are a bunch of hypocrites who shouldn't be allowed to peddle their prejudices in the world of public affairs. The gospel is an out-of-date, discredited fairy story where nobody lived happily ever after. As for Jesus, he may or may not have been a good guy—who knows? Whatever, he comes in handy as a swearword.

But before we despair utterly, let us remind ourselves that we are to be men and women of faith, locked onto and living by God's truth. So, whatever our culture shouts so stridently, whatever appearances may be, we need to go behind and beyond to what God says is in fact the case. And it is there, of course, that we see a gloriously different picture. This is not because of human ability (and insofar as the church became captive to the humanism and pride of secularism, it is just as well that recent events have shaken us out of it: let us repent and put such sin behind us). No, it is all to do with the grace and unchangeable character of God. The world may think it has discarded God and the Christian faith, but God is not so easily dislodged. His ultimate triumph is absolutely assured.

Revisiting the Pre-Constantinian Church

In some ways, we are back where we started. Of course, that is not entirely true. There have been 20 centuries of Christian history, which have indelibly marked much of the world besides shaping the church. In that sense, we cannot go back to where we started. But in other ways, we are perhaps closer to the context of the pre-Constantinian church than we realise.

For the first time in 15 centuries, through most of Europe, the church has neither political nor economic nor educational power. It has a diminishing role in public discourse, though some legal systems and some widely held moral values owe far more to their Christian roots than the church's detractors would care to admit. We find ourselves in the midst of a struggle to conquer and unify the world, though this time less through direct military might and more through technological and economic control. We live in a cauldron of religious pluralism, with institutionalised (as well as popular) opposition to claims to the uniqueness of Christ as the only truth and the only Saviour. We live in cultures where Christianity has been so marginalised that most people could not articulate clearly the core beliefs of the Christian faith, and indeed increasing numbers of men and women live out their lives without ever encountering the gospel in coherent form.

Many Christians from the first three centuries of the church would identify with most if not all of these characteristics. The details may be different, but the general picture bears significant similarities. In particular, and fundamentally, the church in the post-modern West, with rather few exceptions, must come to terms with *weakness rather than power* as the base from which she operates. The early church did not have to be told that: it was their daily experience, vividly underlined through persecution and martyrdom and injustice. The post-modern church is reluctant to face up to her changed circumstances. After all, post-modern culture sees weakness as failure, power as achievement. So then, who finds it comfortable to own up to failure?

Yet here, surely, is precisely where we need the courage to embrace the true paradox of the cross. To follow in the footsteps of the Lord Jesus Christ, we must be prepared to empty ourselves of all power, all rights, all status. It is when we not only *preach* "the foolishness of the cross," but also—far more costly—*live* "the foolishness of the cross" that the power of God is displayed to the world. To be sure, we live not only this side of Calvary, but also this side of the resurrection and of Pentecost. Nonetheless, like the Master, we are called to give ourselves up to the cross;

then God will pour out the blessings of all that followed. If, however, we rush to embrace the triumph of the resurrection and of Pentecost, by-passing the cross, we find ourselves grasping nothing. As it was for the Lord, so it is for us: without death there is no life.

Perhaps if we understood this principle better, we would not designate churches "successful" because they are large or popular or wealthy. This is the language of power. Rather, we would ask, "Are those who come being challenged to lay down their lives for Christ? Is this a community which openly acknowledges its weakness, gives away its wealth, puts faithfulness above popularity, demonstrates dynamic love, and points to the grace and glory of God? Is this a body of people who live out their daily lives in such a way that everything about them declares the gospel of Christ crucified?"

In its earliest years, the Christian community understood these values. Most congregations had a precarious existence, whether or not they actually met in hiding, and the cost of following Christ ensured that few believers could be half-hearted. Since then, down through the centuries, the church has almost always been at its most vibrant where it has not been compromised by official status and political power but has had to concentrate on spiritual integrity. The easing of persecution, the institution of state protection, and the growth of power in society may have seemed a blessing to the church following the Constantinian Settlement in the 4th century. With hindsight, it may be easier to see the many ways in which the church came to be corrupted by power and seduced by wealth and increasingly lost its bearings. While in the mercy of God the church spread in spite of the alliance with political power, and even though there have been movements from time to time flowing from spiritual renewal and reformation, it is sobering to wonder what might have happened had the church consistently and corporately "taken up the cross."

The challenge to us today in the West is to do exactly that.

From the Past to the Present to the Future

Christians, of all people, should take history seriously. The Bible makes that clear, for the Living God has chosen to reveal himself in time and space. From Genesis to Revelation, God shows his dealings with his world from the beginning of time—the start of history—to its close. In the 2,000 years since the church began, God has continued to keep his people at the very centre of what human history is about, as he prepares them for eternity. The study of church history is extremely instructive, as we seek to learn what God has been doing and where his people have taken right or wrong turnings. In particular, biblical Christians will want to examine history in the light of the Scriptures, because God himself has declared that what happened in the past was written to teach us (Rom. 15:4), that is, so that we may in our turn live more fully in accord with his will in the present. Reflecting upon the past—and especially the past in the light of God's Word—will help us to understand where we are now and how we came to be where we are. It will help us to clear our vision and to grow in self-knowledge, however painfully.

However, looking back is only part of the story. In some ways, recognising what was happening in the past from the viewpoint of the present—that is, with the benefit of hindsight—can be easier than either accurately interpreting the present or helpfully anticipating the future. Nonetheless, it is important that we turn now from reflecting upon the past to facing the future. For the church is called to be prophetic as well as historical if she is to be effective. She is called to have her eyes on that sure horizon of the Lord's return and to live in the present in the light of God's declared intentions for the future.

The Humility of Listening

For centuries, the Western church has been in the habit of doing all the talking. In particular, the Western Protestant churches on the one hand and the Roman Catholic church on the other have assumed themselves alone to *be* the church. Other parts of the church, ancient or modern, have tended to be regarded as irrelevant (the ancient churches), heretical (depending on your viewpoint), or immature (the churches of Africa, Latin America, and Asia). Still today in international gatherings, Westerners tend to dominate the talking. While there are complex cultural reasons contributing to this dominance, biblical Christians should model something very different.

If we think primarily in structural and organisational terms and in terms of hierarchy, then it is likely that Western Christians will continue to mirror Western secular values. These tend to include a focus on the need to dominate and exercise power in international relations, be they economic, political, or cultural. After all, Western churches have seniority of age and wealth on their side. Until recently, they had the weight of numbers too. In other words, Western churches have operated from a *power* base. But if we see the world-wide growth of the church as the gracious work of God, and if we truly grasp what it is to be brothers and sisters in the family of God, then we will have a much richer relationship with the church beyond the West. In particular, we will be set free to listen, expecting to learn from Christians in situations far

different from our own. We will expect to learn, because it is the same Triune God who dialogues with them as with us. We are members of the same body.

Such listening is very liberating. It is also extremely instructive. Many of our brothers and sisters in Africa, Asia, and Latin America have had to struggle with issues and realities not addressed in traditional Western theologies. They have not always found the answers to their questions, and sometimes the answers they have found have not been true to the Scriptures. But often they *have* in the grace of God found real answers in God's Word to questions Westerners did not even know were there and wouldn't have known how to answer had they encountered them. This very activity of coming to the Word for fresh insights into fresh problems is sometimes methodologically more familiar to God's people beyond the West. Why? Because in the West we have often lived as if we had all the answers that mattered, whether from the 4th century, the 16th, or the 19th. Now, in the light of new and bewildering contexts, we may know neither the answers nor even how to formulate the questions.

Further, some of the issues which currently haunt us in the post-modern world, such as responding to pluralism, or living without a privileged place in our cultures, or dealing with pervasive pagan spirituality, or having no concept of absolute truth, are issues about which our Two-Thirds World brethren have valuable wisdom. The question is, are we willing to be humble enough to listen? Can we toss our pride aside and ask for the help we so badly need?

Not that there is room for any of God's people—east or west, north or south—to be proud. And even as many Two-Thirds World believers puzzle over the decline of Western churches, they need to recognise soberly that they, too, are often just beginning to experience the impact of third-generation nominalism, syncretism, and the awful corrosion of modernity. Only by the grace of God will they avoid in the near future what we in the West already struggle with. For the forces of globalisation ensure that very few societies indeed are sealed against precisely those forces which have created so much havoc among us. In many countries, quite as much as Christianity, neither Islam nor Communism has been able to withstand subversion via modernity. Global trade, global media, global travel, global ambition, global technology—all these and many more are highways for the expansion of modernity's (and now post-modernity's) empire. And they are almost unstoppable. Short of sealing off a country from all contact with the outside world (as has happened in large measure in North Korea, for instance)—a measure which can only happen in the most repressive of societies—there is no way of keeping modernity at bay. And whether modernity seeps in or floods in, both the harmful and the helpful invade together.

We would be wise to ensure that the grace and humility of listening operate in every direction—north, south, east, and west. Truly, we need one another.

Contextualisation Revisited

The Christian church, as opposed to society in general, does however have a key. And of all Christians, the missionary community should be most aware of this key, for it lies in the practice (and praxis) of contextualisation.

Properly understood, contextualisation is not a theory or a method or a 20th century passing fad. No, it is the dynamic living out of biblical truth in the here-and-now, so that faithfulness and relevance, truth and life, continuity and freshness—

all the amazing contours of God-made-visible in and through his people—are held in God-derived balance with each other. Down through the centuries and all around the world, wherever the gospel has taken root and been genuinely incarnated in this culture or that, contextualisation has taken place. The term may be modern. The practice is as ancient as God's people.

Contextualisation is often misunderstood—or wrongly applied. There are those who so confuse form and meaning that any hint of change from traditional formulations of doctrine or from traditional expressions of worship is immediately branded heresy. Writings and practices from centuries ago are so venerated that the slightest deviation is passionately resisted. But there is a world of difference between recognising how God has used great Christian leaders in their generations and given us a valuable legacy through them, and regarding them as the last word—or a word with almost the weight of eternal Scripture. Augustine, Calvin, Spurgeon, Hudson Taylor—pick your hero where you will, the fact is that if they were speaking and writing in today's world, they would speak and write differently. They would no doubt affirm many of the same things. They would also now address things that were not a concern in their own day and age, and in some areas they might devote rather less attention to issues which burned in their day but do not in ours. There would even be some things they passionately maintained centuries ago which today they would see as wrong, the product of cultural captivity in their own generation.

Contextualisation is not about recapturing some imaginary golden age of the church in the past. Nor, on the other hand, is it about going with the flow of the age in such a way that the church's message and practice are hostage to whatever culture she finds herself in. If Evangelicals (and, even more, fundamentalists) in the past have been especially susceptible to the former, it is arguable today that quite as many in the West have now capitulated to the latter. In our anxiety to be relevant, to woo people for Christ, to demolish barriers to belief, we have too often allowed the world to "squeeze us into its own mould" (Rom. 12:2, Phillips), instead of bringing culture under the authority of God's Word. Because we have not been discerning in relation to many of the claims, values, and practices of modernity and now of post-modernity, we have been, as it were, sucked into a quagmire.

The answer, of course, lies in *critical* contextualisation, carried out prayerfully, humbly, persistently—and with the Word drenching our minds and hearts. It is the Scripture, pondered together by the believing community, through which we must evaluate every part of culture. At the same time, as we are deeply involved in the real life of those within our cultures (we have no authorisation to live in some kind of self-contained Christian ghetto), we will come back to the Scriptures with pressing questions for which we need God's answers. The Western church urgently needs leaders who grasp this need, who will turn away from the secular model of administrator-therapist (preferably combined with a high-profile, "successful" personality, with a show-biz public platform persona), and who instead give themselves to modelling and teaching authentic gospel life distinct from but incarnated within the prevailing culture.

This kind of critical contextualisation, lived out day by day, is costly, exhilarating, radical. Because we have lived for so long unconsciously absorbing the values of modernity—its rationalism and humanism—it will take great courage, often the loneliness of the prophet, to stand against prevailing patterns. The missionary community and the church in the non-Western world have a special responsibility here, for they have both the experience of the struggle to engage in authentic critical contextualisation and also the measure of clear-sightedness and objectivity that comes from a little distance. The missionary community must speak with tears and pain, not arrogance. There are no simple formulaic answers, and the needed changes will surely make us cry out in distress, as well as stretching our faith to the limits. The Western church must listen with tears and pain and penitence. The alternatives are too dreadful to contemplate: a Europe swept bare of churches, as North Africa was long ago, or a form of Christianity so indistinguishable from secular culture as to be totally emasculated.

In one way or another, the time has come for the re-evangelisation of the West. It is a tough mission field, for which we urgently need the very highest skills of critical contextualisation if the gospel is once again to take root.

Roadblocks for the Gospel in the Post-Modern West

Cultures are not neutral. The assumption that they are, frequently favoured in the past and still held in some quarters, is more a product of humanism and a belief in "progress" than of biblical truth. Cultures cannot be neutral precisely because they are a product of human societies, and because of the radical nature of human fallenness, anything that humankind produces will be affected by sin. At the same time, because men and women are made in the image of God and because—however defaced—there are still ineradicable traces of that image in every person, there will be elements of the divine as well as of the demonic in every culture.

The question is, how do we discern what is the product of fallenness and what is the product of grace in any given culture? Such discernment is of very great importance, because the products of fallenness will prove to be roadblocks to the gospel, and the products of grace will prove to be doorways to the gospel. The task of critical contextualisation is not simply to engage in analysis: what is good, what is bad, what is neutral in this culture? Rather, by helping us to discern these differences, contextualisation provides us with important tools: what are the things to affirm? What things may be a "way in" for the gospel? How can we build on them? What are the things to reject as incompatible with biblical truth? How does challenging these things affect evangelism and discipleship? What are the things which are genuinely neutral? Can they be utilised as doorways for the gospel? These things may be at the level of worldview or of beliefs, values, or practices. When cultural insiders and cultural outsiders work on such an evaluation together in genuine and humble partnership, there may be a heightened discernment about a specific culture and a greater understanding of how to work within the culture with both faithfulness and relevance.

The most important roadblocks to the gospel nearly always take one of two forms. They may be so pervasive as to make it impossible to conceive of living within the culture with a particular issue removed. Examples would include ancestor practices in Japan or materialism in the West. (That is not to say that there isn't significant materialism outside the West!) Both of these examples—and many others that could be cited—touch nearly every area of life. The second form of roadblocks may be more hidden, at the level of underlying presuppositions, but extremely influential. For example, in modern culture it was first assumed that absolute truth was to be found in Christian revelation, then that absolute truth was to be found through scientific research, then that absolute truth probably existed but was unknowable. Finally, in post-modern culture the concept of absolute truth is rejected. This has ironically produced the only acceptable absolute: that there are no absolutes.

Closely related to this idea is the belief that there is no "meta-narrative," that is, no overarching story that affects everyone everywhere, nor even one story for any one individual. Instead, there are many fragmented stories—a variety of religions, a variety of myths, a variety of personal preferences—and everyone should have freedom to choose for himself and indeed to choose different stories for different parts of his life. So widely is this personal autonomy embraced and so committed is the disbelief in absolute truth that the gospel becomes both incomprehensible and outrageous: it is, after all, predicated upon Christ as the embodiment of absolute truth and as the exclusive Saviour for all people everywhere in all generations—the absolute meta-narrative, of breathtaking proportions. The declaration of the uniqueness of Christ was foolishness to the Greeks; to the post-modern, it becomes something to legislate against wherever it is possible and to shout down or drown out where it is not.

Moreover, bound up with the rejection of absolute truth is a rejection of the reliable meaning of words. Words only mean whatever you choose to make them mean. If you are the source of a message, you launch it into space, but you cannot insist that your intended meaning is in fact the meaning. It only means whatever the recipient chooses to have it mean—even if that is quite the opposite of what *you* meant. Christianity is, of course, intensely verbal. It is no accident that the Scriptures are called the Word of God and that the

Lord Jesus Christ is the Living Word and the Last Word. God communicates in words, and those words are given divinely intended content which we are not at liberty to change. Our task is to seek to understand what he intended and intends—and our allies are the Holy Spirit on the one hand and the community of God's people on the other. But we are also in our turn to communicate in words, with precision as well as graciousness.

In post-modern culture, the devaluation of words and the substitution of images and subliminal experience (sometimes drug-induced) pose a major roadblock to the gospel. This is far deeper than the growing problem of functional illiteracy (where people who technically are able to read nonetheless refuse to do so, rejecting print in favour of pictures). Here is a culture where communication chiefly occurs below the level of rational understanding and where manipulation by vested interests is easy. Provided the felt impact is a buzz of the senses—excitement, spine-tingling fear, heightened consciousness, adrenaline surges—people become addicted. The mass media, the entertainment industry, and advertising have all understood (and shaped) this shift. Moreover, they have learned how to use their powers for their own benefit (increased markets, changing public opinion, etc.), while deceiving the recipients into believing that they are actually still in control.

By and large, the church has not begun to address this communication shift adequately and certainly not with the balance of critical contextualisation. In some cases, churches have responded by ignoring the cultural shift and by insisting on using words alone, in traditional manner. This not only makes for frustrated evangelism (because people do not hear what you think they should have heard, on the basis of what you have said), but it also

has considerable implications for discipling Christians in a post-print, word-subversive world. In other cases, churches have responded by throwing out word-based ministry (reducing it to vox pops and the four-minute sermon) and rushing to adopt mime, drama, stage spectacles which ape the world of entertainment, fast-paced visual images, and suchlike. However valuable these things may be in a subsidiary role, the problem is that most of them convey imprecise messages, impressions which invite the viewer to invest meaning as he wishes. While this fits neatly with a post-modern mindset, it is incompatible with the "thus says the Lord" of revelation.

Another consequence of rejecting the concept of truth, and especially absolute truth, is the rejection of authority. The moment you abolish an objective external final authority, you begin the inevitable slide towards not simply individual autonomy but anarchy, unless you head instead into dictatorship (which is at base a variant supreme authority). That process may be slowed down by well-established social structures such as government and law, but sooner or later people will despise government and flout the law wherever these conflict with personal wishes. What many people choose to see as simply a philosophical principle becomes all too quickly a matter of the gravest social significance. In those cultures most affected by post-modernism, we already see the accelerating breakdown of law and order, a rejection of any concept of limiting personal freedom for the sake of the good of the community, and the supplanting commitment to hedonism and personal gratification. This process is happening not only in the secular world. It is being mirrored in many parts of the church.

This is an enormous challenge to effective mission in the post-modern context. It is an inescapable part of the Christian message that God requires us to bow to his authority, that we are to submit to the authority of the Scriptures, that we are to submit to one another, and that Christian discipleship is about yielding up claims to personal autonomy while yet accepting personal responsibility. Instead of focusing on self-fulfilment and gratification, we are called on to give ourselves in loving service of others and to be willing to accept pain and loss out of love for God. These are fundamentals which we are not free to set aside.

A final roadblock in the post-modern world is consumerism. The customer reigns supreme, and products must be shaped to suit his wishes. Of course, as we saw above under communication, the producer of the goods may be ruthless in shaping the mind of the consumer so that he wants exactly what the producer wishes to sell. Here, too, the church is having great difficulty. In some cases, congregations have succumbed to the consumerist philosophy. In adapting themselves to offer what people want, they have changed the message. After all, who wants to hear of sin and judgement? Who in a success-oriented culture wants to hear that the very best we can do is so much rubbish when it comes to the Lord's standards of perfect righteousness? How much easier to adopt a message of self-esteem, self-fulfilment, and therapeutic comfort! But the gospel is not a commodity to be marketed, with updated models to suit today's world. The fact that sectors of the church have adopted the language and practices of marketing is a measure of their captivity to contemporary culture.

Bridges for the Gospel

Not everything is doom and gloom! Along with all the sobering challenges to the Lordship of Christ in both modern and post-modern cultures, there are many bridges or doorways for the gospel. These we need to use boldly.

To begin with, most people are not entirely consistently modern or post-modern, and neither modernity nor post-modernity is consistent within itself either. This means that there are frequently "chinks in the armour," cracks in the worldview and the resultant practice, which thoughtful people can be brought to recognise. We need to pay renewed attention to the rather neglected field of apologetics. We need to find effective, confident ways of drawing attention to those inconsistencies and to the biblical answers to them. We need to find the ways in which in our generation the truth of Romans 1–2 is being displayed: men and women cannot entirely escape awareness of God, in whose image they are made. God's Word tells us that the created universe, our own instinctive sense of right and wrong, and our habit of making moral judgements about others all point to truths about God: that he is a personal being, that he is the Creator, and that he is a moral being to whom we are accountable. Like the men and women of Hebrews 11, it is possible to respond to this revelation about God in repentance and faith, even before a person has heard explicitly about Jesus Christ. Alternatively, we may suppress this truth about God, and for that we are held accountable.

In recent decades, after the barren decades of growing scepticism, there has been a renewed recognition that human beings are spiritual beings. Partly this comes from trying to live in a totally materialist framework and finding that it does not fit the facts. It is fascinating, for example, to listen to people in China or the former Soviet Union speaking of the way they still wish for socialism but not the atheistic materialism of Marxism.

On the one hand, this is opening the door to all kinds of spiritual experiences and to regarding any form of spirituality as being as valid as any other. The emphasis may be firmly on experience, which may be thoroughly divorced from truth. At the same time, it is increasingly easy in many parts of Europe, where beforehand there was only cynicism, to talk openly and easily with unbelievers about spiritual matters. Two generations ago, belief in the supernatural was largely the province of cranks and spiritists. Today, there is acceptance that there is a very real supernatural world, though what that world is perceived to be like may be very far removed from the biblical worldview. This has been further complicated by the fact that some Christians have enthusiastically adopted beliefs and practices in relation to the supernatural that are more animist than biblical. There is clearly a great deal of work to be done here, but it would seem that some people, perhaps especially young people, are coming to saving faith in Christ from a starting point of belief in the supernatural.

Along with interest in the spiritual, there is a growing awareness of the environment. While for most people that may be entirely divorced from the Creator, nonetheless that concern readily leads us in conversation straight back to Genesis 1–3. As Christians, we need to repent of the way we have failed in the past to speak with a clear voice about responsible care of God's world. For the most part, Christians along with everyone else have colluded in the greedy exploitation of the environment. It is only quite recently that in the West there have been Christian voices raised in warning and protest and, more importantly, with suggestions of a better way. It is not surprising that many of those most passionately committed to environmental issues are scathing about the church, given its track record. But with

humility and hard work, here is an opportunity to win the trust of a significant sector of the post-modern generation and to build bridges for the gospel. There are also some excellent examples of Christians leading the way in sound environmental projects, and these we should be able to speak of accurately, humbly, with dignity, and pointing to the Lord who is their inspiration.

One of the features of post-modernism is its widespread disillusionment with the answers of modernity. The doctrines of humanism and progress which promised so much have failed to deliver on those promises. Sometimes this failure introduces a good and effective bridge for the gospel. However, in the past the church also frequently absorbed many of the values of humanism and progress, and we need thoughtfully and radically to disentangle ourselves from them before we can speak with integrity to the post-modern generation. On the one hand, we need to recapture a vivid sense of the Lord's return, with all its implications; this, not progress, is the true grid through which we are to view the future. On the other hand, we also need to develop a more profoundly biblical anthropology, establishing within a biblical framework both the glory and the limitations of human beings. We need a clearer articulation of the balance between fallenness (the bad news) and being made and re-made in the image of God (the very best of good news). We need a clearer grasp of biblical blueprints for society as well as for individuals, for the world as well as for the church.

In a culture where many people are asking the painful questions, "Who am I? What is my identity?" Christians above all people should be able to speak of the wonder of knowing our true identity in Christ. This is our ultimate identity, and it is one that is not threatened by family breakdown, by unemployment, or by growing old. Many post-moderns know all too well the precariousness of tying their identity to fragile relationships which may fracture, to physical desirability, or to job and career.

If identity is a bridge for the gospel, so too is purpose. "What am I here for?" is another question which haunts many people. "To shop till you drop" is hardly a satisfying answer. No wonder it leads to despair. After a while, people wake up to the fact that consumerism and entertainment do not adequately deliver on their promises, any more than humanism and progress did in the past. The inescapable hollowness of these pillars of post-modernity sooner or later becomes a gateway for the gospel. Disillusionment can, in the grace of God, become a doorway to hope, the true hope of humankind, the Lord Jesus Christ.

If issues of identity and purpose leave unbelievers sensing their meaninglessness, post-modern life is also intensely lonely. This is inevitable, because God has so created us that it is through relationship with him that we are able to enter into the security of belonging, first to him, then to others around us. Many Westerners are desperately searching for a sense of belonging, of connecting to others at a meaningful level, and yet simultaneously they make that impossible by drawing back from commitment in relationships. Belonging is a product of faithfulness and reliability and commitment, and these are essential cornerstones of God's own character. Perhaps one of the most powerful signs of the gospel in our contemporary Western world is a church—even families—living in committed, faithful love for one another, even through the hard times. This voluntary giving of ourselves to one another, through thick and thin, through pain and sorrow as well as joy, is not just a doorway for the gospel but a great welcoming arch! The Lord Jesus prayed that

his people would love one another and be one, reflecting the loving unity of the Trinity, in order that men and women might believe. That prayer is as vibrantly contemporary in its significance today as ever it was. The quality of our relationships within the Christian family is key to our effectiveness in mission in our weary, hurting West.

Further, the quality of our love for those outside the Christian family is also fundamental to our reaching our societies for Christ. Those who have betrayed others or who have been betrayed frequently (ironically, the pursuit of self-fulfilment will always lead to betraying others in the process) may be shocked when they encounter persistent, forgiving love. The Lord is calling us to live out what we profess to believe. This is counter-cultural indeed.

Back to Ezekiel

We began with an imaginative encounter with Ezekiel, re-packaged for the post-modern world. Many of the themes we have briefly raised in this paper are embedded in that scenario. But as we open our Bibles again to Ezekiel 37, there is a timelessness about the message that we who name the name of Christ need to ponder. God is still in the business of transforming dry bones into dynamic gospel warriors. Just as surely as God's people were in desperate straits in Ezekiel's day, so are we today. Much of the Western church is a jumble of dead bones, despite some places where there is life and God-breathed energy.

In Ezekiel's vision, how did God demonstrate the transformation of those dry bones into a mighty army of servants of the King of Kings? On the one hand, Ezekiel is commanded to preach his heart out, declaring the word of the Lord. How bizarre that must have seemed, how senseless. How can dry bones live? How can dead bones hear? Was Ezekiel talking to the wind? Had there been an audience, he would have been laughed to scorn. That principle is true today too. Living by and declaring the word of the Lord prophetically amongst a continent of the spiritually dead may seem to the observer a fool's game. But it is the way of God and therefore constitutes true wisdom. So on the one hand, God's prophets must speak urgently to the dry bones of his people and then to the post-Christian culture in which we live.

On the other hand, it is God and God alone to whom belongs the power to create life out of death. So as Ezekiel in obedience cries out for life to be given, praying that God in his mercy will do what is humanly impossible, the Lord and Giver of Life transforms the dry bones into vibrant, healthy people. Here is the Spirit-filled, revived people of God, now able to be all that God lovingly designed them to be, to do all that he sovereignly designed them to do.

The key to effective mission in the post-modern West needs to begin with the revival and renewal of the church. Such a church in turn will be able to declare the word of the Lord to the world. And the Lord himself still delights to pour new Spirit-life into his creatures.

Rosemary Dowsett and her husband, Dick, have served with OMF International for more than 30 years, including eight years in the Philippines working with IVCF students and staff. Rose taught for a number of years at Glasgow Bible College, Scotland, where she established a degree programme in missiology. She is currently working on an in-service training programme for all OMF personnel worldwide. She is a writer and travels widely as a lecturer and Bible teacher. She also serves as International Chairman of Interserve International and is a member of the WEF Theological Commission. Rose and Dick have three adult children, two of them married.

Let X = X: Generation X and world mission

RICHARD TIPLADY

IT IS WIDELY RECOGNISED that the West is experiencing a significant cultural and worldview transformation. Estimates of its nature and importance vary, but it is undeniable that new generations are growing up with a worldview radically different from that of their parents and grandparents. The label "Generation X" has been applied to those born more or less between 1965 and 1980. By their attitudes and outlook, this generation, of which I am a member, shows itself to be the first to have been significantly shaped by post-modernity rather than modernity.

Anecdotal evidence of the personal experience of "Xers" shows that we do not find it easy to fit into the culture and structures of much of the contemporary Western church, especially into its organisational forms—including the present mission structures. Just as post-modernity is a reaction against modernity, so much of the Xer outlook is a reaction against the Baby Boomer worldview which preceded it and which currently shapes much of the organisational form and culture of Western society, including the church and its mission structures.

This mismatch has been noted by many Boomers, as well as by the older generations in the world mission community, and it has led to some discussion of the "problem" of Generation X, with attempts to help Xers to fit into existing cultural norms and structures. But what if the problem is not with the Xers? What if the problem is with the culture of the existing structures? If mission agencies, in their structures, procedures, and ethos, reflect the worldview of the generations which formed them, then these are not sacrosanct. Like all cultural forms, they are contingent, relative, and subject to evaluation by other cultural norms and by the Bible.

If Generation Xers do world mission their way, again subject to evaluation by the Bible and by others, but in a way that is true to their own worldview nonetheless, what would it look like? Are new strategies, structures, and methodologies needed? Can the existing structures be changed to allow the Xer worldview to exist alongside others, or are new ones needed?

Motion but No Growth?

One of my favourite stories is that found in the "Missing Chapter" of Douglas Coupland's book *Generation X*, a novel first published in 1991, which charts the life and outlook of three characters, Dag, Claire, and Andy. The "Missing Chapter," though excluded from the novel, became available on the Internet in 1998. This story is set on the asteroid Texlahoma, where it is "always 1974" (if you read the novel, it makes sense—really).

The story concerns the fact that a murderer is at large, "a gruesome murderer who liked to pick on children in particular." The response to this was, "So, naturally, people were upset, and seniors were doubly worried as the number of youngsters paying into their social security kitty was shrinking daily. They screamed for action." Texlahoman society begins to implode, but eventually, through a stroke of luck, the murderer is caught. However, the story ends with the caution: "In spite of the terror Texlahomans endured, and what they might have learned, it remains 1974 there, and it always will. There are no variables in Texlahoma's equation that permit change. There can be motion but no growth."

For me, the power of the story is to be found in noting how the power holders and vested interests of Texlahoma (the "seniors") are threatened by changing circumstances (which admittedly are worrying) and how power is used to maintain the status quo (even when these existing ways are sterile and perishing).

I suppose that many Christians and other observers of the West would accept that our status quo (Western culture) is sterile, even perishing. What does this mean for the Western church, and, in particular, what does it mean for our understanding and practice of world mission? How might the current "power holders" of world mission (i.e., the mission agencies and training colleges) be acting like the "seniors" in Coupland's story?

A Theology of Culture

I want to begin by developing a theological understanding of culture, which is the filter through which I will interpret the trends outlined above. I start with the issue of culture, because there are many different attitudes within the church towards the desirability (or not) of engaging with the surrounding culture(s) in which the church fulfils its mission. So, given that there are many opinions on the matter, it is important that I spell out my position on this issue. You may agree or disagree with things that I say, but it may be helpful for you to know *why* I make some of the comments I do, so that we can at least know exactly what it is we are agreeing or disagreeing about.

"Culture" is a term which describes the worldview, beliefs, values, and behaviour of a particular group of people. It is something that is transmitted from one generation to another. Books and books have been written on how culture works, what it is, and how we should understand human identity in relation to it. For me, the easiest way to understand culture is to think of it as "the way we do things around here." Culture is finite and limited, it is deliberate and chosen, and yet it also exerts a controlling influence on what behaviours, values, and beliefs are acceptable and unacceptable in a society.

However, this is not a paper about the relationship between theology (and the church) and culture in general. I want to address questions raised by one specific culture (Western "post-modern" or "post-whatever" culture) and the implications for mission, which is the purpose for which the church exists. By "mission" I do not wish to imply some mystical doctrine of saltwater, i.e., that "mission" only happens once you have crossed over some "clear blue water." Mission is not a geographically defined activity. It is the church reaching out with God's love in Christ to a fallen world. However, the focus of the organisation I work for, Global Connections, is "world mission" (i.e., cross-cultural mission), so much of my reflection has been developed with this type of mission and its current structures in mind.

My starting point for understanding human cultures is Genesis 1:26-28a: "Then God said, 'Let us make man in our image, in our likeness, and let them rule over the fish of the sea and the birds of the air, over the livestock, over all the earth, and over all the creatures that move along the ground.' So God created man in his own image, in the image of God he created him; male and female he created them. God blessed them and said to them, 'Be fruitful and increase in number; fill the earth and subdue it.'"

All cultures are shaped by human beings, who are made in the image of God and who share (among other things) in God's creative capacity. All cultures, through their beliefs, values, and permitted and proscribed behaviours, are attempts to bring some kind of order and understandability to the complex and chaotic world that we encounter. Cultures are attempts to make sense of the cacophony of reality (control and order are implied

in the "rule/subdue" language of these verses from Genesis). As such, human cultures are good, and the human propensity to create culture is a fulfilment of our created identity.

However, we are no longer simply created in the image of God. Genesis 3 contains the story of human fallenness. Through sin, humanity is now cut off from God, compelled to wander (like Cain) in the cosmos, looking for a home. But although sin is a corruption and a twisting, it has not eradicated the image of God in humanity. The creation mandate for human multiplication, to "fill the earth," which was given to humanity in Genesis 1:28, is reiterated to Noah in Genesis 9:1; Genesis 1:28 also gives us the cultural mandate. Therefore, Cain and his descendants built cities and developed agriculture, the arts, and technology (Gen. 4:17-22), despite the judgement of God upon their ancestor. Humanity is still creative, sharing in that aspect of the divine image, even while fallen.

Thus, human cultures are both good and bad, all mixed up together. Just as human beings are both made in the image of God and also "totally depraved" (which does not mean entirely evil, but instead corrupted throughout by sin, even our good bits), so are human cultures. Some people try to separate cultures into elements that are "good," "bad," and "indifferent," but, just as in my own case, where my weaknesses and failings are so often the flipside of my strengths, so it is with human cultures.

It would be much easier if we could separate out the various elements, embracing the good and rejecting the bad, but fortunately for our sakes, God doesn't do it that way. Jesus' parable of the wheat and tares (Matt. 13:24-30) shows that God will allow good and evil to co-exist until his final judgement. The reason Jesus gives for this is, "While you are pulling up the weeds, you may root up the wheat with them" (v. 29). Trying to make the separation now may result in rejecting something that is good.

Thus, we not only have to live with the different culture(s) of the world; we also have to accept that what seems bad to us (because it is different or a threat) might actually be good. For example, postmodernity has undermined the hubris of modernity, which was and is no particular friend to the Christian faith.

Why Is Contemporary Culture Change So Important?

Every generation is tempted by the delusion that it is unique. Perhaps the reality is that every generation *is* unique, moulded as it is by the life circumstances and challenges that face its members. This theory certainly underlies most of the work done on generational demography, whether by theorists such as Don Tapscott, Bill Strauss, and Neil Howe, or in the seminal article on this issue and the implications for world mission, written by Kath Donovan and Ruth Myors (1997).

I don't make any claims that Generation X is unique in the sense that we are special or more privileged in our understanding of life. Perhaps, however, we are unique in other ways. Management guru Peter Drucker wrote, "Every few hundred years in Western history there occurs a sharp transformation.... Within a few short decades, society rearranges itself—its worldview, its basic values, its social and political structure, its arts, its key institutions. Fifty years later, there is a new world. And the people born then cannot even imagine the world in which their grandparents lived and into which their own parents were born. We are currently living through just such a transformation."

So how should we understand this massive cultural transformation? I would suggest that we can learn a great deal from reflecting on popular culture as portrayed in the media. The media may be great creators of cultural trends, but they are also good reflectors of such trends, market-driven as they are.

"Stay true to what you try to be—your individuality." This line, from a song by current British teen pop sensation S Club 7, is a good starting point. An article in *The Observer* newspaper in April 1999 spoke of the rise of an "I-Society" in Britain, i.e., a generation which has rejected the "me" culture of the 1980s for one which values "individuality, independence, identity, and interactivity." I believe that the issues of individuality and identity are at the core of the questions that contemporary culture (and in particular, Generation X) is asking. The question of identity is found in a lot of current contemporary music, e.g., "Some day I will find, the one who lives inside my mind" ("Dazed, Beautiful, and Bruised" by Catatonia).

Of great importance in creating these issues is the shift to a post-industrial society. In the highly successful British film, *The Full Monty*, a change in lifestyle is forced upon the protagonists by the closure of the steelworks in which they had previously worked. This illustrates a simple fact: philosophers, theologians, and preachers of all kinds need to be aware that people's beliefs and values are often shaped by their behaviour and lifestyles, rather than vice versa. So how might we characterise post-industrial society? It is marked by the change from manufacturing industry to service sector jobs; the change from the factory gate to the shopping mall; the change from production line to workstations in cubicles; the change from machine tools to information technology; the change from terraced housing to executive homes.

Life is becoming more diverse, more fragmented, more individualistic (note the mirth that accompanied the news that Hillary Rodham Clinton's 50th birthday party in 1997 was attended by her 500 "closest personal friends"). The outlook shaped by post-industrial society is one which focuses, as we noted above, on identity, on who we are. In a consumer society, our self-definition often comes primarily from the products we buy and the brands we identify with (Pepsi or Coke, Gap or Levis?). Since we are now looking for individuality—"our" own unique identity, "our" genetic blueprint—then we don't want to look and be the same as everyone else. We want to be distinct, "us." This means that we live in a day not of mass production, but of mass customisation.

Henry Ford, credited with the invention of mass production, famously said of his Model T, "You can have it any colour you want, as long as it's black." I recently visited the Ford U.K. website, which showed that Ford currently offers nine different cars for sale in the U.K. (Ka, Fiesta, Escort, Focus, Mondeo, Puma, Cougar, Galaxy, and Explorer). Taking the Ford Focus alone, you can choose from four body shapes (3-, 4-, and 5-door saloon, plus estate), four levels of specification (CL, Zetec, LX, Ghia), and five different engines (1.4, 1.6, 1.8, 2.0, 1.8tdi), in one of 11 colours. So there are 880 different Ford Focus options, before even beginning to think about interior seat trim or optional extras.

Adverts for the household paint Dulux show a woman stealing some lilac underwear from a neighbour's washing line, or cutting a patch from a yellow hooded top worn by a shaven-headed bodybuilder sitting in front of her on a bus. In both adverts, we then cut to shots of the same woman just finishing some interior decorating, with the room painted in exactly the same colour as the stolen item. In other words, if you can't find the colour you like from the hundreds already on offer in your nearest DIY megastore, then they will mix up another, just for you.

A recent article in *The Face* magazine focussed on household appliances, furniture, and clothing which build on the concept of "beanbag" culture, i.e., objects that mould to your body shape (or lifestyle). However, unlike the original beanbag, the Memo Chair doesn't just adapt to your perfect shape; it retains your imprint. So does the AVO mobile phone, with a shell of rubber which moulds to your grip. Gel shoe insoles have been developed, which adjust to the shape of your foot, and as your foot gets warm, the gel hardens, so leaving an imprint.

This is the key theme of much marketing in the West: whatever suits "you." Personal individuality and customisation to that individuality are the order of the day. This mass customisation of society moves beyond products that we buy to the information and knowledge we receive. Talk of an "information explosion" is common, through the development and expansion of satellite/cable/digital TV, the now-ubiquitous CD-ROMs, and, of course, the Internet.

In response to this, we see the development of tailored communications. "Old" media such as newspapers and music producers are having to adapt to the demands of the consumers of the "new" media, such as the ability to interact with websites and to personalise both the services and content received (thus the Time Warner/AOL merger comes as no great surprise). Similar "tailoring" can be seen in the propensity to talk of "narrowcasting" rather than "broadcasting"; in direct-marketers working with smaller and smaller segments of the population; and in the use of Internet "cookies," which allow websites to identify return visitors, to retain your personal information for future use, and to offer services such as those provided by the Amazon.com website, including recommendations (based on your previous buying patterns) and user profiles ("people who bought this book also bought …").

In this analysis, I suppose I must make reference to the word "post-modern," even though the word is slippery and hard to define. (Note the now-famous quote in the *Independent* newspaper, as far back as 1987: "The word has no meaning. Use it as often as you can.") The commonly accepted definition of post-modernism is "incredulity towards metanarratives" (Jean-François Lyotard). He noted how the leading ideas of Western thought (Marxism, democratic liberalism, Keynesian economics, Christianity), while claiming to offer universal "salvation," offered it in practice only to the few. The as-yet unrealised emancipation of all humanity led in each case to the desire to "conquer" others to its point of view. Thus the freedom offered was not universal and inclusive but limited and exclusive, and it was implicated in violence.

I prefer the description used by the comedienne Lily Tomlin. She has a character called Trudy the Bag Lady, who is helping some aliens from outer space to determine whether, in their search for intelligent life in the universe, Earth might be a likely location to find it. Trudy is not sure it will be. Commenting on her own madness, she says, "I refuse to be intimidated by reality anymore. After all, what is reality anyway? Nothin' but a collective hunch. My space chums think reality was once a primitive method of crowd control that got out of hand. In my view, it's absurdity dressed up in a three-piece business suit. I made some studies, and reality is the leading cause of stress among those in touch with it. I can take it in small doses, but as a lifestyle I found it too confining."

Thoughts on a Generation X Worldview

So how does all this affect our view on life as Christians? What happens when the post-modern disintegration of reality meets the mass customisation of lifestyle and the information tsunami? How is this influence reflected in the Generation X worldview? Here are some ways:

Individuality

We have a major focus on and concern for individuality and identity (who am I?). Since this focus can be created, it leads to insecurity. (If reality is nothing more than "a collective hunch," then my place in that "reality" is in doubt, for how do I know who I am?) This diversification and fragmentation of lifestyle and of society lead to situations where we have more acquaintances but fewer friendships (hence the popularity of "Friends"-type TV programmes).

Flexibility

We see a paradoxical unwillingness to commit too deeply to any one identity. We allow for the concept of self-reinvention. (In *Close Personal Friend*, a film produced in 1995 to accompany the promotion for his book *Microserfs*, Douglas Coupland comments, "Humans are the only animals who can say, 'I'm going to move to San Diego, lose 20 pounds, and grow my hair.'")

Likewise, we don't just deal with information overload by customising the information to our needs. We "surf" the Internet (don't go too deep, or you will get drowned by the information), or we channel-hop while watching TV (a type of parallel-processing or multi-tasking).

Scepticism

In a post-modern worldview, all meta-narratives (constructions of reality) are used by the powerful to maintain their own interests and extend them to the detriment of others. These values encourage scepticism towards all authority holders, secular or religious.

So What About Generation X and Global Mission?

As I think of my generation's involvement in world mission, why is the culture change that we have looked at so important? Because it reflects the culture of an increasing proportion of the population of the Western world, and it will shape the way that the Western church "is" and the way it "does" mission in coming years.

Critique or accept?

The following question will have arisen in some people's minds: Do we just accept the culture change you have described and go with it? Shouldn't the role of the church be to provide a biblical critique of these trends?

I have a number of problems with this particular question:

1. As we noted earlier, cultures are both good and bad (made in the image of God but also tragically broken), and these elements are not easily separable (but are often the flipsides of one another).

2. The language of "critical contextualisation" usually ends up focussing on the "critical" part and not giving too much attention to the contextualisation.

3. I don't see too many comparative critiques of the existing culture of the church and the influence of modernity thereon. After all, there are no totally objective viewpoints, and too often a critique of post-modernity by Christians is based largely on modernist assumptions rather than especially-biblical ones (e.g., the defence of concepts such as "facts" and "absolutes").

4. A critique of my culture is inevitably a critique of me.

I would accept that Generation X and the changes happening within Western culture do need to be carefully evaluated and that this will include a biblical critique. Perhaps this should not, however, be our starting point nor the priority within the global mission movement for the time being. Left to ourselves, Generation Xers are more than capable of critiquing themselves and their cultures. While this is not the goal of this paper, it does not mean that I am unaware of the need for this as well.

I would suggest that a better starting point is to ask what it is that God offers us—a critique or salvation? Of course, judgement is implied in the latter, for if there were no problems with a culture, a worldview, or a person, then there would be no need of salvation. This might provide a fruitful line for reflection of how best to undertake mission in a post-modern culture. We should identify the culture's deepest questions and needs and then consider which biblical/theological themes could answer the quest and bring salvation in its fullest biblical meaning—*shalom* or wholeness.

The generation gap

I want to focus here on the question of how Generation Xers might do mission, rather than how to do mission to them. We might want to begin by asking why contemporary culture change is so threatening to the "power holders" in the Western missionary movement. I suspect that it comes down to a conflict of values. As a result of all we have considered so far, the generation gap is wider now that it has ever been.

For example, in an article in *Details* magazine in 1995, Douglas Coupland noted the Baby Boomers' unease with the Xer attitude: "One would think that the Boomers, coming of age in the '60s, would be thrilled to see the notion of individualism adapting itself to a changing world. Instead, all they see are monsters."

Likewise, Xers are not too keen on the world being bequeathed to them by older generations. "Imagine coming to a beach at the very end of a long summer of big crowds and wild goings-on. The beach bunch is sunburned, the sand shopworn, hot, and full of debris—no place for walking barefoot. You step on a bottle, and some cop cites you for littering ... much like River Phoenix in *Running on Empty*, GenXers have had to cope and survive in whatever territory the Boomers have left behind" (Strauss & Howe, 1991, p. 321).

Whether it's a matter of environmental degradation or mortgaging the future to pay for the present, Xers will have to pay the cost of the consumption inherent in today's lifestyles, without having enjoyed the primary benefit. As the Coupland article mentioned above begins, "You were born in the '60s. Does that mean you'll have to pay for it the rest of your life?"

May I speak to my older mission colleagues?

Please don't patronise us either. There is a lot of talk about the need GenXers have for pastoral care, as if our "problems" can be solved through understanding and patience, until we become more like the older generation. Maybe we are monsters. But maybe we're good monsters, like Godzilla. Coupland ends the article just mentioned with the following: "Andy Warhol once said that he liked sci-fi movies where the monster lays an egg at the end, because it guarantees a sequel. Well, I'm thinking of millions of monster eggs

out there sometime in the future, all hatching small, slimy, horned babies crawling towards some form of truth, tirelessly, en masse, waging war against the forces of dumbness. So please, be a monster."

Maybe we are just what the Japanese have called *shin jin rui*, a "new kind of human being." Maybe we just see the world differently. If so, how will this affect the world mission involvement of the Western church in the coming years?

There appears to be a lack of awareness by many in the current mission sending structures (i.e., the mission agencies) of the culture-bound nature of these structures. The assumption is that because they are the norm, they are OK, even biblical (although it may be more accurate to say that these structures are largely modernist with a few generational tweaks, sprinkled with a biblical overlay). From this vantage point, mission agencies judge post-modern and Xer behaviour by their own values. But surely it is cultural sin to judge the behaviour and attitudes of one culture by the values and beliefs of another. How would we react if we heard someone say to an African or Latino, "Don't live according to your culture. It's worldly. Live in my 'biblical' way"?

Let's be honest. Some missionaries did say that in the past, but would we dare to now? Yet that is often how Xers are made to feel. We have noted that scepticism, individuality, and flexibility are characteristics of the Xer worldview. How might these qualities affect our world mission involvement?

Scepticism

In *Generations*, writers William Strauss and Neil Howe (1991) note that the key difference between GenXers and their preceding generational cohort, the Baby Boomers, is that scepticism has replaced idealism. There are numerous reasons for this.

First of all, Generation Xers grew up with TV, so they were exposed to advertising at a very early age. The latest Royal Mail advert in the U.K. tells us that we are now exposed to 1,500 adverts a day; I read elsewhere recently that Americans are exposed to 3,000 adverts per day. As a result, instead of ceding to mindless consumption, we have learned to be sceptical. We can see through hype, and we subject all truth claims to sharp-eyed evaluation. More recently, advertisers have become aware of this and have tuned their adverts to this new situation. Consider, for example, the following voiceover on an advert for Nike sportswear: "Don't insult our intelligence. Tell us what it is. Tell us what it does. And don't play the national anthem while you do it." Coca-Cola has marketed its Sprite soft drink in the following way: "What soft drink do the world's best snowboarders drink? The same one as the world's worst snowboarders. Image is nothing. Thirst is everything. Obey your thirst." The advertisers don't con us with this approach, but we appreciate the irony.

Xers also grew up experiencing the reality of disappointment. It has been noted that in 1969 our parents' generation saw Neil Armstrong step out of Apollo 11 and walk on the moon, whereas in 1986 we saw primary school teacher Christa McAuliffe blown to pieces in the Challenger Space Shuttle disaster. How will this scepticism affect our view of world mission? I suspect church and mission leaders will see a lack of enthusiasm for ambitious programmes to "complete the evangelisation of the world." We've heard it all before, and we expect that we'll hear it again. What we're looking for is low-key, sustainable, grassroots mission involvement.

A friend of mine has just left his post as director of a large Evangelical relief and development organisation, to work in a small church-planting ministry in an inner-city area. Here's how he describes himself: "... an unashamed Evangelical, reformed, Calvinistic, conservative; strong on the authority, centrality, and sufficiency of the Bible; but craving obscurity, trusting in small communities connected organically in an ad hoc manner, and uninterested in hierarchy, organisational power, and grand strategies."

GenXers don't want to be bamboozled with talk of "the big picture." Whatever "big picture" is presented to us, it will be wrong. The world is too complex, life is too changeable, and God is too mysterious for us to get fired up by that kind of language.

Also, being sceptical of authority, we have a strong sense of the need for justice, along with an awareness and hatred of injustice. We will be stirrers, both within the church and without. I'm afraid others might just find us "rocking the boat" a little.

Flexibility and Individuality

Frustration with Xers is usually expressed in terms of a lack or loss of commitment. My father has worked for the same company for 30 years. For him, that represents security. For me, it sounds like a life sentence.

In their paper "A Generational Perspective on the Future," Kath Donovan and Ruth Myors (1997) demonstrate how the working patterns and values of each generation of missionaries have been shaped by the culture. While the authors worked from an Australian context, their observations can be applied to other Western nations.

For example, the group they refer to as the Boosters (elsewhere referred to as the Builders, GIs, or Silent Generation—born 1920–1950) had their consciousness shaped by the experiences of the Great Depression and World War II. Thus we see their core values of personal sacrifice, flexibility, and long-term commitment to a common cause. Many of these GIs and Silents became missionaries, and their outlook has shaped the spirituality that is often associated with missionary service.

In contrast, the Baby Boomers (born 1950–1965) grew up in the prosperous 1950s (the "Eisenhower" era; the British prime minister of the time famously remarked, "You've never had it so good") and the 1960s, a time of freedom, questioning, and individualism. As a result, their core values are clustered around individualism, self-development, and work. In contrast to their preceding generations, Boomer missionaries feel more able to change mission agency or country of work, but they feel more constrained to remain in the area of ministry in which they are skilled and practiced.

Now this pattern is not necessarily a bad thing. It's actually OK and indeed inevitable, if we accept the reality of our cultural conditioning and its origin in our created nature. Each generation is called to work out what it means to live for Christ in its own era. But it is not called to make any answer it may find to be normative for all the succeeding generations. Why not allow Xers the same freedom to do mission their way, based on their understanding of who they are in Christ—an understanding which is formed in the context of the culture which shaped them?

A heart for world mission

The following is taken from a letter written by an Xer, sent to us at Global Connections in November 1999:

"Today's world is a temporary place. There is hardly a job that comes with long-term security these days, but mission agencies still talk in terms of 'long-term' and 'short-term,' with 'short-term' as somehow lesser. But people live in an environment in which they are expected to move on after a time; otherwise, they are seen as

no longer fresh, in touch, cutting edge. It is seen as necessary movement in order to gain more experience, to be more employable, more relevant to the work. I make no judgements on this state, but feel that we should at least acknowledge it as a fact. Shouldn't we be encouraging mission agencies to support people into longer-term service by allowing them to complete short-term contracts, without then feeling the pressure of either owing the agency or failing the agency? There is a view that says those interested in mission today are not as committed as previous generations because they will not offer their lives in long-term service. I believe this to be incorrect, and I see many who are committed to living out one day at a time for God, reflecting the temporariness of life and its situations. This could actually be seen as a healthier, more honest commitment."

Short-term service doesn't mean that every Xer doing mission will be an inexperienced learner. Instead, they will be able to bring their experience with them, contribute and learn, and maybe then move on, taking that experience elsewhere. As with the letter-writer quoted above, I don't see a lack of commitment to mission among Generation X. What I see is a lack of need or desire to stay with a single organisation, or to remain within structures that feel alien and outmoded. And why should that be wrong? Organisational commitment and commitment to Christ are not synonymous.

This personal flexibility and concern for individuality will affect other core values and concepts currently cherished by the missionary movement. Our motivation for mission will be different, as will our understanding of what mission actually is. We will be able to accept different visions, goals, styles, and so on from different people, and aim to combine the strengths of each into a wider whole. Our communication about mission will have to be tailored more explicitly to the needs and context of each person. I suspect that as Evangelicals we also have a tendency to overcommunicate (this article is probably a good example of that). Perhaps we should aim to be more like Jesus of Nazareth, whose judicious use of stories and parables provides a welcome relief to the information explosion we're experiencing today.

The current structures through which mission is undertaken will probably change a lot. For most of us, structures and hierarchy hold little or no appeal, and a strong desire for a relational way of living will have to be reflected in our work methods. Will Xers change traditional sending structures such as mission agencies, will they abandon them, or will they start their own organisations? The answer is probably "all of the above," for we already observe these trends. The inertia inherent in human nature and cultures will ensure that most organisations stick around, even if Xers don't form the creative heart of them. They will express their own creativity elsewhere.

Since Xers don't want to limit their options, they find it difficult to commit to one organisation. Few are staying with one mission organisation for a long time. The attitude of "stay a short while, contribute what you can, learn what you can, move on," mentioned above, is widespread among my contemporaries. I have also heard the perhaps-unfair-but-genuine question, "Couldn't you do anything else?" being directed towards someone who had spent 25 years working for the same organisation.

Perhaps the core questions are management ones. How do you manage a group of individuals who like to be flexible? How do Xers like to lead and be led? I find it ironic, even sad, that more effort is being put into answering this question in the secular human resources literature than in the church, which seems to be more keen to hold onto its old ways of doing things, rather than asking whether new situations require new ways of working. A starting point for reflection on this subject can be had by visiting the following websites:

www.growingupdigitial.com
www.rainmakerthinking.com
www.generationsatwork.com

The Remaining Challenge

Of course, GenXers will not be the only group doing mission in the foreseeable future. The older generations—the Baby Boomers, the Silents, and the Veterans—make up the major portion of the church. But behind even the GenXers comes the next generation, the Millennials. The challenge that we all face is to retain some kind of unity (or, even better, to try to find some kind of generational synergy) in the midst of this diversity. It won't be an easy task. Neither is it impossible.

Writing in the context of cultural diversity, *The Observer* journalist Simon Caulkin (1999), commenting on Neil Kinnock's task of streamlining the work of the European Commission, noted, "The trickiest, and most interesting, issue of all is a cultural one. Although some companies have tried it, one thing that can't be internationalised is organisational culture." In his book on organisational culture, Charles Handy (p. 68) says something similar: "The first essential, then, of organisational efficiency is cultural purity. To each his own god. Harmony is health. It is when the gods compete within one activity that confusion results, for then the law of cultural propriety is infringed." Robert Flood and Norma Romm (p. 14) note, "Diversity is *desirable*, but … complementarity is not obviously theoretically *feasible*."

And yet there is something in the gospel that says that this adversariality cannot and must not be the case. For the gospel is about reconciliation between God and people and between people themselves. And if God in Christ accepts us as we are, then we too must accept one another as we are—modern, post-modern, pre-modern, or whatever. Reconciliation does not come about by forcing people to fit into one particular mould. We must surely agree with the observation of French post-modern philosopher Michel Foucault, that simply to establish norms of being and behaving is not an adequate solution to diversity. For as soon as a norm is established, it alienates those who do not conform; and conforming is not enough.

Complementarity—finding unity in diversity—is essential. For unity is central to the effectiveness of our mission. Remember Jesus in John 17:23 in this regard: "May they be brought to complete unity to let the world know that you sent me." This tension is not an issue of which the biblical writers were unaware. In the Old Testament, both Ruth and Jonah provide stories which illustrate God's concern for the apparent "outsider," who didn't fit the "norms" of God's people and who could thereby have easily been excluded.

In the New Testament, we see the issue arising in one of the earliest crises to afflict the early church, that is, the demand by Jewish Christian leaders that Gentiles must be circumcised as a condition of salvation in Jesus Christ. Acts 15 describes the decision of the Council of Jerusalem that non-Jews should be allowed to become Christians without submitting to circumcision and the law of Moses. Yet at the same time, James introduced some provisos (Acts 15:19-20), so that the exercise of freedom in Christ should not become a hindrance to fellowship and unity. Paul developed the same theme himself

to help overcome problems of disunity and broken relationships in the churches at Rome and Corinth. In the process, Paul modified the Jerusalem Council provisions even further, with greater liberty in Christ. Might we not transfer Paul's thought in Ephesians 3:10-11, and instead of Jews and Gentiles, think of the generations? The text might read: "God's purpose was to show his wisdom in all its rich variety to all the rulers and authorities in the heavenly realms. They will see this when GenXers and Boomers and Silents are joined together in his church."

This may provide us with a biblical and theological starting point to develop unity in the context of diversity. Not just to "manage" or cope with diversity, but to see it as a strength and to allow each generation to bring its own unique strengths and gifts to the task of mission. Unity has to be more than simply an affirmation of what we have in common (which can so easily reduce to the lowest common denominator). Unity in diversity welcomes and needs the input of each (à la 1 Cor. 12), not just despite ethnicity, gender, or generation, but because of them. We need the specific insights and perspectives of each, for otherwise we are all impoverished—GenXers, Boomers, Veterans.

Drawing to a Close

My concern in this paper has been to focus on mission issues from the perspective of Generation X and to present a perspective of understanding towards us and our idiosyncrasies. I make a plea that we all let X = X and that we be allowed to find our place in God's church and God's mission. At the WEF Missions Commission consultation in Iguassu, Brazil, in October 1999, some of the seniors of the world mission movement were very supportive of our right to find our own answers to our own questions. However, others challenged our thoughts on these issues, asking if we were speaking rhetorically. Some suggested that we were "sincere but misguided" or that we were plain "heretical." They could not allow that we might actually be right. However, I believe that we can make space for diversity, thus allowing each generation to contribute from its strengths and to have its weaknesses compensated for.

The biggest mistake that the Western missionary movement can make is to act as though it is on the asteroid of Texlahoma, and that it is always 1974. Over a quarter of a century on, the world is a different place. In another 25 years, it will be a different place again. Only as we respond to and embrace the changes in our culture, and accept the strengths and gifts of each generation, can the church truly be a place and a messenger of reconciliation, for all generations, in a changing world.

References

Caulkin, S. (1999, July 25). *The Observer*.

Coupland, D. (1991). *Generation X: Tales for an accelerated culture*. New York: St. Martin's Press.

————. (1995). *Microserfs*. New York: Regan Books.

Donovan, K., & Myors, R. (1997). Reflections on attrition in career missionaries: A generational perspective into the future. In W. D. Taylor (Ed.), *Too valuable to lose: Exploring the causes and cures of missionary attrition* (pp. 41-73). Pasadena, CA: William Carey Library.

Flood, R., & Romm, N. *Diversity management*.

Handy, C. *The gods of management*.

Strauss, W., & Howe, N. (1991). *Generations: The history of America's future, 1584 to 2069*. New York: Morrow.

Richard Tiplady is the Associate Director of Global Connections (formerly known as the Evangelical Missionary Alliance) in the U.K. Prior to this, he worked in local church leadership and mission mobilisation. In 1993, he lectured in a theological college in Nigeria. He holds a theology degree from London University and a master's degree in theology from Nottingham University. He is married to Irene, and they have one son, Jamie, who was born in 1992 and whose ambition is to be a monster.

33

From synthesis to synergy: the Iguassu think tanks

ROB
BRYNJOLFSON

ALMOST ALL WHO HAVE attended major consultations participate with a fear that they "plough the ocean," as the South American liberator Simón Bolívar once said in the dismal and difficult time after the deadly revolutionary battles for independence from Spain in South America. The saying comes back to haunt us: "After all is said and done, much more is said than done." What we all desire to see emerge as a result of the Iguassu Missiological Consultation is an enduring legacy, a visible and practical outworking of the discussions, papers, and conclusions. Will there remain something of enduring substance? One element of such a legacy already exists in the form of suggestions and recommendations to the broader missiological community stemming from the think tank sessions that were a key component in the consultation program.

This chapter attempts to synthesize the analyses, suggestions, and recommendations branching from those think tank sessions. Recognized experts participated in each of the 12 topics. Some of these coincided with WEF Missions Commission (WEF/MC) Task Forces already at work. Many of the groups could already identify forums or networks that would sustain the dialogue and would continue working to implement the suggestions. The think tank sessions, then, are the very place we might find real solutions to real problems and contribute lasting efforts directly attributable to the Iguassu Missiological Consultation.

The various topics fell into a natural, progressive organization. The four divisions move from the activity of sending, to strategizing, to issues related to staying, to missiology. Two of the original 12 groups amalgamated, and two others decided not to contribute reports. Below is a summary of the nine reports that were submitted.

Suggestions
Relating to Sending

The church and mission

As history begins with Adam, so mission begins with the church. One team gathered to focus specifically on the local church in mission. Tite Tiénou presented a plenary paper, thus contributing to the consultation a perspective of church and mission from the developing world. This think tank, on the other hand, fretted over an apparent overtly Western perspective. Chaired by pastor John Wood, the group expressed introductory regrets that most members of the missiological community struggle less specifically with issues relating to the local church.

The group determined three important issues that are here presented as recommendations to the missiological community. First, church centeredness is essential to 21st century missiology. John Wood remarked, "If mission ultimately begins and ends in God, it begins and ends experientially in a local church." The experience of mission in the local church, therefore, needs to reassess the ministry, the language, and the training of leaders of the local church.

This think tank reported the need to reassess the ministry of the local church. "There must be a rhythm of worship and mission," we are told. A pattern emerges from Matthew 17. The group of disciples behold the glory of God. They also hear the word of God saying, "This is my Son whom I love; listen to him!" Jesus says, "Fear not," and then he leads the group down the mountain. At the foot of the mountain is a human father in need, who cries out, "This is my son, whom I love. Help him!" The think tank points to this as the "cry of the world."

Wood made a striking observation. Only those who have been to the mountain and returned can help the boy. Some have not gone to the mountain and have neither heard the word of God nor seen his glory. It is also possible to go to the mountain, see and hear the Lord, but never descend to help. "Only those whose lives are marked by the rhythm of worship and mission," we are told, "can be used to bring salvation to a broken world."

This group continued with two more observations that relate to this rhythm of worship and mission. One is that holistic ministries are a necessary concern of the church, but they are inadequate. Too often, the local church engages in mission at a safe distance. Churches need to consider how they can engage the communities they serve, providing local cross-cultural mission. A question for self-assessment is, "Is your neighbourhood glad you're there?" Finally, the group indicated that equipping in gifts misses the mark unless a people match their gifting to the passion that drives their lives. The passion will show us where we are called to minister, and our gifts tell us how to minister.

Organizational and denominational language continues to detract from the greater reality of unity in mission. Reassessment of the church and mission is critical. Shifting the emphasis of language to that of family will affect both where and how mission is done. Asking, "Is the family there?" and, "What is the family doing?" reduces unnecessary competition and the redundancy invoked by asking, "Is the organization there?" Subsequently, this also affects the way the church and missions undertake partnerships and fund-raising.

This suggestion is only helpful to the extent that it can be implemented. The challenge before the mission community in North America, at least, is how to extend influence to the context of the local church. The mission community in North America and elsewhere can develop and use inclusive family language. Perhaps in time the church will follow suit. We are left looking for a more intentional approach to this problem.

The think tank spoke of the need to train pastors in the process of missiological thinking and visioning. They acknowledge, once more, that this concern speaks chiefly to the North American context. "Pastors," we are told, "no longer take the word of mission thinkers and leaders." The result is that missionary activity, without adequate reflection, quickly becomes misguided, uninformed, or not sustainable. An example of such misguided efforts is the local church that presumes a level of cross-cultural sensitivity by merely training and funding a national to reproduce an enterprise that in every way exhibits its foreign origin. The training of pastors in the process of missiological thinking and visioning should assist the movement by developing an awareness of the national alliances and networks already at work, thus avoiding the Adam syndrome ("history starts with us") and fostering partnership and cooperation.

National missionary movements

Sending also requires mobilization. The think tank on national missionary movements provided very helpful suggestions and recommendations for emerging movements. The focus of this group was on both starting national missionary movements and strengthening them.

This team outlined two important aspects of starting a movement. The first relates to the context of the national missionary movement; the latter, to underlying principles behind starting a movement. Movements emerge within a context which, undeniably, needs to be understood. As such, the group has provided for the global missionary community a list of questions that should serve to guide an emerging movement through the process of discerning its own unique context. These questions have been organized into four categories:

1. Observe the movement of God in your country: What is God doing in your country? What is the state of the church in your country?

2. Determine the level of unity in the church: Is there an attitude of co-operation amongst leaders? Does a national Evangelical fellowship or Evangelical alliance exist? If yes, how strong is it? What are the other national platforms for drawing people together?

3. Consider the development of missions to date: Are you a younger sending country or an older sending country? If you are a new sending country, what are the international mission agencies doing? What are people at the grassroots level saying about global mission?

4. Analyze present mission structures and institutions: What are the issues facing the mission sending structures from your country? What are training or educational institutions doing to equip your missionary force?

Offered below are 18 principles this resource group provided as a guide for beginning national missionary movements. Once the context of the new movement has been determined, the principles listed below will assist the development of a strong foundation.

Foundational concerns

1. The Holy Spirit is the primary initiator of a national missionary movement.

2. The centrality of the local church must be affirmed by a national missionary movement.

Leadership

3. Servant-leadership is vital.

4. A nationally accepted platform for gathering is needed.

5. Common, clearly defined outcomes must be developed.

6. The support of a cross-section of leaders is needed.

Attitudes and relationships

7. Consensus must be built.

8. Relationship building is needed between the potential participants of the movements.

9. The national missionary movement should not compete with or duplicate what already exists.

10. The national missionary movement should be an open neighbourhood, not a gated community.

11. Networking with other national missionary movements is vital to success.

12. Key leaders participating in larger international mission conventions/congresses can so impact these individuals that when they return to their country they can catalyze a national missionary movement.

13. National missionary movements must recognize the role of the expatriate and find ways to cooperate.

Other factors

14. Timing is key.

15. Research can be very helpful.

16. Effective information flow is critical.

17. The agenda for the national missionary movement arises from the context rather than from the outside.

18. Start simply.

Strengthening national missionary movements was the other key concern of this reflecting group. Many young movements have blossomed over past years, producing accumulated experiences that may serve to guide those still in process. The group identified and analyzed four critical areas and produced a significant list of suggestions, hints, and examples for each of these. This writer proposes that

this material be circulated widely through electronic media or through bulletins, ensuring its availability to those needing assistance.

First, the national missionary movement needs to set a strong spiritual foundation. Principally, this requires fostering openness to the Holy Spirit's guidance and encouraging dependence on the Spirit. It will also include some form of spiritual "stock taking." Building relationships is the second critical need in strengthening national missionary movements. There are any number of ways to work at relationships. The most helpful suggestion relates to fostering attitudes of acceptance and openness, expanding the circle of involvement disproportionately. Thirdly, a national missionary movement ought to provide significant services to churches and agencies. The perceived value of these services will determine the extent of involvement of those being served. Finally, the stability and maturity of these movements must be achieved. These qualities are not automatic. The timeliness or popularity of an emerging national movement is no guarantee of sustainability or effectiveness.

Missionary training

Sending involves both the church and national missionary movements; it also presupposes an element of missionary training. Research points to the urgency of whole-person training, and the team on missionary training quickly identified this as a common value. The group moved on to consider three specific areas relating to training. The first area dealt with the ongoing needs of trainers. How can trainers keep current? The second area identified a need to develop recognized standards of quality in training. Finally, the session considered how to meet the training needs of tentmakers.

Francophones and Hispanics, among others, utilize a marvelous term, *reciclaje*. In English, we might think of retooling or refreshing. A nurse takes refresher courses to keep abreast of new developments in medicine. No one wants to sit under the scalpel of a surgeon who has not kept current with new techniques. It is not surprising, then, that the missionary trainers gathered on this team determined that keeping current is essential for continual improvement of the quality of missionary training and the effectiveness of trainers.

Brainstorming led to a number of suggestions intent on refreshing or keeping the trainer current. The obvious suggestion came first: to share resources through the development of literature, journals, bulletins, and electronic media. Another suggestion proposed the development of a program for ongoing improvement of the various centers by polling alumni to determine critical areas needing improvement. It was further recommended that reviving the WEF/MC International Missionary Training Associates would foster open communication and consultation between schools. The development of electronic media encapsulates the last two suggestions. The development of an Internet forum provides the means to share contextualized models and curricula and to encourage cooperative curricula development. Furthermore, it would serve to disseminate training resources, including the production of full textbooks, articles, theses, and abstracts, whether by CD-ROM or the Internet, for those centers struggling with the lack of adequate materials. The think tank identified the WEF/MC International Missionary Training Fellowship as a potential broker to act on these recommendations.

The second focus of this resource group was to examine the need for a recognized standard of quality in missionary training. Bob Ferris was asked to summarize criteria already established by the Task Force on Missionary Training. The content of this discussion worked its way into an article and was subsequently published in the International Missionary Training Fellowship Bulletin, *Training for Cross-Cultural Ministries* (Vol. 99, No. 2).

While the think tank group exhibited strong support for the criteria established by the task force, evidence of diverse values in training surfaced. On the one hand, consensus grew for the adoption of the criteria published in the article. On the other hand, it became more apparent that the criteria heightened the distinctions between formal and nonformal training. Representatives from both types of institutions clearly valued distinct methodologies, and though claiming to be working towards the same objective (a trained person), they achieve divergent results. Assuming that these differing approaches are adversaries is a common mistake, when in reality they complement each other.

Inevitably, this signals the need for greater dialogue and partnership amongst the various centers and institutions. It is time to stop comparing the merits of various methods of training and begin to see that whole-person training will encompass informal, nonformal, and formal education. A recommendation was noted that more intentional partnerships in training would allow training centers and formal academic institutions to pursue excellence within their value systems. The nonformal centers must pursue excellence in hands-on training and character development. The formal academic institutions must pursue excellence in the development of foundational knowledge and skills in research and reflection. Missionary candidates, on the other hand, inevitably need both, and satisfying this need can be best achieved through cooperative initiatives on the part of both kinds of institutions.

The final area of dialogue that the team discussed related to the training of tentmakers. The tentmaker has distinct training needs to that of the traditional career missionary and therefore requires training that is adapted to meet his or her specific objectives. One obstacle that such training will face is the variety of definitions surrounding the concept of tentmaking. This topic was directly addressed by one of the think tank sessions. The primary obstacle, however, is the rapid deployment that often affects the tentmaker, making the acquisition of suitable training almost impossible. On the other hand, any training is better than no training at all. A reminder of the importance of lifelong learning or "just in time" learning helped the group see that tentmakers require training on demand and may very well access this training while serving on the field.

One example was cited demonstrating how tentmaker training must address specific needs. "Strategic Coordinator Training" was a Korean model designed for tentmakers who are retooling after a cross-cultural experience. The training that was received focused on how to develop and manage a project.

Suggestions Relating to Strategy

Leaving the issues relating to the pre-field context, we move to concerns affecting the strategic foundation of missions. The urgency of the task, principles of stewardship, commitment to excellence, and our driven call to worship compel us towards higher standards of excellence. For these reasons, we find it imperative that our efforts be effective. Several sessions dealt with issues relating to the strategic deployment of mission resources.

Partnership and cooperation

The partnership and cooperation think tank provided a very helpful analysis of the present situation, demonstrating that partnership is hindered by the problem of two competing models. The group enunciated this concern, saying that it is "more a question of competing models than murky definitions." The popularity of the "P" word does not make clarification an easy task. This observation is perhaps all the more striking in light of the fact that one pre-consultation event offered a one-day seminar on this topic.

Business and family are the distinguishing natures of these two competing models. A comparison of certain characteristics exhibits the dissimilar approach each model will take. The business model views people as stockholders, while the family model sees them as members. Control in the business model is maintained with money, but in the family it is relationships that keep control. In the business model the emphasis is on activities, while the family model values fellowship. Contributions are seen as competitive in the business approach, but they are complementary in the family model. No contribution is devalued even though recognized as distinct. Both models will pursue accountability. However, the business model is one-sided, whereas the family model seeks a mutual accountability.

Reporting for the team, Hugo Morales contributed the following observation: "This dichotomy makes us believe that while one model allows for the efficient accomplishment of kingdom tasks, it does not uphold in its rightful place the characteristics of the second one (family), where it is identified as more than 'doing'; we are to be 'living' kingdom-based relationships, which are centered around people who care for one another and have a vision of ministry that points them in the same direction." The group concluded that a biblical model needs to be developed, with an emphasis that rings true to passages such as Philippians 1:3-6.

The resource group on partnership and cooperation, after analyzing the present situation, moved on to consider hindrances to developing partnership in mission. They observed that diverging agendas, insufficient emphasis on relationships, and the indiscriminate usage of old sponsorship methods hinder the achievement of true partnerships. Figure 1 compares the sponsorship approach to that of partnership.

SPONSORSHIP	PARTNERSHIP
Money	Gifts
Control	Communion
Donation	Participation
Hierarchy	Equality
Imposed vision	Shared vision
Short term	Enduring
One-sided	Mutual
I — You	We
Domination	Cooperation
Dependence	Interdependence
Parent — Child	Peers
Suspicion	Trust
Unhappiness	Joy

Figure 1
Sponsorship vs. Partnership

The group concluded that truly effective partnerships accomplish the determined task primarily through healthy and strong personal relationships. The relationships are sincere, not merely expedient. The result is that both the process and the outcome exalt the mutual relationship in Jesus Christ.

The partnership and cooperation group proposed a single recommendation, with a well-developed agenda for implementation. The recommendation was to convene a task force on partnership and set this group to work on various tasks. First, the task force would need to develop a biblical theology of partnership. Second, the theology that is developed would need to be worked into a partnership handbook. The handbook would spell out the theology of partnership, would be sensitive to divergent contexts, would elicit contemporary models, and would include a best practice checklist and a workable assessment tool. Third, the task force would encourage the development of a curriculum that supports biblical partnership training for institutions of learning and for parties already attempting to develop partnerships. Fourth, a call was made for an international consultation on biblical partnership, well represented from all continents.

Tentmaking

Tentmaking (bi-vocational cross-cultural ministry) has emerged as a singularly significant strategy to reach many of those yet to be evangelized in the world. However, definitions and descriptions, this team reported, continue to lack clarity. Tentmaking as a practice has already emerged and actually has been with us for centuries in one form or another. However, there is no fully accepted definition of who and what a tentmaker is. Furthermore, we lack further description of what a tentmaker does.

The name "tentmaking," though popularized from the examples of the Apostle Paul, Priscilla, and Aquila, does no true justice to the concept. An immediate need for theological and biblical reflection was observed. The present-day concept of tentmaking, though not necessarily at variance with these biblical examples, is certainly distinct. Access is the motivating factor in most cases. Surely, there ought to be other examples found in Scripture of people who served God in ministry while maintaining a vocation?

The team called for clear conceptualization of tentmaking, integrating people in their interactions with daily life. God looks for people intending to use marketable skills to bless the world in which we live. The motivation of the tentmaker ought not to differ from that of any other Christian. The tentmaker might, for example, assist in a church planting project but may not actually be a church planter. Further, tentmaking is more than an excuse to gain access to closed nations. Yet, as a strategy, we cannot avoid the fact that tentmaking has evolved to address the various obvious needs of access. In this regard, we are warned that the nature of tentmaking, while allowing access, will not produce the same mass results that traditional missionary efforts may have done in the past. There is room for neither naïveté nor unrealistic expectations.

Current issues in tentmaking continue to frustrate the task of definition. The resource team identified two concerns that are essentially distinct faces of the same coin. The first problem is one of identity. "It is our estimate," writes Carlos Calderón, "that a large number of potential missionaries are at a loss, without guidance or instruction, as they struggle, balancing God's call to serve him and a 'professional life/upbringing' that has been defined for them as less than 'missionary quality.'"

The second problem relates to the devaluing of vocation. The team suggested that research be undertaken surveying available literature and related subject matter, with the intention of reminding the global church of the significant contribution of tentmaking. The group stated that this material urgently needs to be disseminated in the languages of the newer sending countries, since they offer the greatest potential pool of future tentmakers. Another significant recommenda-

tion is that missions texts begin to treat tentmaking as an integral part of today's missionary strategy and no longer relegate it to the appendix. Finally, missionary evaluation criteria must consider issues relating to the context and nature of tentmaking ministry and not just look at results based on unrealistic expectations.

Media and technology

The unique relationship that media and technology enjoy relative to the future of mission allows them to fall into the category of strategizing. Initially, these subjects were to be discussed by two resource groups, but they came together under one title by mutual accord.

The merged sessions on media and technology clearly identified both elements as mixed blessings. They are essential and useful for the global cause of the kingdom of Christ. Unfortunately, they also carry innate problems and concerns that must be addressed. "An uncritical use of media and technology threatens mission and missionaries."

The group defined three main concerns: spiritual vitality, Christian community, and message integrity. Three danger signs, which this group also contributed, help us understand how these areas become concerns. They come to us in the form of questions for self-analysis. First, what does this use of media or technology do to my general sense of overload and my vitality? Second, what does this use of media or technology do to my face-to-face relationships? Third, how does this use of media or technology color the message we are trying to send?

One of the very significant contributions of this think tank group was a discussion of the biblical concept of wheat and tares. The observation that emerged from the session was that both wheat and tares grow together; hence, there is a mixed blessing. The group developed a

ISSUE	"WHEAT"	"TARES"
Contextualization	Via the Internet, anyone can take a Hiebert course on contextualization.	The course itself is decontextualized in cyberspace.
Power	"Virtual participants" can share in conferences they cannot physically attend.	These "virtual participants" become a new elite in their own countries.
Information sharing	Needs match resources via a missions website.	Information overload occurs, along with bogus virus warnings.
Partnerships	South-South links are formed; a "southern" edition of EMQ is made possible.	English dominates the software and limits the partnerships.
Proclamation	The *Jesus* film on DVD may be included free with all Hitachi DVD players sold next year.	The message is detached from a Christian community or even a Christian individual.
Creative access	Satellite TV is available in the Middle East; Christians can set up a small business on the Internet for creative access.	Careless use of websites and e-mail may lead to persecution.

Figure 2
Key Missiological Issues in Terms of Wheat and Tares

table that compares key missiological issues and the implications rising from media and technology in terms of wheat and tares (Figure 2).

The team on media and technology leaves us with three recommendations, which really are recommended disciplines to reduce the amount of "tares" while growing "wheat." First, it is essential that we keep a Sabbath, so that our spiritual vitality will not wane as a result of the use of media and technology. Second, we need to build relationships in order to combat the depersonalization of technology. And third, we must incarnate the message. No technology can replace the essential and core element of the gospel, which is love.

Suggestions Relating to Staying

Two think tank groups related to issues of remaining on the field. One dealt with issues relating to relief and development affecting many of the missionary receiving countries of the world. The other

group considered the ongoing care of missionaries and how agencies and churches can care for their members.

Relief and development

An observation, immediately obvious but nonetheless striking, offered by the think tank on relief and development states that relief and development will occur whether planned or not. Meredith Long noted that 50% of national missionary workers with the India Missions Association already provide some form of development. They are spurred to action by visible need. Unfortunately, projects and programs receive sporadic starts without clear reflection regarding long-range plans or sustainability.

If such is the case, and should this be a widely shared phenomenon, this think tank recommends that the WEF/MC conduct a survey assessing the training needs of workers who already provide some form of R&D or who are likely to develop some involvement in this kind of ministry. Furthermore, this survey could also identify Christian R&D organizations with needed expertise, in order to broker regional workshops that train workers in specific technical and support needs.

This recommendation underscores the need for networking. Various R&D agencies are now identifying issues and concerns stretching beyond their jurisdictions. A forum that brings together church, mission, and R&D agencies will address common concerns. For example, many now see the strengthening of the local church as a new priority. This task is difficult to achieve, since many R&D agencies develop large-scale projects and rarely relate directly to the local congregation. Networking will improve the coordination of activities while ensuring that identifiable priorities are met. The think tank recommends, therefore, that WEF become involved in the formation of MICAH, which has replaced the International Relief and Development Agency, in order to explore its potential to serve as a forum addressing in teams the multifaceted issues that arise.

The integration of all facets of ministry continues to be a concern for R&D organizations. Biblical values and worldview are crucial to secure integration. Biblical holism is now understood to be foundational to all Christian ministry. It is essential, then, to determine points of convergence between development activities and evangelism. The goal must become the achievement of holism as opposed to distinct complementary emphases. The R&D think tank proposed that this can be achieved when biblical values and worldview become more explicitly part of the ministry projects, thus securing inner change and not merely temporary outward behavioral adjustments. This will result in the diminishing of distinctions between Christian R&D and evangelism. Notable exceptions will remain. Issues of integrity relating to donor obli-

gations and security relating to difficult-access nations may limit direct integration with evangelistic activities.

Member care

Staying implies much more than mere longevity or perseverance in cross-cultural mission. It means fostering the life and ministry of missionaries in ways that release them not only to survive, but also to thrive in difficult contexts. It also includes reducing undesirable or painful missionary attrition. The think tank on member care is a natural link in the chain to address these issues. The concerns of this think tank, however, swell beyond merely staying, with emphasis on such elements as wholeness and effectiveness.

The member care group broached the subject with a two-pronged emphasis. The first was content. Three specific content-related issues were identified by the group. First, member care must occur throughout the life cycle of the missionary. Moments of acute need are easily identified. However, members need care at every stage of missionary service. Second, member care needs to be people centered. This will require that member care be culturally relevant and in line with best practice principles. The last concern is that member care be provided by qualified people.

The second prong of the member care group's emphasis dealt with structures. First, seminars and retreats geared to provide supportive care and spiritual refreshment will become key structures for delivering member care. A second structure is needed to address complicated or long-standing issues. Centers with appropriate facilities are essential for the provision of physical and mental health care. Crisis teams, the third proposed structure, are needed for special care and should be established to provide consulting, training, and services. Finally, the member care team recommended that a suitable structure be developed for further research. Major stressors, observed the group, need to be monitored and researched.

The member care resource group also produced a working model for member care, and they expect to publish an article in detail. The goal of a working model of member care, in the words of Kelly O'Donnell, "... needs to build up three areas: character (virtue/godliness), competence (cross-cultural/professional skills), and compassion (love/involvement) in culturally relevant ways." Further discussions included the need to develop a code of best practice for member care, a consideration of the diversified needs around the world, and a look into the future.

Suggestions Relating to Missiology

The think tank on missiological issues stands alone in this report because it enjoyed strong attendance and keen interest, and its themes were visibly threaded throughout the consultation. A number of key recommendations emerged. The first so strongly represented the pitch and tenor of the plenary sessions that it became the pillar in the contribution of this group. The concluding recommendations are related to the practical outworking of missiology.

This pillar, then, is a call to return to or clarify a trinitarian-based missiology. "Among the issues voiced," reports Bill Taylor, "the need for trinitarian-based missiology has received the most attention from a majority of the participants." Frustration was expressed at the token esteem attributed to the Trinity in mission. The think tank called upon future contributors to ensure that missionary books be written from the perspective of Trinitarianism and no longer offer mere mention of the subject.

This trinitarian-based missiology would have at least a triple focus. The initial focus needs to look biblically and theologically at the unique role of each member of the Trinity relating to mission. "Each divine Person has a distinct and yet overlapping role in creating, revealing, and redeeming." This initial affirmation focus on the Trinity then led to an understanding of community in light of the fact that the Trinity is the primal community. Therefore, community is self-revealing throughout every activity of God, including the life of the church and mission. Questions arose in terms of the missiological application of structures of community and how they relate to our human organizational models. Do our models emerge pragmatically, or are they an expression of the Trinity?

In relation to evangelization, the question was asked: "In what way would this communal model impact our presentation of the gospel, with the epic Story centered not in pragmatic and selfish individualism but rather in shared values of community?" As the church comprehends its trinitarian missiological foundation and as it accepts the implications of the reality of globalization, it must rise to give visible expression to the community of God. "The church by definition must live out the values of trinitarian missiology, for it is the gathered and scattered people of God, each individual and each people with unique contributions, but all shared co-equals and enhancing each other."

The other practical issues relating to missiology were then reported and presented in the form of declarations. The first affirms that missiology must be regenerated. There is now a need for a new missiology to fit a new context. The global missionary community needs to produce this new missiology. A remodeling of old missiology will not meet the needs of the ever-changing world in which we live. On the other hand, this resource team recognized the value of continuity and the regard for work completed in the past.

Secondly, the rise of new missiology must be adaptable. "A creative tension," it was observed, "exists between the universality of the gospel and the contextuality of the different regions." "In creating global missiology, we must not make missiology uniform. Contextuality must be taken seriously." Furthermore, missiology must be approachable. New nomenclature is needed to replace dated and misunderstood terminology and expressions. This is of particular import if the new missiology is to be embraced by the global church. The global mission community, according to David Tai-Woong Lee, "... must use less technical language so that a greater number of reflective practitioners can understand and use the language and process, even as they also create missiology and shape the global missions movement."

Thirdly, missiology must be praxis driven. This requires that both practitioners and theorists of mission must work together in formulating future missiology. There is no other means to secure a missiology that is not speculative and to ensure that it is born out in practice.

Finally, missiology must be inclusive. Two critical areas of concern hover over the vista of missions. New missiology must be sensitive in relation to gender and the different generations that form the global movement. The former relates to the role of women in leadership. Women have contributed a remarkable legacy in the history of missions. Not always were leadership roles accessible in the missions structures, and some agencies started by gifted women eventually were taken over by men leaders. Missiology needs to affirm the gifting of the Holy Spirit in women and allow him to use his servants. Generational

sensitivity is also required if missiology is to rise to the challenge of reaching the world's young and of opening up space for the next generation of mission leaders and missiologists.

The missiological issues resource team concluded with a prophetic word of encouragement that the future of missiology is bright, because we have a God who answers prayer and a global fellowship with which to work. The WEF/MC intends to continue to hear from the global church and mission community with the view to convene a Task Force on Global Missiology.

Final Thoughts

The nine topics summarized here enjoyed significant, creative, and helpful input from the 160 women and men from some 53 nations, reflective practitioners. The international mission community of the WEF/MC now inherits in these recommendations and suggestions a rich, yet practical legacy. Implementing even a portion of these will advance the missionary cause significantly. Let us pray that such is the case, and sooner rather than later!

Rob Brynjolfson along with his wife Silvia and three children call the Americas their home. Silvia hails from Argentina and Rob from Canada. Their overseas experience ranges from church planting to Bible teaching in South America, Spain, and Africa. Presently, they serve as missionary trainers and are the founding directors of Gateway: Training for Cross-Cultural Service, located in Langley, British Columbia, Canada. Rob received an M.Div. degree from Regent College and is completing a D.Min. degree from Trinity Evangelical Divinity School.

Part 6

Listening to mission that rises from community and spirituality

THE GLOBAL MISSIONARY MOVEMENT must revisit and recapture mission that arises from community and spirituality. The WEF Missions Commission in 1996 convened an international consultation that analyzed issues related to missionary attrition. The results of that 14-nation research project were published in *Too Valuable to Lose: Exploring the Causes and Cures of Missionary Attrition* (William D. Taylor, Ed., William Carey Library, 1997). Significantly, the prime reasons for early and painful return from mission service (in both the older and younger sending countries) were not related to inadequate formal training in missions. The significant finding showed that the prime causes were clustered around issues related to spirituality, character, and relationality in the life of the missionary.

Who is responsible to ensure that these qualities are part of the non-formal, "prefield curriculum" of the missionary or of the future pastors of the church? Is it the individual candidate for ministry? Is it the ordaining or sending church? Is it the missionary training programme or the theological institution that claims to train pastors? Is it the sending body (whether agency or church)? Instead of segmenting and fault-finding, would we not profit more by revisiting some of the

historic as well as contemporary models of mission that have risen from intentional communities that emphasize deep spirituality?

It was a missionary friend and colleague, called to the contemplative vocation, who challenged us prior to Iguassu to include this theme in both the program and the book. Her concern was that this component would help counter the contemporary preference for models of formal ministry training that have been exported (primarily from the West) around the world. The unfortunate reality is that most of the current theological education industry—and too many missionary training schools—have bought into the formal model that is historically based on the university. This does not bode good news nor health for the future of the church in mission. Formal training for ministry today is in crisis, and we must both revisit Scripture and learn from these other models of mission. The future of ministry and mission training must be grounded in renewed spirituality and rooted in community.

During the Iguassu Consultation, four of these models (written by Warner, Tiplady, Ekström, and Burns) were presented in their historical order early in the morning, just after worship and prior to the heavier missiological topics. This format helped set a tone for each day. Two other case studies were later commissioned for this book, the Nestorians (Harris) and Copts (Omondi). We are grateful to God for the encouraging number of ministry and mission training programs that are building core components of spiritual formation, character development, and intentional community and relationality into their prefield equipping process.

34

Celtic community, spirituality, and mission

CLIFTON D. S. WARNER

MOST CHRISTIANS in the English-speaking world have recently encountered some bit of artistic or liturgical legacy left by the Celtic Christians. Their crosses, dances, music, and prayers are everywhere. This popularity has to do with the way Ireland, Scotland, and Wales preserved their rich local cultures and traditions—a preservation that attracts Westerners subsumed in a homogenized world and a global culture without local character connecting us to place. We recognize the simple elegance and profundity of their prayers and the lost art of living well as creatures in creation. Their expansive imagination and complex artistry enliven us. Understandably, the Celtic Christian tradition has mostly been recovered and appropriated in private devotion and public worship. But there is another aspect of Celtic Christianity that can inform and reform our vocation as the church. We can also learn from the character of their mission.

Peregrinatio

Celtic Christianity flourished during the so-called Dark Ages, the period when learning ebbed between the fall of the Roman Empire and the Middle Ages. Having developed independently of Rome, Celtic Christianity established its own character and customs, including semi-monastic living arrangements. *Peregrinatio* was one of their unique customs, a combination of asceticism, adventure, and mission practiced by monks who would hear a call to drift the seas, led only by the Spirit of God in the wind of their sails. Where they landed, they started a new community like the one they had left behind. This was a common form of mission.

These Celtic missionaries called themselves *peregrini*, a Latin word that is not easy to translate. They were pilgrims, for lack of a better word, but they were unlike medieval pilgrims. *Peregrini* were voluntary exiles who felt called like Abraham to a land that would only be revealed after the journey had begun, a place to which prevailing winds and currents supervised by God would take them. And it was usually a lifelong commitment. Once, some Celtic monks who drifted ashore in Cornwall were taken to the king, who asked them where they had come from and where they were going. The three men replied that they "stole away because we wanted for the love of God to be on pilgrimage, we cared not where" (De Waal, 1997, p. 2). This quote illustrates that it was both a geographic journey and an interior journey: voluntary exile for the love of God.

Columbanus

Columbanus, a 6th century Irish saint, is a prime example of what we speak of. Columbanus burned with sexual desire in his youth and sought the counsel of a godly woman. Warning him with the examples of Eve, Bathsheba, and Delilah, she gave him some counsel that proved very effective: "Take flight from your homeland." He did. He made his way to the opposite corner of the island and sought the guidance of a few renowned monks. He joined their monastic community in what can loosely be called a monastery. Charismatic and bright, Columbanus soaked up the teaching of his elders and the Scriptures, especially the psalms. He learned them by heart and gained a reputation as a learned man in theology. Eyes must have been on this budding scholar-saint. "Will he become the next abbot? Will he oversee multiple monasteries?"

In his mid-40s, with a secure reputation as one of Ireland's most gifted Christian leaders, he put a request before the presiding abbot: "Dear abbot, may I set sail with some brothers?" The abbot permitted the journey, and having recruited 12 companions, Columbanus set upon the seas to a land God would show him, taking inspiration from Abraham. *Peregrinatio*. It was a voluntary exile for the love of God. Columbanus and his company hit upon the shore of what is now France and pushed into the interior until they came to present-day Burgundy. There they decided to remain. Maybe God spoke to them, or perhaps it was the fabulous wine of the region that kept them there—the Irish were not known to turn down a fine festive beverage. In any case, there they stayed.

That part of Europe was in shambles at the time. The Roman Empire was far beyond the memory of even the oldest generation. For as long as anyone could remember, the area had been hit by wave after wave of attacking barbarians. Corruption, moral decadence, and social-political chaos were the new norm. The church was on the verge of disappearing into a syncretistic religion of Christian-laced paganism. Columbanus and his fellow *peregrini* held up the light of Christ in that particular place and time. They spoke publicly of salvation in Jesus, served the oppressed, cultivated the life of the mind, and established several monasteries in the area, to which thousands flocked over the next 10 years. Throughout the so-called Dark Ages of Europe, other Celtic *peregrini* were being led to other places around Europe, embodying the presence of Christ and leading contagious lives of holy recklessness.

Community and Mission

Celtic Christian concepts of spirituality and community had a distinct character and a distinct influence on their mission. Most missionaries were monks who lived in the semi-monastic compounds. They requested the blessing of the abbot and went out in groups. Typically, the first thing they would do upon arrival was to start a new monastery, just as Columbanus did, which would then serve as the center for prayer, ministry to the poor, and hospitality. Celtic Christians knew of no other way of being a Christian but to be a Christian in community. *Peregrini* were sent from a community, with others, to form the nucleus of a new community.

Spirituality and Mission

Their spirituality likewise shaped their mission. How can it be otherwise if the most clear and powerful message we convey is our life itself, and our spirituality is nothing more than our distinct way of living the Christian life? I will choose four adjectives to describe the spirituality of the *peregrini* and their *lived* life in Christ: robust, ascetic, reflective, and contemplative. They were robust, in that they lived passionately, with an enormous love for life and the created realm. They were ascetic, in that they voluntarily deprived themselves of many comforts, for the love of God. They were reflective, in that they gave serious attention to learning and the life of the mind. This trait one picks up again in their love for creation, for only with a muscular creation spirituality and theology could they deem the things of this world such as art, music, and books as worthy of their sustained attention. Finally, they were contemplative, in that they valued solitude and prayerful meditation. John T. McNeill (1974, p. 157) writes, "The *peregrini* went abroad not to receive benefits but to impart them. They were prepared to accept the hardships of pioneering, asking for themselves only the fellowship of a dedicated community and, in many cases, a private hideaway where they might read their books and commune with God."

Celtic Christianity and Contemporary Mission

Community, creation, reflection, asceticism, contemplation, and a robust embrace of life on earth: these are not the typical values of Evangelical mission. Our pragmatism could use some theological reflection. Our activism could use the reminder that we are not God, a reminder that often comes through the stillness of contemplative prayer. Our mission could use a stronger theology of creation, a theology that would cause us to value life on earth and the earth itself. This means, by implication, that in addition to our concern for people's eternal destiny, we would direct our missional concern toward God's redemption of the physical person, of culture, and even of non-human creation. And all of these things would take place in the context of true community. Our Celtic brothers and sisters in Christ call us to join them.

Christian and pre-Christian Celts gravitated toward the "thin places"—mountaintops and islands where the elements meet. Land and air, land and sea. Boundary places. In our time, we are in a psychological thin place—a new millennium. At such a time, there is value in looking back even as we look forward. When we look back, we remember who we are and learn from our own story. And when we look back to Celtic Christianity, we find that we are all, in one sense, *peregrini*. We are voluntary exiles for the love of God, journeying to a land which we know not, led by the Spirit, in the presence of Christ, protected by the Father, living to the glory of the Three-in-One.

References

De Waal, E. (1997). *The Celtic way of prayer*. New York: Doubleday.

Joyce, T. (1998). *Celtic Christianity: A sacred tradition, a vision of hope*. Maryknoll, NY: Orbis Books.

Lehane, B. (1995). *Early Celtic Christianity*. London: Constable.

McNeill, J. T. (1974). *The Celtic churches: A history A.D. 200–1200*. Chicago: University of Chicago Press.

Stimson, E. W. (1979). *Renewal in Christ: As the Celtic church led "the way."* New York: Vantage Press.

Clifton D. S. Warner currently lives in Vancouver, Canada, where he and his wife, Christine, are students at Regent College. He is studying spiritual theology in the M.Div. program. They have two children, born in Canada. Cliff received his B.A. and M.A. in Spanish philology and linguistics from the University of Texas, where he taught Spanish while serving as a pastor of small groups at Hope Chapel, Austin, Texas. Prior to that, he served as a campus minister with InterVarsity at the same university. If you want more, you'll just have to get to know him.

35

Nestorian community, spirituality, and mission

DURING THESE YEARS when Islam has so captured the minds and hearts of Arabs, it is difficult for Christian believers in the West to imagine a time when Christian communities thrived in the Middle East. Do we remember the first thrilling days of the church in China and India? It is good to look back and celebrate God's faithfulness to the worldwide church and to repeat the stories of the body of Christ's ancient missionary lineage in the East. Reading these chapters of human history, we find galvanizing memories and pose compelling questions of our Christian ancestors and of ourselves.

The theology and spirituality of the Nestorian church can be traced from the 4th century out of Antioch via scholarmonks to the School of Nisibis, which in its day was the best-respected center of learning in Asia. The *Homilies* (496 A.D.), written by Narsai, the scholar-director of the school, tell us that Nestorian theological education was rooted in spiritual discipline, and the school functioned more as a spiritual community than a seminary or Bible school. Along the monastic model, male students took vows for the period of their enrollment, held property and possessions in common, and worked on the campus properties (including a farm) rather than paying tuition. Spiritual discipline was strict. The curriculum was modeled after Theodore of Mopsuesta (350–428 A.D.), who was claimed as the father of Nestorian theology.

Theodore is called "the Interpreter" in the ancient Nestorian church as well as the modern Syrian church for the model of Bible study and exegesis that he pioneered. He taught his students at Antioch that biblical exposition focused on what the Bible literally said, rather than tracing the

PAULA
HARRIS

reader's critical interpretations of the text. This was in marked contrast to Origen of Alexandria, and some other Western church fathers, who read allegorically and opened the Bible to several layers of meaning in the text. Theodore produced literal, text-centered interpretations and raised up a school of students who focused more on hermeneutics than homiletics. The study of the Bible was considered so important that the title of the director of the School of Nisibis was *mepasquana*, which means "interpreter" or "exegete" of the Scriptures.

Most importantly for our purposes, the theology of the school was a missionary theology, modeled not simply on Peter or Paul but on Jesus himself. To his students, director-interpreter Narsai paraphrased Jesus' words, saying, "Your task is this: to complete the mystery of preaching! And you shall be witnesses of the new way I have opened up in my person.... You I send as messengers to the four quarters [of the earth], to convert the Gentiles to the kingdom of Abraham. By you as the light I will banish the darkness of error, and by your flames I will enlighten the blind world.... Go forth! Give gratis the freedom of life to immortality" (Narsai, 1958, p. 165).

We may ask of the Nestorians, who claim Theodore as their theological father and Narsai as their first teacher, who was Nestorius whose name you bear? How justified are the accusations of heresy? Nestorius, for whom the church was named, was a student of Theodore and became a controversial bishop of Constantinople (428 A.D). Nestorius is infamous for being excommunicated as a heretic and banished to a monastery in Egypt. The Nestorian church bears some of his stigma. Catholic critique of his theological positions revolves around two Christological disagreements. First, in a short-sighted attempt to resolve a contro-

versy between Christians who were calling Mary the "Mother of God" and others who called her the "Mother of man," he proposed calling her the "Mother of Christ," which proved to be an extremely unpopular compromise. Secondly, there was a dispute between Nestorius and other Western bishop-rivals on the unity of Christ: Nestorius called him one person (*prosopon*) with two natures (*physis*), human and divine; the Monophysite Cyril preferred one person (*hypostasis*) with one nature (*physis*); the Chalcedon compromise was one person (*hypostasis*) with two natures (*physis*). Several facts are relevant. This theological dispute took place in multiple communities and in translation to multiple languages. At the Council of Nicea, "person" was being translated interchangeably *hypostasis* or *ousia*. One hundred years later, the West was differentiating between *hypostasis* ("person") and *ousia* ("basic substance"), as in the three persons of the Godhead, but one substance. At that point, in the West *prosopon* meant "person," connoting "face" or "appearance," but it was being translated into the Syriac *parsopa* ("permanent personality") by the East (Moffett, 1998, pp. 248-249). Around this time, the Nestorian doctrine of the Trinity was defined as "one divine nature only, in three perfect persons (*quenuma*), one Trinity, true and eternal of Father, Son, and Holy Spirit" (Wigram, 1910, p. 162).

If we ask whether there are other measures of the heresy or orthodoxy of Nestorius and the church which bears his name, the answer must be yes. Scholars from Luther to Samuel Moffett have examined his writings and concluded there was nothing particularly heretical about them (Moffett, 1998, p. 176). Secondly, it is significant that, despite these theological disputes, the Nestorian church and Nestorius himself always subscribed to the historic creeds of the West (Nicea 325,

Constantinople 381, Ephesus, 431 A.D.). When the Nestorian church had occasion to send bishops, archbishops, or other emissaries to Rome or Constantinople, they were received into full communion (after being grilled on their theology) in the Western church and occasionally asked to celebrate communion for the Western leaders. This seems to indicate that the theological differences may have unraveled somewhat during times of face-to-face contact as they communicated in the same language.

The Nestorian missionary model incorporated both professional missionaries (i.e., ordained monks, priests, and bishops) and lay believers who traveled widely as merchants, soldiers, refugees, or the like, spreading the gospel as they went. For example, an early 6th century Nestorian missionary community combined two merchants, a missionary bishop, and four priests. They grew their own food and taught the converts to do so also. They preached the gospel and baptized converts among the Hephthalite Huns (a Turkish people). They learned and wrote down the Huns' language for the first time, translated the Scriptures, and taught the Huns to read and write. We must admire their mission's striking success at integrating evangelism, education, church planting, and even agriculture.[1]

These Nestorian priests, bishops, and monks were all men. Reconstructing traces of women's involvement in this church, during that era in the Middle East and Asia, is a tenuous project. However, a 5th century general synod of the Nestorian church affirmed the rights of all Christians to marry, which may have meant increased influence of women on church matters via their clergy husbands. The reasons cited for this decision were both scriptural and moral. They were based on instructions in 1 Timothy regarding ministerial leaders being "married only once." In addition, it was felt that a strict application of the ascetic rule for those called into church ministry might cause abuse and immorality ("better to marry than to burn," 1 Cor. 7:9). The Persian critique of "weak" celibate clergy may have been a third, cultural reason.

As it took on cultural uniqueness, the Nestorian church continued to grow. From its Persian center in Seleucia-Ctesiphon and then later, Baghdad, the Nestorian church spread down the Persian Gulf and north into Central Asia. As the churches grew, they asked for leaders and ordained clergy to be sent to baptize converts, to teach a more mature theological understanding of the gospel, and to pastor the congregations. Many of the earlier 5th century models of Nestorian mission communities were admirably unified despite great diversity. They incorporated priests and bishops from both sides of theological quarrels described previously, as well as ethnic diversity.

The Arabic Christian community at Hirta (which had an ordained Nestorian bishop as early as 410 A.D. and remained a Christian diocese for 700 years) formed a close community which transcended traditional Arabic tribal differences, calling themselves "servants of God." When persecution of Arab Christians began in 522 A.D., they appealed for political and military help to Ethiopia, the closest Christian power. After mutual skirmishes, an army of 70,000 Ethiopians marched into Yemen, killing so many pagan Arabs and Jews that

---

[1] It should be noted that these Nestorian men weren't the first Christians there. There was a community of Christian women nearby on the shores of the Caspian Sea, which was also written about in 196 A.D. Unfortunately, little historical explanation remains of who they were or which missionaries founded this particular community.

even non-Christians began to tattoo crosses on their hands to escape death. According to Arabic tradition, Muhammad was born shortly after this battle. Observing the results of this model and the later Crusades, we must sadly question the use of violent political power and the close ties between a persecuted church and a foreign government. Other missiological issues arise as well. Despite the admirable unity of the church, why was there never an authentic Arabian base of Christianity? After 400 years, why were the Scriptures never translated into Arabic, and why were Arabs barely literate? Perhaps if Muhammad had encountered a different, more authentically Arabian Christian community, he would have responded differently on his own spiritual journey.

Despite this mixed record, the Nestorian church was a thoroughly missionary church, led by courageous missionary leaders in multicultural societies. The 6th century patriarch Mar Aba was led by a Christian Jew to convert from the powerful state religion, Zoroastrianism. While on trial for his conversion and evangelism, Mar Aba said publicly to his non-believing Persian king, "I am a Christian. I preach my own faith and I want every man [sic] to join it. But I want every man to join it of his own free will and not of compulsion. I use force on no man" (Wigram, 1910, p. 200). If only his wisdom and spirit had influenced the Western church! There was a cost to his courage, but God was faithful. At trial, he was convicted and spent years in prison, but the admiring king commuted his sentence from death to exile. Notably, the king's favorite wife, Anoshaghzad, was a Christian. One wonders, did she influence this decision to free Mar Aba from the death sentence? Lead-

ing mostly from prison and exile, Mar Aba called the Eastern church to spiritual and moral revival, to a renewed study of theological foundations, and to reconciliation. Like other patriarchs, he reaffirmed the historic creeds of the West, including Nicea, as the theological foundations of the Nestorian church. He consecrated and sent the first bishop to the Nestorian community of Hephthalite Huns, mentioned previously.

Some of the most extraordinary achievements of the Nestorian church were in the 7th century, under patriarch Yeshuyab II.[2] In this era, Nestorian missionary monks and priests won converts from the Persian state religion, Zoroastrianism, from Mongol and Korean shamanism, and from Buddhism, Islam, and Hinduism, despite the fact that in many instances it was a capital crime to convert. Responding to the growth and maturity of the church in India, Yeshuyab II consecrated the first archbishop for the church in India. He also authorized the first Christian mission to China, a mission which founded Christian communities all along the trading routes among the Turkish tribes of Central Asia, the Mongols, along the Silk Road, in Tibet and Gansu Province, and finally in the capital of T'ang Dynasty China. This is phenomenal to imagine. When the Pope sent his missionaries, they traveled 1,000 miles from Rome to England, and he could reasonably expect replies from them. In the same time period, when Patriarch Yeshuyab II sent missionary priest Alopen and others 5,000 miles to China, he couldn't even reliably know that his missionaries arrived, much less lead and direct them. Nevertheless, the Nestorian church survived 700 years in China, and at its height there were

---

[2] As an ambassador from the Persian king to the emperor in Constantinople, Yeshuyab was grilled on his theology and received into full communion in the body of Christ. He also negotiated a successful peace between Persia and Constantinople.

Nestorian communities in 11 major Chinese cities, including nearby communities in Korea, Tibet, Mongolia, and other bordering countries. Foreign and indigenous Nestorian priests translated portions of the Scriptures and became influential figures in the T'ang Dynasty courts. The Sui Dynasty (581–618) and early T'ang Dynasty were ruled by mixed-blood Chinese-Turkish emperors. The Turkish-Mongolian mother of the first T'ang Dynasty emperor was quite possibly a Nestorian Christian. But later emperors were thorough nonbelievers. A Buddhist empress, Wu Hou, declared Buddhism the state religion (691 A.D.) and persecuted Christians.

The Nestorian church in China suffered a tragic end, which poses difficult questions for us. How much did the priests' influence with the T'ang Dynasty negatively affect their position? Did their later alliance with Mongol rulers prove problematic as the Chinese responded to foreign dominance? Although there seem to have been many converts, and there were Chinese monks and Mongol bishops, where were the Chinese leaders of the Nestorian church? Only portions of the Scripture, hymns, and Christian texts were translated, but not the entire Bible. In reviewing the fragmentary records that remain, one finds a great deal of orthodox Christian theology but also some Buddhist and Confucian phraseology incorporated into the Christian texts. How much has the translation process been distorted by a syncretized theology? Did the long communication distance from the international Christian community negatively affect the mission churches in China?

In the 8th century, Nestorian Patriarch Timothy held ecclesiastical authority over a church that stretched from Central Asia to South India, from Turkey to Yemen, from the Western Persian/Syrian border to the Eastern Chinese/Korean border. Possibly because of the great distances, the communication difficulties, and his attempt to adapt further to local cultures, Timothy reorganized the church into missionary bishops and local bishops, giving the missionary bishops more independence and authority in their contexts. He consecrated a bishop for the community in Yemen, despite its strict prohibition of Christian evangelism among Arabs. Missionary-minded Timothy prayed openly before a Muslim caliph, asking God that Christians could share the "pearl" of the gospel: "God has placed the pearl of his face before all of us like the shining rays of the sun, and everyone who wishes can enjoy the light of the sun" (Vine, 1948, pp. 125, 270).

Timothy elevated the Indian bishop at Rewardashir into an archbishop and wisely granted the Indian church more independent authority. This church was at most an adopted daughter or sister of the Nestorian church. The Thomas Christians (tracing their evangelistic roots to the Apostle) had had mature churches that were well acculturated to Indian ways when they sought out the wider international church body and requested a bishop from the Nestorian patriarch a few centuries earlier. As the Indian church grew and integrated with the Nestorians, additional Syriac churches had been founded by lay and ordained Nestorians. The Indian church maintained a tenuous balance of reaching out to the wider international body of Christ, while persistently holding onto the traditional Christian roots of their own local church and adapting to local culture. For example, the Nestorian priests initially struggled when the Indian Christians sat cross-legged during readings of the gospel, being more accustomed themselves to stand out of respect for the Scripture. Christianity survived and grew as a minority religion in India in spite of terrible odds.

The Nestorian church survived under the renewal of Persian rule (945–1055 A.D.), the Crusades (1095–1291), under medieval Islam (1000–1258), and well into the Mongol conquest of Ghengis Khan (1162–1227). Large numbers of Mongols were converted to both Christianity and Islam. In 1009 A.D., 200,000 Turks were baptized by Nestorian priests. Several key Mongol queens were Christians, including Sorkaktani (Ghengis Khan's daughter-in-law) who subsequently became the mother of three great Asian emperors— Mongke of the Mongolian Empire, Kublai Khan of China, and Hulegu of Persia. Under these emperors, Christianity mostly flourished. Kublai Khan later wrote to the Pope requesting him to send 1,000 missionaries to China; sadly, only two Dominicans were dispatched with Marco Polo and his uncles, and even those two turned back because of the difficulty of the journey. Other Nestorian monks went separately and served long years in China. Several key Mongol tribes became mostly Christian at that point, including the Uighurs, the Onguts, the Naimans, the Keraits, and the Merkits.

What happened to this missionary church which thrived in China, India, Persia, Mongolia, and Arabia? Did the Islamic conquest prove fatal? No, the Nestorian church survived Islamic domination for hundreds of years as a minority religion.[3] They continued to win converts to the gospel and to grow new communities, in spite of always being a smaller overall percentage of the population than Christians were in the West. They survived encounters and persecution with the powerful Asian religions of Islam, Hinduism, Buddhism, Confucianism, Zoroastrianism, and Shamanism. At times, the church succeeded in becoming indigenous, with lo-

cal leaders educated in their own language and traditions; at times, it significantly did not. Some scholars have suggested that the Nestorians overly contextualized their methods and that this contributed to their disappearance.

It is notable that the Nestorian church survived despite the fact that in this millennium the great Asian empires ruled by Persians, Chinese, Mongols, or Arabs never had a Christian emperor similar to Constantine in the West. However, many of these pagan emperors had Nestorian Christian queens or queen mothers, so we must wonder about their influence on political decisions about church matters. Nestorian church leaders made strategic alliances with political rulers and their consorts, which sometimes served the church and its purposes and sometimes hurt it. There is no one simple missiological answer as to why this church survived so long, only to retreat into an inwardly focused state church in Iran, Armenia, and the hills of Kurdistan. But the fact remains that it did retreat from its missionary priorities and ceased to obey Jesus' command and promise to all Christian disciples that "you will be my witnesses ... to the ends of the earth" (Acts 1:8).

Around the time of the Islamic conquest, two apologists, a Nestorian Christian and a Muslim, debated their faith. Towards the end of the long public debate, the Christian confessed, "But now the monks are no longer missionaries." Samuel Moffett adds, "If Christians were no longer evangelizing and the monasteries were no longer producing missionaries, the decline might well be fatal. And yet, after 300 years of Islamic rule, the church of the *dhimmis*, though separated, battered, limited, and self-wounded, was

---

[3] Both the Persians and Muslims allowed Christians a degree of freedom and self-rule within self-contained Christian communities, called *melets* in Persia, and *dhimmis* under Islamic rule.

still surviving and still undefeated as part of what Christians call 'the body of Christ on earth'" (Moffett, 1998, p. 361).

References

Isichei, E. A. (1995). *A history of Christianity in Africa: From antiquity to the present*. Grand Rapids, MI: Wm. B. Eerdmans Publishing Co.

Moffett, S. H. (1998). *A history of Christianity in Asia: Vol. 1. Beginnings to 1500* (2nd ed.). Maryknoll, New York: Orbis Books.

Narsai. (1958). Statutes of the School of Nisibis. In A. Vööbus (Ed. and Trans.), *Papers of the Estonian Theological School in exile, Vol. 12*. Stockholm, Sweden: ETSE.

Neill, S. (1982). *A history of Christian missions*. New York: Penguin Books.

Saeki, P. Y. (1951). *The Nestorian documents and relics in China* (2nd ed.). Tokyo: Maruzen.

Vine, A. R. (1948). *The Nestorian churches: A concise history of Nestorian Christianity in Asia from the Persian schism to the modern Assyrians*. London: Independent Press.

Wigram, W. A. (1910). *A history of the Assyrian church, A.D. 100–640*. London: Society for Promoting Christian Knowledge.

Paula Harris currently provides leadership in program development, missiology, and multi-cultural relations to the Urbana Student Mission Convention, which is sponsored by InterVarsity Christian Fellowship. Paula is also a single mother of two biracial children and a graduate student at Fuller School of World Missions. Before coming to Urbana, she served as a language instructor in Quiquihaer, China, with English Language Institute, and then developed and directed evangelistic lingua-cultural exchange programs in Ukraine with InterVarsity Missions. Paula studied at Wheaton College, Illinois, and the University of Wisconsin, Madison, under their graduate program in English and literary criticism.

36

Moravian community, spirituality, and mission

THE MORAVIAN CHURCHES date their commitment to world mission from 21 August, 1732. Over the next 150 years, this movement, centred on the original Moravian community at Herrnhut, in Saxony, Germany, sent out a total of 2,158 missionaries. These missionaries displayed a distinct form of spirituality and community, which provided a model to the emerging Protestant mission movement of the early 19th century.

The roots of the Moravian community are to be found in Pietism, which was a late 17th century renewal movement within the Lutheran church in Germany. Protestant theology (both Lutheran and Reformed) had become as formal and arid as the Roman Catholic scholasticism it had originally reacted against. By contrast, Pietism focused on a relationship with Jesus Christ, not on dry, correct orthodoxy. A disciplined life was more important than sound doctrine, and piety and the fear of God replaced irrelevant intellectualism. Personal conversion and experience superseded a satisfaction with nominal Christian allegiance. As such, the Pietists preceded the Evangelical Revival in Great Britain and North America by some 50 years or more.

As well as developing a faith which engaged the heart rather than the mind, Pietism was responsible for stimulating a new interest in missionary outreach. In Lutheranism, the religion of the people was the choice and responsibility of the state. The Puritan theocratic vision meant that church and state, if not co-terminous, were at least closely allied. In both cases, missionary work was easily seen as the property of the civil and ecclesiastical hierarchy. By contrast, the Pietists taught that missionaries were to go out under the direction of Christ and the Spirit alone, irrespective of political con-

RICHARD TIPLADY

siderations. As such, mission outreach became a matter in which the "ordinary" person could be interested and participate. This breakthrough was to have profound implications for the life and vision of the Moravian community, to which we now turn.

The Moravian community was formed in 1722, when Count Nicolas von Zinzendorf, who had been nurtured in Pietistic circles, allowed a group of persecuted religious refugees from Moravia to settle on the family estate in Saxony. The new community was named Herrnhut ("The Lord's Watch"), from Isaiah 62:6-7. Herrnhut developed its own form of Pietism, with a deep devotion to the crucified Christ and an absolute, unconditional surrender to his will.

The community's missionary interest was stirred by a number of factors. Some of the community, while in Denmark, met a slave from the West Indies. Zinzendorf himself, while in Copenhagen in 1732, heard that the Lutheran mission to Greenland was in danger of being abandoned. This information was in fact wrong, but it spurred Zinzendorf to call on the Herrnhut community to support this mission. Thus was the decision made, and it mobilised a new missionary movement, almost unparalleled in passion and commitment, which would in turn have a significant impact on the later Protestant missionary movement.

The Moravians' experience, together with their distinctive take on spirituality and community, contributed to the following aspects of their missionary methodology:

Mission as a "Popular" Movement

We have already noted the democratising influence of Pietism on Christianity. Intellectual ability was not deemed necessary in order to follow Christ, for Christianity engaged the emotions and the will, rather than the mind. By the same token, mission was not an activity reserved for the interest of the ruling elite.

The Moravian missionaries exemplified this way of thinking, in that the Herrnhut community was largely composed of uneducated peasants and artisans. Not that they disdained preparation for mission, but they saw their settlements as "proved seminaries" for missionaries, and even as late as 1818 they rejected a proposal to form a separate training school for missionaries.

In 1793, the Moravians informed the newly created BMS that "learning, and what the world calls accomplishments, we have not experienced to be of much use," and in 1795 the LMS were advised that, among non-Europeans, a craft was more appropriate than theological learning, as the Moravian missionaries already knew the Bible, and they prayed for the constant guidance of the Holy Spirit.

This "democratisation of mission" was also a characteristic of the early British and American "faith" missions of the late 19th century, which saw themselves as releasing for mission the "neglected forces of Christianity." They also saw the new "mission halls" as functioning as training grounds, in much the same way as had the Moravian communities.

Mission as Communal Action

The Herrnhut community was self-supporting, and it was expected that this model would be followed by their missionaries wherever they worked. The tension inherent in such a dual role, in that missionaries might be diverted from their core calling, was recognised. One check on this was that each Moravian mission community lived "as one family," with a common cash account, so as to restrain any member who might be so tempted out of self-interest.

The BMS drew on this model in its early days and recommended it to William Carey, Joshua Marshman, and William Ward in Serampore, India: "You will find it necessary to form what you proposed, a kind of Moravian settlement; as otherwise we do not see how they can be supported."

Strict discipline was another characteristic of the Moravian community, and the LMS lamented in 1796 that "we have not, like the Moravians, disciplined troops, but a hasty levy of irregulars ... and we are not to expect the subordination kept up in their missions."

A Martyr Mentality?

The Moravian missionaries seemed to specialise in going to remote, difficult, and dangerous regions. In the first 20 years of the movement, they could be found working in Greenland, the West Indies, the Arctic Circle, North America (among the Native Americans), Suriname, South Africa, Algiers, Ceylon, China, Persia, Ethiopia, and Labrador.

Perhaps their early experience of persecution and migration gave them a special sensitivity and empathy towards those who were marginalised and who might otherwise be overlooked.

"Christ Crucified and Nothing Else"

The above quotation, taken from 1 Corinthians 2:2, might be the most significant and lasting contribution of Moravian spirituality to missionary practice. We have already noted how this was a hallmark of the Herrnhut community, and after an initial false start, it became their distinctive message and one which influenced the whole of the later Protestant missionary movement.

Moravian missionaries arrived in Greenland in 1733 and worked alongside the existing Lutheran mission (albeit not without some tensions). At first, they followed the Lutheran style of preaching and sought to prove the existence and attributes of the one God (i.e., to "preach idolatry out of them") and then to enforce obedience to the divine law. As the Lutherans had already found, this attempt (which could be said to be based on Hebrews 6:1) made no significant impact on the indigenous shamanism.

In 1740, the Moravians reported their first convert, who had been "solidly awakened by the doctrine of Jesus' sufferings." They believed that the Holy Spirit had revealed this emphasis to them, and thereafter it became their approved method and message.

It led to some interesting experiments in contextualisation. Zinzendorf advised his missionaries in Greenland not to speak of Christ as a sacrifice, since the autochthonous shamanism knew no such concepts. Zinzendorf also is reputed to have said, "If the greatest need of the heathen is a needle, then we should call our Saviour a needle." Such attempts were vital, if the focus of Christ was to be maintained but also be meaningful at the same time.

It is possible, despite their mutual antagonism, that David Brainerd was influenced by the Moravian missionaries who worked within a few miles of him in Pennsylvania in 1744. The Moravians claimed that while he used "the usual method of preaching ... by connected arguments," he was ineffective, whereas when he "ventured straightaway to preach to them simply the Saviour," he and other Presbyterian ministers were "astonished by ... such a large and quick awakening."

The fifth clause of Carey, Marshman, and Ward's "Form of Agreement" (composed in 1805 to outline their methods in detail) refers to the Moravians specifically in this regard: "It is a well-known fact that the most successful missionaries in the world at the present day make the atonement of Christ their continued theme. We mean the Moravians. They attributed all their success to the preaching of the death of our Saviour...."

In summary, we see that the Moravians, by their communal lifestyle and their spirituality, established a model for missionary work which was not just successful in itself, but which had a profound influence on the emerging Protestant missionary movement of their century and the next.

In the contemporary era, when much of the focus of missiological thinking concentrates either on ecclesiology or pneumatology, it is perhaps also important to retain the Moravian emphasis on Christology.

Richard Tiplady *is the Associate Director of Global Connections (formerly known as the Evangelical Missionary Alliance) in the U.K. Prior to this, he worked in local church leadership and mission mobilisation. In 1993, he lectured in a theological college in Nigeria. He holds a theology degree from London University and a master's degree in theology from Nottingham University. He is married to Irene, and they have one son, Jamie.*

Jesuit community, spirituality, and mission

OF THE SEVERAL missionary models in the history of the Catholic church, I have chosen to consider some elements about the Jesuits and then to describe the way their spirituality and community life converted into concrete action in mission.

Ignatio de Loyola (1491–1556), a Spanish soldier, founded the Jesuit Order in 1534. He was wounded in a battle, and during his convalescence he experienced a religious conversion. After a period of intense prayer, he wrote a book called *Spiritual Exercises*, a kind of manual to bring people closer to Christ, with emphasis on the devotional life. According to John Veltri (p. 2), in his explanation about the writings of Ignatio during the months of prayer, he "noticed how God led him to pay attention to the diverse 'voices' inside of him, to the movements of consolation and desolation in his heart and spirit. He gradually learned to discern the sources of these desires, thoughts, and movements of the heart and spirit: which of them came from God and which of them drew him away from God, and most importantly, which of them he should act upon." Loyola found six other men who joined him in his spiritual efforts, and by vows of poverty, chastity, obedience to the Pope, and pilgrimage to Jerusalem, they started a new religious society. In 1540, Pope Paul III approved the organization of the order.

Loyola was a contemporary of Martin Luther and John Calvin and could be compared with them as a reformer within the Catholic church. "For Luther," says Latourette (1975, p. 843), "the path led to revolt from Rome and to the Protestant Reformation. For Loyola, there came an enhanced devotion to the Papacy and a discipline and an organization which were the major new force in effecting and shaping the Catholic Reformation."

BERTIL
EKSTRÖM

Innovations

The Jesuits introduced numerous innovations, breaking with medieval practices of penitence, fasts, and common uniform and choral recitations. Key words to characterize the Jesuits were mobility, adaptability, and flexibility. Their openness to society and to the changes taking place in their new times allowed them to become involved in a great variety of ministries in many parts of the world. The society grew rapidly, and in a few years the mission-driven Jesuits were found in many places, especially in Latin America, Asia, and Africa. Their missionary purpose was clear, and as a result of relative independence from the political authorities (e.g., the King of Spain), they had some freedom to demonstrate that priority. They served directly under the authority of the Pope, and obedience to him was one of their core values. One of the more famous Jesuits was Francis Xavier (1506–1552), who was a missionary to several places in Asia, particularly India and China.

The Jesuits described part of their mission "to advance souls on the way of Christian life and doctrine, to propagate the faith by public preaching and expounding Holy Scripture, to give the *Spiritual Exercises*, to do works of charity ... and to try to bring spiritual consolation to the faithful by hearing confession" (Latourette, 1975, p. 847).

Jesuit Spirituality

The understanding of spirituality among the Jesuits is based on Loyola's writings. The Society of Jesus should follow the example of Jesus "in a life of prayer and in a continuous search for how best to live as an authentic human being before a loving God." Veltri (p. 3) calls this an incarnational spirituality, giving practical action to the gospel values. In the same way that "Jesus preached forgiveness of sins, healed the sick and possessed, and gave hope to the poor and to those socially and economically outcast," the Jesuits should minister in their society.

But Ignatio argued that this spirituality is also realistic. It is a daily struggle between good and evil, and there must be a sensibility to what kind of works should be done for the best of the people and what God's will is for the concrete situation.

Ignatio's "Prayer for Generosity" is a good example of what he meant:
"Lord, teach me to be generous.
Teach me to serve you as you deserve;
To give and not to count the cost,
To fight and not to heed the wounds,
To toil and not to seek for rest,
To labor and not to ask for reward,
Save that of knowing that I do your will."

The Jesuits in Latin America

The first Jesuits came to Latin America in 1549, less than 10 years after papal approval of the order. They stayed until 1767, when they were expelled from Spain and from all the colonies because of the conflict between the missionary church and the colonial Hispanic civilization. Pope Clement XIV abolished the order in 1773, but it was reestablished in 1814 by Pope Pius VII.

In their work in Latin America, the method used by the Jesuits was that of the *tabula rasa* ("blank slate"). They assumed that the indigenous tribes needed to start from scratch, both in their religious life and in the organization of their society. That did not hinder the Jesuits from using some of the cultural expressions of the native peoples. The famous *reducciones* ("reductions") were, in many places in Latin America, their main project. The communities included school education, agriculture, cultural events, religious life, and catechism. Like the Celtic orders, all was done in a combination of spirituality and community, shown in missiological practice. One key idea of the *reducciones* affirmed that it was possible to live a community life, sharing everything and building a just and harmonious society. It was a kind of community development, where the Amerindian peoples participated in the administration and benefited by the growth. Of course, that was a problem for the Spanish colonizers to accept. They wanted the Indians to work for them as slaves and not to be their equals in any sense. So the Jesuits were forced to abandon their missions, and the *reducciones* were destroyed either by the *conquistadores* or by themselves in the absence of the leadership of the friars.

Methodology

Pablo Deiros (1992, p. 290), Argentinean Baptist church historian, cites Fernando Mires' book, *Colonization of the Souls in Hispano America*, synthesizing the methodology of the Jesuits in the following points:

1. They studied and learned the indigenous language (the Guarany).

2. They assured that the *reducciones* were isolated from the Spanish cities.

3. They tended to respect the basic political relation between the leaders (*caciques*) of the indigenous tribes.

4. They won over the Indians by helping them to develop their artistic activities (music, handicraft, painting, etc.).

5. They practiced the religious "accommodations" as Francisco Xavier had done in India.

6. They practiced a kind of economic accommodation, improving the system used by the Indians.

According to the French historian Clovis Lugon (1977), the Jesuits founded a Christian Communist Republic in Paraguay, so strong were their emphases on common ownership and on the sharing of outcomes by all individuals in the community.

Their defense of the indigenous people is a rich lesson for us today. Bartolomeu de las Casas, a Dominican, had earlier shown the way. The Jesuits took the Indians' side against the Spanish and Portuguese *colonizadores*. They gave the Guaranies human status and value as people created by God.

Paternalism and Superficiality

But there were also weaknesses in the Jesuit form of work. They forced the Indians into a kind of community life that they were not used to, and when the Jesuits had to leave, those model societies were dispersed and, in some cases, destroyed. The paternalistic way of acting never allowed the Indians to take over the responsibility for the community. Stephen Neill (1982, p. 203) makes the following commentary about the work of the Jesuits in Paraguay: "The weakness of all this great enterprise was that the Jesuits did so little to develop a sense of initiative and independence among their flock. They seemed to wish rather to have around them docile children than to train adults for self-government. They had complete control of the situation for more than a century; in that time they never brought forward a single candidate for the priesthood and developed no order of religious women or nuns."

Another problem was the superficial way that the Indians had received the Christian faith. Although different from their own experience of renewal and strong spiritual experiences, the Jesuits seem not to have had the same concern for deep spirituality among the new converts. The focus was more on orthodoxy than on real conversion (Deiros, 1992, p. 358). The result was a superficial and nominal Christendom, typical of many places in Latin America to the present day.

Holistic Mission

What we learn from the Jesuits is that spirituality can lead both to an active participation in the society and a holistic practice of the gospel. Their sense of community life was not limited to themselves, but rather they wanted to share their Christian principles with others. Only in mission could the spiritual and community life be meaningful. We can criticize the Catholic Orders in general and the Jesuits in particular for not having the right approach to the gospel and not preaching faith in Jesus as we understand it. They can also be charged for their ways of doing things and imposing the Catholic beliefs on the indigenous tribes. But we cannot deny that they had a deep concern to reach their own unreached peoples and to establish a holistic model of life that we very often lack in our mission work today.

References

Deiros, P. (1992). *Historia del Cristianismo en America Latina* [The history of Christianity in Latin America]. Buenos Aires, Argentina: FTL.

Dussel, E. (1981). *A history of the church in Latin America: Colonialism to liberation.* Grand Rapids, MI: Wm. B. Eerdmans Publishing Co.

Ekström, B. (1995). *The Paraguayan culture: The syndrome of the pombero.* Academic paper. São Paulo, Brazil: FTBSP.

Jesuits. (1992). *The new encyclopedia Britannica. Vol. 6.* Chicago, IL.

Latourette, K. S. (1975). *A history of Christianity: Vol. II. Reformation to the present* (rev. ed.). New York: Harper & Row.

Lugon, C. (1977). *A República "Comunista" Cristã dos Guaranis (La Republique Communiste Chretienne des Guaranis) – 1610/1768.* Rio de Janeiro, Brazil: Paz e Terra.

Mellis, C. (1976). *Committed communities: Fresh streams for world missions.* Pasadena, CA: William Carey Library.

Neill, S. (1982). *A history of Christian missions.* New York: Penguin Books.

Veltri, J. *Presentation of the Jesuit spirituality.* In the web page managed by Rev. Raymond Bucko of the Department of Sociology and Anthropology at Le Moyne College, the Jesuit College of Central New York.

Bertil Ekström was born in Sweden and with his wife, Alzira, they have four children. Ekstrom is a missionary kid who has lived in Brazil since he was four years old. A Baptist pastor and seminary teacher, from 1991 to 1995 he was president of the Brazilian Association of Cross-Cultural Agencies, and from 1997 to 2000 he has served as president of COMIBAM, the Latin American continental missions network. He serves on the Executive Committee of the WEF Missions Commission. He is a staff member of Interact, a Swedish Baptist mission, and is affiliated with the Convention of the Independent Baptist Churches of Brazil. He has a master's degree in theology from the Theology Faculty of the Baptist Seminary of São Paulo.

38

Coptic community, spirituality, and mission

HOW WAS IT THAT the Coptic church was able to endure years and years of a harsh regime bent on obliterating it? Its survival can be greatly attributed to the monastic communities within the church that conserved its spirituality and flavor, thus enabling the church to carry out missions both within and outside of Egypt for the length of time that it did.

It is understood by many that the Coptic church was the first to take Christianity to Ireland through the monks of the Monastery of St. Mena. From Ireland, Christianity spread to the rest of the British Isles—Wales, Scotland, and England. This constituted the earliest outreach by the Coptic church in missions that served as a precursor to their future missions. The Coptic church is said to have been founded by the Apostle Mark as the church of Alexandria and Libya, the first among the Pentapolis churches which extended from Barka eastwards to Tunisia during the first Christian century. In the 4th century, the church had two Bishops in Libya. Today there are two churches there—one in Tripoli and the other in Bani-Gazi.

In the time of St. Athanasias (4th century), the Coptic church was established in Ethiopia, and its first bishop, St. Fremontious, was consecrated in A.D. 329. The church in Nubia was also established, which remained under the pastoral care of the Coptic church until the revolution of the 19th century. Meanwhile, they remained under the Pope of Alexandria, along with the Nubian, Libyan, Ethiopian, and Pentapolis churches. With Jerusalem, today they compose the See of St. Mark.

The pages of the Coptic chronicles are littered with detailed accounts of religious harassment motivated by religious intolerance. The spread of Islam during the 7th and 8th centuries in Egypt affected the Coptic church, though it neither

FRANCIS OMONDI

obliterated her nor totally quenched her missions drive. With the coming of the Muslim rule in Egypt, the church came under very harsh rule. Laws were developed concerning places of worship, depending on the conquest and the terms of treaties. Conversions, construction of new churches, and the erection of synagogues were forbidden. However, limited restoration of worship places was permitted with certain restrictions. From the beginning of the Islamic conquest, Christians had been forced to cede to the Muslims half of their churches, which then became mosques. Muslims imposed restrictions on the use of bells, on burial ceremonies, and on construction of worship places.

Destruction policies were also carried out against the churches, monasteries, and convents. For instance, when Mohammed al-Mudabbin arrived in Egypt as a minister of finance in A.D. 861, he tripled the *jyzya* (taxes paid by Christians) and ordered churches to be pillaged. The *diwah* (money and alms) intended for the bishopric and the monastery were confiscated. Monks were imprisoned, while patriarchs who were unable to pay the taxes demanded from the Coptic episcopate fled from place to place and went into hiding. As long as Muslims have ruled Egypt, the hold on Christians there has not changed as such. Yet in spite of these difficulties, the church has been able to develop a focus on mission.

Entering Our Days

The contemporary mission movement in the Coptic church is embedded in the story of Bishop Antonios Marcos, the bishop of Africa affairs in the Coptic church. In the decade of the 1950s, the churches began outreaches that catapulted them into greater service in missions. In a youth meeting at St. Mary's Church in Faggala, Cairo, a servant made

an appeal for volunteers who would be willing to serve in the outlying villages outside Cairo and in the farming areas where no one went. As a high school student involved in the youth programs of the church, Marcos went out to serve, unaware that he was sparking the beginning of a mission movement within the Coptic church. He showed a keen desire to serve in the region, although his fellow servants were not in favor of reaching out to the cultures in which they had not been raised. Nevertheless, during the outreaches in the villages, they learned how to understand these different cultures so strange to them and to discern the kind of entrance they should seek so that their mission and services would be accepted. These were the key lessons:

1. Listen well and observe carefully before drawing any conclusions.

2. Understand the mind of the people and their way of thinking before doing anything that may conflict with their customs and belief. This will avoid initial rejection.

3. Learn their own language. You will thus win their hearts, because the people's tongues are very dear to them. Once you speak to them in their own languages, their hearts will open, and they will listen to you.

The way these young Christian workers to the villages came to the level of the local people was crucial. They were not seeking to change their cultural life as much as they wanted to transform their spiritual life. They were able to gather people in community around the Word of God, from children to youth to adults, in a real atmosphere of fellowship. This resulted in spiritual joy—the joy of praising and singing, of comfort in prayers, and of belonging to one body.

After Marcos served in the villages, he enrolled in the university to study medicine. There every book he read and every movie he watched about mission work in Africa stirred him. He soon confessed a desire to serve in Africa, which was seen at that time as a strange spiritual ambition for his generation.

The church was trying to upgrade the standards of the pastoral service to the people and to prepare new priests and servants in the same fields. Even missions began to be considered part of the pastoral work of the church. But the church recognized that they did not have the ability nor the experience nor sufficiently equipped servants to serve people of other cultures. Without any clear direction, Marcos finally chose to serve as a tentmaker in Ethiopia. As a medical practitioner, he found doors opened to him to meet people's health needs as well as spiritual needs. Ironically, he had earlier not wished to go to Ethiopia, knowing that the church there had its own patriarch, bishops, and institutions. He had wanted to serve among a people who knew nothing about the Lord.

So Marcos went to Ethiopia with the blessing of the church, but with the understanding that he was on his own to meet his needs. Thus began what in subsequent years became a new missions outreach of the modern Coptic church in Africa beyond the borders of Egypt and south of the equator.

In Ethiopia, Marcos had a remarkable career. He was greatly loved by the people and even offered citizenship: he had become so identified with the culture, the people, and the church that they considered him Ethiopian. He returned to Egypt soon after the Ethiopian Revolution of 1974. There he entered the monastic life with the monks of Baramose Monastery. The monastic life was saturated with prayer, meditation, the practice of psalmodic praises, and long vigils into the night hours. This spiritual community became a source of great spiritual energy for the church and the launching pad for further missions into Africa.

It was during this time in the monastery that the increasingly tragic news about the difficult situation throughout Africa stirred the hearts of the monks towards the peoples of Africa. The thought that there was no Coptic mission serving these peoples was distressing to them. The continent and its people began to fill their prayers, though they had no way of following through beyond prayer. The Western churches of Catholicism and Protestantism had arrived in Africa as early as the 15th and 18th centuries, respectively. Yet the Coptic church, which had had no influence, was now beginning to cast its mission vision towards Kenya, Uganda, Tanzania, Zambia, and the Congo.

First, they had to recruit missionaries to serve the needs across Africa. This led them in the 1960s to inaugurate the Institute of African Studies in the theological college of the Coptic church. In the 1970s, scores of young men to be sent to Kenya, Uganda, Ghana, and Zaire were trained in a monastic approach to dogma, theological history, canons, and traditions in order to shape them for service.

The challenge of poverty was inevitable as these missionaries served in the context of Africa. But the Coptic missionaries found they could equip the people to meet their own needs by training them in handicrafts and practical skills by which they could become self-supporting. This should be understood in the context of a church that itself had little financial capital to help alleviate the poverty in which they found themselves.

Coming to a Close

The Copts initiated their modern African ministries at a time when other missions had already claimed great exploits in the region where they were working.

Therefore, they decided to focus on raising up indigenous churches in areas that lay far off the beaten tack. One of their unique contributions was to establish monasteries which in turn became centers of training and of spiritual formation for the people.

This monastic-centered approach to mission, which also shaped the early Irish missionaries of previous centuries, has once again flowered within the Coptic church. It is now bearing good fruit within the nations of sub-Saharan Africa. The ancient faith once delivered to the Copts of Egypt by the Apostle Mark continues to bear fruit to the honor and glory of the Triune God.

Francis Omondi and his wife Anne have three boys. They serve with Sheepfold Ministries, a Kenyan Mission agency that plants churches among unreached people groups (especially Muslims) in East Africa. They are involved in training and sending cross-cultural church planters. Francis founded Sheepfold Ministries while a student at Kenyatta University in Kenya (1988), and he has directed the organization for the last 12 years. He is an ordained priest in the Anglican Church of Kenya. He holds a degree in education and economics from Kenyatta University. He is a WEF Missions Commission Associate.

39

Brazilian Antioch community, spirituality, and mission

BARBARA BURNS

THE ANTIOCH MISSION, Brazil's first interdenominational national missions agency, was born within the context of a Bible school in the interior of the State of Paraná.

In the late 1960s, a charismatic revival swept churches in several regions of Brazil. In the north of Paraná, several churches under the leadership of Jonathan Ferreira dos Santos, a newly graduated Presbyterian pastor, adopted the renewal and began experiencing miraculous church growth and vitality. Within a few years, over 30 young men and women felt called to full-time ministry and went to Pastor Jonathan for help. They were already engaged in evangelism, preaching, teaching, and miraculous healings and deliverances from Satanic forces; they acutely felt the need to band together for prayer and for gaining more Bible knowledge and practical skills.

Pastor Jonathan and his wife invited the women to live in their house, and he rented a neighboring house for the men. Thus began their studies and life together. Because the numbers rapidly increased, Pr. Jonathan was able to get a piece of property for a school as a donation from the city of Cianorte. On the weekends, everyone had ministry assignments. During the week each day after classes, students and teachers cleared the forest, laid bricks, and built their own school. By 1970 there were over 100 students.

This school was not for adolescent students. Students were not invited by someone to learn to be future ministers. They were already active, seeking the Lord for help and spiritual growth. This led to a community developed through their own efforts, with the guidance of Pr. Jonathan and other leaders who were joining him.

When I arrived at the school in 1971, I was amazed at the vitality of prayer, at the practice of preaching in every available place, at the miracles, and at the togetherness of a student-run school. Students prayed together, often all night or early in the morning. They all participated in church planting teams. They prayed for the sick and oppressed and possessed. They fasted. They worked in the garden, cleaned toilets, cut the grass, ran the office and kitchen teams, and monitored the dormitories. Class-bound theory was offered within this active community context.

Up until the early 1970s, the school's missions vision remained limited to the 400 km radius around Cianorte. A census taken in the early 1970s revealed that 20% of the population in the region was Evangelical,[1] due in part to the Bible school's practical ministry.

In 1972, several factors led to an enlarged missions vision and outreach. Leslie Brierly (a World Evangelization Crusade missionary) visited the school and showed missionary slides. Robert Harvey, also of WEC, became acquainted with Pr. Jonathan and begin influencing him toward world mission. Missions began to be taught in the classroom, and eventually a course on cross-cultural missions was included in the curriculum.

In spite of these influences, most of the students were still doubtful and critical of the idea of cross-cultural missions. Then one morning, during the devotional period of a missions class, the idea of missions caught fire. One of the skeptical students started to pray. Suddenly he began crying and knelt down on the rough cement floor, asking God to forgive him for not accepting missions as part of God's plan for the churches and for his own life.

Within seconds, the entire class was praying and crying. Other classes heard the prayers and came to join in. The whole school community prayed until noon. Because it was a spiritual community and not a traditional formal school, it was all right for the students to pour out their hearts together. It was all right to hear from the Lord. God could speak to these students and shake them out of their traditional outreach limits and make them see his love for the world.

Within a short time, a vital missions movement had sprouted. Watered by occasional critically important God-sent outside forces, it blossomed into a world-wide outreach which continues to grow even now.

The school, which, after some low points, has regained its original number of students, continues with a missions emphasis, offers a master's degree in missions, and continues a mission prayer ministry. The school's denomination has its own missions agency with several missionaries world-wide.

Of wider significance was the birth of the Antioch Mission in 1975. A new graduate, who had been touched by the new cross-cultural missionary emphasis in class, was sent to Mozambique in 1974 to work with drug addicts. After a short time, he was caught in the middle of the Marxist revolution and was imprisoned, along with his American colleagues. When the students and teachers in Cianorte heard of his imprisonment, they were electrified—some to scoffing and criticism, others to prayer and brokenness.

A small group began to pray for their friend Clesius each day at a set time, and God began to speak to that group and show them that it was not just for Clesius that they must pray, but for Mozambique,

---

[1] This number is from memory, and the exact date of the census is uncertain.

for Africa, and for the world. In one meeting, they joined hands in an emotional moment and vowed to give their lives for missions. They decided on that day to form an organization that could inform and challenge the churches to send and support missionaries and to pray for Clesius and future Brazilian missionaries. They even decided on a name—the Antioch Mission.

To that original group came Pr. Jonathan and Pr. Decio de Azevedo, the Antioch Mission's first elected president, along with many others. The Mission was legally organized and registered in 1978, and in its constitution declared: "The Antioch Mission is an Evangelical, interdenominational Association, ... with the purpose of announcing the glory of God among the nations and of making disciples of our Lord and Saviour Jesus Christ, inspired in the work of the Holy Spirit in the New Testament church in Antioch, which, having been born through missionary effort, became a missionary church. The Antioch Mission desires to help Evangelical churches fulfill their missionary responsibility in the world, participating in the spiritual and material support of those sent."

The Mission eventually moved to Londrina and then to São Paulo, each time broadening its sphere of influence. Churches began to hear about missions, and schools were challenged to help prepare cross-cultural missionaries. In 1977, the Mission started its own training school, with one student and one teacher; it now has a full-blown seminary and missions training program. Over 150 missionaries have been prepared and sent to the field.

The Antioch Mission was also involved and influential in the formation of an Association of Brazilian Cross-Cultural Missions Agencies (AMTB) and has been active in leadership in the AMTB over the years.

(The AMTB sees the need for cooperation and mutual help between agencies.) From the AMTB came the Association of Brazilian Missions Teachers (APMB), an active association which offers consultations and missiological literature to missions teachers.

From spirituality and community to mission. That is exactly what happened and in that order. Can one exist without the other? The Antioch Mission came from a spiritual community and has sought to create wider spiritual and missionary communities. It continues to operate as a community model, with students and teachers living together to learn and to minister, just as in Cianorte, but now with a nationwide and world-wide outreach.

Barbara Burns was born in Pasadena, California, and was raised between Palm Desert, California, and Prescott, Arizona. Moving every year between the two places gave her the first exposure to an aspect of good missionary training! Her educational background includes the West Suburban Hospital School of Nursing, Chicago; Arizona State University, BSN; Denver Seminary, MREM; and a D.Miss. from Trinity Evangelical Divinity School in 1987. Over the last 23 years, Barbara has served as a missions teacher across Brazil in a diversity of schools. For six years she was the Executive Secretary for the Brazilian Association of Missions Teachers. Currently she is the Educational Coordinator for the Centro Nordestino de Missões missionary training program in Brazil. She is an Executive Committee member of the WEF Missions Commission.

Part 7

Accepting serious commitments

WE CONCLUDE THIS PUBLICATION with a diverse commentary on the Iguassu Affirmation by eight colleagues from seven nations. All were present in Brazil: Prado, Wood, Ross, Fountain, Girón, Stamoolis, Anyomi, and Castillo. They offer their own personal and diverse perspectives on this document. They represent women and men, pastors and missionaries, practitioners, theologians, and missiologists from North and South, East and West. They represent gifted and godly colleagues from the borderless church of Christ. They represent the reflective practitioners who offer such promise to the future. They each speak to different aspects of the Affirmation that touched them personally. In so doing, they refract the light of the glorious diamond of our global Evangelical missiology.

Drawing to a close, the final word comes to challenge the reflective, passionate, and globalized practitioner. Suggestions and recommendations are made to continue the process that was initiated at Iguassu and that is now presented in this missiological volume.

But much remains to be done. We invite and challenge the leadership of our borderless church of Christ. This specific word is directed to local church and denominational leaders, to students and faculty of the theological education

institutions and missionary training centres, to the missionary sending structures and member care networks, and to the national, regional, or international missionary movements and networks. We cannot afford to live and serve with a spirit of autonomy and independence. May our global Evangelical movement be known by that unique and Spirit-empowered combination of action and reflection, study and strategy. Let us remember and emulate the superb example of that great reflective practitioner, the Apostle Paul: evangelist, missionary, church planter, team leader, strategist, missiologist, theologian, and author.

To the Triune Father, Son, and Spirit alone be the high glory!

40

The Iguassu Affirmation: a commentary by eight reflective practitioners

FOLLOWING IS THE TEXT of the Iguassu Affirmation, as in chapter 2, but here the sections are interspersed with comments from eight reflective practitioners. The following commentators were selected:

- Pastor from the Two-Thirds World: Oswaldo Prado, Brazil
- Pastor from North America: John Wood
- Practitioner/missiologist from the South Pacific: Cathy Ross
- Practitioner/missiologist from Europe: Jeff Fountain
- Practitioner/missiologist from Latin America: Rudy Girón
- Missiologist/theologian from North America: Jim Stamoolis
- Practitioner/missiologist from Africa: Seth Anyomi
- Practitioner/missiologist from Asia: Met Castillo

The Iguassu Affirmation
Preamble

We have convened as 160 mission practitioners, missiologists, and church leaders from 53 countries, under the World Evangelical Fellowship Missions Commission in Foz do Iguassu, Brazil, on October 10-15, 1999 to:

1. Reflect together on the challenges and opportunities facing world missions at the dawn of the new millennium.

2. Review the different streams of 20th century Evangelical missiology and practice, especially since the 1974 Lausanne Congress.

OSWALDO PRADO
JOHN WOOD
CATHY ROSS
JEFF FOUNTAIN
RUDY GIRÓN
JIM STAMOOLIS
SETH ANYOMI
MET CASTILLO

3. Continue developing and applying a relevant biblical missiology which reflects the cultural diversity of God's people.

We proclaim the living Christ in a world torn by ethnic conflicts, massive economic disparity, natural disasters, and ecological crises. The mission task is both assisted and hindered by technological developments that now reach the remotest corners of the earth. The diverse religious aspirations of people, expressed in multiple religions and spiritual experimentation, challenge the ultimate truth of the gospel.

In the 20th century, missiology witnessed unprecedented development. In recent years, reflection from many parts of the church has helped missions to continue shedding paternalistic tendencies. Today, we continue to explore the relationship between the gospel and culture, between evangelism and social responsibility, and between biblical mandates and the social sciences. We see some international organizations—among them World Evangelical Fellowship, the Lausanne Committee for World Evangelization, and the AD 2000 and Beyond Movement—that have begun a promising process of partnership and unity.

Increased efforts at partnership have been catalyzed by an emphasis on methodologies involving measurable goals and numerical growth. Flowing from a commitment to urgent evangelization, these methodologies have shown how our task might be accomplished. However, these insights must be subject to biblical principles and growth in Christlikeness.

We rejoice in diverse missiological voices emerging around the world, but we confess that we have not taken them all into our theory and practice. Old paradigms still prevail. Participation by and awareness of the global church, as well as mission from people of all nations to

people of all nations, are needed for a valid missiology in our time.

Our discussions have invited us to fuller dependence on the Spirit's empowering presence in our life and ministry as we eagerly await the glorious return of our Lord Jesus Christ.

In the light of these realities, we make the following declarations.

Commentary by Oswaldo Prado

The meeting promoted by the WEF Missions Commission in Brazil, in October 1999, was remarkable. Besides happening in a Third World country, the moment couldn't have been more propitious because we were about to conclude another stage of missions history—the Second Millennium.

With an objective of proclaiming Christ in a fallen world, which is subject to all kinds of social and economic differences, the meeting echoed the passion of everybody's heart. From the perspective of a pastor who lives in a country where a few own too much and the majority live with practically nothing, how does one live and also spread to the whole world the kingdom of God? Thinking about these matters has had an enormous impact on my heart, for I have ministered for 20 years in a local church in the metropolis of São Paulo.

Iguassu raised other questions: How do we reconcile the Brazilian expatriate missionary heritage, which has often been paternalistic, with the fact that because we were poor we received not only qualified missionaries but also financial resources during a great part of the 20th century? Are we capable of fulfilling the mission now without foreign resources? Also, how are we to explain the growth of the missionary movement in these last years, which has characterized the church of Latin America, Africa, and some places in Asia?

What we realized at that memorable Iguassu meeting was that the 160 mission leaders in attendance, some of them pastors, were open to listening to what the Holy Spirit would say at that critical moment of history. Those who came from nations with long missionary traditions, as well as those who have experienced a missionary church in their countries for only a few decades, gathered together to reflect on the challenges of a relevant study of missions as it relates to a new millennium.

Commentary by John Wood

It is a privilege to have been among those who gathered in Foz do Iguassu on October 10-15, 1999, for the WEF Missions Commission's missiological consultation. My perspective is that of a white, North American pastor of an affluent suburban congregation. I carried two overarching concerns to the consultation. First, how can independent-minded, entrepreneurial Evangelicals express the unity for which our Lord fervently prayed the night before his crucifixion—a unity so winsome and visible that it will validate the gospel (John 17:21, 23)? And second, how can affluent Christians truly partner with Christians of limited financial resources without reinforcing patterns of dominance and dependence? The time spent in worship and fellowship with brothers and sisters from around the world was a particular pleasure. The papers and workshops were stimulating. The daily Bible teaching of Ajith Fernando was challenging and convicting to one accustomed to the comforts and assumptions of American life.

The Iguassu Affirmation produced by the conference bears all the marks of what it is (a paper written by a small, culturally diverse committee and edited by the entire assembly acting as a committee-of-the-whole) and of what it is intended to become (a working paper to be taken into different cultural contexts as a starting point for further missiological reflection). It is filled with good things, but many of them are buried treasure because, until one reaches the section entitled Commitments, there seems to be neither a compelling and clear outline guiding the presentation, nor a clear statement of the themes being discussed, but merely a collating of good things that ought to be said or of topics offered for further reflection. On closer look, however, there is an internal structure in the first two sections that helps someone like me better appreciate the early sections of the Affirmation.

The opening paragraph of the Preamble gives three reasons for the consultation having been convened. The paper then turns to the global context in which we serve. To a world facing ethnic, economic, and ecological crises and religious pluralism, "we proclaim the living Christ." The Preamble is almost entirely Christological in its focus, with only one reference to "the Spirit's empowering presence" and none to God the Father, while the three following sections of the Affirmation are self-consciously trinitarian. The paper would be stronger and more internally consistent, I think, if the Preamble established a trinitarian foundation for what follows. However, I suspect that the Christological focus is in response to the problem of religious pluralism that denies the uniqueness of Christ.

Five themes begin to emerge in the Preamble that receive fuller treatment in the Declarations and Commitments, namely, the ultimate truth of the gospel and the following four needs: the need for holistic missions, for increasing partnership and unity among Evangelical organizations, for a biblical critique of missiological methodologies, and for a greater diversity of "missiological voices" shaping our reflection. Because these themes are addressed more fully in the sections that follow, the paper would, I think, be stronger if the Preamble omitted its third, fourth, and fifth paragraphs (beginning with, "In the 20th century, missiology witnessed …" and ending with, "… for a valid missiology in our time"). The Preamble would then focus on the cultural contexts in which we do missiological reflection and would set the stage for what follows: "In the light of these realities, we make the following declarations."

Commentary by Cathy Ross

I gladly present my personal interaction with the Iguassu Affirmation. I write this from the perspective of a privileged white woman, who has lived and worked in the Democratic Republic of Congo (formerly Zaire) as a CMS mission partner and who now teaches missiology in Aotearoa/New Zealand.

I applaud the efforts of the WEF to bring together mission practitioners, missiologists, and church leaders from all over the world to reflect on mission in this new era. However, as a woman, I was shocked and disappointed at how few women were at the consultation. Of the 160 participants, 19 were women. Where were the women? There are approximately twice as many women as men working in mission around the world, so it is indeed lamentable that so few attended a consultation such as this. The Preamble rightly states, "Old paradigms still prevail." How true this is when it comes to hearing and experiencing women's perspectives on mission.

The Preamble also states, "In recent years, reflection from many parts of the church has helped missions to continue shedding paternalistic tendencies." Thankfully, we are coming to the realization that the centre of gravity for Christianity has shifted and is now to be found in the South

rather than the North. We are slowly beginning to realize the essential nature of partnership between North and South and that we in the North (or West or whatever designation you prefer—Aotearoa/New Zealand fits neither!) desperately need the insights, challenges, and vitality of our Christian sisters and brothers from the South to enlarge and enliven our faith and witness.

Equally essential is the nature of partnership between men and women in mission. It is glaringly and painfully obvious that we as Evangelicals are lacking the insights, the vision, and the heart of women in mission. In the Republic of South Africa, they speak of "affirmative action appointments," so that marginalized groups can enter spheres which were open only to whites in the apartheid era. If only the Evangelical world could enable similar affirmative action for women in mission, so that just as we were created in the image of God to complement one another, we could listen and learn from one another in the fullness of the body of Christ.

Commentary by Jeff Fountain

Our departing plane rose and banked over the gigantic Iguassu Falls, the awesome natural backdrop to our consultation. From the air, I could clearly see the great watershed where the broad, brown river plunged suddenly into the gorge below, with some 265 wild torrents of foam gradually merging into a chocolate ribbon winding on downstream through the dark green tropical vegetation.

That image remains indelibly imprinted on my mind. And since my return to Europe, it lingers as a striking metaphor for the occasion of the consultation. The great watershed of the millennium transition loomed large during our deliberations. We were conscious that the new century would bring unprecedented challenges and opportunities. The last decade of the 20th century had warned of white water approaching. The rate of global change had increased dramatically. A major break with the familiar past was imminent. While the round figure of 2000 was an arbitrary milestone of history with no particular eschatological significance, it happened to coincide with mega-shifts in culture, communications, politics, economy, and beliefs. Historians would likely look back on this millennial turnover as a great historical discontinuity.

For those of us at the consultation from Europe, that was especially true. Marxism had imploded, and Christendom's long millennium of power and privilege was rapidly nearing its end. Increasing numbers of Europeans were now post-Communist, post-Christian, and post-modern. What would the New Europe look like in the opening decades of the new millennium?

This was a crucial moment to consult and evaluate and seek God's wisdom together. How would the Evangelical missions movement negotiate this approaching turbulence? So then, how does the Iguassu Affirmation reflect our state of readiness, as the world Evangelical mission community, for the changes rushing headlong towards us?

As stated in the Preamble, "Old paradigms still prevail"—and, we might add, they die hard. Futurologist Patrick Dixon warns that those stuck in last century's paradigms risk being labeled "pre-millennialists"! Whatever our eschatology, it is imperative that we all make the transition to "post-millennial" paradigms. It would be a Y2K tragedy of major proportions if the Evangelical community remained in a time warp.

Commentary by
Rudy Girón

The first thought that comes to my mind when I think of the Iguassu Consultation is Proverbs 15:22, "Plans fail for lack of counsel, but with many advisers they succeed." The Affirmation that came out of the discussion of 160 missiologists, practitioners, missionaries, theologians, and others is really a product of corporate wisdom. Women and men from 53 nationalities, representing a great variety of theological, missiological, and denominational positions, were present that week. So we can look at the Iguassu Affirmation as a good attempt to express a corporate missiology. The Affirmation was a challenge to achieve with such diversity of cultures, ages, perspectives, and languages represented in that event.

Commentary by
Jim Stamoolis

One of the main reasons the Iguassu Affirmation will be a pivotal document for the missiological community lies in its approach to the contemporary situation. Taking full cognizance of the historical and social factors that have shaped and continue to shape the practice of missions, the Affirmation demonstrates that it is rooted in the historical continuum. It is in interaction with and in critical reflection on the prevailing methodologies of mission that the Affirmation attempts to define the new paradigms. While the document betrays its origins as having the stamp of a committee rather than the seemingly smooth hand of a single author, it is remarkable in its even-handed approach to very complex issues. The drafting process, involving three full drafts that were presented to the entire consultation and a marathon revision session lasting three and a half hours, ensured that many viewpoints would be heard. As a member of the drafting committee, I had a sense of cooperation and interaction that I had scarcely believed possible.

As the Preamble amply demonstrates, before moving on to a new formulation, we must give recognition to the factors that have shaped the present paradigm or, perhaps more properly, the present paradigms. Economics and politics have always been an issue in missionary work, yet at times it has been deemed unspiritual to acknowledge their power to shape mission practice. What tended to happen in the course of European missions from the time of the Counter-Reformation on was for missionaries to use the economic and political structures as vehicles for mission. While there often was criticism of economic and political exploitation, the situation in a post-colonial environment requires the mission agencies to understand the neocolonial pressures that impact the gospel, both in the sending countries and in the receiving countries.

Mission is not just social science applied to a religious environment, but the social sciences can shed light on the application of the gospel. Context is all-important for mission. One of the strengths of the Affirmation is that the document is deeply rooted in the realities of history as well as the present situation. This is particularly evident in the Commitments section that lists member care along with the expected topics such as spiritual warfare. The Affirmation is an accurate assessment of the current situation of mission and an attempt to speak a prophetic word about the challenges ahead for the missionary enterprise.

Commentary by
Seth Anyomi

The Iguassu Affirmation in mission history may be viewed as a watershed—the great divide between an old and new era in missions. The venue of this historic WEF Missions Commission gathering in Brazil,

a Two-Thirds World country, signifies the recognition the world is placing on the new direction of the global missionary movement. As a millennium makes an exit and another is ushered in, for us who participated in this significant meeting, the experience was more than words can describe.

The Preamble underlines the unity forged by the global community of practitioners, missiologists, and church leaders from the 53 countries gathered. The challenges and opportunities were viewed through the lens of this togetherness. The review of the past centered upon unity in diversity. The future focuses on the different peoples and cultures united by a common biblical missiology, contextualized in these various cultural domains. Jesus is declared as the living reality and answer to the complexities of our world.

Commentary by
Met Castillo

I am honored to interact with the Iguassu Affirmation. I do so from the perspective of an Asian mission leader with the Evangelical Fellowship of Asia and as a missiologist and practitioner at the same time.

I was privileged to be one of the 160 participants in the Iguassu Missiological Consultation, representing the Missions Commission of the Evangelical Fellowship of Asia and the missions movement in the Philippines. I believe that from the inception of the plan, there was an honest attempt to secure a fair representation from the younger sending churches as well as the older sending countries.

I appreciated the three-fold purpose of the consultation, but I was more interested in spending adequate time reflecting together on the challenges and opportunities facing world mission. I also sensed a great deal of freedom and objectivity in the discussions. There was, of course, the tendency for the English speakers to respond more quickly than those whose mother tongue is not English, but the atmosphere was non-threatening. Reflecting together was the key.

The relevance of Christ as the message of missions must never be diminished. Christ is the unchanging message to a fast-changing and diverse world. The uniqueness of Christ must be proclaimed without apology in polytheistic Asia.

We have gone a long way on the road to partnership in missions, but a lot more has to be done, particularly in the areas of how we partner and whom we partner with. A common perception is that partnership appears to be a game of the "big players." While this type of partnership could serve as a teaching model and a source of encouragement for the "small players," it is certainly one-sided and tends to be exclusive. Strategies and methodologies are often minted by Western missiologists and then transported to the rest of the world. The small players often become implementers. But Iguassu produced a resounding voice calling for interdependent partnership that involves the global church.

Declarations

Our faith rests on the absolute authority of the God-breathed Scriptures. We are heirs of the great Christian confessions handed down to us. All three Persons of the Godhead are active in God's redeeming mission. Our missiology centers on the overarching biblical theme of God's creation of the world, the Father's redeeming love for fallen humanity as revealed in the incarnation, substitutionary death, and resurrection of our Lord Jesus Christ, and ultimately of the redemption and renewal of the whole creation. The Holy Spirit, promised by our Lord, is our com-

forter, teacher, and source of power. It is the Spirit who calls us into holiness and integrity. The Spirit leads the church into all truth. The Spirit is the agent of mission, convicting of sin, righteousness, and judgment. We are Christ's servants, empowered and led by the Spirit, whose goal is to glorify God.

We confess the following themes as truths of special importance in this present age. These themes are clearly attested to in the whole of the Scriptures and speak to the desire of God to provide salvation for all people.

1. Jesus Christ is Lord of the church and Lord of the universe.

Ultimately every knee will bow and every tongue confess that Jesus is Lord. The Lordship of Christ is to be proclaimed to the whole world, inviting all to be free from bondage to sin and the dominion of evil in order to serve the Lord for his glory.

2. The Lord Jesus Christ is the unique revelation of God and the only Savior of the world.

Salvation is found in Christ alone. God witnesses to himself in creation and in human conscience, but these witnesses are not complete without the revelation of God in Christ. In the face of competing truth claims, we proclaim with humility that Christ is the only Savior, conscious that sin as well as cultural hindrances often mask him from those for whom he died.

3. The good news of the salvation made possible by the work of Jesus Christ must be expressed in all the languages and cultures of the world.

We are commanded to be heralds of the gospel to every creature so that they can have the opportunity to confess faith in Christ. The message must come to them in a language they can understand and in a form that is appropriate to their circumstances. Believers, led by the Holy Spirit, are encouraged to create culturally appropriate forms of worship and uncover biblical insights that glorify God for the benefit of the whole church.

4. The gospel is good news and addresses all human needs.

We emphasize the holistic nature of the gospel of Jesus Christ. Both the Old Testament and the New Testament demonstrate God's concern with the whole person in the whole of society. We acknowledge that material blessings come from God, but prosperity should not be equated with godliness.

5. Opposition to the spread of the gospel is foremost a spiritual conflict involving human sin and principalities and powers opposed to the Living God.

This conflict is manifested in different ways, e.g., fear of spirits or indifference to God. We recognize that the defense of the truth of the gospel is also spiritual warfare. As witnesses of the gospel, we announce that Jesus Christ has power over all powers and is able to free all who turn to him in faith. We affirm that in the cross, God has won the victory.

6. Suffering, persecution, and martyrdom are present realities for many Christians.

We acknowledge that our obedience in mission involves suffering and recognize that the church is experiencing this. We affirm our privilege and responsibility to pray for those undergoing persecution. We are called to share in their pain, do what we can to relieve their sufferings, and work for human rights and religious freedom.

7. Economic and political systems deeply affect the spread of God's kingdom.

Human government is appointed by God, but all human institutions act out of fallenness. The Scriptures command that Christians pray for those in authority and work for truth and justice. Appropriate Christian response to political and economic systems requires the guidance of the Holy Spirit.

8. God works in a variety of Christian traditions and organizations, for his glory and the salvation of the world.

For too long believers, divided over issues of church organization, order, and doctrine—such as the gifts and ministry of the Holy Spirit—have failed to recognize each other's work. We affirm, bless, and pray for authentic Christian witness wherever it is found.

9. To be effective witnesses of the Holy God, we need to demonstrate personal and corporate holiness, love, and righteousness.

We repent of hypocrisy and conformity to the world, and we call the church to a renewed commitment to holy living. Holiness requires turning from sin, training in righteousness, and growing in Christlikeness.

Commentary by Oswaldo Prado

One of the points which especially caught my attention was the firm commitment to the fundamentals of Scripture. In the beginning of the Christian era, the church sought solidification of its faith through many credos and confessions. In contrast, the 20th century was marked by the sudden growth of pluralism and religious syncretism. The Brazilian Evangelical church is an example of the 20th century realities. Although we are experiencing numeric growth never seen before, sometimes we may wonder when entering a church building if we are there to adore the true God or just to feel some "spiritual experiences."

The meeting at Foz do Iguassu showed the singularity of Christ and his power over the world and the church. We could not help but see that we are a Christian church. We must not let go of the absolute statements of high faith in the Scriptures. These statements have enormous relevance to the Third World church. Because this church is still young, it suffers the temptation to expand much more through business strategies than biblical ones.

The character of the Latin American church is also a result of its economic and political environment. Especially in the 1970s and '80s, Brazil and other countries experienced totalitarian army governments, which worsened social distinctions and resulted in poverty and social injustice. Our meeting in Iguassu recognized that these situations also affected the expansion of God's kingdom. We now need the Holy Spirit's direction in fulfilling our mission, interceding for our political leaders, and developing concrete plans for evangelization aimed at the welfare of our citizens.

There are two things in favor of the Third World church. First, the church has known how to survive through all kinds of suffering. Second, it readily shares its meager possessions for the expansion of the gospel among people not yet touched by the good news.

Commentary by John Wood

The opening statement of the Declarations leaves no doubt that this is an Evangelical document by strongly affirming the authority of Scripture. It then follows with a note of sweet catholicity by observing our indebtedness to consensual orthodoxy. (I take "the great Christian confessions" actually to refer not so much to the lengthy and detailed Confessions of the Reformation that too often divide Evangelicals, but rather to the great Ecumenical Creeds of the early church that unite us.) The Declarations section then affirms for the first time the trinitarian nature of missions and centers missiology on the biblical themes of creation, fall, redemption, and consummation. The first paragraph closes with another statement on the work of the Holy Spirit.

The form of the Declarations then changes to a cataloging of nine biblical and missiological "themes" confessed "as truths of special importance in this present age." I am a bit puzzled at the structure of the presentation at this point. It would seem either that the first paragraph, narrative in form, should be broken down into a list of themes that would then flow into the following nine, or that the nine should be presented in a narrative form that flows out of the first paragraph. Nor is it entirely clear to me why only these particular themes are declared or why the words, "We confess," are used of the Declarations and the words, "We declare," are used of the Pledge.

Nevertheless, there is an unstated, underlying logic to the themes. They declare, in order: the Lordship of Christ, the uniqueness of Christ, the gospel of Christ to the whole world, the gospel of Christ to the whole person, opposition to the gospel, suffering for the gospel, Christians and social structures, Christians and unity, and Christians and holiness. These declarations are prophetic in calling each of us, regardless of one's cultural context, to a costly declaration and application of the whole counsel of God to our own lives and to every part of life, especially in the places where principalities and powers are opposing the spread of God's kingdom. There is a strong and compelling appeal for the wedding of a rigorous Christian mind and a vigorous Christian heart.

Commentary by
Cathy Ross

As Evangelicals, we wholeheartedly endorse these declarations. How good to see the person of the Holy Spirit affirmed as the agent of mission, which reminds us that the Holy Spirit may indeed do surprising and unexpected things in mission. No matter how much we strategize, God is the author of mission, and we know God delights in surprises. How appropriate to be reminded that we are "Christ's servants" and not harbingers of a particular culture, worldview, or political system, although we confess it has sometimes seemed like that.

I am encouraged by the emphasis on the holistic nature of the gospel in the fourth declaration. So often we have pursued and enforced a Greek dualism between spirit and body, to the detriment of God's mission and the good news we proclaim.

It is this holistic nature of the gospel and its concern for justice which is good news for women. Consider the following statistics: "Women form 35% of the world's paid labour force, head up 33% of all households, make up 95% of all nurses, perform 62% of all work hours, and yet receive just 10% of the world's income and own 1% of the world's property.... Women make up 70% of the poor, 66% of illiterates, 80% of refugees, 75% of the sick."[1]

We see the urgent and pressing need for women's issues to be heard and addressed by Evangelicals in mission. It is indeed a question of working for justice for those who are suffering outright injus-tice. The gospel is good news for everyone, but women as a group are marginalized, oppressed, and alienated—perhaps more than any other group. Even secular governments realize this. The government of Aotearoa/New Zealand will match aid agencies' donations by four to one for any project which targets the welfare of women. May we as Evangelicals be at the forefront of any initiative which brings not only justice but also healing, wholeness, and newness of life to marginalized groups.

In the seventh declaration, it is good to see Evangelicals encouraging a realistic awareness of and involvement in economics and politics, under the guidance of the Holy Spirit, as an appropriate part of mission. Too often, we have abrogated our responsibility in this area and let blatant injustice continue, as long as we have had the freedom to "preach the gospel"!

Commentary by
Jeff Fountain

In the first place, much of the Iguassu Affirmation is reaffirmation. Developments in the last decade had rendered such midstream corrections necessary. While the historic Lausanne Congress in 1974 had made ground-breaking progress in clarifying the interface between evangelism and social involvement, Lausanne II in Manila (1989) had been followed by new emphases which had sometimes stressed breadth at the expense of depth. Some had urged an all-out effort towards closure before the century's end. Others in Europe had responded to that call with caution. James Engel, in an article quoted by Bill Taylor in the opening address, warned of "misguided strategies based on paradigms of world evangelization that have lost their mooring in all that Christ taught about the kingdom of God."

---

[1] Long, J. D. (1997, June 17). The plight of women. *Monday Morning Reality Check.*

The Declarations affirming the holistic nature of the gospel (see 4, 6, and 7) help restore biblical balance to our understanding of the mission mandate.

Commentary by Jim Stamoolis

The strong Evangelical statements of the introductory paragraph mean that the document stands in the tradition of other Christian confessional documents. Scripture, the Trinity, and the role of the Holy Spirit are appropriately highlighted. These are given to be undisputed points among Evangelicals. It is especially important to identify the Holy Spirit as the agent of mission, lest any consider mission to be primarily a human enterprise.

The Affirmation demonstrates that there is an integral connection between the foundation of mission and theology. There is no sense of a missionary enthusiasm that is not clearly rooted in biblical theology.

When the document comes to the issues that the consultation believed needed special emphasis, the key points are listed that are necessary for mission in the 21st century. These topics would form the basis for further study and reflection. They are a catalogue of the subjects for books and monographs, written from different cultural perspectives, which should form the basis of missiological thinking. Much has been written on some of these topics in English and other European languages. What is needed is reflection from other parts of the church, so that all may benefit from the experience of Christians in other settings.

The dual focus of the first declaration, that Jesus Christ is Lord of the church and the universe, correctly points out that if he is not Lord of both, he cannot be Lord of either. The confession of Christ as Lord of the church must include the confession of his Lordship over the entire created

order. The second declaration follows logically, in that Christ must then be the only Savior of the world because he is Lord of all. Therefore, all must have the opportunity to know who their true Lord is. These are the essential pillars of the missionary mandate, and without them there is no redemptive mission, only humanitarian relief work. Therefore, holistic ministry flows out of the redemptive mandate.

The spiritual nature of the conflict is clearly pointed out. It is not a matter of mere intellectual consent; rather, the spread of the gospel is a spiritual battle. The realization of the reality of suffering and martyrdom is an indication that the battle cannot be fought by armchair strategists sitting in comfortable surroundings. The essential focus on prayer for sisters and brothers who are undergoing persecution reminds us again of the dual realms of the physical and the spiritual. Later, in the Commitments, there is a call for the development of a theology of suffering which will serve the entire church.

The call to halt the division over traditions and organizations is most appropriate. It is not a call to structural unity of organization, but rather a call to a unity in the Holy Spirit. There is nothing that would advance the cause of Christ more than ongoing demonstrations of the real spiritual unity all Christians share by virtue of their relationship to the Lord Jesus Christ and the indwelling presence of the Holy Spirit. Charismatics who have felt excluded from the mainstream of Evangelical life need to be welcomed as sisters and brothers. The church among these communities is growing rapidly, and there needs to be a willingness to discern the work of the Holy Spirit within the various traditions. While the experience of church life differs from situation to situation, the reality of the presence of the risen Christ, as mediated through the indwelling Holy Spirit, should give confidence of the ability of the Spirit to work in both old and new Christian traditions. The Affirmation's call to affirm, bless, and pray for authentic Christian witness could be the single most powerful force in manifesting the reality of Christ that the world has ever seen.

The call for holiness for effective Christian witness is always in season. There was never a period in the history of the church when holiness was not an important component. In spite of outward prosperity, the lack of holiness has marred the testimony to Christ throughout the centuries. The temptation to various types of sinful behavior only reinforces the spiritual nature of both the Christian life and Christian mission.

Commentary by Seth Anyomi

The affirmations that follow the missionary review highlight the pillars of the Evangelical faith: the Lordship of Christ over not only the church but the entire universe, his uniqueness as God incarnate and the only Saviour of the world, and the efficacy of his work which made possible the good news of salvation. These affirmations all underscore the urgency of giving expression to Christ's message in every tongue and culture.

The fact that we are to be heralds of the gospel to every person on the face of the earth cannot be overemphasized. What is most important also is the language and form in which the gospel is communicated. This declaration helps to clarify misconceptions about the origins of Christianity. Up to today, A.D. 2000, Christianity is still being referred to as the "white man's religion" in Africa.

The Affirmation further declares the relevance of the gospel to every human need, whether physical or spiritual. This brings hope not only to impoverished parts of the world, but also to a spiritually, socially, and culturally corrupted world, regardless of nationality or ethnicity.

The fact that in the cross God has won the victory points to a distinctive definition of spiritual warfare, its process, and its universal assessment. Christ is the man of war and the victor in every spiritual battle.

Neglected subjects in Christian doctrine, "suffering, persecution, and martyrdom," were brought to the forefront. This made sense of the pain, humiliation, and tragic imposition on Christians in many parts of the world. A call to identify, offer assistance, and join in every effort to bring freedom and justice to oppressed Christians worldwide was also a call for Christians to become truly the body of Christ, where all suffer when one suffers.

There was a reminder that world governments and economic systems originate from God. Therefore, their success and sustenance as such rest upon the faithful prayer support and involvement of Christians worldwide.

The eighth declaration restates the Great Commission, which if paraphrased would read, "Go into every person's world" and make disciples of all nations. This simplifies and explains the diversity of ministries and Christian organizations having one common goal of bringing a Christian witness within one's given sphere of operation.

The ninth point of the Declarations is of particular interest to African Christians. Even in pagan societies, holiness and expressions of love in communal living are highly esteemed. The gods are said to react violently to any act of impurity, injustice, or deliberate wickedness. An emphasis on the doctrine of holiness, love, and righteousness will register well with the church in Africa.

Commentary by Met Castillo

I wholeheartedly support these affirmations. Mission theology as rooted in the God-inspired Scriptures can never be overstated. There is a need to ground practitioners and leaders in a biblical theology of missions. Doing missions is often based on a few verses of Scripture picked out from here and there, thus missing the whole picture.

It is good to emphasize a Christocentric mission theology as expressed in the first three themes. This is in line with time-tested Evangelical tradition on soteriology. Salvation through faith in Christ is the foundation of mission theology that puts the "go" on our feet. It is the bedrock that withstands religious pluralism in our world today.

The holistic nature of the gospel is adequately and clearly stated, but how to communicate this gospel to the non-Western, phenomenal mind in order to gain acceptance remains a real challenge to many practitioners. We who claim to be Evangelical and missions minded need to work on this some more.

It is when we proclaim the whole gospel to the whole person that we encounter opposition and experience suffering or even martyrdom. The gospel confronts evil to the core, and evil will not tolerate the gospel in society.

Commitments

We commit ourselves to continue and deepen our reflection on the following themes, helping one another to enrich our understanding and practice with insight from every corner of the world. Our hearts' desire is the discipling of the nations through the effective, faithful communication of Christ to every culture and people.

1. Trinitarian foundation of mission

We commit ourselves to a renewed emphasis on God-centered missiology. This invites a new study of the operation of the Trinity in the redemption of the human race and the whole of creation, as well as to understand the particular roles of Father, Son, and Spirit in mission to this fallen world.

2. Biblical and theological reflection

We confess that our biblical and theological reflection has sometimes been shallow and inadequate. We also confess that we have frequently been selective in our use of texts rather than being faithful to the whole biblical revelation. We commit ourselves to engage in renewed biblical and theological studies shaped by mission, and to pursue a missiology and practice shaped by God's Word, brought to life and light by the Holy Spirit.

3. Church and mission

The church in mission is central to God's plan for the world. We commit ourselves to strengthen our ecclesiology in mission, and to encourage the global church to become a truly missionary community in which all Christians are involved in mission. In the face of increasing resistance and opposition from political powers, religious fundamentalism, and secularism, we commit ourselves to encourage and challenge the churches to respond with a deeper level of unity and participation in mission.

4. Gospel and culture

The gospel is always presented and received within a cultural context. It is therefore essential to clarify the relationship between gospel and culture, both in theory and practice, recognizing that there is both good and evil in all cultures.

We commit ourselves to continue to demonstrate the relevance of the Christian message to all cultures, and ensure that missionaries learn to wrestle biblically with the relationship between gospel and culture. We commit ourselves to serious study of how different cultural perspectives may enrich our understanding of the gospel, as well as how all worldviews have to be critiqued and transformed by it.

5. Pluralism

Religious pluralism challenges us to hold firmly to the uniqueness of Jesus Christ as Savior even as we work for increased tolerance and understanding among religious communities. We cannot seek harmony by relativizing the truth claims of religions. Urbanization and radical political change have bred increased interreligious and ethnic violence and hostility. We commit ourselves to be agents of reconciliation. We also commit ourselves to proclaim the gospel of Jesus Christ in faithfulness and loving humility.

6. Spiritual conflict

We welcome the renewed attention given in recent decades to the biblical theme of spiritual conflict. We rejoice that power and authority are not ours but God's. At the same time, we must ensure that the interest in spiritual warfare does not become a substitute for dealing with the root issues of sin, salvation, conversion, and the battle for the truth. We commit ourselves to increase our biblical understanding and practice of spiritual conflict while guarding against syncretistic and unbiblical elements.

7. Strategy in mission

We are grateful for many helpful insights gained from the social sciences. We are concerned that these should be sub-ject to the authority of Scripture. Therefore, we call for a healthy critique of mission theories that depend heavily on marketing concepts and missiology by objectives.

8. Globalized missiology

The insights of every part of the church are needed, and challenges encountered in every land must be addressed. Only thus can our missiology develop the richness and texture reflected in the Scriptures and needed for full obedience to our risen Lord. We commit ourselves to give voice to all segments of the global church in developing and implementing our missiology.

9. Godly character

Biblical holiness is essential for credible Christian witness. We commit ourselves to renewed emphasis on godly living and servanthood, and we urge training institutions, both missionary and ministerial, to include substantive biblical and practical training in Christian character formation.

10. The cross and suffering

As our Lord called us to take up our crosses, we remind the church of our Lord's teaching that suffering is a part of authentic Christian life. In an increasingly violent and unjust world with political and economic oppression, we commit to equip ourselves and others to suffer in missionary service and to serve the suffering church. We pursue to articulate a biblical theology of martyrdom.

11. Christian responsibility and the world economic order

In a world increasingly controlled by global economic forces, Christians need to be aware of the corrosive effects of affluence and the destructive effects of poverty. We must be aware of ethno-

centrism in our view of economic forces. We commit ourselves to address the realities of world poverty and oppose policies that serve the powerful rather than the powerless. It is the responsibility of the church in each place to affirm the meaning and value of a people, especially where indigenous cultures face extinction. We call all Christians to commit themselves to reflect God's concern for justice and the welfare of all peoples.

12. Christian responsibility and the ecological crisis

The earth is the Lord's, and the gospel is good news for all creation. Christians share in the responsibility God gave to all humanity to care for the earth. We call on all Christians to commit themselves to ecological integrity in practicing responsible stewardship of creation, and we encourage Christians in environmental care and protection initiatives.

13. Partnership

As citizens of the kingdom of God and members of Christ's body, we commit ourselves to renewed efforts at cooperation, because it is our Lord's desire that we be one and that we work in harmony in his service so that the world will believe. We acknowledge that our attempts have not always been as equals. Inadequate theology, especially in respect to the doctrine of the church, and the imbalance of resources have made working together difficult. We pledge to find ways to address this imbalance and to demonstrate to the world that believers in Christ are truly one in their service of Christ.

14. Member care

Service of the Lord in cross-cultural environments exposes missionaries to many stresses and criticisms. While acknowledging that missionaries also share the limitations of our common human-ity and have made errors, we affirm that they deserve love, respect, and gratitude. Too often, agencies, churches, and fellow Christians have not followed biblical guidelines in dealing with cross-cultural workers. We commit ourselves to support and nurture our missionary workers for their sakes and for the gospel witness.

Commentary by Oswaldo Prado

Recognizing the strategic importance of the Brazil Consultation in Foz do Iguassu, during the week we raised some themes which may be used for our own reflections and practices in a new millennium. Some of these have great relevance for the shepherding of our Third World church.

One issue was grappling with the church/mission equation. Unfortunately, many have sought to disconnect the church from its missionary duty, thereby blinding the church to its priority vision, which is to spread the glory of the Lord among all peoples. Our Brazilian ecclesiology is still fundamentally ethnocentric, and we are forced to meet the demands of our denominational organizations. In addition, our missionary heritage in many cases did not challenge us with a commitment to world mission. Thus, the pastors and leaders of missions of the local church often need to undergo an apprenticeship under a new paradigm in which the church and mission walk together.

Another area which we Brazilians will take home from Iguassu is the sincere and open dialogue that took place among those who work in the arena of mission study and reflection, along with the pastors who work primarily with missionary action. We regret that too often in the past we walked alone, when actually we should have depended on each other. We are a church which needs a foundational mission study for missionary work. Also, those who are on the mission field must be valued much more.

For a long time, the church in Brazil, as well as in many other parts of Latin America, has received unfiltered theologies and structures coming from North America and Europe. In some cases, this has been healthy, but in other cases there have been serious problems. Our meeting in Brazil raised the theme of spiritual warfare. We recognized that spiritual warfare is present in most of our churches and that it has become a divisive issue on each pastor's agenda. We know that today Christians are carelessly using this area of spiritual conflict without proper care and scriptural support.

For us as Latin American pastors, there was great value in reflecting on the presence of deep suffering in the Christian life. Our church has tended to exclude all kinds of pain and suffering, leading Christians to believe that such themes are not part of the Christian life. These extremes are the result of imported theologies, which teach material prosperity as a sign of a healthy spirituality. Nowadays Christians have a tendency to abandon their communities at the first sign of struggle and suffering. Our meeting, fortunately, recovered the cross and suffering as an integral part of the Christian life and gave us new strength to meet the tragedies in an oppressed world.

Commentary by John Wood

While this section is consistent in structuring its presentation and clear in stating its themes, it is not as clear why several of the themes already dealt with under the Declarations are now taken up again in a different order without reference to what has gone before. However, the Commitments do propose a commendable and necessary missiological project of continuing reflection "with insight from every cor-

ner of the world." This section is very strong in content, addressing the need for reflection both in traditional areas of Evangelical strength (e.g., trinitarian foundation, biblical and theological reflection, church and mission), as well as in areas where we have been weak (e.g., gospel and culture, spiritual conflict, Christian responsibility regarding economics and ecology). This section will serve my own congregation's world missions team as an excellent foundation document for further reflection.

I believe, however, that the two central sections on Declarations and Commitments would be stronger if they shared an internal structure or if the one flowed logically out of the other. They read as if written by two different committees not working closely enough with each other.

Commentary by Cathy Ross

The Commitments are a rather eclectic collection, although most arise out of the Declarations. I look forward to more detailed study on the nature and role of the Trinity in mission and on what a deeper understanding of the Trinity might mean for us in our practice of mission and how we live in community in God's world.

The second commitment, calling for a deeper theological and biblical reflection on mission, is timely for Evangelicals, when many institutions seem to be diminishing their commitment to the study of cross-cultural mission in favour of other disciplines. May we have the humility to listen and learn from our sisters and brothers in other cultures and contexts as they theologise in their communities, so that we may truly reflect the worldwide body of Christ.

I appreciate the positive approach to culture seen in the fourth commitment. May we rejoice in all the good things of God's world, realizing that God created culture and that the gospel not only critiques elements in any culture, but also enhances certain elements of culture. I pray that this commitment may also extend to our Evangelical subcultures across the globe, so that we do not become entrenched in our own favoured positions but allow other perspectives to breathe new life into our particular contexts.

The commitments, which urge godly character and servanthood as well as the call to suffering, are pertinent reminders for us in the West that the way of Jesus is indeed the way of the cross. May we eschew triumphalistic and comfortable approaches to mission and practise radical servanthood. It is good to hear Evangelicals opposing policies that serve the powerful. May God give us not only the discernment to work out who the powerless are for us in our context, but also the grace to serve these people.

At last, we have an Evangelical declaration which deals with the environment and urges us to protect the integrity of creation! This is a huge commitment that requires advocacy and purposeful action from us in the West.

How we long for a true partnership of equals as we work in mission! Can it happen? Perhaps we in the West need to be silent for a time. Perhaps we need to sacrifice our plans and strategies so that true partnership can happen. Perhaps we need the humility to remain silent, stand still, and receive in humility from our sisters and brothers from the rest of the world. Could we do it? What would happen if we did?

Commentary by
Jeff Fountain

As the millennial watershed approached, church leaders across the European continent were being faced with an undeniable truth: Europe had now become the Prodigal Continent. Europe was out of phase with church growth exploding in Asia, Africa, and Latin America. Once synonymous with Christendom, Europe was now becoming a desperate mission field itself.

Missiological insights traditionally reserved for "the foreign mission field" needed urgent application in our European cities and neighbourhoods. It is no coincidence that one of the most widely read and quoted European churchmen in the last decade was a former bishop in India, Lesslie Newbigin. He clearly saw that Europe was at an historic crossroads. For the first time ever, Europeans had tried and rejected in turn each of the three broad categories of worldview: animism, theism, and materialism. Post-modernity was a clear rejection of the last. Newbigin warned that when Europe forgot the Book that told the story that brought the hope that had transformed culture after culture on the continent, Europe would revert to her Eastern roots of animism.

The Commitments listed in the Affirmation present a serious and urgent agenda for us Europeans. We must see expressions of the church emerge that relate effectively to post-Christians (praise God for the impact of Alpha groups in many European countries!), post-Communists, post-moderns, and that growing urban population sector, post-migrants (the children of immigrants who have never had any Christian influence in their upbringing). Such expressions will involve heavy wrestling with the themes of the gospel and culture, pluralism, and even spiritual warfare.

We must go back to the future, recovering models from the past which impacted pagan societies the first time round with an attractive expression of the Christian faith—such as the Irish Celts, whose culture-redeeming, life-affirming communities became the building blocks for the new order we now know as Western civilisation.

The commitment to partnership, while not new, takes on a novel twist for Europeans in the light of the historic shift in the centre of gravity of the global church to the South and East. One of the consultation jokes was that for many Two-Thirds Worlders, partnership with Westerners was like dancing with elephants! But we Europeans today are spiritual lightweights when it comes to church planting, experience in cell churches, gifts of faith and vision, relating to immigrants, recognising and understanding animism in contemporary guises, and engaging in spiritual warfare. Our missionary God has begun to send Asians, Africans, and Latin Americans to partner with us in Europe—and we desperately need their help!

A major personal takeaway was the reminder that the cross and suffering are part of authentic Christian life. Sometimes an emphasis on marketing strategies and measurable success has clouded our awareness that God's ways are not ours, that resurrection life only follows death, and that historically the blood of the martyrs has been the seed of the church.

How God works through shakings and sufferings has been clearly demonstrated in recent events in the Balkans. Despite waves of anarchy that sent Western missionaries packing, Albania, the world's first atheistic nation, became a missionary-sending nation in the closing months of the century. Evangelical Albanians are now helping Muslim Kosovars to rebuild their shattered land, and they have helped plant over 20 new fellowships in the six months since the last NATO bombs fell. We can continue to expect the "surprises of God"—even in 21st century Europe!

Commentary by Rudy Girón

Observations on Commitment 6

Of the many elements that we might discuss, I would like to focus my attention on points number six and seven of the Affirmation Commitments. As a practitioner in missions and a Pentecostal missionary, I find the elements implied in the sixth commitment quite relevant to my reality. Spiritual warfare is something that comes to our doorway every day. Definitely it is a subject that needs to be addressed in a biblical and balanced way.

For a long time, Pentecostals have been rightly known as those who experience and minister within the reality of spiritual warfare. In relatively recent years, other authors, especially non-Pentecostal writers, have become acquainted with the issues of spiritual warfare or have experienced a spiritual awakening in their ministry. Intrigued by their experience, they have started to theorize and then write about spiritual warfare. Applying psychology, anthropology, sociology, and some practical experience to their findings, they have emerged with new understanding and theories about spiritual warfare. For traditional Pentecostals, many of these newer "revelations" are rather common. At the same time, some of them are exaggerated. We Pentecostals are amazed at how these newer spiritual practitioners are able to theorize about what we have been practicing for decades! Until recently, traditional Pentecostals never had the interest, the opportunity, or the means to write about their experience. That does not mean that they do not understand the subject. On the contrary, they know by experience what it means to engage in spiritual warfare against the dark forces and also about releasing the supernatural power of God in our world and ministry.

There has been an over-fascination with the mystical elements that are implied in spiritual warfare. This is true not only of Christians, but also in our general societies. Many movies about the supernatural, demonology, voodoo, vampires, and all sorts of spiritual evils have been produced by the secular film industry. Many novels written by Christian authors have rewarded both the writers and their publishers with handsome financial profits. These realities prove that there is a spiritual awareness of the ongoing warfare of the spirit.

Yet the seriousness of this issue did not emerge as it should have at the Iguassu Consultation, for only one presentation on the subject was made, and that one was from a Christian anthropological standpoint. Nevertheless, the fact remains that understanding the nature of spiritual warfare is something with which we must deal seriously if we want to reach those who are without Christ, regardless of culture or nationality. The battle we face is not just a political, financial, and intellectual one. We face serious spirituality issues in our society today. Spiritual warfare needs to be seriously studied from a missiological standpoint, using the Scriptures as our foundation.

We also must give more room to those who have spiritual warfare knowledge and experience, who know how to engage the evil powers, and who have lived victoriously over the years. Despite the fact that many of these practitioners may not be able to explain intellectually all the details of such a battle, this should not exclude them from the dialogue. It seems to me that there are not many practitioners of spiritual warfare present in consultations like ours in Iguassu. Therefore, we are left with those who know the issue only from the more theoretical side of the coin. This is an issue that must be dealt with in future consultations. It would be very productive to convene a specific missiological consultation on this issue, involving missiologists, anthropologists, missionaries, and theologians from all branches of Pentecostal and non-Pentecostal traditions.

When it comes to spiritual warfare, especially in what is called the "mission field" (which is truly now everywhere), we are aware of the need that we missionaries have to recognize that we are not just fighting against human intellectual, political, or economic forces. We are truly battling against evil cosmic forces. There is a spiritual realm in which we are engaged, and we need to be prepared both intellectually and spiritually. Many missionaries are returning earlier than expected to their homes and sending churches, frustrated and discouraged. The causes are complex in most of the cases of preventable attrition. Nevertheless, we believe that behind the obviously recognizable causes, there may be spiritual elements that are part of an evil warfare confronted by most missionaries, and we need to consider this reality carefully.

Before becoming a cross-cultural missionary in Russia, I had worked in many ministerial positions, both in my country and outside my country. However, when I became a full-time missionary working outside my common "territory," I experienced uncommon spiritual battles. If we are not spiritually prepared to deal with such battles, we may be defeated without even knowing what the reason for our defeat was. Sometimes we cannot explain intellectually what is going on, but we know, as Paul knew, that our battle is not against flesh and blood, but against "the rulers, against the authorities, against the powers of this dark world and against the spiritual forces of evil in the heavenly realms" (Eph. 6:12). This is not an easy battle; it is spiritual warfare.

The Iguassu Affirmation calls for a serious biblical consideration of the issue, and rightly so. We need to revisit the Bible to discover and evaluate the cosmic spiritual realities that the early church confronted from its inception. We need to come afresh to the biblical text, carefully examining our theological preconceptions, and discern with honesty the biblical and current worldviews, along with the reality of this massive spiritual battle. Beginning with Jesus, who confronted Satan in the early stages of his ministry, right to the end of the apostolic era, the church was already engaged in a great spiritual battle. Today we see the need for the church worldwide to be prepared to engage in spiritual warfare. Our missiology will be incomplete unless we examine our concepts of spiritual warfare.

Observations on Commitment 7

This statement referred to strategies in missions. It was unfortunate that almost none of the major missiologists that represent the so-called "managerial missiology" were at Iguassu. I do not blame the organizers of the consultation for this absence, for I believe they tried. Perhaps it was mainly due to reasons on the part of those who represent these missiological emphases. That left us again in Iguassu with only an unbalanced side of the coin. If some of the missiologists who have produced a vast field of data regarding the unreached people groups of the world had been present at Iguassu, they would have enriched the consultation. Articulate proponents of this perspective could have spoken on behalf of the methods and statistics used to promote missionary awareness in the local churches and could guide us on the field itself.

These statistical and sociological tools that explain part of the spiritual reality of our present world have been a great resource and a great blessing to many of our

Two-Thirds World missionary movements. We acknowledge that when it comes to setting goals for reaching the unreached, we run the danger of losing track of the deep spiritual challenges presented by the unbelieving world. We have the tendency to reduce that reality to mere numbers and oversimplifications. But that does not mean that the entire contribution coming from these well-respected leaders and organizations is useless or that it can be dismissed simply as "managerial missions." Even more serious is the fact that those who attack all the good elements of a statistical approach to missions usually do so from a position of intellectual advantage. But many of these critics possess limited practical experience of the realities of this world.

As a missions mobilizer in Latin America, I can testify to the great blessing it has been to our church to have statistical and social sciences information to enlighten and shape our understanding of the Great Commission. The emerging missionary movements from the Two-Thirds World have been founded with much intercessory prayer. That prayer has been greatly informed by the abundant data gathered under the strategic vision of those who have worked hard to determine the numerical realities of the spiritual condition of the world. All of us can recognize the blessing of having the objective numbers of Barrett, Johnson, Pate, Winter, and others. None of us can deny the great impulse that the innovative concept of the 10/40 window has brought to our missionary enterprise. People who never before thought about spiritual needs in other parts of the world suddenly have been moved by the realities they have discovered through this "managerial" approach.

It is important to mention that missiologists from academia have the tendency to present the Great Commission in such sophisticated theological jargon that the common Christian (who wants only to understand how to contribute to the Great Commission) is simply lost. Those of us who have preached in the great pulpits, as well at the simple pulpits of *barrio* churches, know how effective it is to translate the biblical mandate of making disciples in all nations, when we can show what a "nation" means and how many of them are still unevangelized. I always keep in mind Matthew 9:36, where when Jesus saw the multitudes, he had compassion on them. A well-known missiologist once said, "Understanding leads to compassion." Jesus saw the crowds and grasped their spiritual needs. We need to see through reliable statistics to the realities of this world. I agree with that Presbyterian pastor from the beginning of the 20th century when he said, "We need to preach missions with the Bible in the right hand and with the statistics in the other."

I recognize that when it comes to strategizing, we can run the risk of simply reducing mission to attainable numerical goals. Also, we are well aware that mission is not simply sharing the gospel, but it includes a holistic approach to the full needs of the person. Those of us who have been involved in what is called "managerial missiology" have found these emphases to be a great blessing as we spread the missionary vision throughout our Latin American continent. Yes! We affirm the need to avoid an oversimplification of the mission or a reductionism in our scope of missions. Nevertheless, we voice our concern that in applying the epithet "managerial missiology" to all statistical strategizing, we may mislead the global missionary movement and deprive the church of very valuable tools that have blessed many of our churches worldwide.

Again, I join my voice with the appeal of the Iguassu Consultation that we avoid an oversimplification of missiology, especially of the Great Commission, by reducing everything to numbers and to managerial strategies. We must be careful not to conclude that those who produce, use, and spread statistical information are seen only as the ones who reduce mission to mere numerical elements.

What might be a healthy attitude and step to take? We must return to the trenches of the rural and *barrio* churches and there test our missiological jargon. Then we will realize that unless that jargon is explained and illustrated, whether or not we include elements of "managerial missiology," nobody will understand what the Great Commission means. Let us keep a balanced approach to all the elements that combine to formulate a relevant missiology for our 21st century.

Commentary by Jim Stamoolis

When the Affirmation reaches the Commitments, it sets out the theological and missiological agenda for the next several decades. As noted with the Declarations, the points of the Commitments are without a doubt the areas that should form the areas of writing and reflection for practicing missionaries, professors of mission, and graduate students. Each point could provide the seeds for many master's theses and doctoral dissertations. These writings need to be done in the various linguistic and cultural contexts of mission, not only in the traditional missiological centers of the Western churches. It would be interesting to see how the various cultural traditions handle topics such as the Trinity or spiritual conflict.

The global missionary enterprise is mature in many respects, but it needs to encourage the younger churches to find their own voices and to break out of traditional models of interpretation. To some, such words sound alarming, if not heretical, since they believe that the basic exegetical work has been done. Nevertheless, the Affirmation is correct when it points out the shallow and inadequate use of the Bible, along with the tendency to be selective in using the witness of the biblical text. It is critical that this commitment not be lost or ignored. The Western church needs the witness and exegetical observation of those from other traditions to unlock the depth of God's revelation to humankind. The Bible has been read through a Western filter that has been unable at times to distinguish the biblical worldviews from the cultural presuppositions coming from the Enlightenment. A pertinent example would be the acceptance of spiritual activity in the New Testament era by Evangelical theologians, but their unwillingness to understand how demonic activity affects people for whom the link between the material world and the spiritual world still exists.

The call for partnership is important, since it comes out of the theological and missiological framework of the Affirmation. It places the problem exactly where it needs to be if real progress is to be made, that is, in the area of theology and not just pragmatic practice.

The practical concern for the human agents of the missionary enterprise is commendable, in that there has historically been a dual tendency to place the missionary on a pedestal of honor but to ignore the real human needs of the worker. The call to deal realistically with these fellow servants of Christ in a biblical manner is timely. There needs to be a revised commitment to pastoral care if the missionary movement is to witness effectively to the reality of Christian community.

Commentary by Seth Anyomi

United by a common vision and call to disciple the nations, crucial Commitments were made to ensure an effective, faithful communication of Christ to every culture and people. Upon these Commitments the WEF Missions Commission members charged themselves with the responsibility of impacting their respective nations, regions, and spheres of influence.

The African church undoubtedly would welcome a renewed emphasis on God-centered missiology. Many African traditional societies such as the Ashantis already hold God as a Trinity, symbolized in the three-pronged symbol of *nyame*, meaning God. The reminder by the Affirmation would surely reinforce the understanding of the trinitarian foundations of mission.

Regarding the topic of biblical and theological reflections, the approach for the church in Africa may differ from that of most of the world. This is because the majority of African Christians are still illiterate. Whereas the issue of Bible doctrine may not mean much to the average African Christian, they derive their strength from devotion to closeness with God through a consistent and in-depth prayer lifestyle.

Regarding the issue of church and missions, a gradual rather than radical approach may better suit the need of the African church. Up until about two decades ago, all of Africa was a mission field. The African church was not taught about her place in world evangelisation. Many thus saw world missions as a reserve of the "rich" Western church. However, in recent times certain African nations have begun to send out missionaries. These sending churches and agencies may well serve as models and catalysts for the rest of the continent.

With the African church plagued with the virus of syncretism, an open discussion and resolution to the subject of the gospel and culture will be welcome news. A clear distinction would need to be drawn between a people's indigenous culture, biblical culture, and doctrine.

Most African Independent Churches sprang up across the continent in reaction to the deep Westernisation of the gospel. The missionaries of old saw everything in the African culture as evil and paganistic, and so even the good elements of the culture, like our mode of worship, were not allowed in the church. The African Independent Churches broke away from the missionary established churches, but they went to another extreme by seeing only good in the African culture, culminating in the syncretistic crisis. A commitment to transform the evils in every culture by the gospel and to strengthen the good elements is indeed refreshing news.

Pluralism is an African reality. Amidst myriad tribal, family, and household gods, the uniqueness of Jesus Christ as the only Saviour must be strongly emphasized. His deity, his message, and his redemptive work must be highlighted to forestall all opposition to the gospel of Jesus Christ. That "urbanization and radical political change have bred increased interreligious and ethnic violence and hostility" is true in every sense in the African context. A change in government in Nigeria, for instance, saw a Christian President ascend the corridors of power, breaking a long tradition of Muslim leadership. The democratic era has given rise to Muslim governors seeking to institute the Sharia law in their states. This has resulted in severe clashes between Christians and Muslims, leading to the loss of lives and property.

In Ghana, urbanisation has caused conflicts between traditional African religion adherents and the church in Accra, the capital. The "Ga" traditional authorities want everyone in the city to obey their laws concerning a ban on drumming and noise-making during certain periods of the year. They argue that their gods are offended by such activity during that time of the year. This has not gone over well with the many other tribes and Christians resident in the city who do not subscribe to this paganistic requirement.

Africans clearly understand spiritual warfare, since they naturally seem to be closer to the spirit world. Where the African church may need instruction is in the area of faith as the only basis for spiritual warfare. Christ has already fought and won the battle with the devil over sin and death. The believer's warfare is therefore one of abiding faith in the victorious and all-conquering Saviour.

In planning strategy in missions, we must look to the Scriptures rather than to academic knowledge for our basis. To the African church, this focus is indeed good news, since it means that the church is not at a disadvantage. Whereas many in the African church are familiar with the Scriptures, not as many are highly educated.

Africa is part of the global Christian community. An understanding of this fact may be cultivated by placing emphasis on Christ as the foundation and head of the true church. All believers are members of this one body, be they Asians, Americans, or Africans.

Cultural norms and values clash with Christian ones, especially in societies where people live in fear of instant retribution when their deities are offended or provoked. This contrasts with the fear that Christians have for our God—a fear which originates from love and devotion to God, rather than an aversion to punishment.

As regards the doctrine of the cross and suffering, the African church may find it easier to accept suffering as a reality than their colleagues from the West, who are not so used to such a lifestyle. Most of Africa lies in the shadow of poverty, famine, and tribal warfare. The average African would die for his land. It is therefore easy to explain why it may be expedient for him to die for his God.

Sophisticated issues such as the world economic order and the Christian's responsibility are quite remote to the average African Christian. In a context where peasant farming and mere subsistence are the norm, such exalted themes will remain outside their reach for many years. Educated African Christians may cooperate with the Western hemisphere to find solutions to these global issues.

The issue of partnerships requires more clarification within the African church. Inter-church or intra-church cooperation within African localities is no problem. This is part of the communal culture. But when this extends to the West, then we run into difficulty. What kind of partnership could exist between unequals in terms of economic, educational, and technological advancements? The challenge is to find ways to forge equity between inequities. Most of us agree that the Lord mandated interdependence rather than dependence.

The issue of member care is not a problem to the African missionary. The community cares for its own and extends the same to strangers in their midst. The only problem might be a willingness of every missionary, national or foreign, to integrate into the serving community.

Commentary by Met Castillo

The list of 14 commitments is an excellent attempt to identify and describe the various areas that require serious attention and study. It was a job well done, considering the diversity of minds, backgrounds, and experiences of the participants. I am sure there are more than 14 themes, but if we take time to look at these, I believe we will acquire an understanding of missions that will result in our taking the Great Commission more seriously.

I would like to comment on three of the 14 themes. First, church and mission. I have no problem with the church in mission. I believe in the missions-involved church, and we must do everything possible to enhance its effectiveness. But in my part of the world, a great deal of confusion arises over the relationship between the church and mission. The problem stems from the dichotomy of the church and mission organizations in doing missions. I bring this to the fore simply to state the need for a more thorough discussion on this issue.

Second, gospel and culture. This is an area that requires serious study and consideration. To many in the younger sending churches, this is something very new. To others, a study of culture is often synonymous with compromising with the "weapons of the flesh." Still others look at this area as taboo. But it is time we view culture as the means through which God communicates to man, for man sees reality through his cultural spectacles. He views the gospel through his values and worldview. We cannot disassociate man from his cultural background in our attempt to lead him to faith in Christ.

Third, globalized missiology. The missiology of the global church, whether older or younger sending churches, has to be forged to a strong missiological concept in order to develop a strategy that will enhance the work of missions in the new millennium. Third World churches are gaining new experiences that help them to become mature and capable. The experiences of the older and younger sending churches should converge into one source of information for missiologists and practitioners around the world.

Pledge

We, the participants of the Iguassu Missiological Consultation, declare our passion as mission practitioners, missiologists, and church leaders for the urgent evangelization of the whole world and the discipling of the nations to the glory of the Father, the Son, and the Holy Spirit.

In all our commitments, we depend on the Lord who empowers us by the Holy Spirit to fulfill his mission. As Evangelicals, we pledge to sustain our biblical heritage in this ever-changing world. We commit ourselves to participate actively in formulating and practicing Evangelical missiology. Indwelt by the Spirit, we purpose to carry the radical good news of the kingdom of God to all the world. We affirm our commitment to love one another and to pray for one another as we struggle to do his will.

We rejoice in the privilege of being part of God's mission in proclaiming the gospel of reconciliation and hope. We joyfully look to the Lord's return and passionately yearn to see the realization of the eschatological vision when people from every nation, tribe, and language shall worship the Lamb.

To this end may the Father, the Son, and the Holy Spirit be glorified. Hallelujah!

Amen.

Commentary by Oswaldo Prado

The Iguassu Affirmation recognized that we cannot underestimate the task that was given to each of us as pastors, mission students, missionaries, or leaders. As members of Christ's church, we are called to proclaim the gospel of the kingdom to all the world. This requires a serious discipleship which produces a healthy church within a holistic world missionary vision. We must take care to perform such a task by depending continuously on the presence of the Holy Spirit. He gives us the assurance that one day people of all races, languages, tribes, and nations will stand before Jesus declaring, "Worthy is the Lamb, who was slain, to receive power and wealth and wisdom and strength and honor and glory and praise!" (Rev. 5:12).

Commentary by John Wood

The high point of the conference for me was the final communion service at which we signed the Pledge, declaring our passion for the "evangelization of the whole world and the discipling of the nations to the glory of the Father, the Son, and the Holy Spirit." I will not soon forget the joy of looking around at my sisters and brothers of different colors from different cultures speaking different tongues, a sweet foretaste of "the eschatological vision when people from every nation, tribe, and language shall worship the Lamb."

While the document lacks the elegance and internal consistency of having one gifted author compose the original draft and do the final editing, what it gains is the value of expressing the cries and whispers of many voices from diverse cultures. It is truly a consensual document and, as such, will hopefully find favor and stimulate dialogue among Christians of many cultures who continue to "reflect together on the challenges and opportunities facing world missions at the dawn of the new millennium."

Commentary by Cathy Ross

To the Pledge, I joyfully say: Amen! May we go in the name of Christ!

Commentary by Jeff Fountain

With the Iguassu Falls well behind us, now comes the application. We celebrated the "privilege of being part of God's mission in proclaiming the gospel of reconciliation and hope." Yet the one who offers hope leads. Let's be honest—are we, God's people in Europe, really leading? Are we seen by our fellow Europeans as offering hope? As I write these words, the Pope has just made an unprecedented apology for the sins of the Catholic Church through the ages. May we Evangelicals have the same courage to be honest about our failures to demonstrate the gospel of reconciliation and hope; about our shortcomings in seeking the welfare of our "city of exile"; about abdicating our role and responsibility as salt and light in society. May we earn a new name as "the people of hope" as we accept the challenge of helping to shape the New Europe. May God visit us with mercy, vision, and creativity as we gather as leaders from across the continent in Budapest for the Hope for Europe congress, HOPE 21, April 27 – May 3, 2002.

Commentary by Jim Stamoolis

It would be a work of God if not only the 160 participants of the Iguassu Consultation, but all who are engaged in the proclamation of the gospel could agree with the Affirmation and undertake under the guidance of the Holy Spirit to transform the missionary enterprise.

Commentary by Seth Anyomi

The Pledge that concludes the Affirmation is both collective and individual. For both the WEF Missions Commission body, which has the task of getting the message out, and for individual Christians with divine accountability, there is an inner motivation to make a difference and to impact the next generation.

Commentary by Met Castillo

I join the rest of the participants in endorsing the Pledge. Yes, let's go for it— that the world might know Christ in their hearts.

Oswaldo Prado and his wife, Sirley, have two children and are missionaries with OC International (Sepal, in Brazil). Before joining OC, Oswaldo pastored the Independent Presbyterian Church of Ipiranga in São Paulo, Brazil, for 20 years. He is currently the Coordinator for Vision and Strategy of the Brazil 2010 Project, advisor to the Secretary of Missions of the Independent Presbyterian Church of Brazil, and Vice-President of the Dr. Paul Pierson Global Mission Center in Londrina, Brazil. Oswaldo has a bachelor's degree in theology from the Independent Presbyterian Seminary, and he is working on his master's in missiology at the South American Theological Seminary in Londrina. He is author of the book From the Call to the Field. He is a WEF Missions Commission Associate.

John Wood, grateful husband of Marianne and father of three children, is the Senior Pastor of Cedar Springs Presbyterian Church in Knoxville, Tennessee. He holds degrees from the University of Massachusetts and Gordon-Conwell Theological Seminary, and he has studied at the Hebrew University in Jerusalem. John frequently speaks at conferences for churches and mission organizations such as World Vision and SIL, and he serves on the boards of a number of schools and organizations, including the National Association of Evangelicals and WEF's North American Council.

Cathy Ross completed an M.A. in French and German from Auckland University before going to study with her husband for two years at All Nations Christian College in U.K. They then spent time in Rwanda and Belgium prior to working with the Anglican Church in Zaire/DCR. During their time there, Cathy was involved in the diocesan TEE programme. On her return to New Zealand, she worked half time as the Auckland Representative for the Church Missionary Society. She is married to Steve, and they have three young children. She is also the National President for Tertiary Students Christian Fellowship, and she serves on the NZCMS Council and the New Zealand Anglican Missions Board. She has a CDRS, Dip.Tchg., B.D., and is working on her doctorate on the role and contribution of CMS missionary wives to New Zealand in the 19th century. Cathy is currently the Director of the School of Global Mission, Bible College of New Zealand.

*Jeff Fountain is regional director for Youth With a Mission in Europe and oversees 160 operating locations in 34 European nations. Originally from New Zealand, Jeff studied history at Auckland University and later worked as a journalist and then for Inter-Varsity Fellowship. Jeff came to Holland in 1975 after working in Canada and married his Dutch wife, Romkje. Together they have three sons, and Jeff is now a naturalised Dutchman. He has been one of the initiators of Hope for Europe, a pan-European alliance of networks and partnerships spreading the hope of Jesus Christ throughout European life and society. Jeff also leads Centrum's Heerenhof, a multi-functional centre of YWAM for ministries of renewal, re-evangelisation, and reform in Dutch society. He has actively promoted the DAWN vision in Europe and initiated VisNed, the contextualised DAWN movement in Holland. He edited a missions reader published by Kingsway in 1985 called **The Final Frontier**.*

Rodolfo "Rudy" Girón, a Guatemalan, was graduated as an architect from the San Carlos University of Guatemala. God called him to full-time ministry at the age of 28, and he has been an evangelist, pastor, and educator in his denomination, the Church of God, Cleveland. For seven years he served as president of COMIBAM International, and he was a member of the Executive Committee of the WEF Missions Commission. In 1997, he and his wife were sent as missionaries to Moscow, where he is the president of the Eurasian Theological Seminary, an institution that serves the nations of the former Soviet Union. He and his wife, Alma, have four adult children.

*Jim Stamoolis was born in the United States of Greek immigrant parents and was raised in the Greek Orthodox Church. While studying engineering, he was evangelized by a student from Guyana. Completing his B.S.I.E., he earned an M.Div. and a Th.M. in systematic theology from Trinity Evangelical Divinity School. He and his wife Evelyn served in theological education and student ministry in South Africa, and he earned a Th.D. in missiology at the University of Stellenbosch. His dissertation was published as **Eastern Orthodox Mission Theology Today**. In 1981, Jim was appointed IFES Theological Secretary and traveled internationally among student groups. From 1989 to 1998, he was Dean of the Graduate School of Wheaton College. He is currently Executive Director of the WEF Theological Commission. He and Evelyn have three sons.*

Seth Anyomi and his wife, Christiana, have four children. Trained as a teacher in Ghana, Anyomi later did further undergraduate study (B.A., Oral Roberts University) and a doctorate in educational administration from the University of Tulsa, Oklahoma. He and his wife pioneered the work of the African Christian Mission in Ghana. They have planted a number of churches and currently run a day care center, a Christian school, a vocational school for girls, a missionary training institute, and two medical clinics in Ghana. Since 1990, Anyomi has served as President of the Ghana Evangelical Missions Association. He is a WEF Missions Commission Associate.

Met Castillo and his wife, Ina, are the parents of three adult children. Together they served as pioneer church planters to tribal people of northern Philippines. Met has also been a teacher, editor, and author, and he is the founder and current President of the Great Commission Missionary Training Center. He served from 1983 to 2000 with OC International, based in Singapore and Manila. Met has been the coordinator of the two Asia Missions Congresses in his capacity as Executive Director of the Evangelical Fellowship of Asia's Missions Commission. He did his initial ministry studies in the Philippines, then went to India (Union Biblical Seminary) and the U.S. (Asbury and Fuller), where he received his D.Miss. from Fuller Theological Seminary. He is a member of the Executive Committee of the WEF Missions Commission.

41

Drawing to a close: inviting reflective, passionate, and globalized practitioners

WILLIAM D. TAYLOR

WE ARE POISED at an historic moment in the flow of both *chronos* time and *kairos* time. One the one hand, we rejoice in the borderless church of Christ, present in all of the political entities of the world as well as in thousands of people groups.

I underscore a deep conviction, stated in the preface to the Iguassu Affirmation (see page 15): "We are profoundly thankful to our Lord for those who in recent decades have sustained the passion for world evangelization. There are many women and men, organizations and movements which have done all in their power to focus our attention on the unfinished task, to understand the vast unreached world of peoples and cities, and to underscore the vital necessity of obedience to Christ's final charge to the apostles. For this we are grateful, and we are indebted to them."

In light of this statement, as we gaze out over our vast unreached and under-reached world, we commit ourselves anew to the proclamation and incarnation of the fullness of the Great Commission. Inasmuch as it is in our power, we want to provide a genuine and appropriate opportunity for all people in the world to consider and respond to the claims of Christ. Nevertheless, the fact is that the unreached worlds (primarily due to historical, geographical, cultural, and spiritual factors) are tough to reach. We also accept the challenge of the cities, of the poor, of the children at risk, of the educated sophisticates of our world, and of the power groups in cultures and nations. We must establish and nourish an incarnational Christian presence in the multiple and overlapping worldviews of our globe, whether pre-modern, modern, or post-modern.

We recognize the huge challenge for the re-evangelization of the West, a task so eloquently articulated by Rose Dowsett in this book and referenced by other authors. This massive combined global arena for the gospel requires an understanding of God's heart for the nations, for from that trinitarian artesian well flow the waters of motivation, truth, message, hope, transformation, and expectation for the future.

The preface to the Affirmation goes on to affirm (page 15), "We are also grateful to God for the growing body of women and men who are seriously reflecting on just what it means to do biblical missiology in this complex world. Just as the epicenter of the global church has shifted from the North to the South, in the same way the epicenter of creating and doing theology and missiology is changing. We rejoice in the former shift and realize that the second one invites us to greater missiological partnership."

The five selfs of the church of Christ lie before us: the older three, self-supporting, self-governing, and self-propagating, and the newer two, self-theologizing and self-missiologizing. The Iguassu Consultation as well as this book sprang from all five of these, but in particular the last two. And so we now come to the end of this missiological book feast. The diamond of globalized missiology has been at least partially revealed, and we see its refracted beauty. We must now lay out some of the serious and practical missiological tasks that point us to the future. We speak directly to the reflective practitioners—those women and men, younger and older, less and more experienced, who combine heart, body, and mind in their passion for God and the world he has created.

An Agenda for the Missiological Future: Doing Missiology

We return to Escobar's definition of missiology (page 101): "... an interdisciplinary approach to understand missionary action. It looks at missionary facts from the perspective of the biblical sciences, theology, history, and the social sciences." How might we engage in this serious and profitable task as we look to the future?

The more common approach is for us to operate individually, doing missiology solo, maybe teaching or presenting these reflections to a group or conference, then perhaps publishing them. This seems to be the hallmark of the way modern theology and missiology have been done for a long time. The extreme models would be the "ivory tower" scholars, who study, cogitate, teach, and write from a distance. The fact is that this kind of person is caricatured, especially by the extreme activist (another caricature), who reputedly has no interest whatsoever in the more serious reflective task.

Casting aside these extremes, would there not be an alternative approach to the individualized work style? What might missiology look like when done in the context of the community of faith, where there is individual work but also the engagement of the corporate team? These communities or teams of reflective practitioners can be most diverse. They include theological and missiological students together in the task, or husbands and wives, or a formal class completing an assignment in a theological institution. They could be pastors and thinking laity of a local church or denomination. They could be teams of faculty in schools. They could be teams of women and men in mission societies around the world. They could be specialized teams from the national, regional, and international networks of our Evangelical world.

However, all of these missiological groups would exist and serve with a strong commitment as a community that also is engaged in quietness, prayer, and active worship of the living and Triune God. In that doxological context, they are observing, reading, studying, talking, arguing, challenging, modifying, presenting, and publishing. They are in service to God and the church of Christ.

Whether the missiological reflection is done individually or in the context of community, it must be carried out in the broader arena of engagement with the historic families of faith that flow from orthodox Christianity. Evangelicals must engage and learn from those bodies of the historic Christian family of Christ which have such different trajectories. For example, what can we learn from the substantive theological foundations laid down for all Christians by the early Orthodox Fathers? What insight can we acquire from the Roman Catholic monastic missionary orders—female and male? What of the other streams of our rich, liturgical church history?

What can the independent churches learn from the denominations? Ironically, many of the denominations of Africa, South Pacific, Latin America, and Asia were started by missionary organizations that in their "home country" were neither churches nor denominations. What can these independent mission structures learn from the denominations that grew up out of their faithful evangelism and church planting?

What can non-charismatics and charismatic Pentecostals learn from one another? Has the supernatural nature of the Christian faith been stripped of its power due to an overly rational and logical gospel that was carried around the world?

What does it mean to be a practicing supernaturalist operating under the empowering presence of the Spirit?

Focusing on Different Categories of Missiological Concern

First, there are issues that emerge from national or regional contexts. This agenda becomes clear as we read and evaluate the two sections of this book written by 16 authors representing diverse geographical and cultural perspectives. I underscore here only a few of these critical themes that are specific to those arenas, whether the country is vast or small. In Asian nations, there are issues of ancestral worship, ministry in the context of religious pluralism, persecution of Christians, authority structures of culture, the new materialism, and economic prosperity. In Africa, similar issues emerge, but others are distinct, such as spiritism and syncretism within African traditional religions, Christian nominalism, and the legacy of Western missions and their influence on the younger mission movement. In Latin America, questions include, How will Evangelicals grapple with the crisis of nominalism in their churches? How will they face the newer challenge coming from the revival of pre-Columbian worship amongst Latin American indigenous peoples? Christians in nations of the West struggle with their own complex set of topics: the re-evangelization of their people; church and missions cast in the mold of modernity but living in an increasingly post-modern world; and issues of gender in the Christian community. The island nations of the Caribbean and South Pacific have their own particular issues. The Middle East, cradle of our faith, provides a complex spectrum of challenges, particularly for Evangelicals, who are a precarious minority within a minority.

Secondly, there are issues more general in nature, with global implications, requiring the service of the international community of reflective practitioners. We do well to revisit the Iguassu Affirmation in order to identify these critical themes and concerns. We can also review some of the major papers of the second section of this book, such as the chapters by Samuel Escobar, Paul Heibert, Antonia van der Meer, Chris Wright, David Tai-Woong Lee, and Alan Roxburgh. What are we going to do with our understanding of truth, hermeneutics, and ethics? What about issues of authority, suffering and martyrdom, and the nature of the Great Commission? Significantly, the crisis of Christian nominalism appeared as a critical concern in all of the regions. Holistic mission cannot be relegated to the second tier of missiological importance.

What do we do with the concerns and diverse positions on the issue of eternal destiny? At Iguassu, one of Chris Wright's footnotes on this subject provoked a great discussion in the smaller working groups as well as in other informal gatherings that week. We must revisit this vital theme, opening the arena of discussion to the different convictions sustained within our Evangelical community of faith. The World Evangelical Fellowship has a core doctrinal statement. That framework offers the freedom of diversity as long as one operates within that biblical foundation.

What about the export/import business in missions, primarily (but not exclusively, for the same mentality is found in other regions of the world) from the West to the rest of the world? Church, mission, and educational structures, theological categories, and ways of understanding and doing missiology and theology have been taken around the world with the unspoken assumption that they are the right and only way of doing things in the life of the church and its mission. Another set of issues: What will we do with the reductionisms of modern missions? Are they all equally true and important? Are these oversimplifications simply a concern of missions from the West, or are they of global import? It certainly becomes a global problem when we realize that the minimalist emphases have been exported around the world due to the enormous communications resources of the West.

What does the church in the West have to learn from the church in non-Western nations? What can the "older church" in the West learn from the practicing supernaturalism and the ministry of the Spirit in the life of the non-Western churches? How can the church around the world best prepare to grapple with the increasing waves of persecution and suffering? What does it mean to be the global body of Christ in these contexts? Where is our theology of martyrdom? Who is best qualified to prepare and strengthen in this arena? Probably it will not be those whose Christianity has been lived out in broad freedom, with government protection of their religious liberty. Those who have suffered must be the teachers, and the rest of the church listens and learns.

While Paul Hiebert's chapter focuses on spiritual warfare and worldview, he has some significant and challenging remarks on the three major categories of doing theology: systematic, biblical, and missiological. Particularly intriguing were Paul's footnotes on the foundation and nature of systematic theology. What would it look like if we opened up the categories of systematic theology beyond the commonly (at least in Europe and North America) accepted ones? What are the implications of theology done primarily from a missiological perspective? And what would a zero-based theology and missiology look like if we were able to start the process from scratch, as if nothing had been done before? Admittedly, this is impossible in its fullness, but the potential is there for startling new understandings about God, Scripture, truth, creation, and culture.

What might a missiology look like for the post-modern world, a reality not limited to Western nations? At Iguassu, the younger participants grappled with their own understanding of a hermeneutic and missiology by and for their generation, so shaped by the most recent tectonic changes of culture and worldview. There was a degree of healthy tension between them and some of the older participants who simply did not understand the challenging statements of their younger brothers and sisters. This missiology of the future must be articulated by the younger generation of mission leaders, but they in turn must invite the gracious input of the older colleagues. And the leadership structures, organization, and publishing houses must open space for this younger expression of Evangelical missiology. This also is missiology done in community.

Perhaps a more extensive note might be made regarding trinitarian missiology. Already a number of writers have addressed this theme, either as a segment of their chapters or in major presentations, such as Ajith Fernando's expositions, Alan Roxburgh's chapter, and the observations by Samuel Escobar.

Trinitarian missiology has a multi-faceted focus. The most obvious is the biblical and theological study that identifies the specific role in mission played by each member of the Godhead. Each Person has a distinct and yet overlapping role in creating, revealing, and redeeming. What Ajith Fernando did in Iguassu is a prime example of exegesis that identifies the unique contribution of Father, Son, and Spirit, and then examines the church as the manifestation of trinitarian missiology

on earth. What would it look like if teams of reflective practitioners engaged in the task of understanding these distinct roles of the Godhead? Have some of our Christian bodies emphasized one member of the Trinity at the expense of the others?

A second dimension looks at the Trinity in the context of community. The Trinity is the first community; it is an eternal community; it is a community in which each Person defers to the other's uniqueness. This community is self-revealing in history and in the life of the church. In this light, new questions would emerge. For example, what is the united role of the Trinity in creation, revelation, and redemption? In what ways do they operate together and not separately? What are the practical outworkings of the fact that each member of the Three cedes to each other, honors and enhances each other, releases each other to his specific role in divine realities? This is so eloquently revealed in Anton Rublev's 14th century Russian icon. The three figures appear as very similar angels, but upon clear examination they are truly distinct, with the head of each slightly bowed to the other's, deferring to and honoring each other.

Missiologically, we must also ask in what ways individualism and authoritarian leadership in church and missions are truly Christian, especially when they apparently ignore collegiality or the rest of the body of Christ. This is an international problem, not limited to just one culture or nation. What's more, does our Christian concept of community come primarily from pragmatic human organizational models, or does it emerge from the model of the supernatural Trinity? In what way would this communal model impact our presentation of the gospel, with the epic Story centered not in extreme individualism and personal decisions, but rather in shared values of community? Already some of our colleagues from India are discussing the implications of this gospel presentation to their vast nation. The church by definition must live out the values of trinitarian missiology, for the church is the gathered and scattered people of God, with each person having unique contributions to make but all sharing as co-equals and enhancing one another.

A Commitment of the WEF Missions Commission

In October 1999, the Iguassu Consultation initiated a process. In the course of that week, a representative team of seven men and women listened to their colleagues, edited and wrote, listened again and revised, and then finally drafted a seminal statement of nine declarations and 14 commitments. That document was affirmed by the participants just prior to an extended service of worship and holy communion. The Iguassu Affirmation has now become a working document and has already been translated into Spanish, Portuguese, French, German, and Korean. It has been studied, critiqued, and criticized in different contexts around the world: from theological institutions to missiological classes, from churches to individual mission agencies, from national to regional mission leader gatherings.

But the global missiological challenge is vast as we look to the future. We in the WEF Missions Commission cannot and will not serve alone. We need the national, regional, and international networks to work with and in this missiological community. Whether the World Evangelical Fellowship's Theological and Missions Commissions, the Lausanne network, or the new Great Commission Roundtable—we all must come together to avoid duplication and confusion and to converge on the missiological task with our combined resources and commitments. The Spirit of God has created a huge platform of Christian centers around the world. This platform requires an open space of equals around the table of agenda and discussion of practical outcomes and decisions. It also invites the stronger financial centers and organizations of the Christian world to ensure that these varied global voices are heard in venues, media, and publications.

A word to the missiological stakeholders, those who have a true commitment to and need of a re-examined, biblical, and global missiology. These include Christian leaders in the missionary movement, mobilizers and activists as well as the reflective ones; it includes churches and denominations, administration and faculty of both theological institutions and missionary training centers, as well as mission sending structures. I repeat, we desperately need each other at this moment of crisis and opportunity around the world. We must develop strategic alliances as we do our missiology—whether at the level of grassroots ministry or in teams of reflection that lead us to a revised praxis. Let us come together to serve together.

Drawing to a Close

As we gathered at Iguassu, we had to ask ourselves, "Why another international gathering? Why another consultation? Why another book? Why more missiological reflection?"

We are bombarded on a daily basis with an unending flow of fast-breaking secular and religious news. This vast, 24-hours-a-day, immediate, global, and detailed news is overwhelming. We simply cannot absorb and evaluate it all adequately. It comes from multiple sources, all claiming equal importance, from flashpoints to trends. We cannot keep up, and the result is a gradual numbing of our Christian consciousness. We also have vast theological and missiological libraries and printed resources. On top of that, we now receive unprecedented information through the Internet and CD-ROMs—all ready to serve the church around the world.

Yet for all of the intense mobilizing, strategizing, activity, and mission events of the last 20 years, there was the realization that we were entering the new century with little actual, substantive interaction between theology and missiology, between practitioners and scholars, within the context of equal input by all the diverse voices of the global Evangelical church. In an age when the ancient and new pluralisms unleash a bewildering array of competing spiritualities and religious options, it behooves us as Evangelicals to ground our practice upon strong theological underpinnings and reflections. At the same time, we need to come together as equals and dialogue "around the table," thus allowing our missiology to be shaped by the interaction of our diverse viewpoints and cultural realities. By doing this, we will participate in the new paradigm that emerges for the century unfolding before us. No longer can or should one part of the body dominate or dictate to the rest. Our encounter at Iguassu was a foretaste of the mutual interdependence of equals that awaits us as we are willing to model ourselves after that self-same dance of the Trinity where each member, in self-giving love, honors and enhances and defers to the others.

May God give us wisdom of discernment as we serve the living and Triune God, as we serve the church around the world, and as we serve our hungry and pain-wracked global human family.

I close, presenting again for reflection and self-searching the prayer from Jim Engel which was given at the end of our first chapter (Engel & Dyrness, 2000, pp. 24-25).

A Prayer for Renewal and Restoration

Heavenly Father,
our Lord and giver of life,
forgive us for the extent to which
we have naively succumbed
to the spirit of the age,
for our preoccupation with
false measures of success,
for a sense of triumphalism
which replaces
humble dependence on you,
and for our blindness in avoiding
those parts of your Word
which do not fit neatly
into our theology.
We humbly confess our total
dependence on you
as the Lord of life.
Let us see a lost world afresh
through your eyes
and give us discernment
through your Spirit.
Share with us your priorities
and give us the courage to be
responsible stewards
of our obligation
to take the whole gospel
to the whole world.
Speak, Lord, for your servants
are listening.
To you we give all glory,
honor, and praise.
Amen.

References

Engel, J. F., & Dyrness, W. A. (2000). *Changing the mind of missions: Where have we gone wrong?* Downers Grove, IL: InterVarsity Press.

*William D. Taylor is Executive Director of the WEF Missions Commission and has coordinated the ministries of the MC since 1986. He was born in Costa Rica of missionary par-*ents and has lived in Latin America for 30 years, 17 of them with his family as a long-term missionary with CAM International, serving on the faculty of the Central American Theological Seminary. Married to Yvonne, a native Texan, he has three adult children who were born in Guatemala. He has edited **Internationalizing Missionary Training** (1991), **Kingdom Partnerships for Synergy in Missions** (1994), and **Too Valuable to Lose: Exploring the Causes and Cures of Missionary Attrition** (1997). He co-authored with Emilio Antonio Nuñez, **Crisis and Hope in Latin America** (1996), and with Steve Hoke, **Send Me! Your Journey to the Nations** (1999). He also serves as visiting faculty at seminaries in various countries.

Index

DATE DUE